THE
POWER
OF
WOMEN

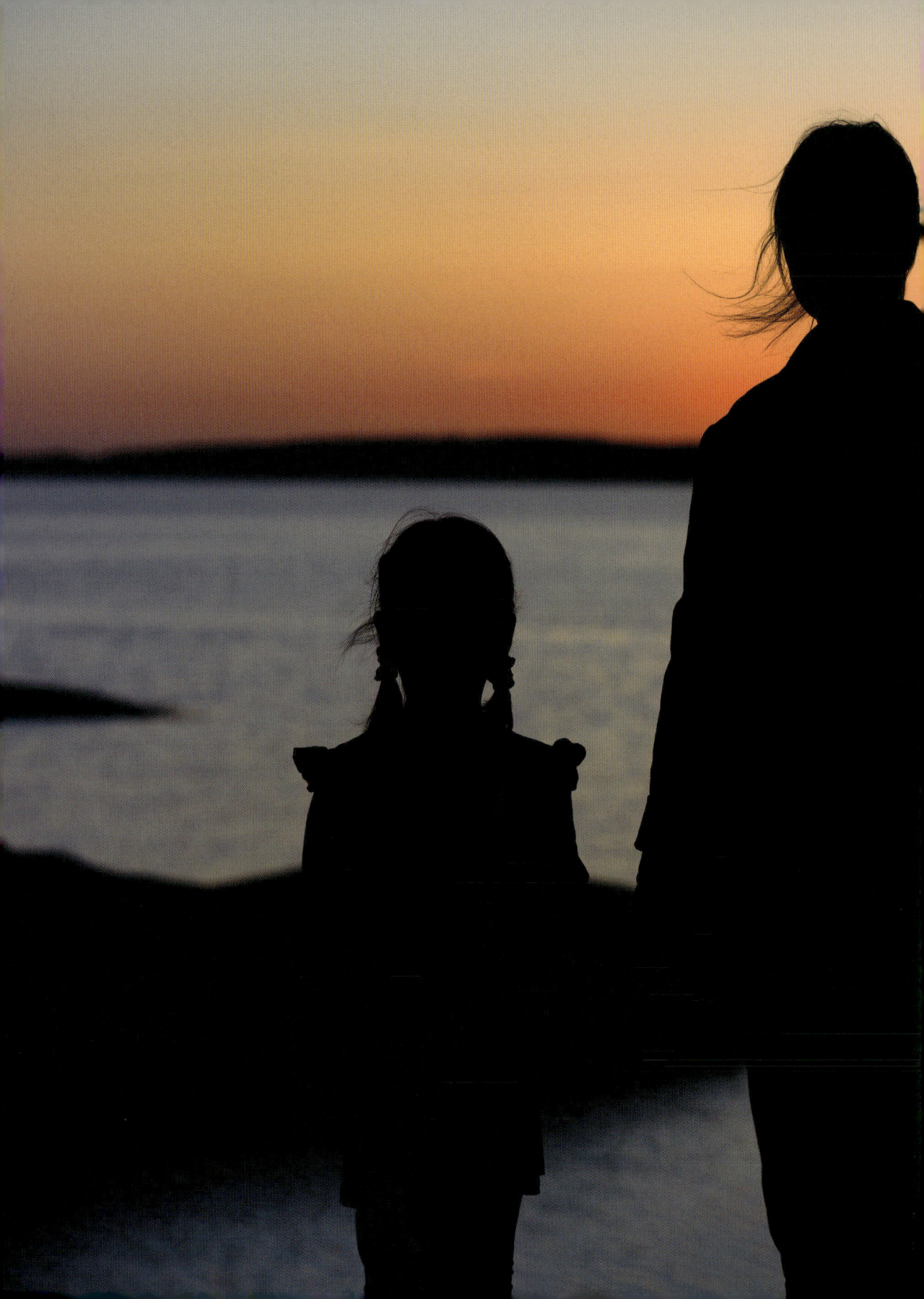

THE **POWER** OF **WOMEN**

AN ATLAS OF BEAUTY BOOK

MIHAELA NOROC

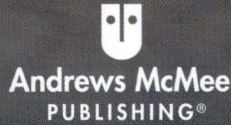

Andrews McMeel
PUBLISHING®

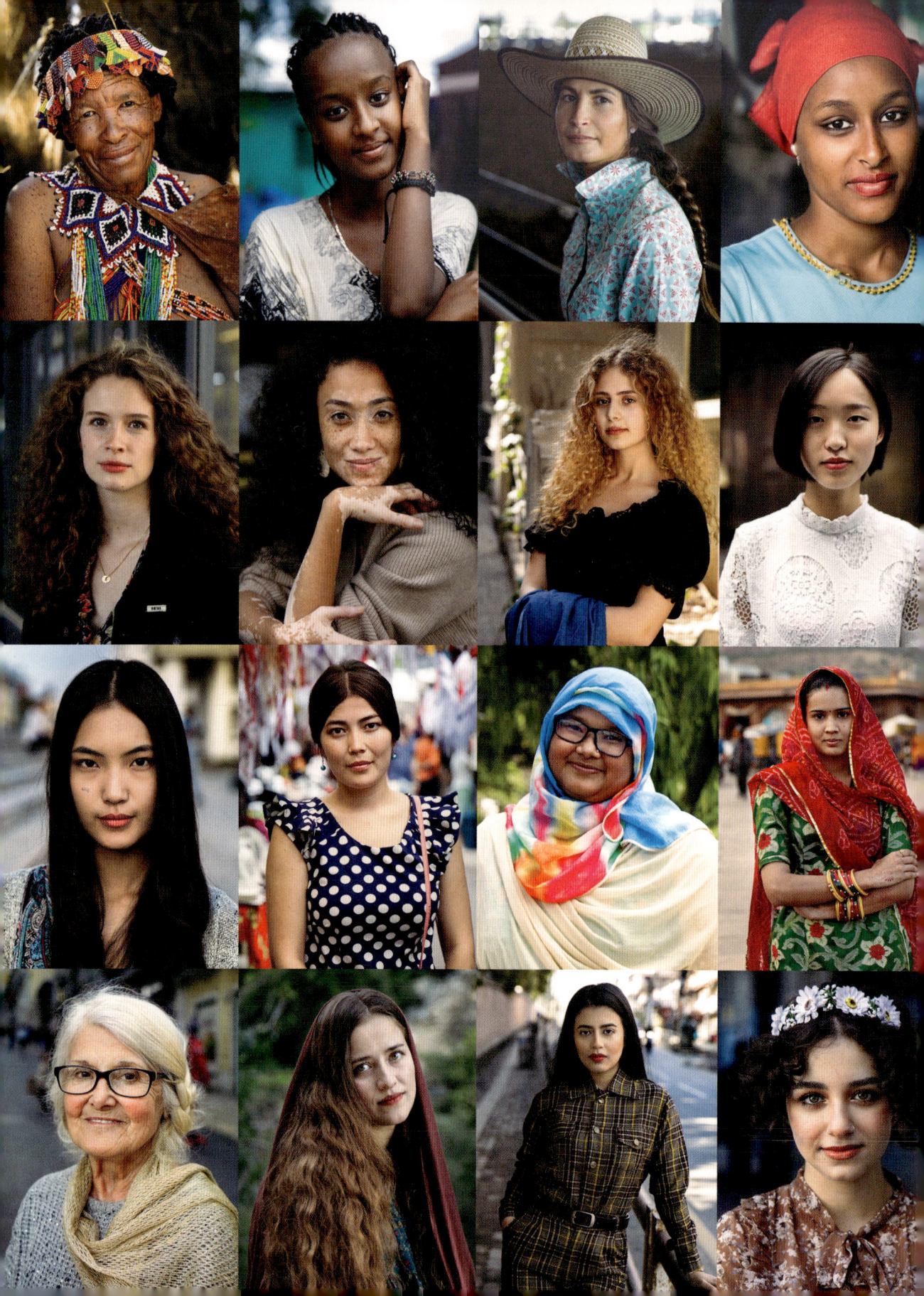

INTRODUCTION

It's been almost twelve years since I began traveling the world and photographing women. In 2017, I gathered some of my photos and stories in a book titled *The Atlas of Beauty: Women of the World in 500 Portraits*. The feedback was incredible, and soon people started asking for more.

This new book—completed eight years later—took significantly longer to make than the first. It's more than a simple continuation; this new volume is a book of its own with a deeper and more mature approach. In these past eight years, many things happened defining who I am today. On a personal level, I lost loved ones. At the same time, I became a mother.

Soon after the release of my first book, my daughter, Natalia, was born. It was an immense joy that I had never felt before, but I also felt more responsibility and fear than ever. I found myself questioning whether I could continue traveling the world and working on my project. And there were many other questions: Was my duty as a dedicated mother to change my life completely and stay home beside my daughter? Or, on the contrary, should I continue my work in order to be the best example and inspiration? In the end I found the answer.

Throughout the years that followed, I made every effort to work on the project while bringing Natalia with me whenever possible. Being next to her every single day in the beginning was essential to me, and I knew how much she needed me, too.

The first time I had to leave her at home felt agonizing. It happened during a journey close to a war zone. I remember hearing gunfire while photographing women there, but the biggest challenge by far was being separated from my daughter for the first time.

Fortunately, my husband helped enormously whenever I had to work on the project. Without him, I couldn't have continued to travel the world.

Balancing work on this new book with my role as a mother proved to be the greatest challenge of my life. Yet the women I met around the world taught me that challenges are part of your evolution, so I knew I had to continue. While working on *The Power of Women*, I've grown a lot as both an artist and a human being. I began focusing more on the stories of the women I met. I strived to find their unique qualities, go deeper, and capture a wider range of diversity.

Speaking of diversity, this beautiful word has been overused in the past decade. It's become almost cliché. Look around—everyone talks about diversity, but genuine diversity is rarer than ever. I don't want this book to be part of a fleeting trend that praises diversity just to be popular. If people see this volume in a hundred years, I want it to feel as relevant then as it is today. I believe the true spirit of humanity transcends time and space and exists in countless facets that defy standardization.

While working on this book, I tried to visit vastly different environments. From neighborhoods in Baghdad to posh streets in Manhattan, and from traditional villages in Peru to modern districts in Tokyo, *The Power of Women* showcases a vast spectrum of womanhood. In a way, it is an encyclopedia of incredible women, but I prefer to call it an Atlas of Beauty. Because, ultimately, beauty is what unites us all, despite our differences.

I've traveled the world and met women of all ages and backgrounds: progressive and traditional, with and without children, corporate employees and artists, and athletes and housewives. These years have been a profound learning experience. That's why, besides the stories of the women I've met, I'm also sharing some of my own experiences in this book.

You may be wondering why I decided to call this second volume *The Power of Women*. I believe that all the women featured in this book—and all the women of the world—have their own unique power. The power of women, for me, isn't tied solely to strength. A woman is powerful even when she cries and feels weak and vulnerable. Because the power of women encompasses a vast spectrum of qualities.

During all these years of travel, I have discovered thousands of ways in which women use their unique power for good causes, which ultimately reveals what I call beauty. And I hope this book will be an inspiration for those who are in search of their authentic self and their own beauty.

Some stories from this volume will sadden you, while many others will make you smile, but this varied blend ultimately defines our complex planet as well as the complex human spirit. In an increasingly divided world, I hope this collection of photos and stories will be perceived as a manifesto for love, knowledge, and hope. Now it's time to start the journey.

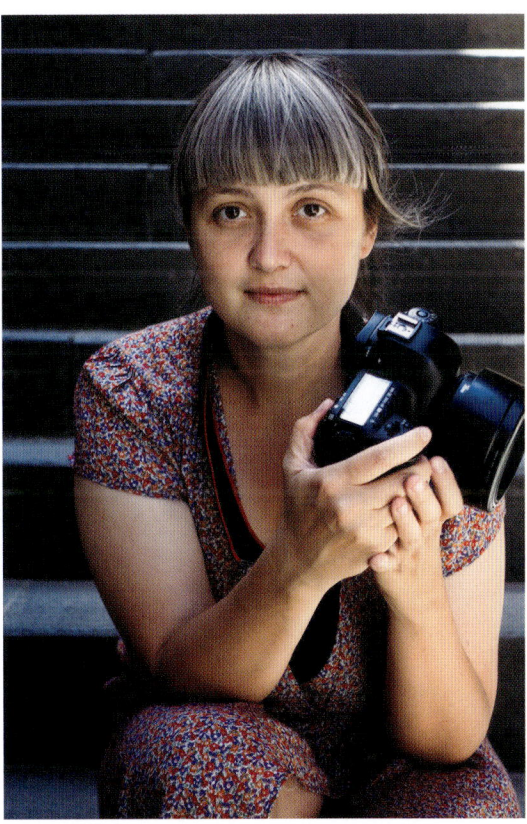

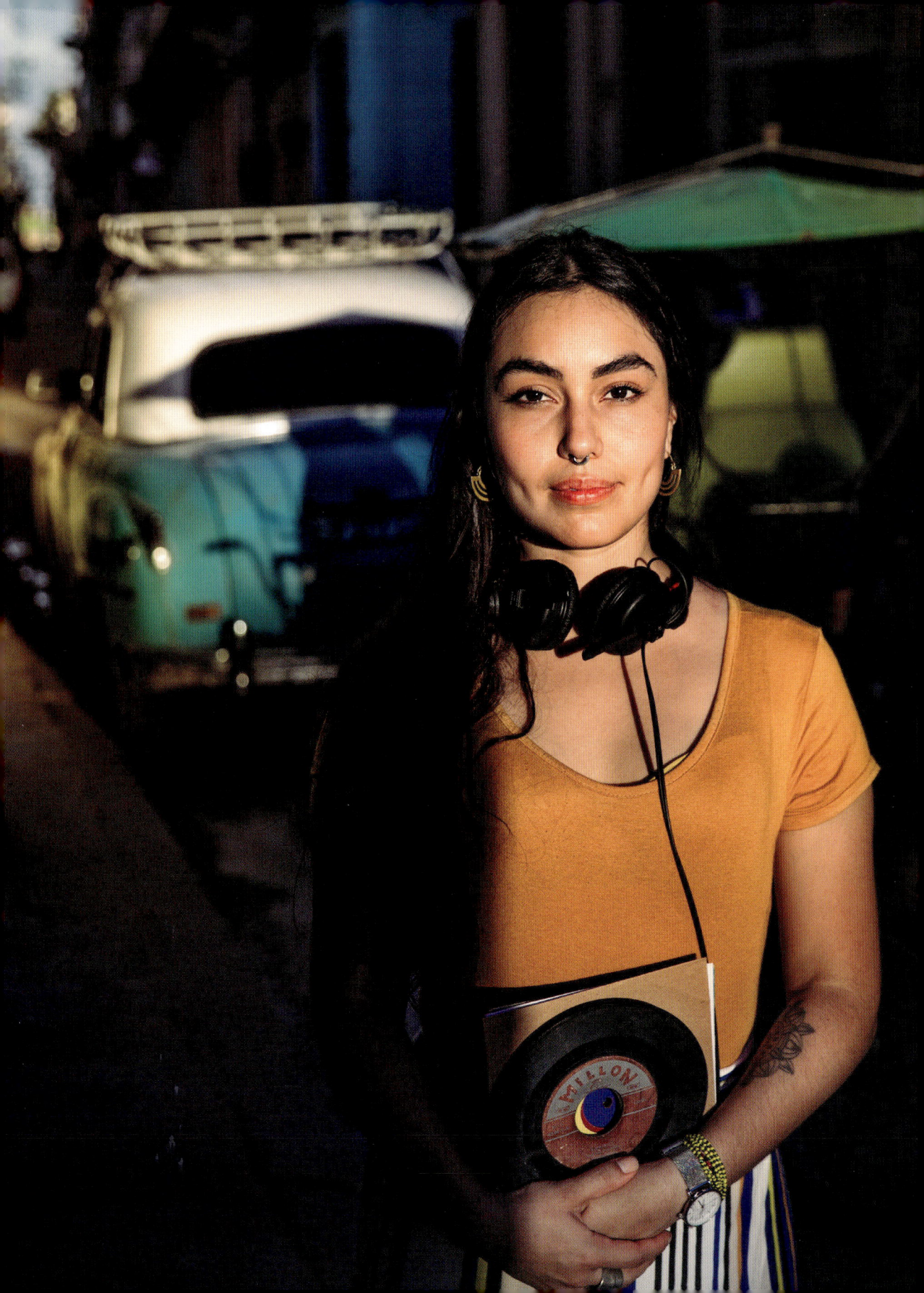

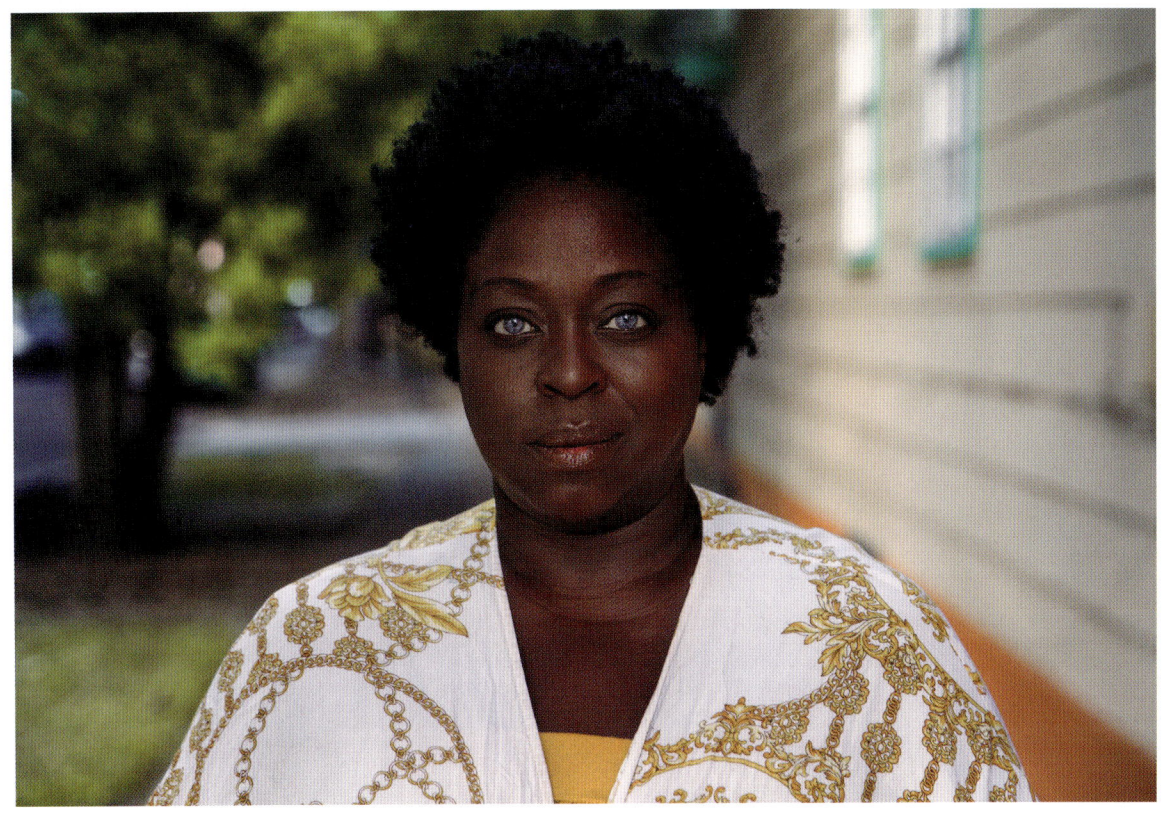

NEW ORLEANS, UNITED STATES *(Above)*

I was walking on the magical streets of this city when I heard a magical voice. When I went closer, I saw two magical eyes. Her name is Alicia Renee, and she is a singer-songwriter.

HAVANA, CUBA *(Opposite)*

Cami Layé Okún is more than a DJ. For many years, she has been going door-to-door around Cuba to talk to people about the music they love and to collect old records from them.

She has been mixing this music in surprising ways, animating dance floors with tropical, tribal, and Latin rhythms while bringing lost, forgotten music back to life.

Cami is the kind of DJ who never consumes alcohol or drugs before or during performances. Her passion and joy are more intense than anything. Born to a Bolivian father and a Cuban mother, Cami is in love with diversity, and music is her way of bringing together the beautiful cultures of the world.

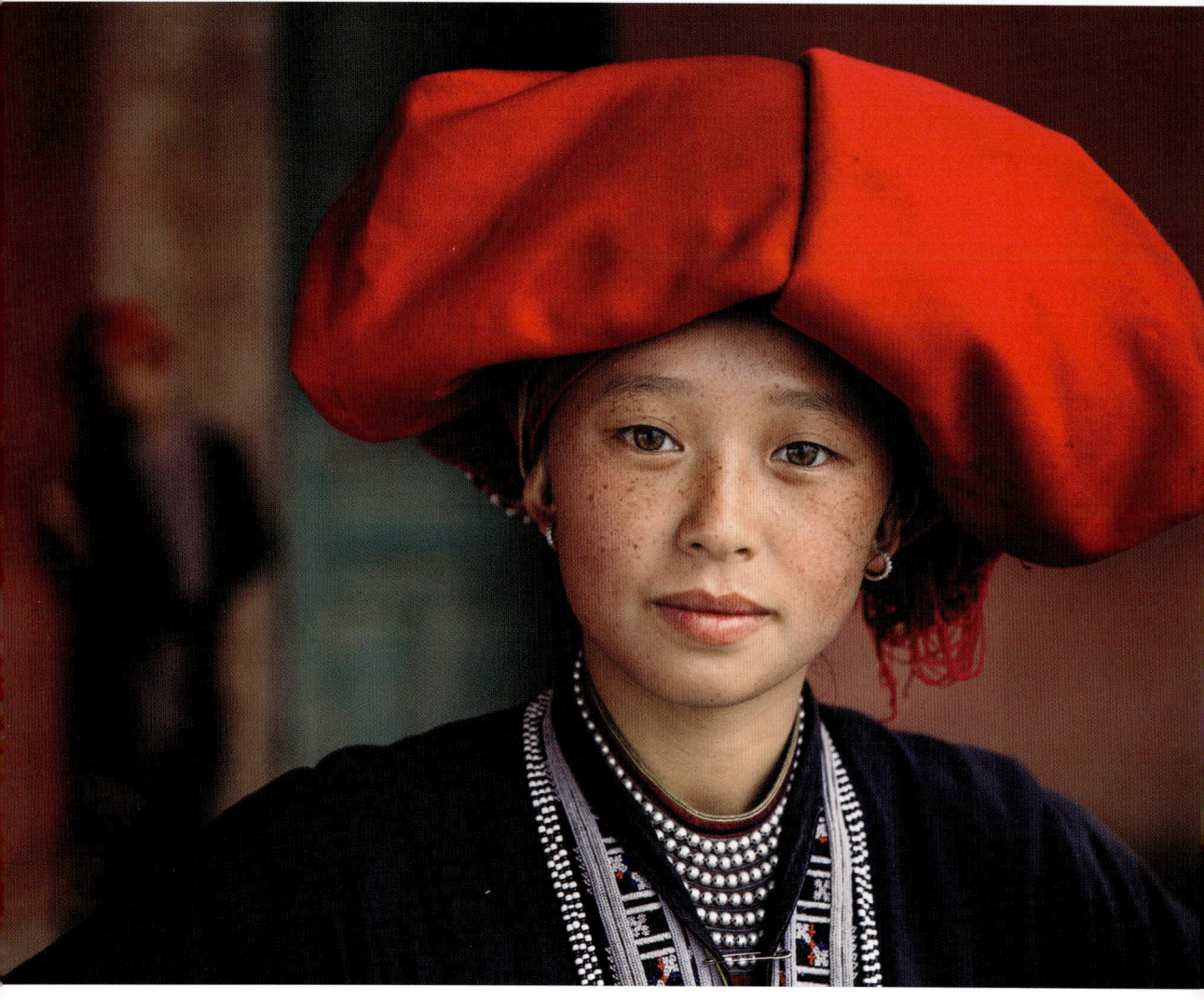

NORTHERN VIETNAM

Ta Mai lives in a small village and is part of an ethnic group called Red Dao. In her community, women wear this kind of red turban only after they get married. Ta Mai got married when she was only sixteen. Now she's twenty and already has two children. That's common in her community. What is uncommon is that she had a love marriage.

The lives of these fascinating people are complicated. They mostly live off agriculture, eating only rice and a few vegetables every day. And still they wear beautiful handmade clothes that take months to weave. This might seem impractical for people in many parts of the world: struggling to survive while dedicating so much time to craft and beauty. But I believe that any human being needs authentic beauty, and those who have a simple life are sometimes closer to it.

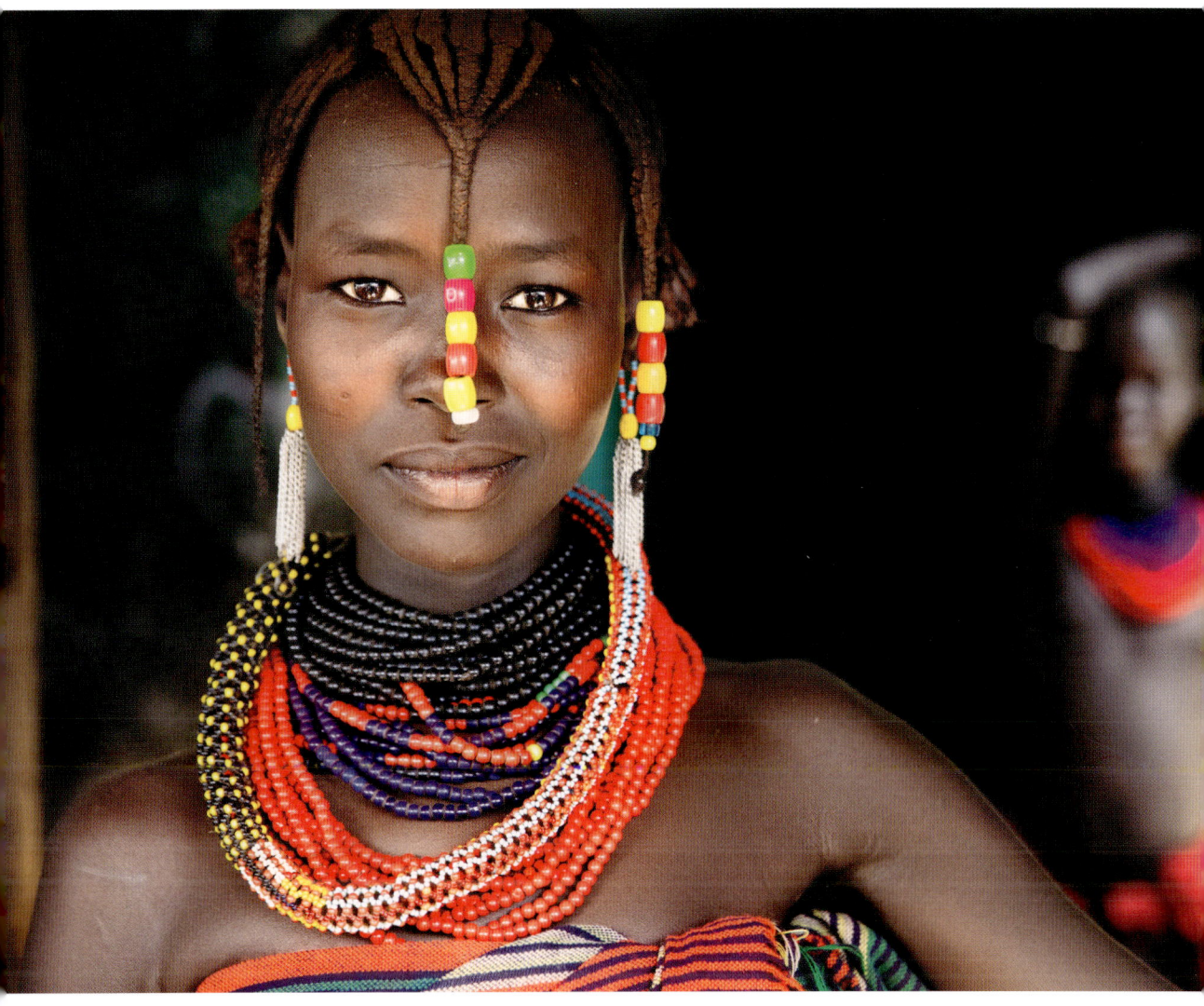

OMO VALLEY, ETHIOPIA

Kaale, an ethnic Daasanach, is part of an agropastoral community. Despite their challenging lives as nomads, the Daasanach people place great importance on their appearance. The women's hairstyles not only showcase their beauty but also serve as markers of their marital status. In Kaale's case, her distinctive hairstyle reveals that she is unmarried.

Some would say this is a part of the captivating story of humanity. Others would say that, on the contrary, this is not empowering at all for the twenty-first century. In the end, our world is a complex tapestry with thousands of nuances and thousands of differing opinions.

REYKJAVÍK, ICELAND

Ragga is a force of nature. She's been a part of a unique expedition at the south pole, she's driven huge trucks with tourists on glaciers, she's worked with mountain rescue teams and as an EMT, and now she works as a firefighter—all while being a dedicated mother, too.

Growing up with her three older brothers, Ragga was never treated differently by her parents despite being the only girl and the youngest in the family. Perhaps this kind of education is one of the reasons why Iceland is considered the best country in the world when it comes to gender equality.

Ragga told me that even here, in the most equal place on Earth, there are still some prejudices regarding women working in male-dominated fields. But, as you can imagine, nothing will ever stop this extraordinary woman from following her path.

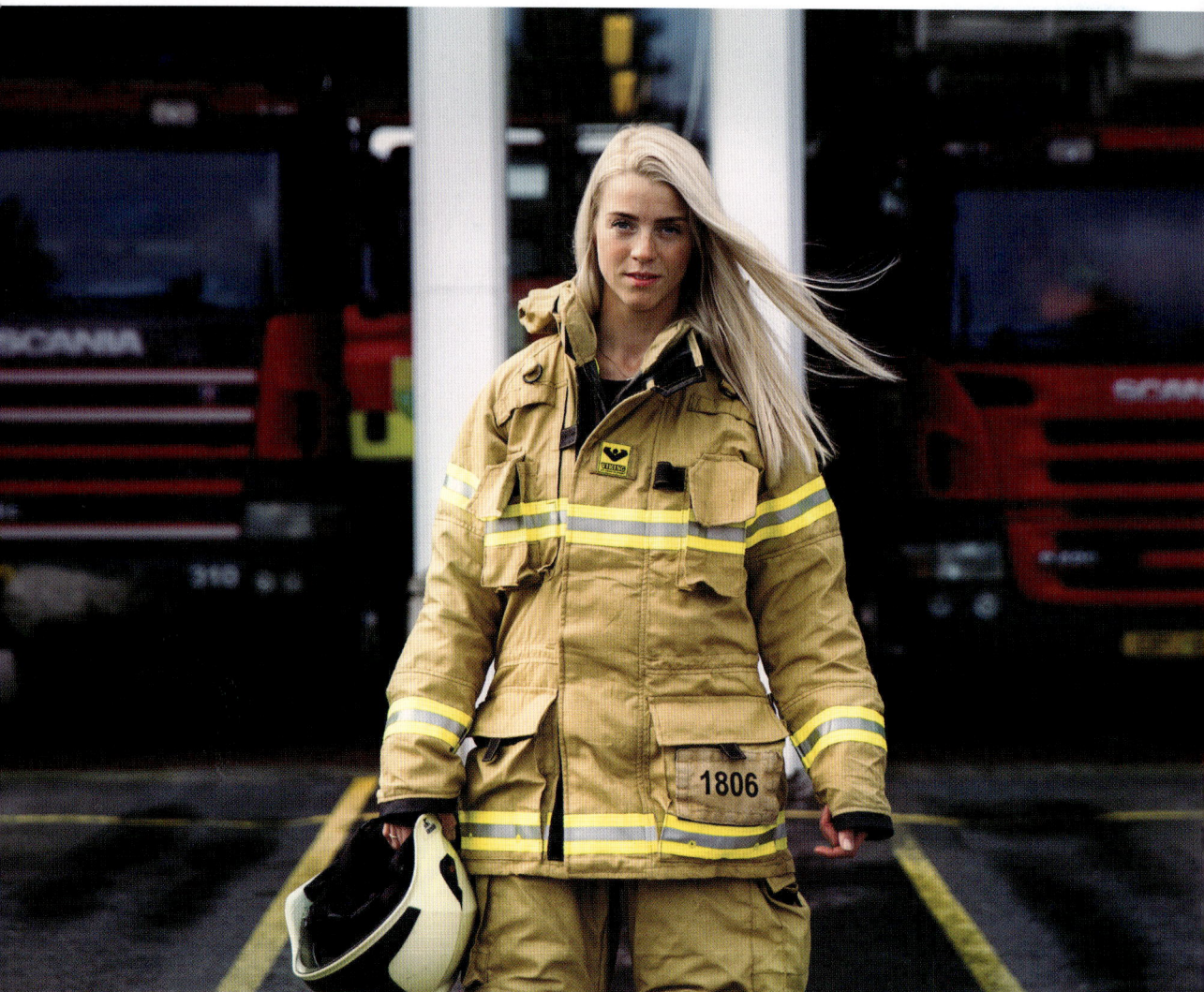

ABU DHABI, UNITED ARAB EMIRATES

Against all prejudices, Amna Al Qubaisi fell in love with sports cars during her childhood and became the first Emirati female racing driver. Her journey was far from easy. She lives in a conservative society in which many people believe that this field is not appropriate for a woman, but she has managed to succeed anyway. At the young age of twenty-one, she has already built a prolific career.

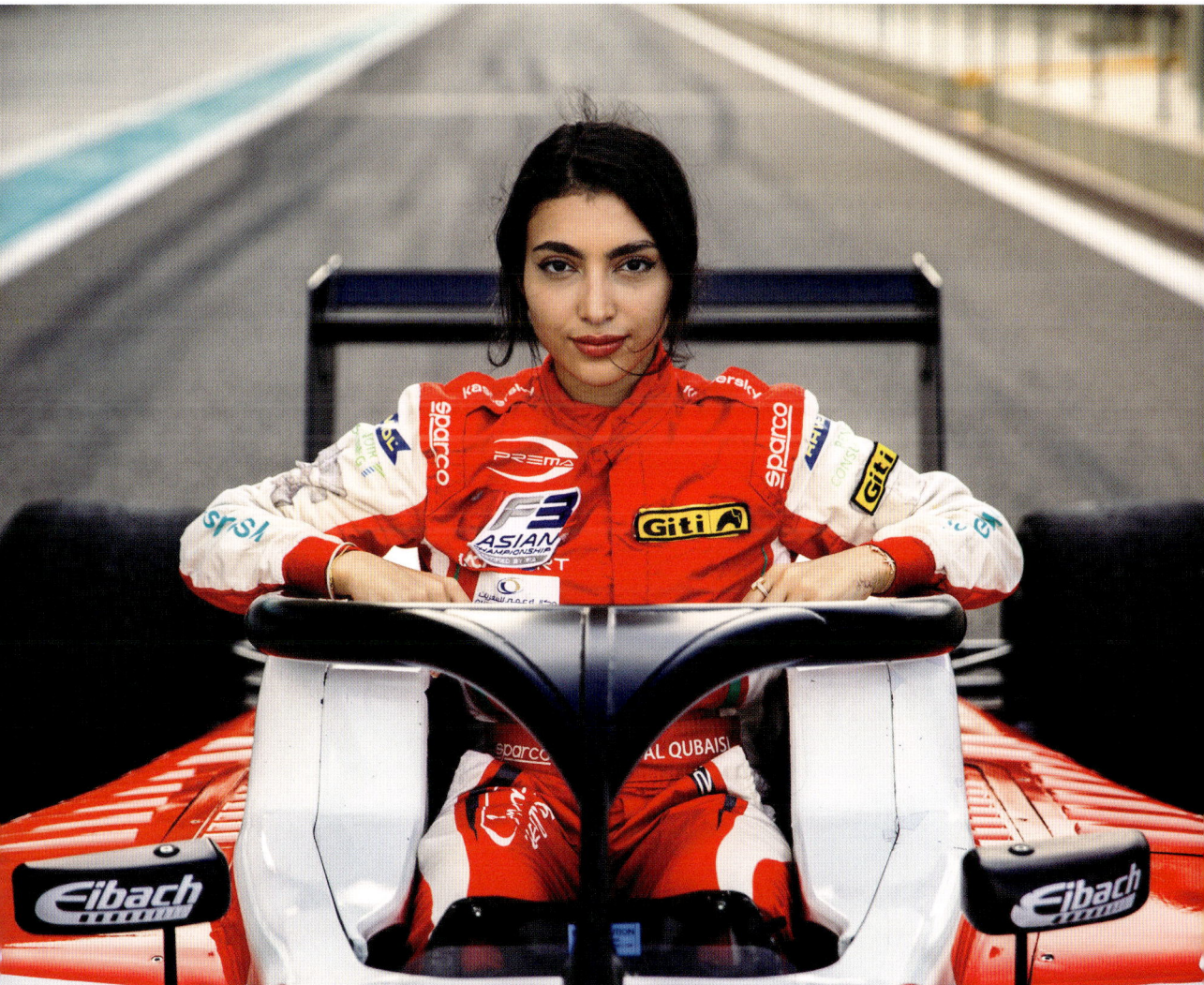

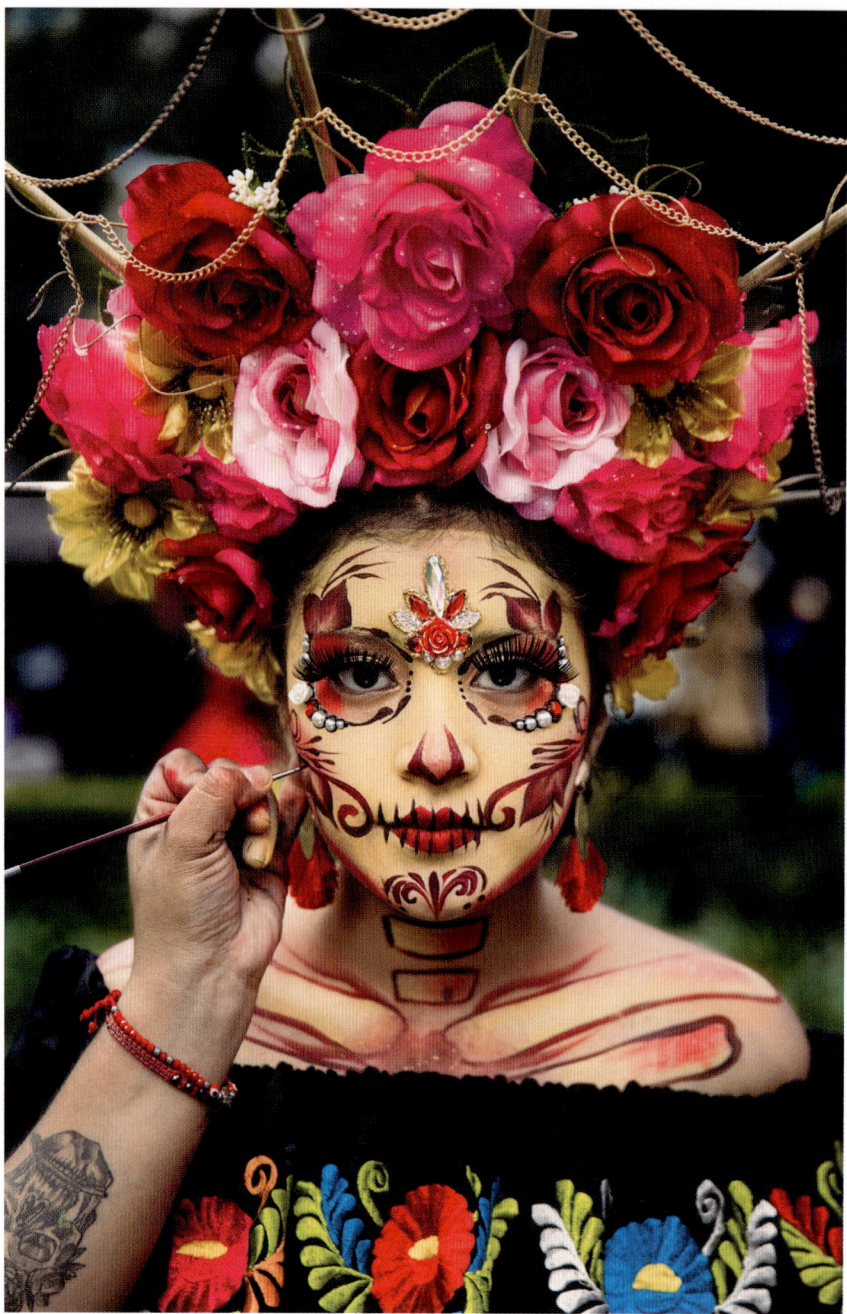

MEXICO CITY, MEXICO

Meet Paola as she gets her makeup done for the Catrinas parade during *el Día de Muertos* ("the Day of the Dead"). During this holiday, families honor their loved ones who have passed away. Many people wear complex makeup like Paola. They also decorate graves and build elaborate home altars with various offerings for the deceased, such as flowers, food, and paper decorations.

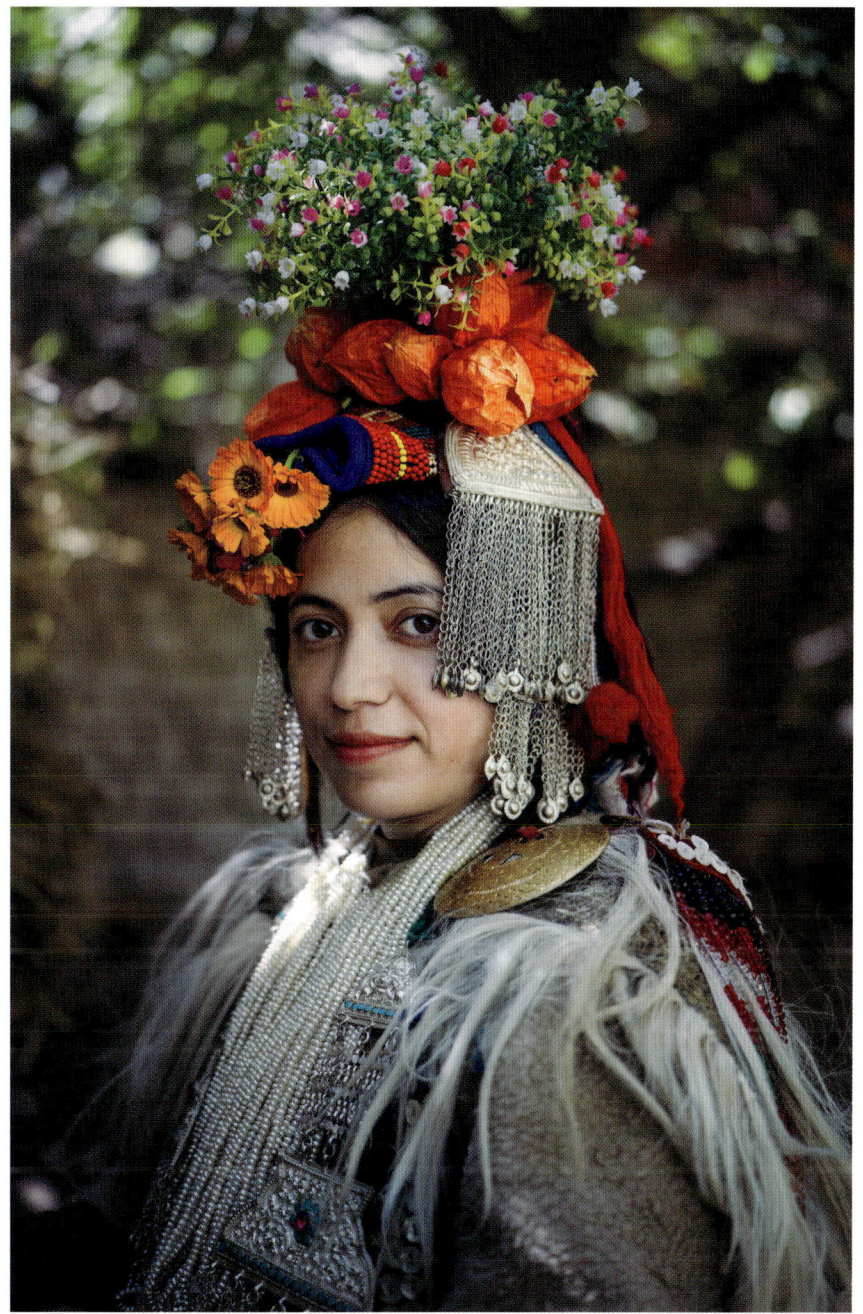

LADAKH, INDIA

Zamngmo moved from her village to a city for studies. However, during vacations, she returns to this picturesque village. When festivals and special events take place, she always wears her traditional outfit, as do most Brokpa people, or Aryans, as they prefer to be called. Wool forms the base of the garments, which provides warmth and durability in the high-altitude climate. The silver ornaments and gems, beautifully combined with flowers, make this outfit something unique in the world.

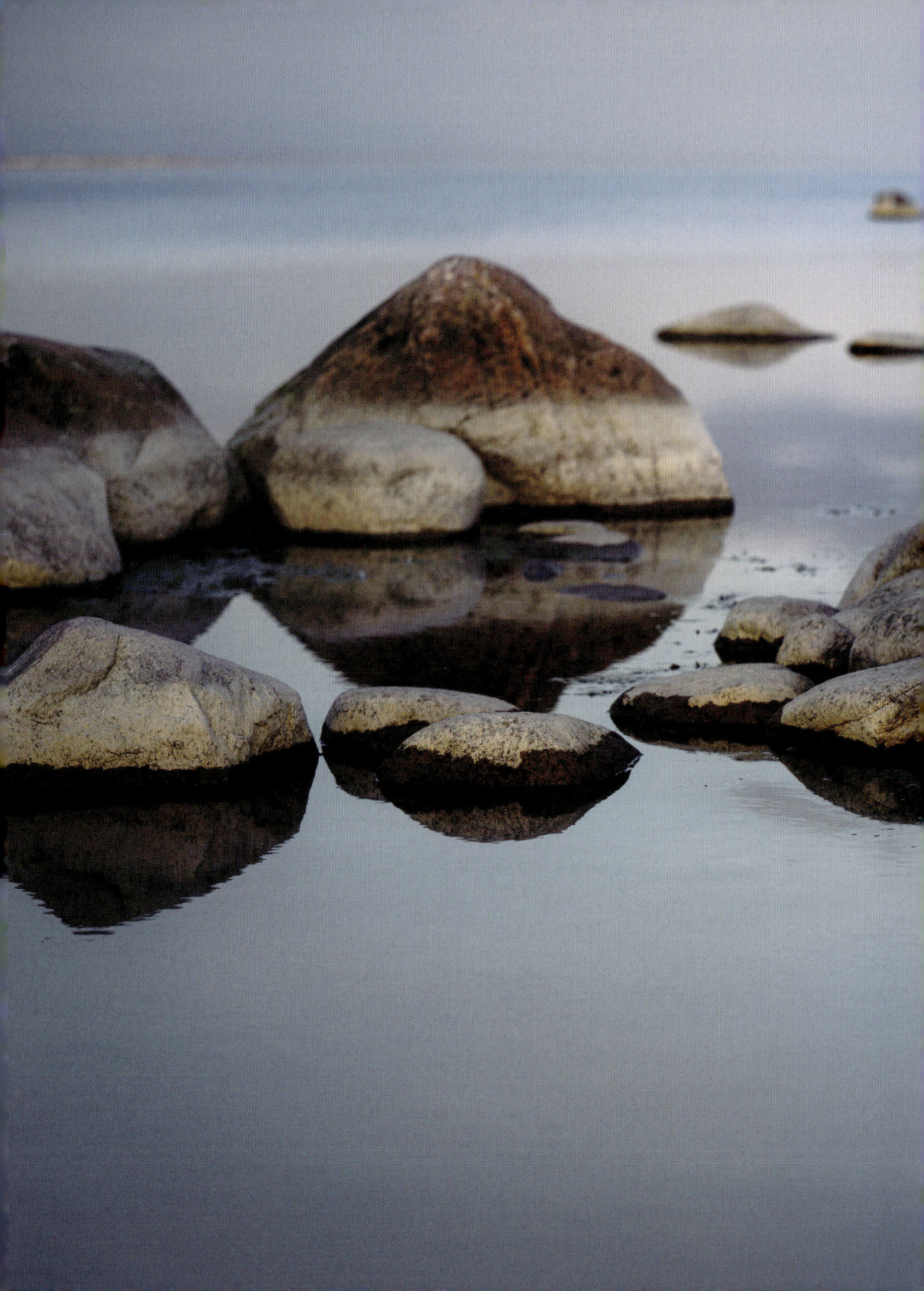

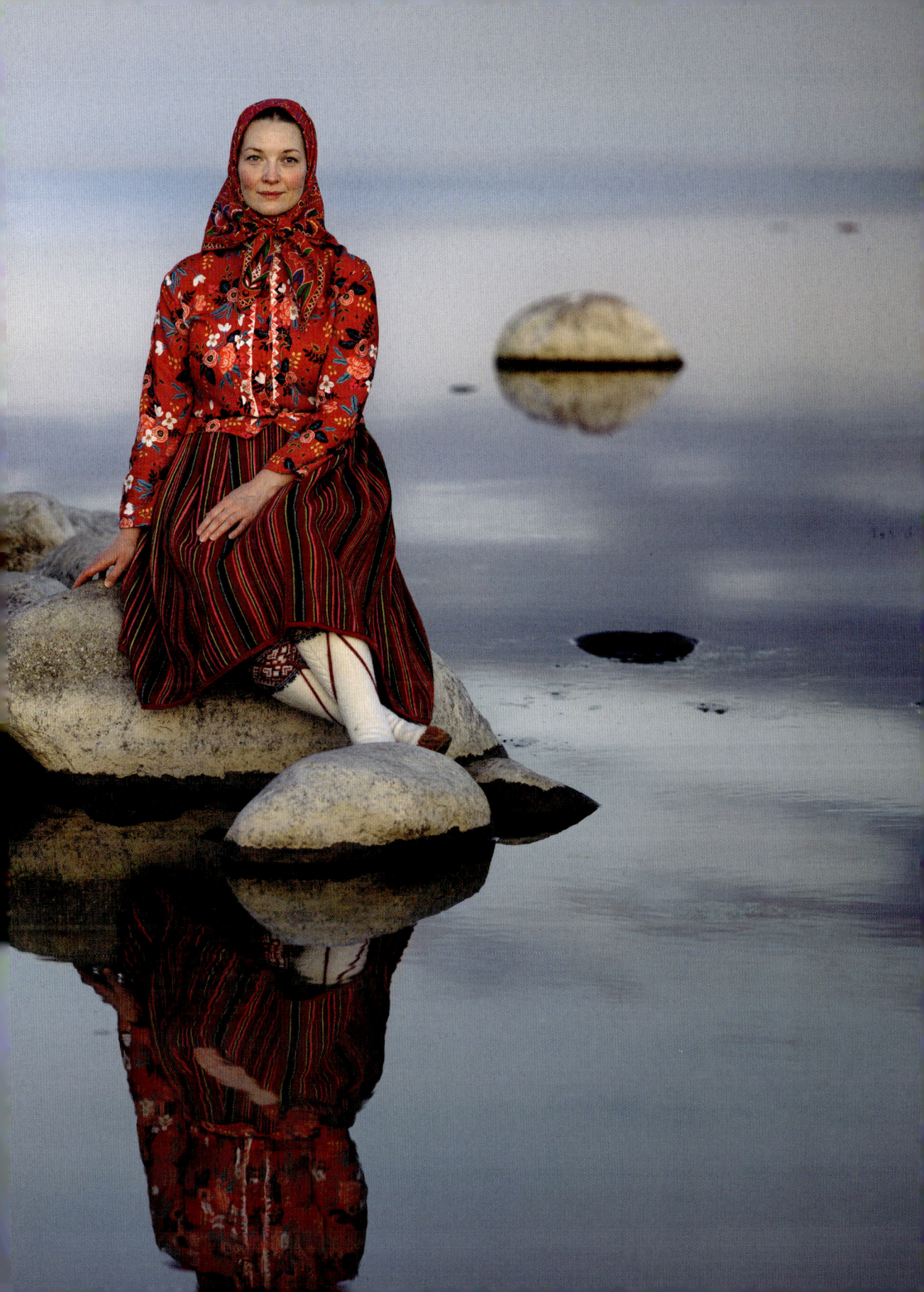

KIHNU ISLAND, ESTONIA *(Previous spread)*

Kihnu is not just a splendid island; it is also considered by some to be Europe's last surviving matriarchy. In a place where men were often away at sea, women always ran the show and kept the vibrant traditions.

During the communist regime, Silvia's parents had to move from Estonia to Canada. Although Silvia was born in Canada, her love for her roots brought her back to Estonia. She now lives on Kihnu Island, where some of her ancestors lived. She works to preserve and promote the culture of this traditional and fascinating place.

MIŃSK MAZOWIECKI, POLAND *(Opposite)*

Wirginia, known as DJ Wika, brings dance floors to life with her vibrant personality. At eighty-six years old, her enthusiasm and optimism are boundless.

Throughout her life, Wirginia has witnessed significant suffering. Seeing the horrors of World War II and then dedicating her career as a teacher to support children with disabilities and troubled backgrounds instilled in her a deep desire to bring joy to the world.

It was after retirement and the loss of her husband that she discovered DJing, and today she is an experienced DJ with hundreds of shows under her belt. Her mixes appeal to all ages, creating a beautiful bridge between generations.

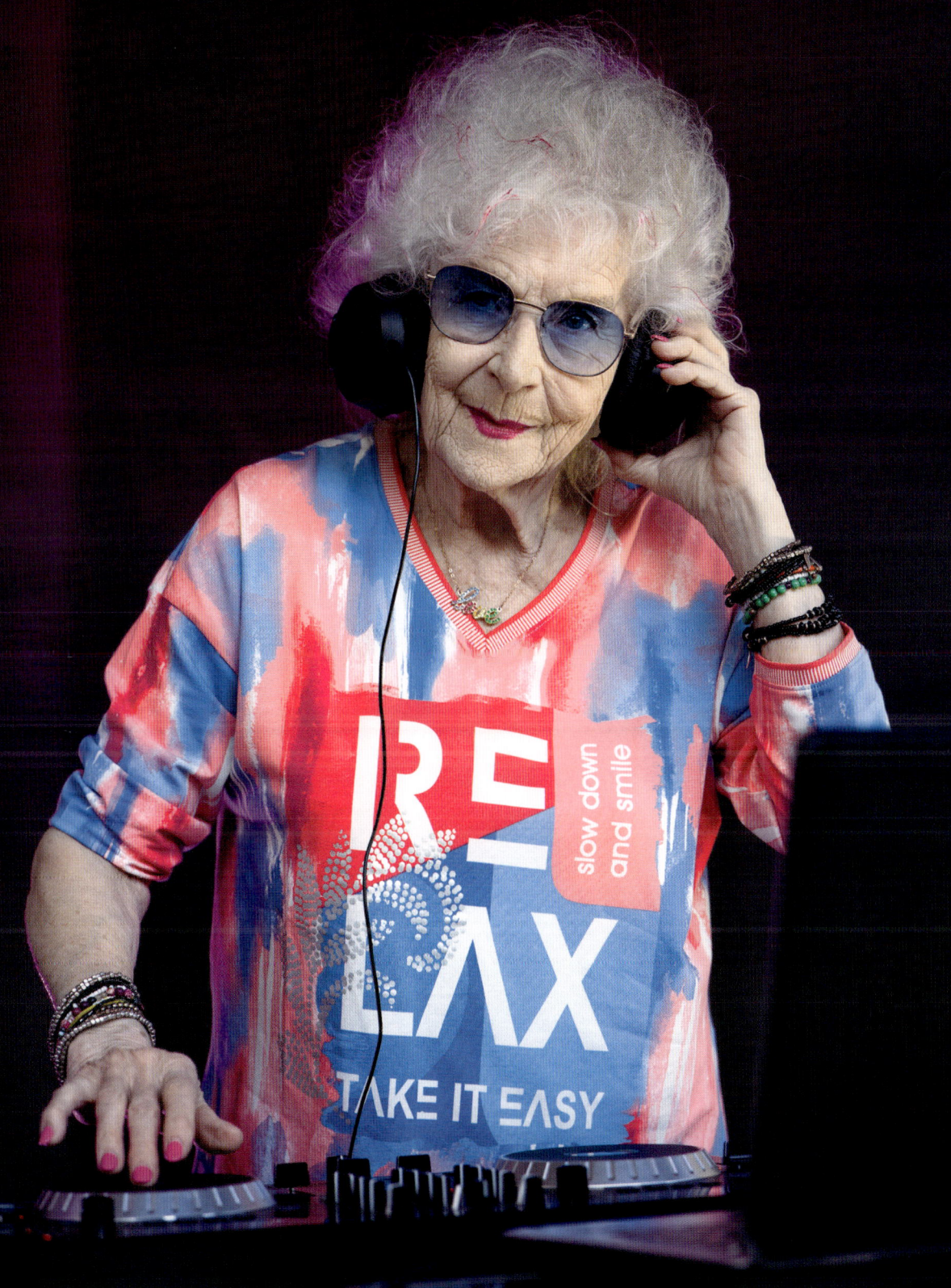

ISLAMABAD, PAKISTAN

Since childhood, Kamila Aazeen Husain wanted to dedicate a big part of her life to meaningful causes. She started volunteering and teaching underprivileged kids when she was only thirteen years old.

When she was seventeen, she and a colleague founded a nonprofit that provides education to children of families living below the poverty line. One year later, she founded an animal shelter with her sister. Since then, Kamila has raised funds, helped hundreds of children, and rescued more than one thousand animals. She's still very young, but her achievements are already impressive.

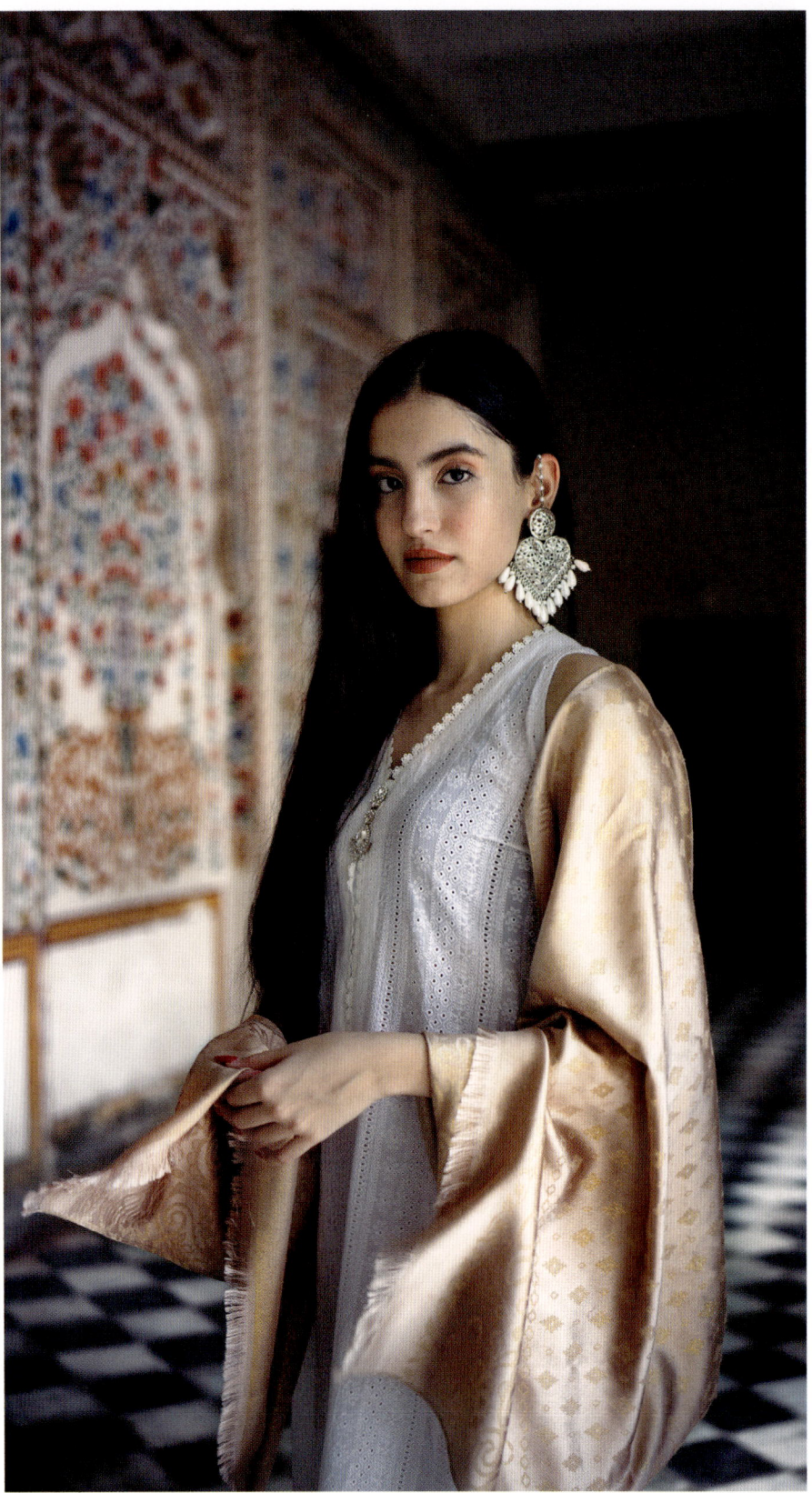

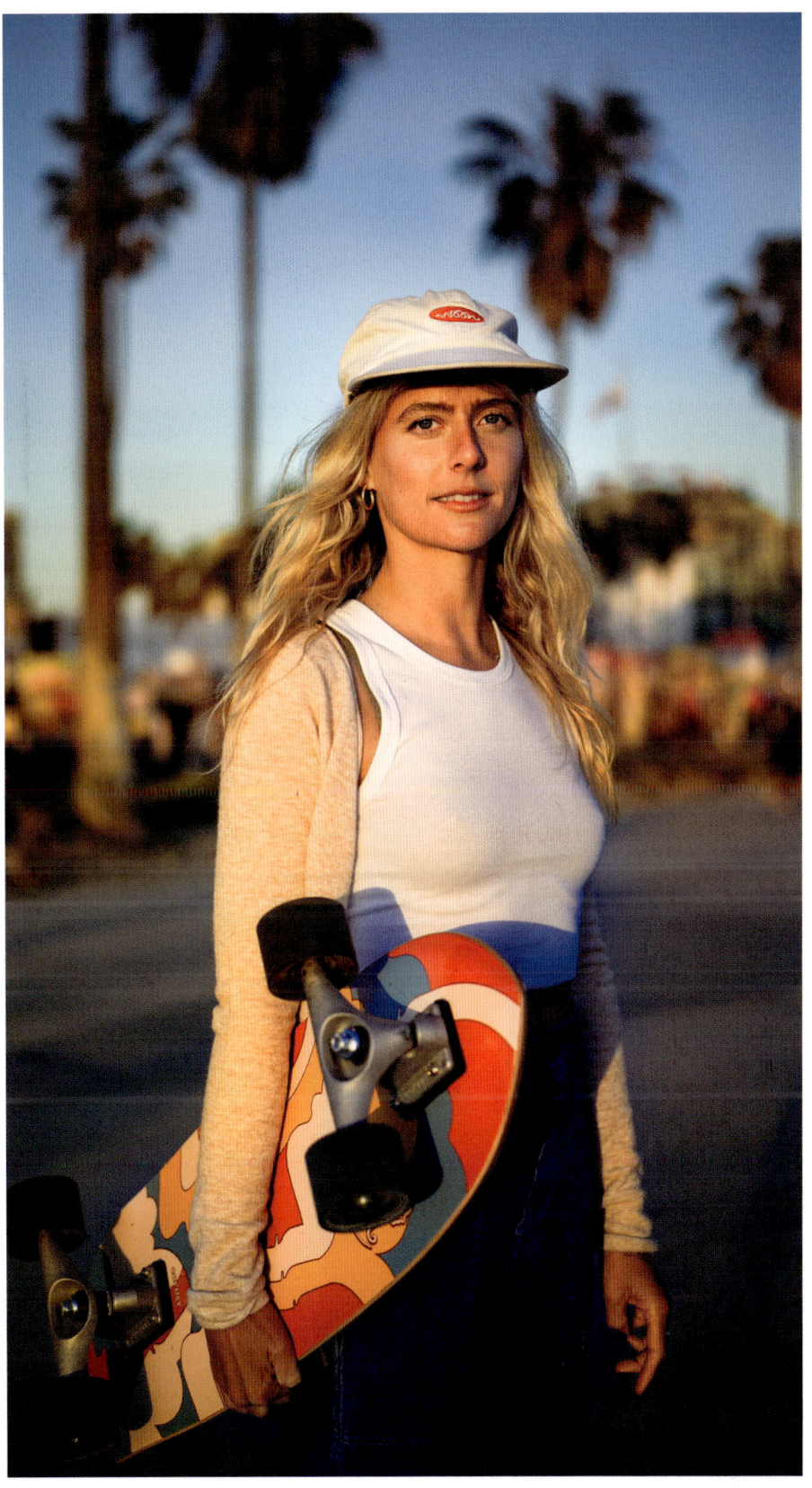

LOS ANGELES, UNITED STATES

Lucy Osinski has led a very captivating life. She began as a ballerina, then became a farmer, and later worked in the film industry while also doing a lot of surfing. However, her biggest passion is skateboarding, which eventually became the central focus of her life.

Lucy is the cofounder and CEO of a community called GRLSWIRL that empowers girls through skateboarding. What started as a small group of founding women has evolved into a global force with hundreds of thousands of online members. Through her work, Lucy aims to promote skateboarding as a way to break barriers, unite women, and enhance their lives.

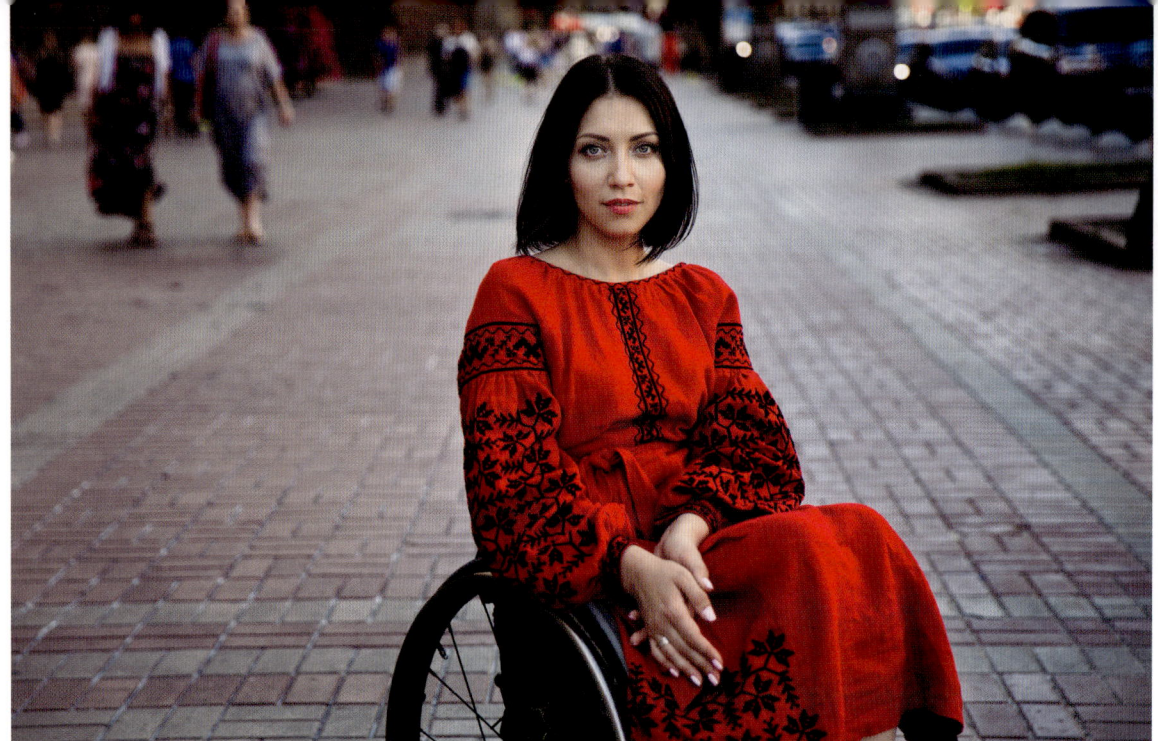

KYIV, UKRAINE

Uliana Pcholkina and her brother were raised by a single mother. Her brother was born with a disability, and Uliana herself became paralyzed at the age of twenty-one after a terrible road accident.

Uliana endured immense suffering, but she told me that her mother suffered even more. Witnessing her mother's devastation served as Uliana's motivation to gather strength and move forward.

She embarked on a new journey, becoming a Para-Karate champion and then a television presenter, which made her mother smile again. At the time when I met her, she was providing guidance to others who had recently experienced similar accidents. Unfortunately, terrible new challenges followed for Uliana.

During the early days of the war in Ukraine, she was trapped in her Bucha home, surrounded by heavy bombardments and armed attacks. Confined to her wheelchair, escape was impossible. Fortunately she survived, and today she remains strong and determined, continuing to make a difference in her homeland by assisting other people with disabilities who are grappling with the horrible consequences of war.

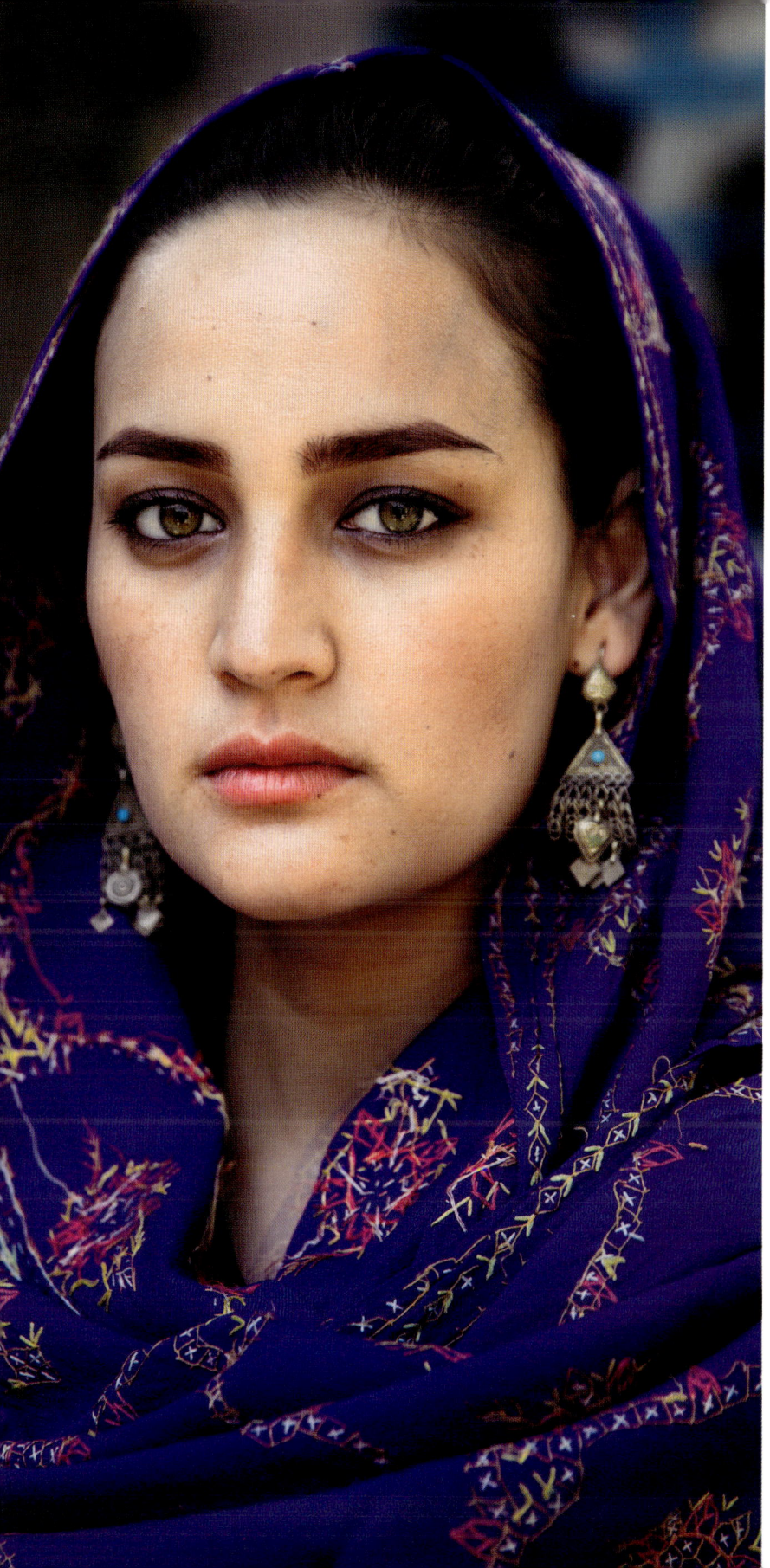

KABUL, AFGHANISTAN

I vividly recall the day I met Jamila. While photographing her, the sound of gunshots echoed in the background. I was so stressed, but she remained remarkably calm since gunshots were unfortunately a common occurrence in Kabul during that period.

Jamila grew up in a family of eight siblings and had to start working at an early age to support her loved ones. At the time we met, she was working in an office and enduring a two-hour commute each way every day. However, her true passion was acting. She participated in various projects, including independent films and photo shoots, whenever she had the chance.

A few weeks after our meeting, Kabul and the rest of Afghanistan fell under the control of the Taliban. From that moment, almost all Afghan women found themselves in a desperate situation—but for Jamila, an ethnic Hazara with an artistic background, the danger was even greater. Fortunately, Jamila managed to escape the country by first fleeing to Pakistan and then traveling to Bangladesh. Her escape alone could be the subject of a separate story.

After arriving in Bangladesh, Jamila tirelessly searched for ways to fulfill her dream and pursue an acting career. Recently, she received her letter of acceptance to a foundation acting course at the prestigious Juilliard School.

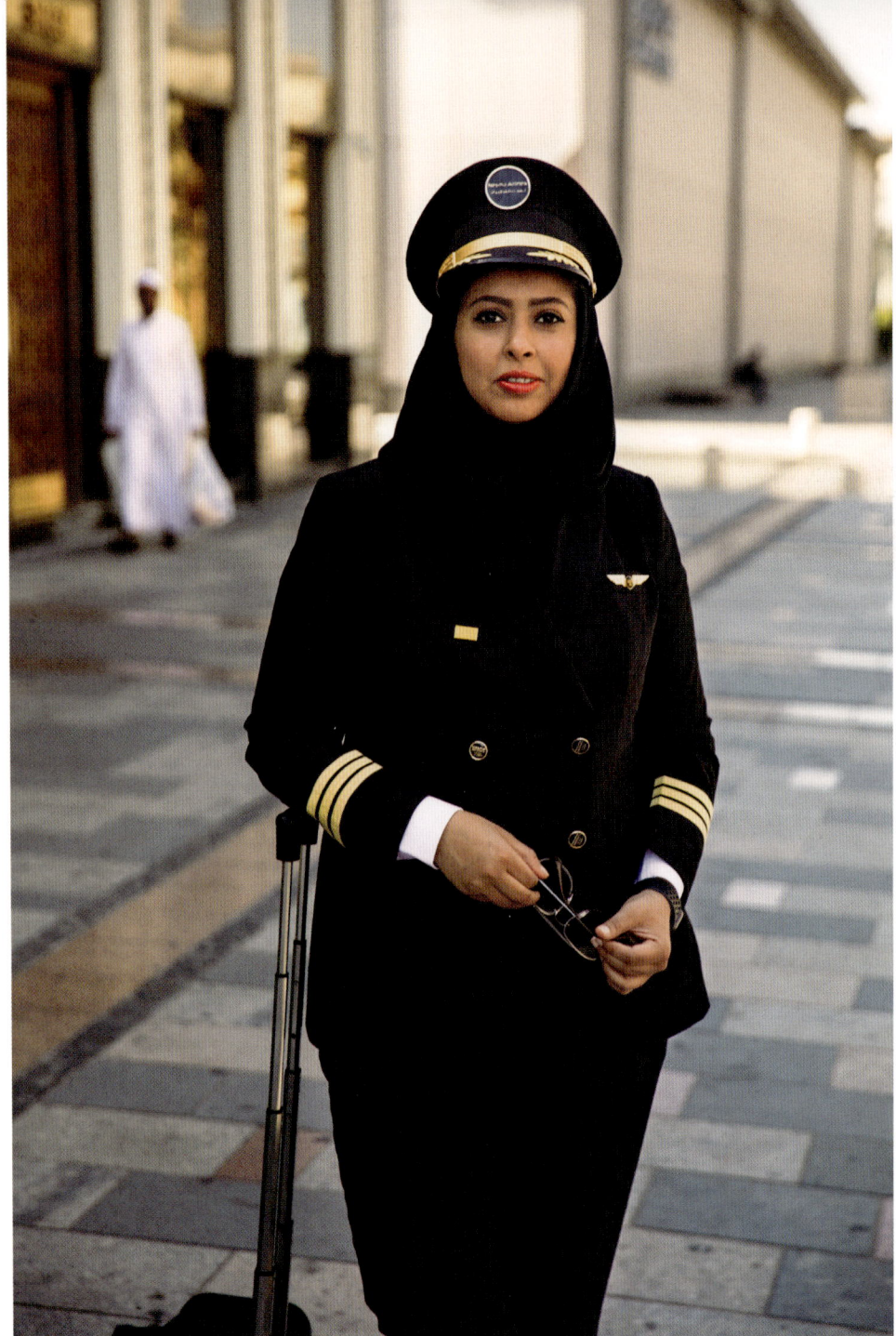

JEDDAH, SAUDI ARABIA

Yasmeen Al Maimani is the first woman in Saudi Arabia to become a commercial airline pilot. In a country where women were not even allowed to drive cars a few years ago, Yasmeen dared to dream big. She trained rigorously for years and patiently awaited an opportunity— something that seemed impossible at the time. When Saudi Arabia's policies shifted and opened doors for women in aviation, Yasmeen was ready to fulfill her dream. After her first flight as a pilot, tears of happiness flowed down her face.

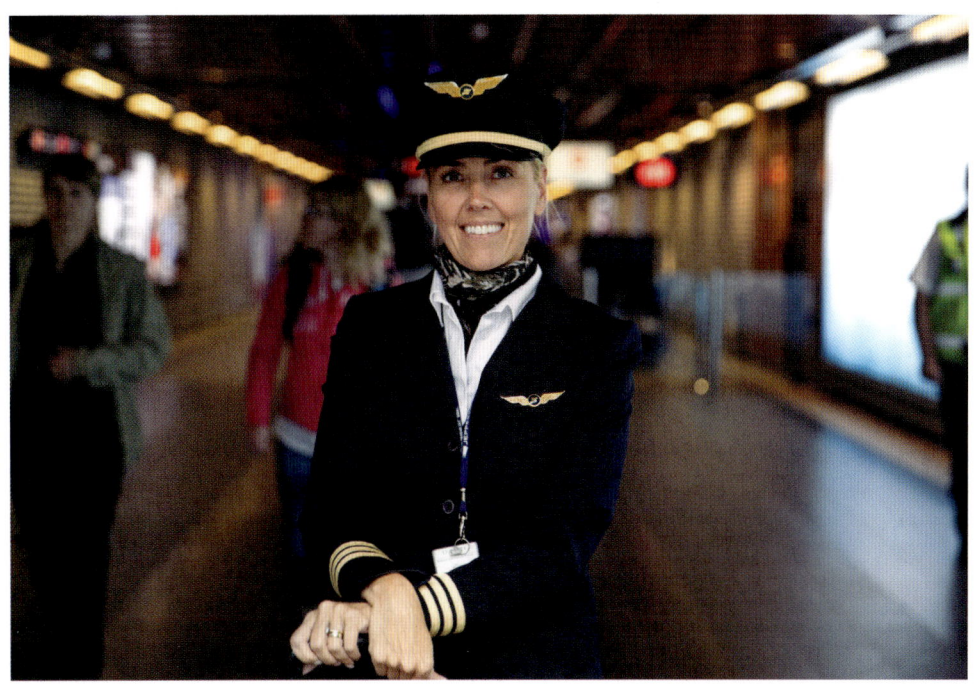

REYKJAVÍK, ICELAND

Laufey, an experienced pilot, was returning from a long trip when I noticed her in the airport.

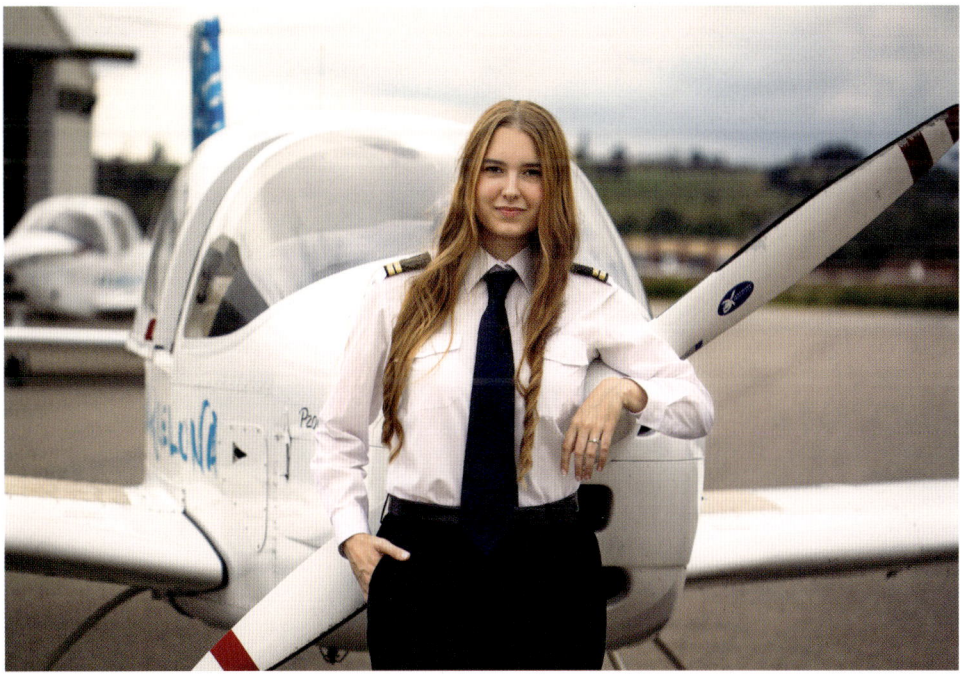

BARCELONA, SPAIN

When I met her, Gemma was training intensively to become a pilot. It's great to see more and more women pilots all over the world.

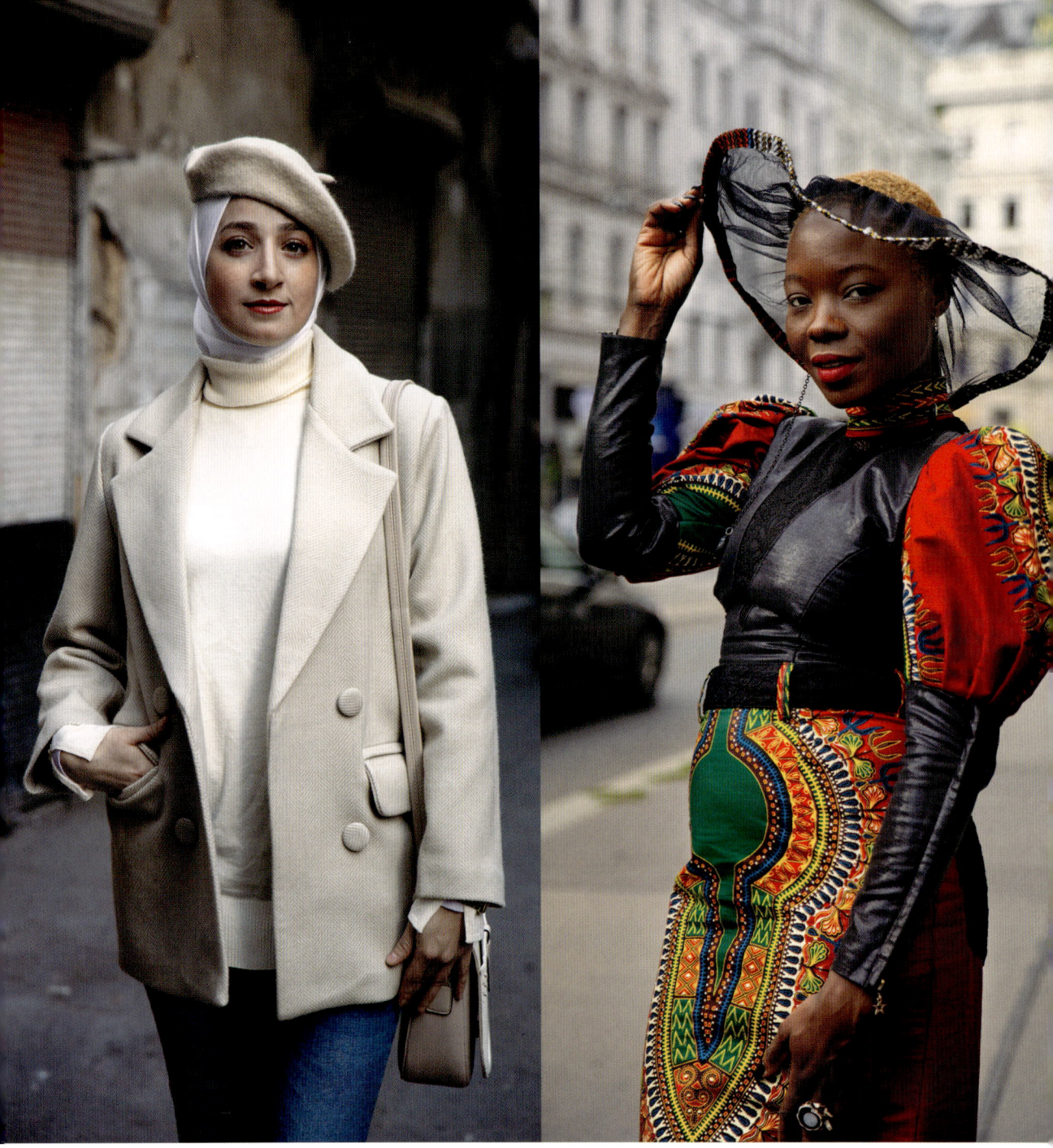

DAMASCUS, SYRIA

Fatema is a surgeon.

VIENNA, AUSTRIA

Barbara is a fashion designer and entrepreneur.

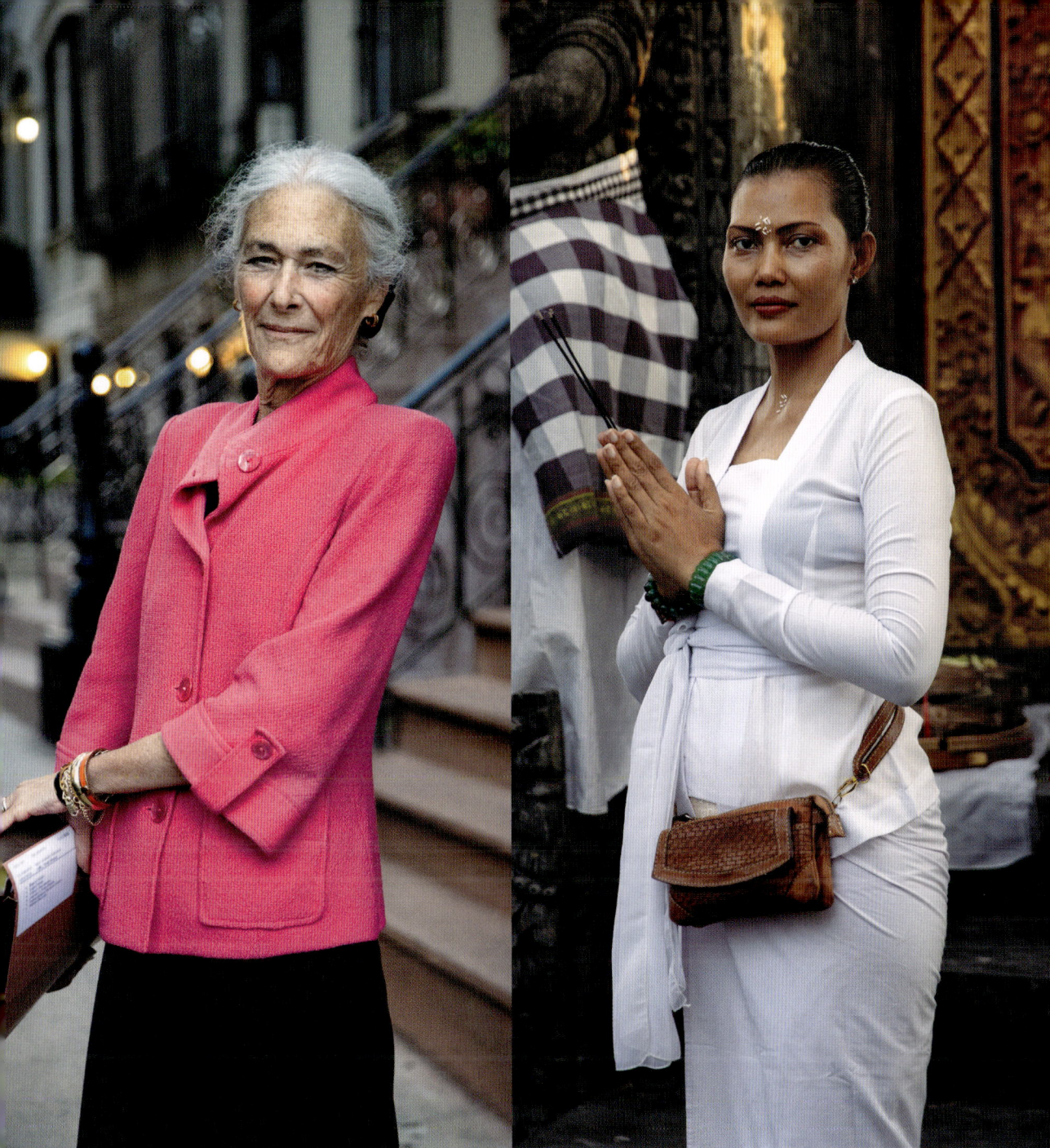

NEW YORK CITY, UNITED STATES

Virginia is a lawyer.

BALI, INDONESIA

Nilawati is a Hindu priestess.

BUCHAREST, ROMANIA

Oana's story is a long and painful journey from darkness to light.

It was a Friday in 2015. That terrible day started for Oana Rotariu like any other Friday. She went to work and, later, to dinner with her fiancé. They decided to go to a club for a concert and were enjoying the performance until the tragedy unfolded.

At 10:32 p.m., a fire broke out in the club. With around four hundred people inside, panic ensued as everyone rushed toward the one tiny exit. In the chaos, many fell, and the exit quickly became blocked. Those who made it outside started helping others escape. Oana and her fiancé were far from the exit, and the fire was rapidly spreading. Her fiancé shielded her with his body. Somehow, they managed to escape the building, but not without life-threatening injuries.

The tragic fire claimed the lives of sixty-four people and left one hundred and fifty injured. Many of them—including Oana's fiancé—are remembered as real heroes who selflessly saved lives by sacrificing their own.

Oana was in a coma for forty days with very slim chances of survival. Miraculously, she defied the odds and awoke from the coma—only to learn that her fiancé passed away and that her recovery would be a difficult and uncertain one. She still had a huge motivation to fight for her life: the two loving parents by her side who were determined to save their only child no matter what.

Oana embarked on a long journey of rehabilitation in hospitals. She underwent many surgeries, but her progress astounded the doctors. After two years of immense struggle, she began to see a glimmer of light at the end of the tunnel.

Oana had to relearn basic motor skills before she could reintegrate into society. Every day presented new challenges, but in her new life, she discovered that even the impossible was possible. Today, she works as an IT business analyst and loves to travel. She blogs about her experiences and inspires others to embrace their own beauty despite any imperfections.

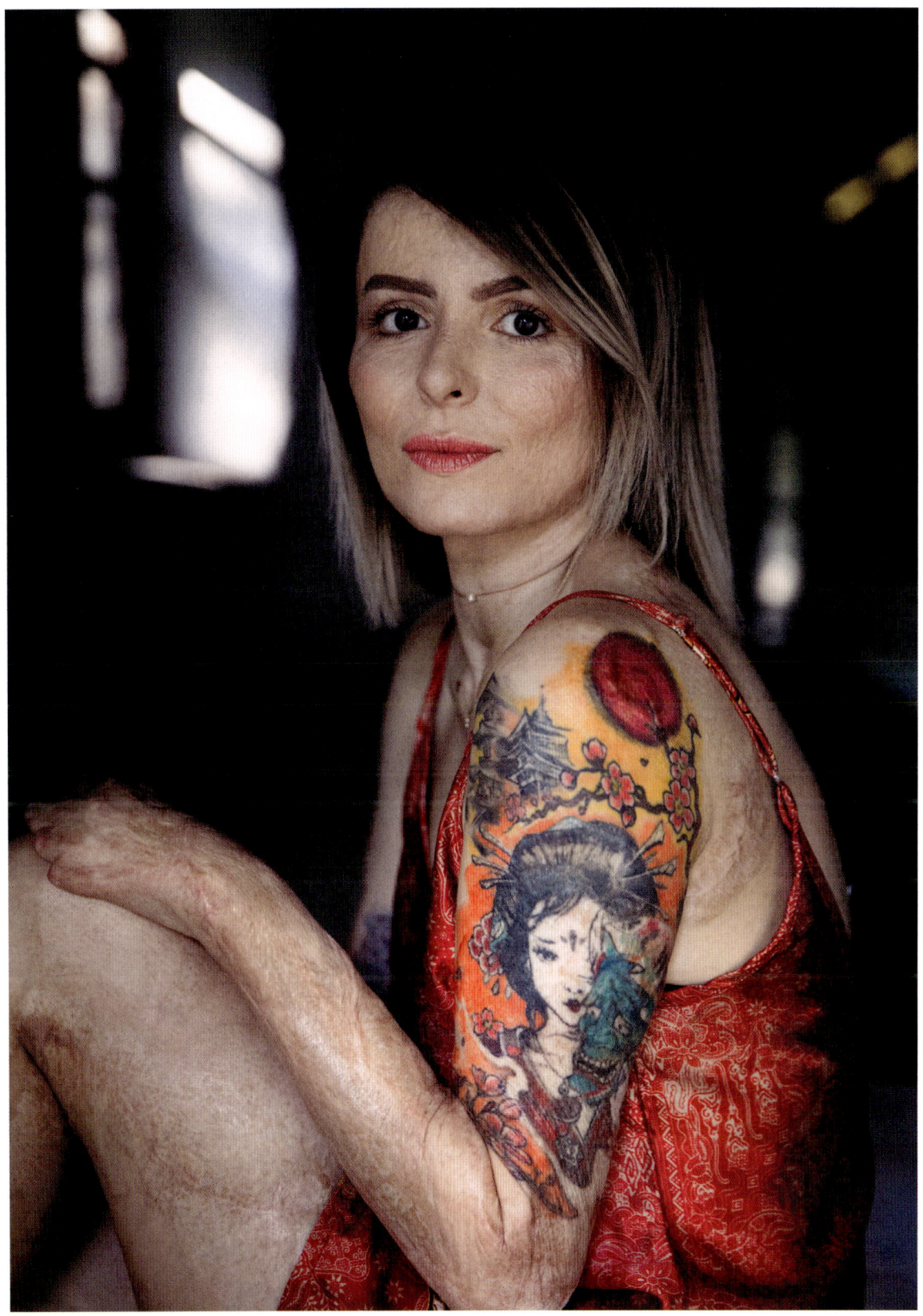

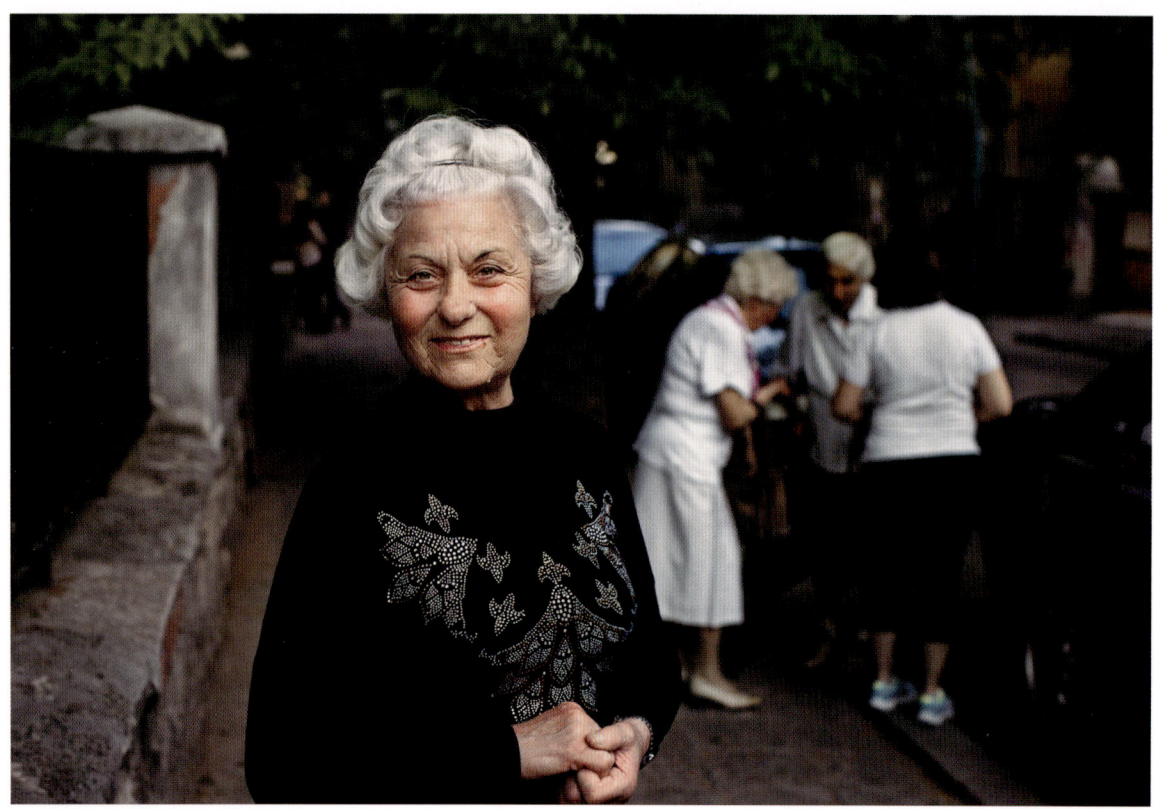

PLOVDIV, BULGARIA (Above)

Margarita taught violin for most of her life. Music gave her the strength to carry on after terrible nightmares, like when she lost her husband and only child.

After she retired, she had to find a new way to bring music into her life. She started teaching free private violin lessons to her neighbors. You can see a few of them behind Margarita in this photo. They were all out for a concert that day.

BEIRUT, LEBANON (Opposite)

I spotted one lone woman fishing among a group of men, and I had to find out her story. Shuruq is retired, and fishing actually makes a difference for her. It especially did so during those days when Lebanon was affected by a terrible economic crisis.

Even so, more than anything, fishing is and has always been a hobby for Shuruq. She likes to be alone with her fishing rod, to feel the breeze and hear the waves, while enjoying a cigarette. She watches the sunset, then heads home to share the fish with her cats. It's the simple pleasures that can make a difference during difficult times.

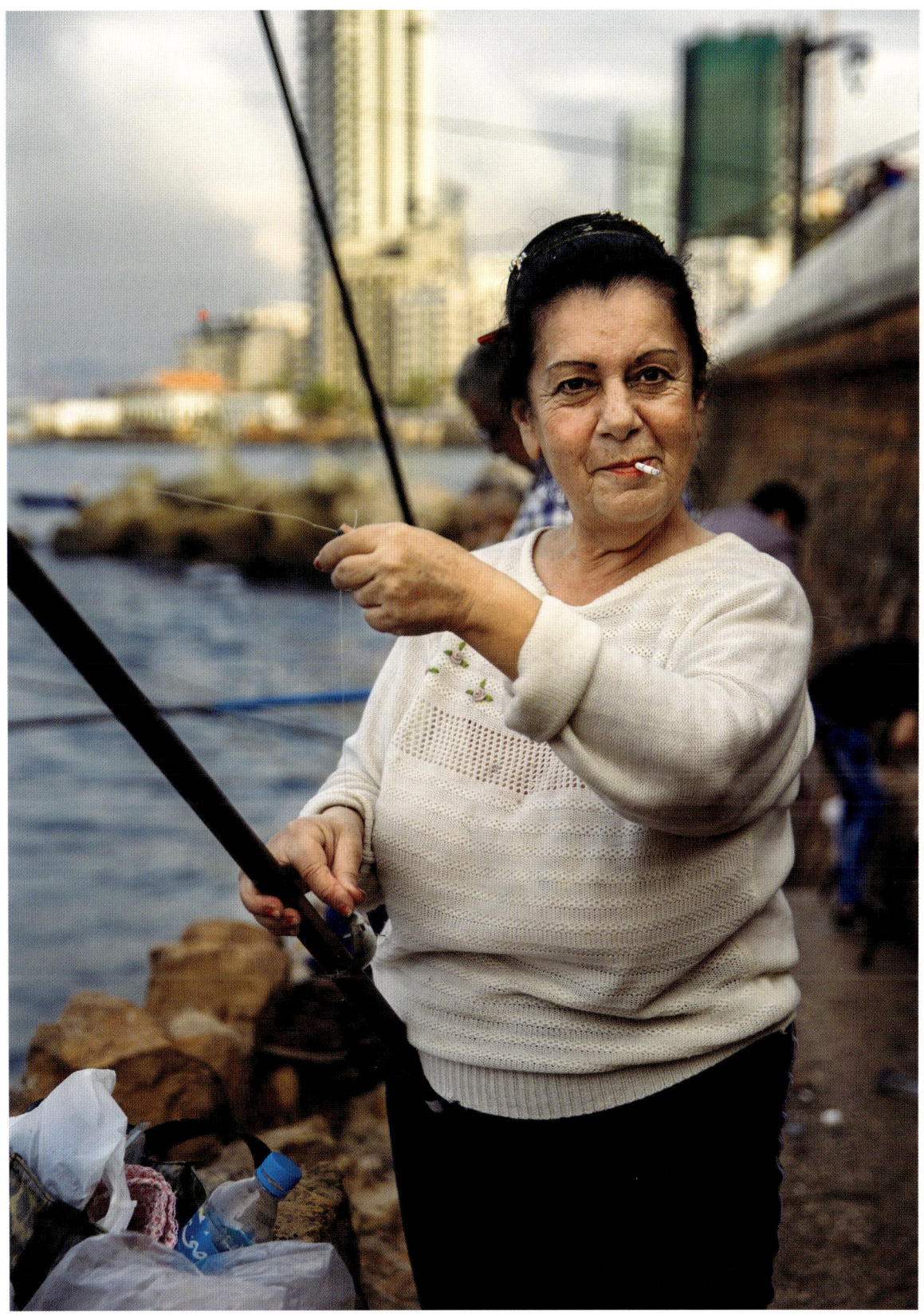

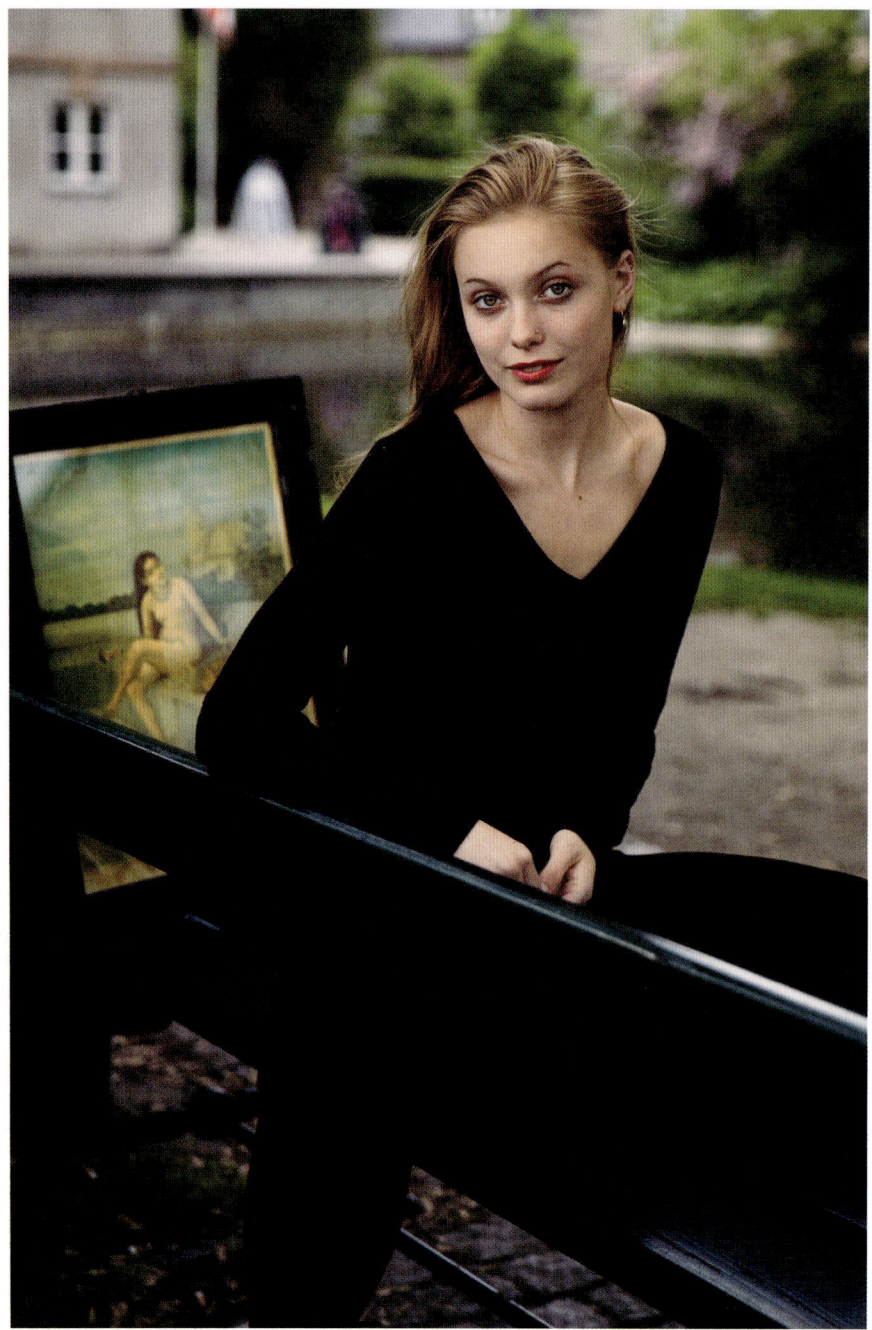

COPENHAGEN, DENMARK

When I met Laura at a flea market, she was buying a painting. I noticed a resemblance between her and the enigmatic woman in the painting, and I wanted to capture the moment and find out more.

Laura told me that, over the years, she's been through many health struggles, and art was always her best therapy.

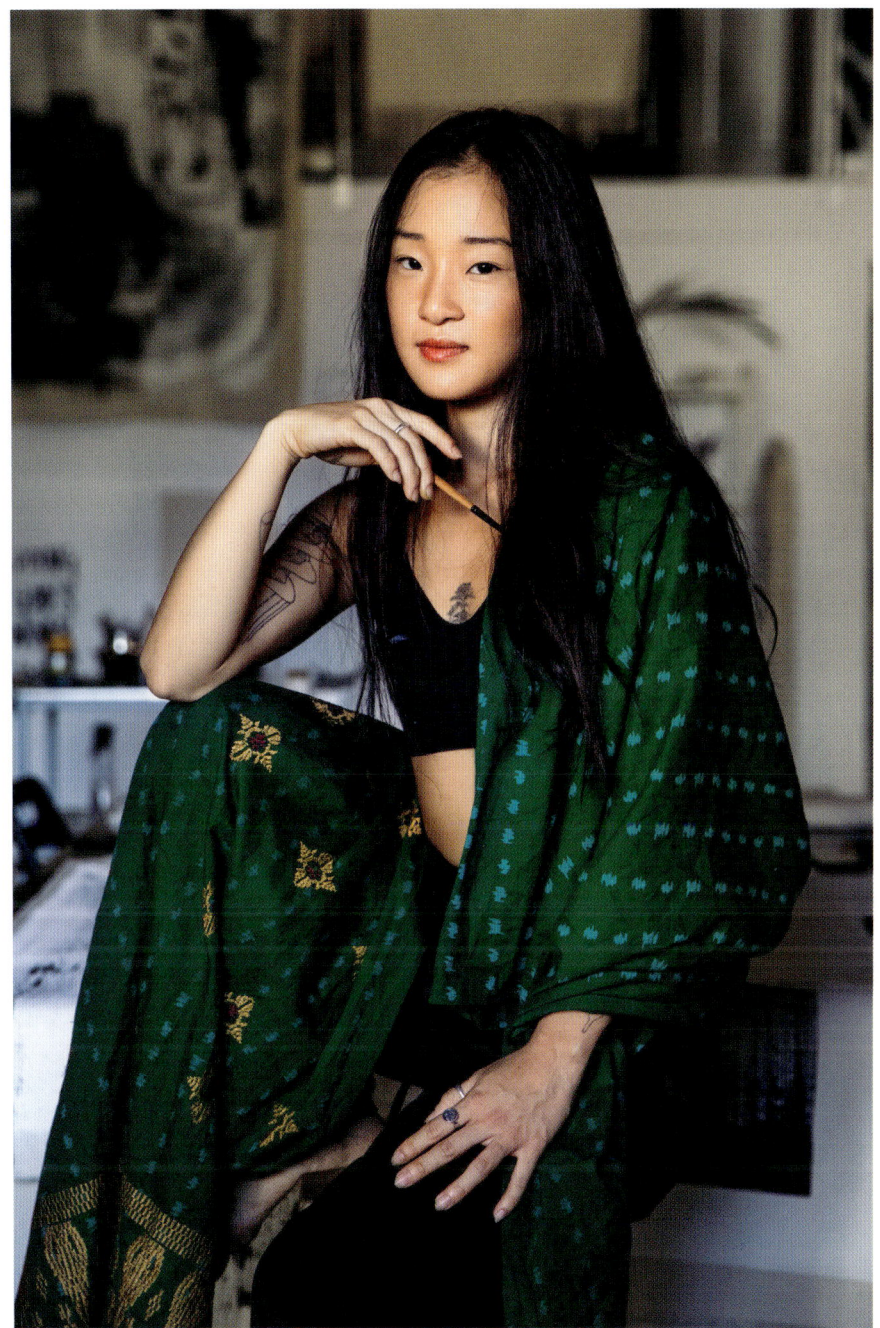

TORONTO, CANADA

Born in South Korea, Dahae moved to Canada with her family when she was eleven. Her parents made efforts to send her to prestigious schools and were convinced of the path she needed to take to secure her future. But Dahae is a free spirit and had different plans. She followed her calling and became a respected interdisciplinary artist or—as she likes to call it—a visual philosopher.

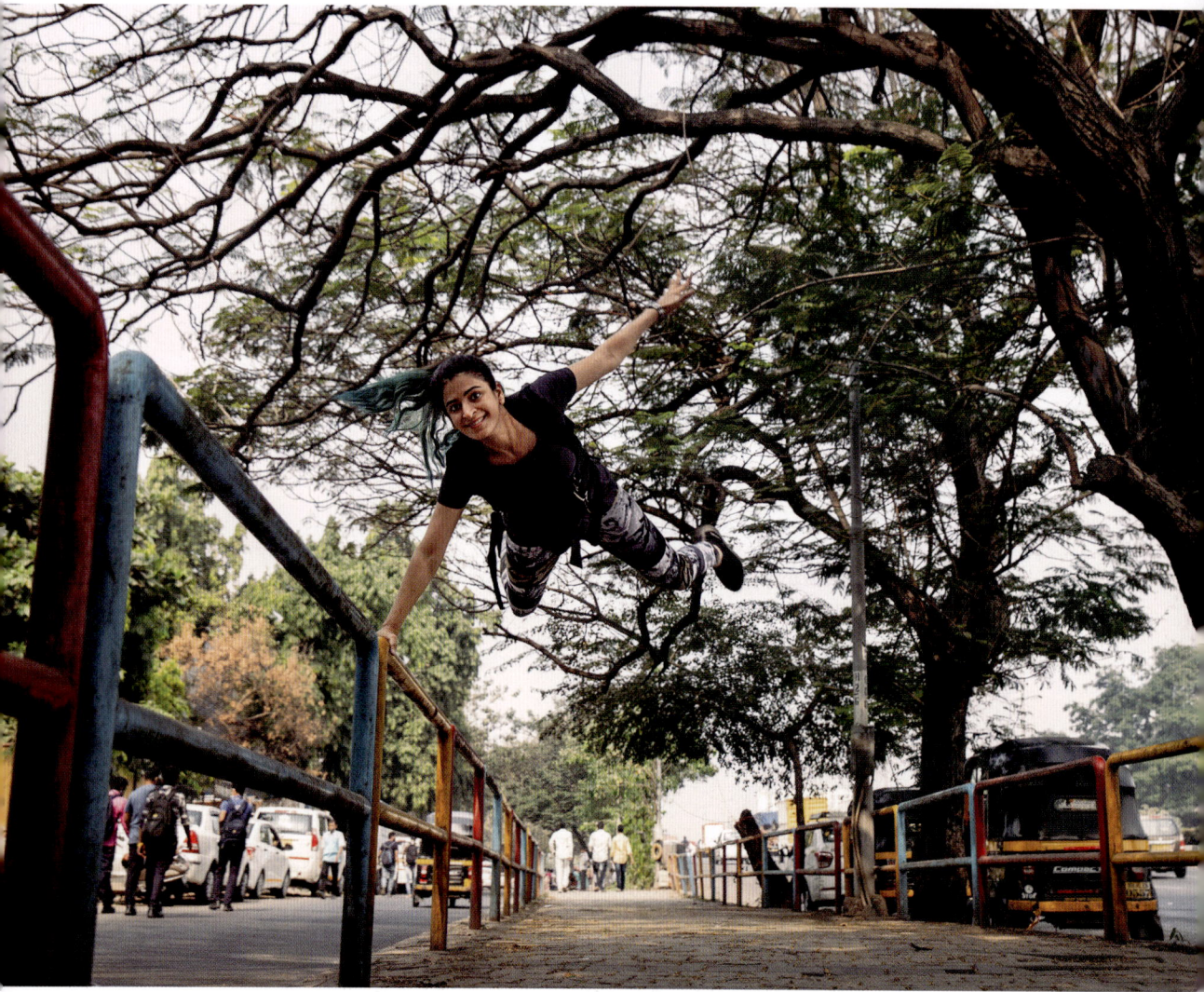

MUMBAI, INDIA

Sanober Pardiwalla is a professional stuntwoman. During adolescence, she was already a gymnast, an excellent swimmer, and a black belt in karate, and she had started to perform her first stunts for movies. In the following two decades, she had the chance to be a stunt double for some of the greatest Bollywood actresses.

When she started her journey in the Indian film industry, the concept of a stuntwoman didn't exist—there were only stuntmen. But Sanober has worked in more than two hundred movies, jumping off high cliffs, making spectacular dives under the water, simulating car and motorcycle crashes, and defying all challenges inside movie sets—and outside them.

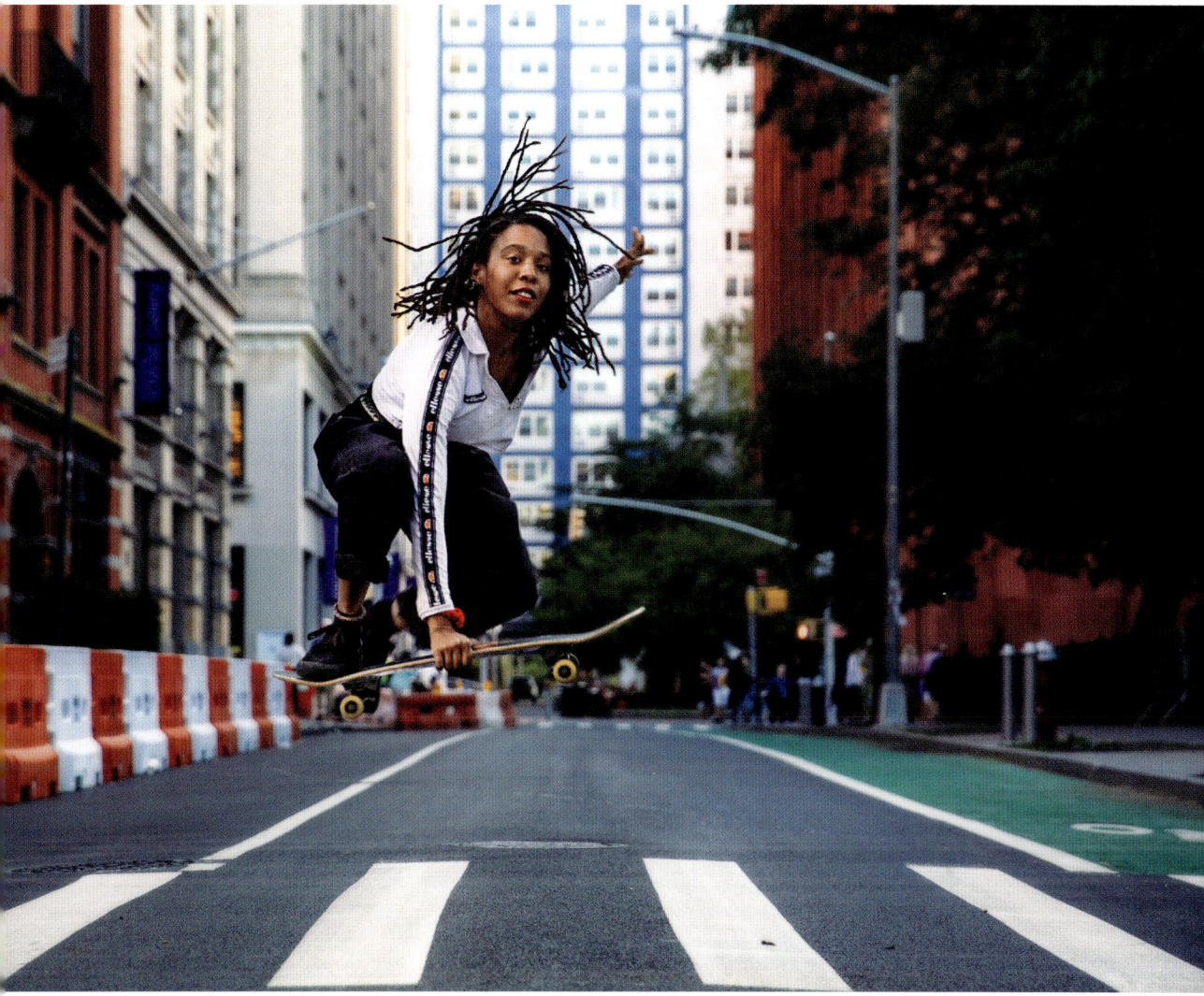

NEW YORK CITY, UNITED STATES

For Kava Garcia Vasquez, skateboarding is not just an entertaining activity and a means of transport. More than anything, it is a means for change.

After university, through a one-year grant, she traveled the world and conducted comprehensive research about how women around the globe are empowered through skating.

When she returned home, Kava used her knowledge to cofound a community called Bronx Girls Skate to celebrate and grow women's skateboarding—not just in the Bronx but way beyond.

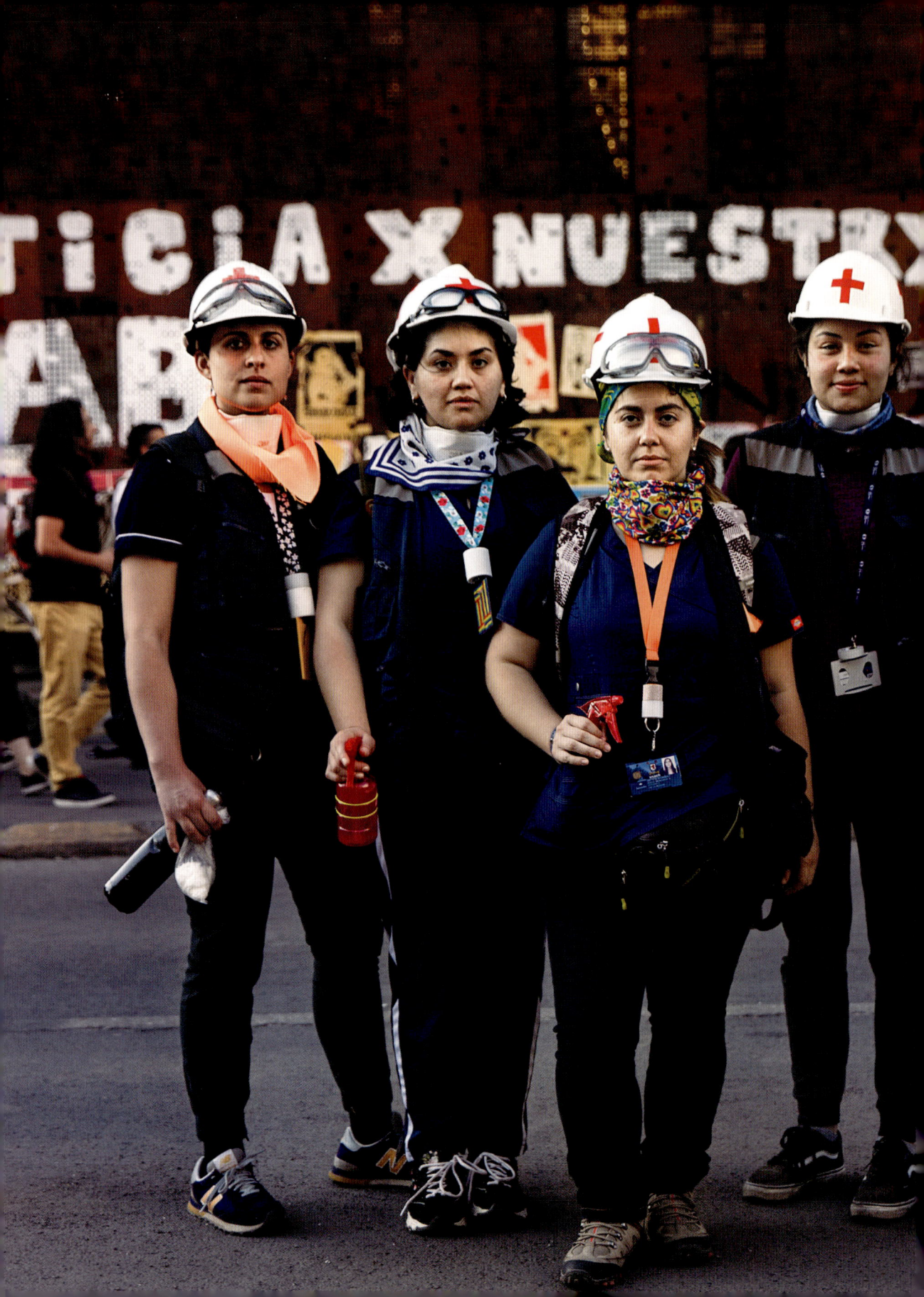

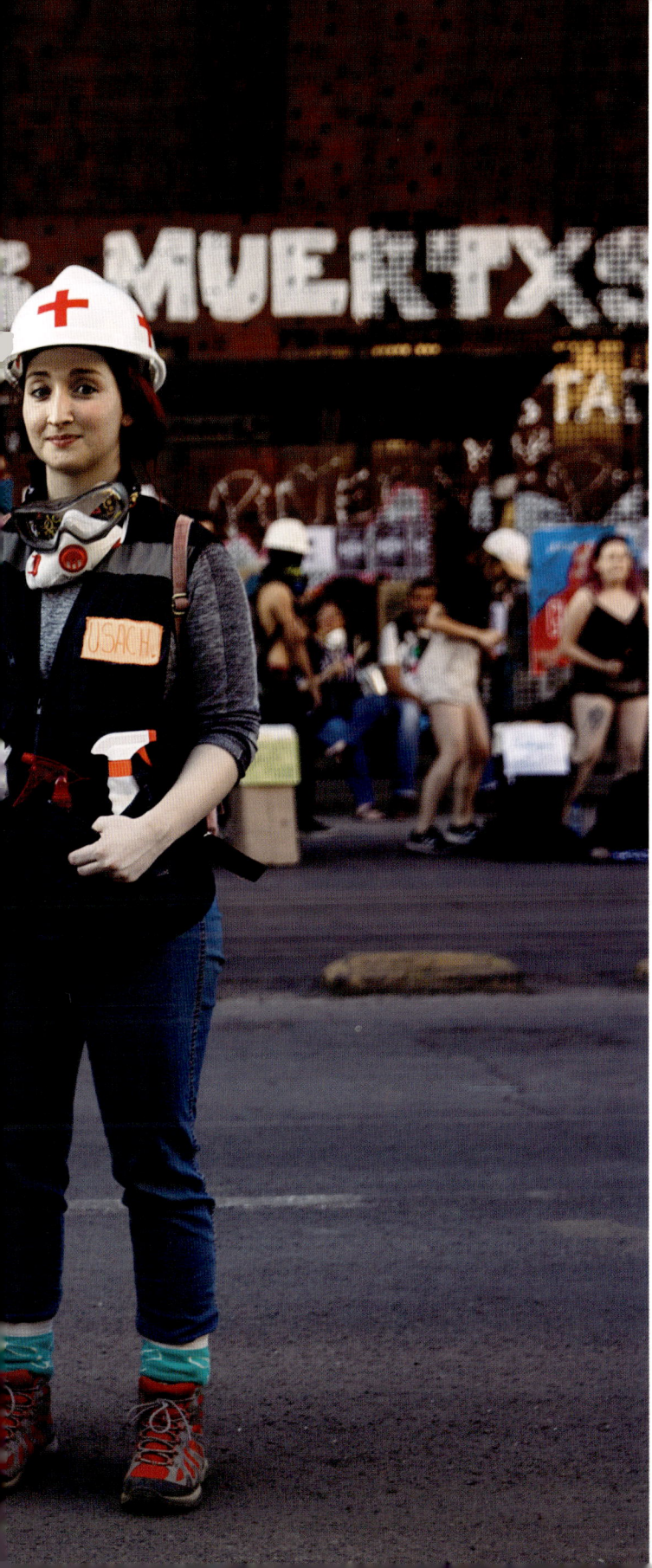

SANTIAGO, CHILE

In 2019, I spent two weeks in Chile's capital, witnessing episodes of the country's worst civil unrest in thirty years. What started as a small demonstration against the rise in public transport fares transformed into a huge wave of protests against poverty and inequality.

Many people died during the unrest, and tens of thousands were injured around the country. Many were shot by police pellet guns and lost their eyes. In the middle of these clashes between protesters and police were groups of volunteers, medically trained, who were risking everything to help those in need. They were saving lives and eyes.

Amanda, Javiera, Rocio, Maria José, and Francesca were all medical students on a dangerous mission since the beginning of the protests. They were witnessing incredible violence, but they were fearless. No wonder people started to applaud them when I took this photo. Even in the darkest moments, real beauty shines.

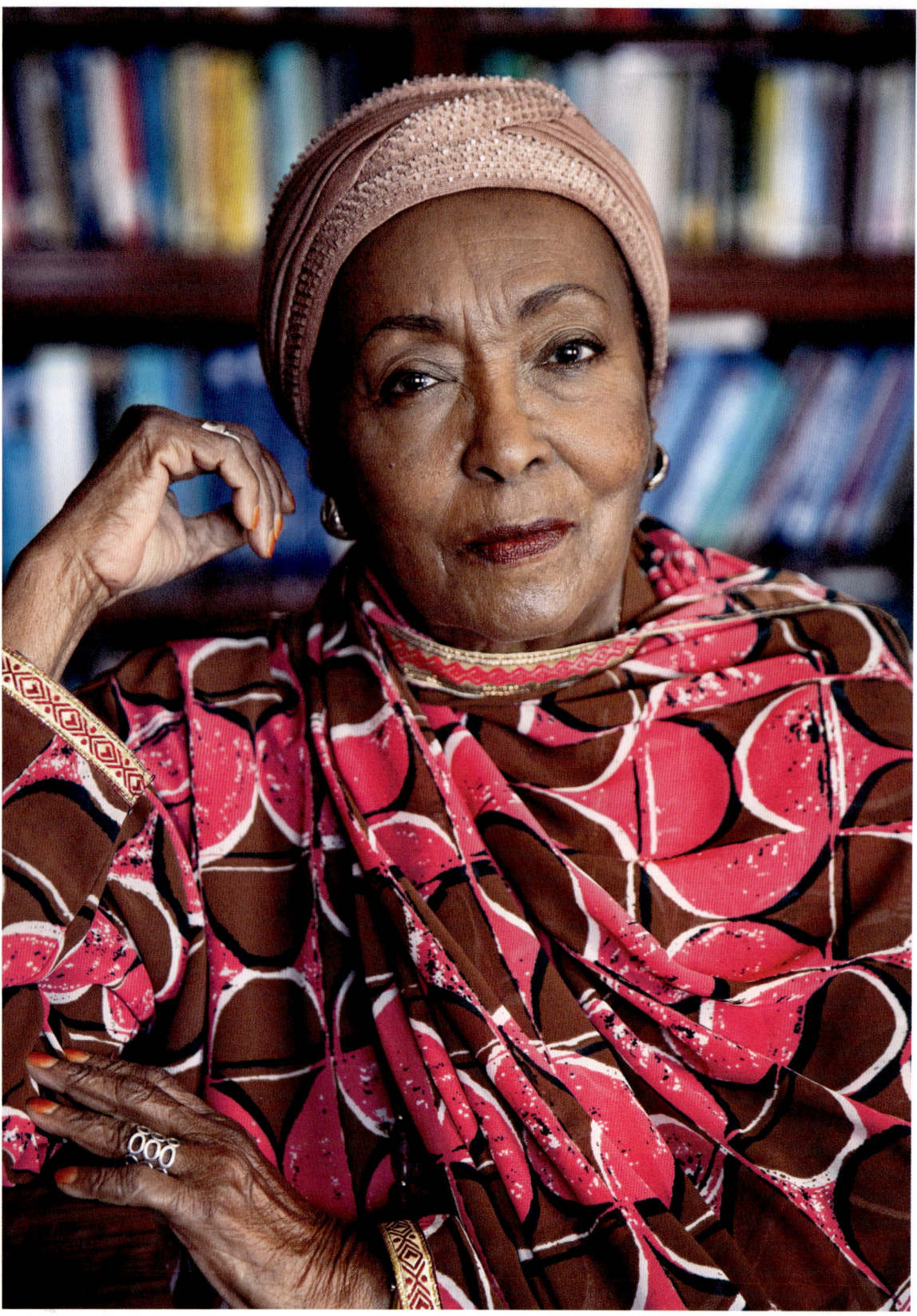

HARGEISA, SOMALILAND

Edna Adan Ismail is an activist and pioneer in the struggle for the abolition of female genital mutilation (FGM). FGM is a widespread practice in many parts of the world and involves the cutting or removal of the external female genitalia. Right now, there are more than two hundred million women from thirty countries who have been subjected to one or more types of FGM.

FGM is typically carried out on girls before they reach puberty, ranging from infancy to adolescence. It is usually initiated and carried out by women, who see it as a source of honor and who fear that failing to have their daughters and granddaughters cut will expose the girls to social exclusion.

Edna herself experienced the trauma of FGM. Her father was an eminent doctor who totally opposed the practice. When Edna was eight years old and her father was on a business trip, her mother and grandmother arranged the procedure, fearing that the little girl would be stigmatized and considered unfit for marriage later.

The consequences of FGM can range from immediate complications, such as severe pain, bleeding, infections, and even death, to long-term health issues, including chronic pain, urinary problems, childbirth complications, and psychological trauma. Wanting to prevent other women from undergoing the same trauma she did, Edna trained as a nurse and midwife in the United Kingdom. Afterward she returned to her country, where she worked relentlessly to eradicate the practice.

For decades, Edna has been actively educating communities, conducting awareness campaigns, and providing support and resources to those affected by FGM. She established a maternity hospital that offers essential maternal and child health-care services free of charge, saving thousands of lives.

At eighty-five years old, Edna resides in the hospital, devoting every moment of her life to supporting those in need. It was there where I had the honor of photographing her and expressing two heartfelt words: "Thank you!" Thank you, Edna, for making this world a better place.

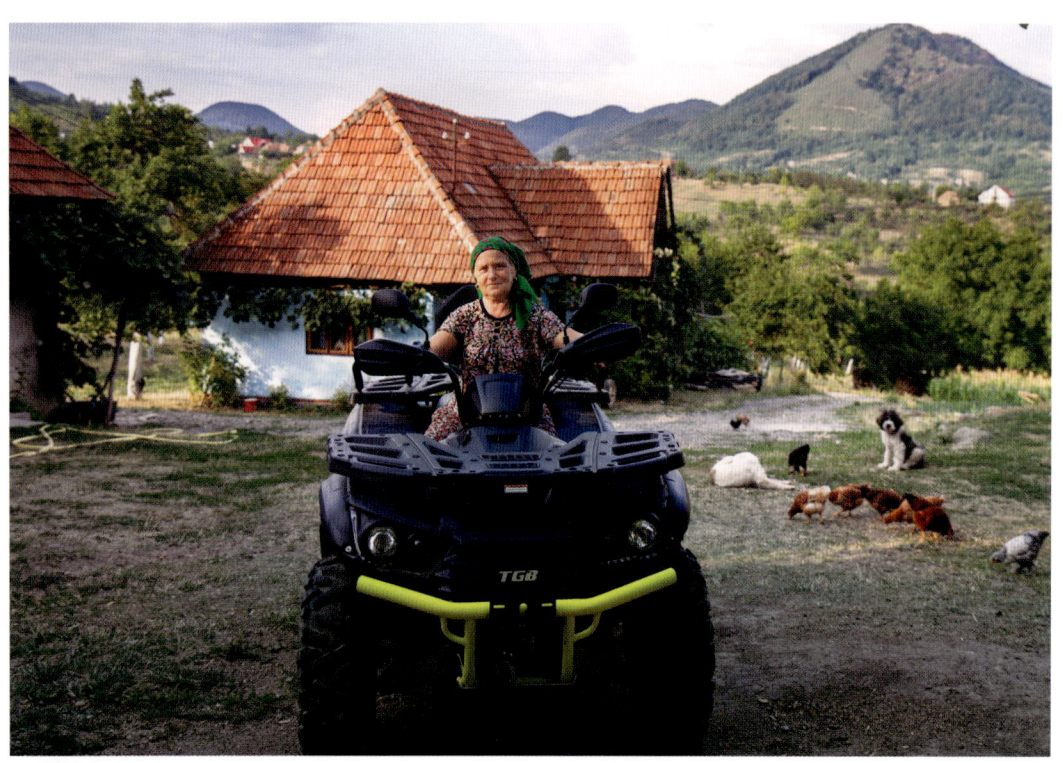

SATU MARE COUNTY, ROMANIA

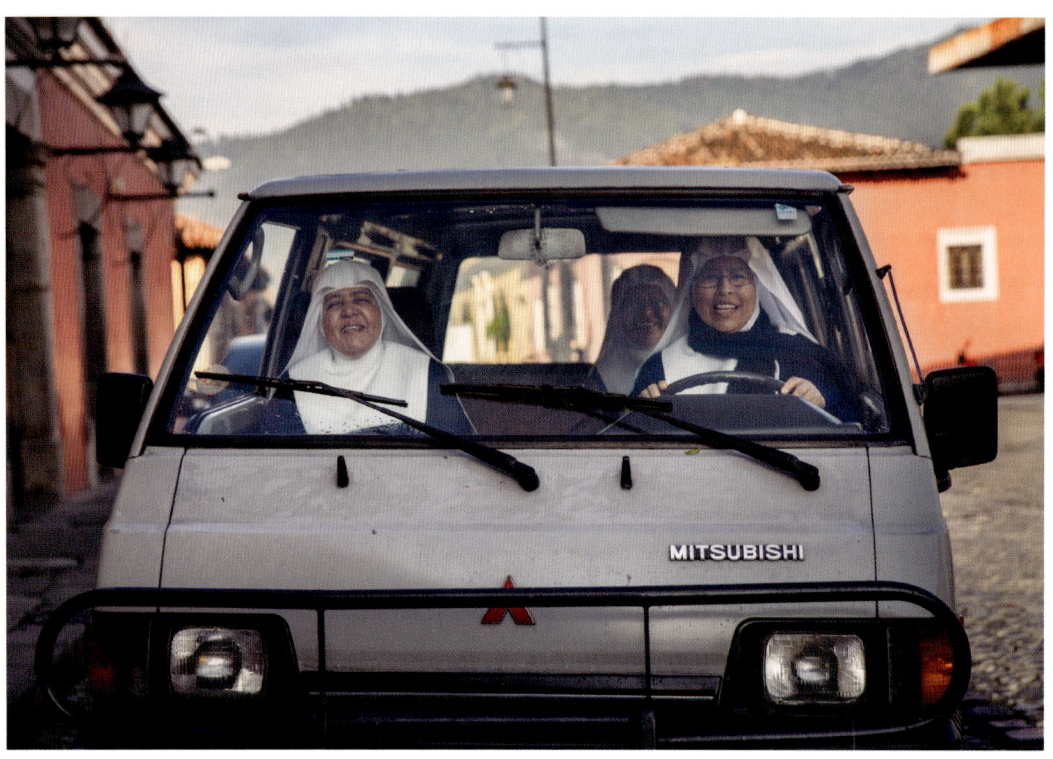

ANTIGUA, GUATEMALA

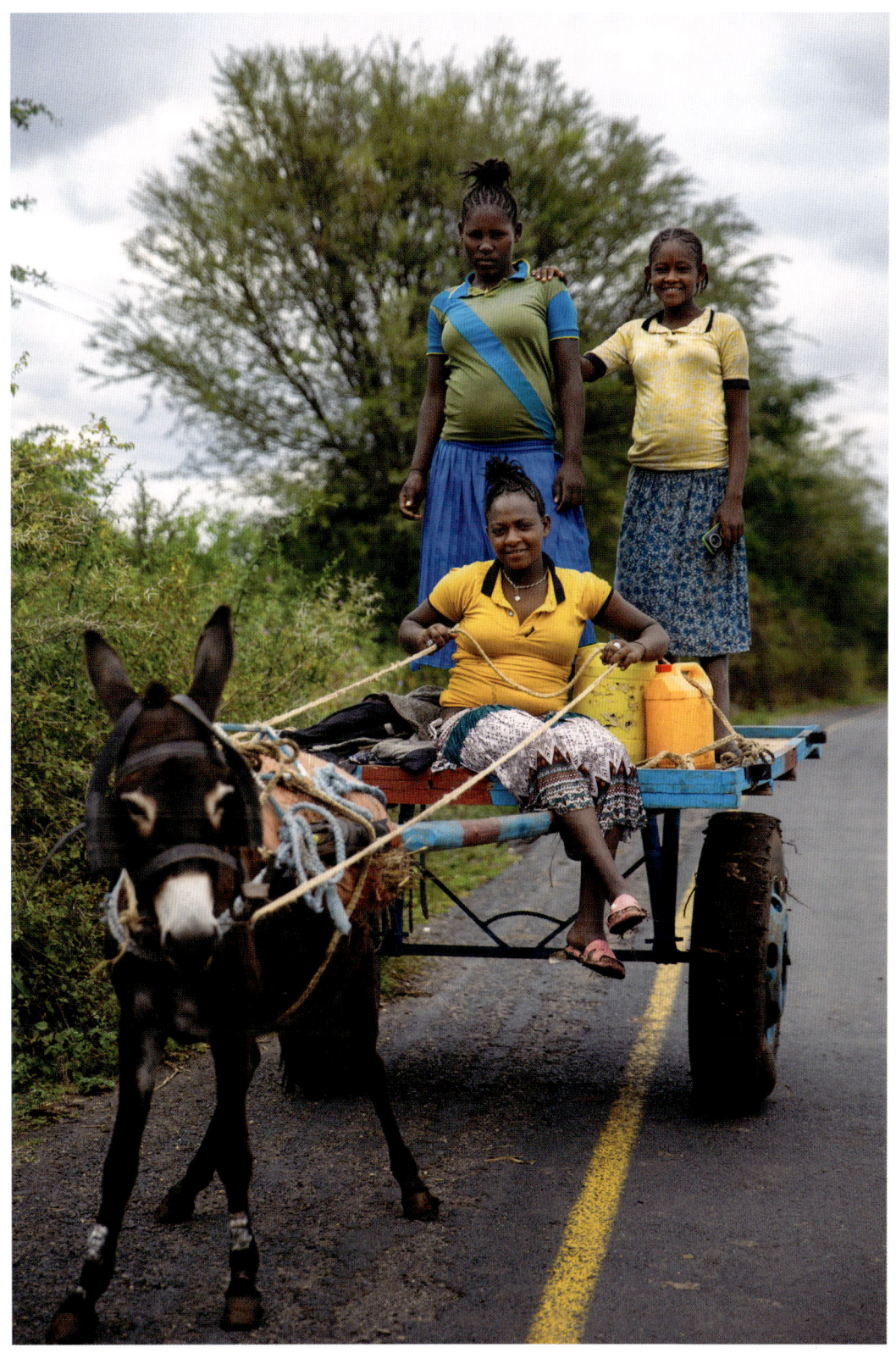

CENTRAL ETHIOPIA

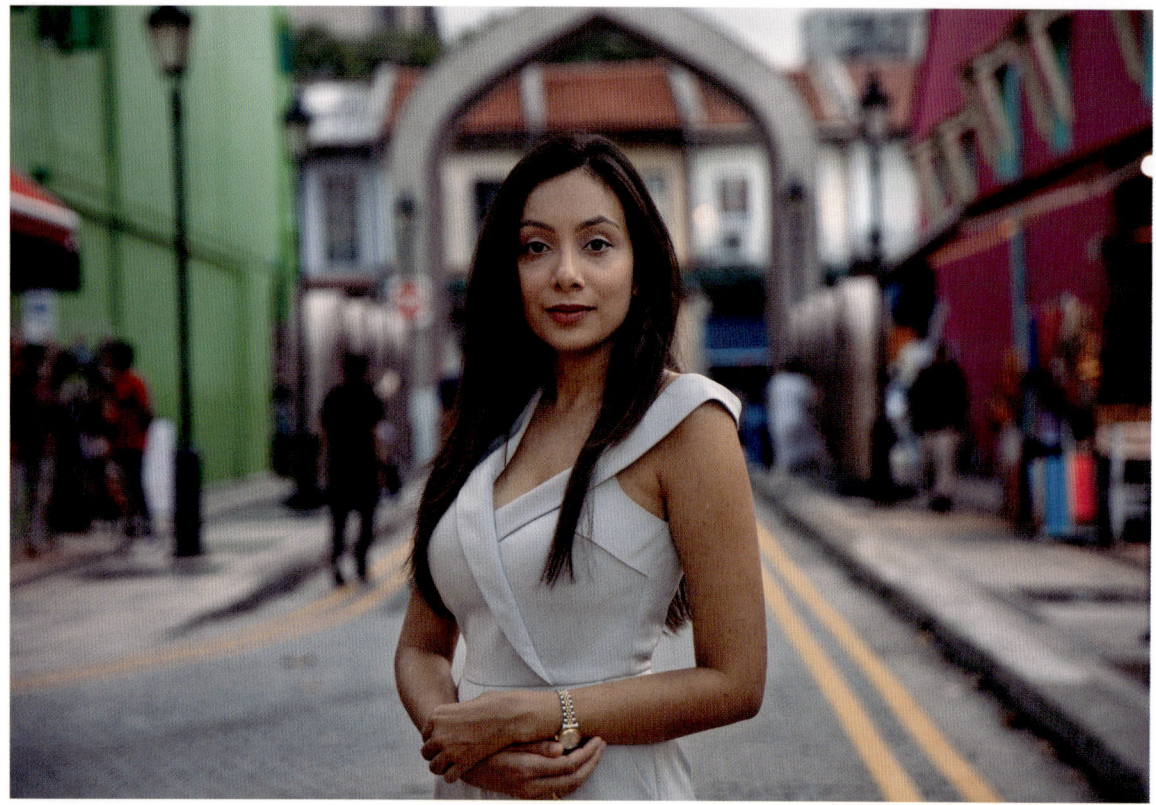

SINGAPORE

Shivangi Bagri is the founder of TruCup, a company that produces menstrual cups. In many parts of the world, women cannot afford to purchase tampons or menstrual pads. The menstrual cups produced by Shivangi's company can provide them with a more affordable and sustainable alternative. Beyond that, menstrual cups are better for women's health and for the environment.

Shivangi shared with me heartbreaking stories about young girls who are forced to miss school due to lack of access to menstrual products. Or women who need to use dangerous alternatives like ash to protect themselves during their menstrual bleeding.

Despite walking on a path filled with taboos and constantly encountering reluctance to adopt this revolutionary solution, Shivangi is determined to educate and empower women around the world about the benefits of menstrual cups. She's donated tens of thousands of menstrual cups to communities in need, empowering thousands of women and changing the world one cup at a time.

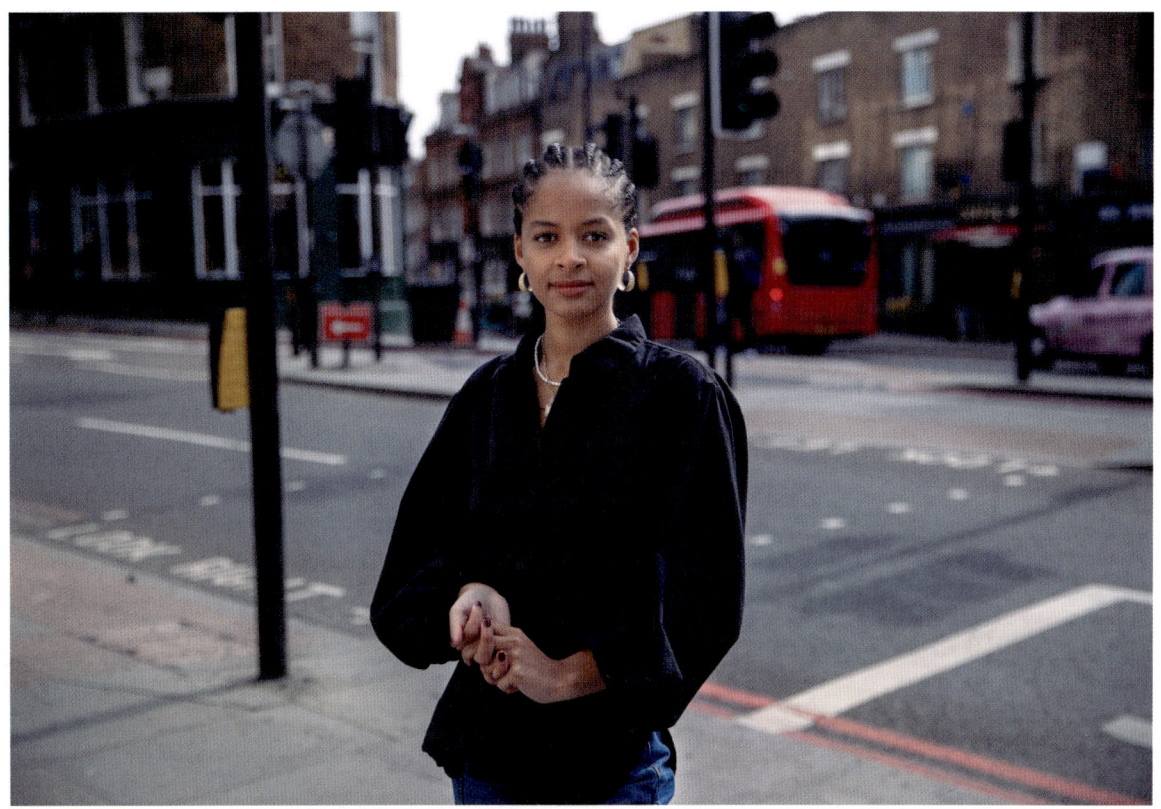

LONDON, UNITED KINGDOM

Josephine Philips is a young entrepreneur with a vision for the future. She successfully launched a business straight out of university that was sparked by her interest in sustainable clothing and her studies in physics and philosophy.

Determined to move away from fast fashion, Josephine embraced secondhand clothes. However, she encountered a challenge: finding specific sizes for these unique items.

This challenge inspired her to create an app called SOJO, which connects customers with local seamstresses. Through a bicycle delivery service, clients' clothes are sent to local seamstresses for alterations and repairs before being returned. It's like food delivery, but for clothing repairs. Her business is amazing but also practical and sustainable from front to back.

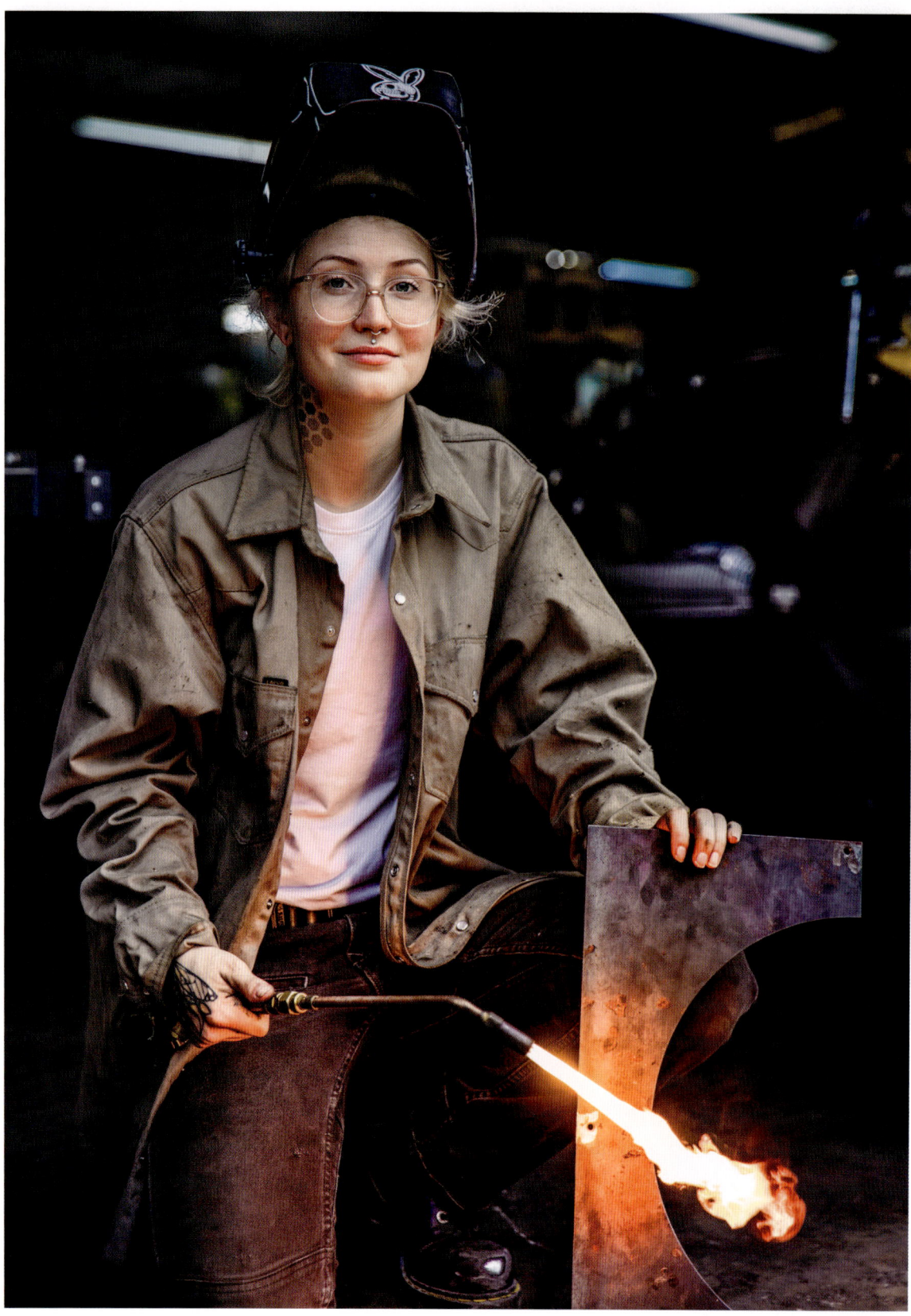

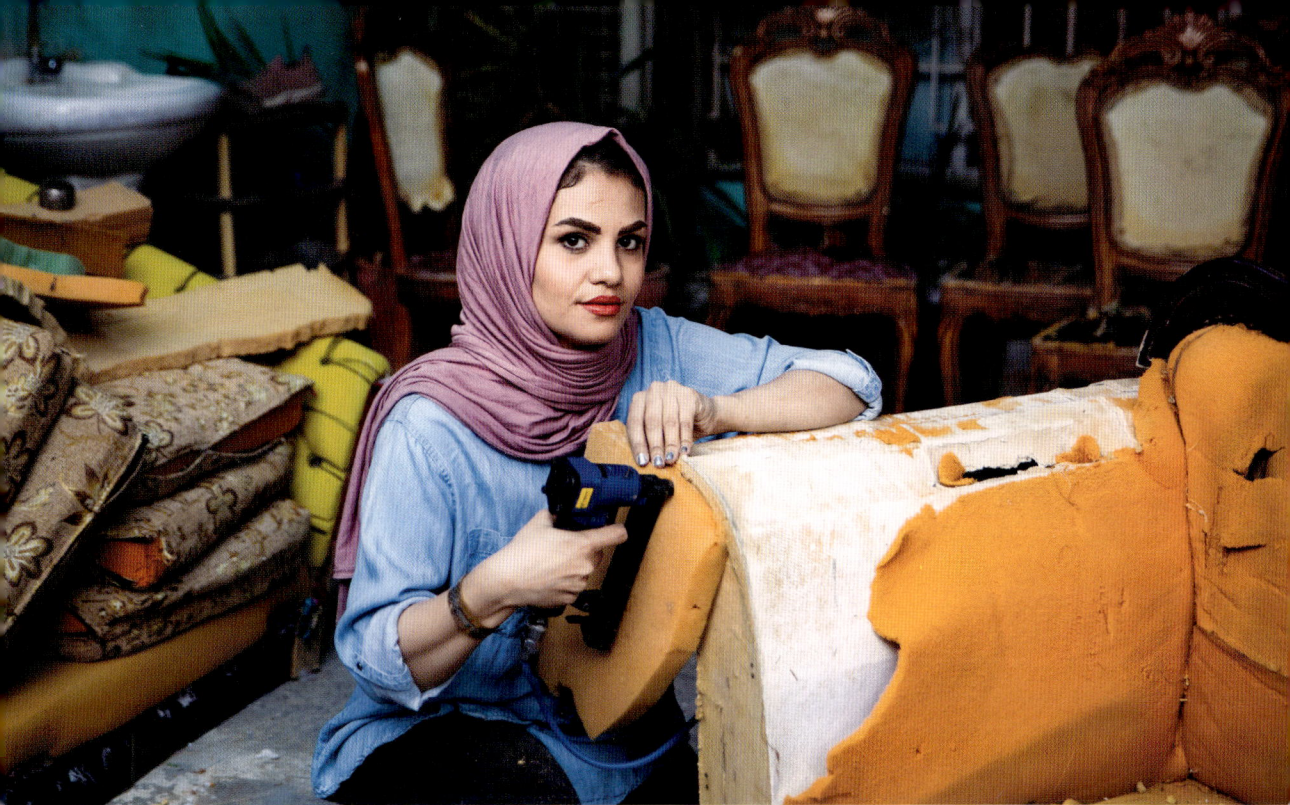

BAGHDAD, IRAQ *(Above)*

Noor grew up in a country devastated by conflicts. She was also always surrounded by conservative people. Despite these obstacles, she managed to become a skilled and respected carpenter.

It all began when Noor decided to learn how to create her own furniture out of necessity—the cost of buying it was too high. The results were spectacular, and, over time, she established her own workshop in her courtyard. Initially, many people around her were unwilling to accept that a woman could be a carpenter, but her husband remained consistently supportive. Today, Noor works tirelessly to fulfill orders while also taking care of her four children. She dreams of one day opening a small carpentry school for women.

It is rare to witness a woman crafting and repairing wooden objects anywhere in the world. However, to witness such a sight in Iraq is truly astonishing.

AUSTIN, TEXAS, UNITED STATES *(Opposite)*

Courtney was only seventeen years old when she had to start working to support herself. She tried many, many different jobs. She was a waitress, a barber, a waxer, a bread packager, a day care manager, a horticulturist, and a landscaper, and now she is a welder.

At her new job, Courtney finds herself surrounded by a myriad of sparks. Yet, within her, there is also a spark that ignites from time to time and pushes her forward whenever she feels like she doesn't belong in a place.

She had disappointments and depressions along the way, but for now she finally feels that she found the right job. Today, Courtney is twenty-six, and all her colleagues are men, but she proves that a strong and courageous woman can do any kind of job and defy all stereotypes.

KYOTO, JAPAN *(Below)*

Sasaki and Tachibana were walking hand in hand through the streets of their city when I noticed them. Their bond is truly impressive. They told me they have been best friends since they were five years old.

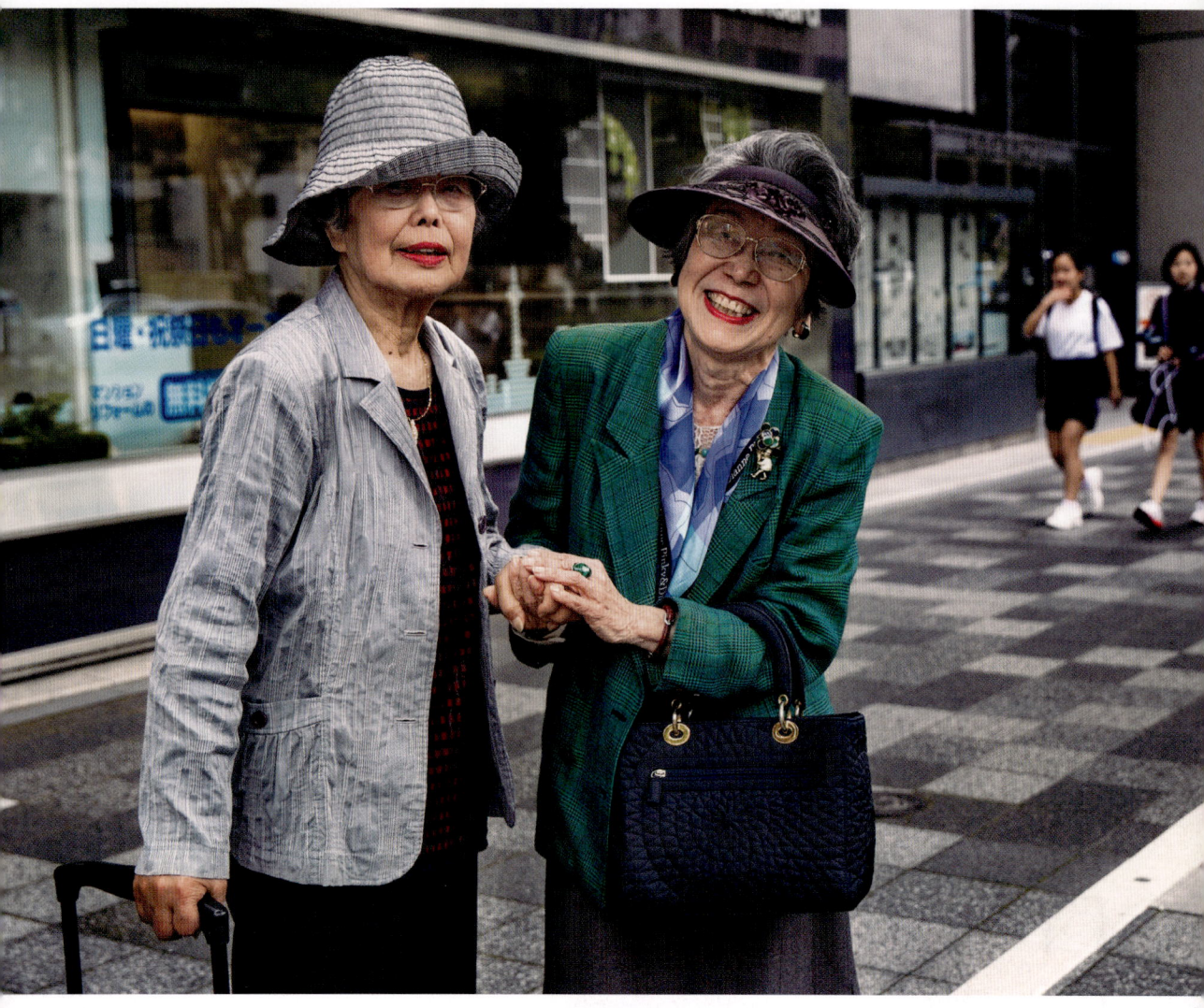

ANTIGUA, GUATEMALA *(Opposite)*

Carmen and Jorge met almost seventy years ago. They first encountered each other at a party, where he invited her to dance. Since that moment, they have been inseparable.

Known as *los Abuelitos Alonso* ("the Alonso Grandparents") in the local dancing community, Carmen and Jorge have spent their entire lives dancing together and exploring various genres of music. They shared their motto with me: "We live to dance, and we dance to live." It all makes sense.

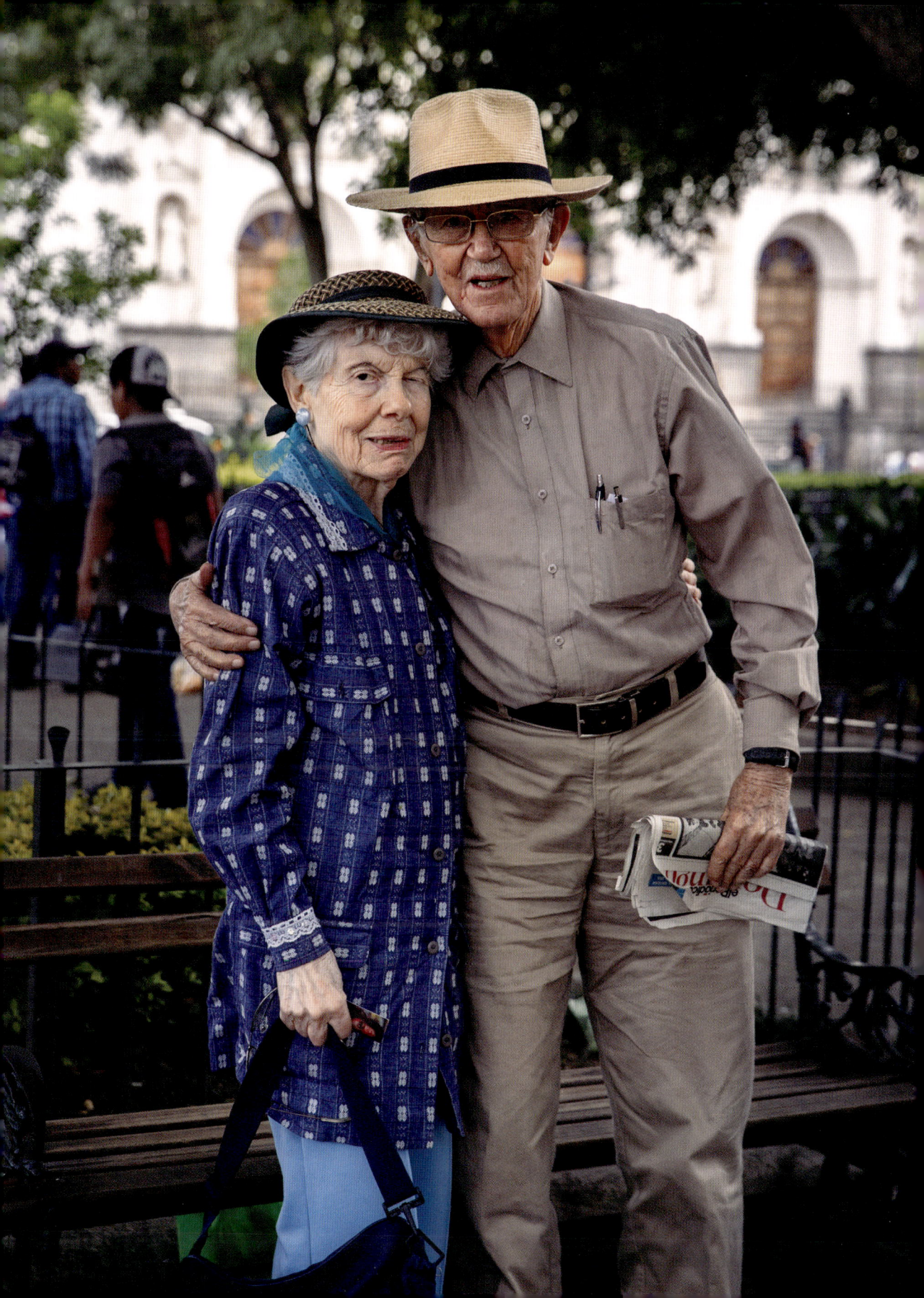

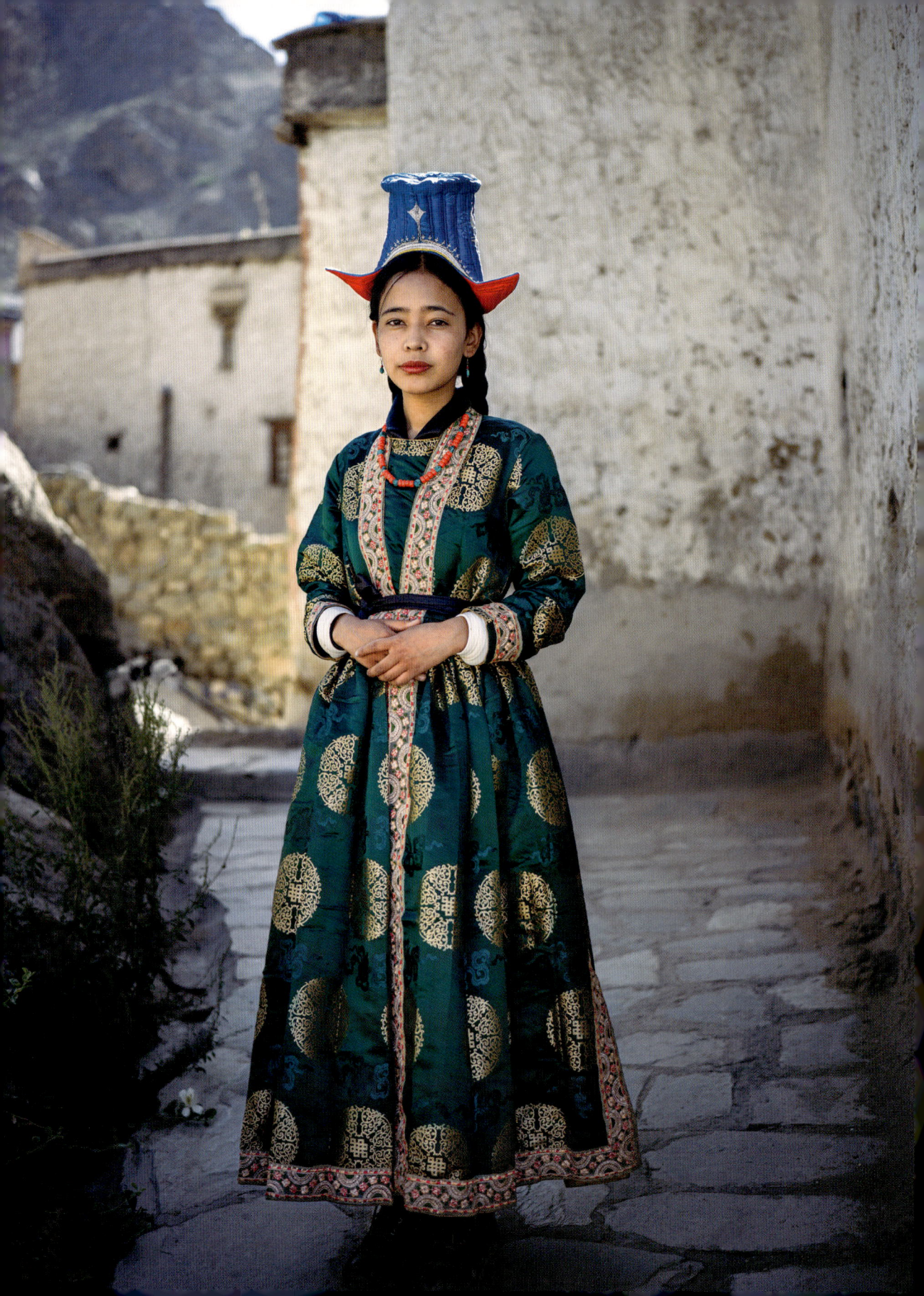

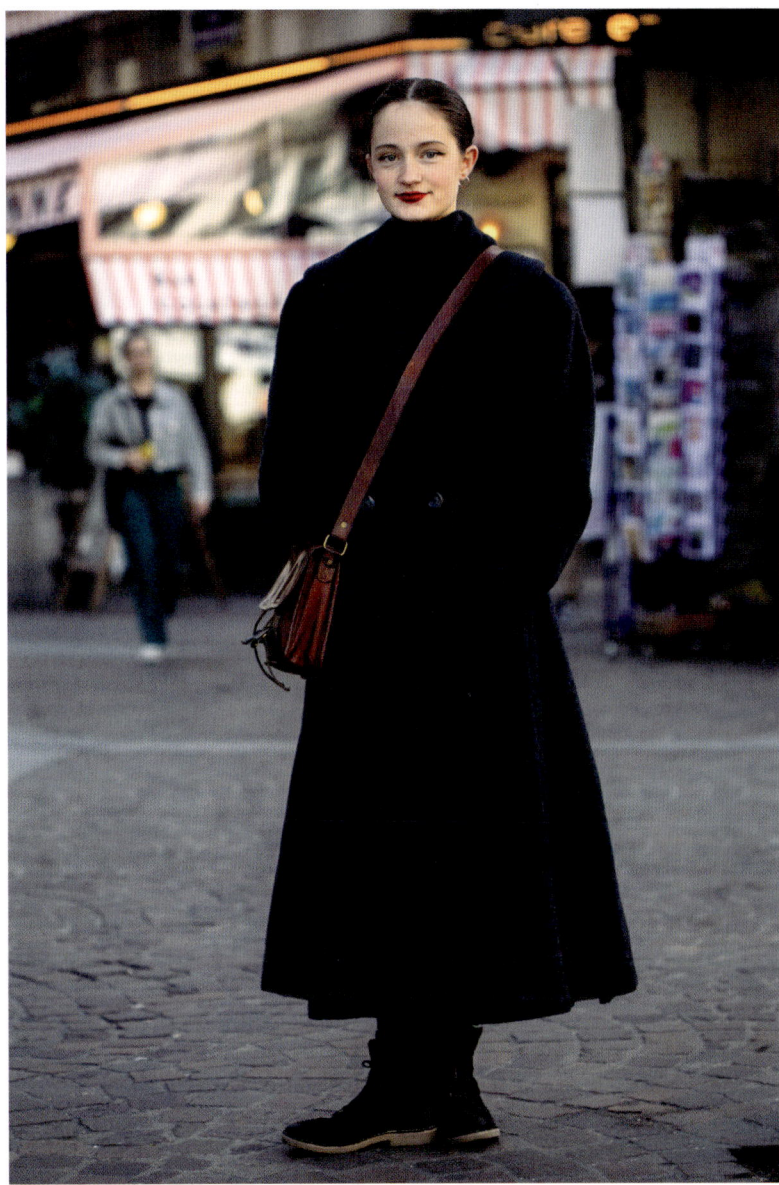

PARIS, FRANCE *(Above)*

Emilie, a fourth-generation seamstress, is passionate about vintage fashion and wears it every day. Her family's tradition in sewing has taught her to see the beauty and craftsmanship of these old clothes.

LADAKH, INDIA *(Opposite)*

Richen, an economics student, is part of the first generation that adopted modern clothes in this area. However, on special occasions, she is proud to wear her Ladakhi traditional costume. Her hat is called a *tipi* and is made of brocade.

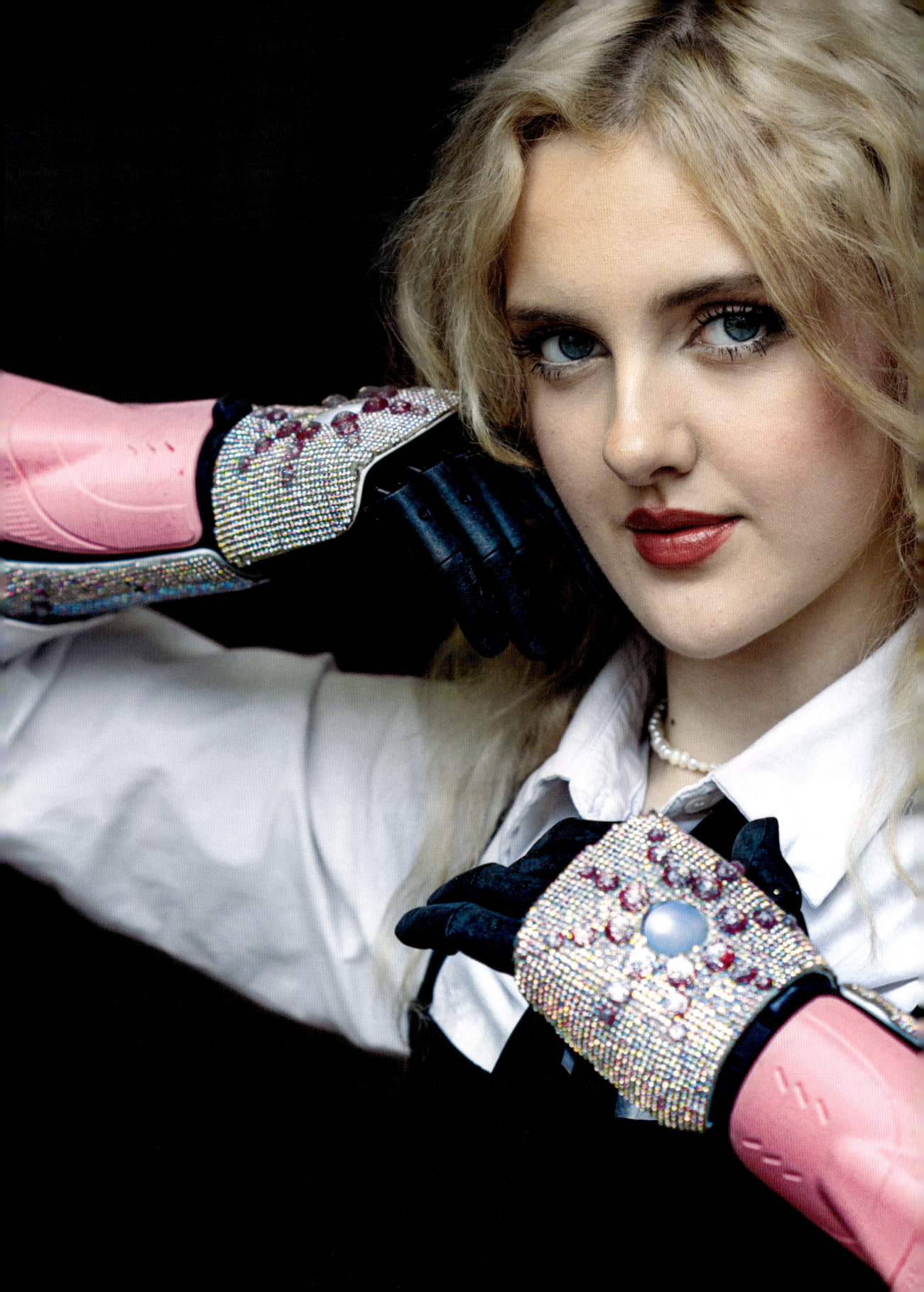

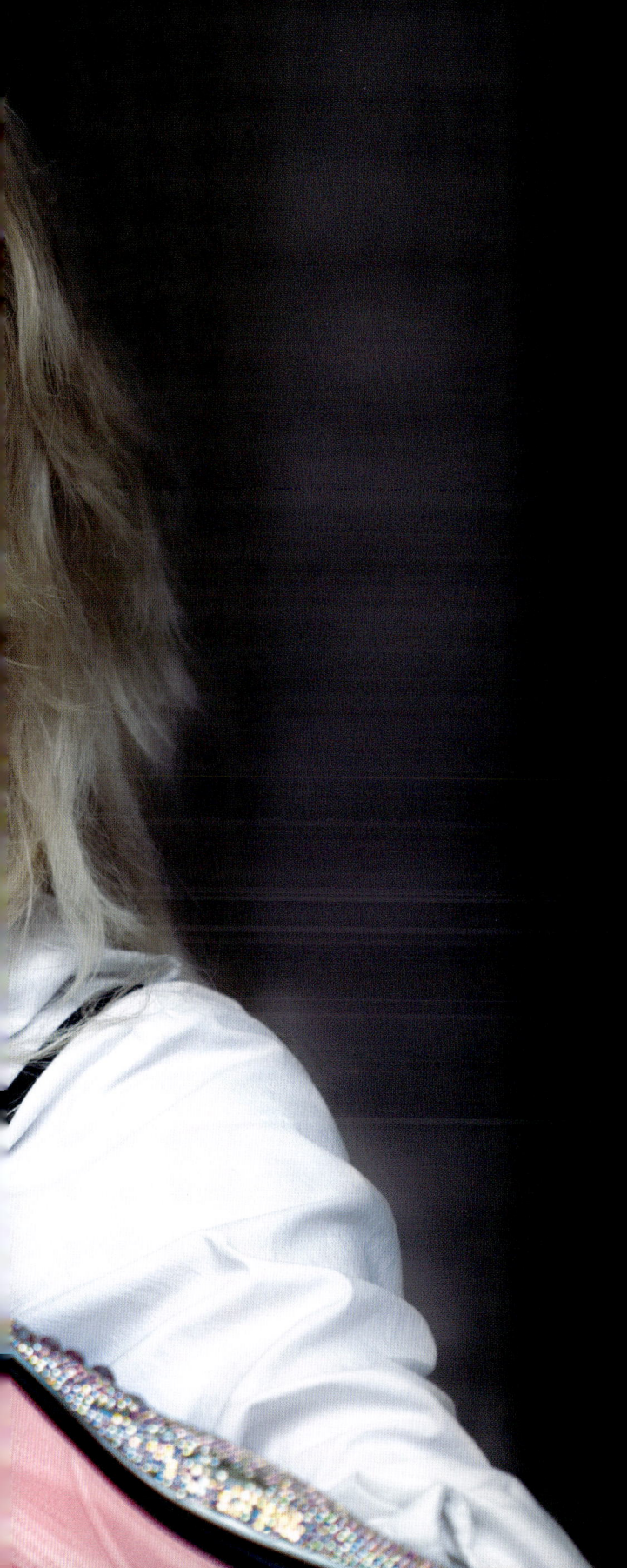

LONDON, UNITED KINGDOM

For me, Tilly Lockey is a superhero. Not in movies or magazines but in real life.

When she was a baby, Tilly fell ill with what doctors believed to be a simple ear infection. Her mother had doubts about the diagnosis. When a rash appeared on Tilly's skin, her mother knew they needed to rush to the hospital. Tilly was diagnosed with meningococcal septicaemia, a very severe infection. The doctors told her parents that she was likely to die. But against all odds, Tilly survived after a complicated operation to have her arms and toes amputated.

In the beginning, Tilly used simple prosthetic arms, but her mother constantly researched for better options. That's how she discovered a company called Open Bionics that was looking for people like Tilly to trial a revolutionary prosthetic arm. When she was eight, Tilly was chosen to participate in the trial, and her life changed completely.

Tilly's new bionic arms enabled her to perform complex tasks that had seemed impossible. In time, her mission became clear: to promote body positivity and self-love while also raising awareness about prosthetics and meningitis.

Today, Tilly is a singer, actor, TV presenter, inspirational speaker, and beauty vlogger. She's also fundraising for meaningful causes and is working with scientists to turn medical devices into fashion accessories.

Tilly transformed something that was once seen by society as a huge disadvantage into a celebration of beauty, diversity, and strength. It seems like a miracle, but that's what superheroes do.

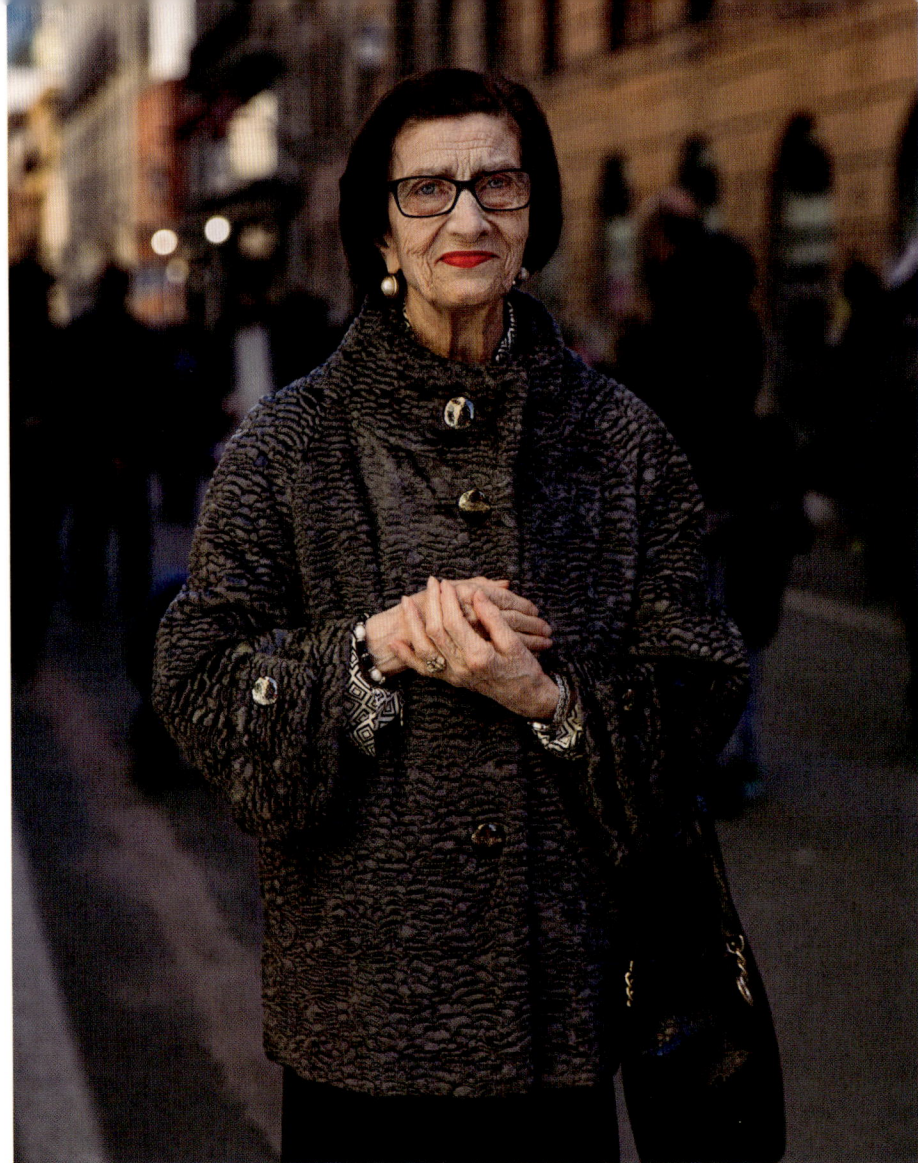

PALERMO, ITALY

I met this lovely, elegant lady on the historic streets of central Palermo in Sicily. In this traditional part of Italy, both family and faith in God hold great importance.

Giovanna lost her mother when she was only ten years old, during the Second World War, so she had to take care of her four younger brothers from a very young age. Later on, she became a mother herself and raised three children. When I met her, she was deeply worried about one of her daughters who was dealing with a serious illness.

Giovanna's life has had its share of ups and downs. She has faced the loss of family members and friends, yet she has never lost her faith and elegance. It seems that her faith has given her strength and hope, while her elegance has provided a sense of normality during challenging times. When it was time to say goodbye, she took my hands, looked at me kindly, and said something in Italian. I believe it was "May God bless you."

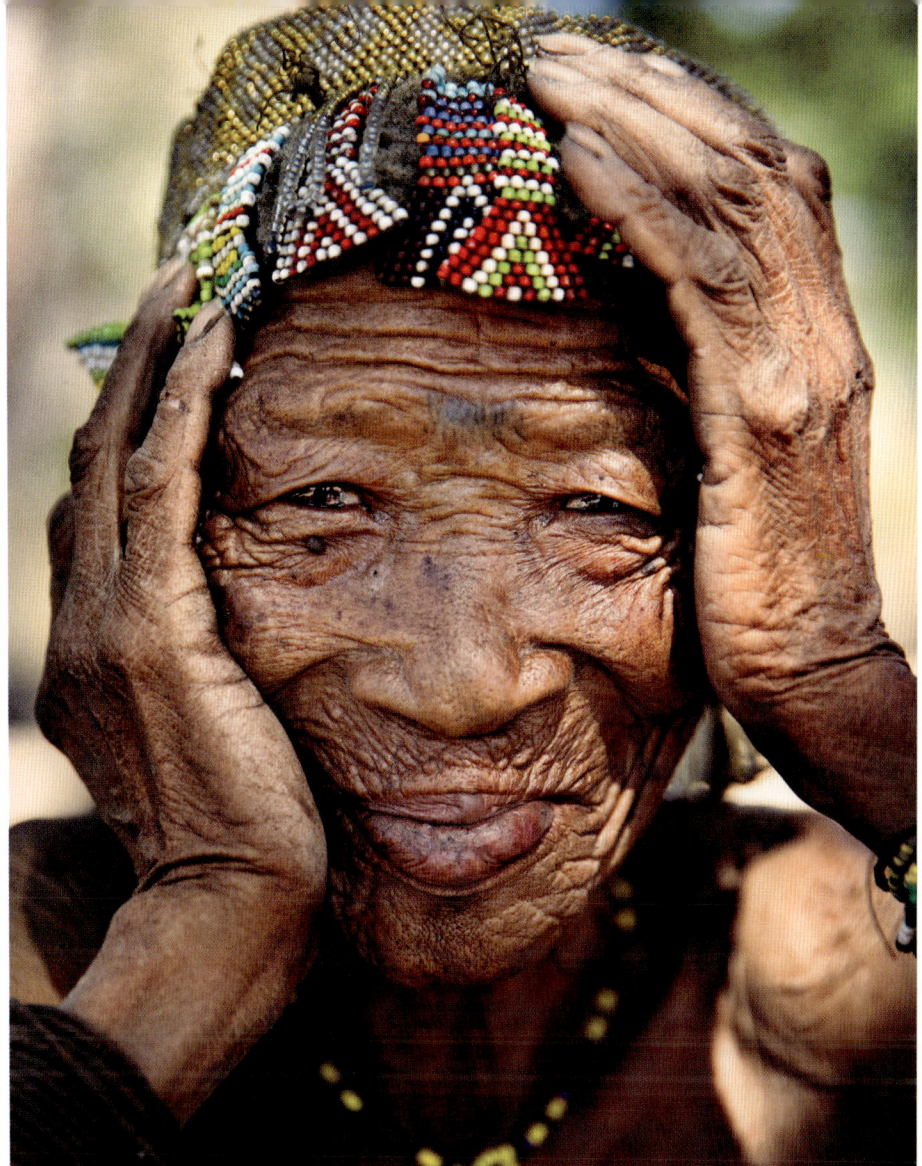

NORTHEASTERN NAMIBIA

|Koce is the oldest in her community, and she's part of one of the oldest tribes on Earth: the San peoples. That's why her name can barely be transcribed through modern alphabets. |Koce lived for most of her life in a community of hunter-gatherers. They were experts in medicinal plants, they enjoyed total freedom, and they used to live like their ancestors thousands of years ago.

The so-called modernization programs of the government forced them away from their original lands and from their traditional way of living. Today, they are mostly farmers and are confined to a small territory, living a difficult life they never wanted.

|Koce still remembers her old life very well and how much she loved to run. At her age, she's not able to run anymore, but she still loves to sing and dance. Her husband used to be the healer of the community, and she helped him during rituals by singing and dancing. What a fascinating woman, and what a complex story. Looking at her, I somehow see the whole story of humankind.

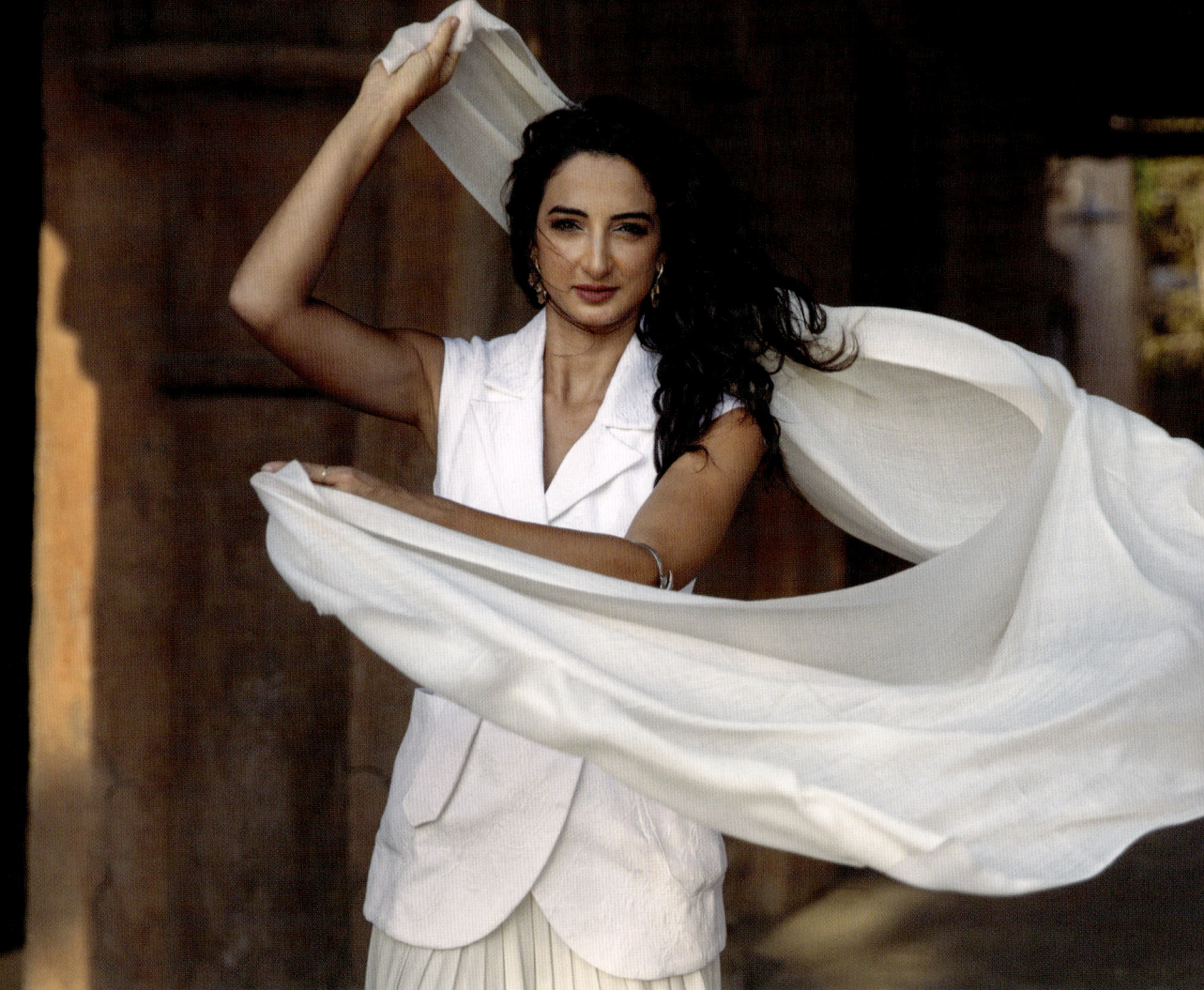

DUBAI, UNITED ARAB EMIRATES

Raha Moharrak is the first Saudi woman to climb Mount Everest as well as the highest mountains on each of the seven continents. Convincing her family to support her dreams was a challenge as tough as the mountains themselves.

Back in her twenties, Raha was living in the United Arab Emirates and starting a career in graphic design when she learned about an expedition on Mount Kilimanjaro. She didn't have any experience with mountains, but she felt she would like to join the adventure during her vacation. She clearly remembers the day she called her father to ask if she could do the climb. His response was a very clear "No."

But that "no" made her aspirations even stronger. She thought, *The fact that I'm from a conservative country doesn't mean I can't climb a mountain.* So she spent hours crafting an email to her father, pouring her heart out and describing the importance of his support. Days passed without a response, leaving Raha feeling devastated. But then a short message arrived: "I love you. You're crazy. Go for it."

Fueled by her father's newfound support, Raha's passion for mountaineering blossomed. After conquering her first peak, nothing could stop her on her path to becoming one of the greatest female explorers.

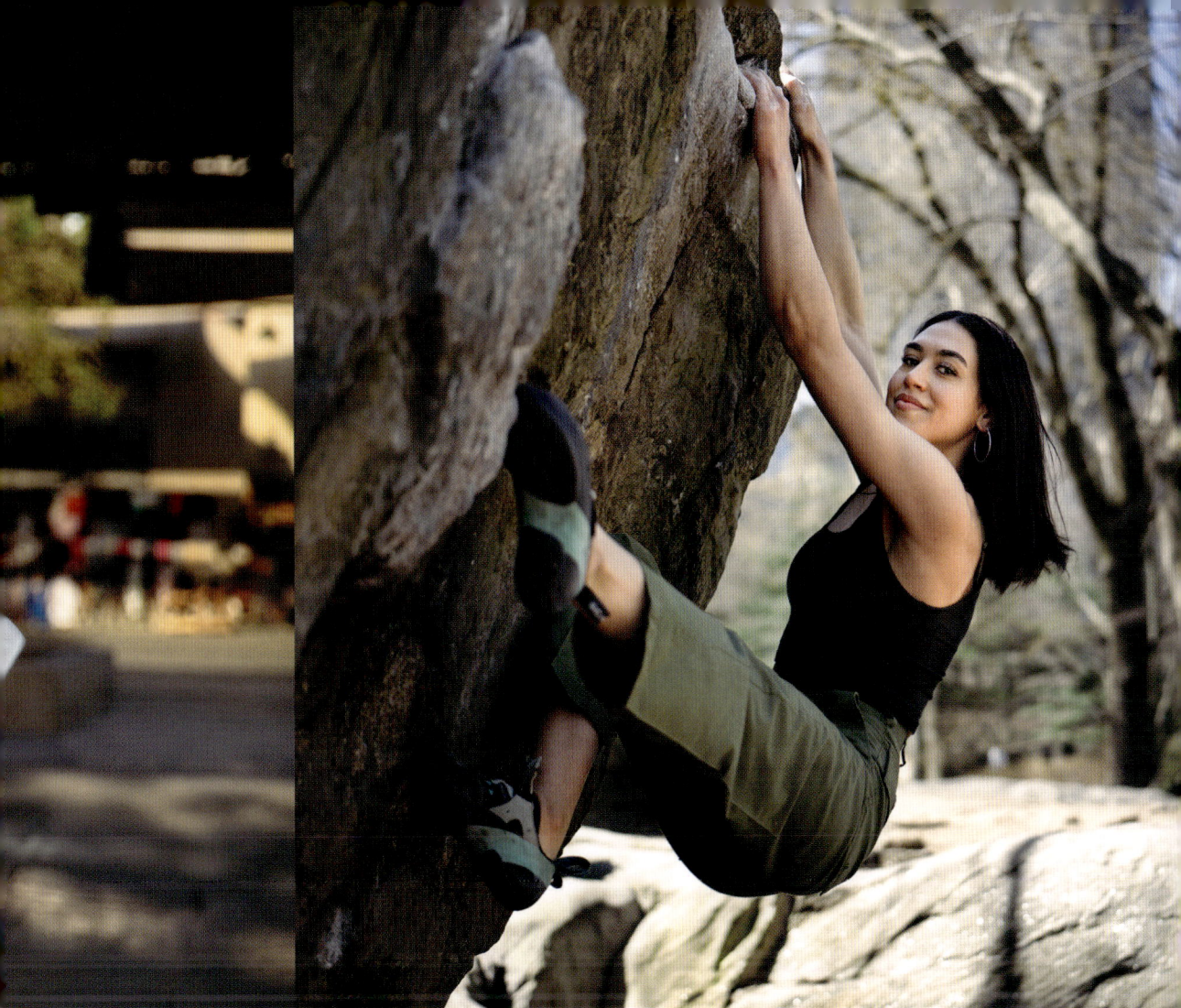

NEW YORK CITY, UNITED STATES

Isabella Rojas is a climber with almost twenty years of experience. I photographed her around the small rocks in Central Park, a place she often visits for bouldering fun. However, her climbing career has taken her to different parts of the world on very challenging routes.

Isabella also loves to share her knowledge as a climbing and bouldering instructor. She knows from her own experience how much children can evolve, both physically and mentally, through climbing. On the rocks, the body is working at its full capacity, while the mind focuses solely on the present by finding unique solutions every second.

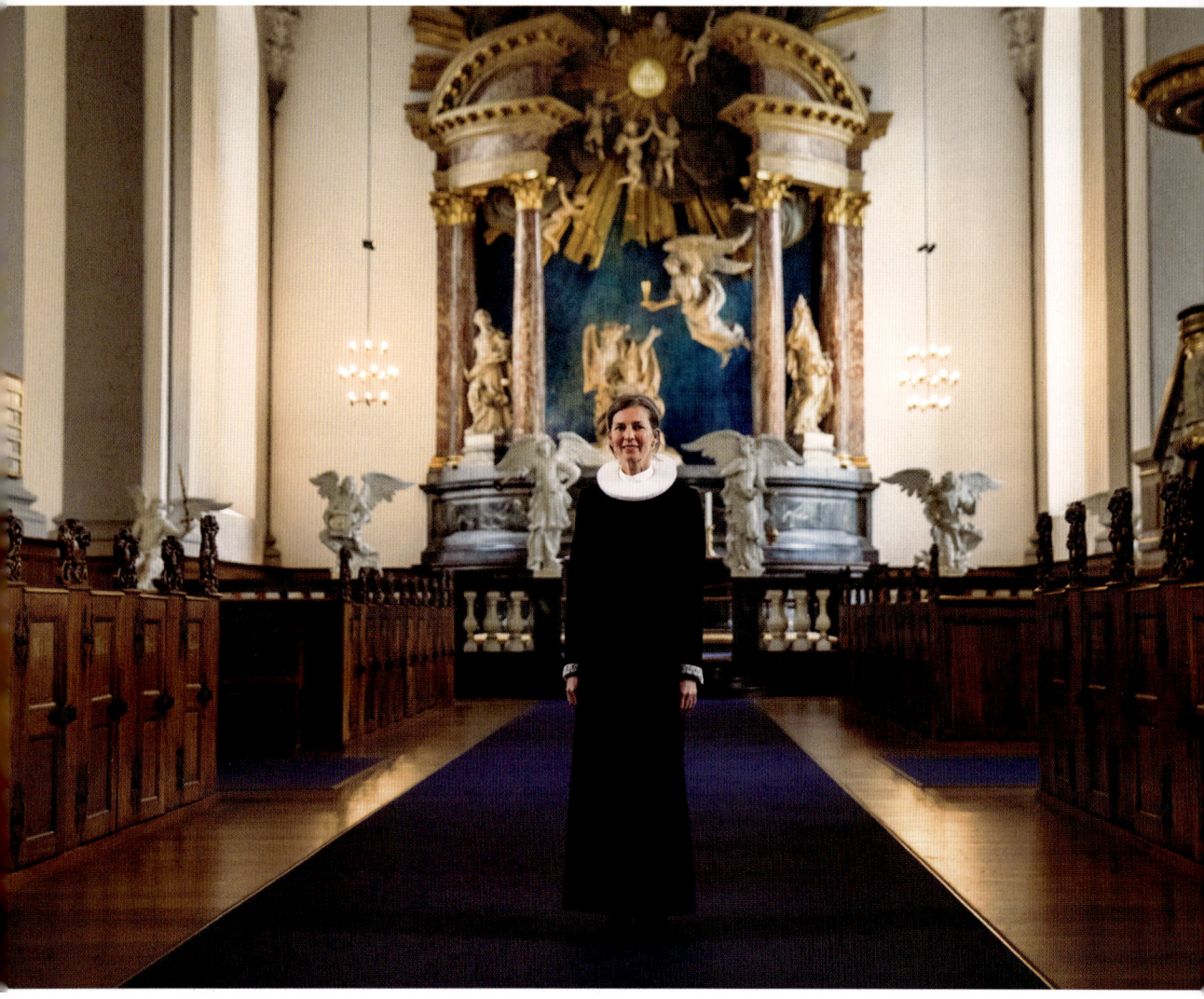

COPENHAGEN, DENMARK

Marlene serves as the parish priest of this cathedral. It belongs to the Evangelical-Lutheran Church in Denmark, which is the established, state-supported church. I met her at the end of a long and exhausting day for her—right after a funeral. Despite the exhaustion, she kindly agreed to be photographed and shared her experience as a female priest. It was interesting to learn that although women were first ordained as priests in Denmark in 1948, they now constitute the majority of priests in the country.

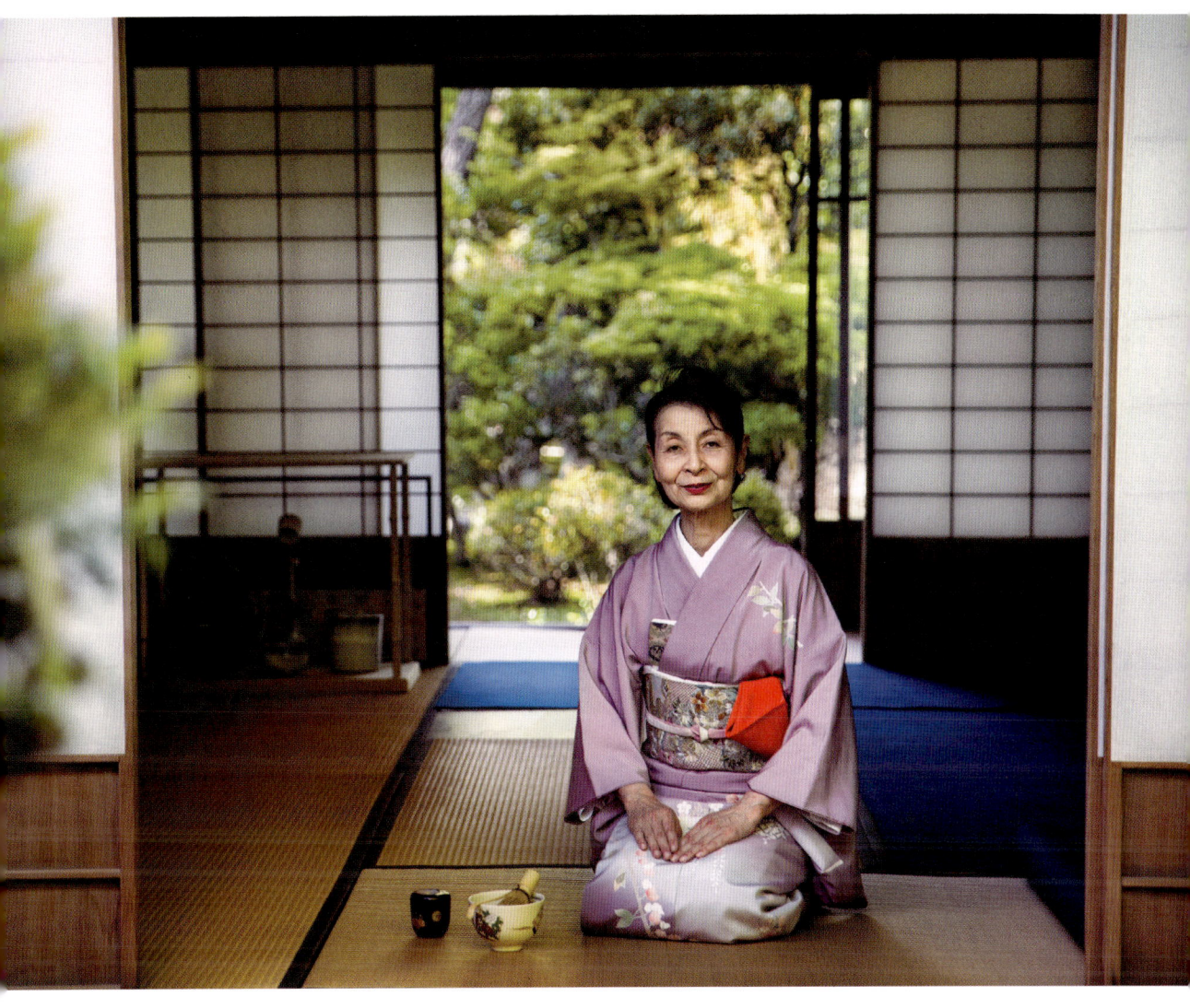

KYOTO, JAPAN

Mieko lives in this ancient city that served as the capital of Japan for more than one thousand years.

Mieko spent most of her life working as an English teacher. However, after retiring, she discovered a new way to share her knowledge and became a tea ceremony teacher. She learned this captivating art from her mother and now enjoys introducing it to foreigners who have an interest in Japanese traditions.

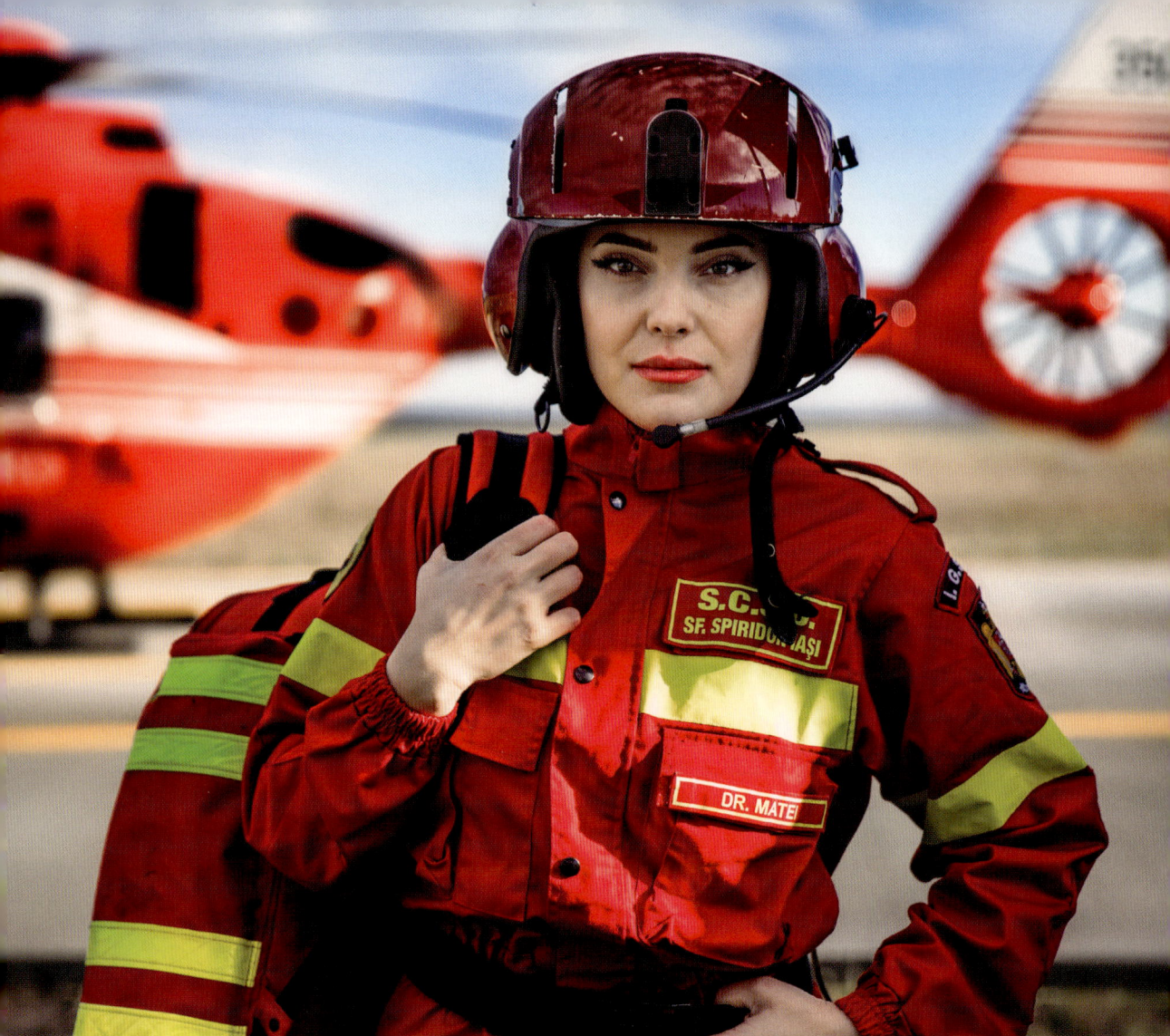

IAŞI, ROMANIA

As a doctor in emergency medicine, Giorgiana has seen it all. She has watched children die, then had to be the one to tell the tragic news to their parents. She lost colleagues and friends in a helicopter crash. She witnessed the hell in 2020 while working in Covid-19 intensive care units. But while experiencing so much pain, she saved hundreds of lives. And that gave her the strength to go on.

Women make up the majority of frontline health-care workers globally. Our world has many brave heroines like Giorgiana.

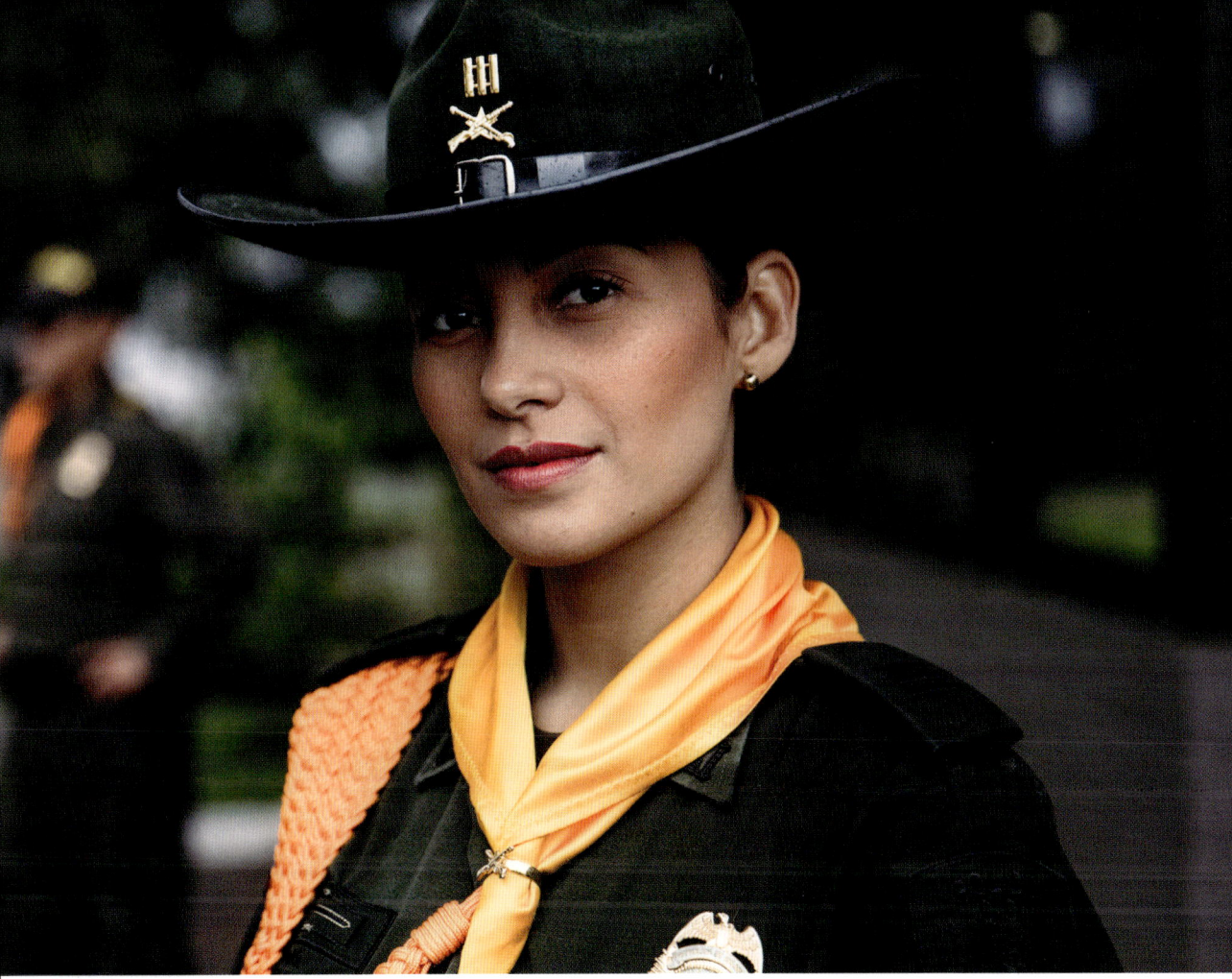

MEDELLÍN, COLOMBIA

Maybe no police force in the world has faced as many challenges as the one from Medellín during the times of Pablo Escobar. Nataly grew up during this time and decided she wanted to fight for peace and justice as a police officer.

Nataly's father was a police officer, too. She was only four years old when her dad was murdered while on a mission against Pablo Escobar's cartel. Today, Nataly is a captain in the Colombian police. She has sixty subordinates, most of whom are men. It must be much harder for a woman to gain the respect of such a team, but Nataly has prepared for that since she was a little girl.

Things are better today in Medellín thanks to fearless people like Nataly and her father. We call these kinds of people brave and courageous, but I also like to call them beautiful.

ISFAHAN, IRAN

Marzieh is one of the strongest women I've ever met. In 2014, she was driving around the streets of her city. Two men on a motorcycle approached her vehicle while she was stopped at a traffic light. Shockingly, one of them threw acid on her face before quickly fleeing the scene.

Despite the presence of video cameras surveying the street, the police never managed to catch the perpetrators. Similar attacks occurred in Isfahan that year—all targeting women who did not conform to conservative dress norms. Many Iranians believe that these attacks were orchestrated to discourage women from embracing more liberal outfits.

Today, Marzieh tirelessly works to raise awareness about these horrific attacks and advocates for a ban on the sale of acid. She cried while recalling the memories of that horrible day. But it didn't stop her from sharing her story. She finished with a smile. It was the smile of a powerful woman who found the strength to overcome her suffering and the courage to fight for her cause, so this would never happen to another woman.

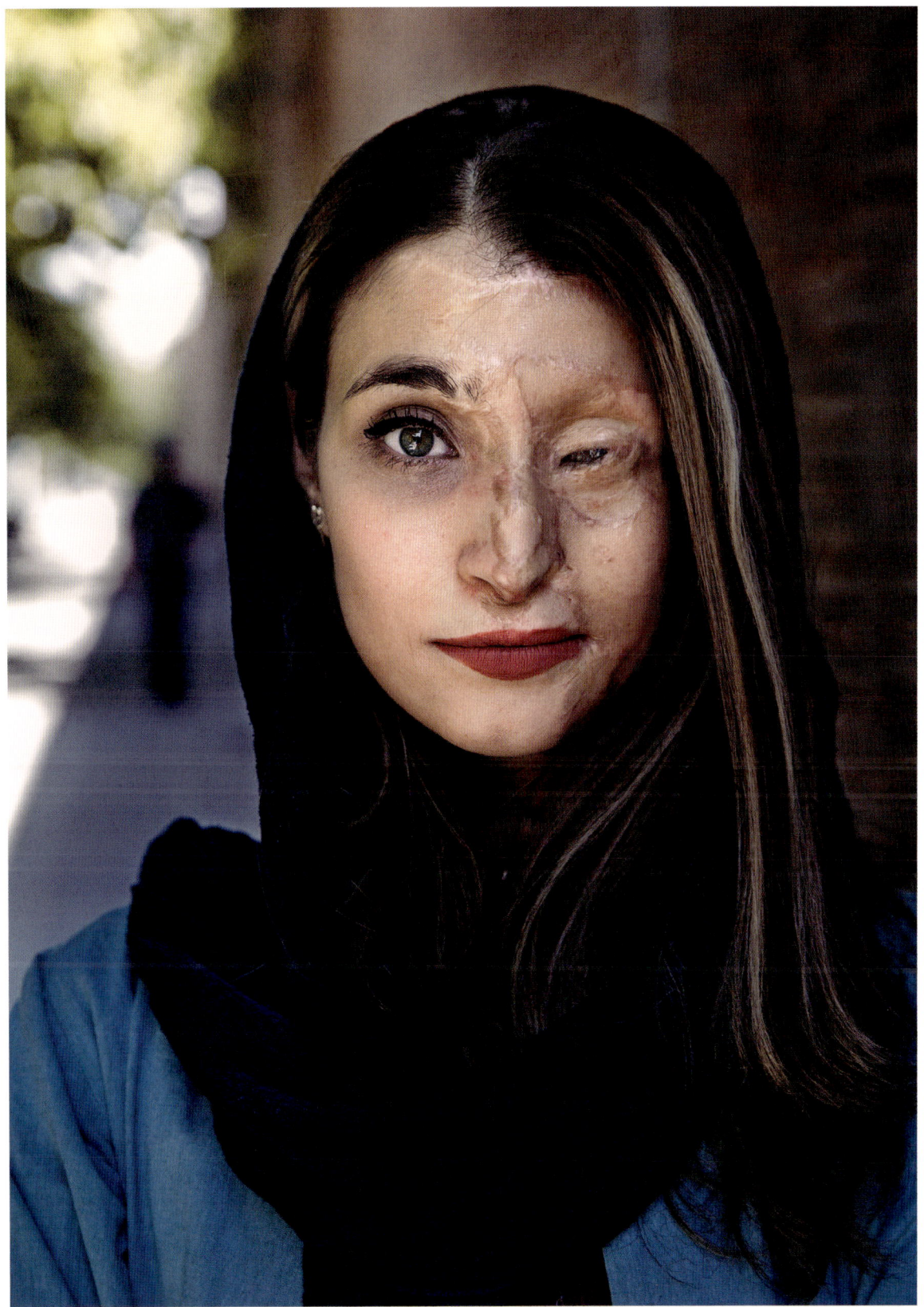

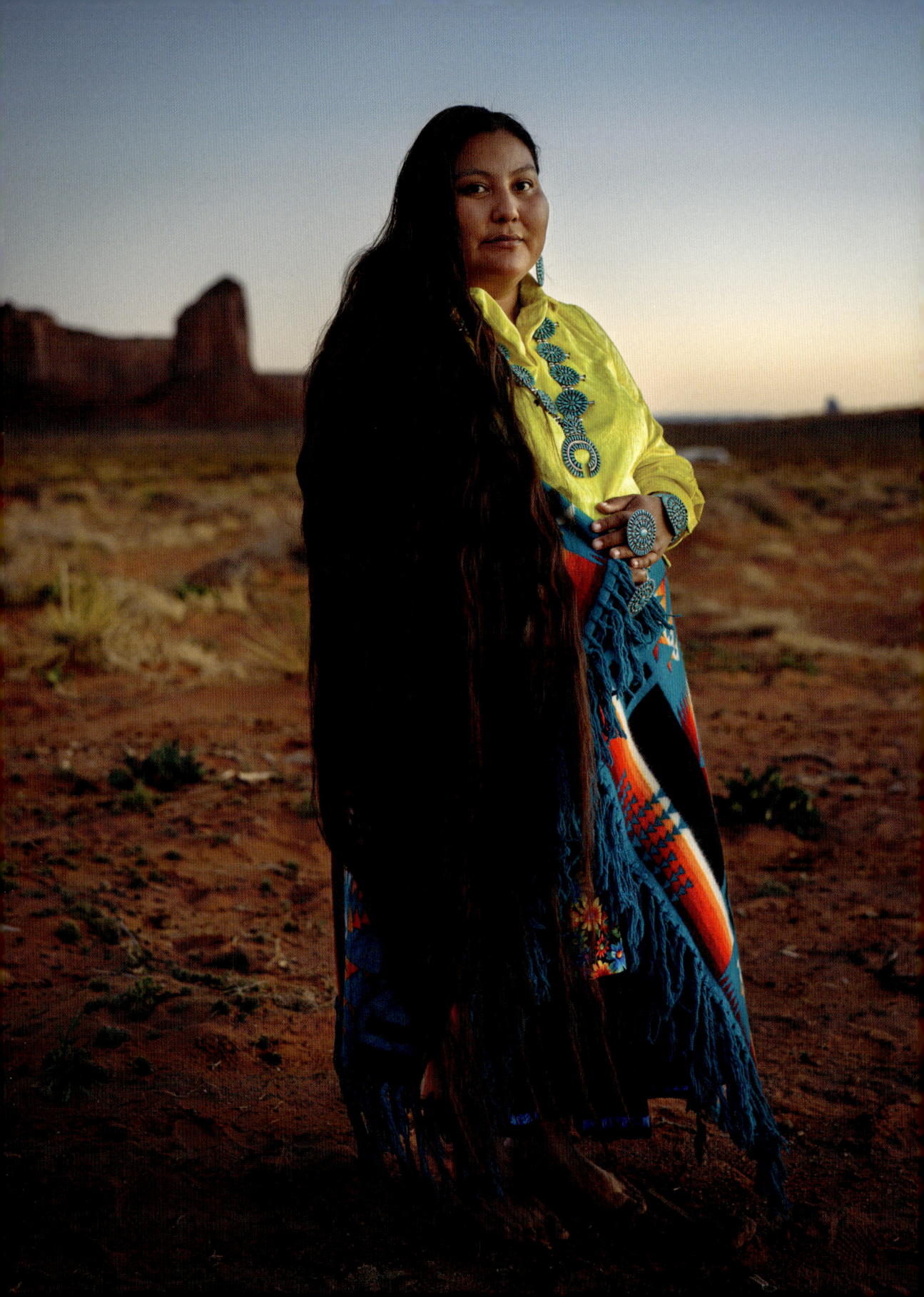

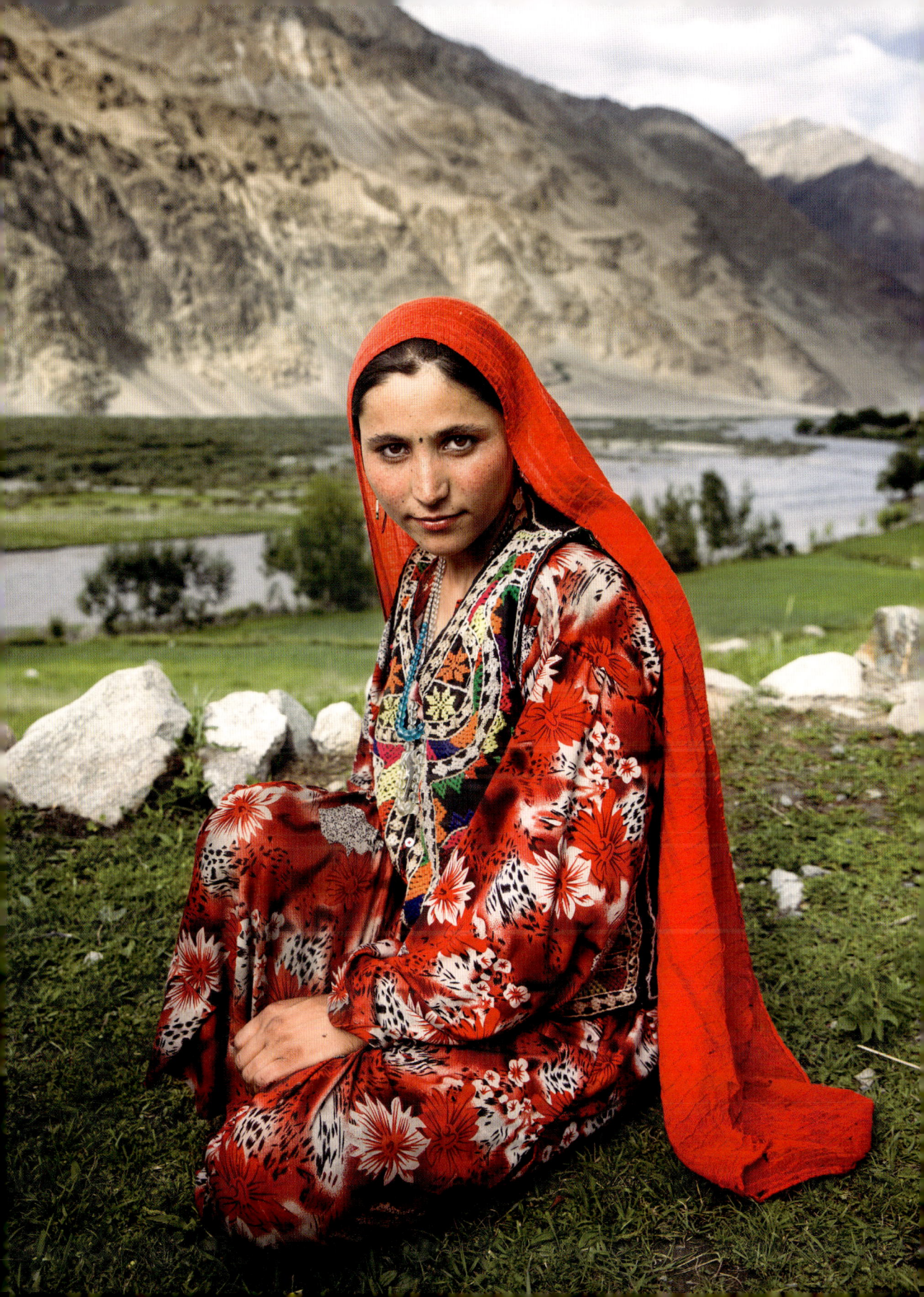

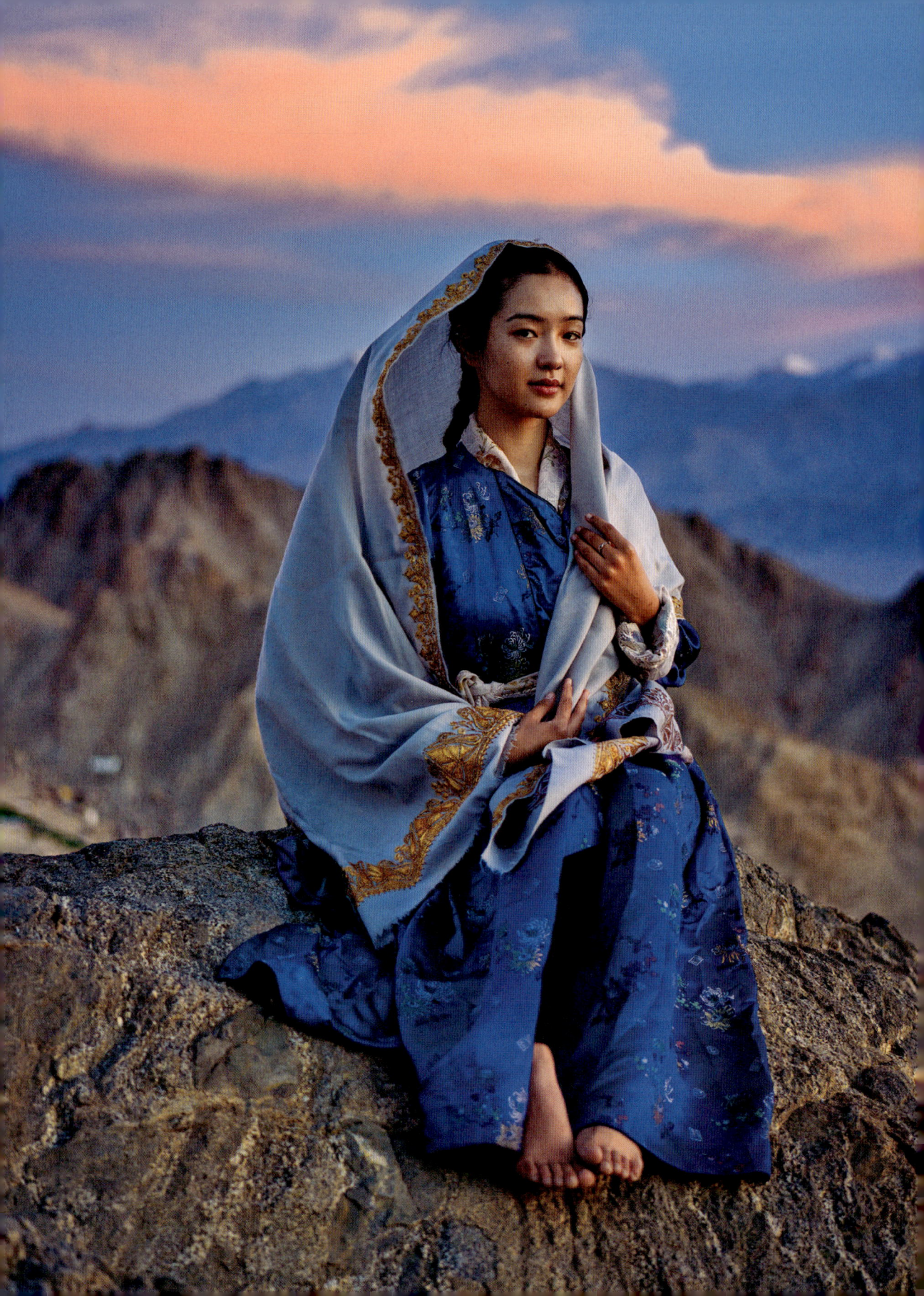

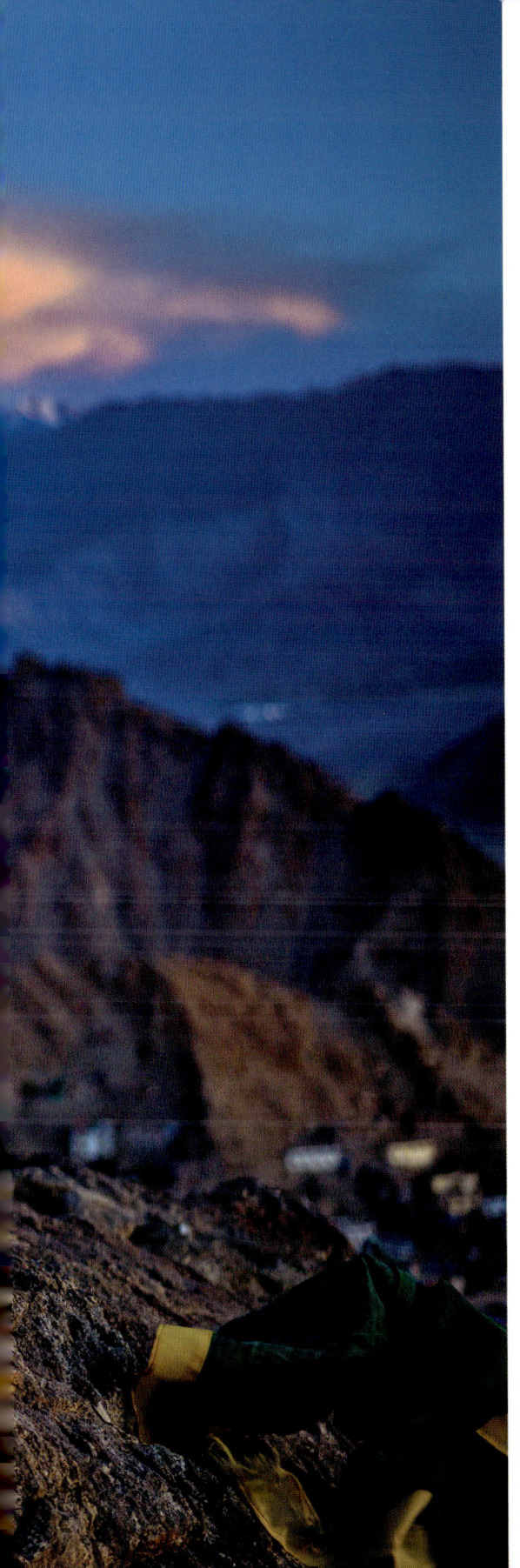

MONUMENT VALLEY, UNITED STATES *(Previous spread, left)*

Shanythia is a Navajo silversmith living in the spectacular Monument Valley. Following tradition, she cuts her hair only when she loses a close relative. She has performed this ritual once: when her grandfather passed away.

I spent a day in Shanythia's courtyard, which was truly captivating. Interestingly, her courtyard sits precisely on the border of two states—symbolizing the complex history of her people. Half the courtyard is in Arizona, while the other is in Utah. It is amazing to see people like Shanythia who, despite so many challenges, uphold ancient traditions and remain deeply connected to their roots.

NORTHERN AFGHANISTAN *(Previous spread, right)*

This woman lives in one of the most remote areas of the world. In this part of Afghanistan, people have not experienced many lifestyle changes over the past hundred years or so. Because of the steep mountains, this region has remained extremely isolated. Shopping is not common here, so most people make their own clothes and eat what they grow.

LEH, INDIA *(Left)*

Insha wanted to show me her favorite place in her hometown, and that's how we ended up here just before sunset. The Himalayas and the surrounding mountain ranges are home to incredible ethnic diversity. These majestic mountain ranges have helped preserve ancient traditions, languages, and ethnicities for centuries. I feel privileged that I still have the chance to capture some of this valuable heritage in my photos, but for how long, I wonder?

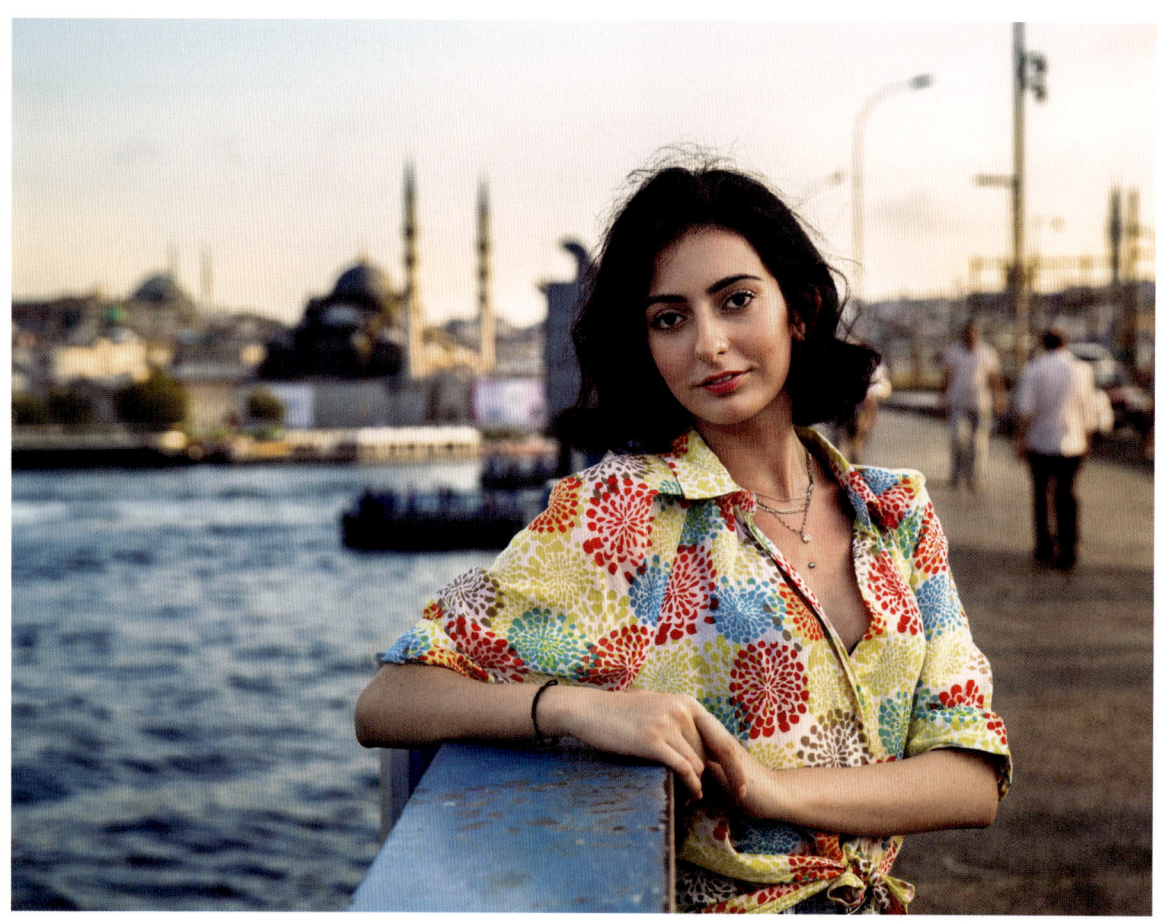

ISTANBUL, TURKEY

Tutku faced many heartbreaking moments in her life, but her positive spirit always gives her the strength to move forward. Tutku started working for a living at an early age, after her father became paralyzed. Her determination paid off, and a few years later, she became a chef. Yet she continued to face hardships along her journey.

One day, Tutku suddenly lost her hearing. She sought medical help from multiple doctors, but her case seemed hopeless. "I remember standing on my balcony and closing my eyes. I told myself that if I opened my eyes and saw even a single bird in the sky, it would mean I would hear again. Tearfully, I hesitated to open my eyes for a while. But when I finally did, I saw two birds."

After some time, Tutku received an innovative hearing implant that partially restored her sense of sound. Now she can work again as a chef, but her hearing is weak, which is a huge challenge in a busy restaurant. Tutku never complained when we met. On the contrary, she expressed deep gratitude for every second of her new life.

KOBLENZ, GERMANY

Cindy Klink is a deaf performer, meaning she brings songs to life in sign language. Like Tutku, she has a cochlear implant that provides her a sense of sound.

Because of her deafness, Cindy has experienced discrimination since childhood. Her parents, who are also deaf, were always there for her. Cindy's desire to become a musician and actress was constantly mocked outside her home. But she didn't really care about what others thought of her. She focused on following her dreams.

Today, Cindy stands on stages and performs songs in sign language. Her movements sometimes look like a dance—a true performing art—which creates a unique experience for her audience whether they are deaf or not. Music can be experienced on a completely different level.

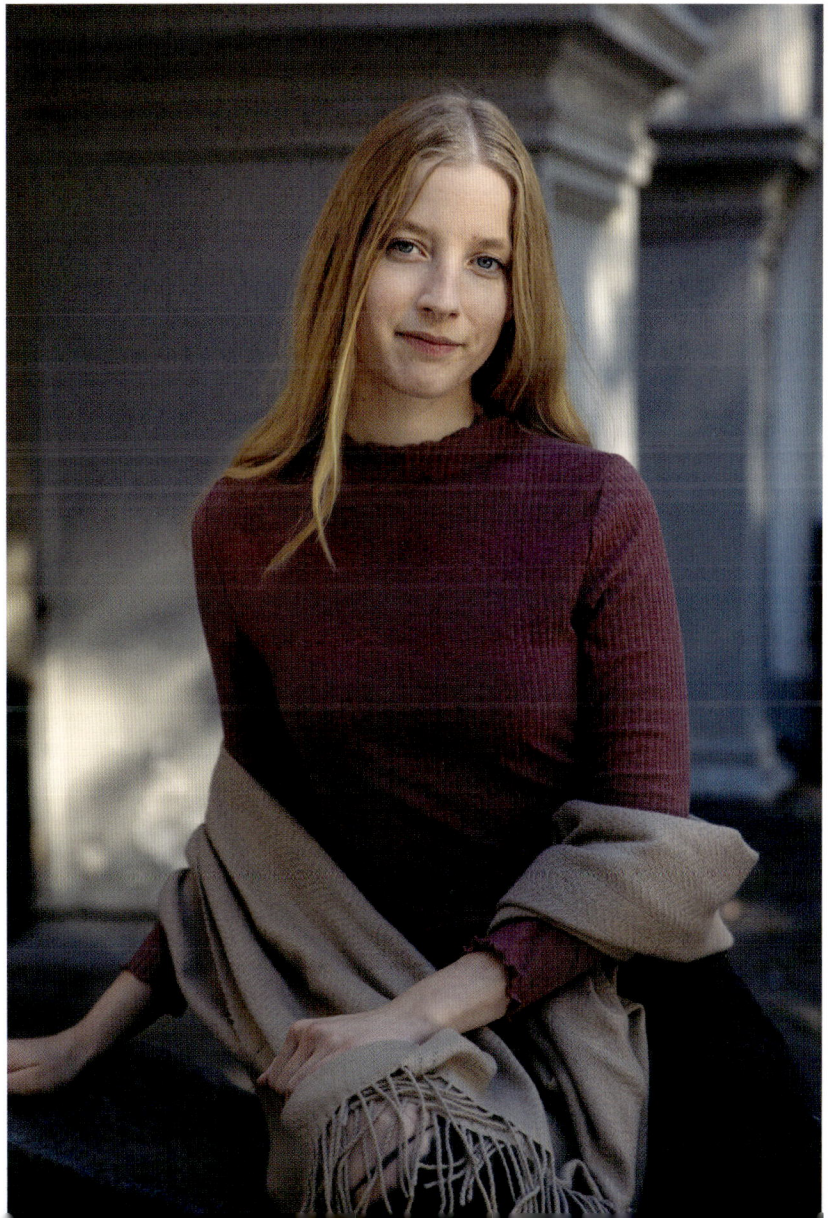

MIAMI, UNITED STATES

Danié Gómez-Ortigoza is an artist, and braiding is her medium. Having grown up in Mexico, Danié has been fascinated by braiding for as long as she can remember. Her grandmother taught her the secrets of this fascinating tradition as a way to celebrate her mestizo, or mixed, heritage.

After living in five countries and understanding the complexity of the world, Danié began using braiding as a means to connect people and cultures. Today, her braiding practice extends beyond mere hairstyling; it has evolved into braiding rituals and circles.

In Danié's braiding circles, women come together to form a ring, intertwining their hair and symbolizing the power of womanhood. As Danié likes to say, she is on a mission to trace the invisible thread that braids us together.

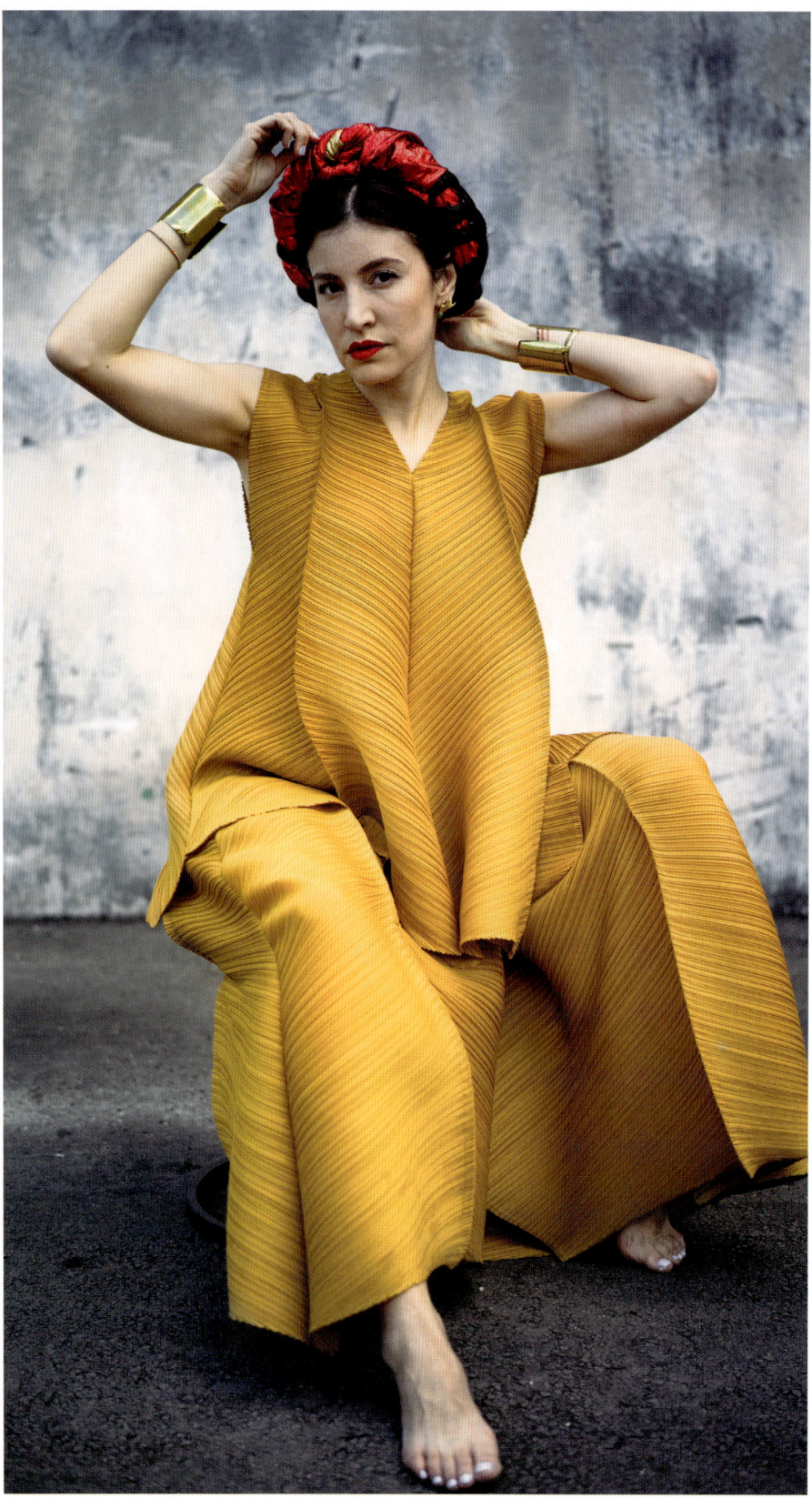

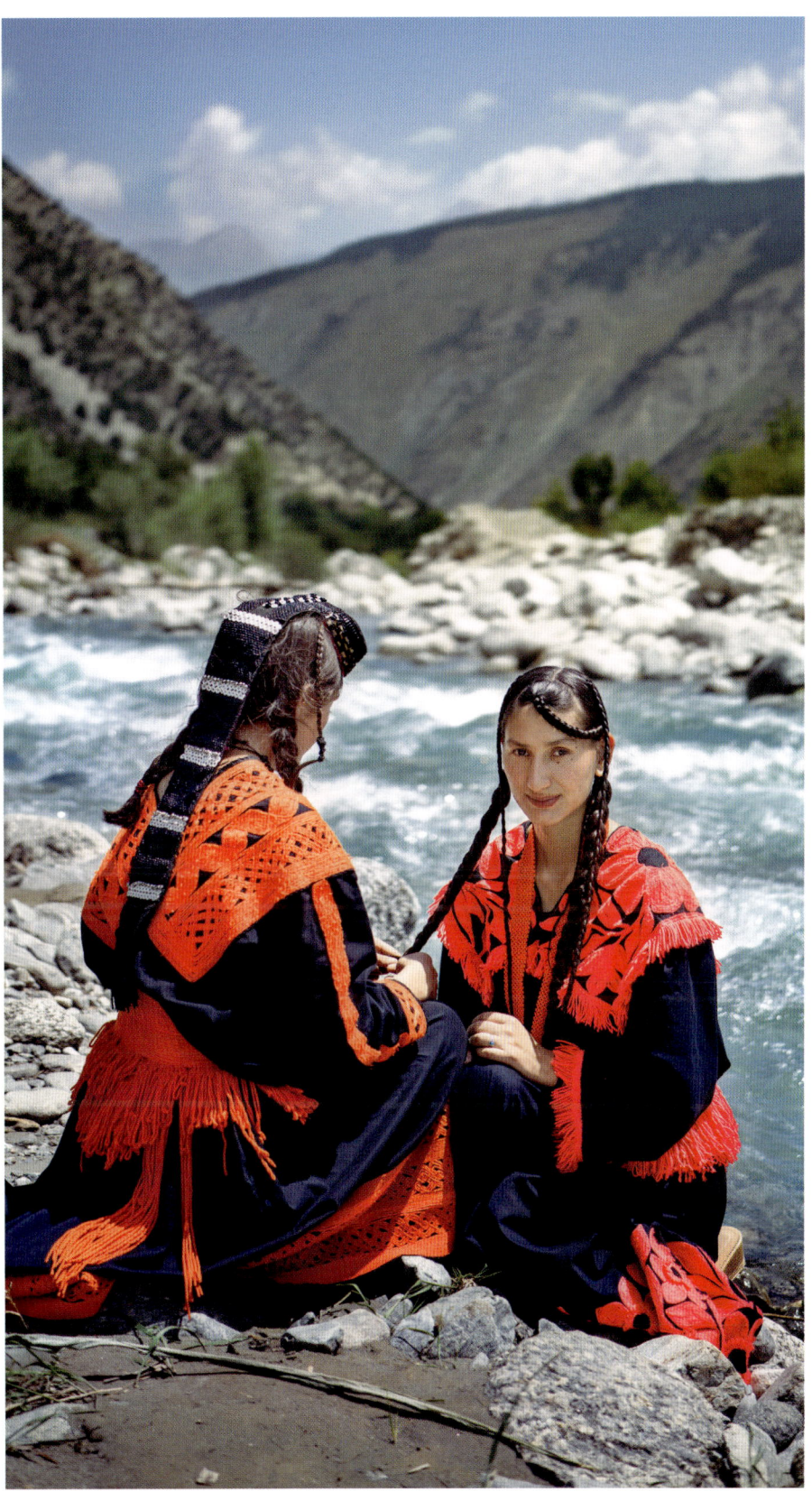

NORTHERN PAKISTAN

Due to living in a very traditional environment, Kalash people have a remarkably distinct culture.

Parsikla studies medicine in a city a few hours from her village. During vacations, when she returns home, she loves to immerse herself in Kalash traditions. As soon as she arrives, she goes to the river to wash and braid her hair. Then she dresses in traditional clothing like all women in this community.

For Parsikla, it's not just about following traditions. More than anything, it's about her profound love for her origins. Parsikla's commitment to her Kalash heritage is an example of the deep connection that people all over the world share with their roots.

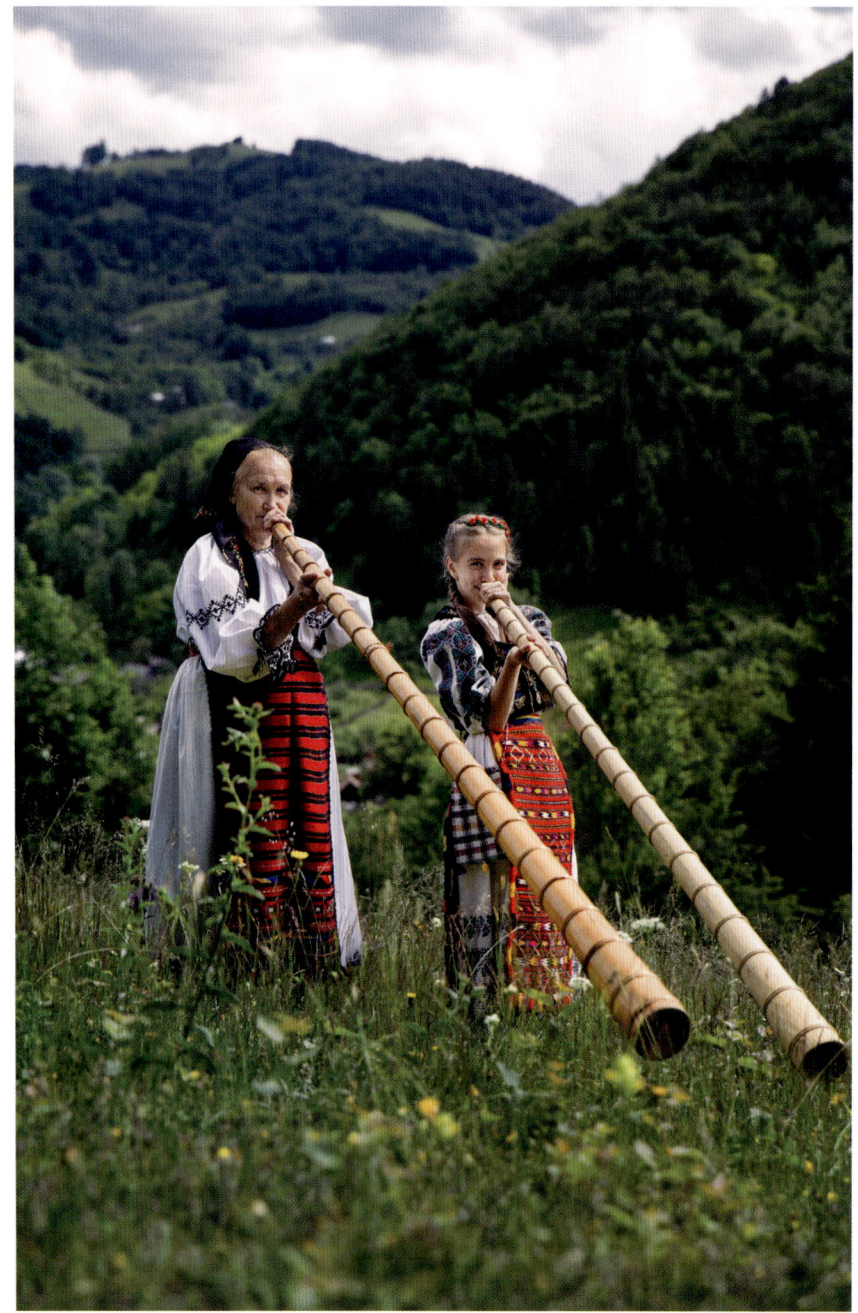

APUSENI MOUNTAINS, ROMANIA

Mariana Gligor began playing the tulnic, a long wooden horn, seventy years ago.
Throughout her life, in addition to being an accomplished player, her mission has
been to pass on this tradition to future generations. Here she is teaching Ana Maria
the secrets of this ancient instrument. The tulnic is quite heavy, which requires
strength to hold as well as lung power to play, but Ana Maria is thrilled to be a
part of this amazing heritage.

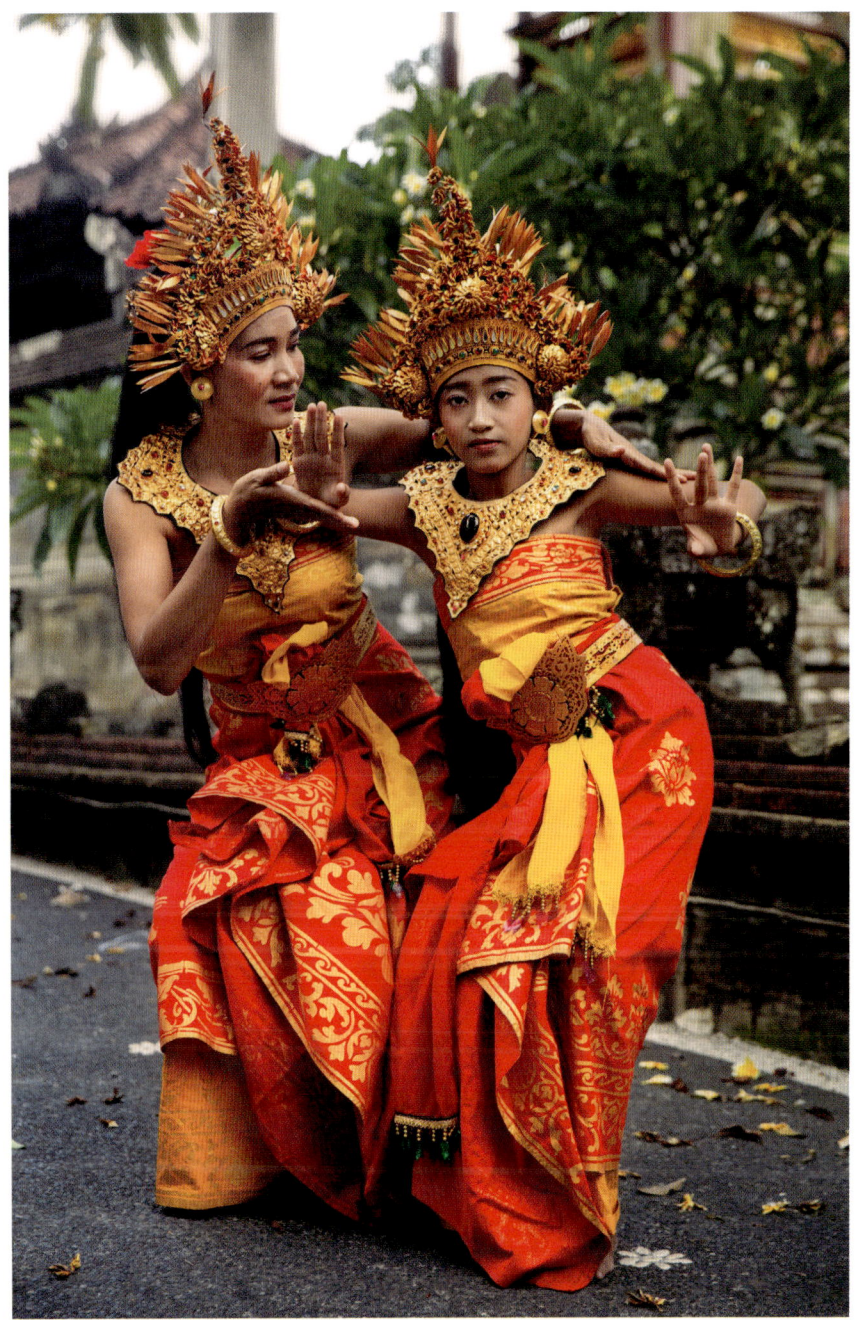

BALI, INDONESIA

Here a mother teaches her daughter a traditional Balinese dance. For hundreds of years, Balinese people have performed this unique dance that expresses complex stories and symbolism while, most importantly, passing tradition down to the next generation.

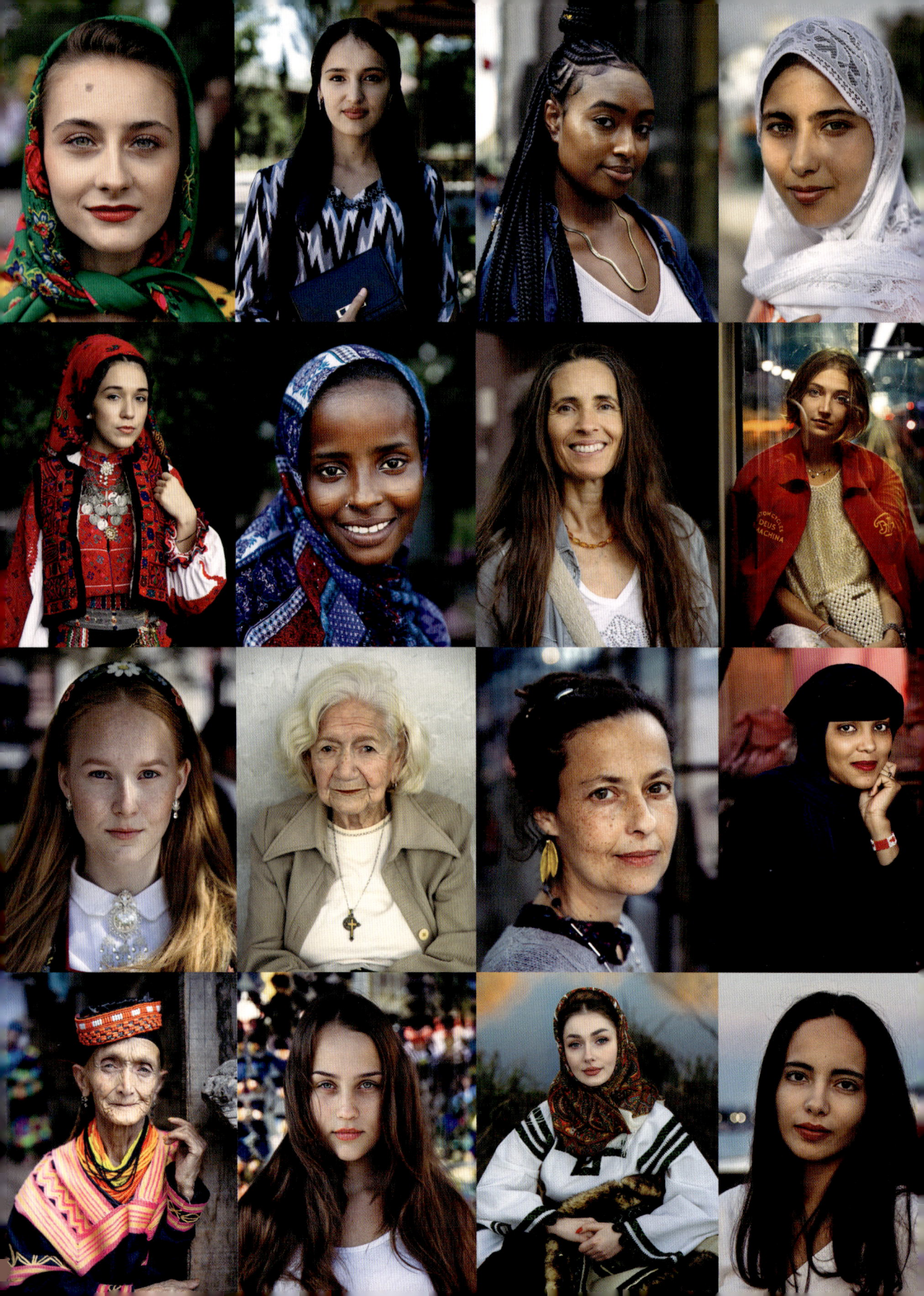

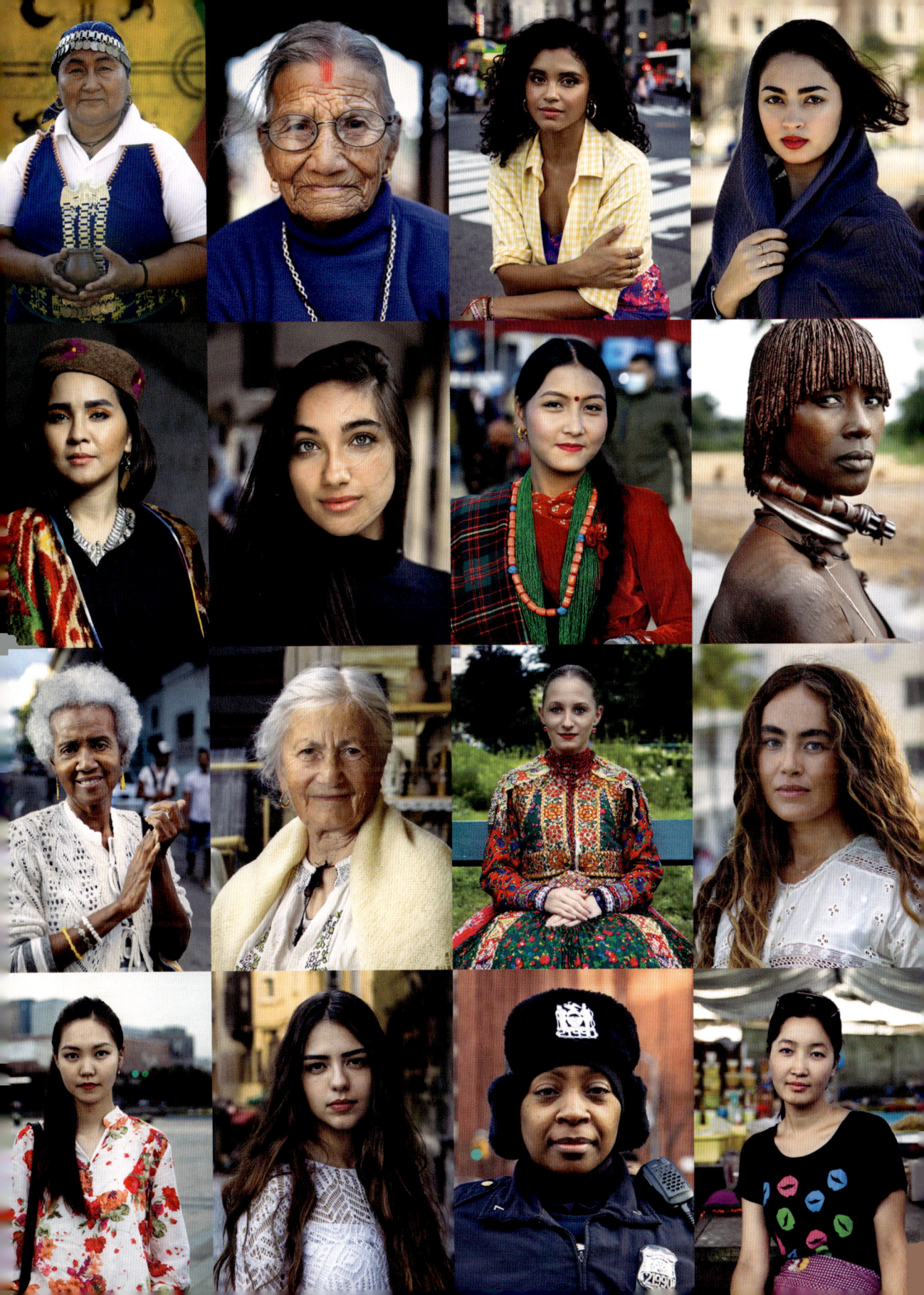

BEAUTY

I'm somewhere in the world, in a community affected by poverty, visiting a market very early in the morning. Suddenly, I see a girl, about fifteen years old, sleeping in front of a tent on a sidewalk. There are more tents with entire families living in them. The girl feels my steps on the sidewalk, and she opens her eyes. Her gaze meets mine with a kindness that words fail to capture, accompanied by a smile that is so genuine and sincere. She just woke up in front of her tent, where she lives with her family. They even pay rent to live on that sidewalk, so they can be next to the market where they earn a living. But she smiles at me.

Her power to offer such warmth amid challenging circumstances strikes me deeply. That's pure beauty to me. We start talking, and I find out she's a smart and educated girl—she goes to school while also helping her parents in the market. If I were in her shoes, sleeping on a sidewalk and seeing a foreigner with an expensive camera first thing in the morning, I wouldn't have that same power to smile so kindly. Envy or anger would probably fill my mind. But so many of the women I've met possessed a power to which I can only aspire. For me, this embodies true beauty.

However, beauty extends beyond kindness alone. True beauty lies in the sum of our qualities and how we use them for positive purposes. In other words, using your power for good. Maybe you don't have this girl's remarkable power to be kind in the face of hardship. Neither do I, for sure. But every single human has their own abilities. Use yours positively. That's where true beauty lies.

In my public presentations, I often do an experiment in which I ask the audience to search for the words "beautiful woman" online. You can try this, as well. Almost all the results are similar: seductive looks, perfectly symmetrical features, and almost no diversity at all. But on the streets of the world, things are different.

Unfortunately, millions of women around the planet suffer from this standardization of beauty created by the media. They feel the pressure to look a certain way or behave in a certain way. I was bulimic and anorexic during my adolescence, and I know the pain so well.

Often during my travels, women refused to be photographed just because they didn't feel beautiful. I managed to convince some of them that it's not true at all. But others simply couldn't accept that they could be a part of a project about beauty. I probably could have made another book from all the refusals.

As a mechanism to tackle the problems created by this narrow standard of beauty, some argue that beauty is irrelevant. But I disagree. Beauty is a topic of widespread discussion and cannot be ignored. Instead of dismissing beauty, my aim is to redefine it. Of course, I'm just a small drop in a gigantic ocean, but that's how things change in the end—drop by drop. I think we must broaden our perspectives; we must open our eyes and look around more deeply. We must discover beauty in people around us, like this girl in the market, and ultimately, we must discover beauty in ourselves.

In a world grappling with so many problems, the media's narrow definition of beauty won't solve anything. However, the real beauty that resides within all good human beings has the power to make a real difference. As Prince Myshkin's saying goes, "Beauty saves the world." And in a world filled with conflicts and division, only real beauty can make a positive change.

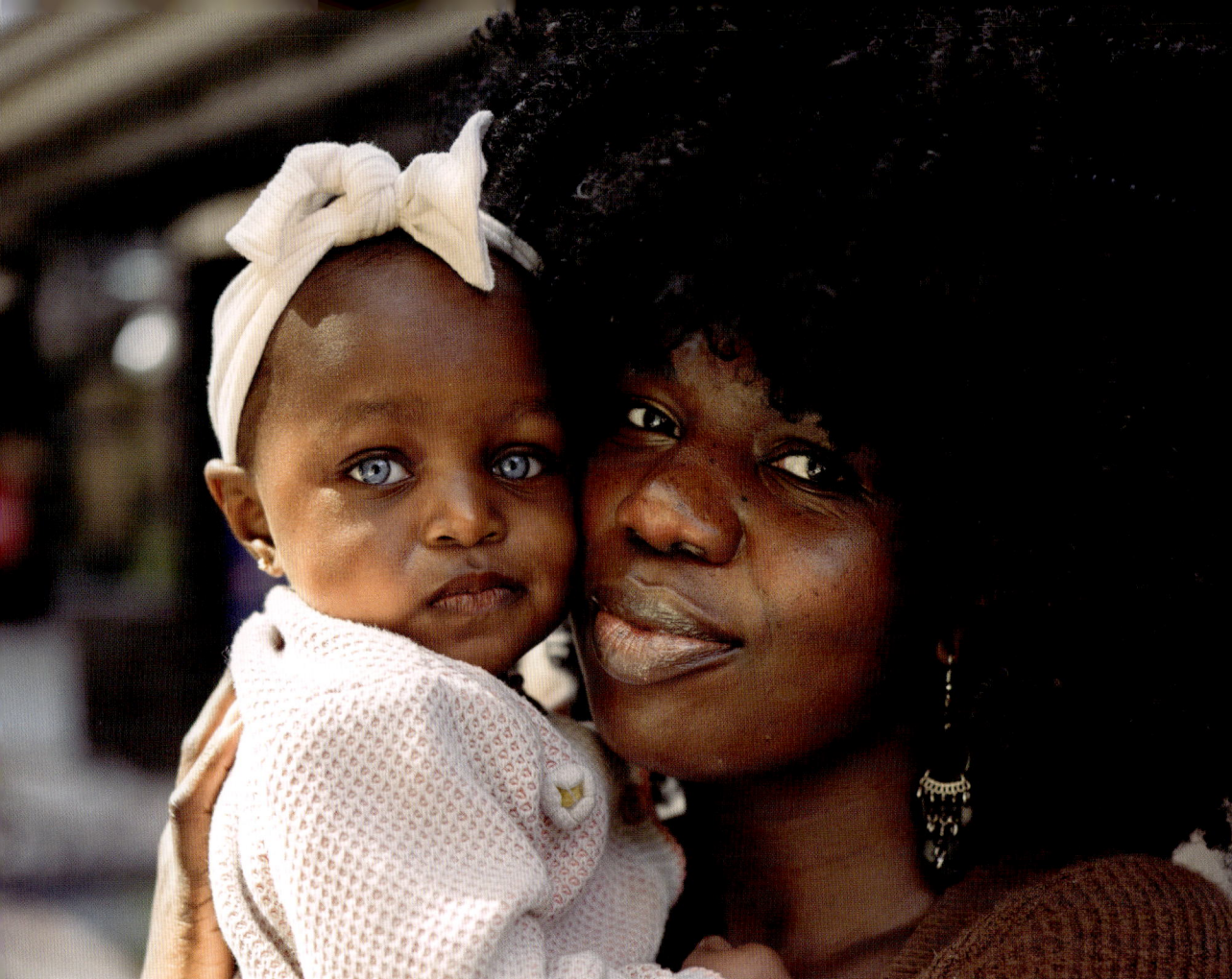

SALT LAKE CITY, UNITED STATES *(Above)*

When a civil war broke out in Liberia, Cheryl Neufville's parents decided to relocate to the United States. Cheryl was born in Boston, studied dance in college, and eventually decided to change paths.

Many years ago, Cheryl's great-grandmother was the midwife of her village in Liberia, and Cheryl grew up hearing fascinating stories about her. Inspired by these childhood memories, Cheryl also became a doula, providing much-needed support for many mothers—not just at home but also in Africa, where she worked as a volunteer. She met her husband there, and that's how little Naomi was born.

Cheryl has noticed that, in the United States, African American women face many more challenges during pregnancy than the average woman, and she wants to change that through her work. She's even more motivated now that she has a daughter to inspire.

VIENNA, AUSTRIA *(Opposite)*

Annika comes from a small mountain village and is studying midwifery. She believes every woman needs a warmhearted and trustworthy presence when giving birth, and she wants to be that presence.

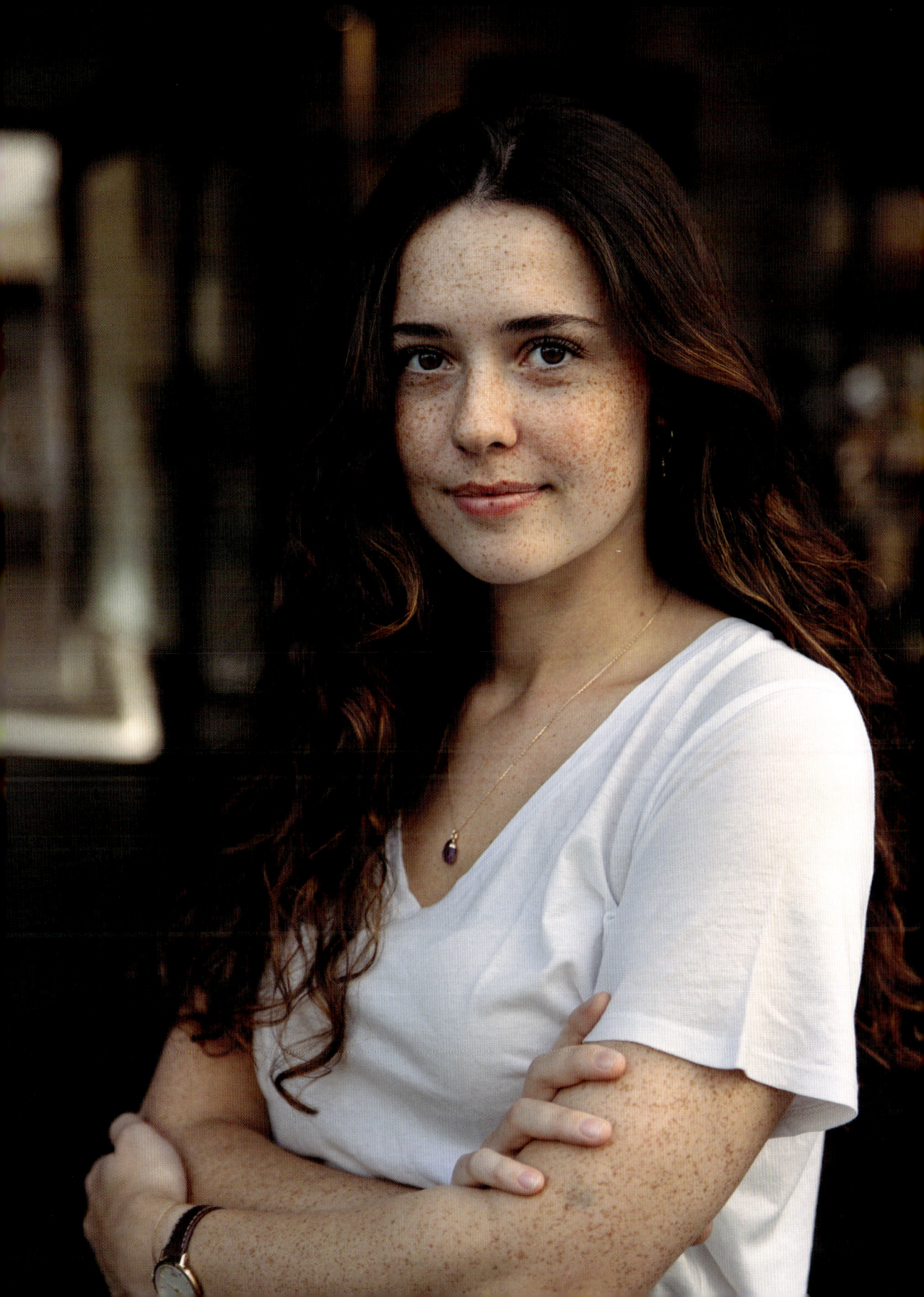

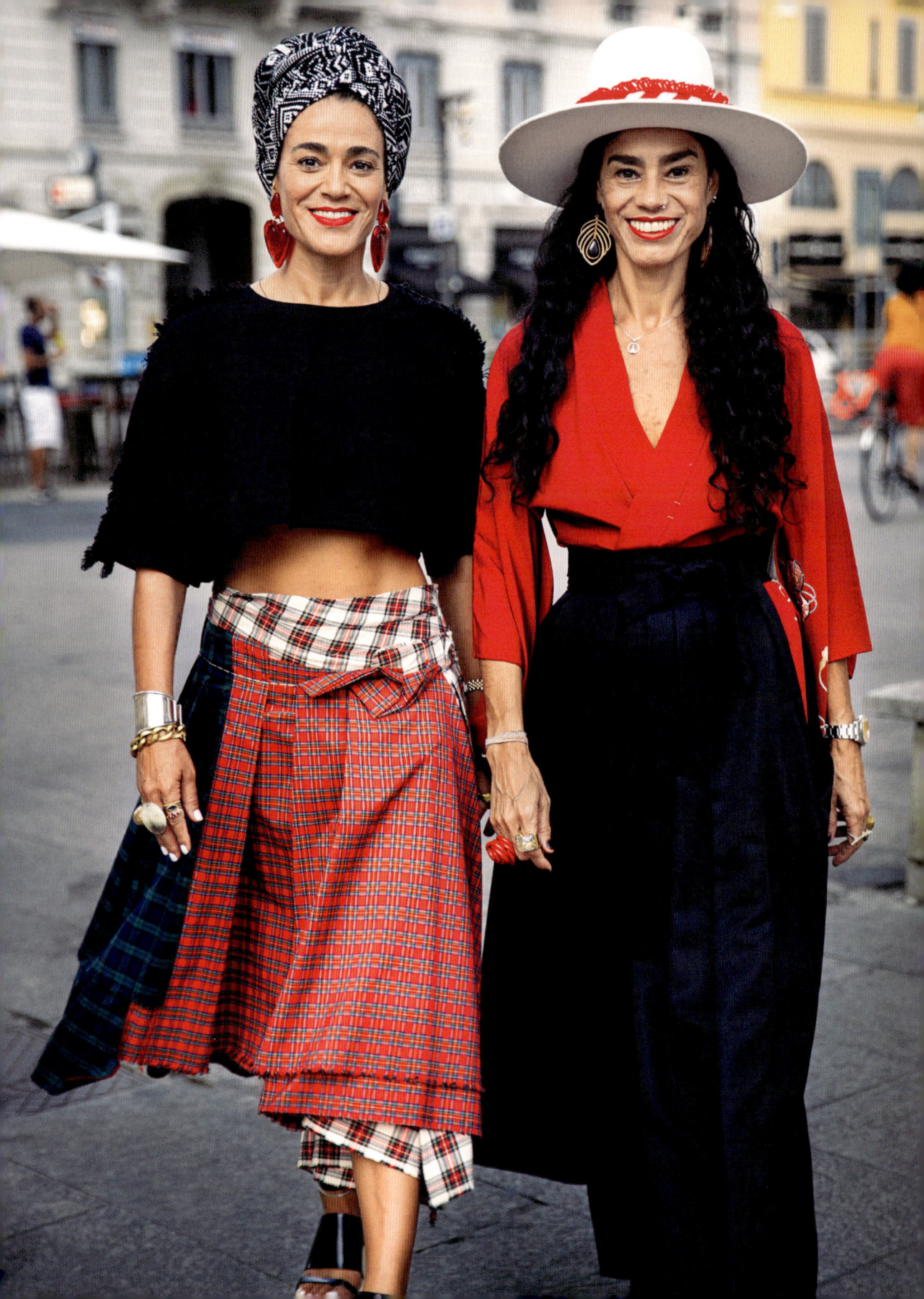

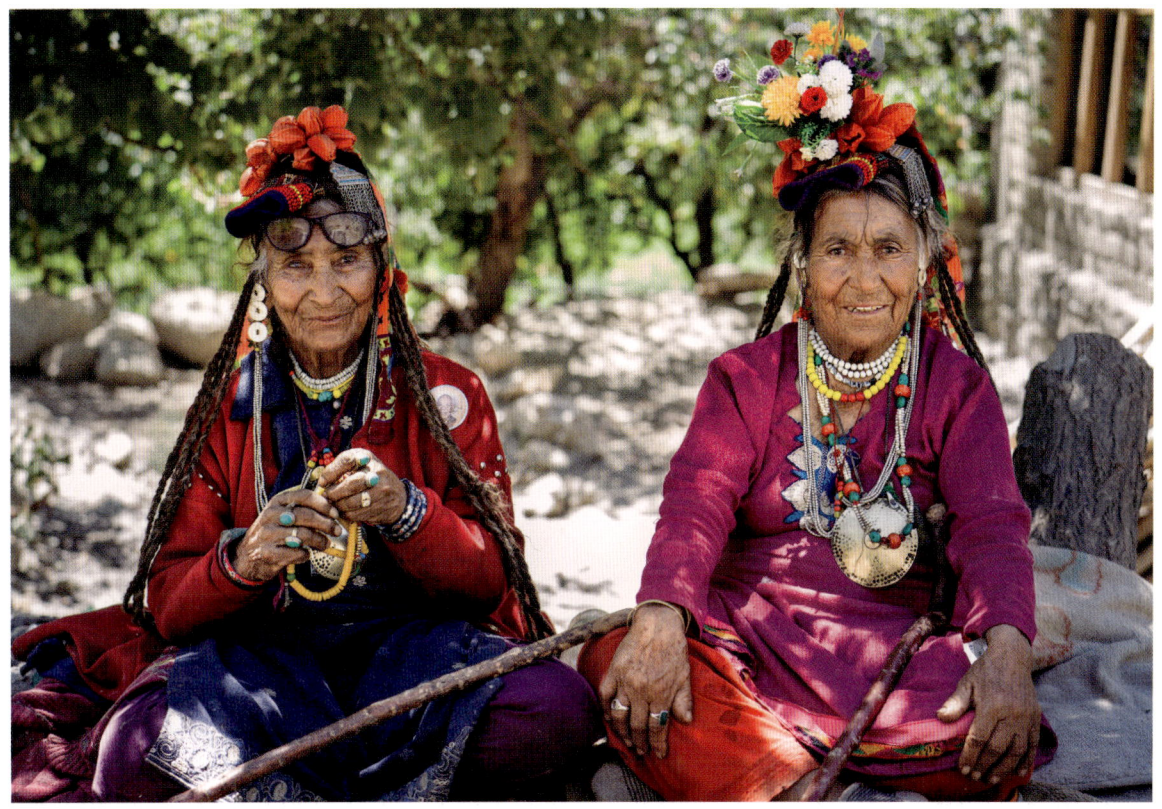

LADAKH, INDIA *(Above)*

This is how these two sisters dress every day. When I noticed them, they were relaxing and enjoying the sunny day next to their homes. Here, television and the internet aren't common pastimes. Instead, relaxation means sitting beside the main road and observing village life.

MILAN, ITALY *(Opposite)*

Meet Adriana and Luciana, two sisters who were born in Brazil but who have lived in Italy for almost twenty years.

After raising five children between the two of them, and as they were approaching their fifties, they decided to explore their biggest passion: a love of color as expressed through fashion.

Adriana and Luciana, known as the Toledo sisters, are successful stylists today, which proves there's no recipe nor ideal age for following your dreams. They defy standardization every day, not only through their spectacular designs but also through their own inspiring story.

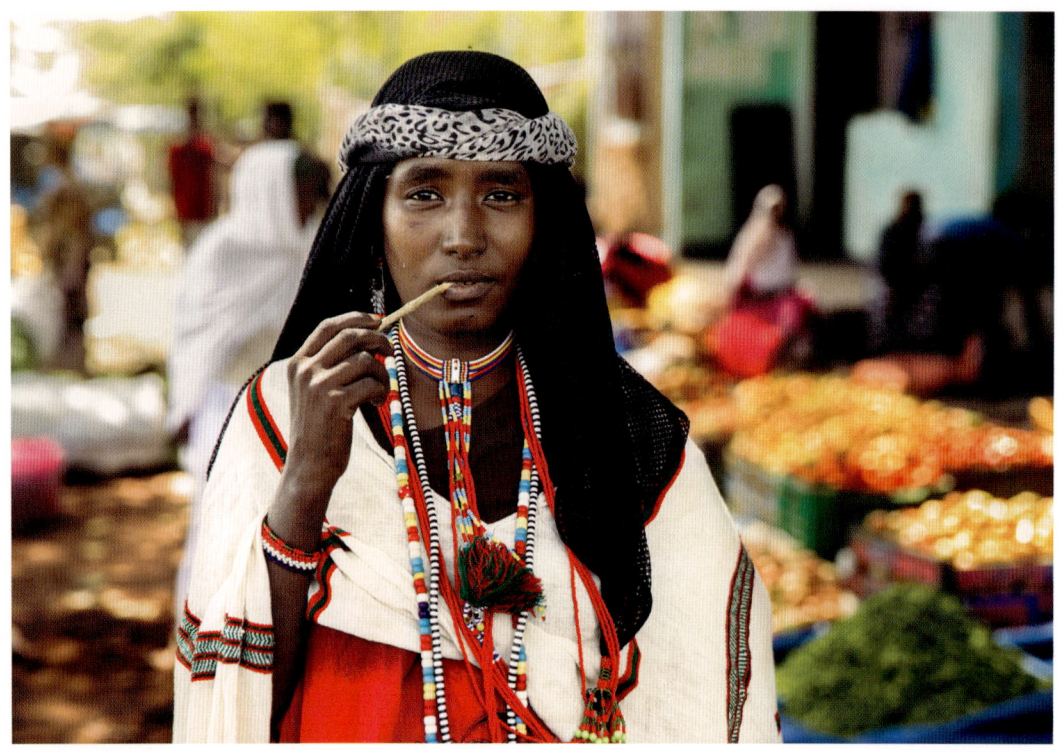

METEHARA, ETHIOPIA

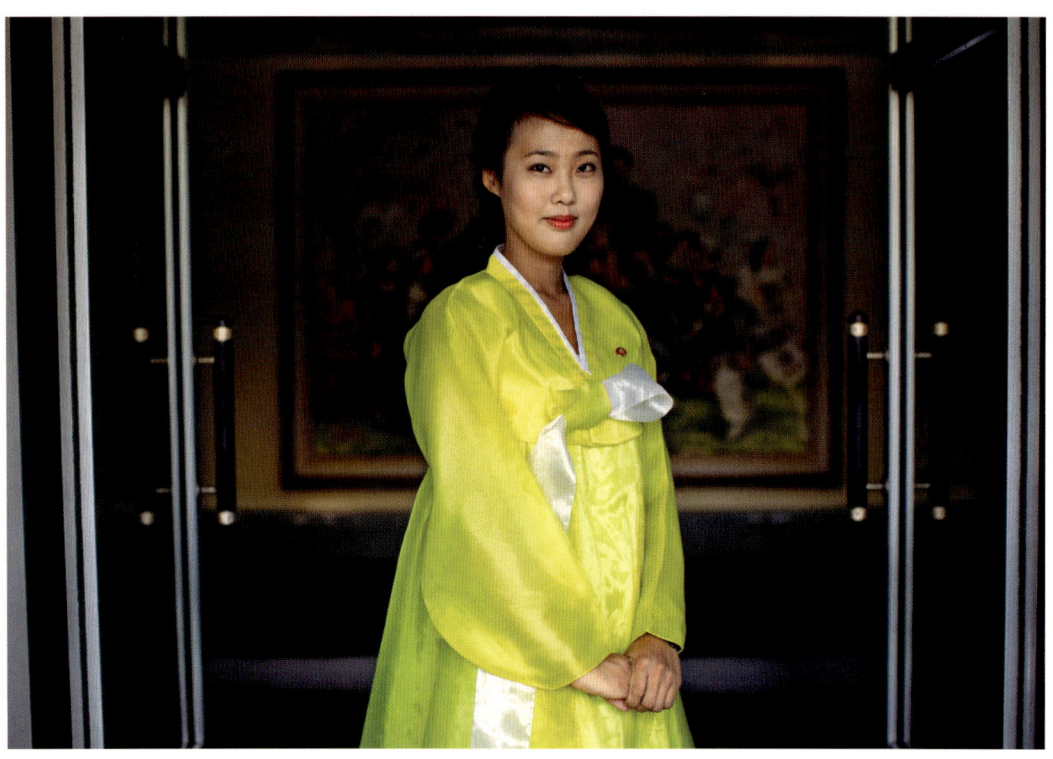

SINUIJU, NORTH KOREA

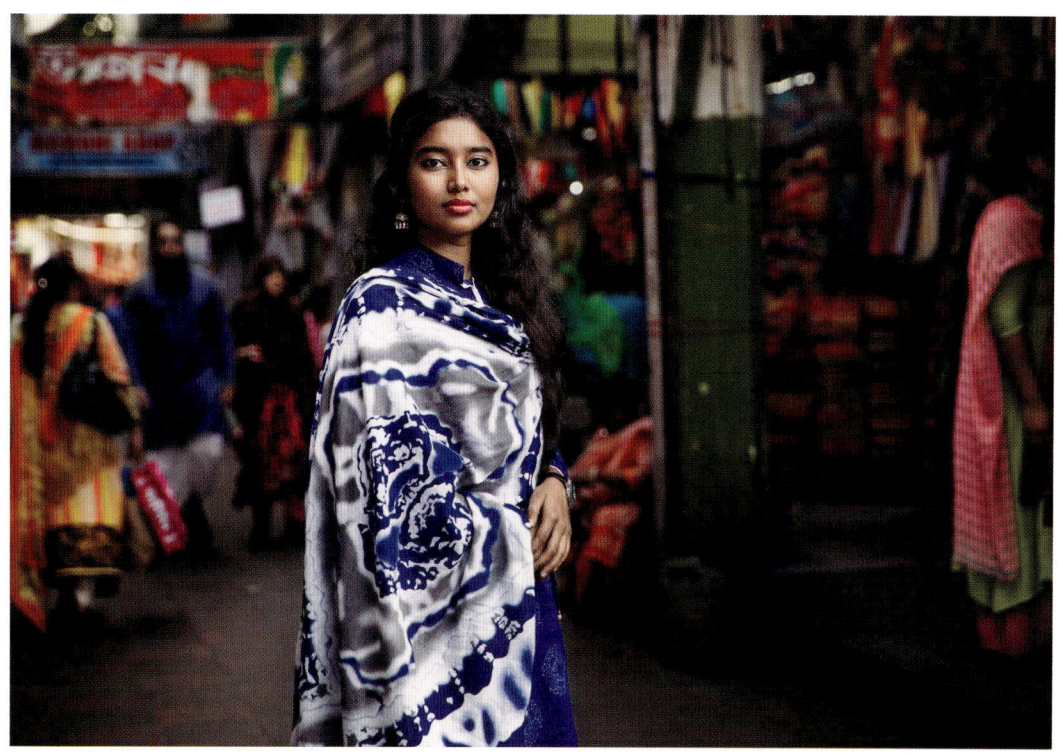

DHAKA, BANGLADESH

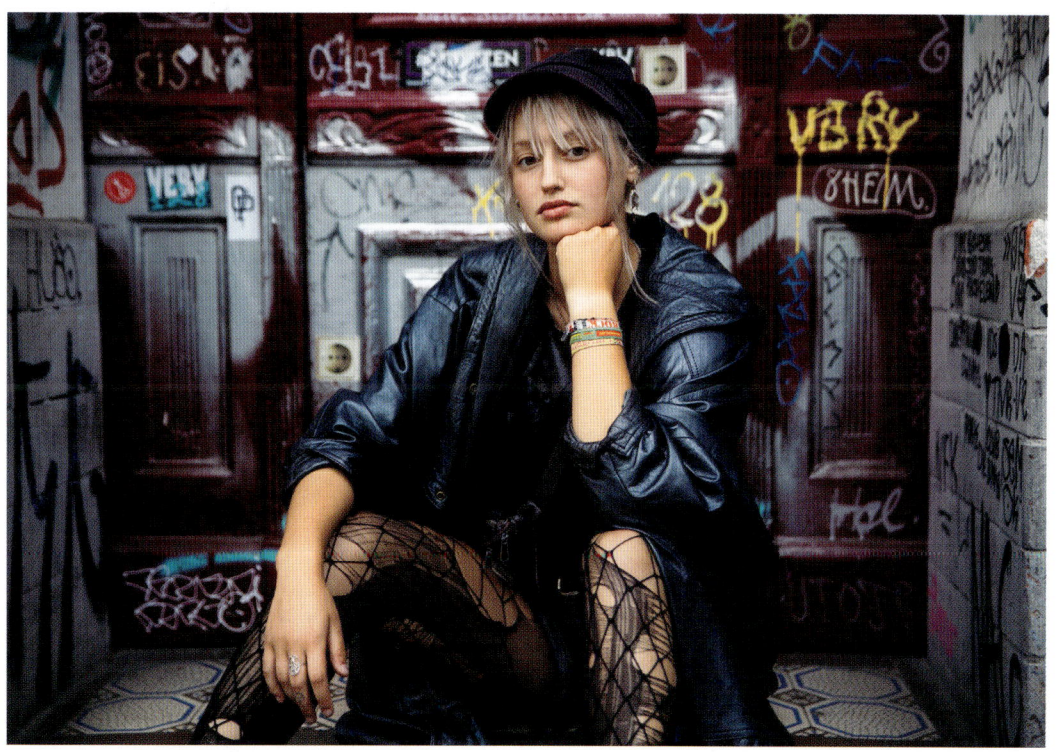

BERLIN, GERMANY

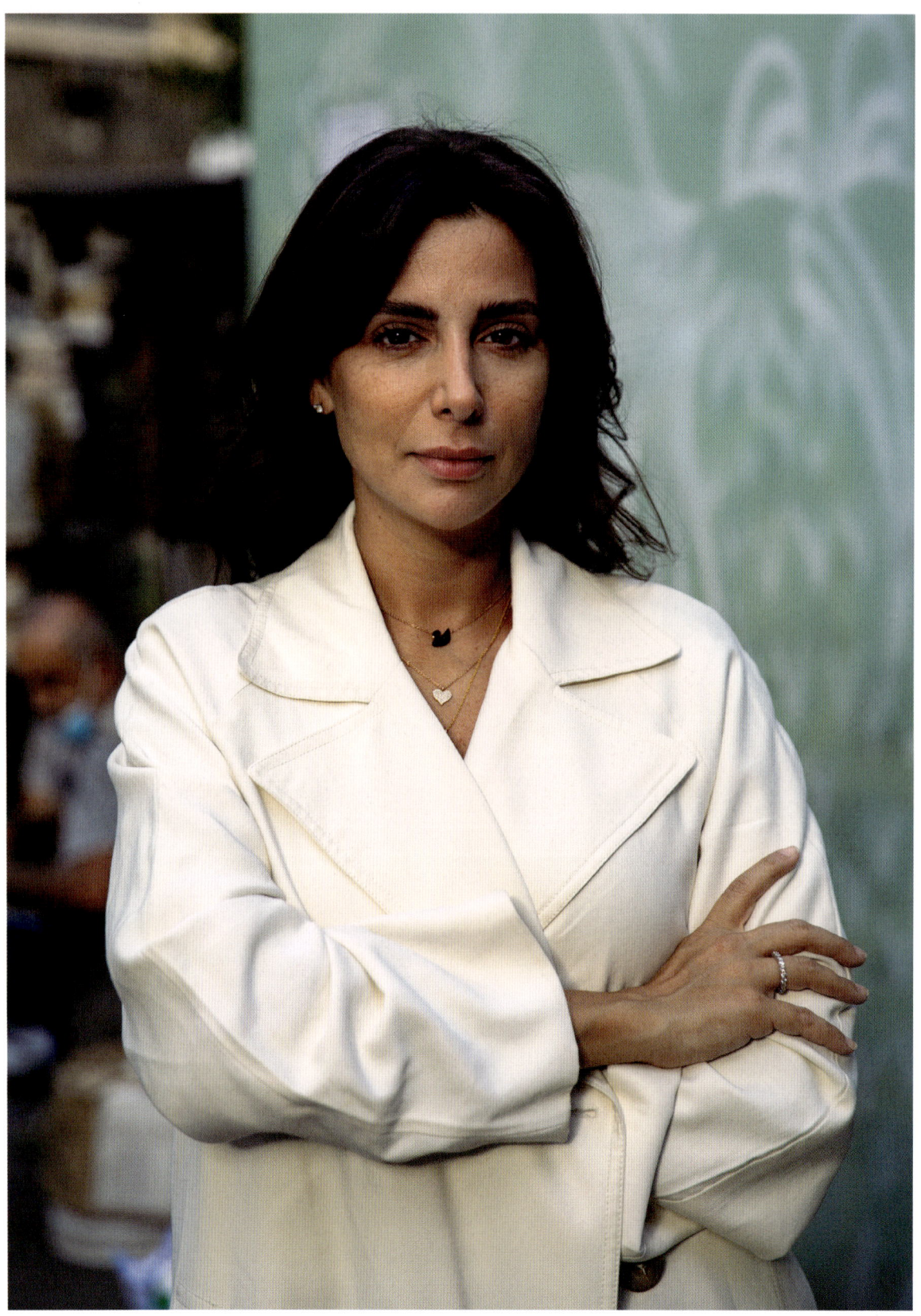

COLOMBO, SRI LANKA *(Below)*

Sonali's work is dedicated to those in suffering—a dedication born from her own experiences. While photographing her, I noticed a scratch on her hand. She told me how she twice wanted to take her own life.

For those around her, Sonali always had a perfect life. She was great at school, and that was all that mattered to her family. She graduated in medical bioengineering and held prestigious jobs. But there were always many struggles inside. She suffers from bipolar disorder and has had many moments in her life when she didn't find a motivation to continue. She began harming herself when she was eleven, and, despite trying various antidepressants, she found little relief.

What proved most effective was speaking openly about her struggles and listening to others facing similar challenges. So, she decided to dedicate most of her time to helping those in need. Today, Sonali works for the World Health Organization and also for SheDecides, a global movement that fights for women's rights. In the end, I think curing others' suffering is the best cure for your own suffering.

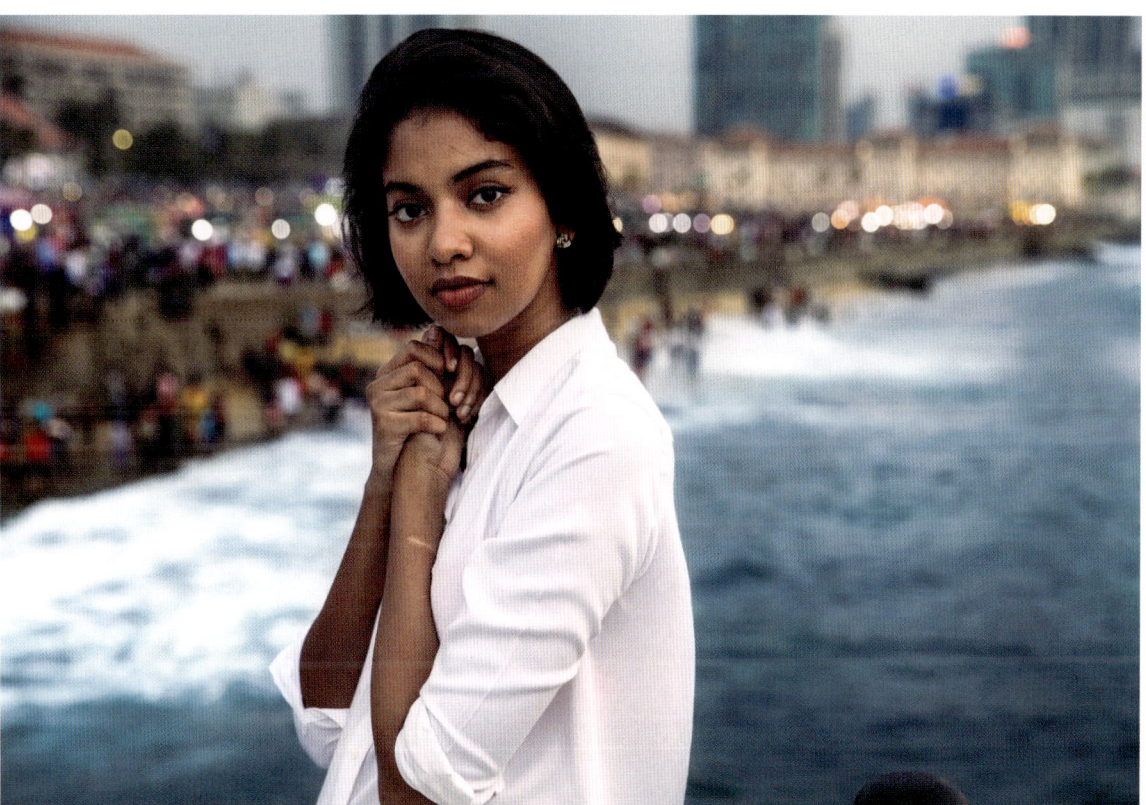

BEIRUT, LEBANON *(Opposite)*

Mia Atoui is a psychologist and the cofounder and president of Embrace, a mental health organization that offers free therapy and operates a suicide prevention hotline. In a country devastated by different crises, Mia has saved many lives through her extensive work in suicide prevention.

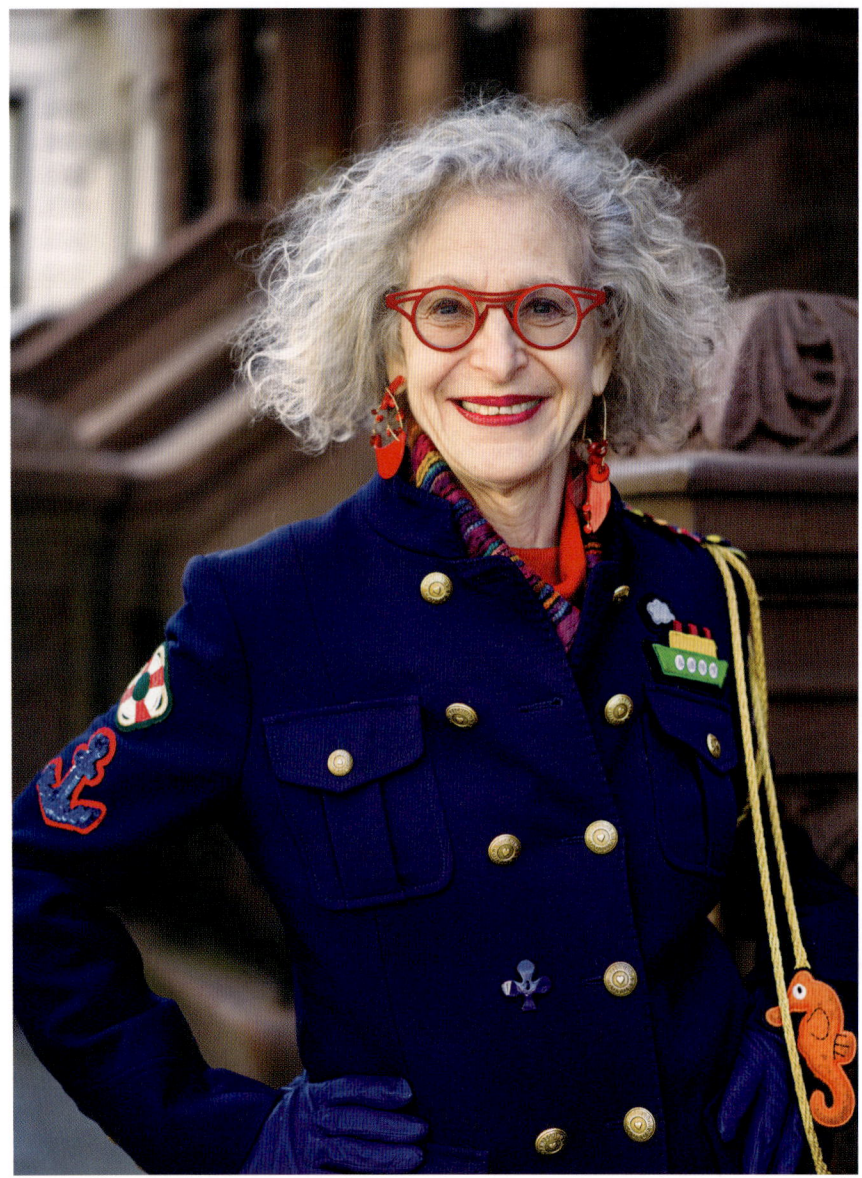

NEW YORK CITY, UNITED STATES

Dayle had a long and prestigious career as a lawyer. After retirement, she finally had enough time to focus on her biggest passions: dancing, visual arts, and fashion.

A few years ago, she created a fashion blog that promotes independent designers, which proves that style and joie de vivre know no age.

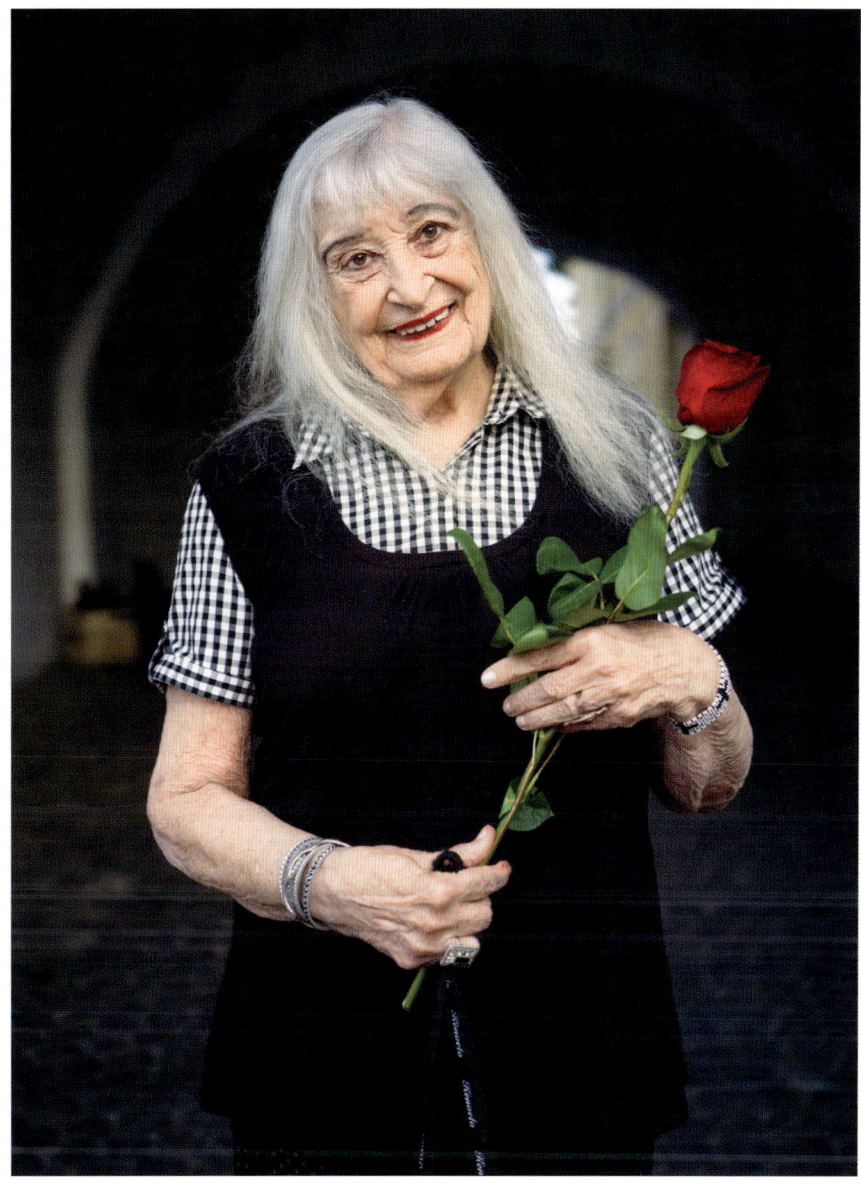

SIBIU, ROMANIA

Nora Iuga, a ninety-two-year-old poet, writer, and translator, was touring her country to promote her latest poetry book when I met her.

During the communist dictatorship—marked by strict censorship in this part of the world—Nora faced prohibition because of the erotic content of her poems and her free, nonconformist style.

Love has been the central theme of Nora's work as well as her life. She cherished her husband, her son, and her friends, as well as her country. She loved all her pets. She also loved smoking, drinking vodka, and nudism. Talking to her for a couple of hours felt like one of the most genuine and inspirational conversations I've ever had.

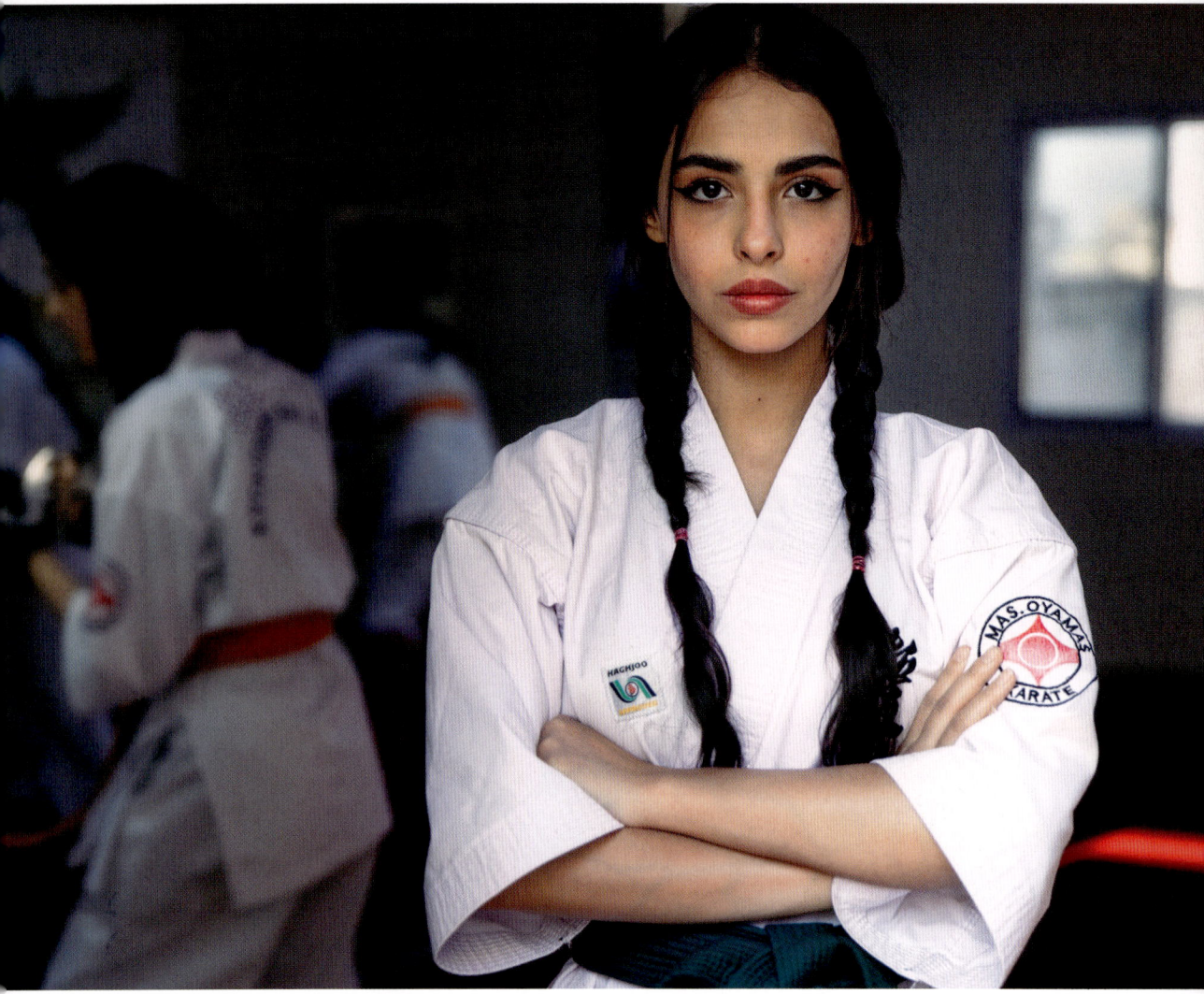

BAGHDAD, IRAQ

A few years ago, Jannat Thaaer decided to take self-defense lessons after she was attacked on the street by a thief. She chose Kyokushin, a full-contact style of karate. However, when she initially started, she found herself surrounded by male classmates, which led her father to hesitate about letting her participate.

Despite the challenges, Jannat persisted and quickly became an exceptional fighter. She began sharing pictures of herself as a fighter on social media and soon received many messages from other women who wanted to follow the same path.

Today, Jannat has her own Kyokushin class dedicated to women. She has more than thirty students who come to practice this tough full-contact style. I was fascinated to witness one of the classes. I saw fierce women with very different backgrounds, both conservative and liberal, fighting with determination and united by a shared ambition to break boundaries.

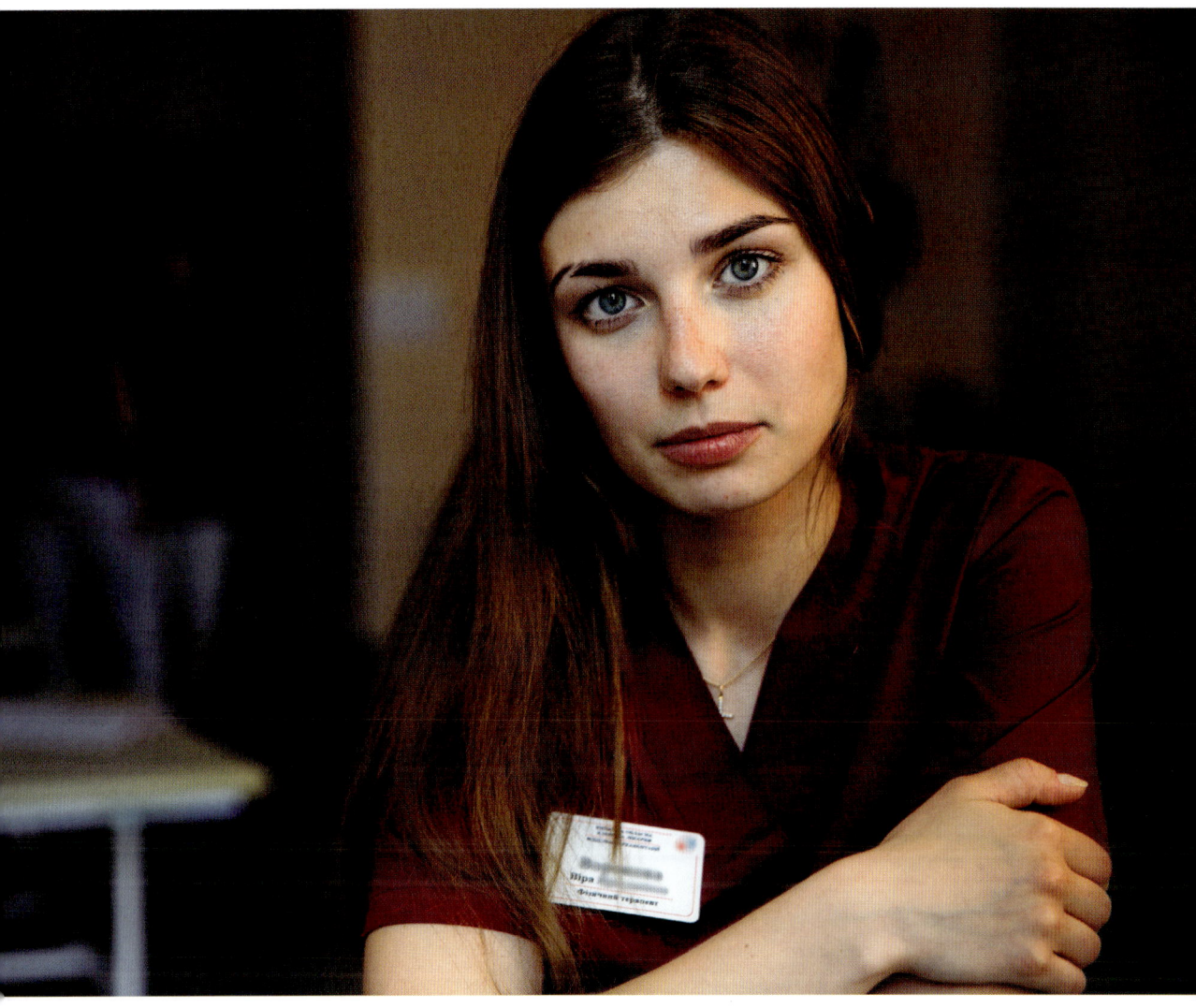

KYIV, UKRAINE

I photographed Vira, who is a physiotherapist, in 2018. She told me that many of her colleagues left the country in search of more opportunities and better incomes. But she decided to stay, knowing the Ukrainian health-care system was in desperate need of specialized personnel. When we met, she had a modest income but was committed to build a better future for her country.

Unfortunately, a few years later, Ukraine was devastated by war. More than ever, the country needed people like Vira. She continued to remain there, working tirelessly to support her people.

DUBLIN, IRELAND *(Below)*

Growing up with dyslexia, a learning difficulty that affects reading and spelling, Clara was always surrounded by mistrust and misconceptions. However, she proved her teachers wrong and excelled in languages while becoming one of the best in her class.

When she had her first boyfriend, people told Clara that she needed to lose weight to maintain the relationship. She went through long periods of depression and took a lot of pills but ultimately found the best cure for herself was learning not to care about what others think and say.

She noticed that many people believe losing weight leads to happiness, but she realized that happiness follows different paths. Through self-teaching, Clara broke free from all the misconceptions and discovered that the best sources of joy lie within her.

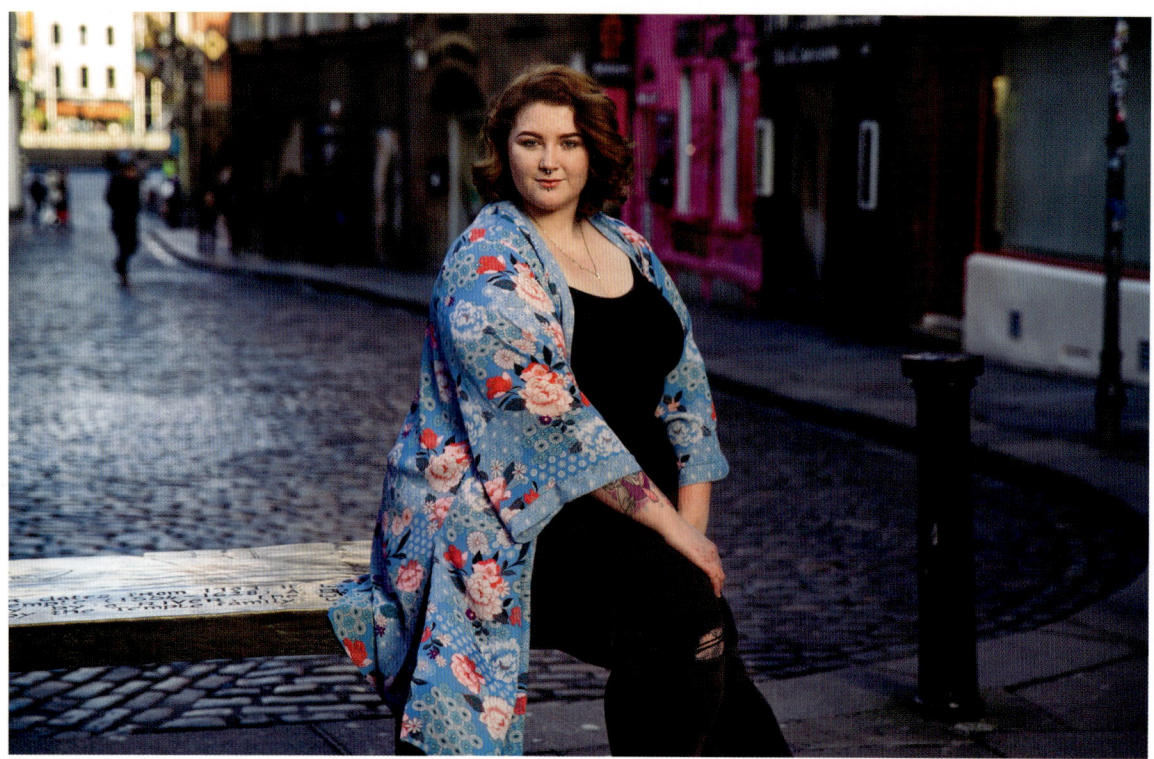

BHAKTAPUR, NEPAL *(Opposite)*

I told her that I liked her hand tattoos, and she invited me for tea and a bowl of rice. Her name means "full of love," and maybe love is exactly the secret to her longevity. Purna Maya is ninety-seven years old, or, as she likes to say it, she's "three till one hundred."

Purna Maya has always lived on this tiny street in this town. During chilly days, she likes to sit in the sun in front of her house, watching and talking with the neighbors. She's like the granny of the neighborhood—everybody knows her. She gave birth and raised six children here as well as many grandchildren.

The world has changed much, but Purna Maya is still living here on the very same street. She finally has the chance to rest and enjoy the sun after a long and intense life.

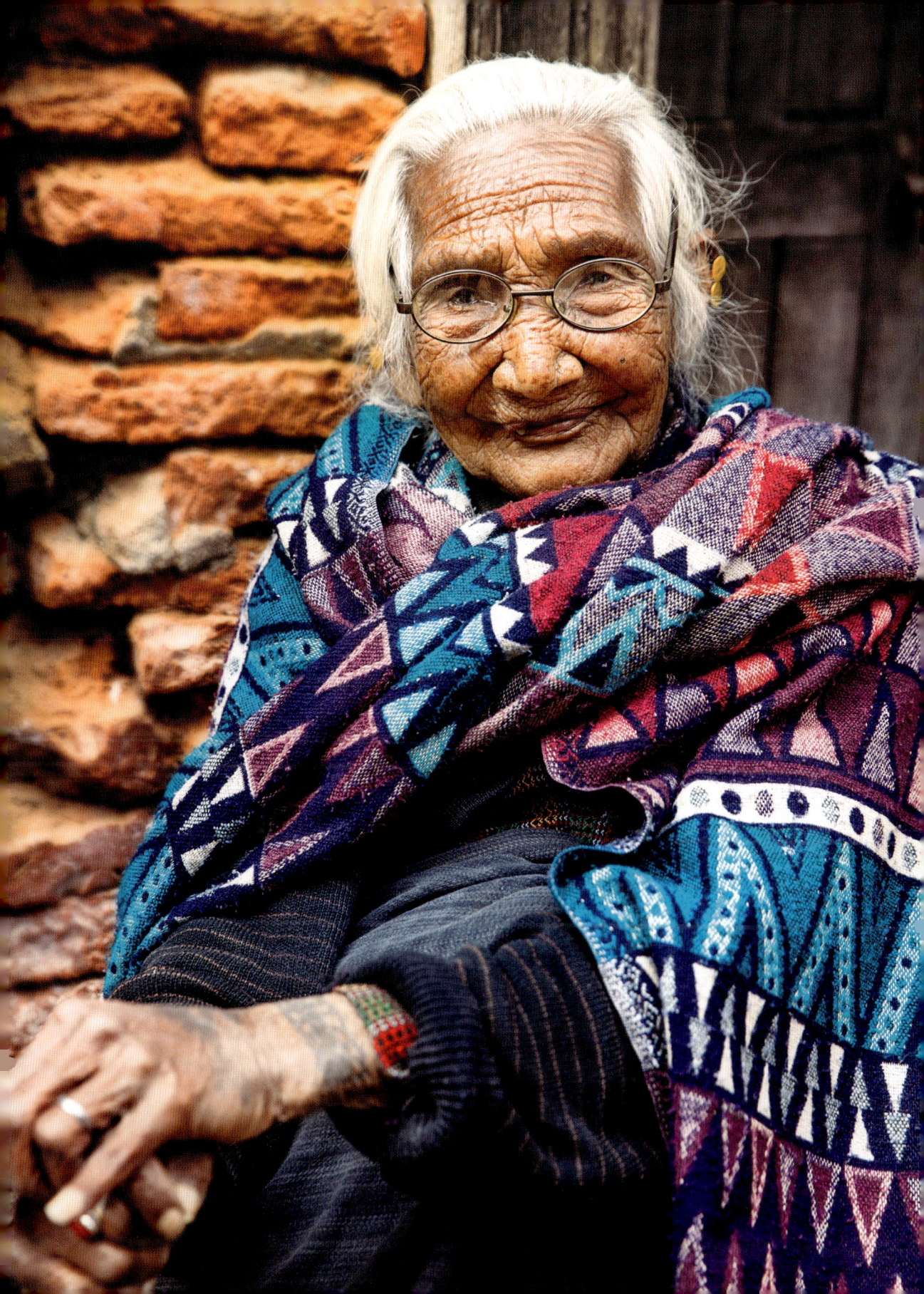

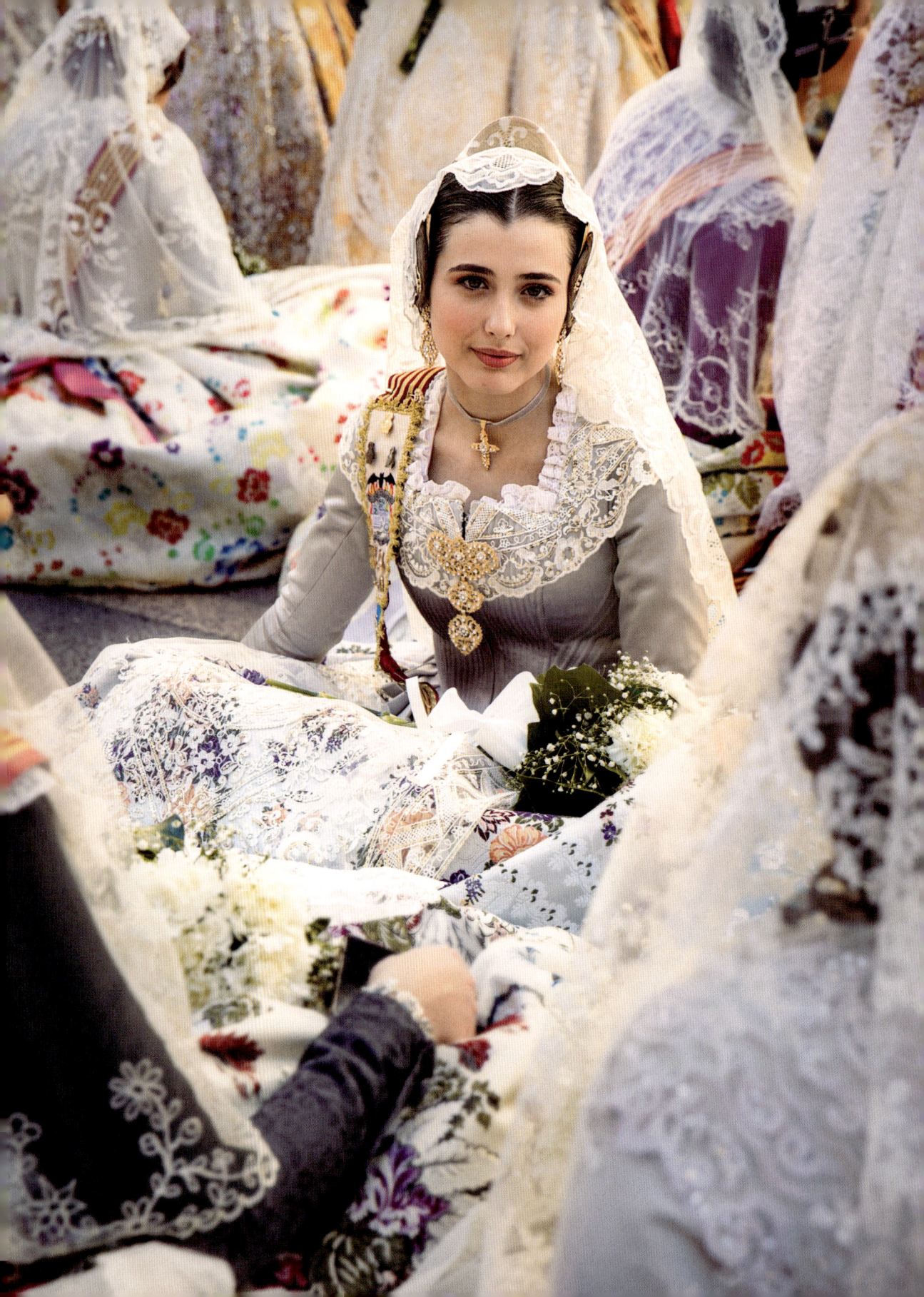

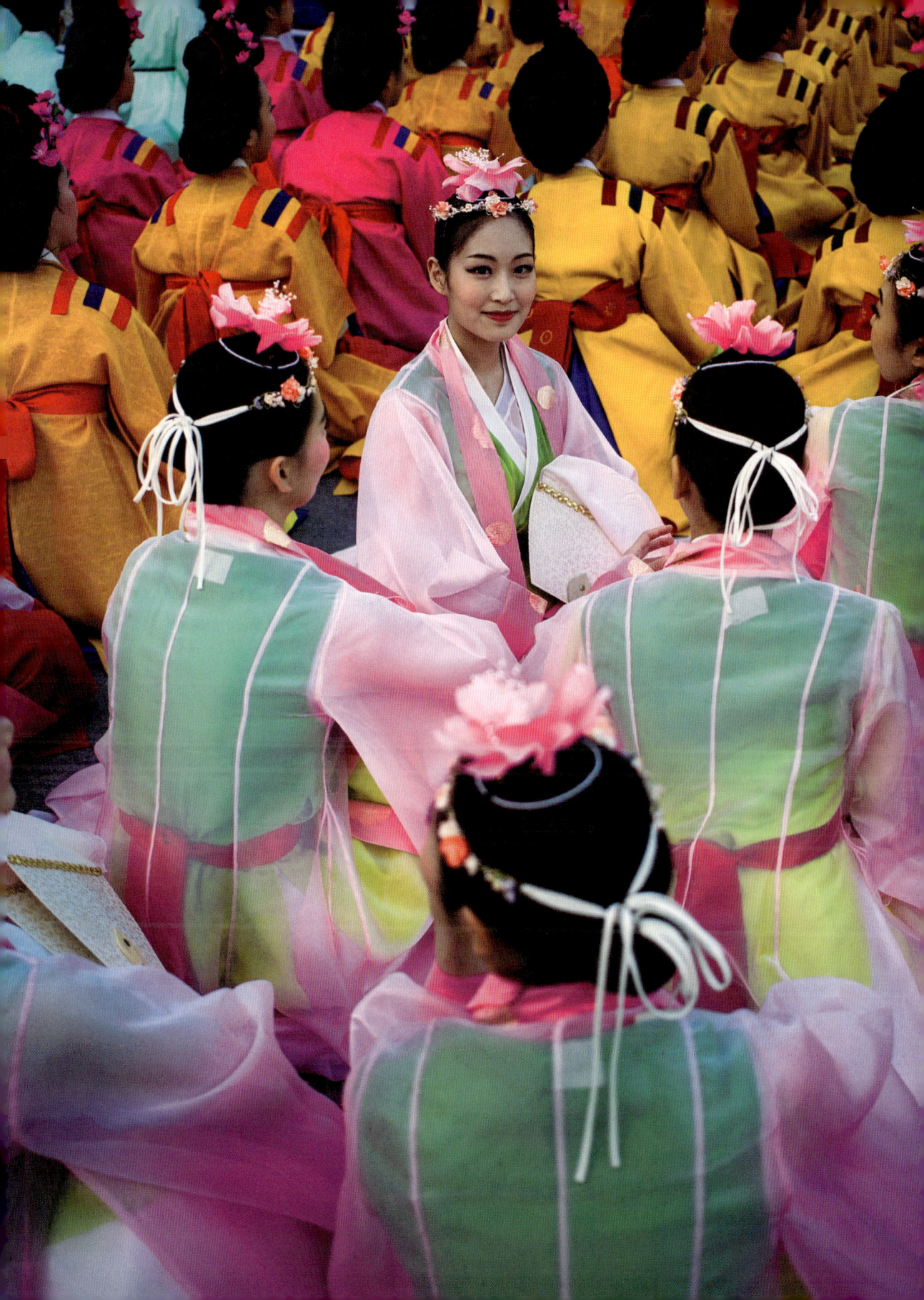

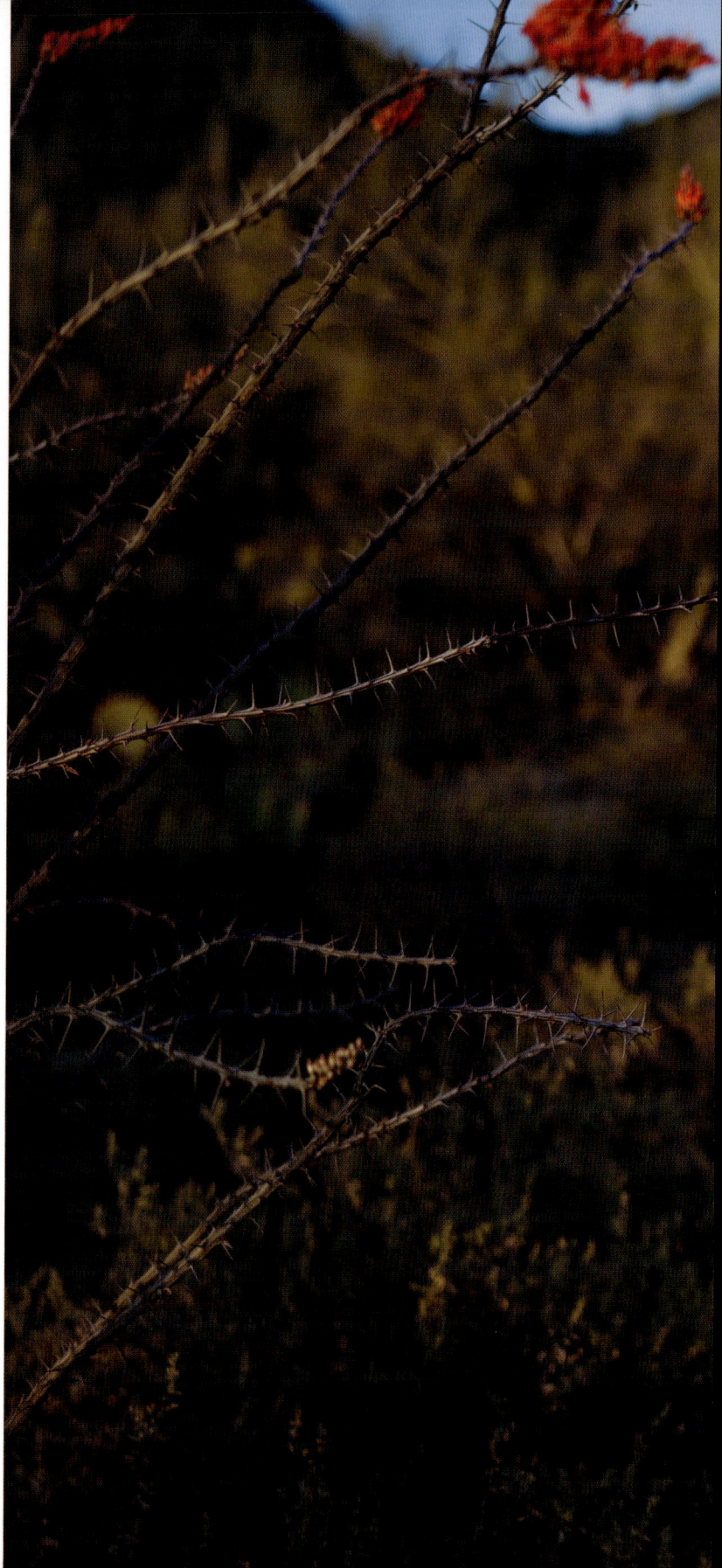

VALENCIA, SPAIN

(Previous spread, left)

I photographed Marta during Las Fallas, one of the most intense celebrations I have ever witnessed. This festival, featuring fireworks, parades, and huge statues, has a history of centuries.

Hundreds of women with incredibly complex hairstyles wear spectacular dresses and exquisite jewels while parading around the city. They are called *falleras*. Being a *fallera* is a complicated task. It takes year-round preparation, and it's all over after just a few days of celebration. But that feeling of being in a fairy tale must be unique.

SEOUL, SOUTH KOREA

(Previous spread, right)

This is a festival in another part of the world. I captured this photo during the K-Royal Culture Festival.

ARIZONA, UNITED STATES

(Right)

I photographed Stina in the Sonoran Desert. This magnificent place is home to more plant species than any other desert in the world, some of which are exclusive to this region.

Stina Swesey, an herbalist and the founder of a small business, passionately crafts skincare products that honor the plants and traditions of folk herbalism. While she has studied plants in different parts of the United States, she chose to return to her birthplace to establish a deep connection with the captivating flora of this unique desert.

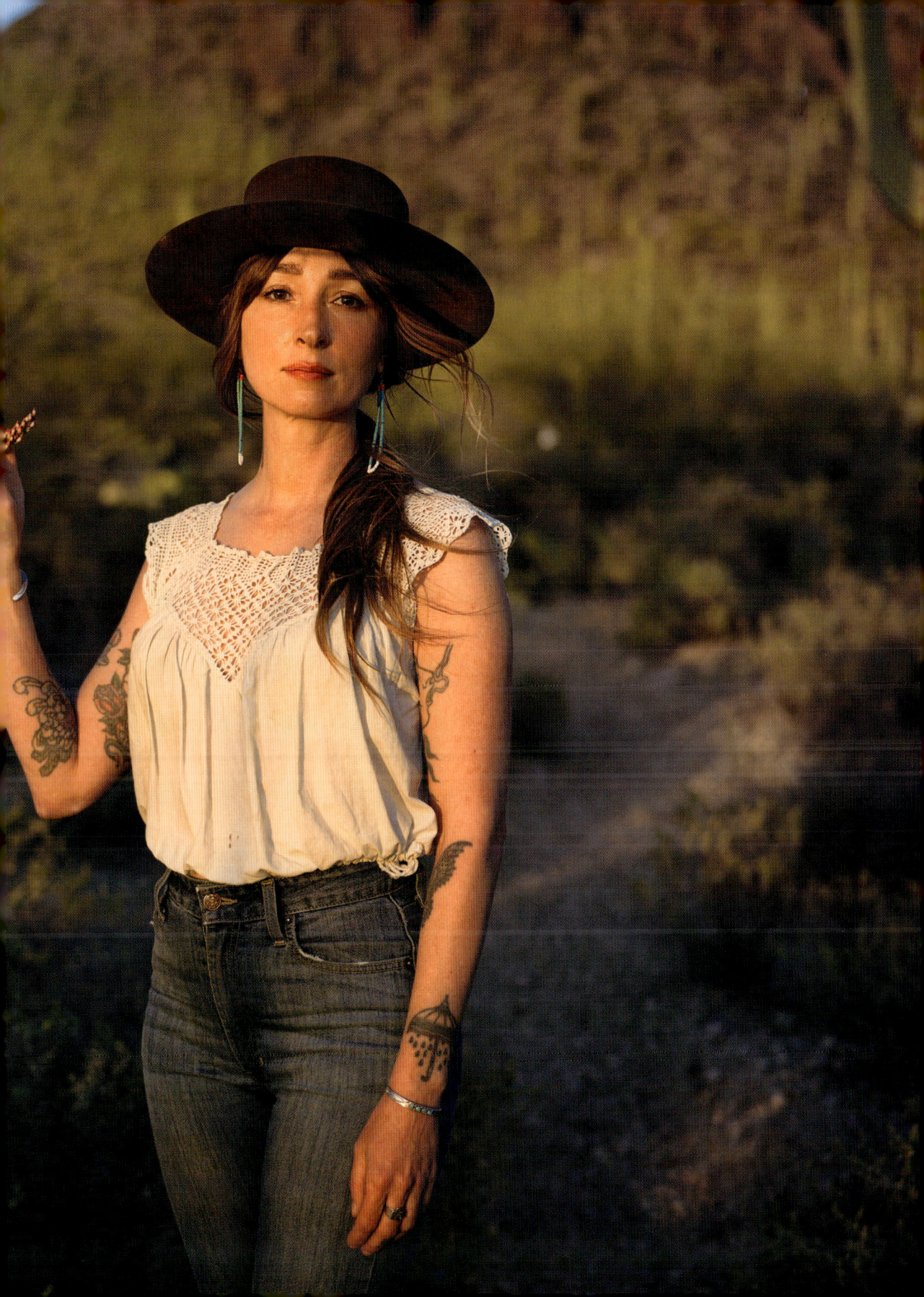

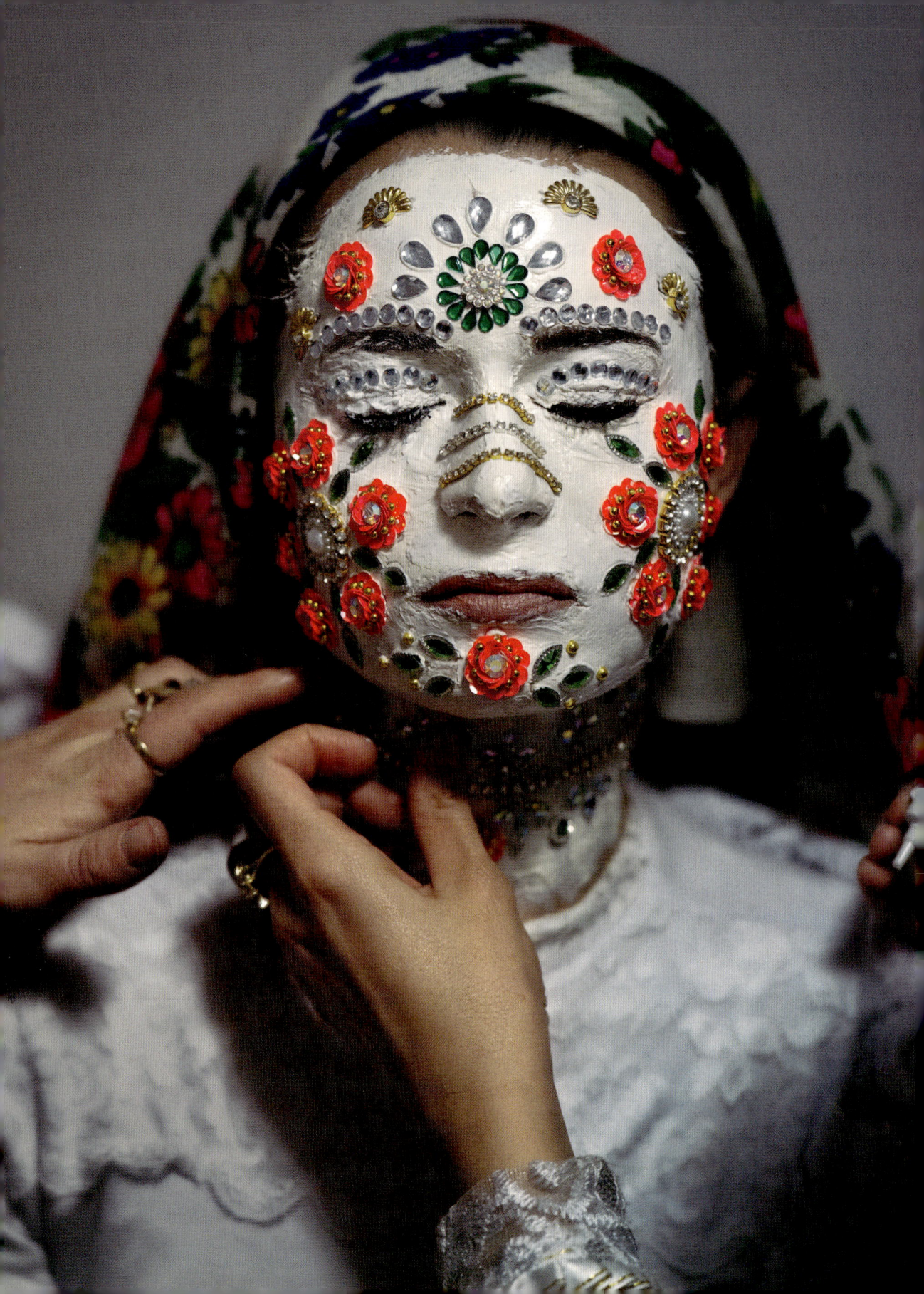

SOUTHERN BULGARIA *(Opposite)*

This is Aisel on the second day of her wedding, as she takes part in a captivating ritual known as *gelina*. Aisel is from Ribnovo, a remote Muslim village nestled high in the mountains of southern Bulgaria.

In this traditional village, the entire community takes part in the splendid wedding festivities, which typically last two days. The culmination of the celebration involves the painting of the bride's face. This significant moment takes place in a private setting, away from male eyes, with a few older women skillfully crafting the mesmerizing decoration.

The meaning of this ritual is hard to trace. Some believe it's a way to protect the bride. Following the *gelina* ceremony, the bride proceeds to her husband's home and is accompanied by the entire community. Upon arrival, both spouses receive a blessing from the imam, which marks the beginning of their new life together.

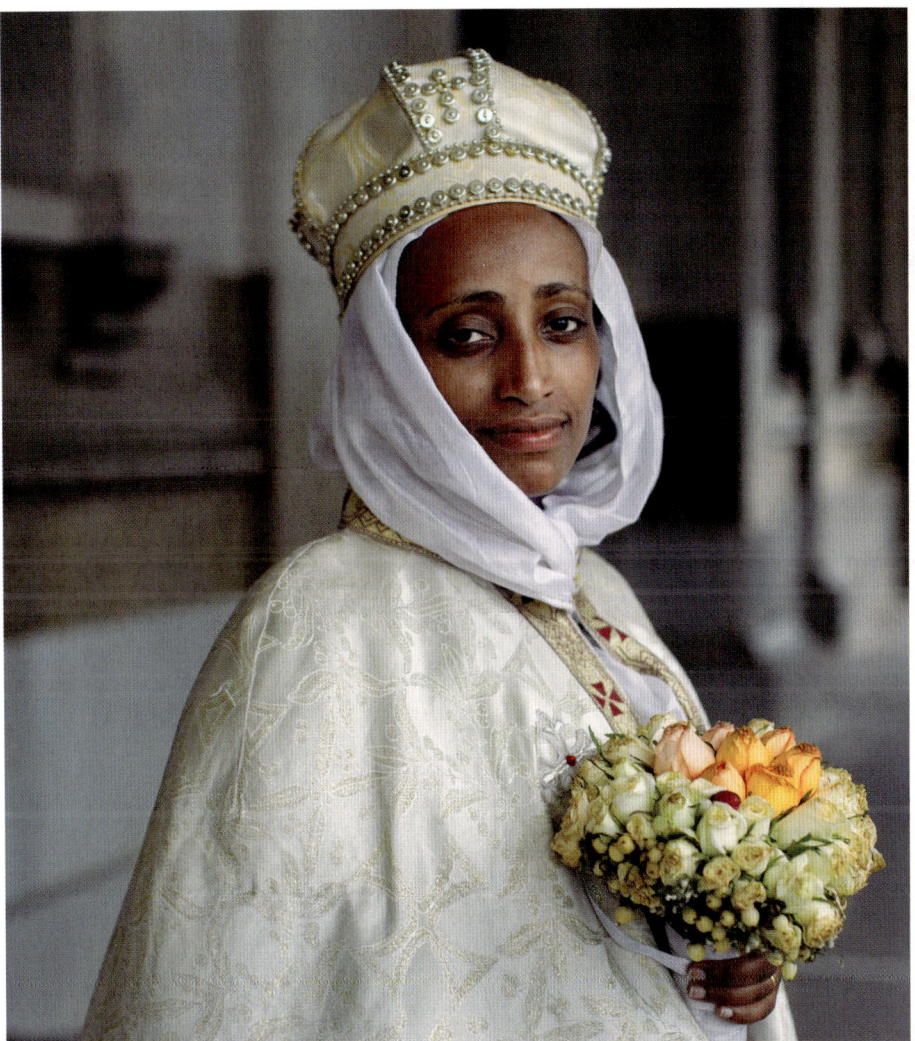

ADDIS ABABA, ETHIOPIA *(Above)*

I photographed this bride next to a church right after her wedding ceremony. In Ethiopia, during Christian Orthodox weddings, the bride and groom wear crowns, as they symbolically become the king and queen of their household.

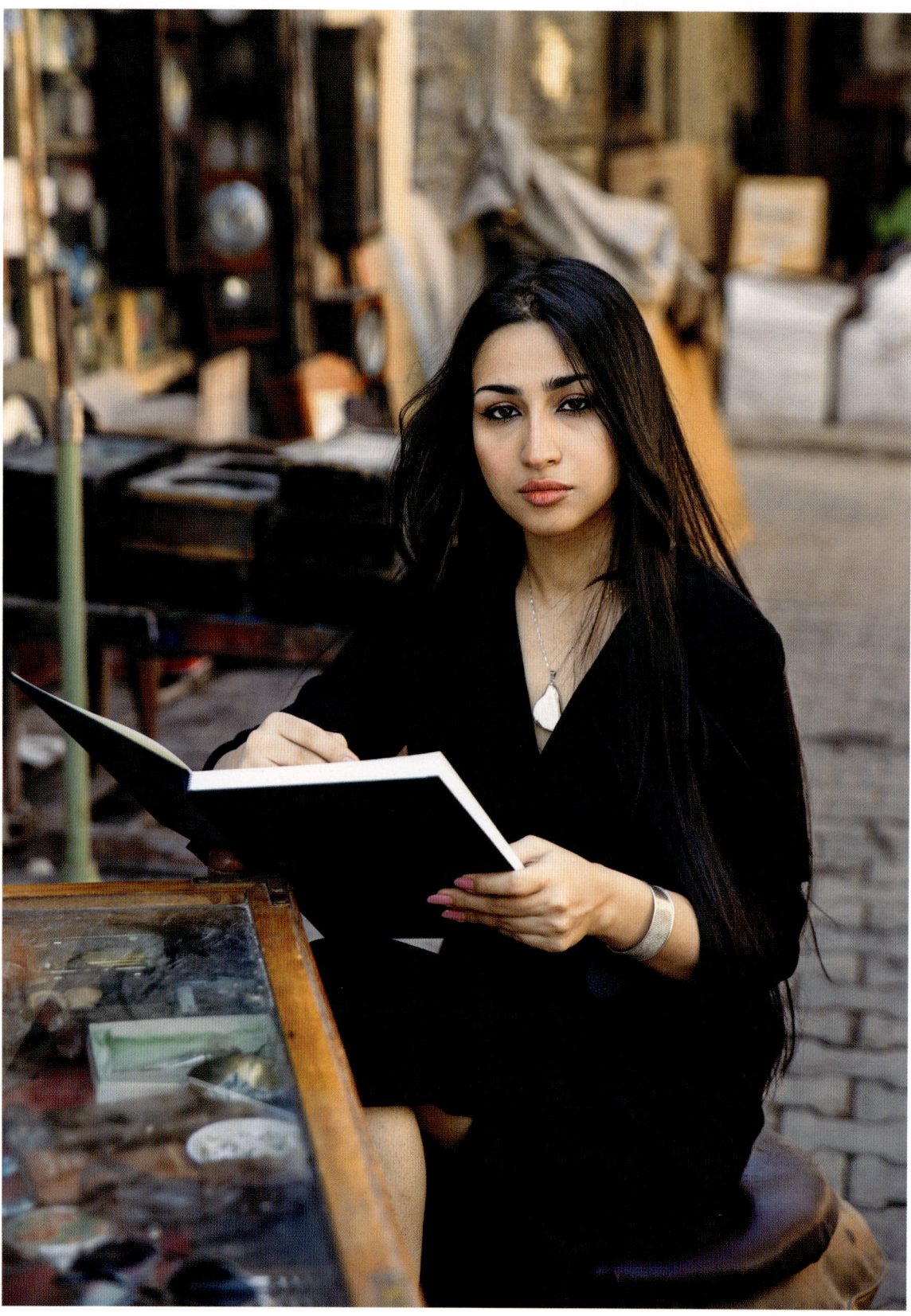

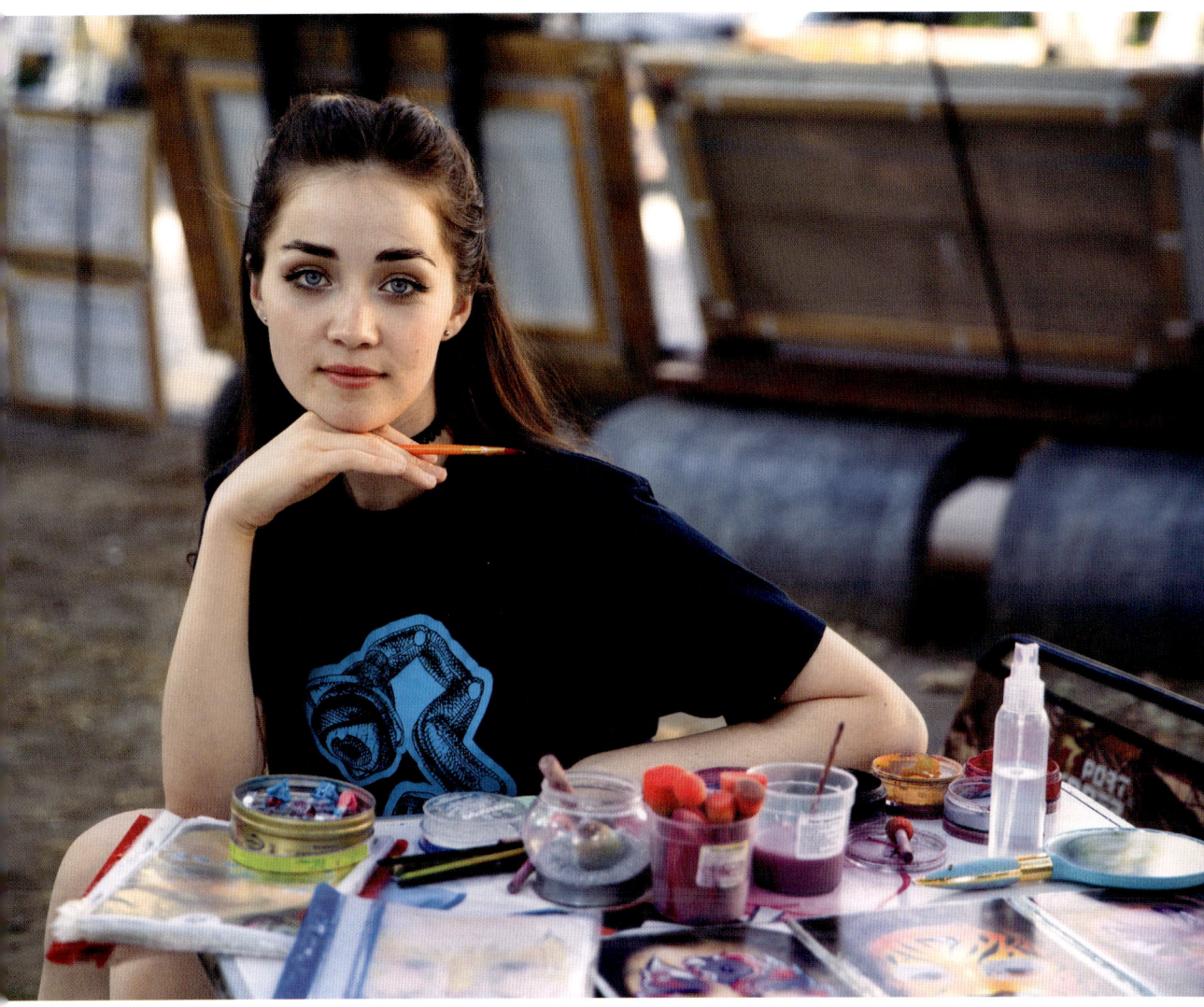

CHIȘINĂU, MOLDOVA *(Above)*

During the week, Liliana paints on canvas since she studies painting at the university. On weekends, however, she paints faces to make a living and enjoys the company of children.

BAGHDAD, IRAQ *(Opposite)*

Tabarak is a painter and sculptor. She remembers a time during the war when it was difficult to get clay for her sculptures, so she'd go to the backyard and use the soil for her work.

CLUJ COUNTY, ROMANIA *(Below)*

I noticed Katalin in the alley of a small village inhabited by ethnic Hungarians. This lovely woman was holding some herbs from her garden. She was eager to offer them as a gift to another lady from the village.

When I look at Katalin, I see a whole generation of Eastern Europeans who have been through difficult times but have learned to see the beauty of simple pleasures.

As children, they witnessed the Second World War at its epicenter. Then came an abrupt and painful transition to communism and cruel dictators, followed by another abrupt transition to capitalism. But there was also a lot of happiness in their lives, because they valued even the littlest of things. Maybe that's why this small bundle of herbs looks like a treasure in Katalin's hands.

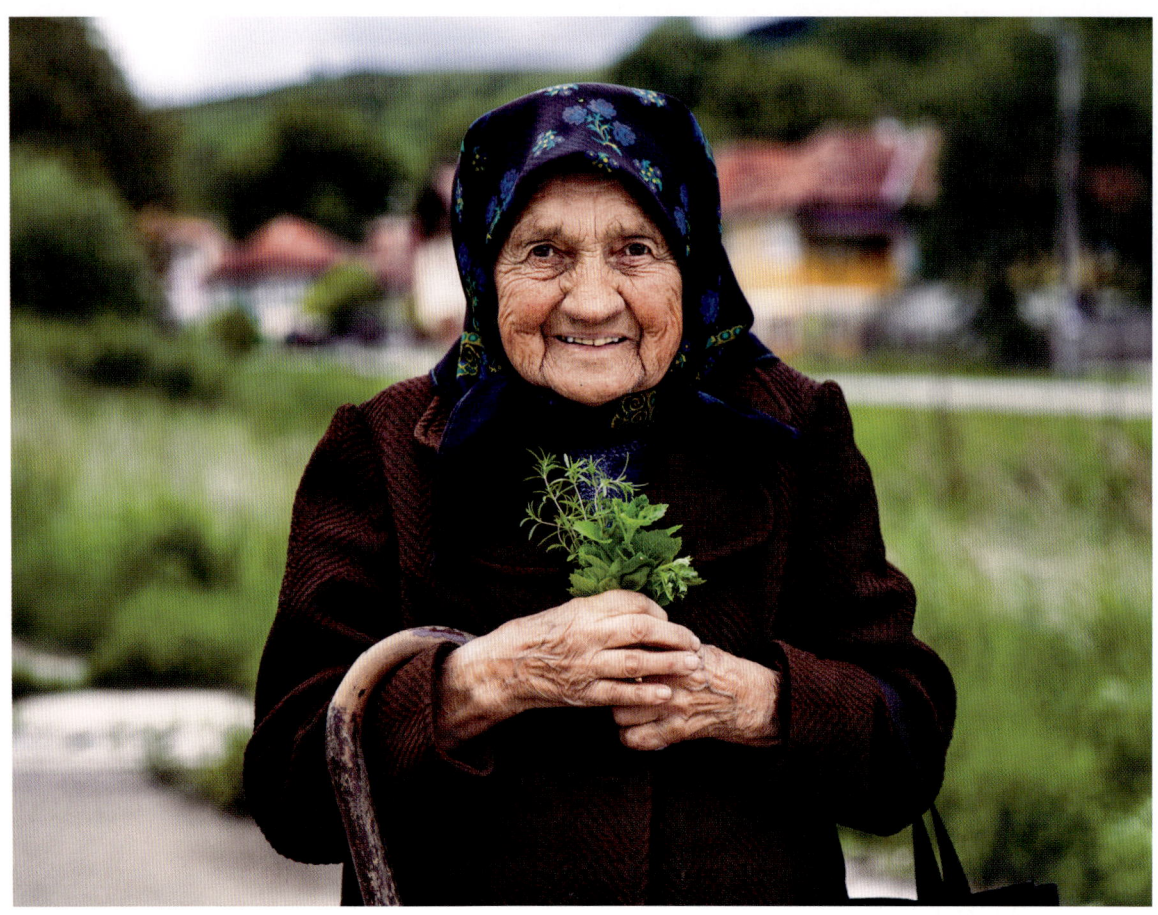

KOLKATA, INDIA *(Opposite)*

It was a misty, magical morning when I noticed a Hindu ceremony taking place on the ghat, the steps along the Hooghly River. After carefully filling her pot with water, Sandra stepped out of the river and kindly consented to be photographed.

Sandra had previously made a wish that came true. That's why, on the day we met, according to tradition, she was collecting water from the river to take it to a temple a couple of miles away, where she would offer it to Lord Shiva. As I photographed her for a few seconds, I could feel waves of pure happiness and harmony emitting from her.

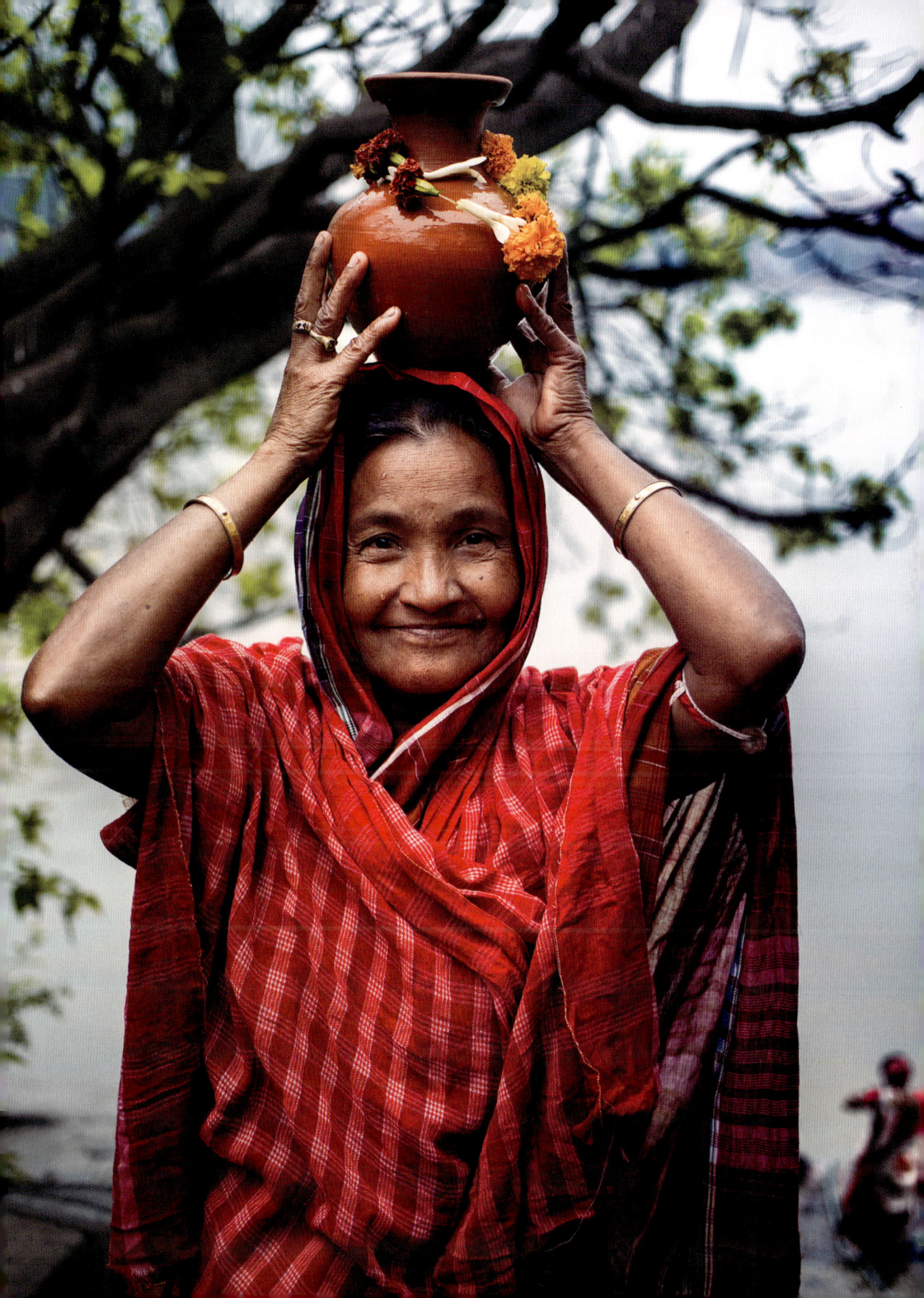

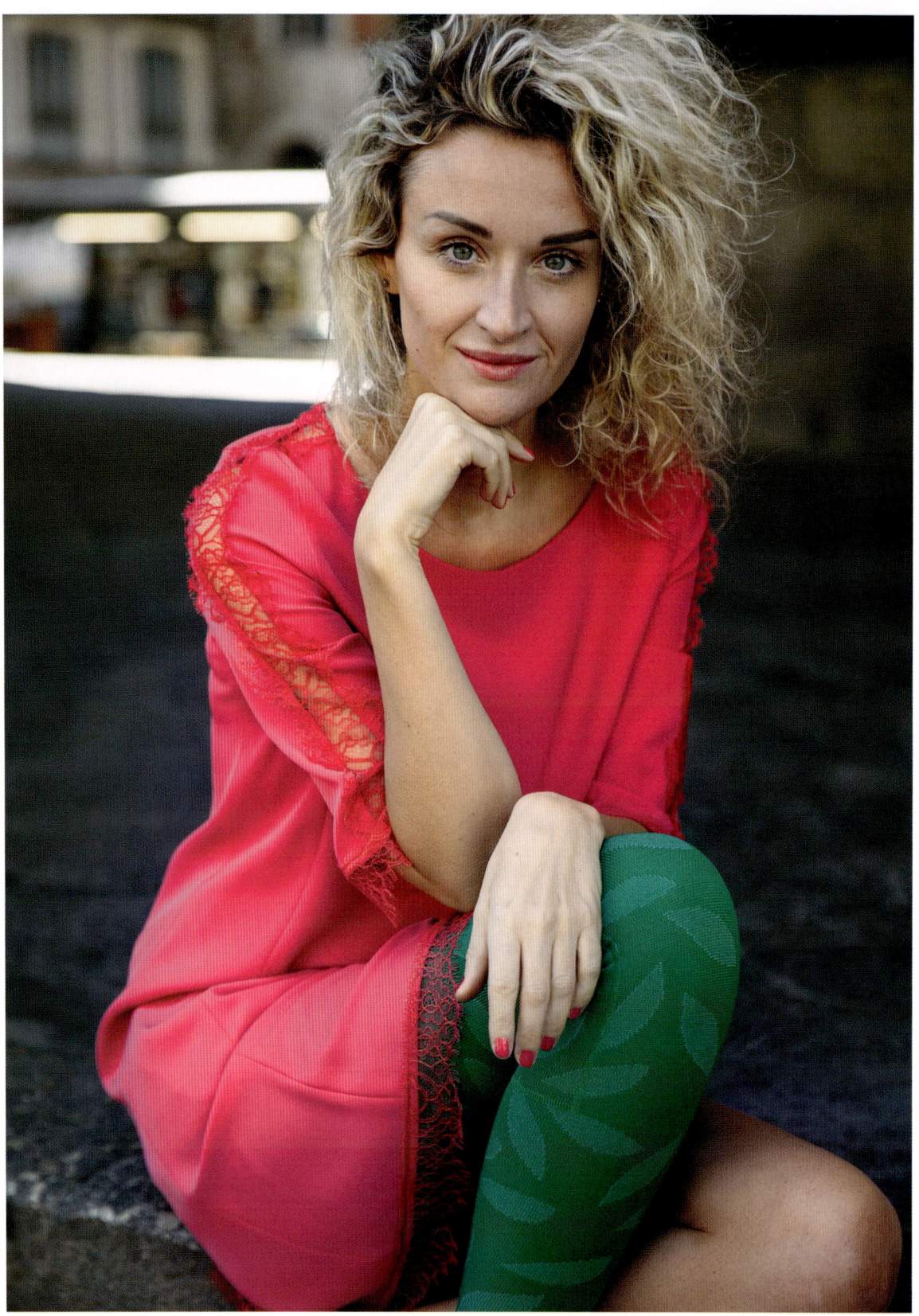

Many Ethiopian women display a great sense of style despite their daily challenges. Iftu, a member of the ethnic group called Oromo, came to this small town from her village in search of work.

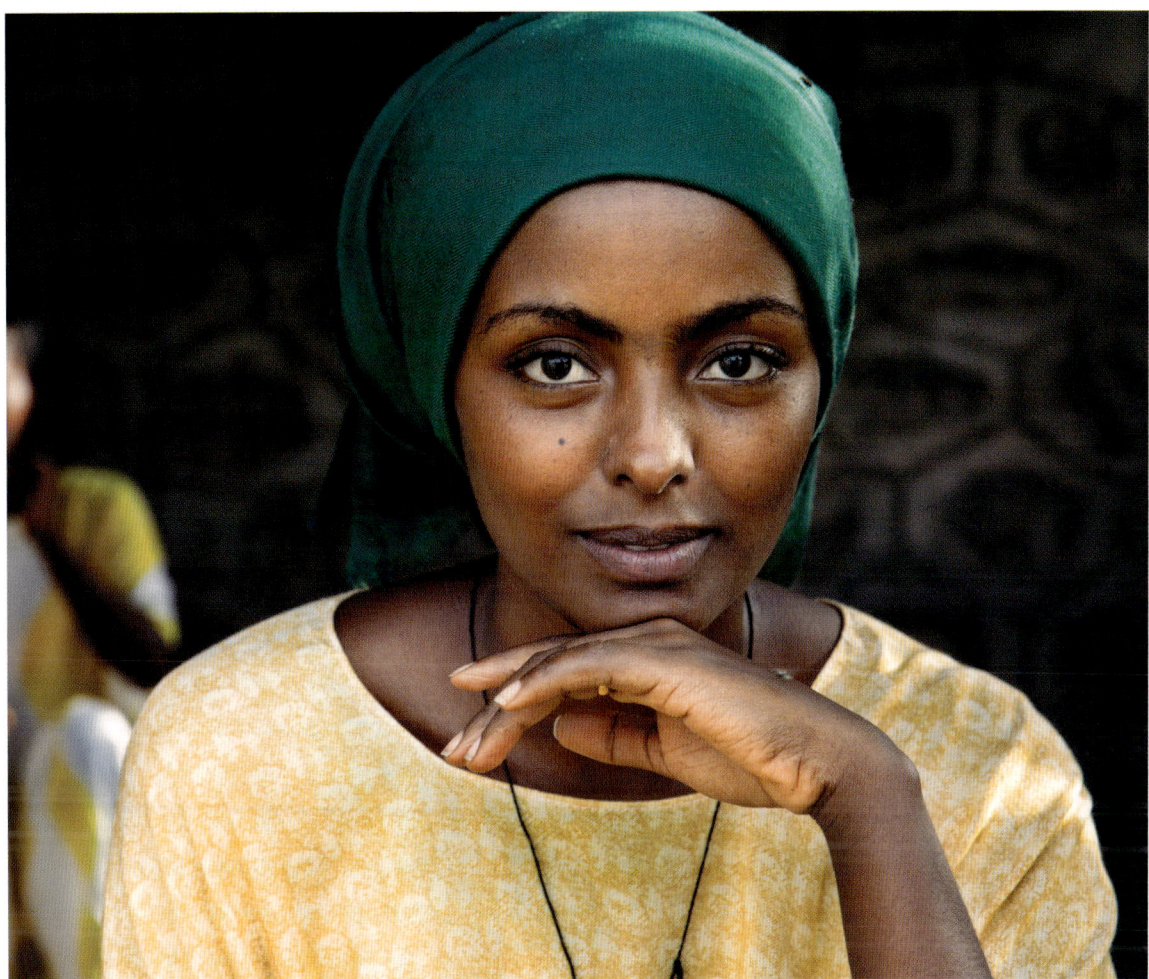

MILAN, ITALY *(Opposite)*

When Anna Maisetti was twenty-two, she was diagnosed with skin cancer. After surgery, she was left with a lifelong condition called lymphedema. Now she must always wear a special compression sleeve to prevent her foot from swelling and becoming inflamed.

In the beginning, she felt depressed about her new reality and tired of coping with the challenges of the condition, and she was always trying to hide her bandage. But after a while, she had an idea that changed her life. What if she stopped hiding the bandage and transformed it into a stylish accessory? What if she transformed lymphedema from a source of shame into a symbol of self-expression?

Anna founded a community and wrote a book about her experience of living with lymphedema. Today, she has many bandages in different colors. She matches them with her everyday style and inspires thousands of other people who live with the same condition.

Despite the challenges of lymphedema, Anna decided to color her life and make the most of it.

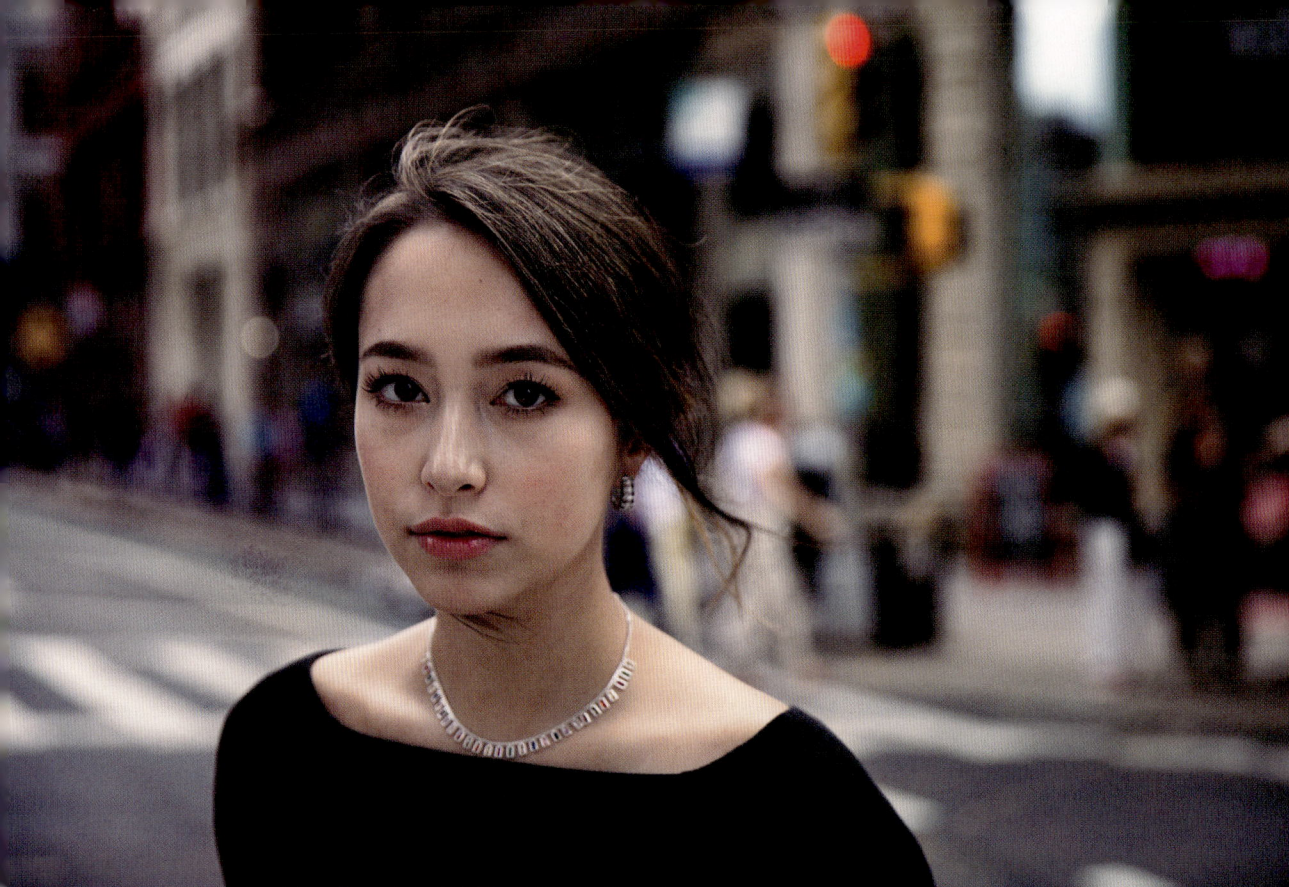

NEW YORK CITY, UNITED STATES

Ann Makosinski is a brilliant scientist on a path to becoming an artist, too. She grew up in Canada and is of both Filipino and Polish descent. She inherited her passion for science from her scientist father. When other children were playing with dolls or toy cars, she was playing with cables and electronic parts. Not long after that, she started to build her first inventions.

During childhood, she often visited the Philippines, her mother's homeland. A friend there, who was living in a place without electricity, told Ann how she'd fail at school because she didn't have enough light to study after dark. This friend was only one of millions of children in this situation. That's how Ann came up with an innovative idea: to create a convenient flashlight powered by the heat from your hand—no batteries, no charging. For her invention, Ann won in her category at the prestigious Google Science Fair at just fifteen years old.

When I met her, Ann was developing a line of toys to help children learn physics. She was giving speeches about her amazing experiences. And she was also taking acting classes. She dreamed for a long time of developing her artistic side, although this came as a surprise to most of her family and friends.

She believes that art and technology should work together, hand in hand. For example, she says, a device with great technology is nothing without great design. And, indeed, art and science are closer than ever today. People like Ann are using both art and science to build a better world.

SHIRAZ, IRAN

I met Ramina Torabi many years ago. Back then, she was dreaming of a more liberal life. A free spirit, she was deeply passionate about style, fashion, and culture.

After I posted her photo on social media, many Iranians were captivated and wanted to know more about her. She then moved abroad and started a blog about fashion, style, and the life of an Iranian woman in the diaspora. Over time, she became a real star for the Iranian people, her deep love for Persian culture and Persian people defining her every step.

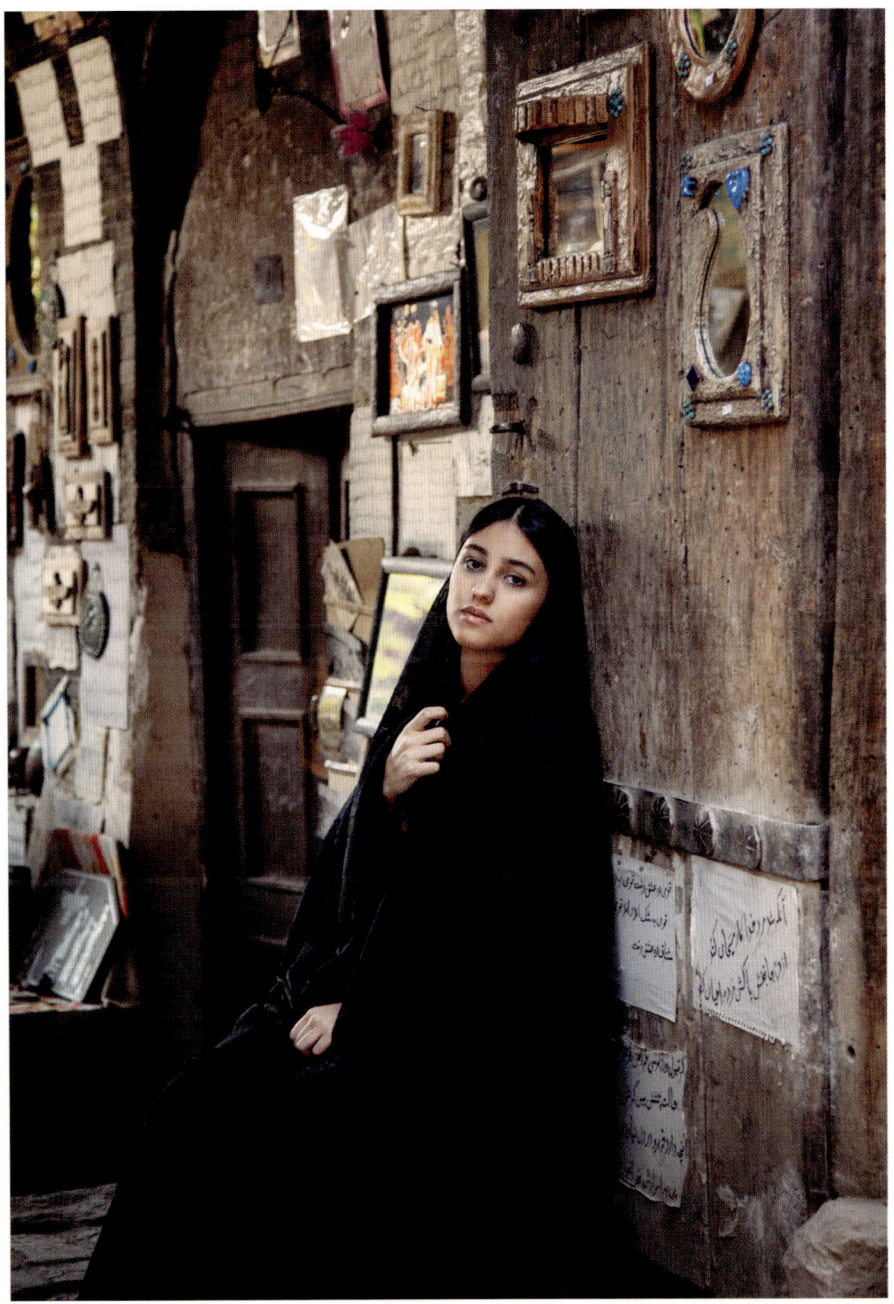

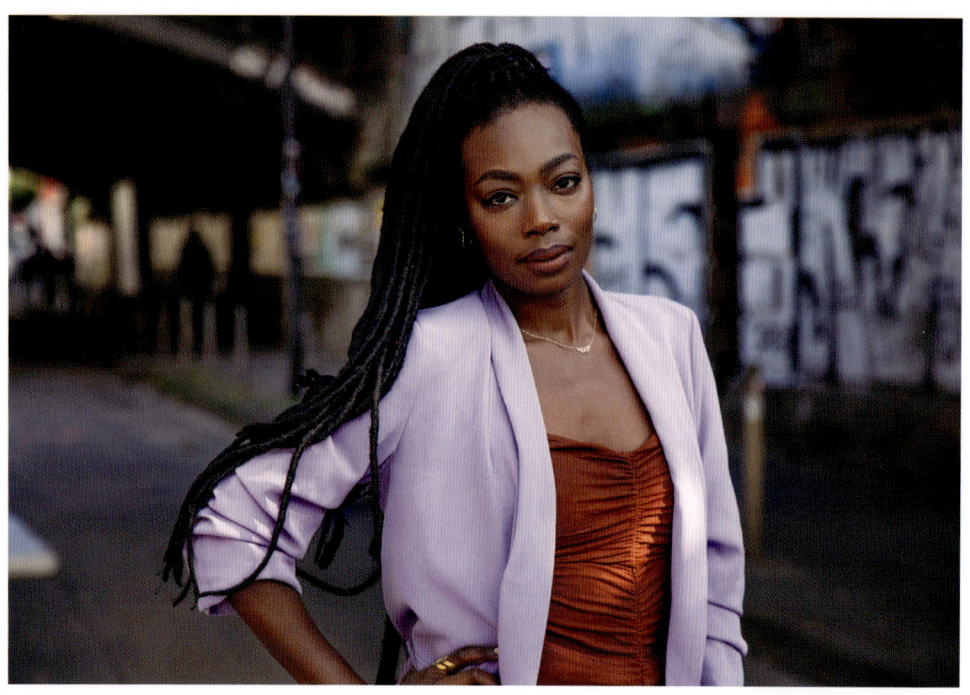

Melane Nkounkolo is a singer, a songwriter, and a music producer with an eclectic approach.

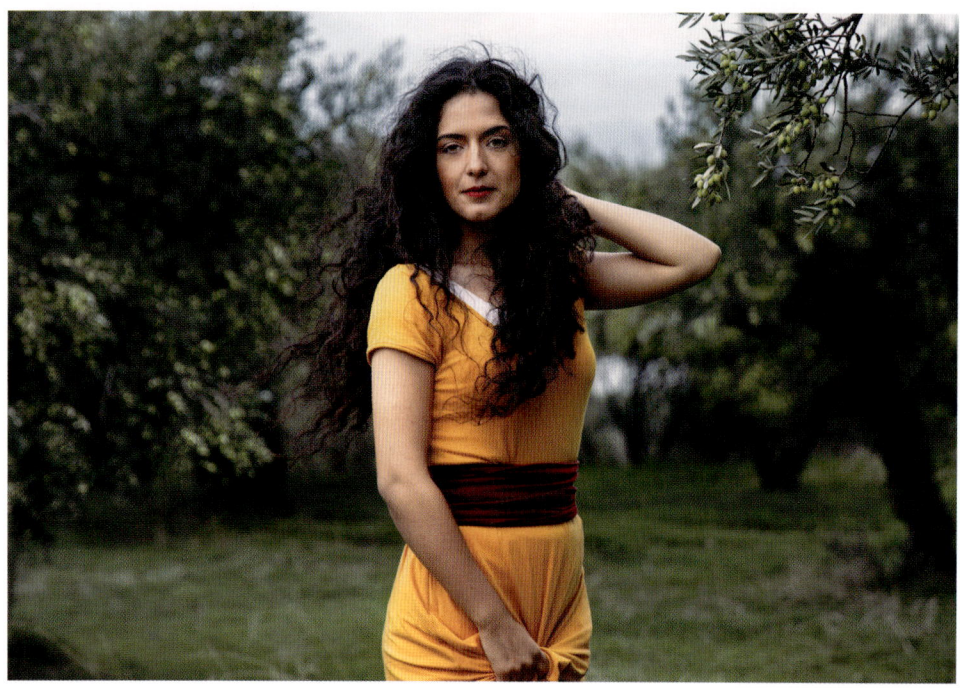

HERAKLION, GREECE

Evangelia Orfanoudaki is a storyteller, captivating children with beautiful shows filled with fascinating tales. Her name means "bringer of good news" in Greek—a perfect fit for her work.

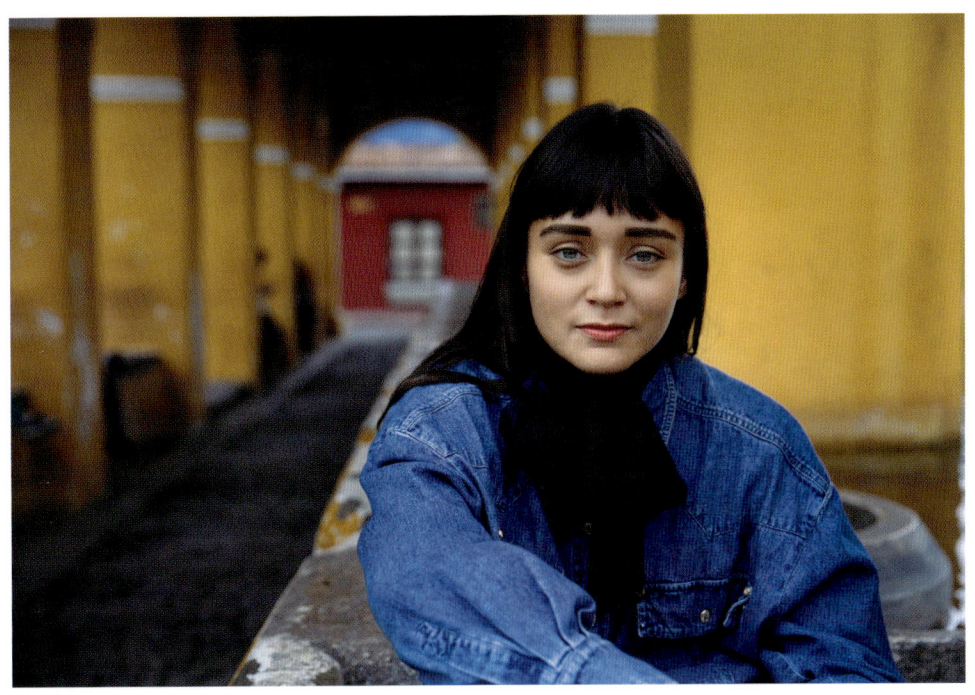

ANTIGUA, GUATEMALA

Alexa Maithé is a Honduran visual artist.

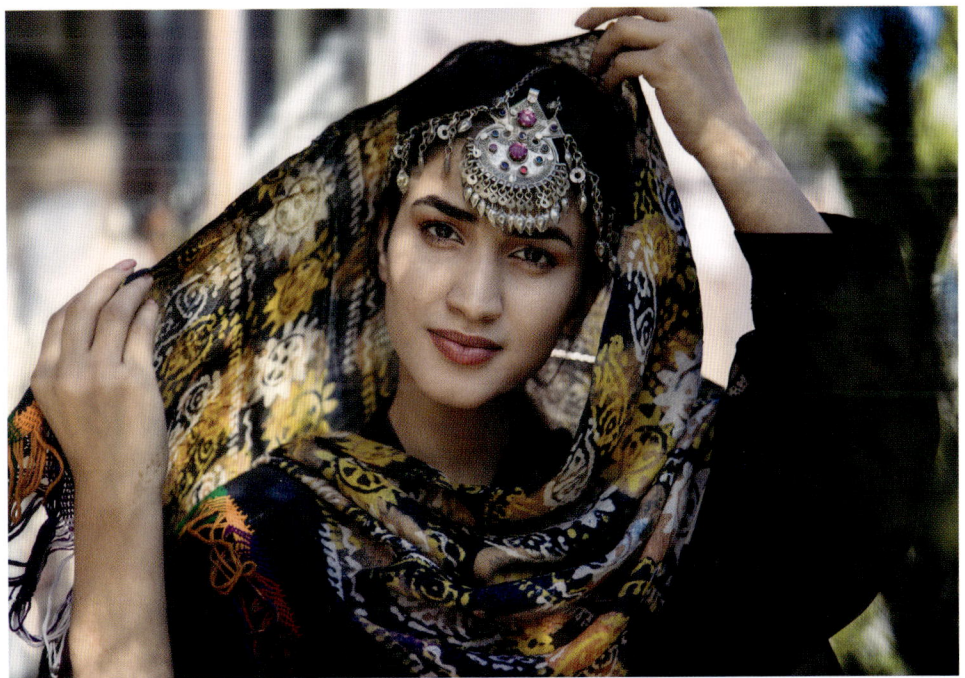

KABUL, AFGHANISTAN

Mahal Wak is an award-winning actress and activist. As an actress, she's played many roles while dressed in traditional Afghan outfits.

ANDES MOUNTAINS, PERU

While pregnant, Juliana suffered a severe accident on the steep, narrow paths around her isolated village. By a miracle, the baby survived. But Juliana was forced to move to the nearest city because of her medical condition. She continues to live there with her son.

Juliana comes here, to her native village, as often as possible and hopes that her medical condition will someday allow the two of them to move back. She loves her village, she loves the mountains, and she feels that this is the only place where she and her son can connect with Pachamama—the most important goddess revered by Indigenous people of the Andes, also known as Mother Earth.

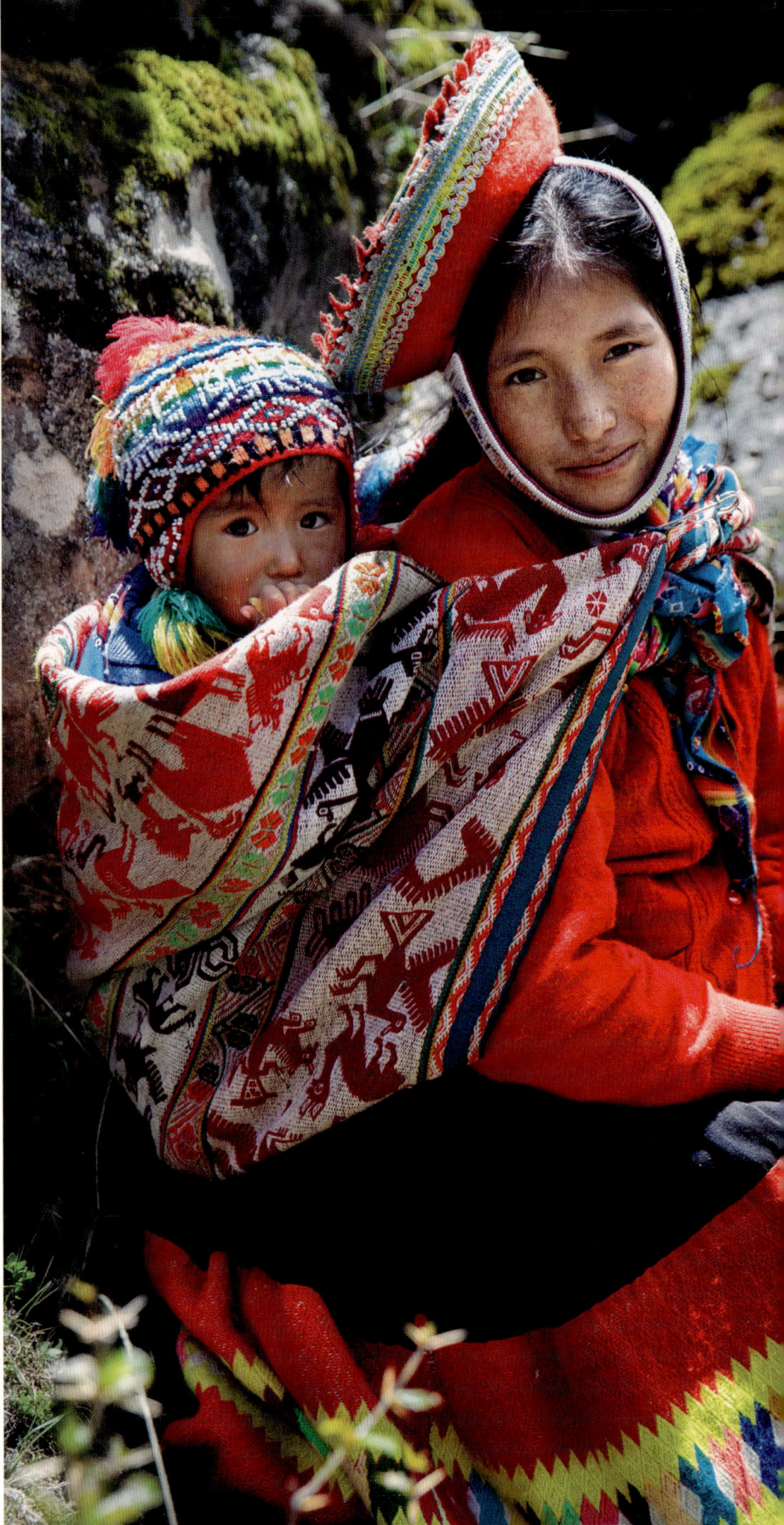

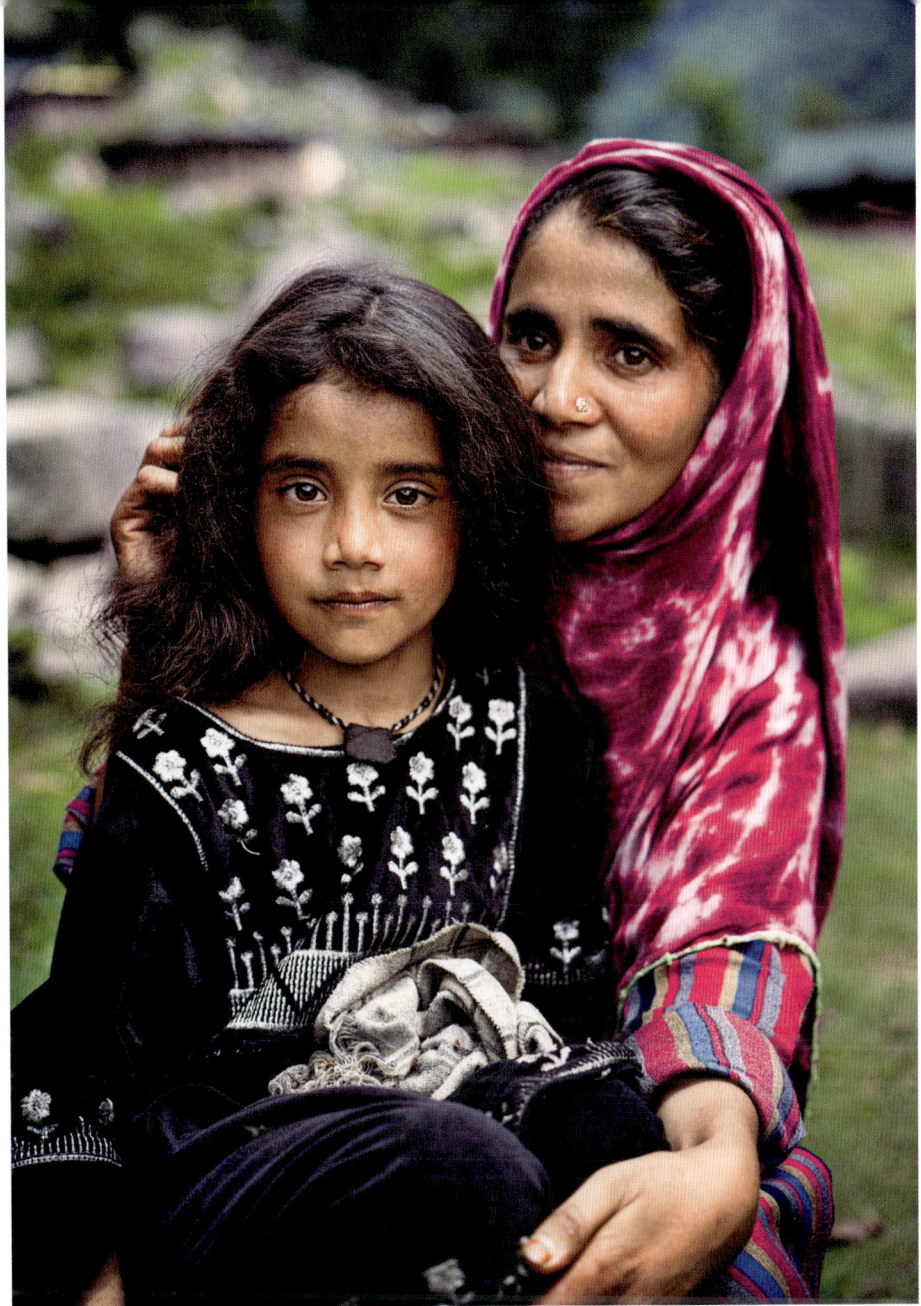

INDIAN-ADMINISTERED KASHMIR

Kashmir, a region with a captivating ethnic diversity, is home to many fascinating communities. Parveena and her daughter Rubeena are part of an ethnic group known as Gujar.

During the summer, they live high in the mountains alongside their cattle, surrounded by the beauty of nature. However, as winter approaches, they migrate to the warmer valleys.

The life of these people is challenging, but, like many traditional communities, they maintain a deep connection with spirituality, which gives them strength and hope. For instance, little Rubeena wears a *ta'wiz* around her neck, a special amulet containing a few verses from the Quran.

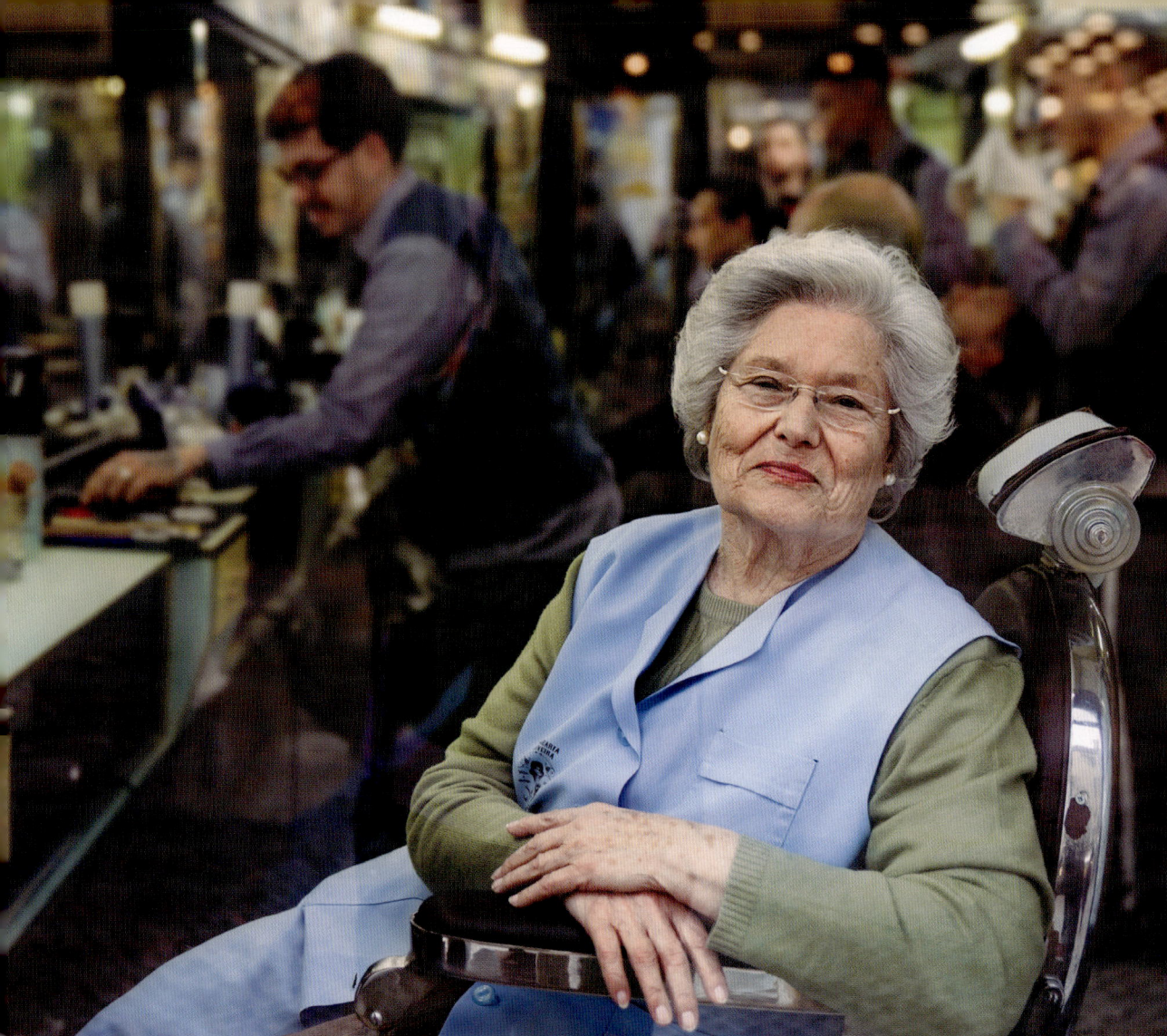

LISBON, PORTUGAL

Paula was eighty-four years old and full of energy when I photographed her. Just three years earlier, she had overcome breast cancer and was now living life to the fullest.

I noticed her in the barbershop where she worked as a manicurist. Although she's retired, she was working because she couldn't stand to be inactive.

On this day, Paula was the only woman in a room full of male clients and employees, but she was perfectly integrated and respected. At eighty-four, her hands moved with dexterity and her soul glowed.

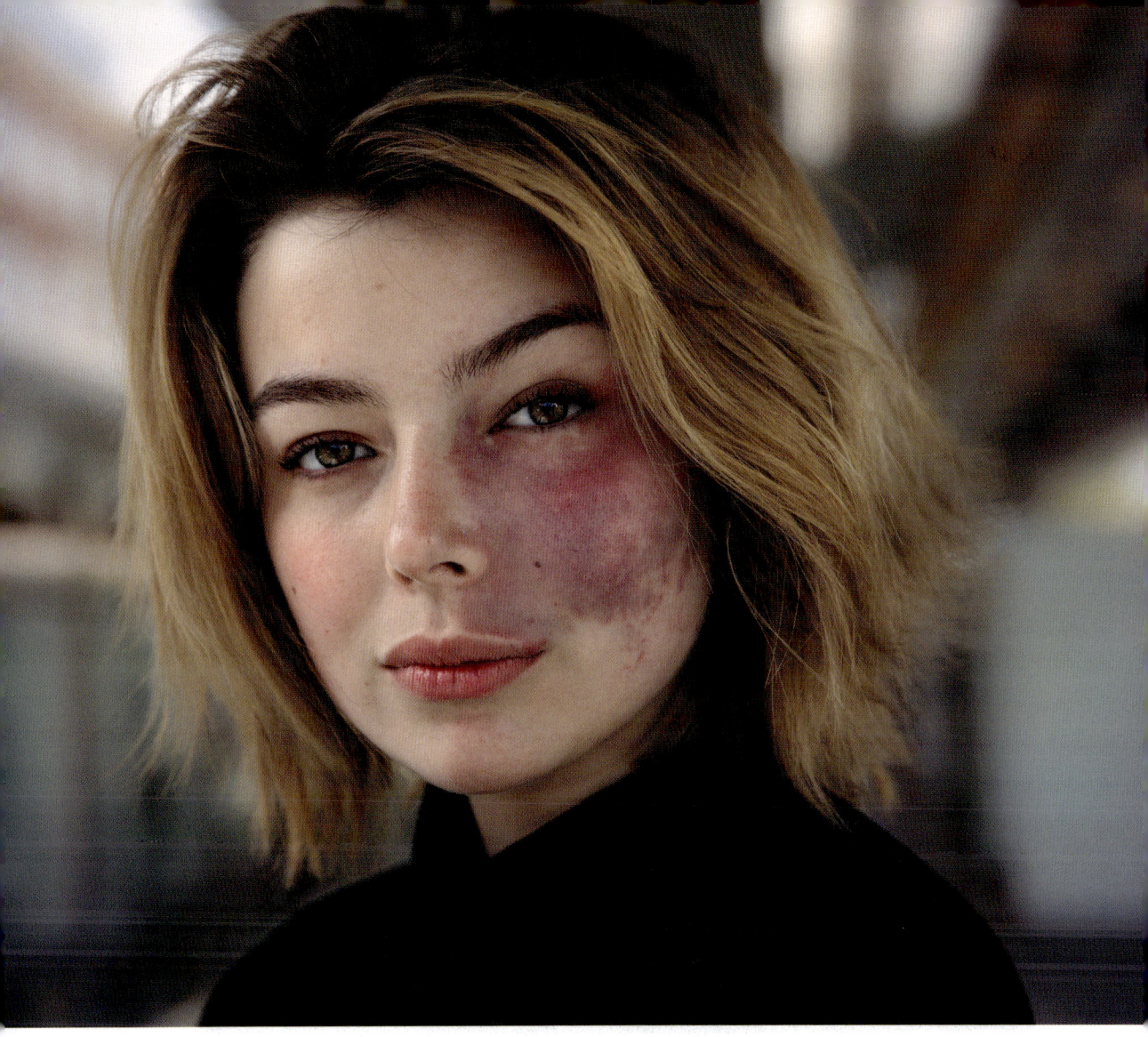

COPENHAGEN, DENMARK

I noticed Nikka, who is of Croatian heritage, on the streets of this beautiful city. She was delighted to be photographed and relaxed while talking about her birthmark. Nikka is one of the many women of the world who taught me how important it is to be yourself.

NORTHERN CALIFORNIA, UNITED STATES

Gillian Larson is riding her horses through the most remote and wild places in the United States. She has a degree in biology, and her incredible expeditions blend a love of the outdoors with respect and care for her amazing horses.

After navigating the many challenges of the wilderness during her long expeditions, she shares the routes and the information so others can enjoy these fabulous experiences, as well.

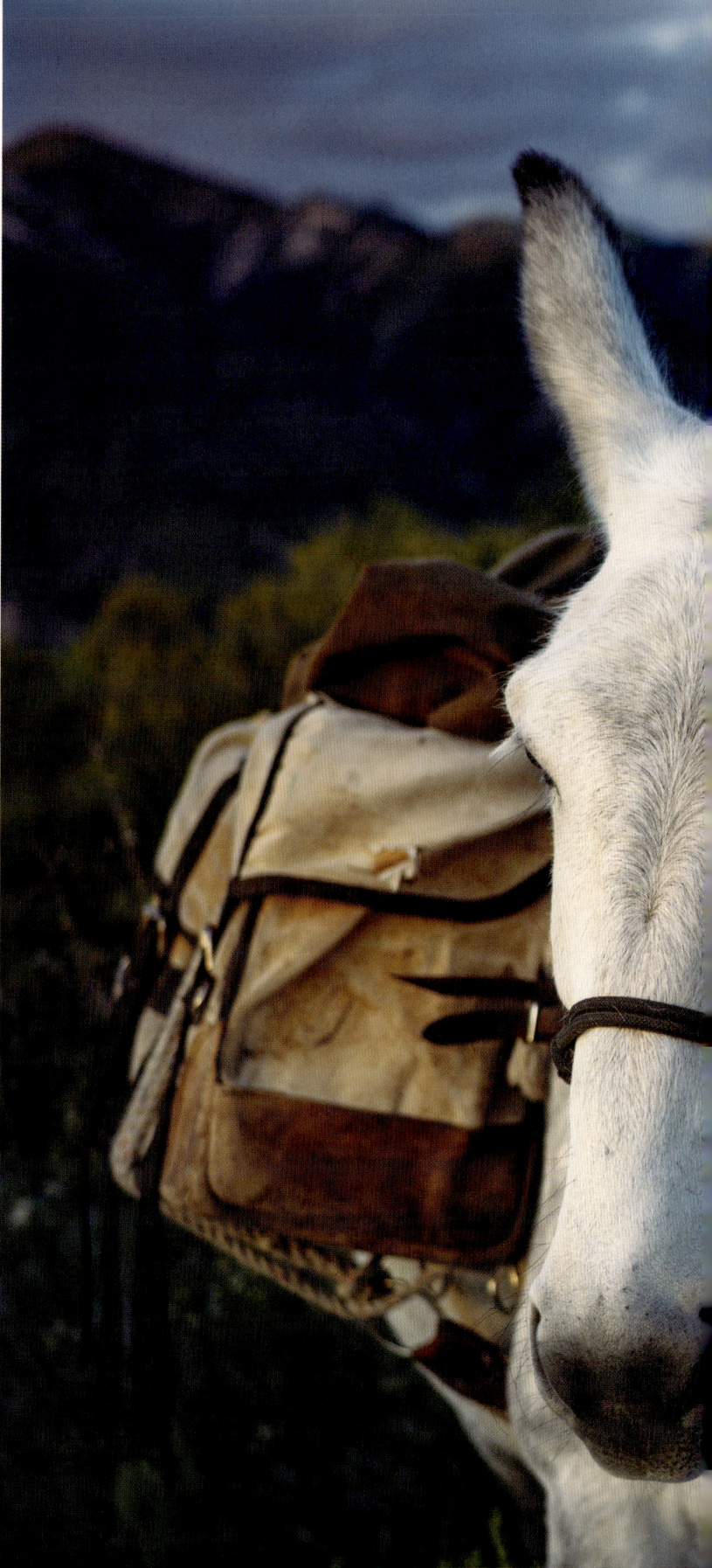

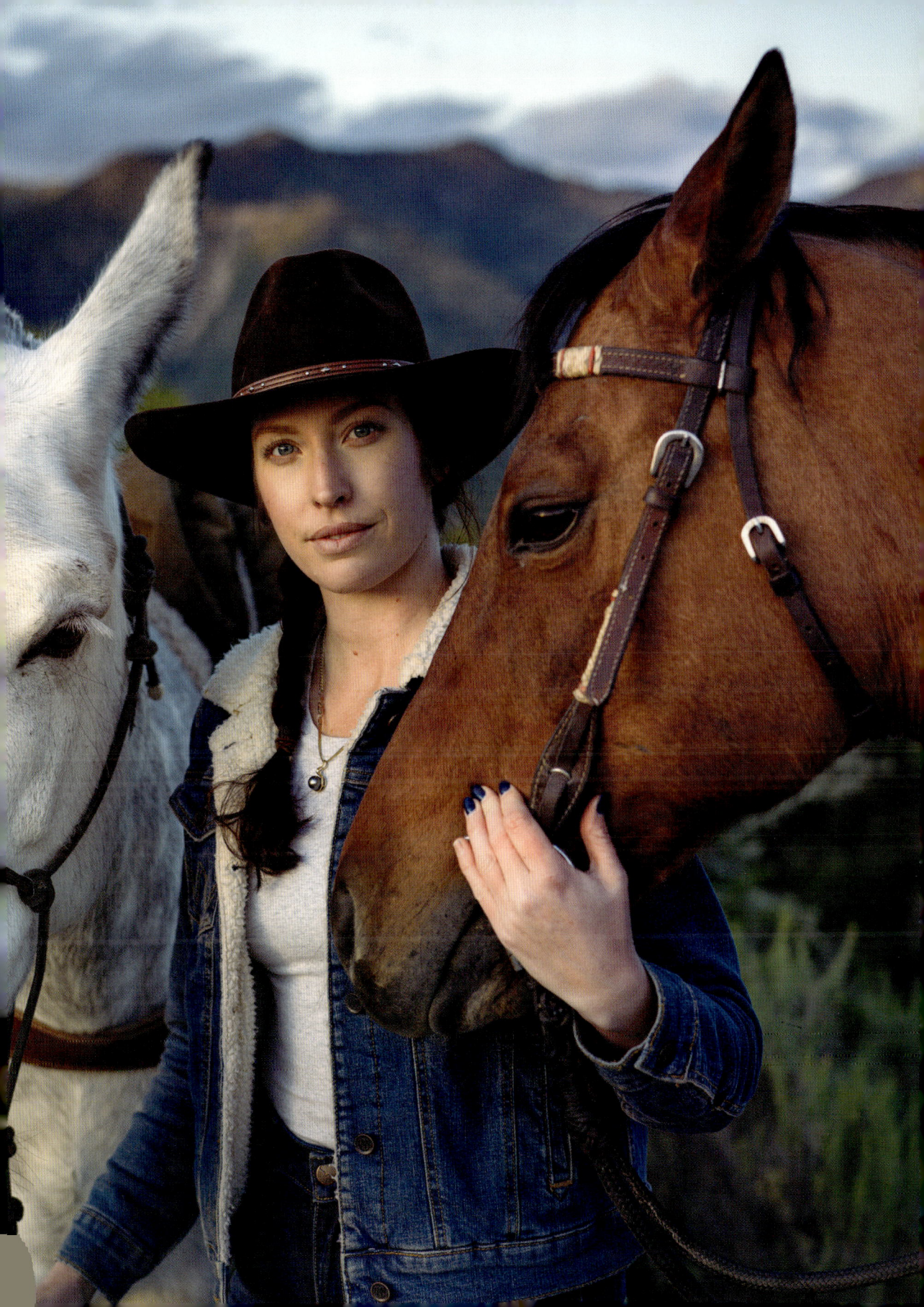

IAȘI, ROMANIA

Irina Catighera loves to live a vibrant life and enjoy the diversity of the world. So far she has been to almost one hundred and forty countries—mostly on her own. Although she first traveled outside Romania in her thirties, exploring the world has quickly become the passion of her life. She had challenging and intensive work as a gynecologist, but she traveled as much as she could on her days off.

When I met her, she held two jobs. She told me that she even takes loans to support some of her journeys. She is now focusing on more challenging destinations— leaving the comfortable ones for later, when she will be older. Irina, the world inspires you, and you inspire us.

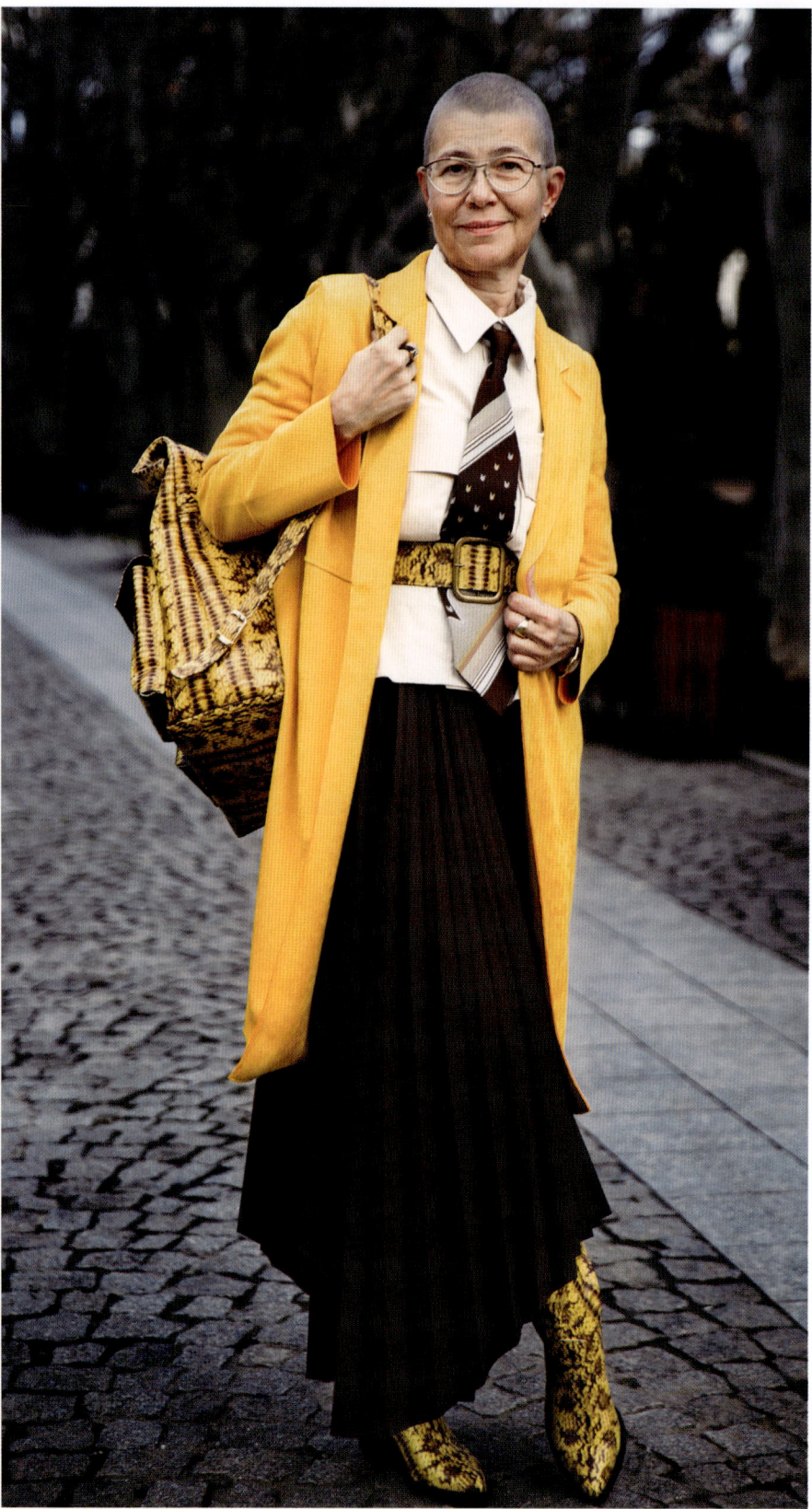

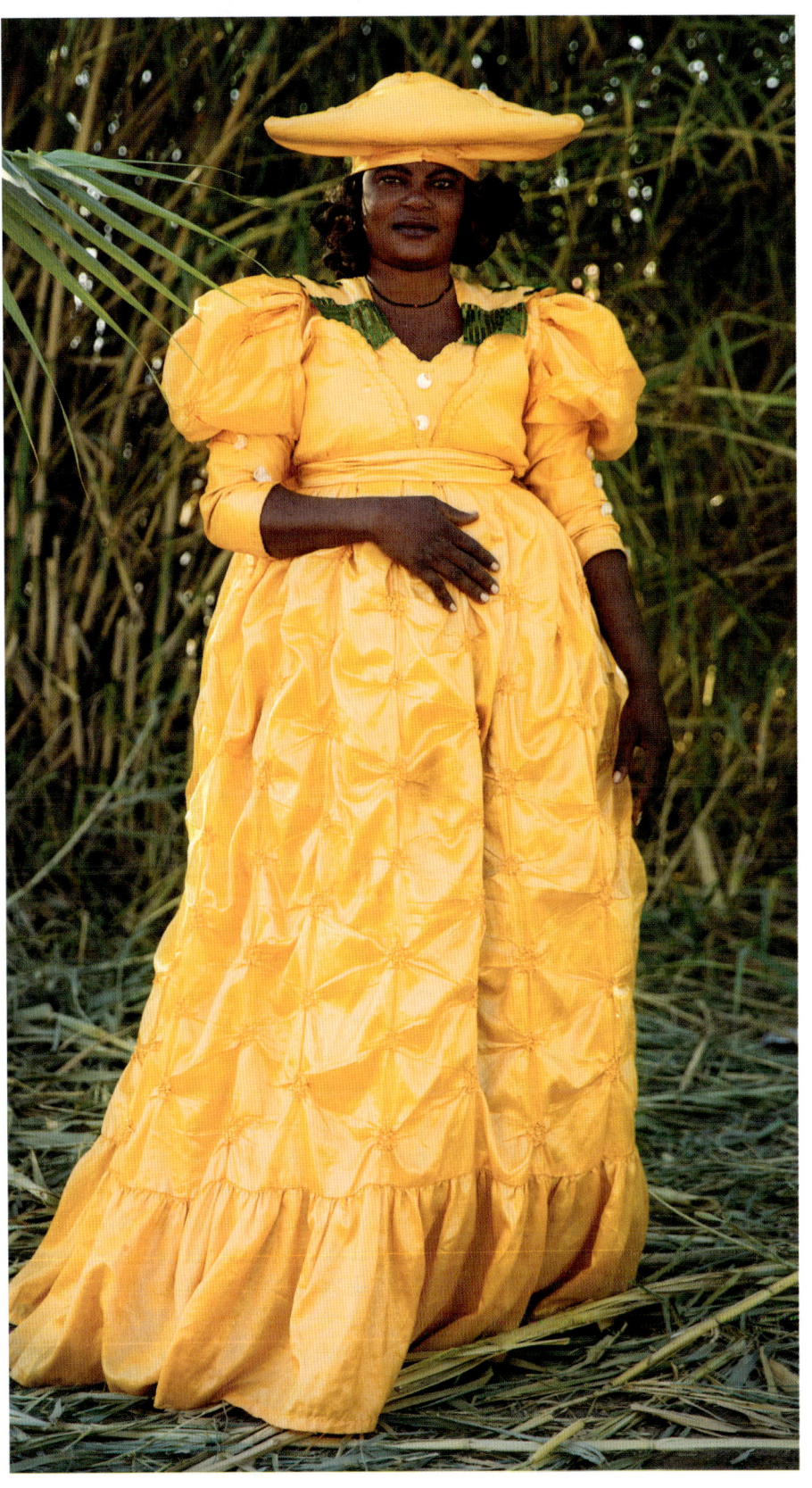

OPUWO, NAMIBIA

Izabella wasn't returning from a celebration but from her job, where she works as a secretary.

The outfits of Herero women are incredibly vibrant and spectacular. They wear a type of splendid dress called *ohorokova* in every moment of their lives. But behind these vibrant colors, there's a story of suffering and resilience.

During the Herero genocide in the early twentieth century, many Herero women were killed or forced to flee their homes and abandon their traditions. As a symbol of protest and resilience against colonialism, Herero women retained only the basics of European dress, adapting it and making it uniquely their own. The spectacular headpiece, for example, is called *otjikaiva* and symbolizes the horn of cattle—the animal most revered in Herero culture.

For me, Izabella and all Herero women wearing *ohorokova* are the living embodiment of defiance and beauty.

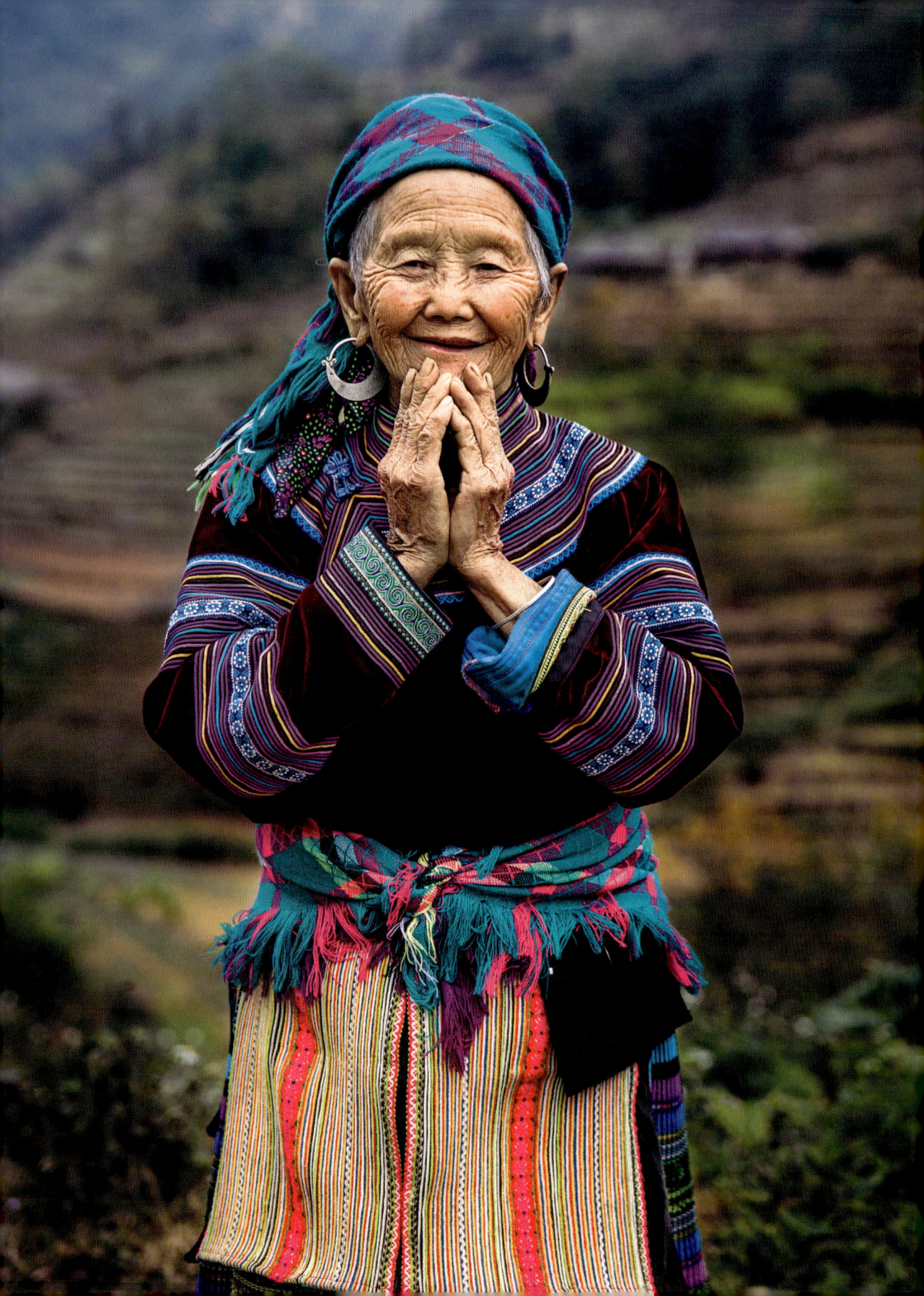

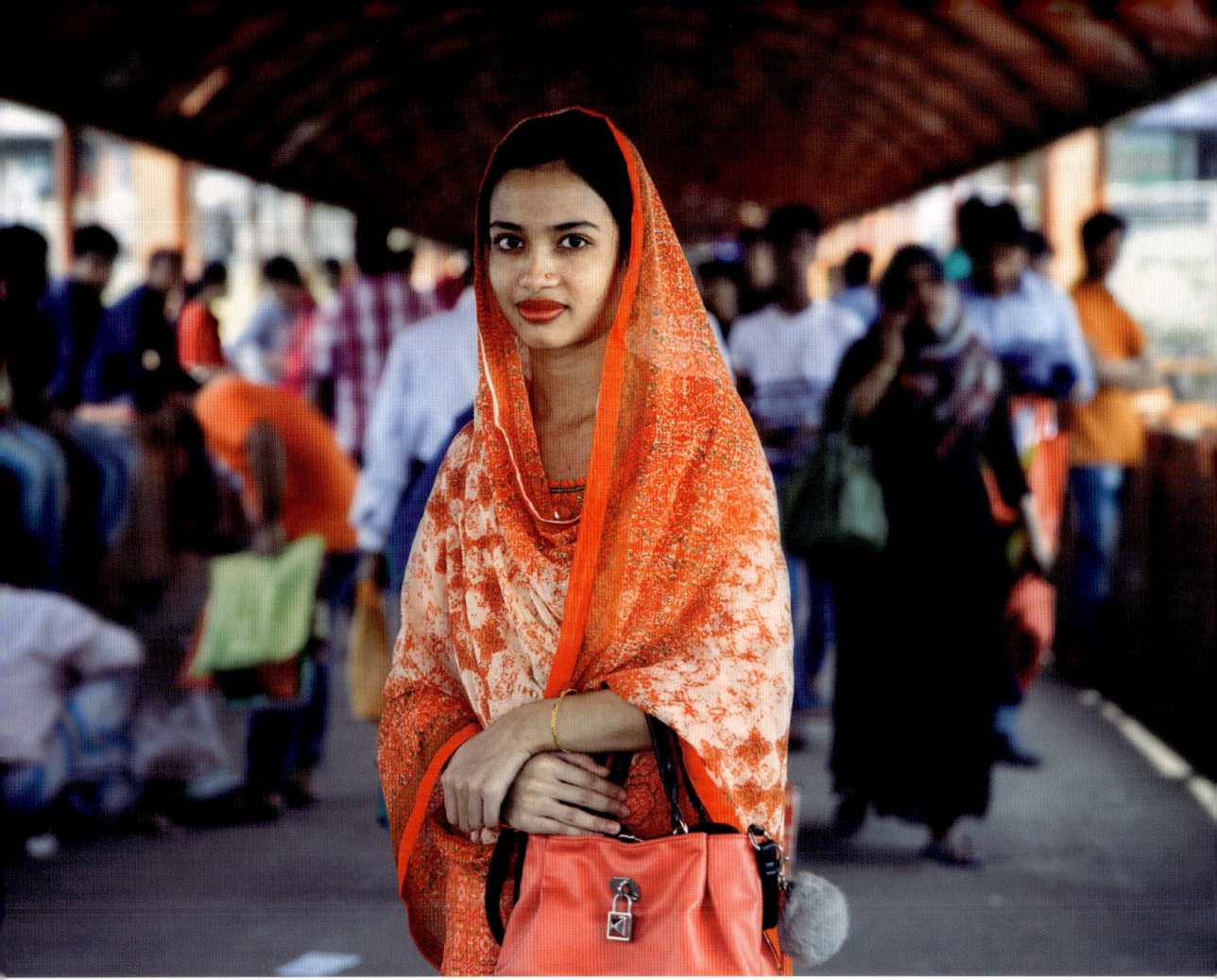

DHAKA, BANGLADESH *(Above)*

I met Rehana on a bustling pedestrian bridge where thousands of people, each with their own stories, cross every day. Rehana's story is about love. She married the man she loves against the will of her family, who preferred an arranged marriage. She chose a very challenging path in a part of the world where arranged marriages are the norm in many families.

NORTHERN VIETNAM *(Opposite)*

Di is eighty-six years old and part of an ethnic group called Hmong. Despite all challenges, she told me she'd had a very beautiful life with her beloved husband and their five children. Fifteen years ago, her husband passed away, and since then she has never taken off these earrings, which were made by him. Beauty shines everywhere, and so does love.

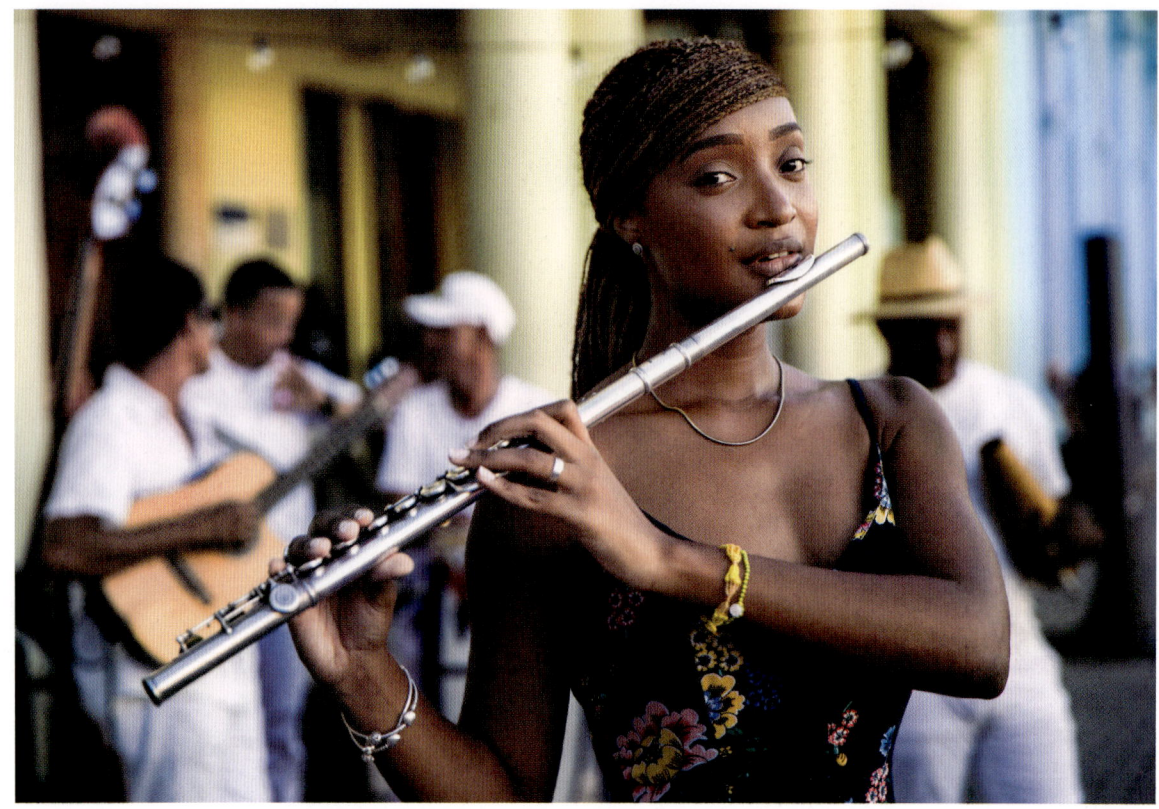

HAVANA, CUBA

For a musician, the competition is incredible in Cuba. Nowhere in the world will you find such a substantial community of extraordinary musicians. To make it to the top, besides talent, you need years and years of practice.

I met Yansa on the colonial streets of Old Havana, where she was playing with her band at a terrace. Here the best music is on the streets, at terraces, and in bars—it's not only in concert halls.

Yansa has played the flute since she was eight years old. While most of the other children were outside playing, she was inside, practicing hard despite the heat and her fatigue.

She told me that all the sacrifices were worth it. Today, she can make a decent living from doing what she loves most. She also supports her parents financially. She knows how much they did for her, and now she's happy to help them, too.

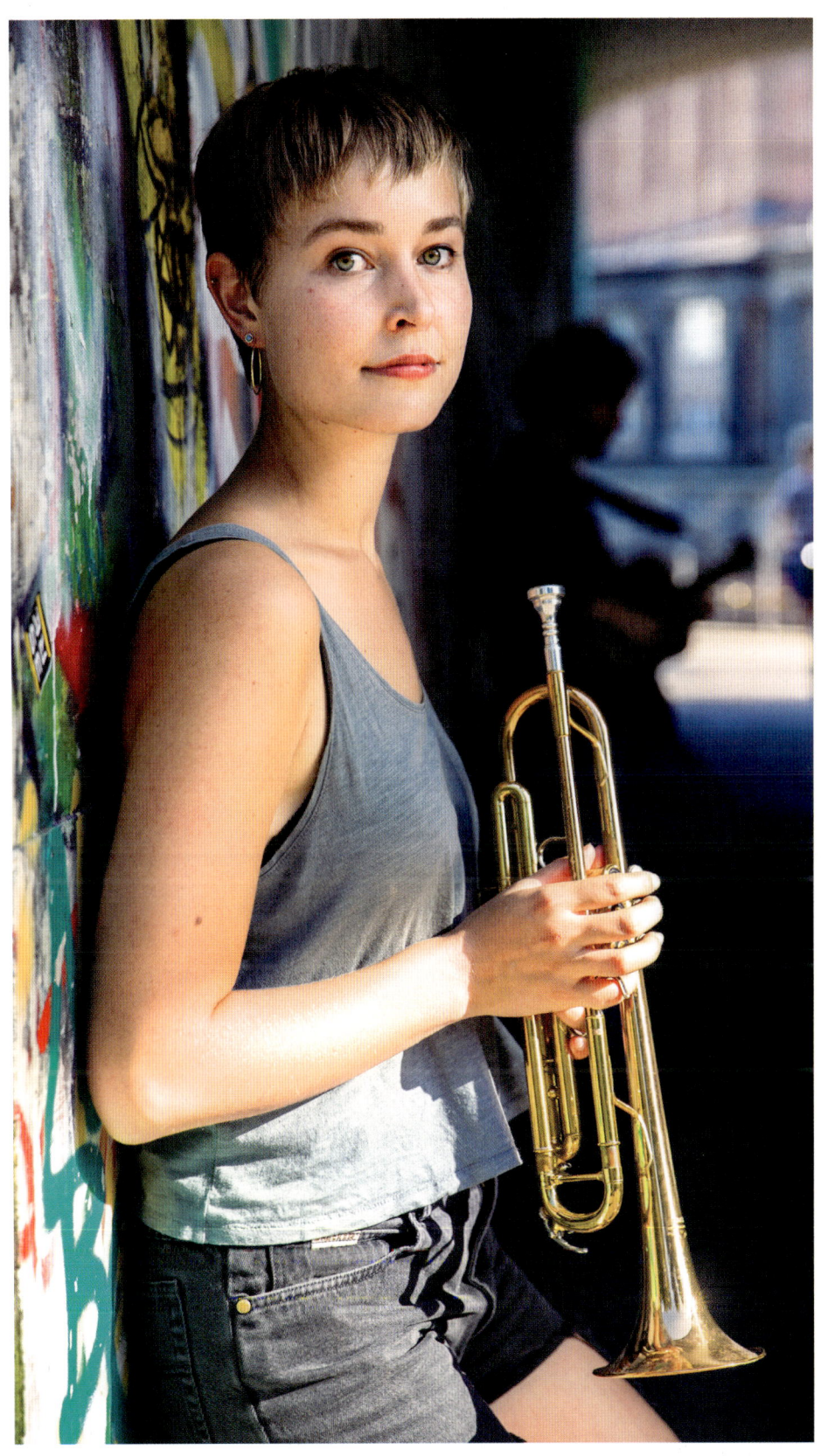

BERLIN, GERMANY

Maaike is from the Netherlands and was visiting Berlin for vacation. She missed playing her trumpet, so she decided to have a little show in a park.

Maaike started playing the trumpet when she was eight years old. After high school, she considered following in her mother's footsteps and starting a more stable career in a corporation. However, she soon realized that the trumpet is her life, so she continued with musical studies at her university.

She knows that she took the more difficult path, but she's doing what she loves most.

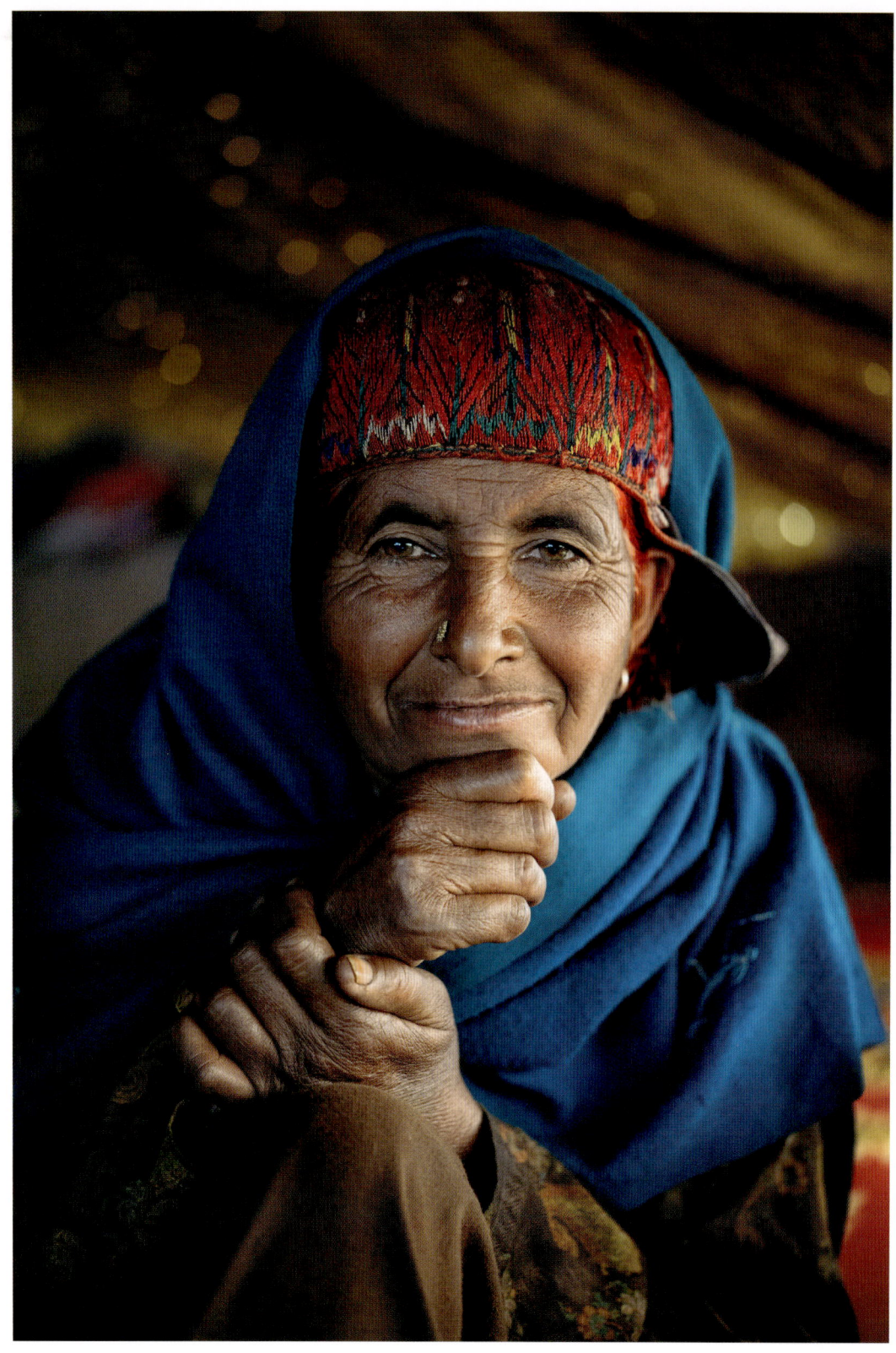

NORTHERN INDIA

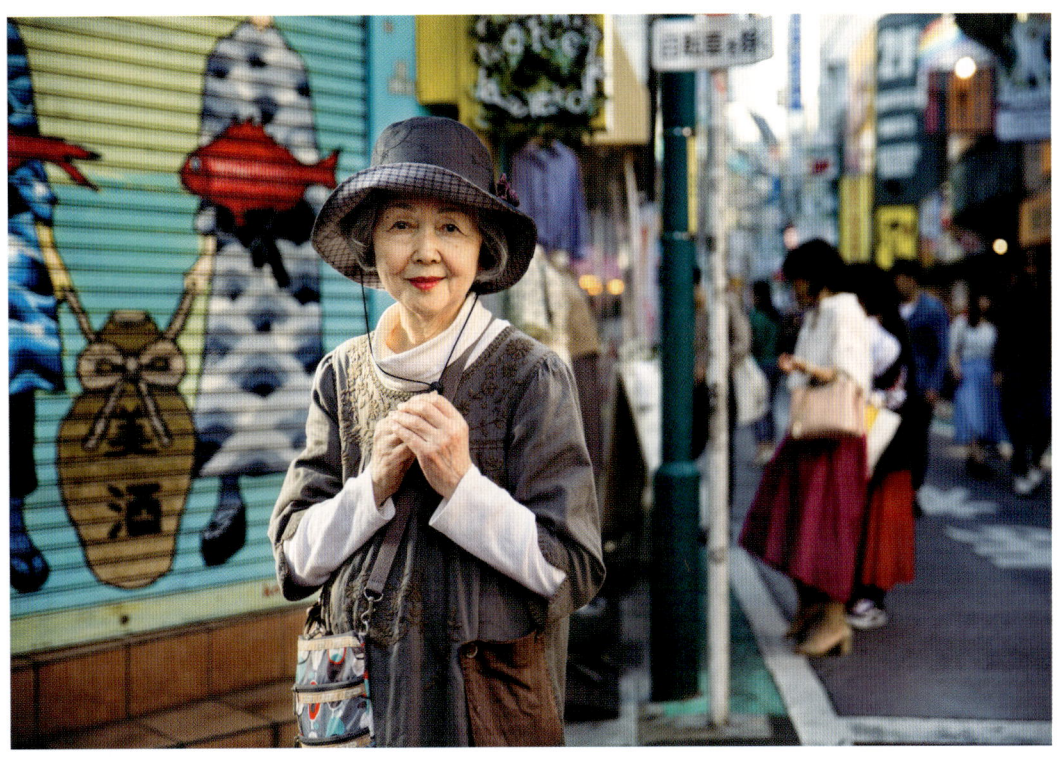

TOKYO, JAPAN

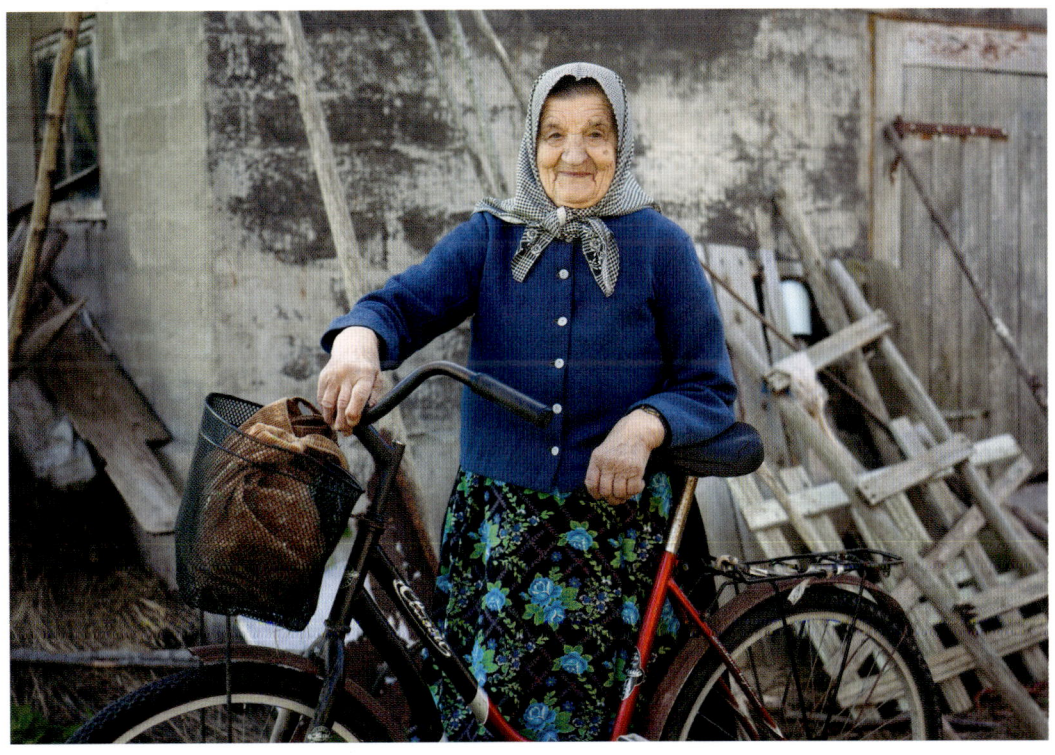

KIHNU ISLAND, ESTONIA

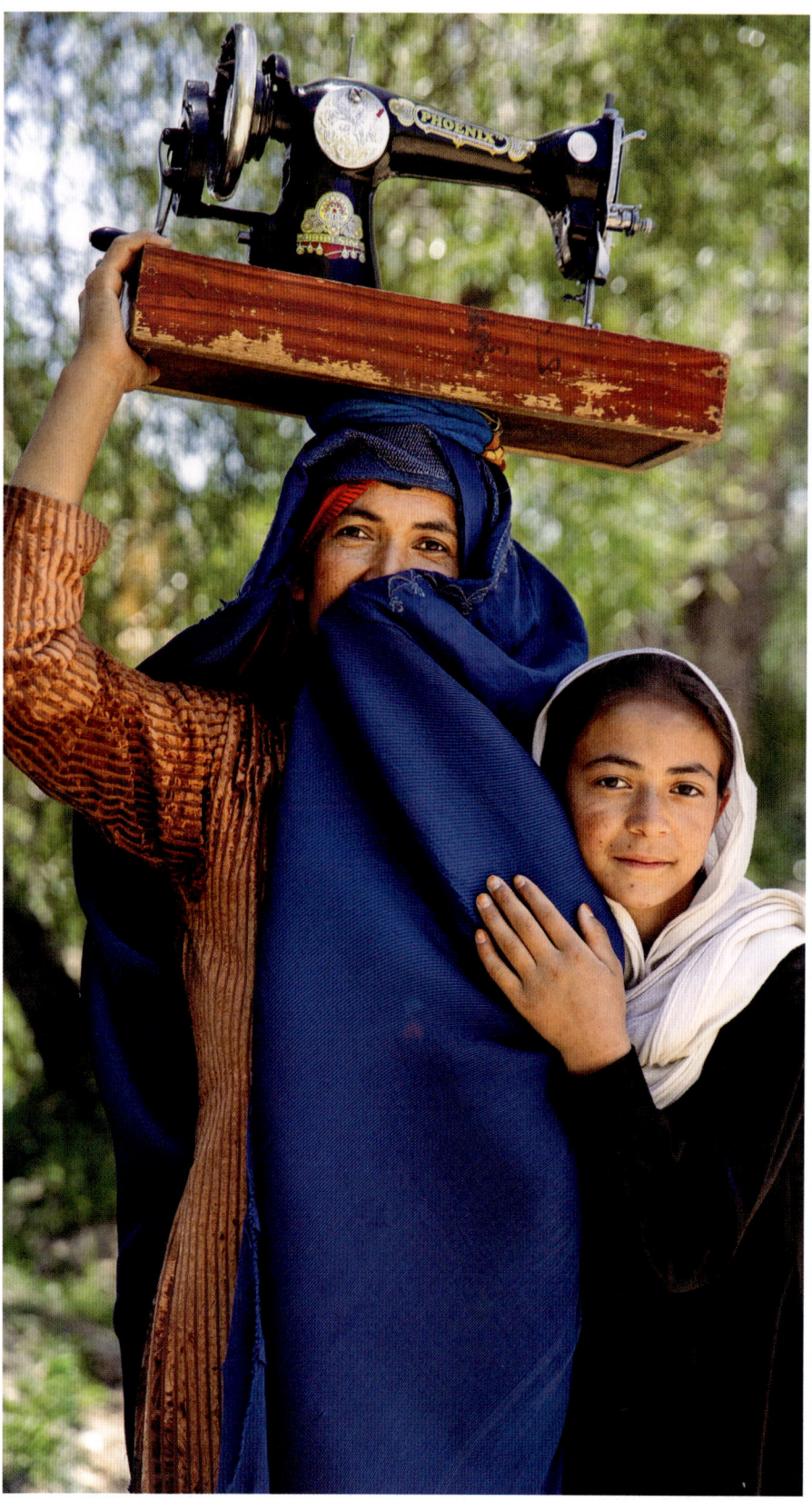

NORTHERN AFGHANISTAN

Fatema was on her way to get her sewing machine repaired, accompanied by Arezo, one of her four daughters. The sewing machine is vital for their family, as they are skilled tailors who specialize in making burqas similar to the one Fatema herself wears.

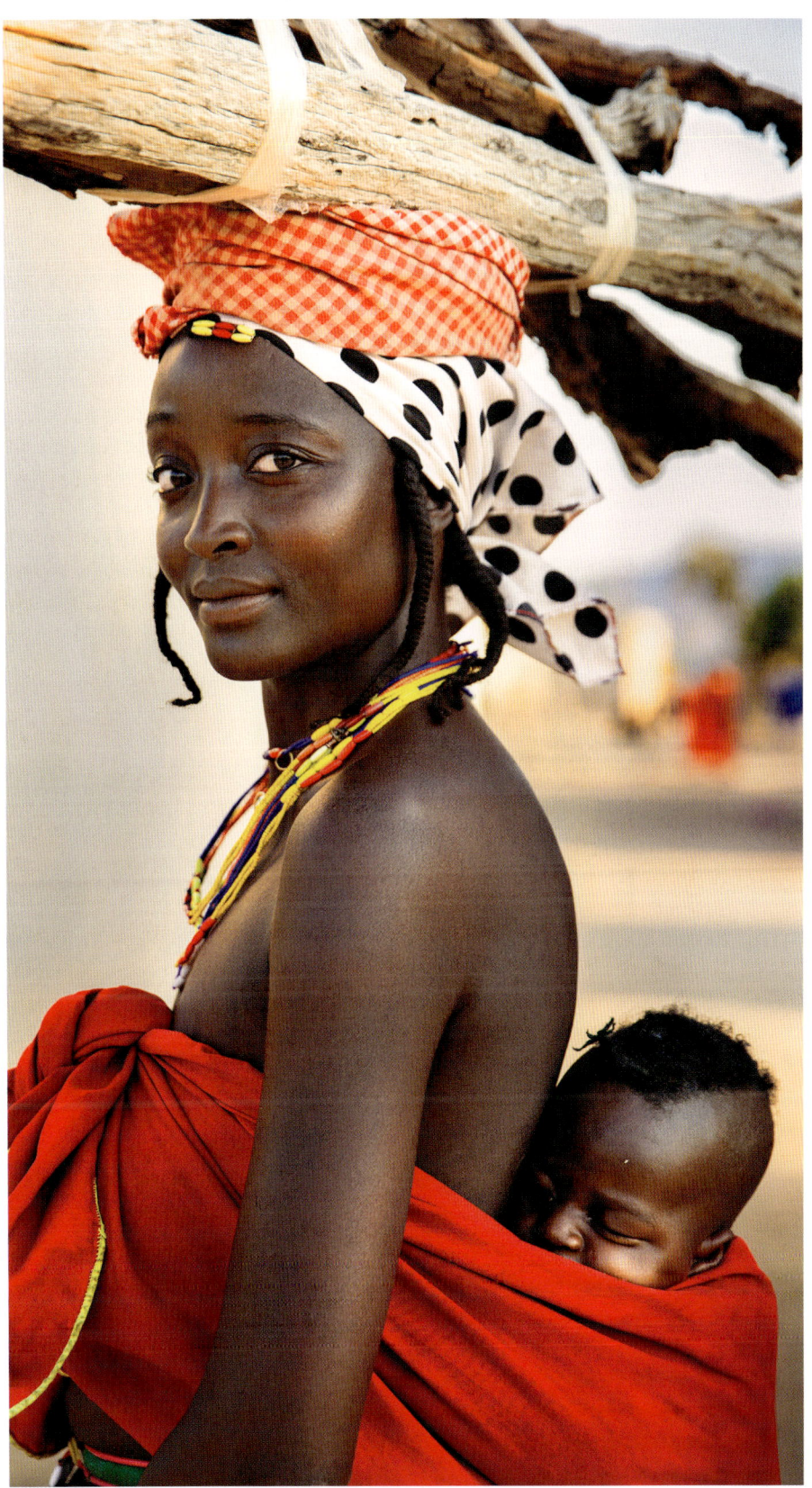

OPUWO, NAMIBIA

Tuazikirapi and her little boy are ethnic Zemba. Following tradition, her son will be given a name only after a special ritual is performed around a holy fire. In this part of the world, fire is an essential part of the culture for both spiritual and practical needs.

Tuazikirapi carries firewood on her head every single day—even now, when she has just become a mother. Zemba people came here as refugees from the neighboring Angola, and selling firewood became their only way to make a living.

Women like Tuazikirapi and Fatema, who live their lives with dignity and hope despite all challenges, are usually unknown—but, for me, they are real heroes.

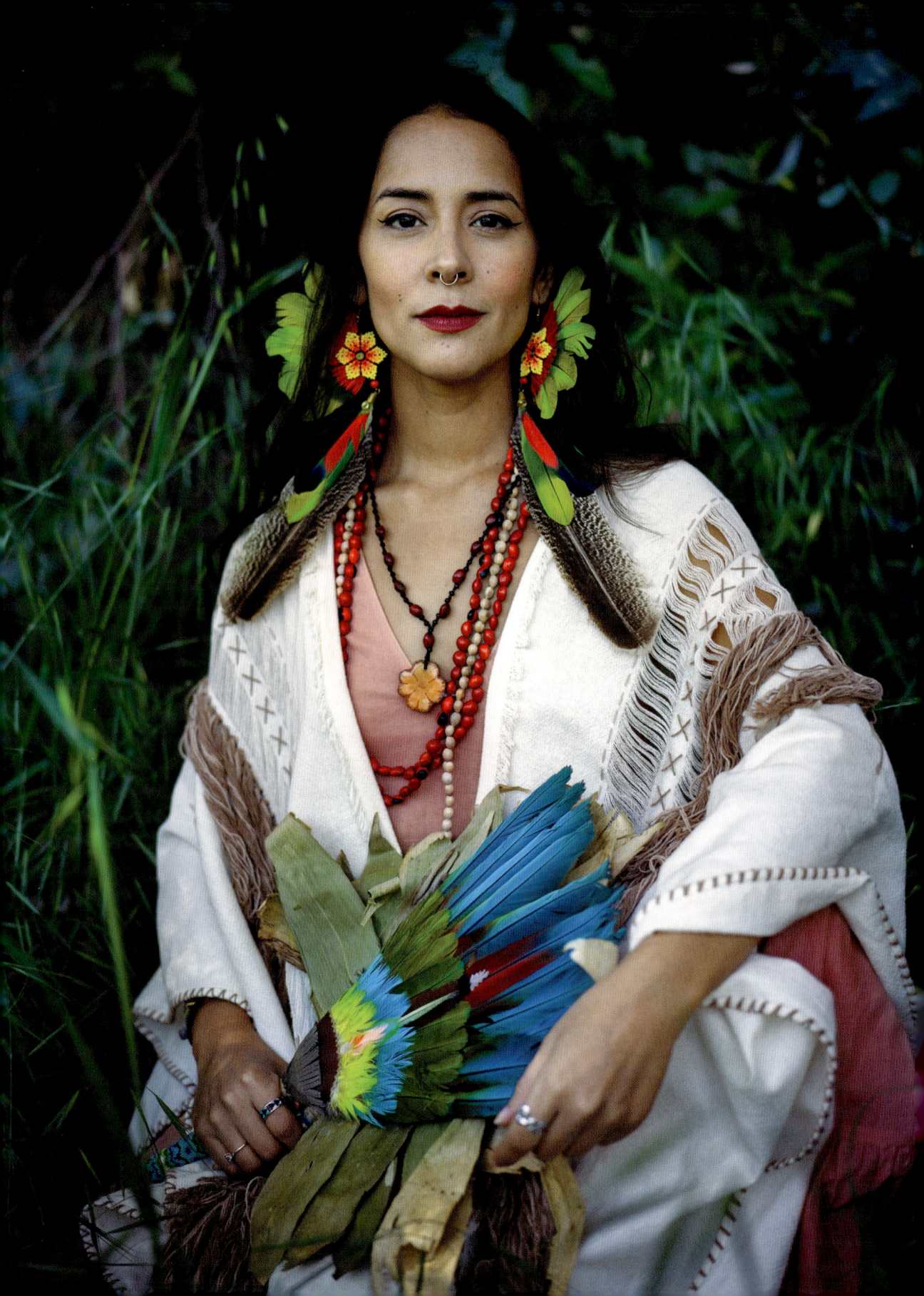

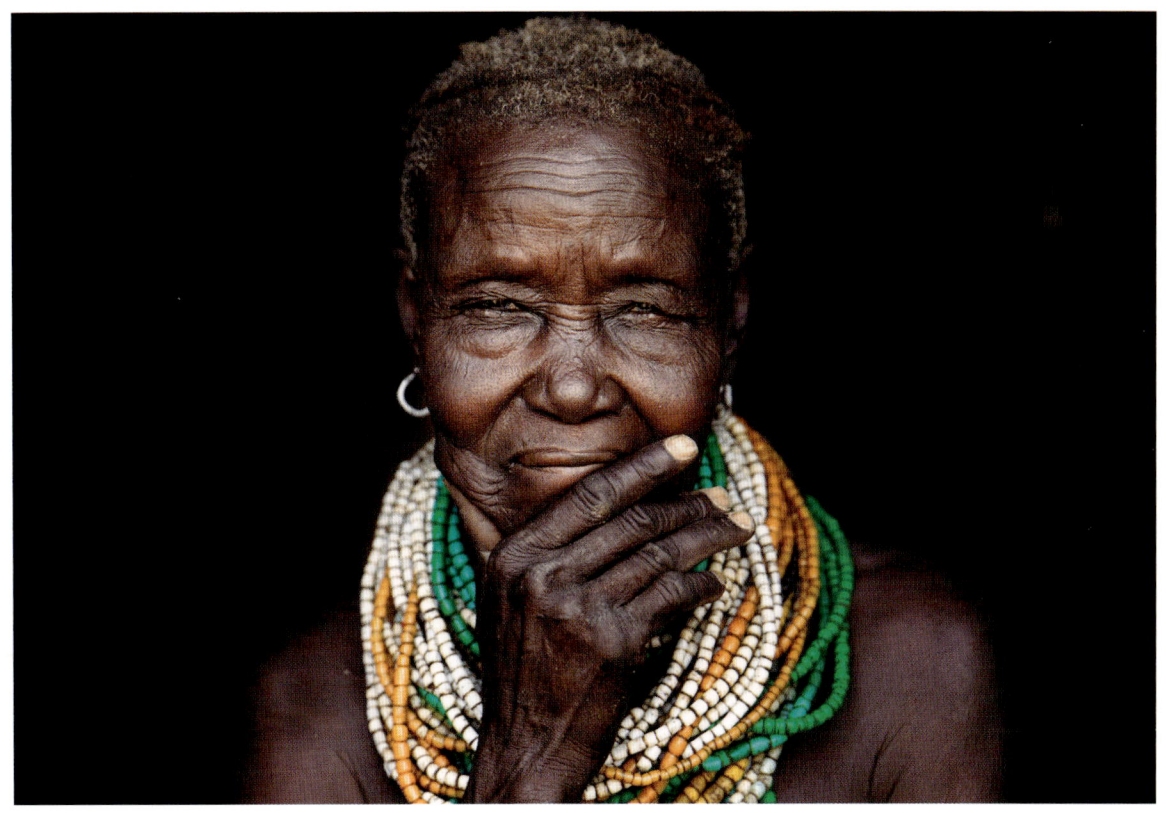

OMO VALLEY, ETHIOPIA *(Above)*

This valley is the home of many different ethnic groups, each living much as they did hundreds of years ago.

This amazing lady is Nasuru, an ethnic Nyangatom. As the midwife of her village, she has assisted in hundreds of childbirths. She told me that death is something very common, and her own example says it all. Of the ten children she gave birth to, only five survived.

Even after witnessing so much death, Nasuru continues to celebrate life, with her wise and charming eyes never forgetting to smile.

CALIFORNIA, UNITED STATES *(Opposite)*

Deep in the jungle of Peru, Daniela Riojas met shamans who completely changed her life. Her spiritual journey brought her to different parts of South and North America.

She has been under the guidance of different Indigenous elders and collected rare traditional wind instruments while also exploring and celebrating her own Indigenous ancestry. Today, she lives in California and organizes complex ceremonies, offerings, and retreats.

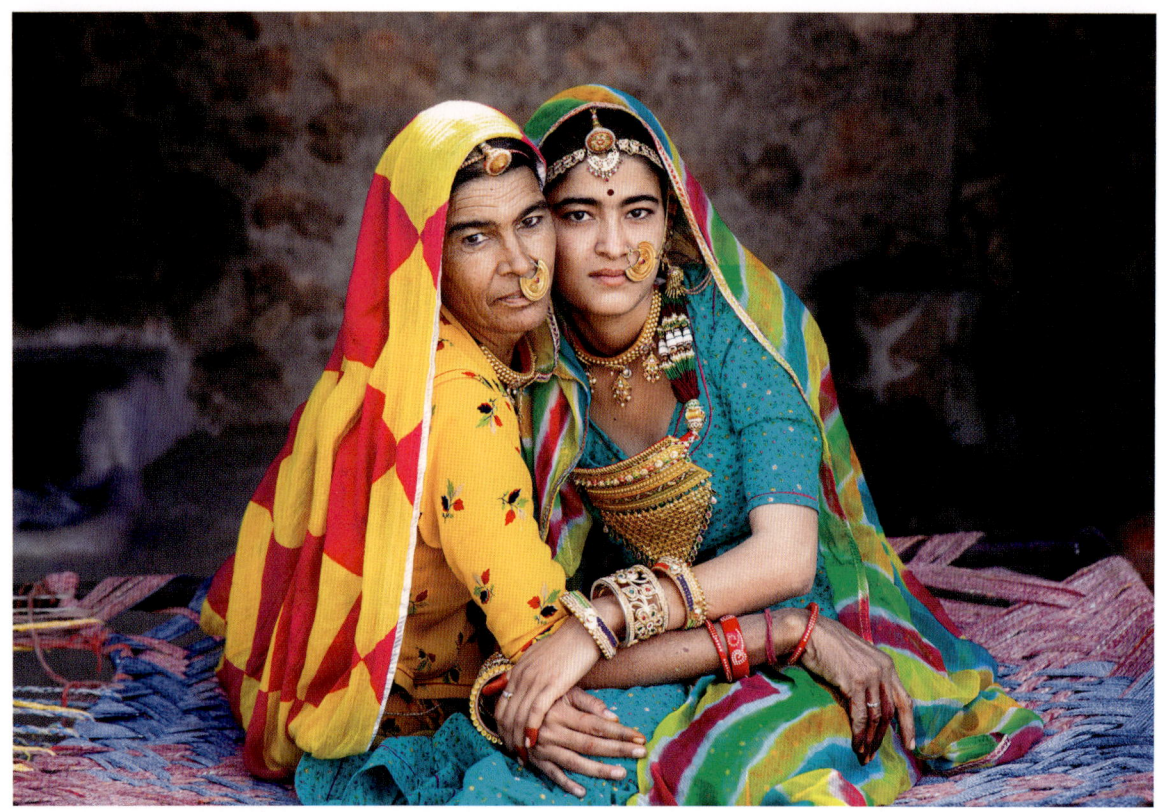

NORTHWESTERN INDIA *(Above)*

The connection between mothers and their children transcends country and culture, and that's why I love to capture it all over the world. Luni and her daughter, Nikitha, are part of a Hindu community called Bishnoi, and they live in the Thar Desert.

On one hand, I was so happy to capture this connection in this special part of the world, surrounded by colorful and spectacular traditions. On the other hand, I was sad to be away from my own daughter for a few weeks. In the end, love comes with all kinds of other feelings—not just happiness—and mothers know that best.

BERLIN, GERMANY *(Opposite)*

The love of a mother knows no age. When I met them, Tanja was taking care of her daughter, Katja, during her treatment for bone cancer. Although it was a very tough moment in their family, I was impressed to feel so much love and harmony in their home, with both making the most of every moment spent together. With her mother by her side, Katja fought with optimism and got better and better after our meeting. I'm sure that love was an important part of the treatment.

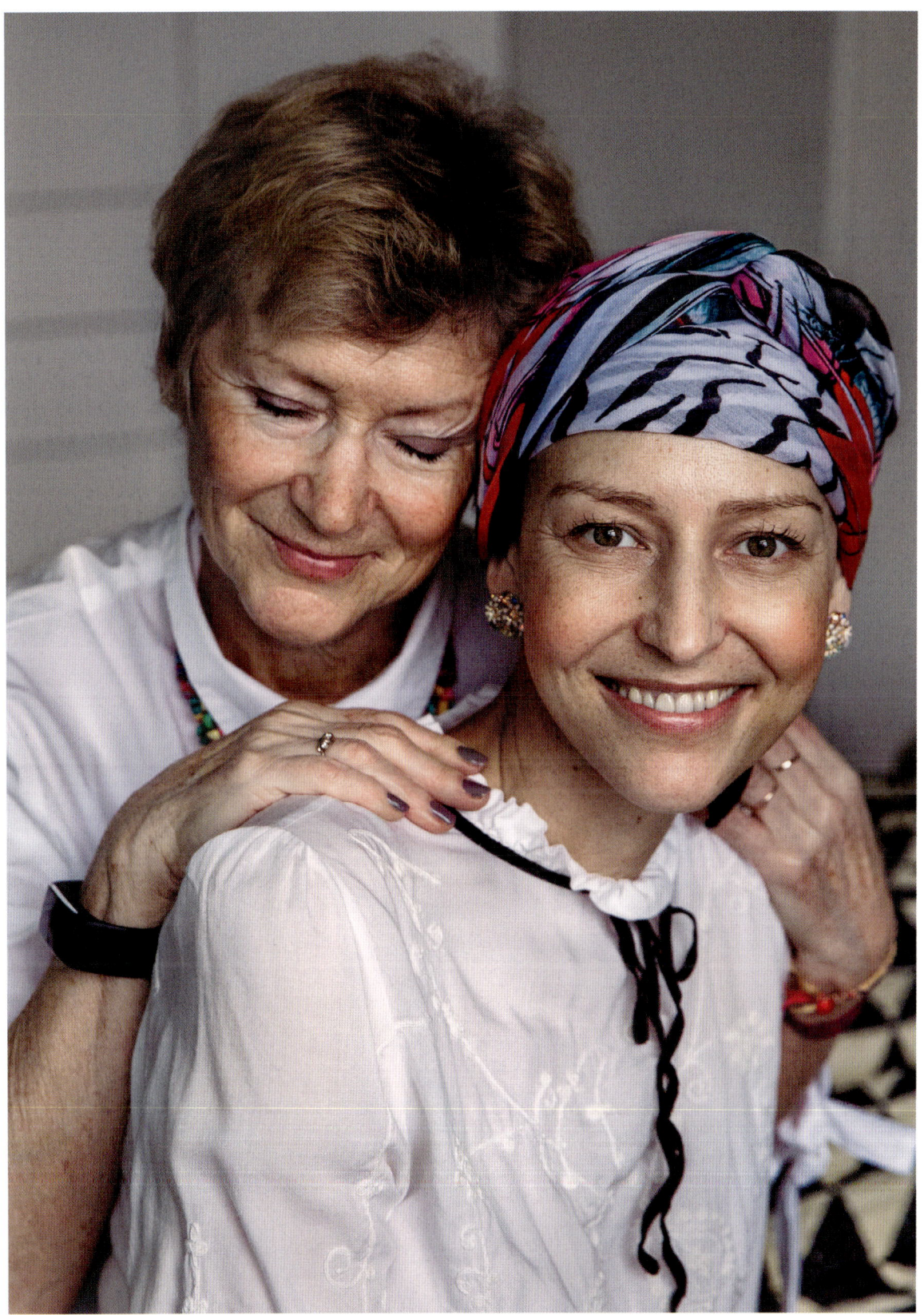

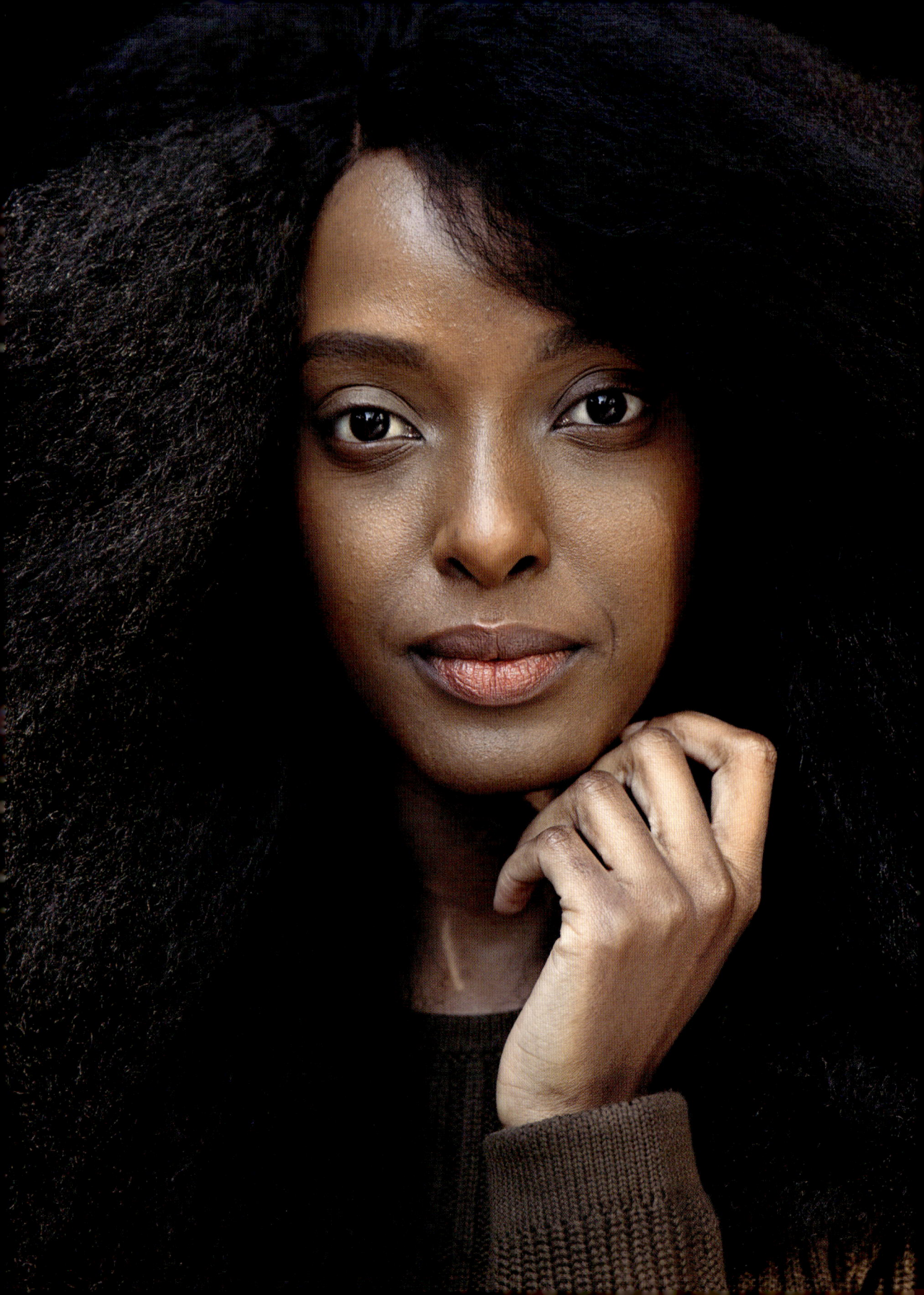

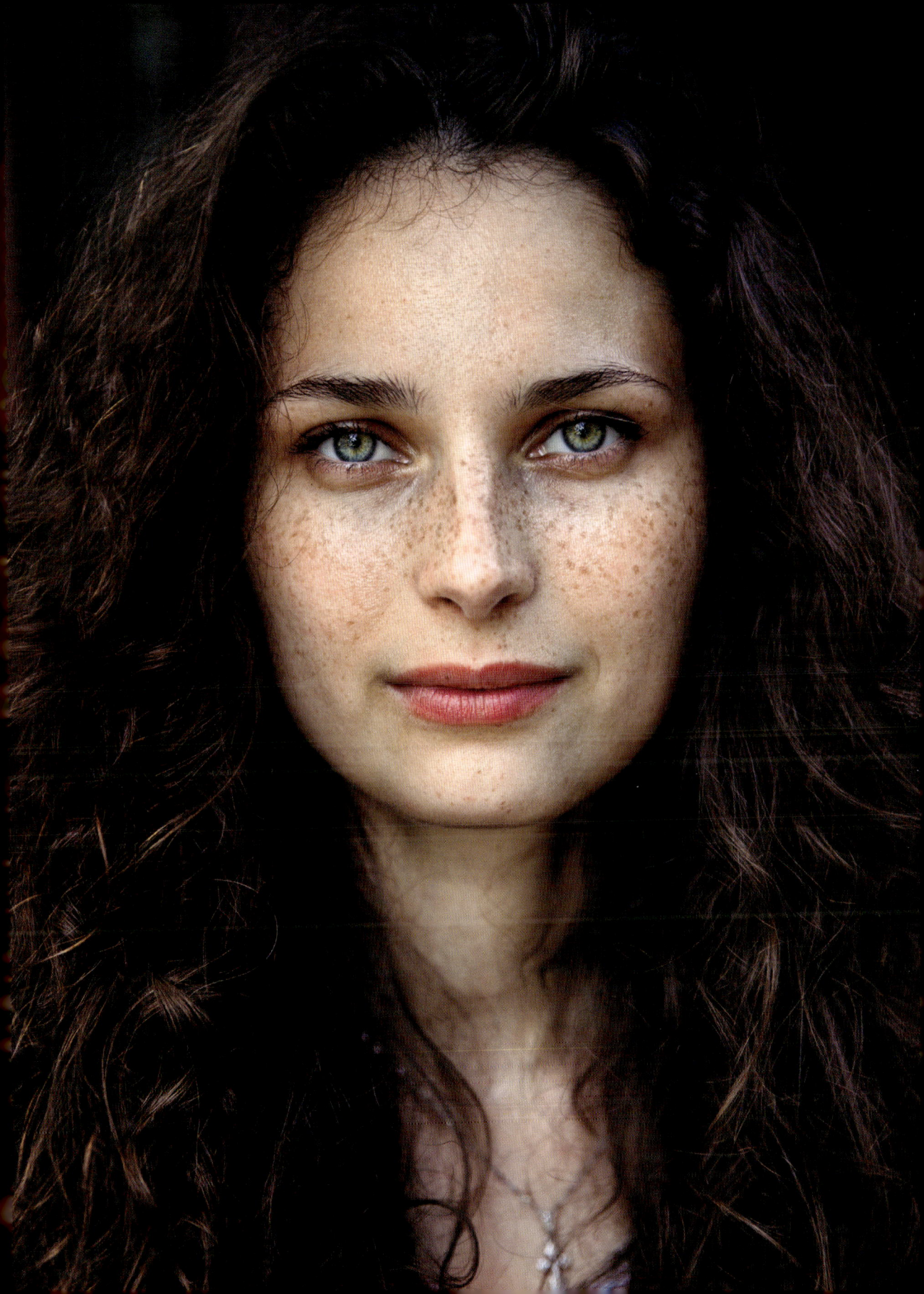

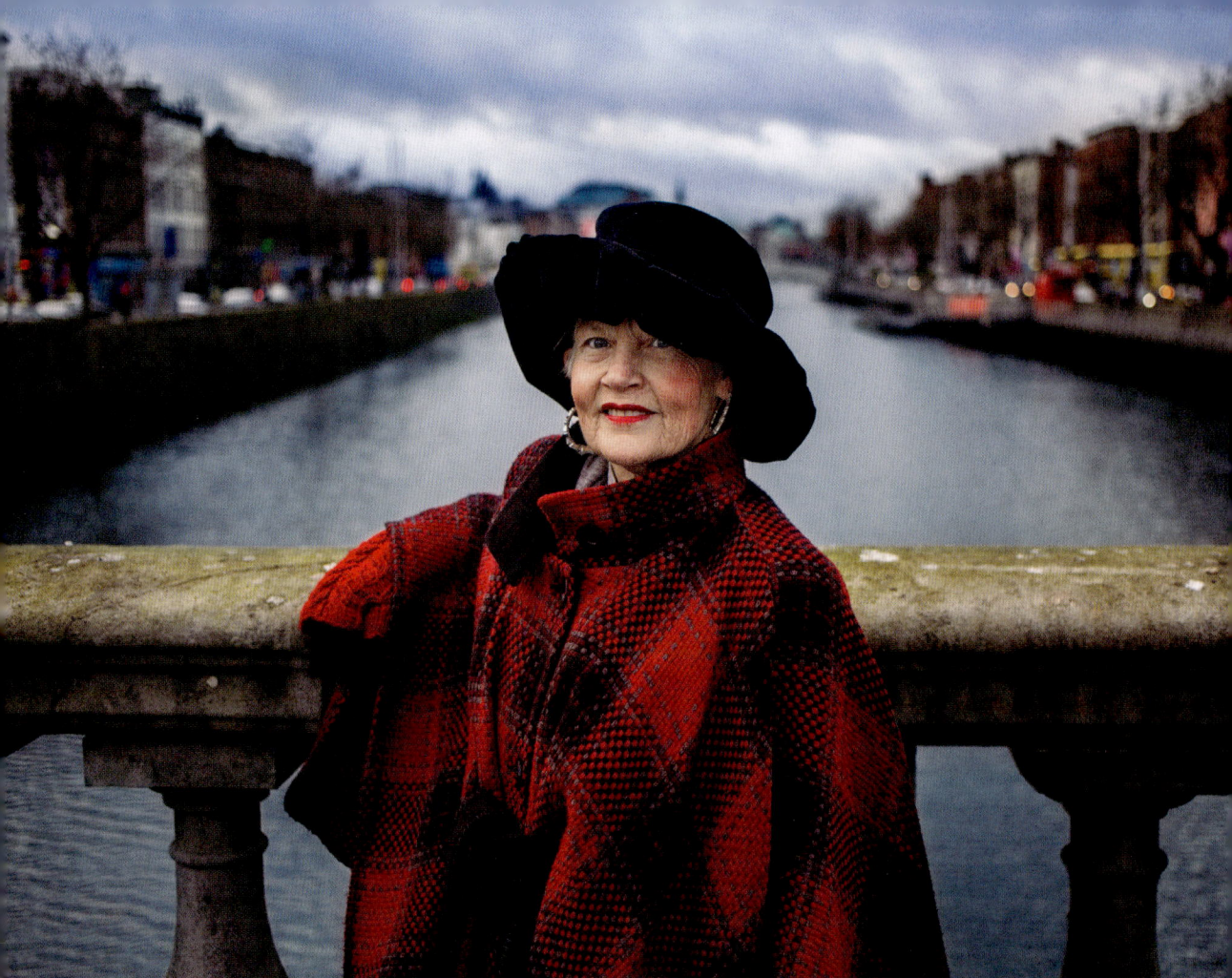

DUBLIN, IRELAND

Shirley is from the United States, but she travels to
Ireland once a year. She adores the country and tells
me it is the place where she feels closest to the sky.

LONDON, UNITED KINGDOM *(Previous spread, left)*

Eva was going to a job interview when I noticed her.

CHIȘINĂU, MOLDOVA *(Previous spread, right)*

Nadia was coming from work when I met her.

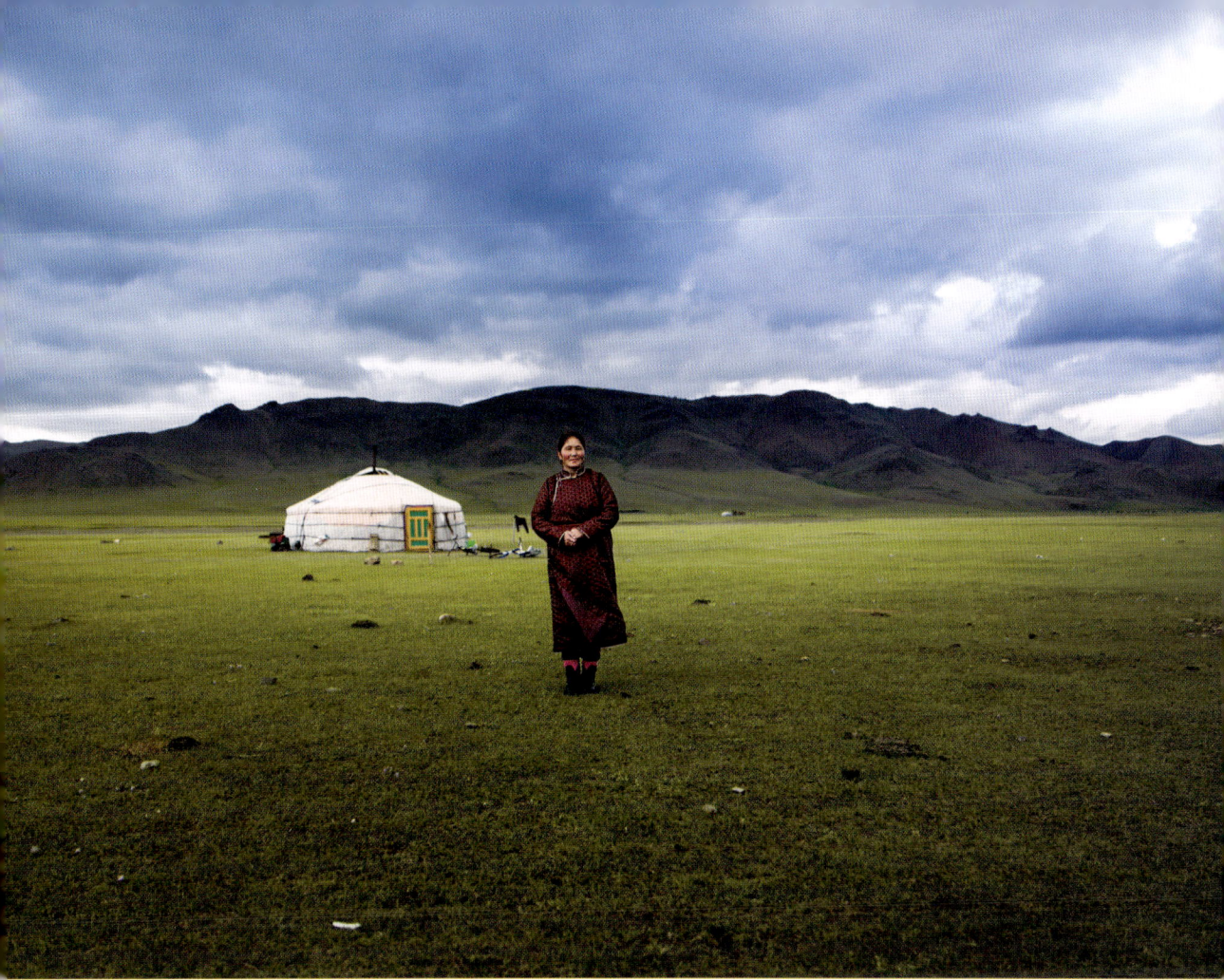

MONGOLIA

In Mongolia, you'll also feel close to the sky. In this vast steppe, you can sometimes drive for hours before you'll finally see the yurt of some nomads. They always wear a *deel*, which is an item of typical Mongolian clothing resembling a robe.

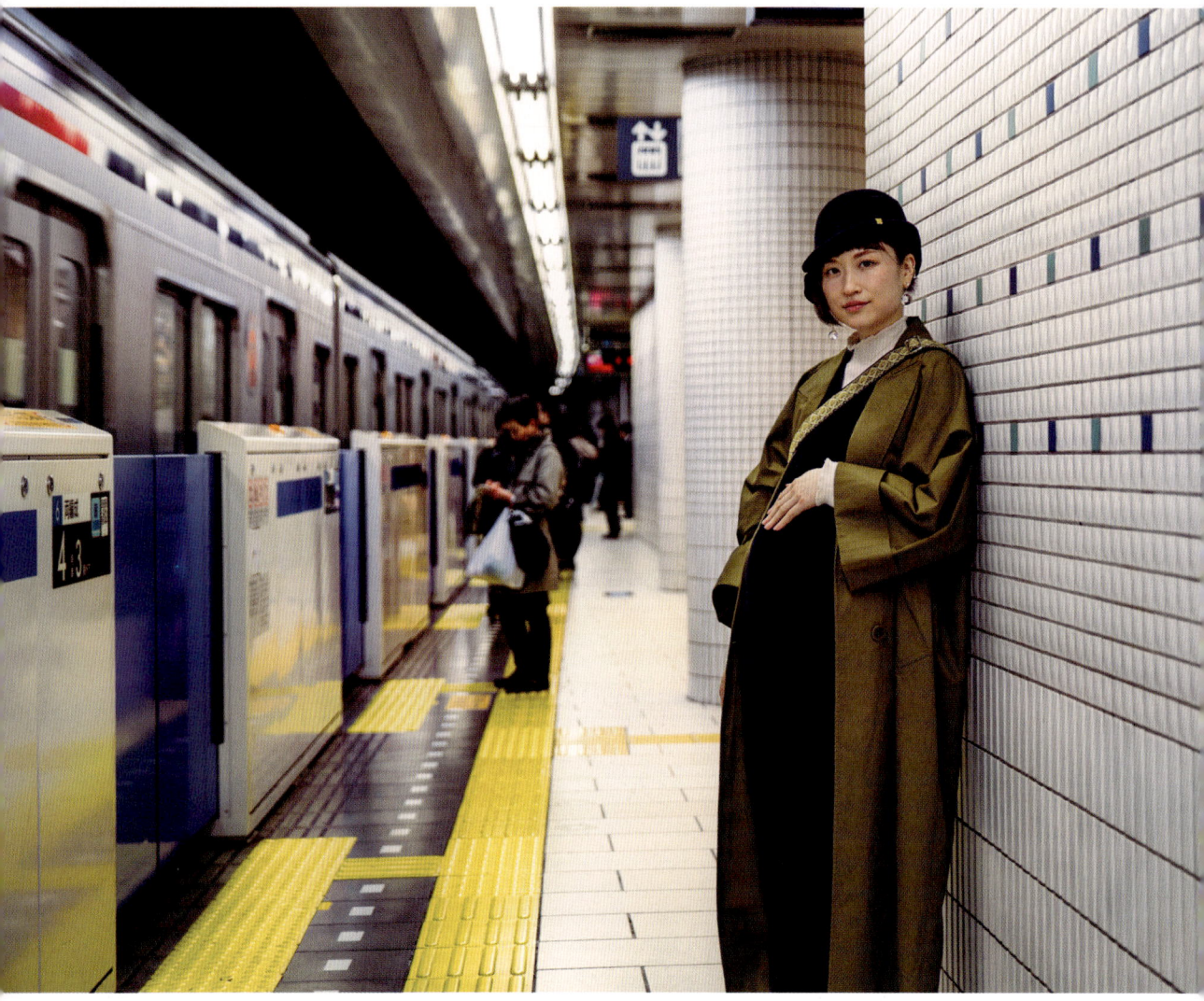

TOKYO, JAPAN

Shoko, eight months pregnant, was waiting for a train when I met her. She is a hip-hop dancer and teacher, and she was excited about becoming a mother very soon.

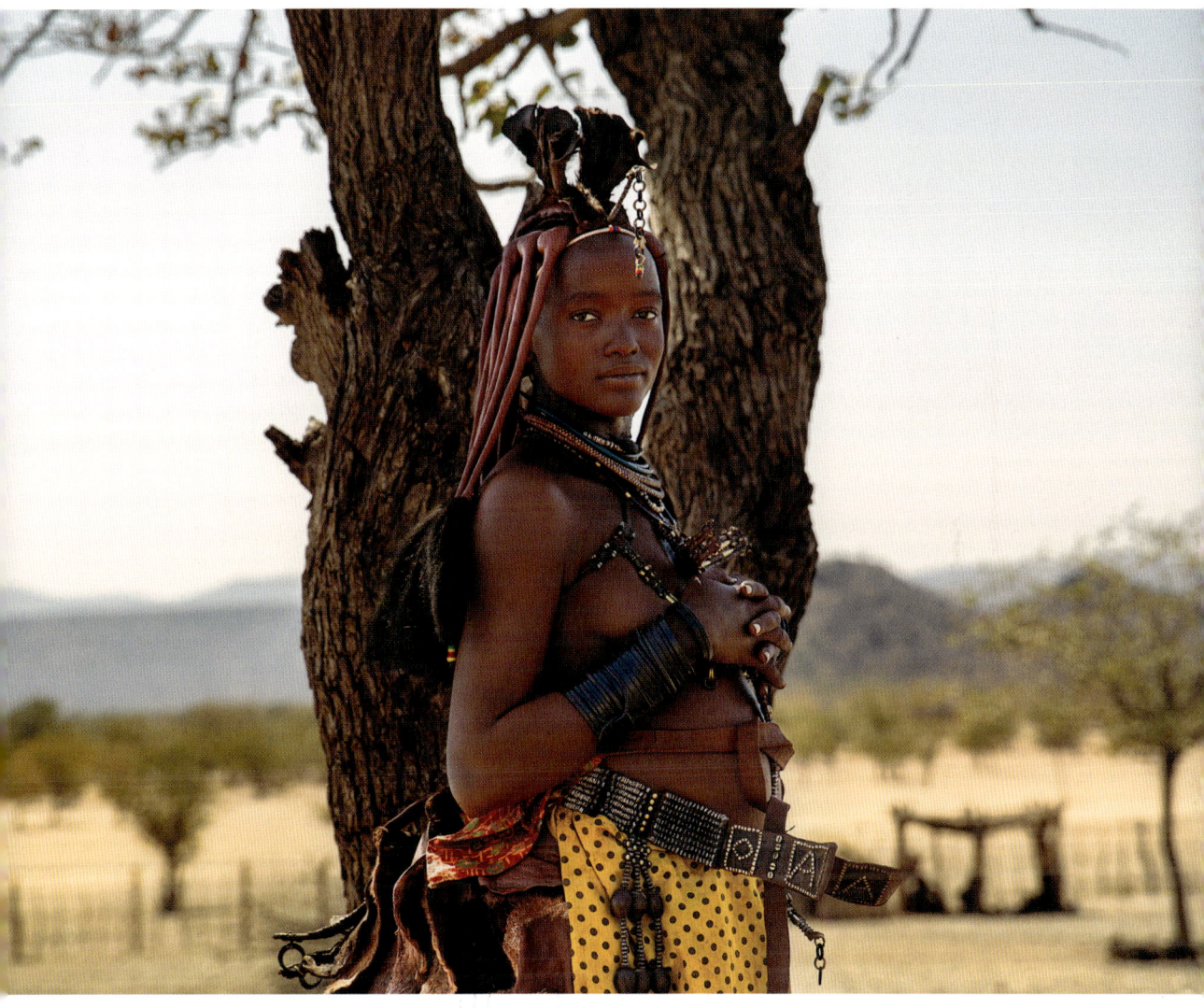

NORTHERN NAMIBIA

In another part of the world, Uatjete was pregnant with her first child. She was not worried at all about the birth—all women here give birth at home. The Himba have a special connection with nature, which probably gives them confidence despite all challenges.

The Himba are famous for covering themselves with *otjize,* a mixture of butterfat and ochre pigment. Otjize is like a magical potion in this harsh desert climate. First, it cleanses the skin over long periods, so there's no need for water. Second, it protects from insects. Third, it works as a perfume because it contains aromatic resin of a plant called Commiphora. Fourth, it gives the skin a distinctive texture and an orange look, which is a sign of beauty. And last but not least, it's used for hair styling to create very complex designs. Uatjete will soon teach her child this natural way of living—it's how these people have lived for thousands of years.

JEDDAH, SAUDI ARABIA

Women in combat sports are faced with prejudices all over the world—even in liberal places. But Halah Alhamrani does this in one of the most conservative places on Earth.

Halah has been in love with combat sports ever since she can remember. She started training intensively at the age of twelve. She practiced jujitsu, Muay Thai, boxing, and kickboxing.

As a child, she was diagnosed with attention deficit hyperactivity disorder (ADHD). Sports were the key factor that disciplined her. Her passion became her escape from the anxiety of being misunderstood, and she wanted to encourage more women to find empowerment through combat sports. In 2003, she opened the first gym dedicated to women in Saudi Arabia in her own home. She named it Flagboxing. Today, Flagboxing has many locations all over the country, and its slogan—"Fight like a girl!"—perfectly describes Halah's philosophy.

She believes that women are strong in their own right and don't have to imitate men to prove their strength. Her own example says it all: a dedicated and gentle mother, a successful entrepreneur, and a fierce fighter—coexisting identities within one fabulous woman.

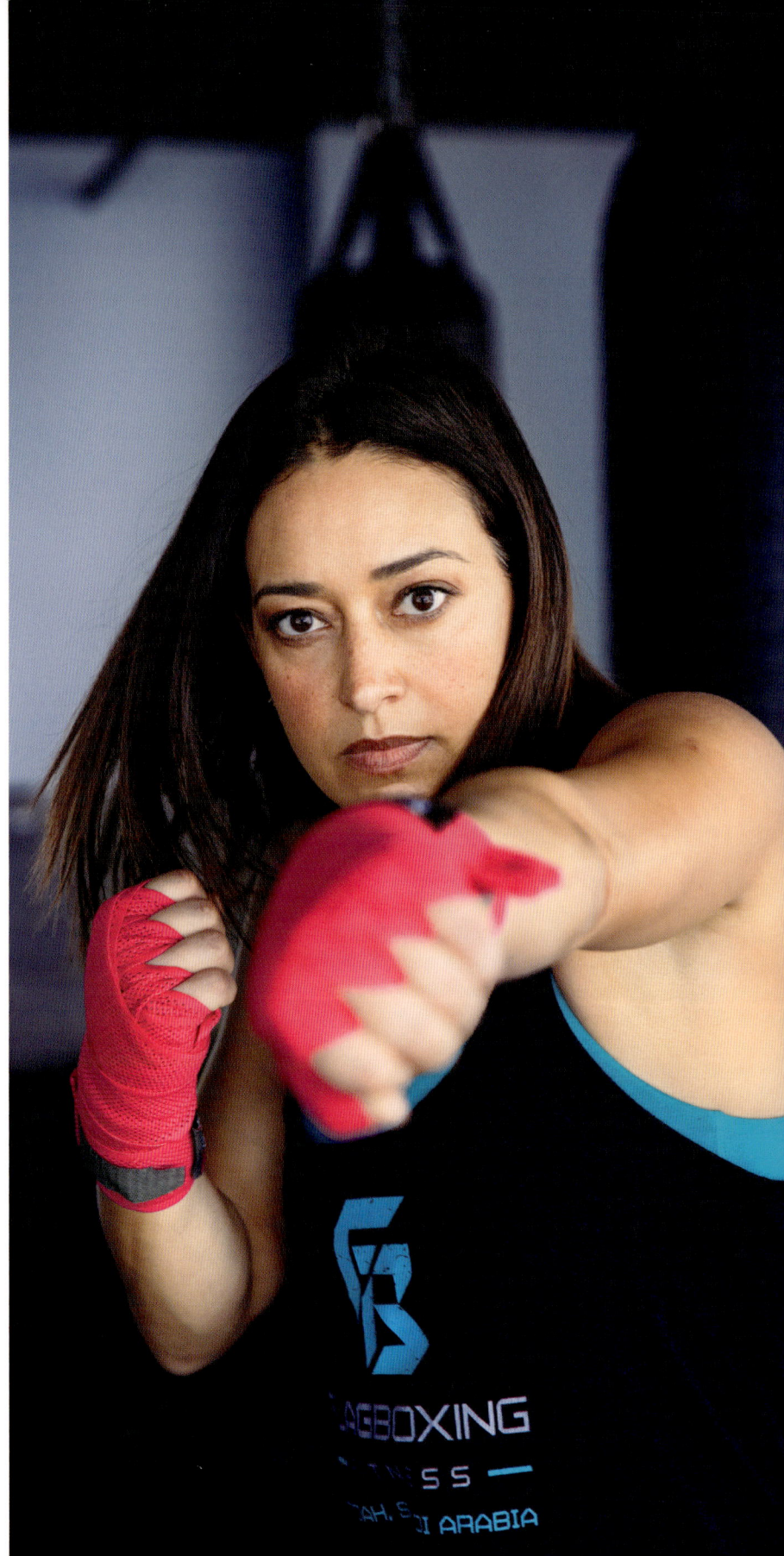

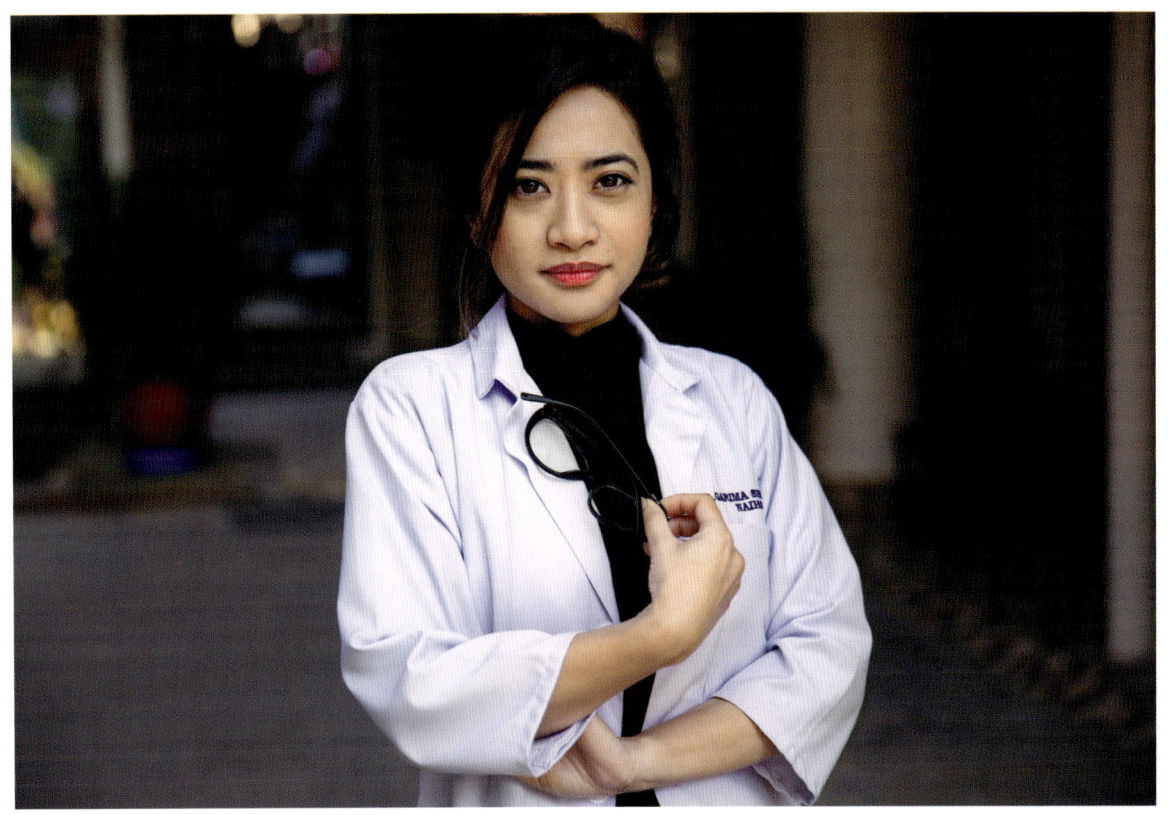

KATHMANDU, NEPAL

In her first years as a doctor, Garima Shrestha met many women from rural communities who were victims of *chhaupadi*. This idea of menstrual taboo prohibits women and girls from participating in normal activities while menstruating. During their menstruation, women are considered impure and banned from the house. They have to live in a so-called menstrual hut next to their homes in poor conditions without any menstrual hygiene products. More than that, in some communities, women who have just given birth must stay in the hut with their children for up to two weeks.

Devastated by these stories, Garima decided to act. She founded SHE Nepal, an organization aiming to fight taboos around menstruation and women's health by changing old mentalities. More than that, Garima's organization makes sanitary pads easily accessible in rural parts of the country. For the first time in their lives, many women in rural communities across Nepal finally have support.

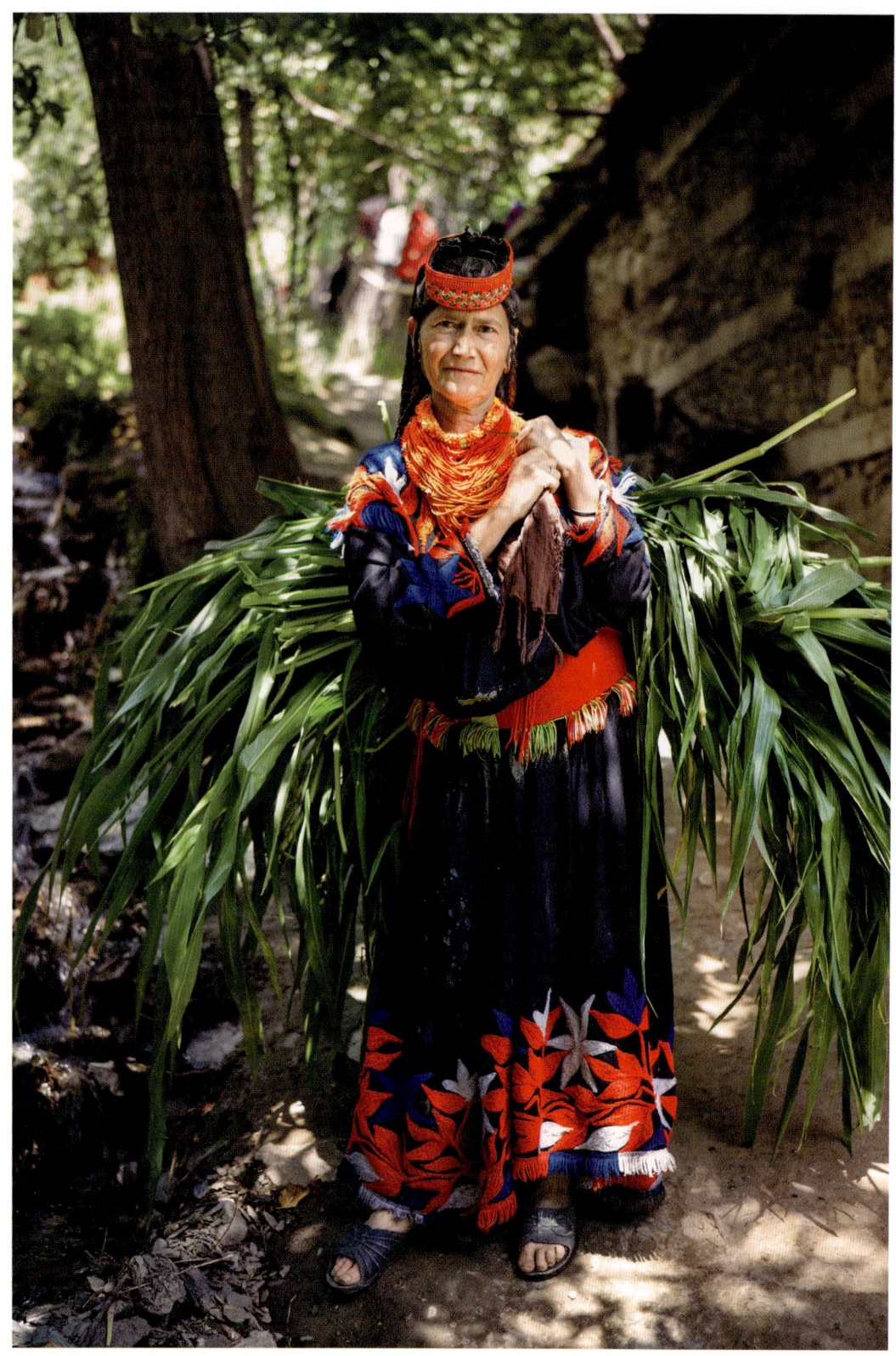

KALASHA VALLEYS, PAKISTAN

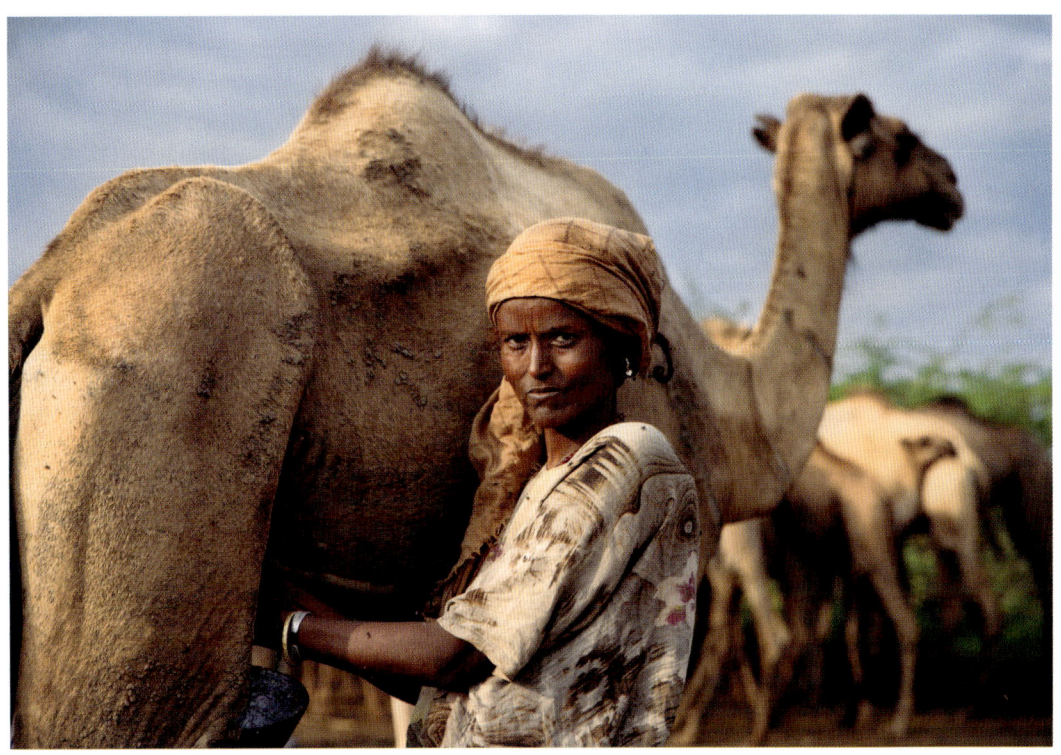

AWASH, ETHIOPIA

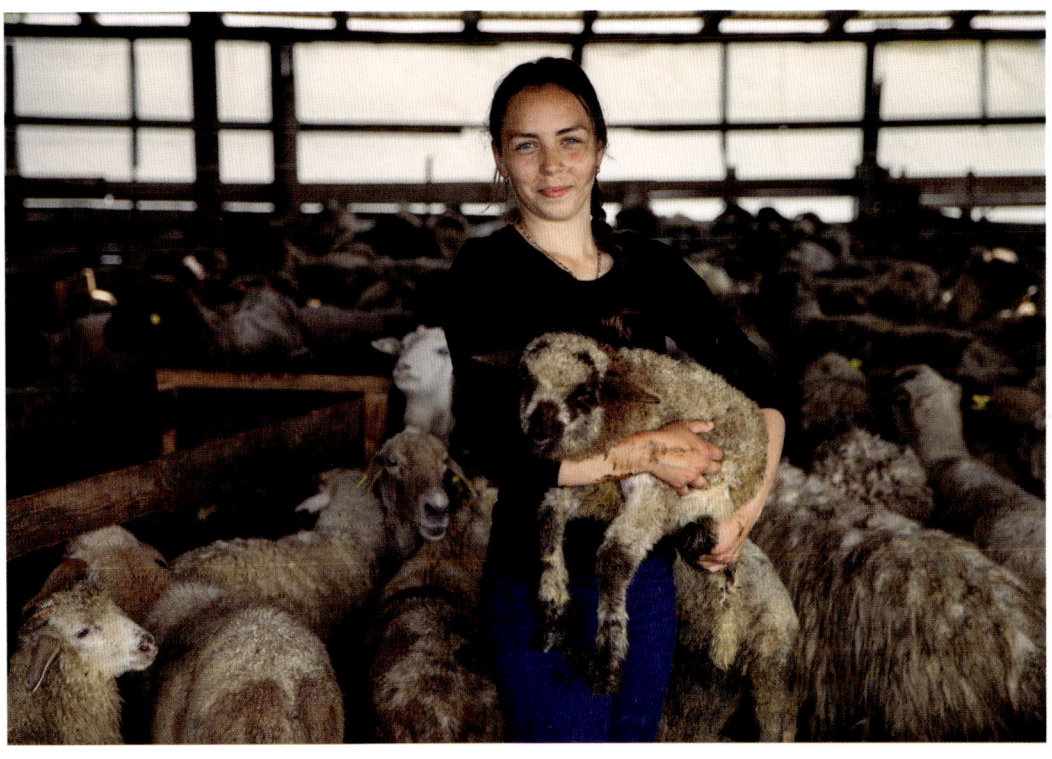

TIMIȘ COUNTY, ROMANIA

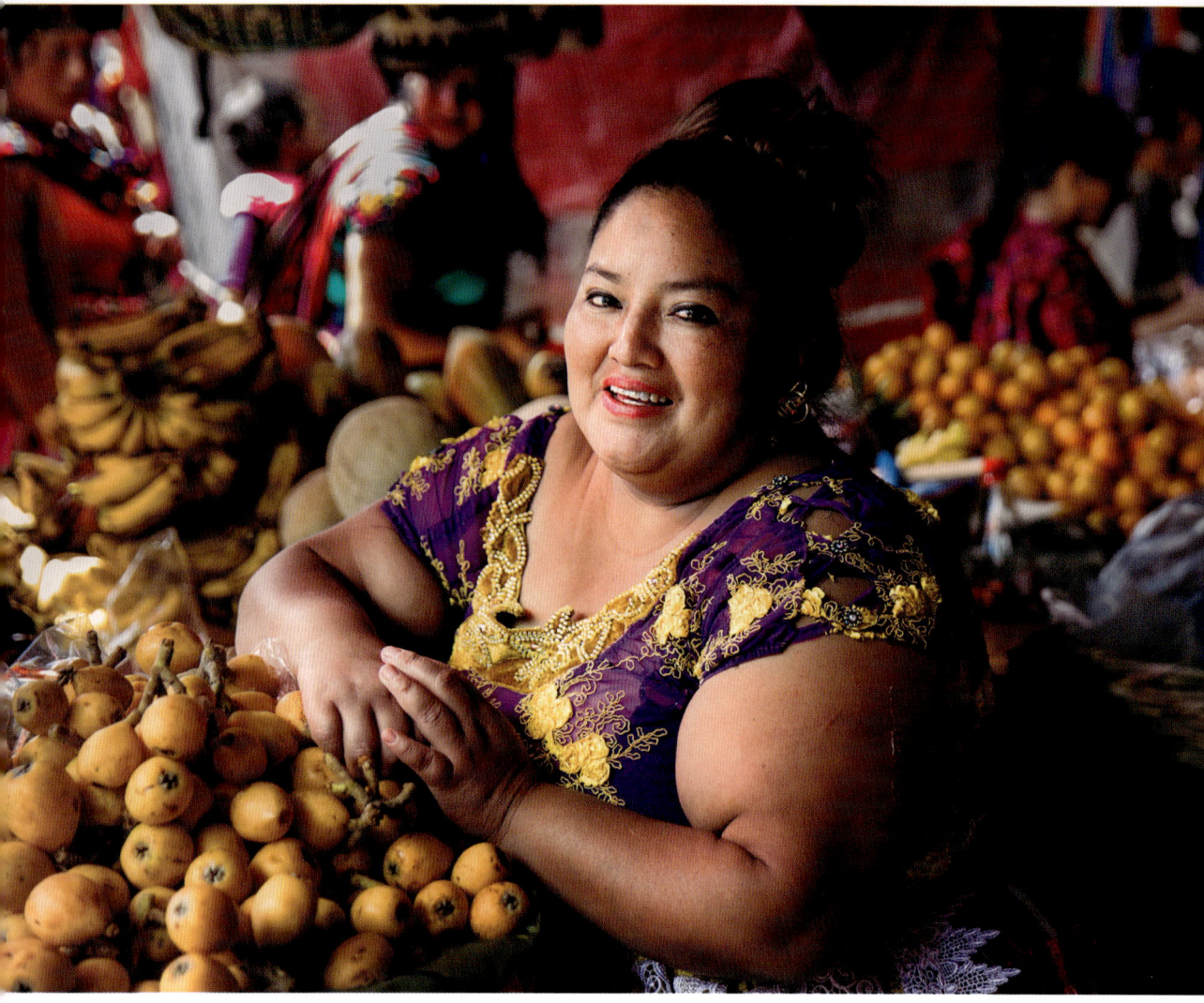

CHICHICASTENANGO, GUATEMALA

Micaela was selling these sweet, delicious fruits called loquats when I noticed her in the market of this small town. If you look at a loquat tree, you'll notice that these fruits grow in many small clusters—exactly like families. And Micaela's story is one about family.

Micaela told me proudly that she was a seller in this market before she was born. That's because Micaela's mother was already working here while pregnant with her. Micaela became the oldest of ten siblings. Being the eldest, she not only helped her family at the market but also acted as a second mother to her brothers and sisters.

Was this a burden for her? On the contrary. In many traditional parts of the world, people have very hard lives. But it's the connection with their families and with local traditions that gives them the strength and the bright spirit to see the beauty of life.

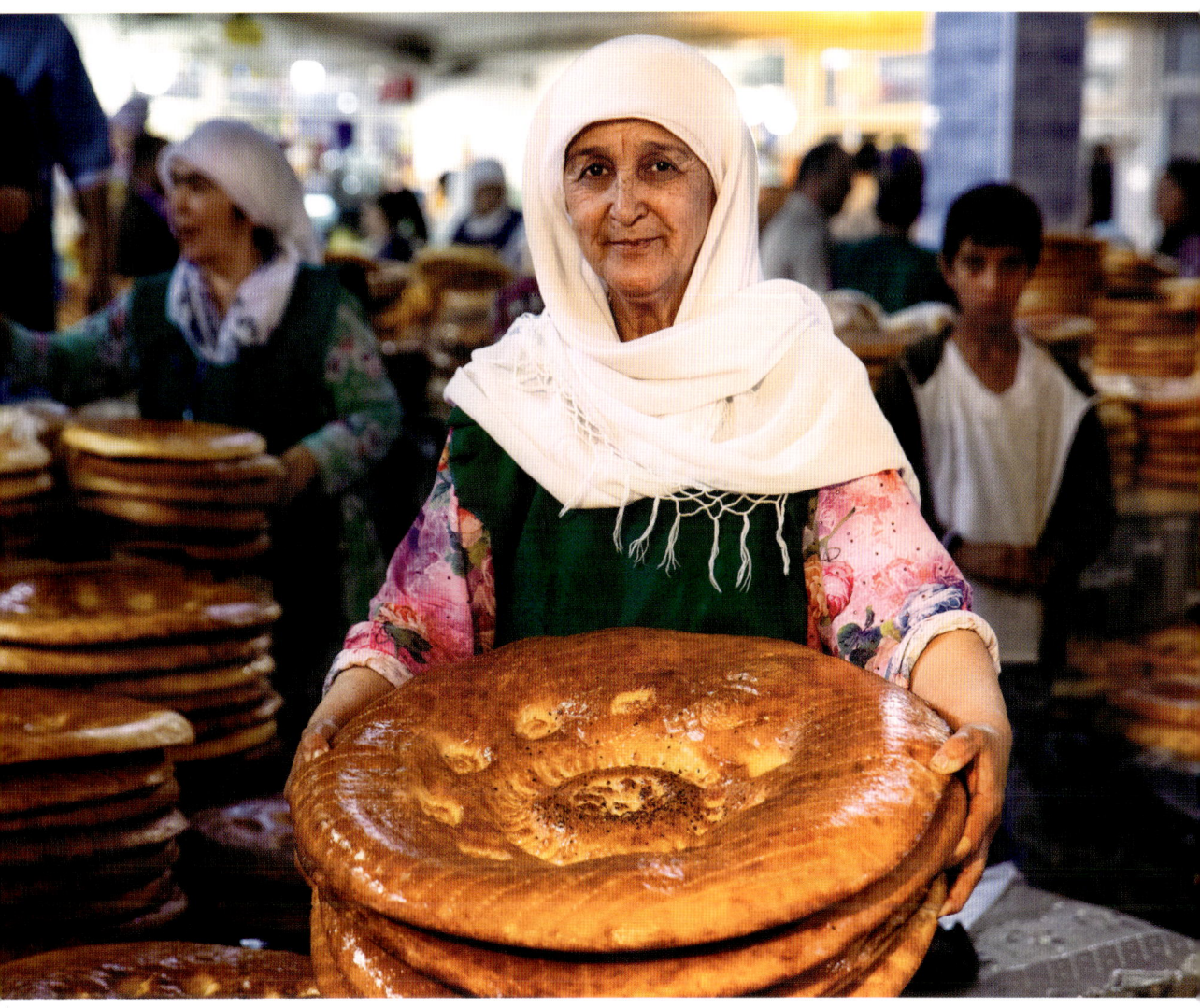

DUSHANBE, TAJIKISTAN

There are few places in the world where bread is so appreciated and celebrated like in Central Asia. It feels strange to describe bread as being beautiful, but not here. And believe me, it's not just beautiful—it's also super tasty.

Robia has been selling bread in this market for decades. Her son and her husband are baking it in a traditional clay oven while her grandson helps her at the stall. This bread was specially made for Eid al-Fitr, the big Muslim celebration that marks the end of Ramadan.

With each bread sold, Robia is one step closer to her simple yet impressive dream: to be able to send her grandson to university.

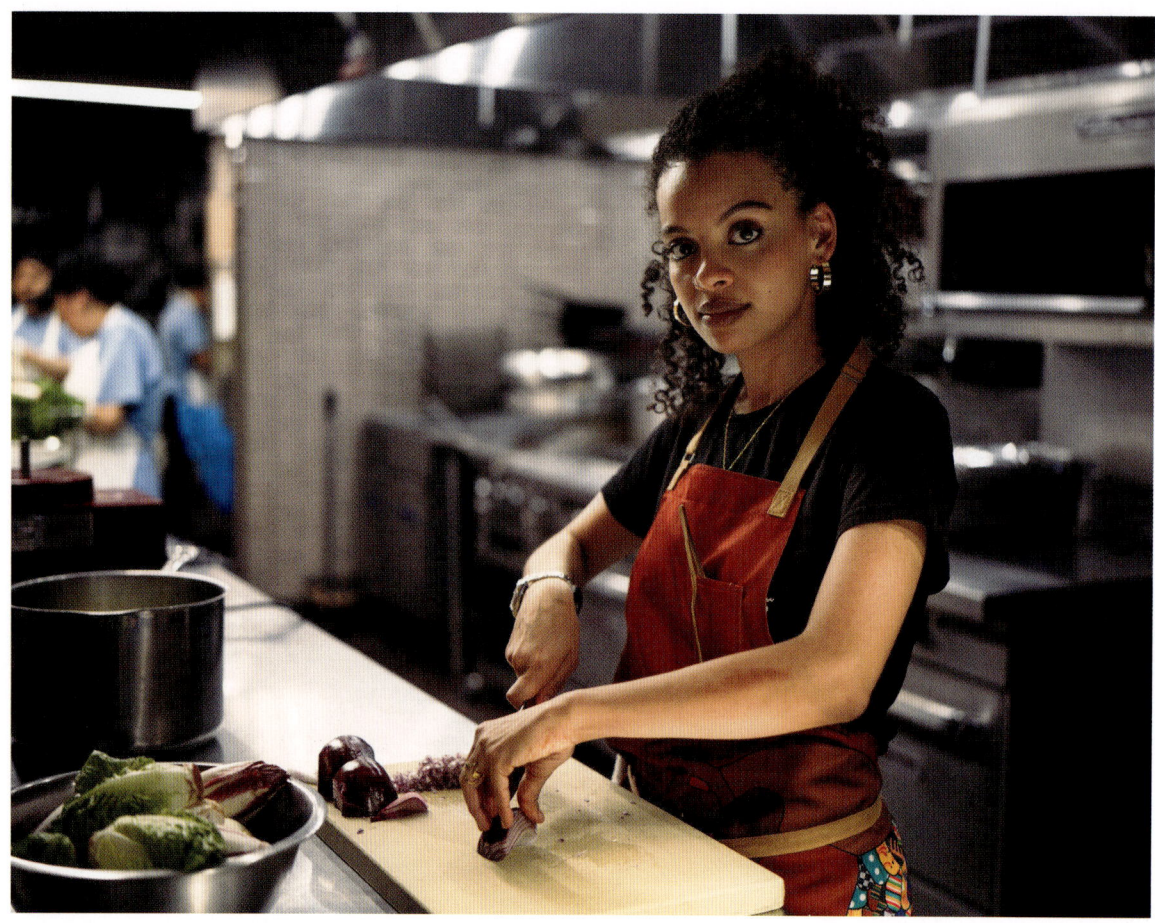

NEW YORK CITY, UNITED STATES *(Above)*

Fariyal Abdullahi moved from Ethiopia to the United States when she was sixteen. After getting a bachelor's degree in psychology, she decided to switch career paths. Fariyal traveled around the world, visiting eighteen countries, eating, cooking, and learning about the cultures of our planet.

Upon her return to the United States, she studied at one of the most prestigious culinary schools and then worked at some of the best restaurants in the world. I photographed her in the seafood-focused restaurant in NYC where she's an executive chef. It was interesting to find how proud she is about her Ethiopian heritage and to witness how she incorporates her past into some of her dishes.

COLOGNE, GERMANY *(Opposite)*

Lorena Morato was born in Brazil. After a tumultuous childhood, she moved to Spain on her own at age nineteen. She became a squatter and joined a group of political activists. For four years, all her belongings fit into one small bag as she moved from one abandoned building to another. Eventually she started learning the art of tattooing and moved to Germany.

Initially practicing on her own skin, Lorena now owns a prestigious tattoo salon, and she's well known for her unique inkwork as well as her beautiful paintings. Her inspiration comes from nature, spirituality, her Brazilian roots, and her own intense life.

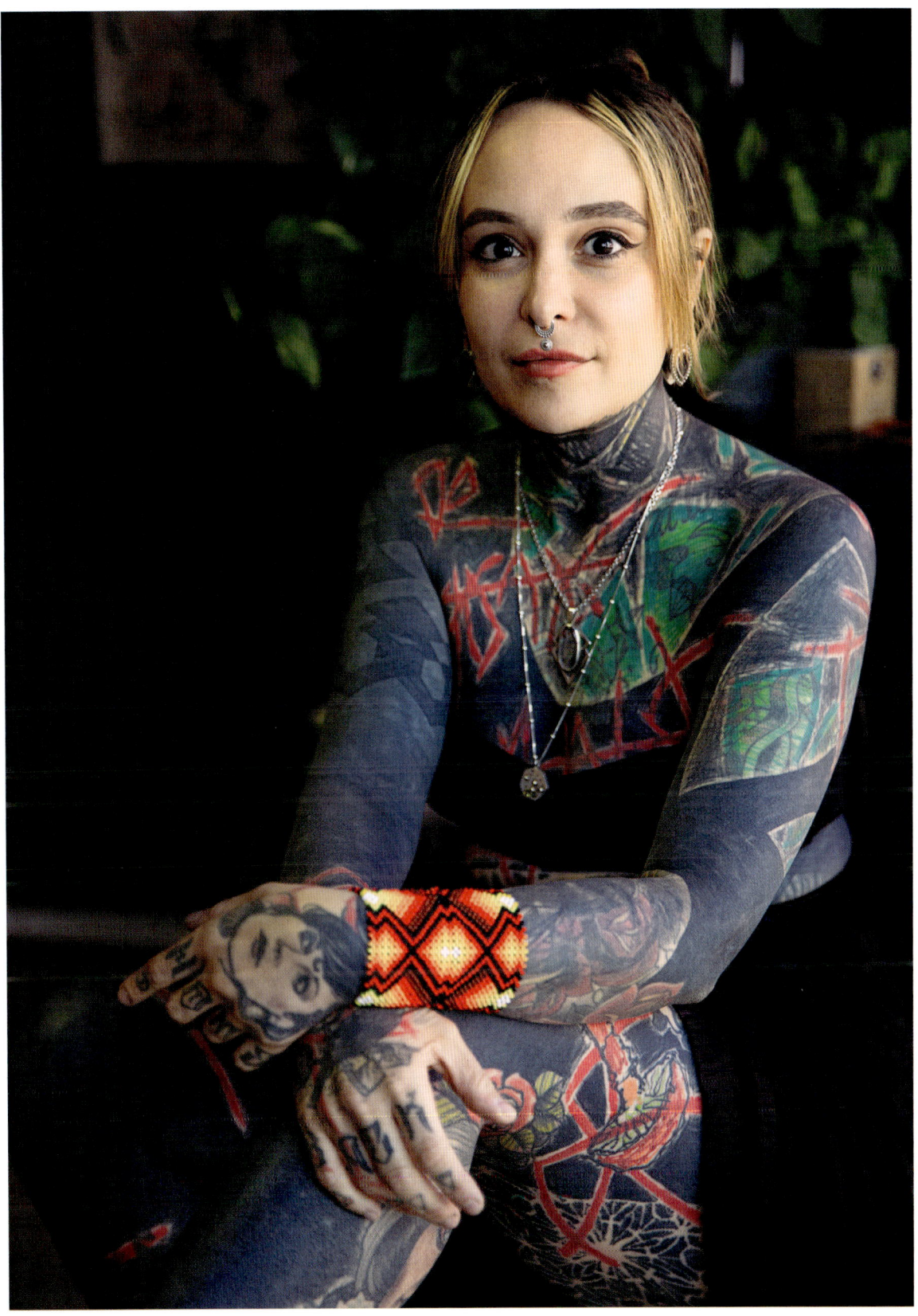

ANDES MOUNTAINS, PERU

Aide lives in a remote village nestled in the Andes Mountains of Peru. There, at over four thousand meters, life is harsh. By contrast, the daily clothing of the locals is incredibly sophisticated and colorful and takes a tremendous quantity of work to make. Some women, like Aide, decorate their hats with fresh flowers every day. It was fascinating to find out that these flowers are not just beautiful but also serve as natural perfume.

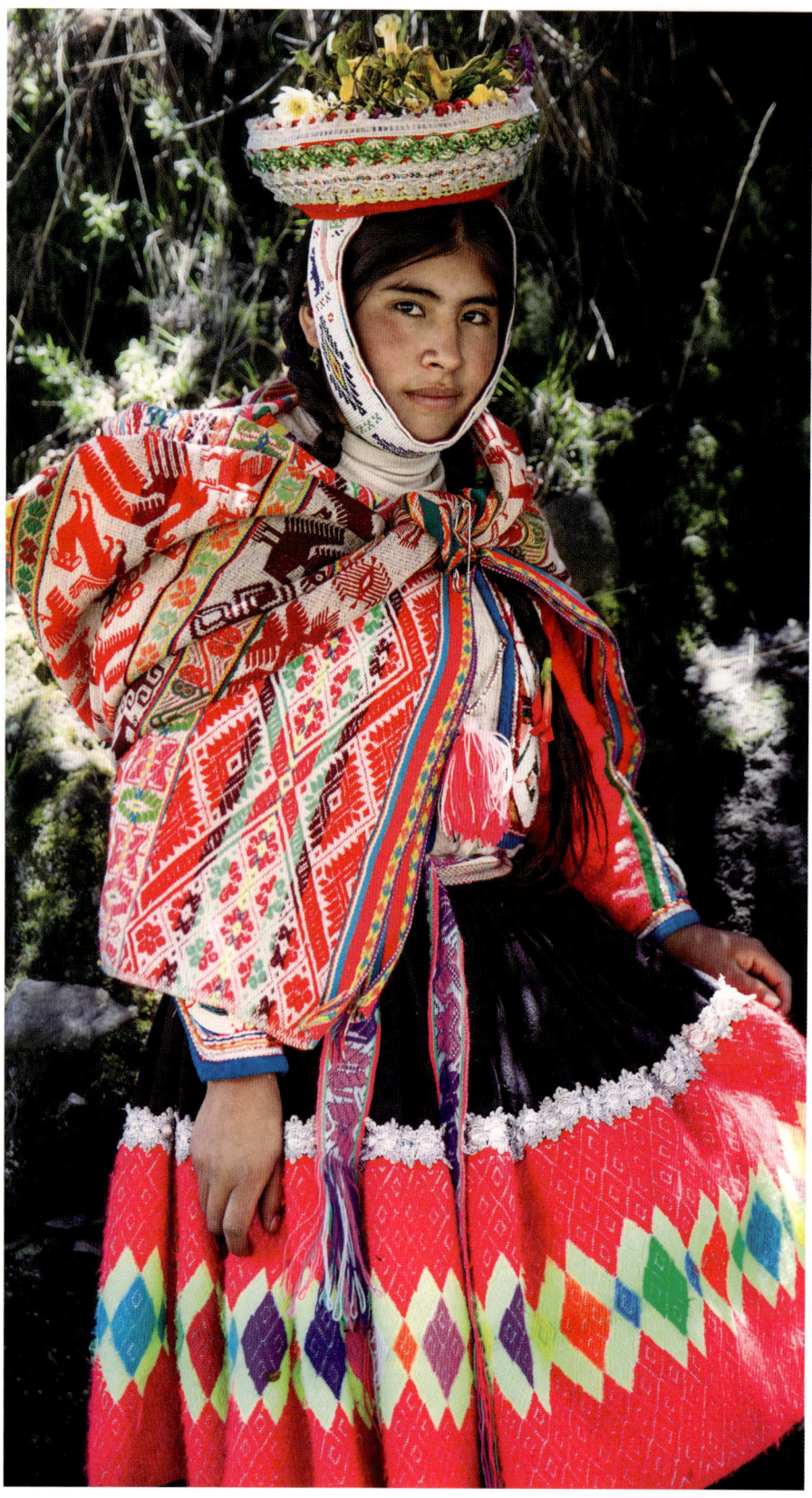

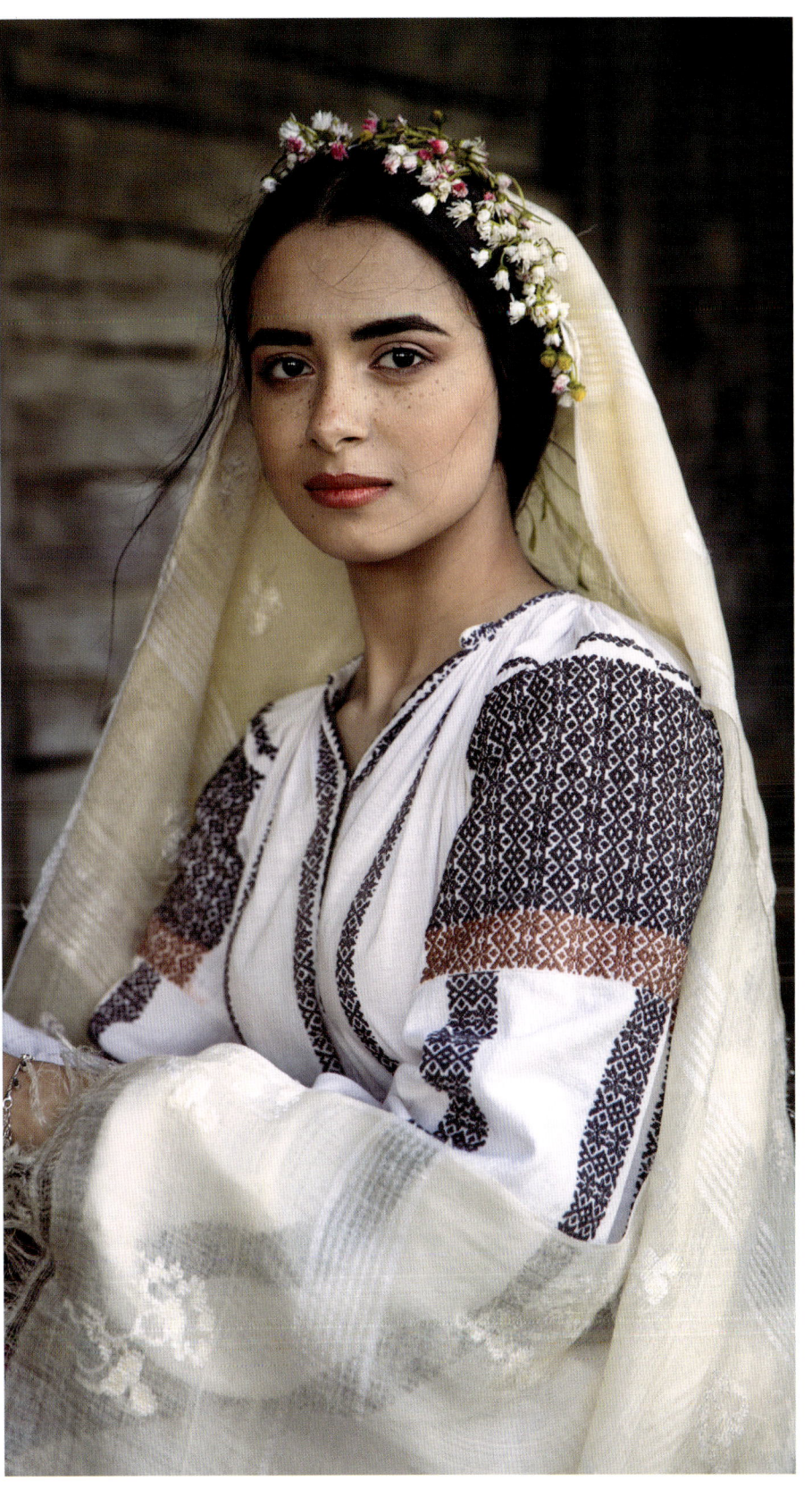

HOBIȚA, ROMANIA

Ștefania lives in a village renowned for its traditions. Nearly one hundred and fifty years ago, just a few minutes away from Stefania's house, one of the greatest sculptors of the twentieth century was born. Constantin Brâncuși was influenced by the local wood carving tradition and later became a pioneer of modernism while earning the title of patriarch of modern sculpture.

Today, Ștefania is a member of a traditional dance group in the village. She inherited this beautiful old outfit from her grandmother. Apart from her passion for folk culture, she also loves technology and is preparing to study robotics. Like Brâncuși, she values the past while keeping her focus on the future.

Indeed, traditions and progress can coexist harmoniously. I believe this is the key to a better world.

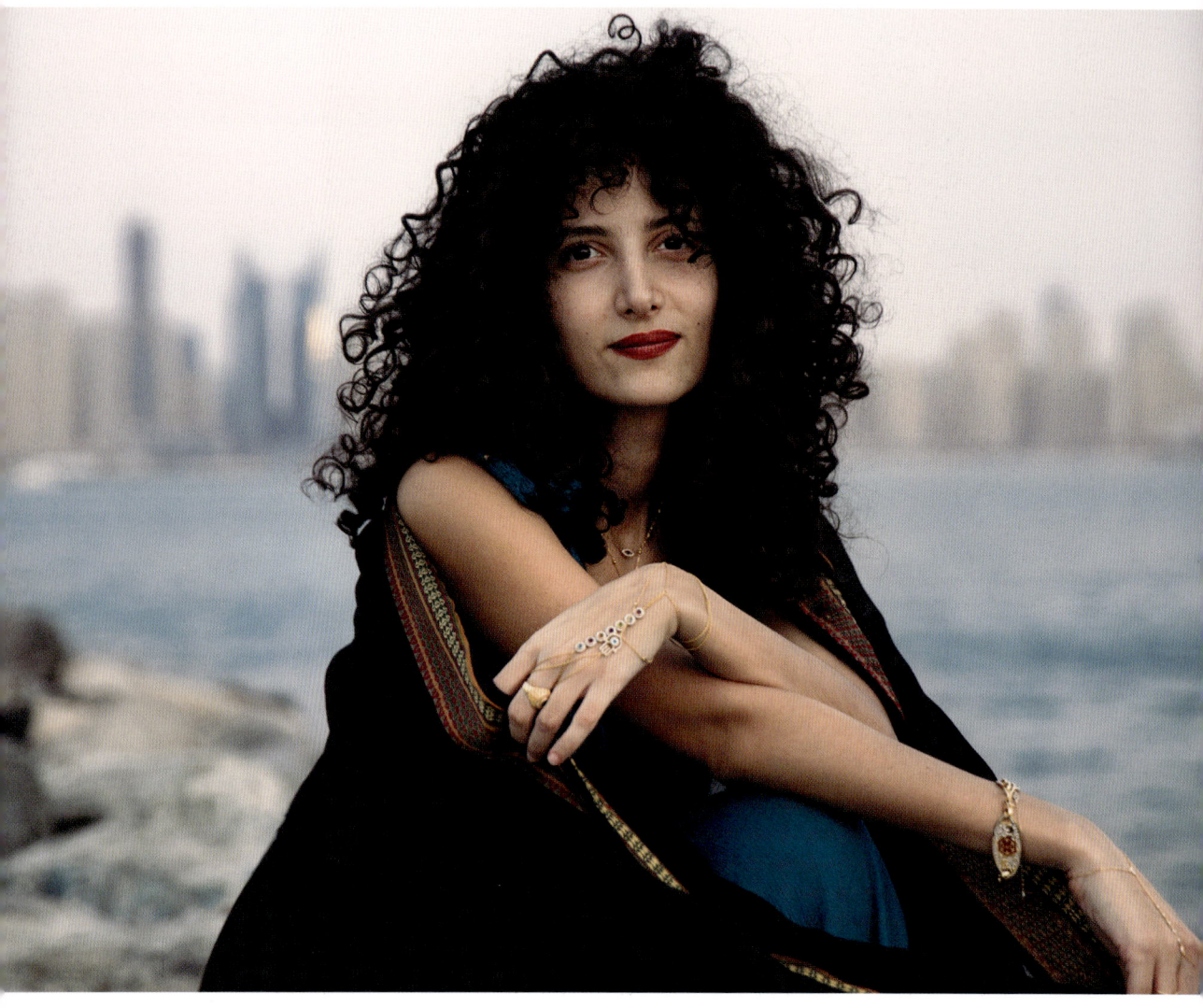

DUBAI, UNITED ARAB EMIRATES

I photographed Amira with her city in the background. There was a sandstorm in Dubai that day, but suddenly the atmosphere became peaceful. And peace is what Amira is looking for after many years of struggles.

When she was eight, Amira was diagnosed with lupus, a complicated autoimmune disease. At the moment, she needs to take about twelve pills per day. She always wears a medical alert bracelet in case she faints.

It doesn't stop her from doing amazing things. She created the first lupus support group in the Emirates so people can share their struggles and live a better life. She is also a successful lawyer, a yoga teacher, and a dance performer.

Finding peace amid the storm seems impossible. But not for brave people like Amira.

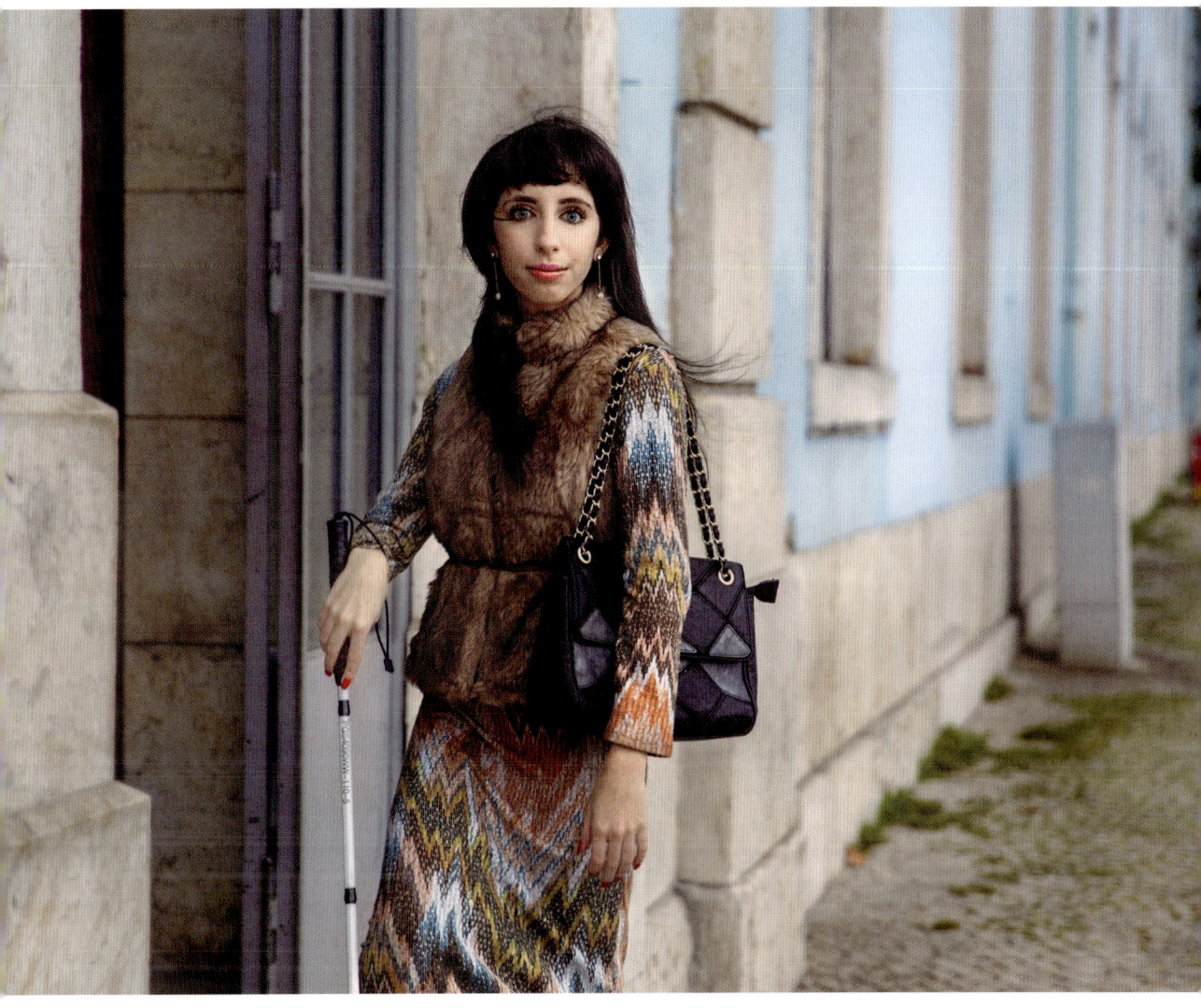

LISBON, PORTUGAL

Anna was on the way to meet some friends when I noticed her. She shared with me that she lost her vision when she was only two years old, but she never lost her lust for life. She told me we have only one life, so we should celebrate it every day. And that's what she does.

Every day, Anna dresses elegantly because she loves styling. Her mother describes the clothes to her, and Anna then creates the outfits based on her mother's descriptions. Another passion of hers is traveling. She told me how fascinated she is to feel the air, the sounds, and the atmosphere of each new destination.

On the professional side, Anna has a master's degree in psychology and loves to work with children. It's fantastic when inspirational people such as Anna choose to work with little ones. It's people like her who can best shape the future of the next generation.

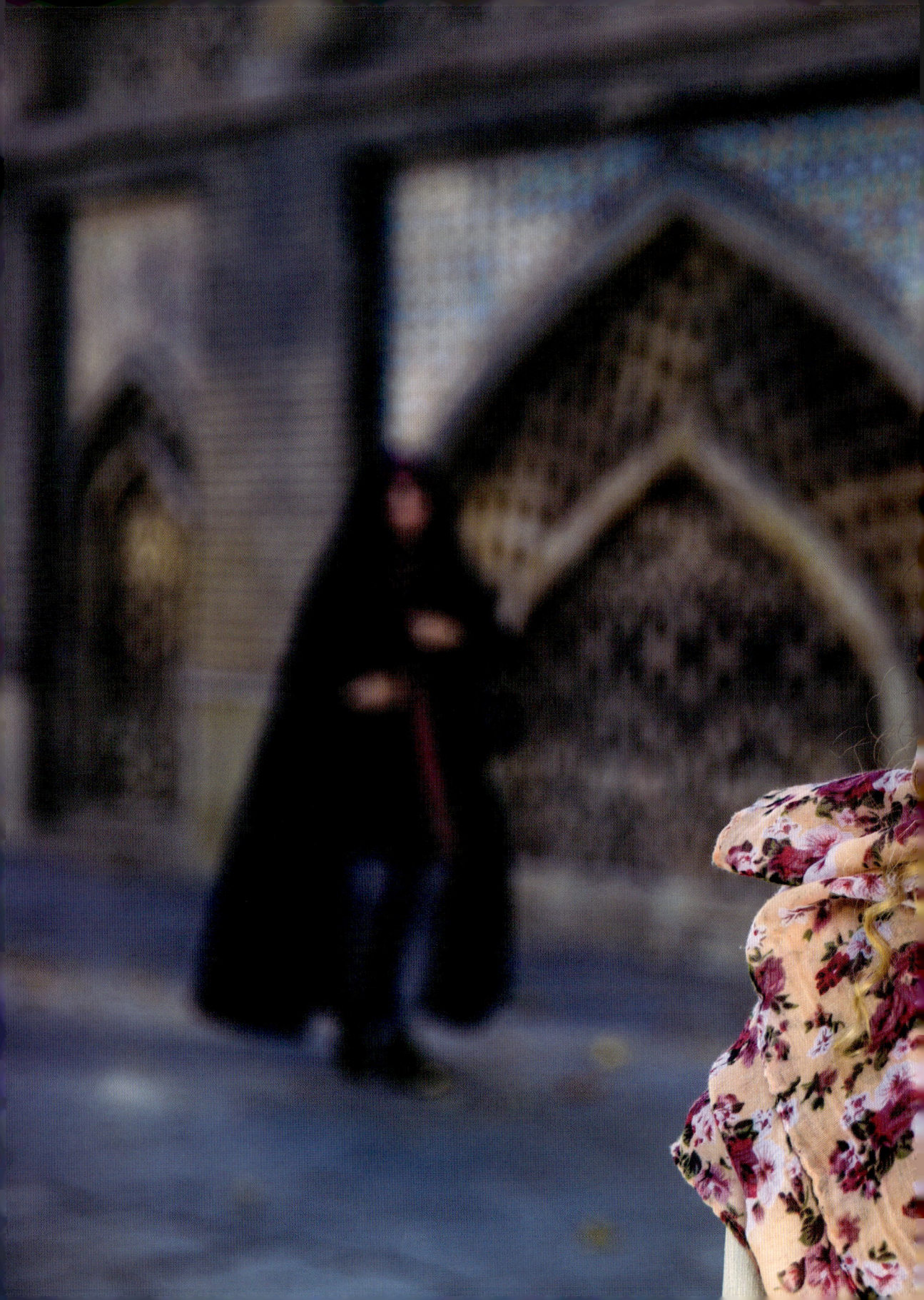

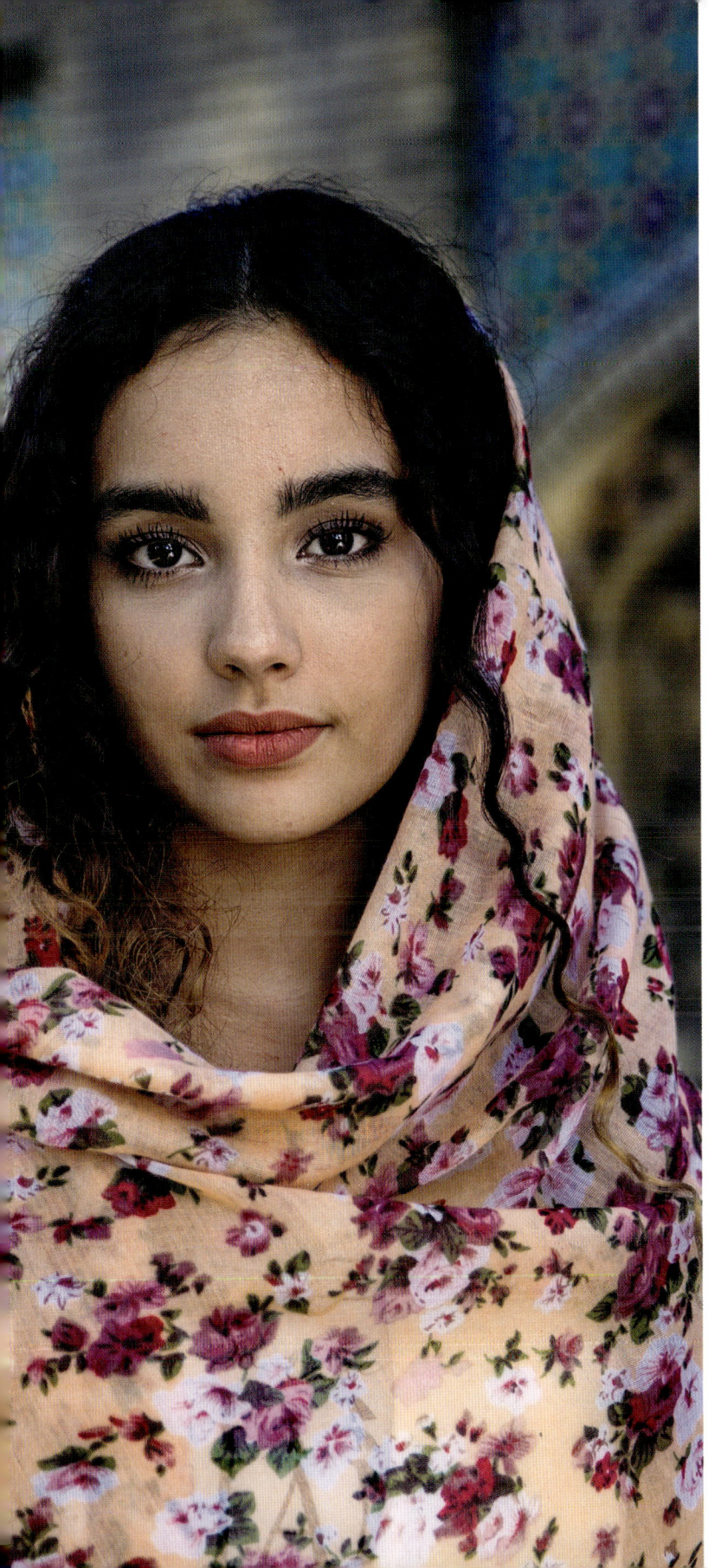

TEHRAN, IRAN

Farnoush has studied violin since her childhood. When I met her, she was both nervous and excited, because she was preparing for her first concert.

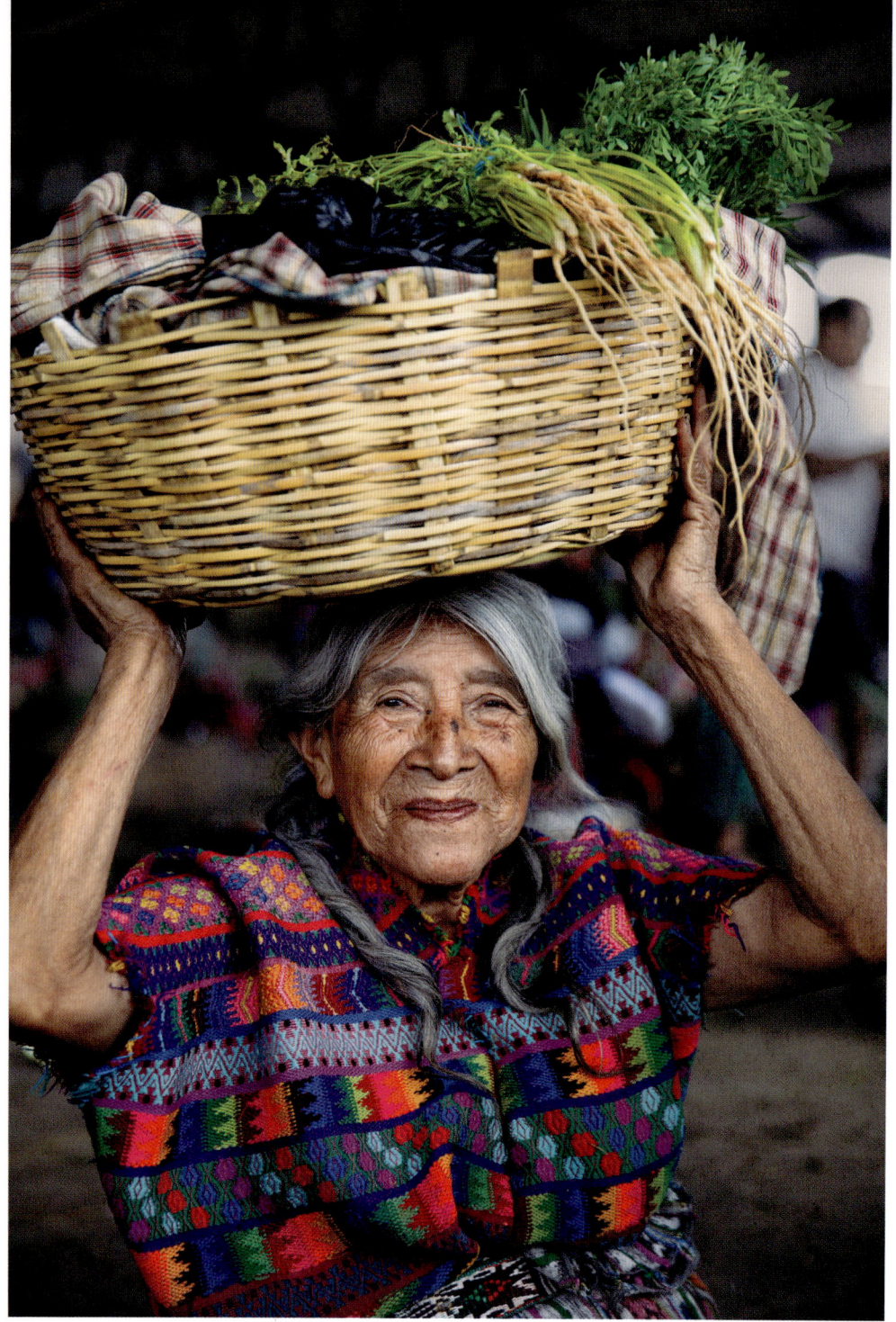

ANTIGUA, GUATEMALA

Fidelia has carried firewood from the forest since she was a child, while also raising eight children. For the past twenty years, she's pursued a new line of work, and now she sells her homegrown vegetables at this market. At eighty years old, she feels fortunate to have this work—work that is not nearly as demanding as her previous job carrying wood. Fidelia's story exemplifies how our perspective shapes the way we perceive and enjoy our own lives.

KOLKATA, INDIA

Every morning before sunrise, Gauri comes to the flower market to buy splendid garlands. Then she crosses the huge Howrah Bridge over the Hooghly River during her long walk to a Hindu temple, where she will sell the garlands to people who come there to worship.

It's exhausting work, but Gauri is happy that she can afford to send her three daughters to school and offer them a brighter future.

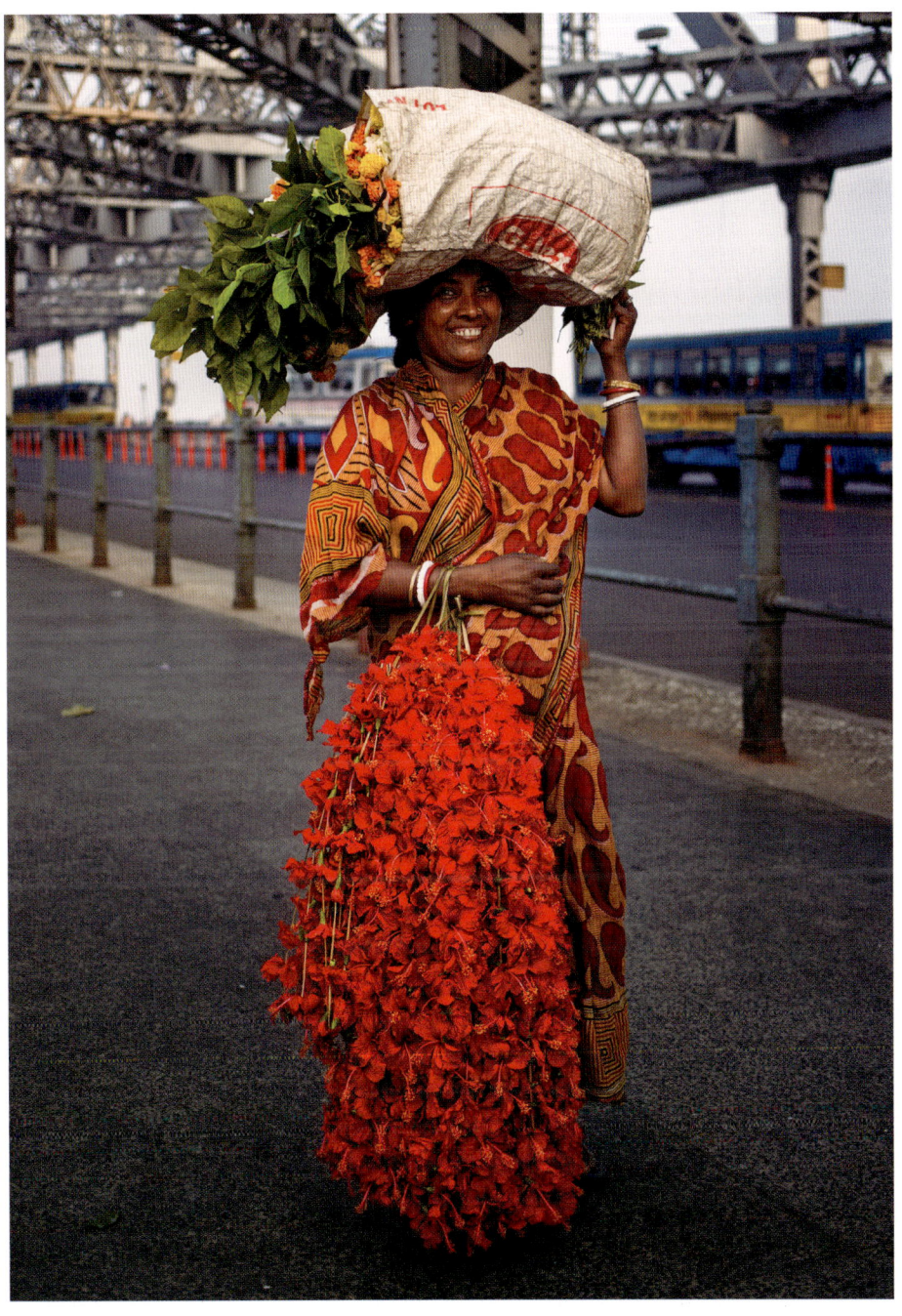

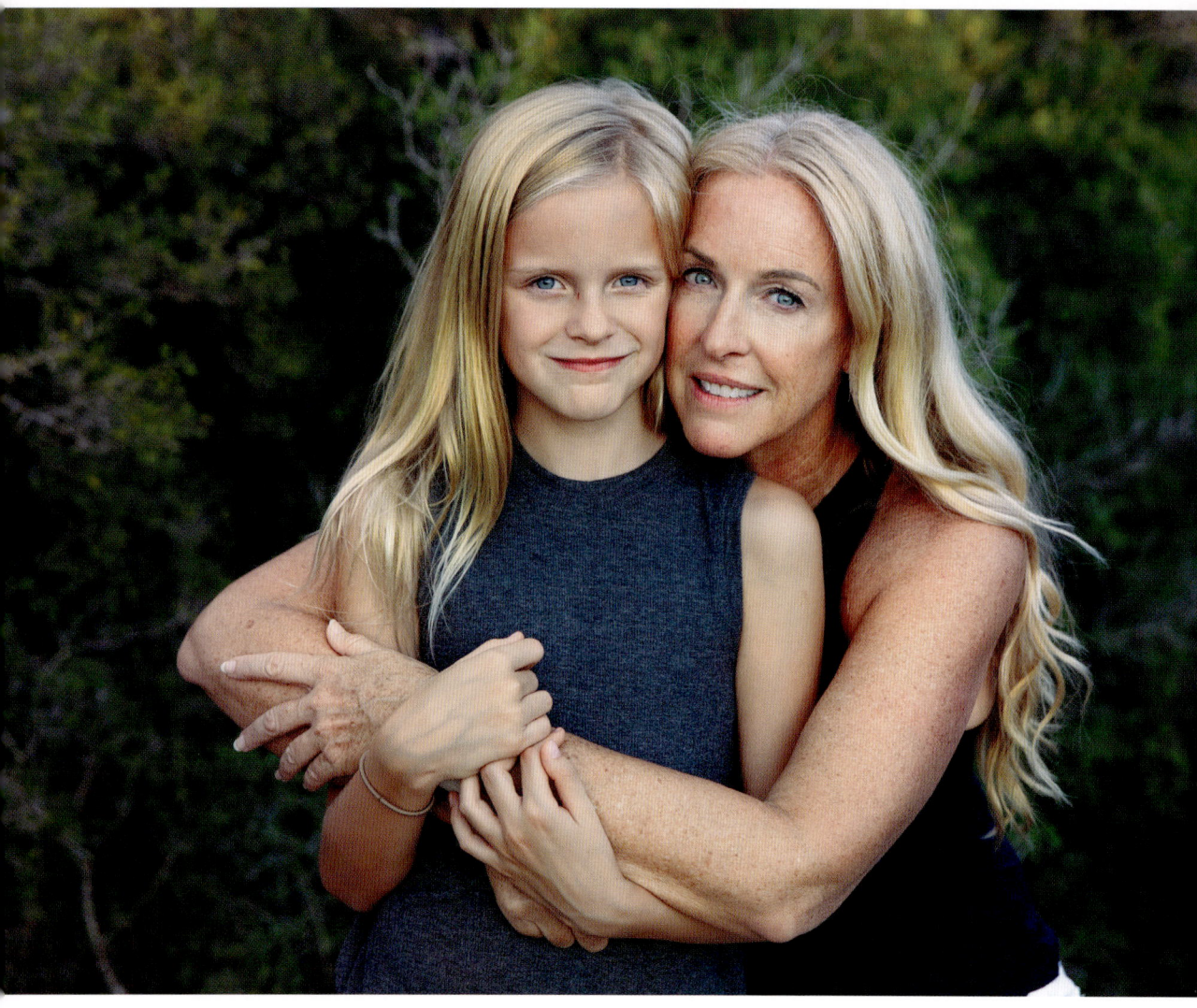

AUSTIN, TEXAS, UNITED STATES

From the first moment I met Montannah Kenney and her mother, Hollie, I could feel their beautiful relationship and profound bond. As a new mother myself, they immediately became a great inspiration for me.

Montannah and Hollie are an incredible team and have faced many challenges. Both are in love with mountains and enjoy traveling the world to experience new heights. When she was seven, Montannah became the youngest girl in the world to climb Mount Kilimanjaro, Africa's highest peak. She wanted to honor her father, who passed away when she was very young. "There, on the peak of the mountain, I felt closer to heaven, closer to Dad. I blew kisses to him so he knew I was there."

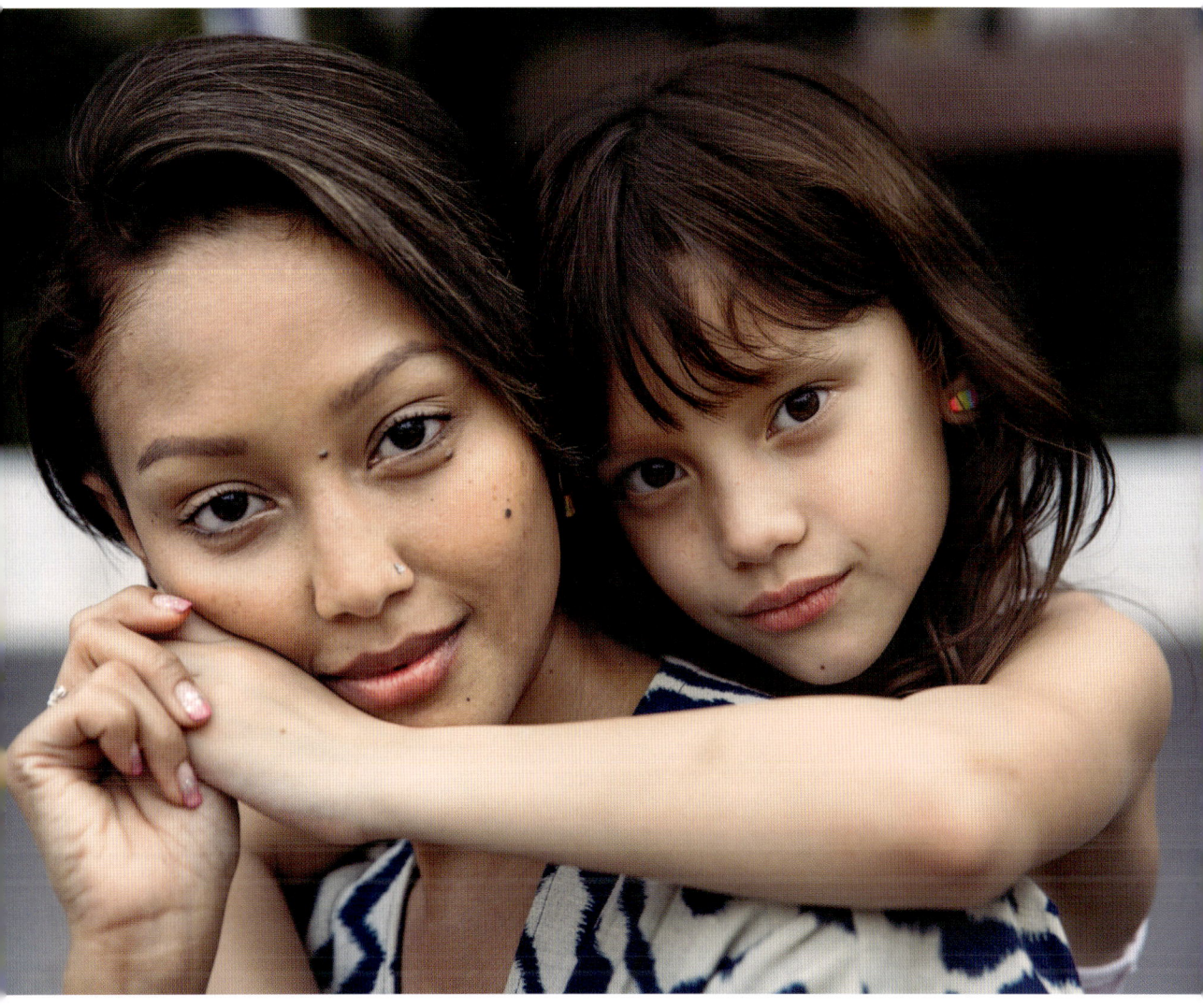

BANGKOK, THAILAND

So much diversity in one single family. Miah, the mother, was born in Singapore and is of Indonesian, Malay, and Chinese heritage. Haley, the daughter, was born in Thailand and has Dutch heritage, as well.

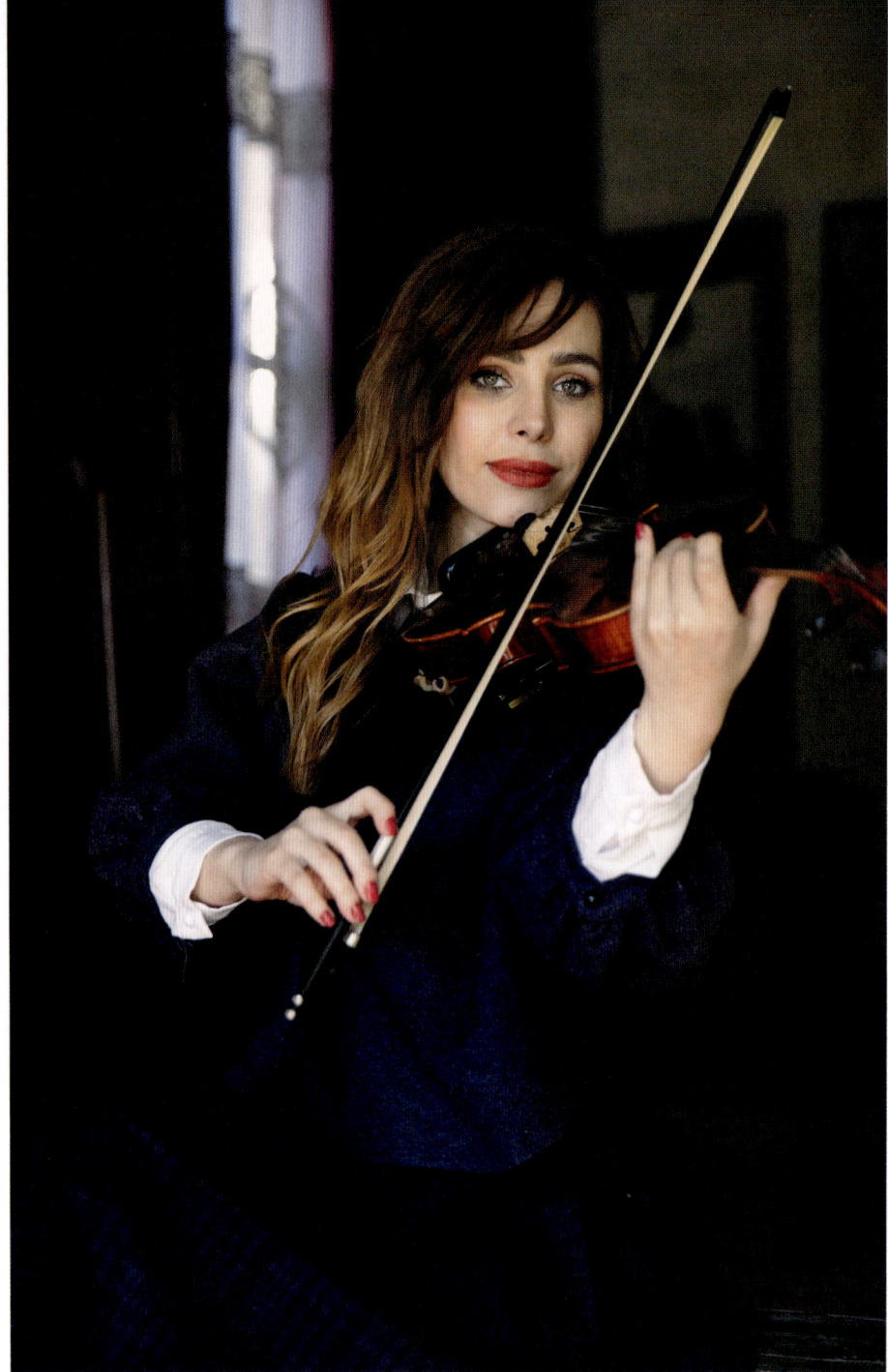

DAMASCUS, SYRIA

Dima Khierbeck clearly remembers a day, a few years ago, when she was practicing inside the opera house and counted twenty-seven bombs that fell nearby. A few hours later, when she went out of the building, she saw the dead body of a colleague from the opera staff.

Humans invented music, but we also invented bombs, and that's the story of our contradictory nature. And I'm wondering if there will eventually be a day when, everywhere in the world, the splendid sound of music will prevail over the horrific sound of bombs.

KABUL, AFGHANISTAN

How many artists would risk their lives every day to create? Sahraa Karimi is a film director who was living in Kabul when I met her—one of the most dangerous places on Earth at that moment. She was the only woman in the country with a PhD in cinema and also the first woman to be the general director of Afghan Film Organization. She grew up during the Taliban rule, when girls were not even allowed to go to school. Her father was a teacher, so with his help, she continued to study at home. Later, she received asylum in Europe and worked hard to be accepted to study film.

After completing her studies, she gave up a comfortable life in Europe and decided to return to her war-torn country. Through her films, she aimed to empower Afghan women and offer a new perspective of them—one different from the clichés portrayed in international media. When we met, the Taliban were gaining more territories and had added Sahraa to one of their kill lists. However, she remained committed to continuing her fight for her country through filmmaking. She didn't have a gun; she had only her camera to shoot with.

A few weeks after our meeting, the Taliban captured Kabul. Fortunately, Sahraa managed to escape the country so she could continue to use her powerful voice from abroad.

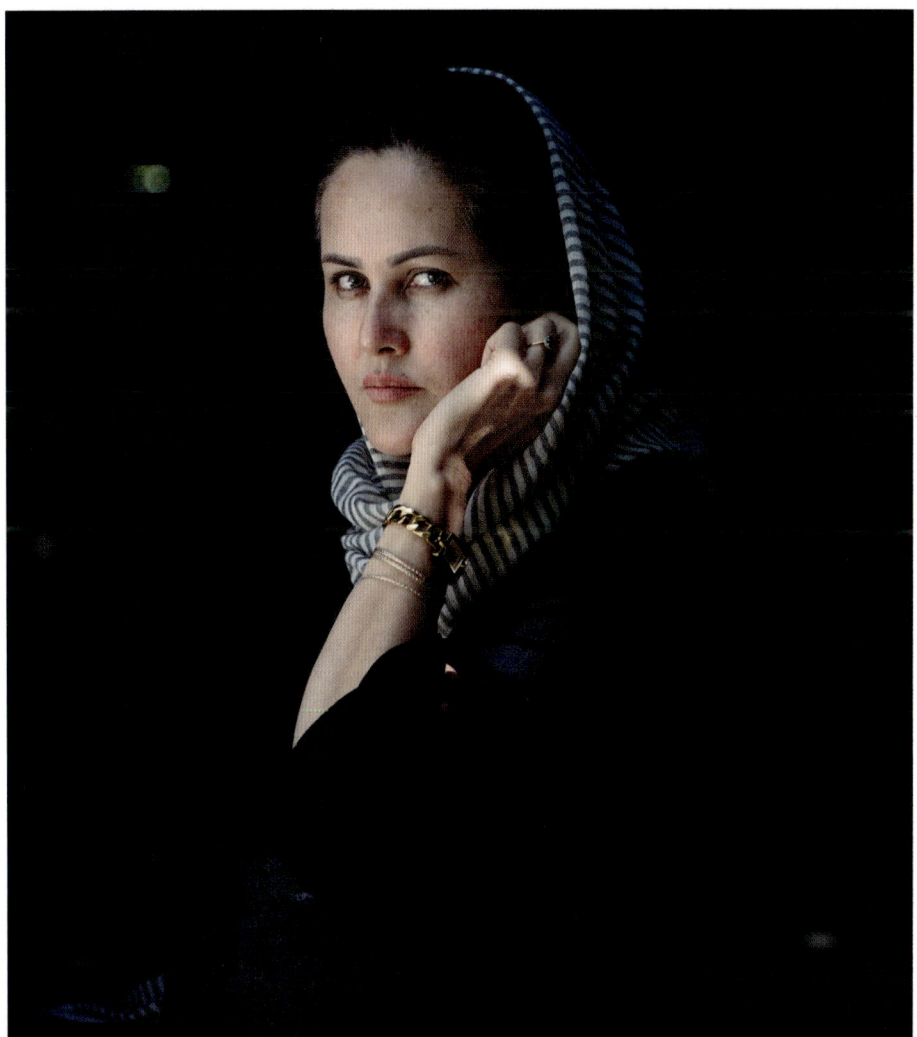

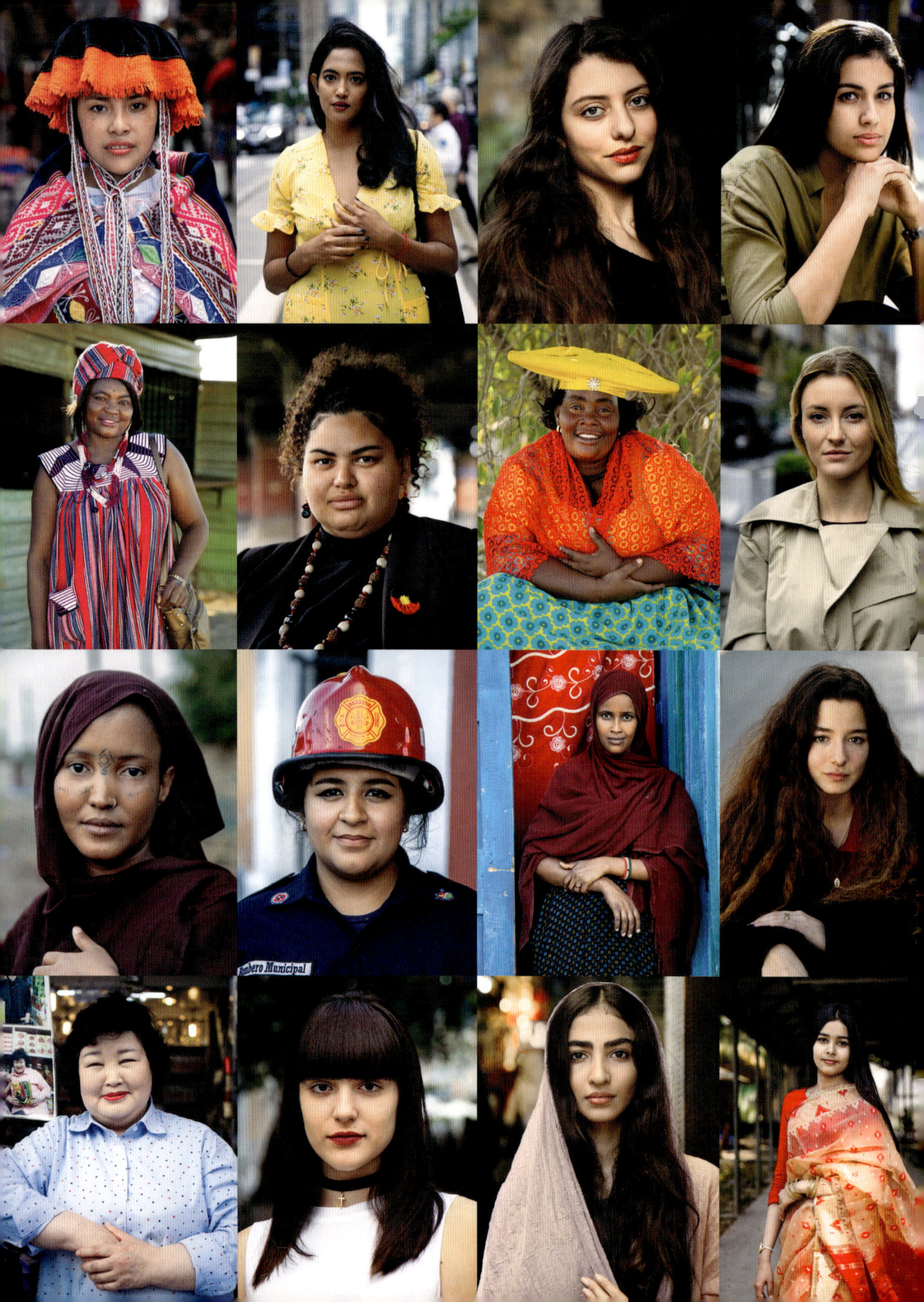

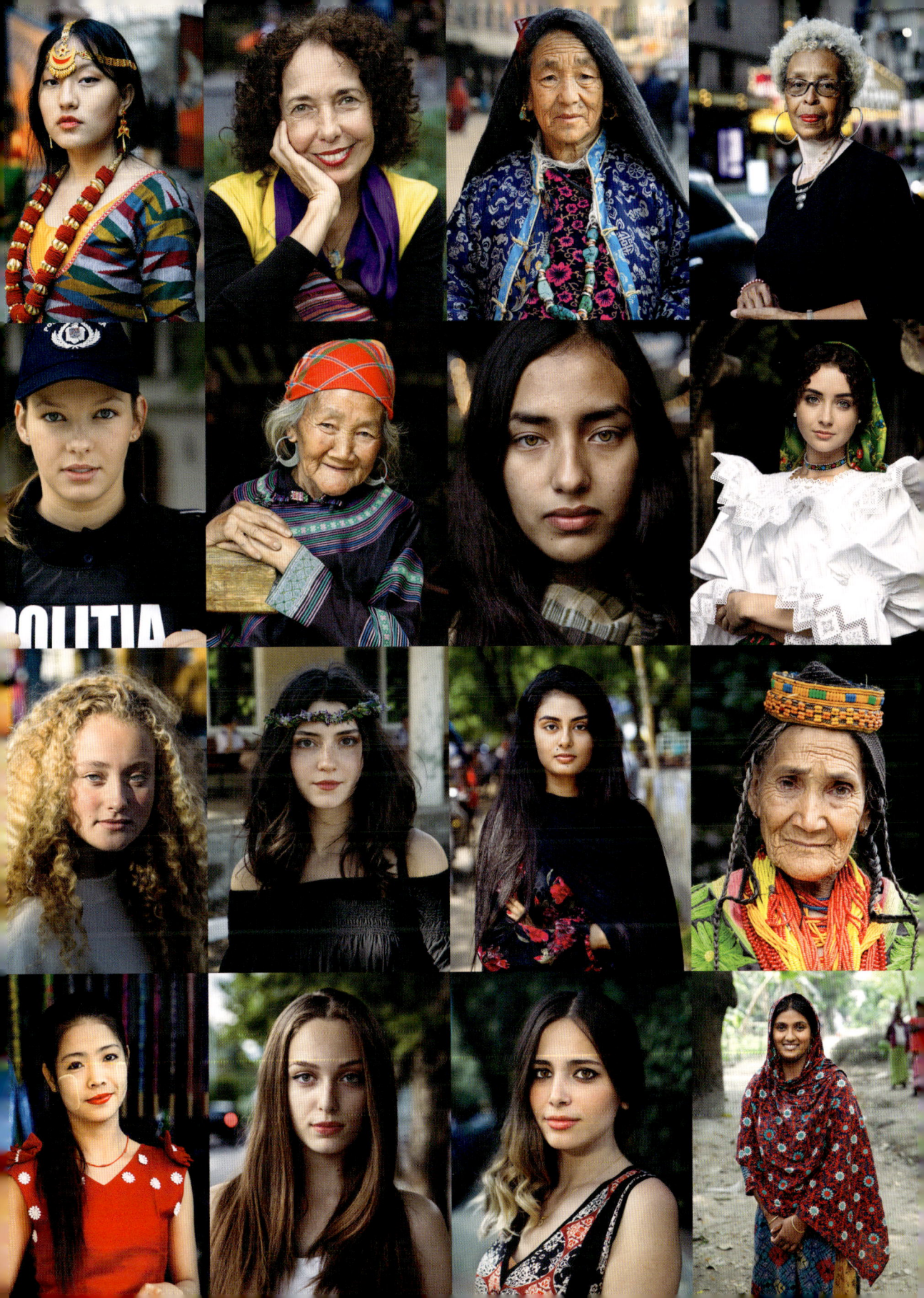

COURAGE

I'm in one of the most crowded cities in the world. I see hundreds and hundreds of people around me, rushing. It's a tough day for me. Every woman I approached today refused me. And I'm so nervous about approaching another stranger. The language barrier adds another layer of difficulty. Many women here don't speak English and, even with my phone's translation app, they often seem pressed for time. They probably think I want to sell them something, or they simply don't trust me. In the end, a woman accepts to be photographed. Her portrait and her beautiful story make me feel like I'm flying.

Years of approaching women on the street haven't erased the occasional waves of fear. From the outside, it seems like it's just a brief conversation with a stranger. But anyone who's tried it knows how overwhelming it can feel.

Many photographers who approach strangers tell me they feel the same fear, they feel their hearts pumping out of their chests. And they ask me, how do I do it, and what is my secret? Well, there's no secret in my case. I also feel nervous most of the time, and I also feel my heart beating loudly just before I start speaking with a stranger. But I do it. I simply do it despite the fear.

And that's not my only fear related to my project. I'm afraid of flying, and it feels like I'm dying every time I'm in a plane. The same goes for car and bus rides with reckless drivers. But despite these fears, I've flown hundreds of times, I've taken many cars with crazy drivers because there were no alternatives, and I've approached women on the streets in all corners of the world with my heart in my throat.

During all these years, while hearing hundreds of stories and living my own story, I realized that courage isn't about the absence of fear but about facing it. Yes, some people are simply fearless—they were maybe born like that. But for most people, that's not the case.

Therapists, coaches, self-help methods—they can all be valuable tools. But some fears may never fully vanish. And many times, these fears are a huge roadblock on the path to our dreams. They hold us back from harnessing our power, from sharing our unique beauty with those around us, and from building a legacy.

For me, there's no magic potion that gives you courage. It's about taking action, facing your fears, and climbing the wall to see what's behind it. Because beyond each episode of fear, there may be light, and there might be a triumph that makes it all worthwhile.

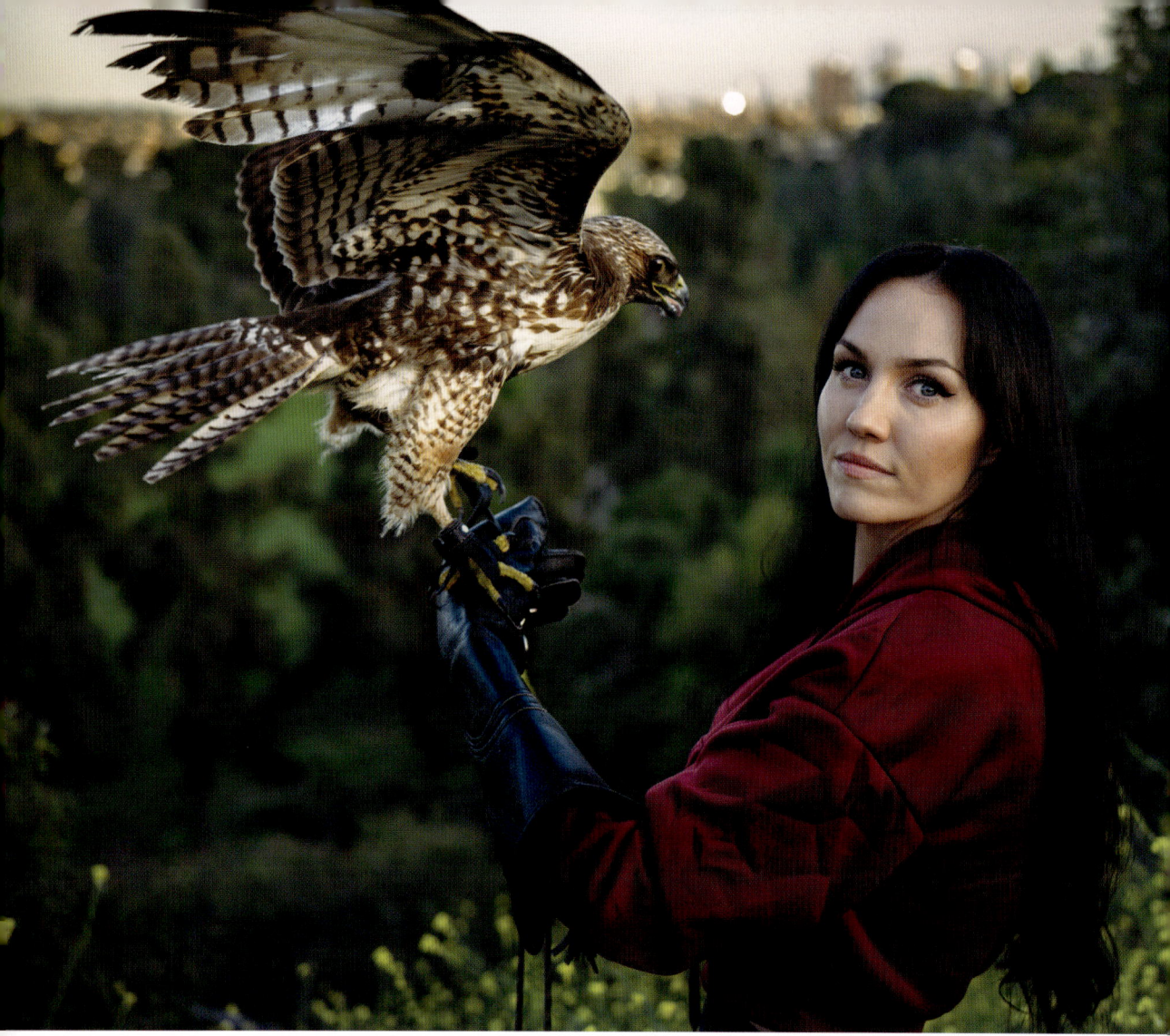

LOS ANGELES, UNITED STATES

Alura McNeely is a falconer. She saves hawks, raises them, and releases them. She also takes care of a fascinating owl. She is the mother of two girls, and I was amazed to find out how great it is to raise kids with birds at home. Alura is actually doing therapy with her birds for children who face difficulties, and the results are exceptional.

Alura's own childhood was difficult, but once she discovered falconry, she knew it would be her path. In the beginning, male falconers told her that a woman can't be a falconer, but soon she proved them wrong.

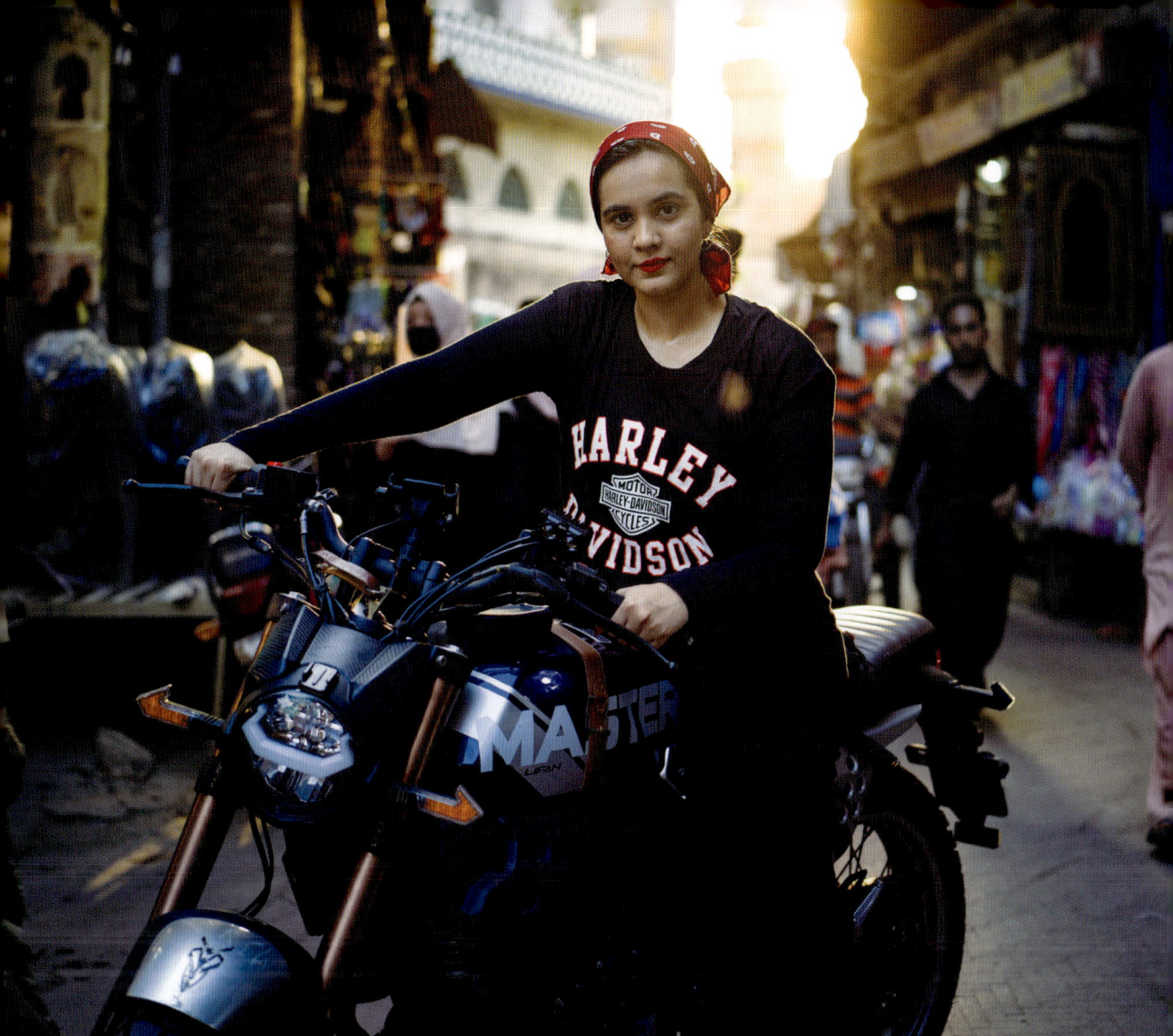

LAHORE, PAKISTAN

I photographed Zenith Irfan on the busy streets of her city. As I looked around, I could see that people were quite surprised to see a woman confidently riding a powerful motorcycle.

Zenith is actually the first Pakistani female motorcyclist to ride across her country. Zenith's father had a similar dream; he wanted to travel the world on a motorcycle. Tragically, he passed away when Zenith was just ten months old, leaving her with a void that only riding could fill. Inspired by her father's aspiration, Zenith gradually developed a deep love for motorcycles.

Initially, she learned to ride so she could navigate the chaotic traffic while commuting to her high school. Later, she met a community of male motorcyclists and, after hearing their stories, started to dream about riding across Pakistan. She clearly remembers how one motorcyclist told her that, as a woman, she would never be able to do so. However, Zenith had a dream to fulfill. In the end, nothing could stop her.

For Zenith, riding is much more than a means of transport. It is a way of connecting with her father, discovering herself, and discovering her homeland. She now has a new goal: to start a touring company and help more women follow their passion for riding motorcycles.

MAWLAMYINE, MYANMAR

Eindra is selling flowers in the central market of her town. Every day, she wears this paste on her face called thanaka. This cream, which smells a little like sandalwood, is made by grinding tree bark and mixing it with water.

Thanaka has been extremely popular in Myanmar for millennia. Almost all women apply this paste to their faces and bodies. Not only is it a beauty aid; it also provides a cooling sensation as well as protection from sunburn.

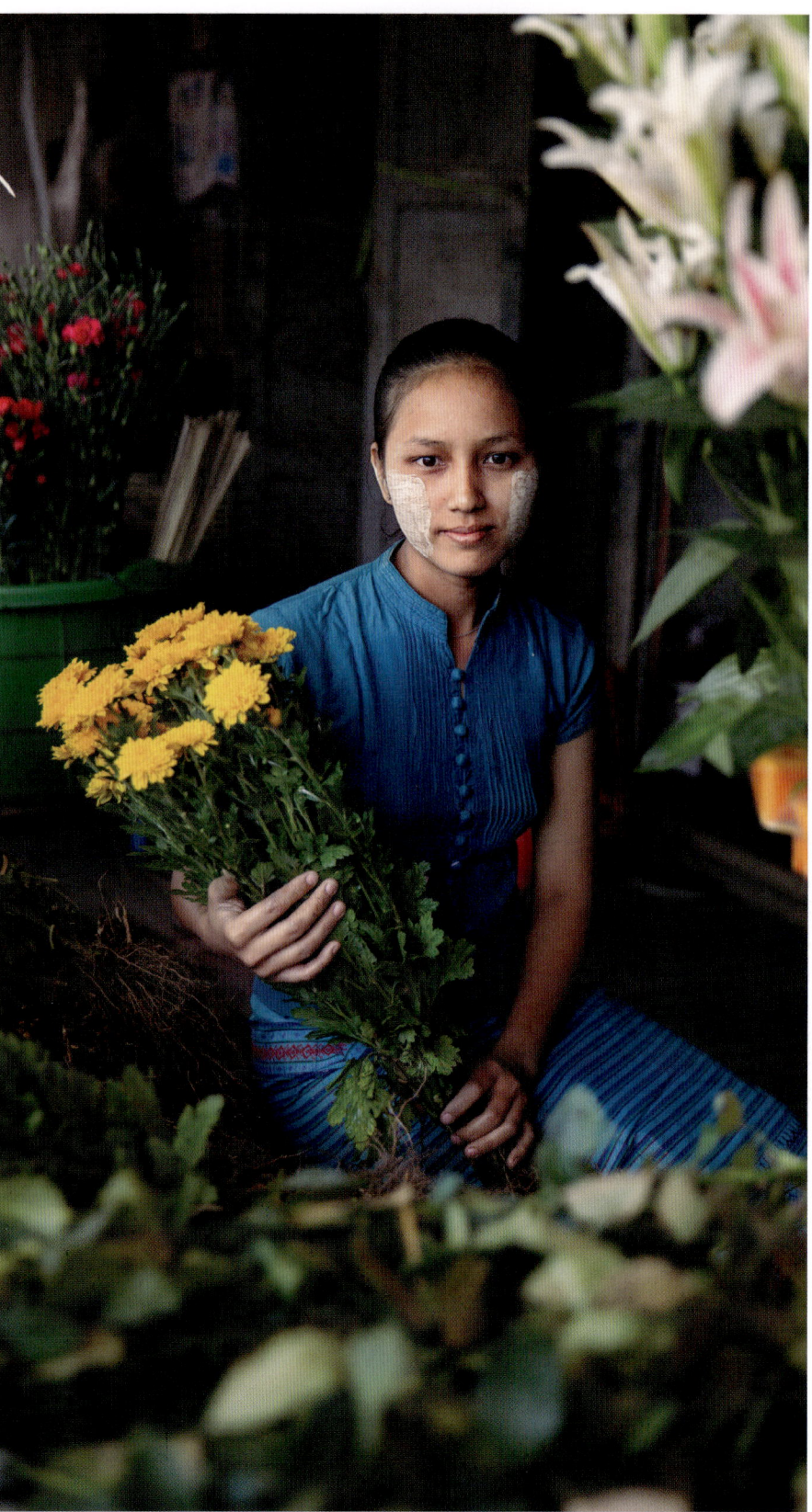

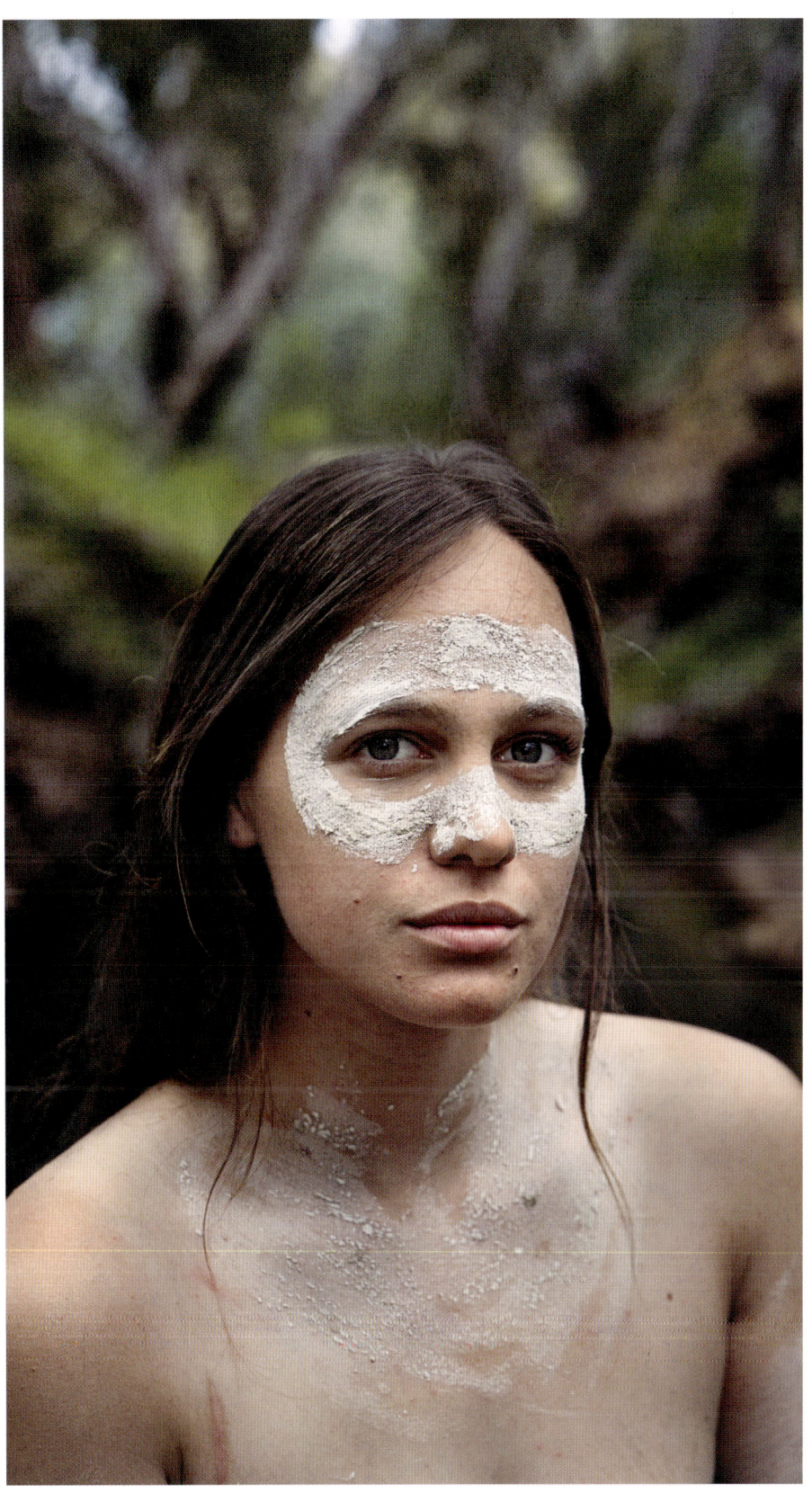

MELBOURNE, AUSTRALIA

Kirra was born to an Aboriginal mother and a Croatian father, yet she was primarily raised by her mother within a Yamatji-Bunuba Aboriginal family. Today, she plays professional Australian football—a sport as tough as American football. She also serves in the Australian Army while being a dedicated mother.

She feels that her Aboriginal upbringing defines her most, and that's why she wanted me to photograph her with her face painted with ochre. She was raised in this fascinating culture, and now she wants to inspire more Aboriginals to follow their dreams.

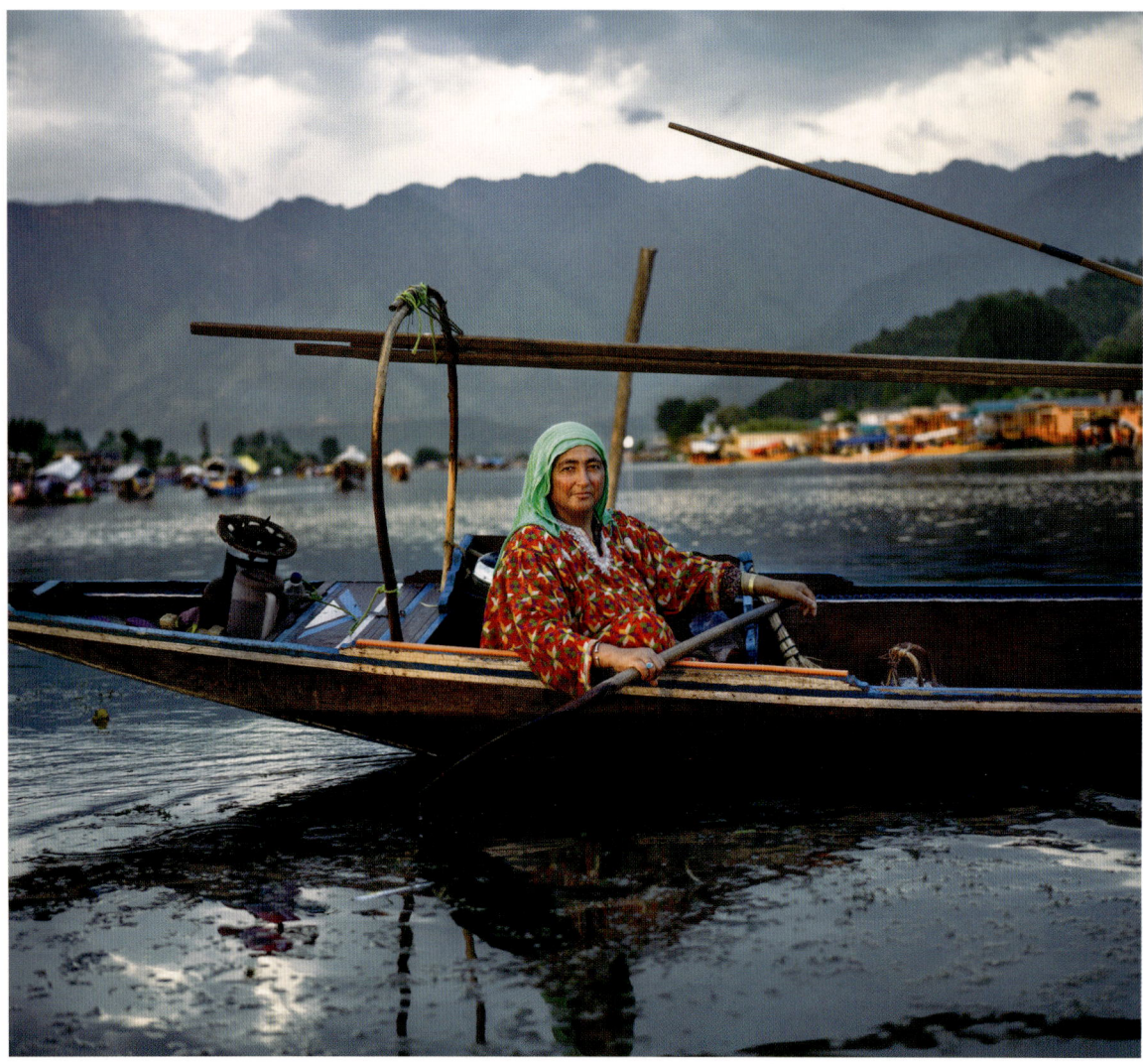

INDIAN-ADMINISTERED KASHMIR

Sundar lives in a small fishing community on the shores of the splendid Dal Lake. Every evening, she and her husband go fishing together in their shikara, a traditional Kashmiri boat. They spend the whole night on the lake. In the morning, they return to shore and head straight to the market to sell their catch.

They always carry with them a kangri, a traditional heater used in Kashmir. On chilly nights, they light charcoal in the kangri and place it under their long, traditional clothes to stay warm. On warmer nights, they simply use it to light the charcoal for their hookah.

Life is not easy for Sundar, but this is how her community has lived for hundreds of years. Their shikara, their kangri, and their clothes are not just simple objects—they are precious symbols.

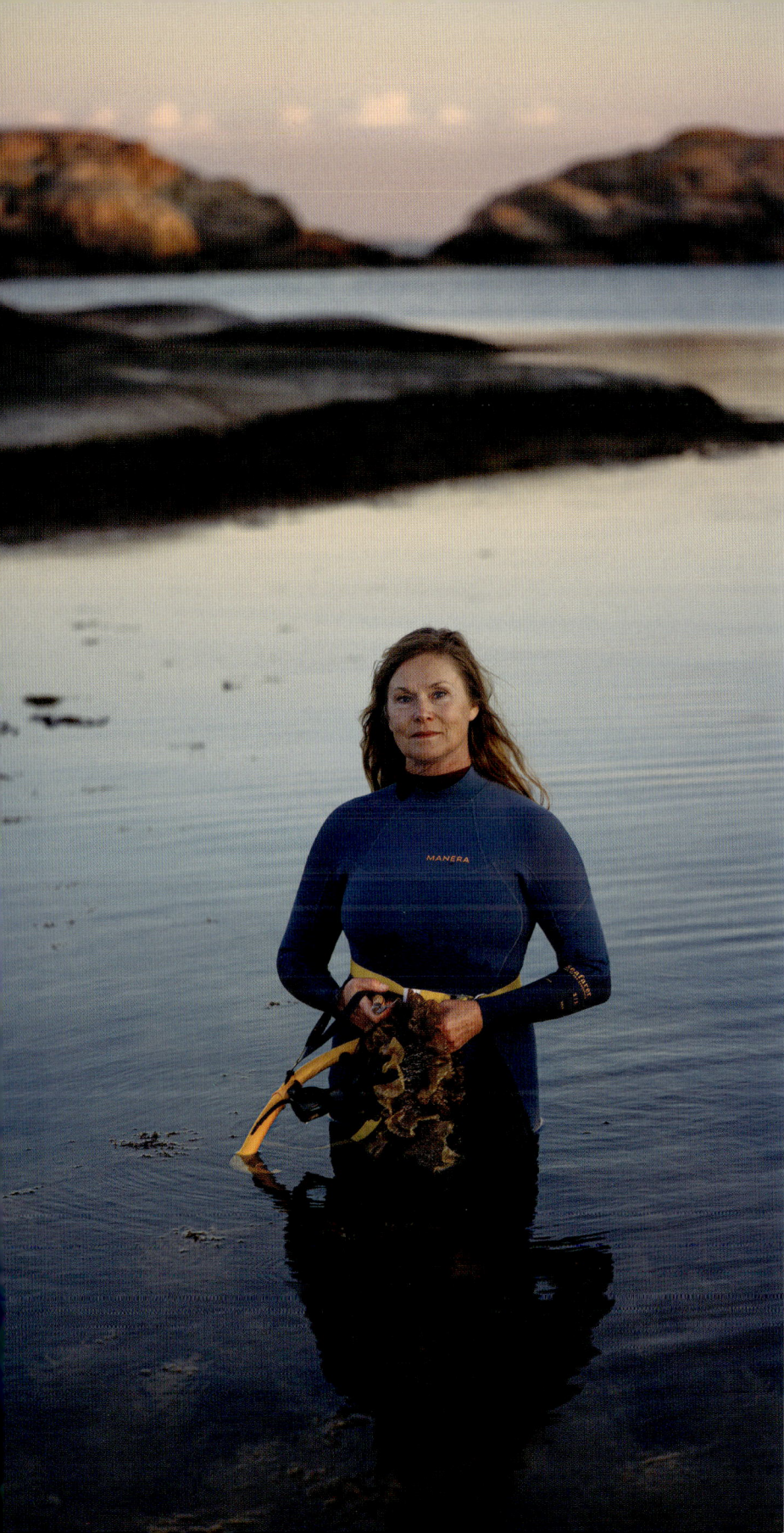

GREBBESTAD, SWEDEN

Meet Linnéa Sjögren, a passionate seaweed diver and founder of Catxalot, a company dedicated to this unique underwater ingredient. Very few people know the secrets of this fascinating algae, which come in hundreds of species, perfect for every kind of food, from cakes and salads to complex dishes!

Linnéa has spent years sharing her knowledge through seaweed-picking courses, while also supplying fresh seaweed and beach plants to restaurants. Linnéa teaches people how to pick it responsibly to ensure it keeps growing back, while also advocating for cultivating seaweed, which is a sustainable way to grow food.

Before meeting Linnéa, I didn't know anything about the fascinating seaweed, so all this experience felt like a revelation.

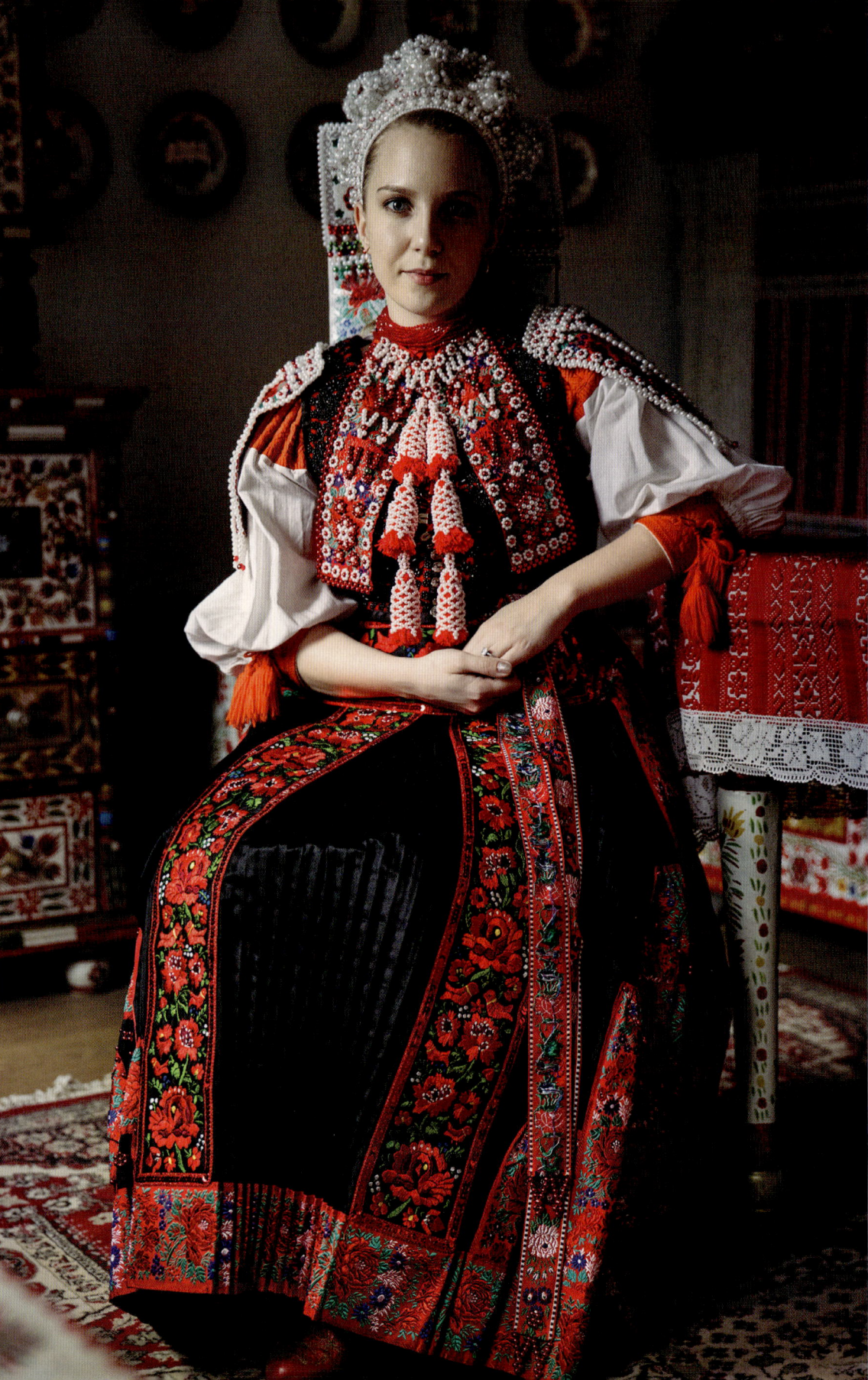

KULOB, TAJIKISTAN *(Right)*

This kind of embroidery is called Chakan and is widespread in this country in central Asia. The art of Chakan is part of the UNESCO Intangible Cultural Heritage list. Maliks, Nizoramo, and Sharafnisa learned how to make these splendid complex handicrafts from their mothers and grandmothers and then taught the art to their daughters.

I personally feel privileged that I live in a time when I can still witness these incredible traditions.

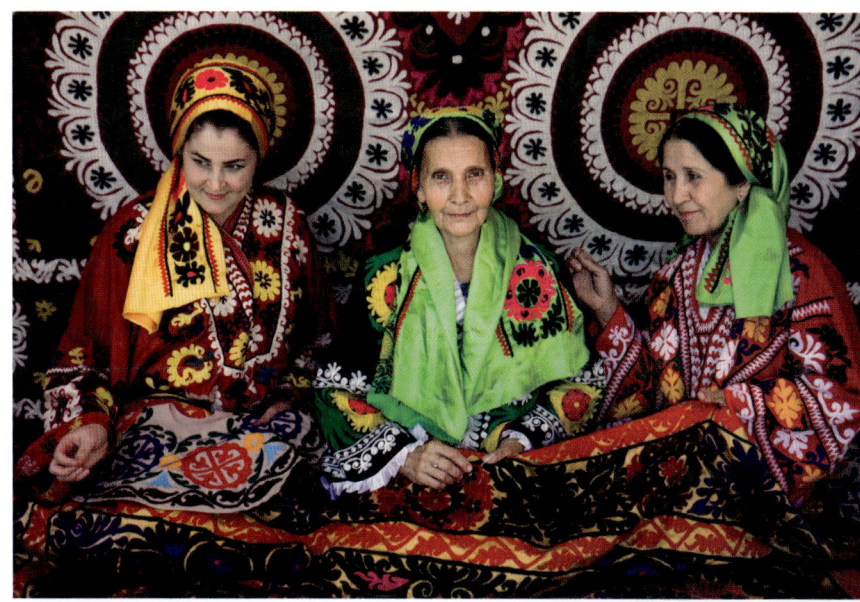

ANDES MOUNTAINS, PERU *(Right)*

In this remote village, which sits at an altitude of more than thirteen thousand feet, all women are experienced weavers—they begin practicing the craft at age eight. Despite being a small and isolated community, women here never suffer from loneliness. They spend most of their time together, working, chatting, and having fun. While traveling the world, I have realized that, usually, the larger a community is, the more isolated its members tend to be.

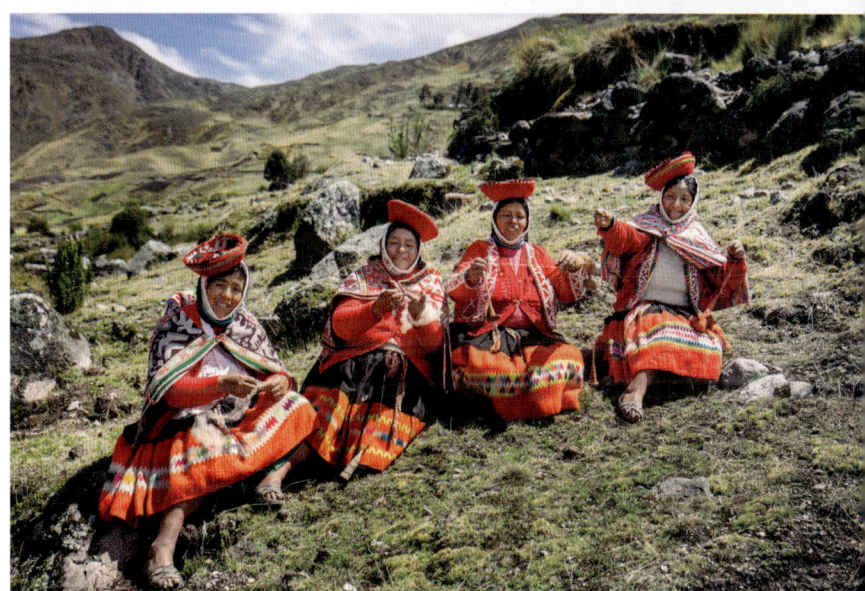

CLUJ COUNTY, ROMANIA *(Opposite)*

Zsuzsa is an ethnic Hungarian. When she was a little girl, she dressed traditionally every Sunday to attend the church where her father was a priest.

In some Eastern European villages, houses have a special room where valuable traditional dresses, linens, and housewares are kept and exhibited. In the old times, these were the trousseau, or dowry, for brides.

The world has changed. Zsuzsa is an IT specialist and lives in a big and modern city. But she still visits her parental home in this small village, and she wears the beautiful outfits inherited from her ancestors. It's a way to honor not only her family but also her passion.

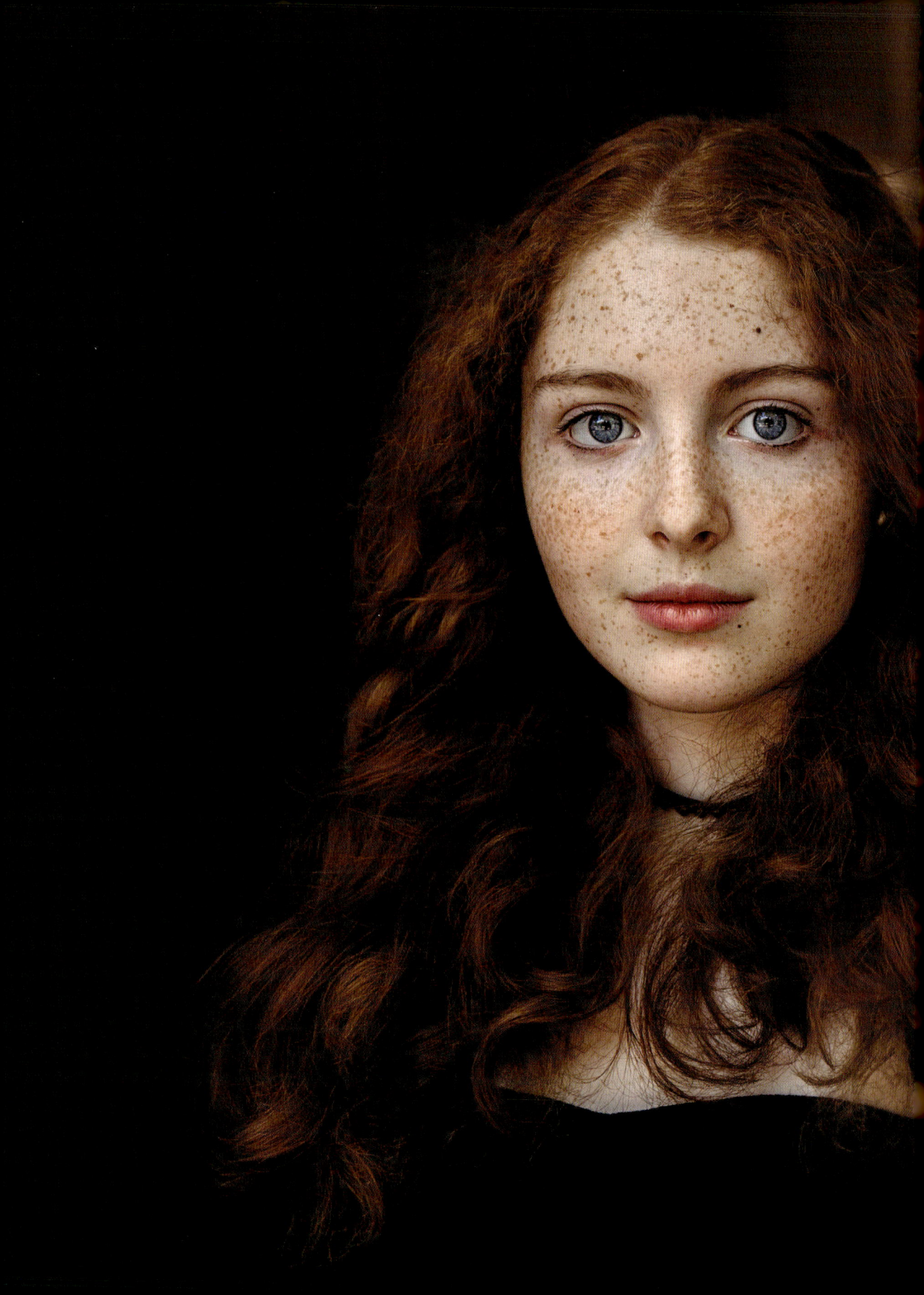

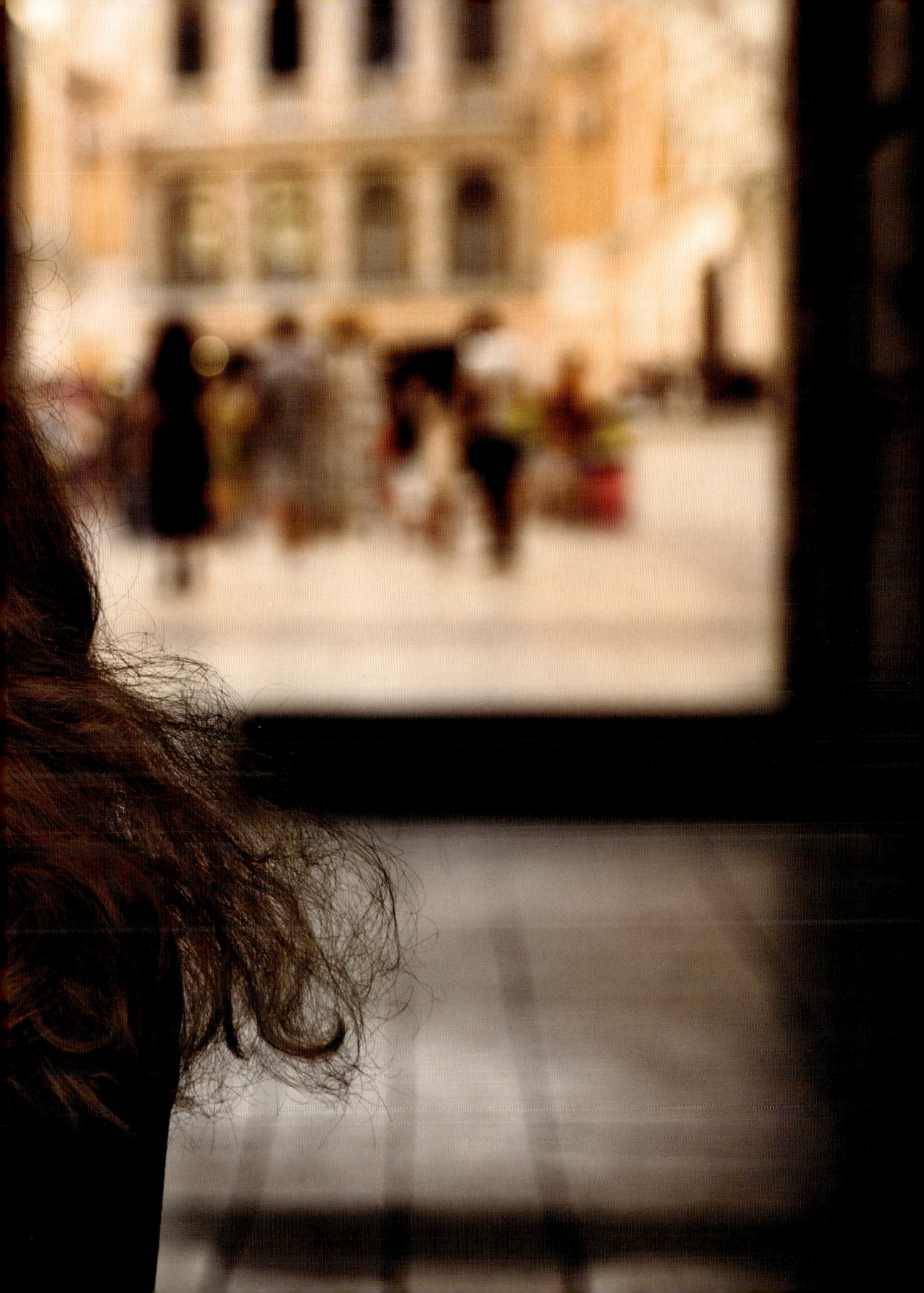

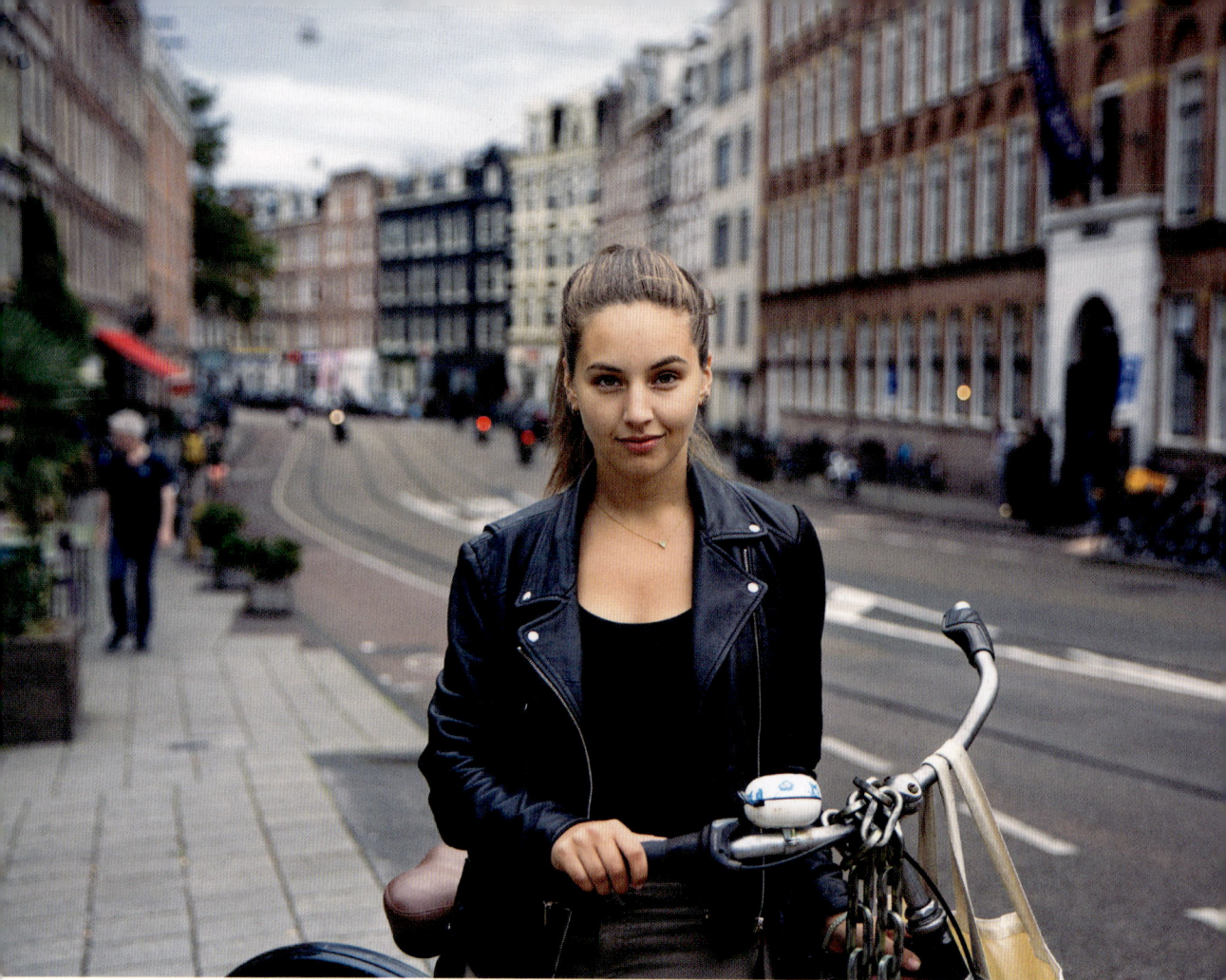

AMSTERDAM, NETHERLANDS

For more than a decade, Debra Barraud has been navigating the streets of her diverse city, photographing thousands of people and collecting their unique stories. Through her project, which is called Humans of Amsterdam, she aims to capture the essence of what makes each human being special and unique.

ODESA, UKRAINE

(Previous spread)

It was a peaceful and serene summer on the streets of this picturesque city long before the war began in Ukraine. Alina was enthusiastic about starting her studies in architecture.

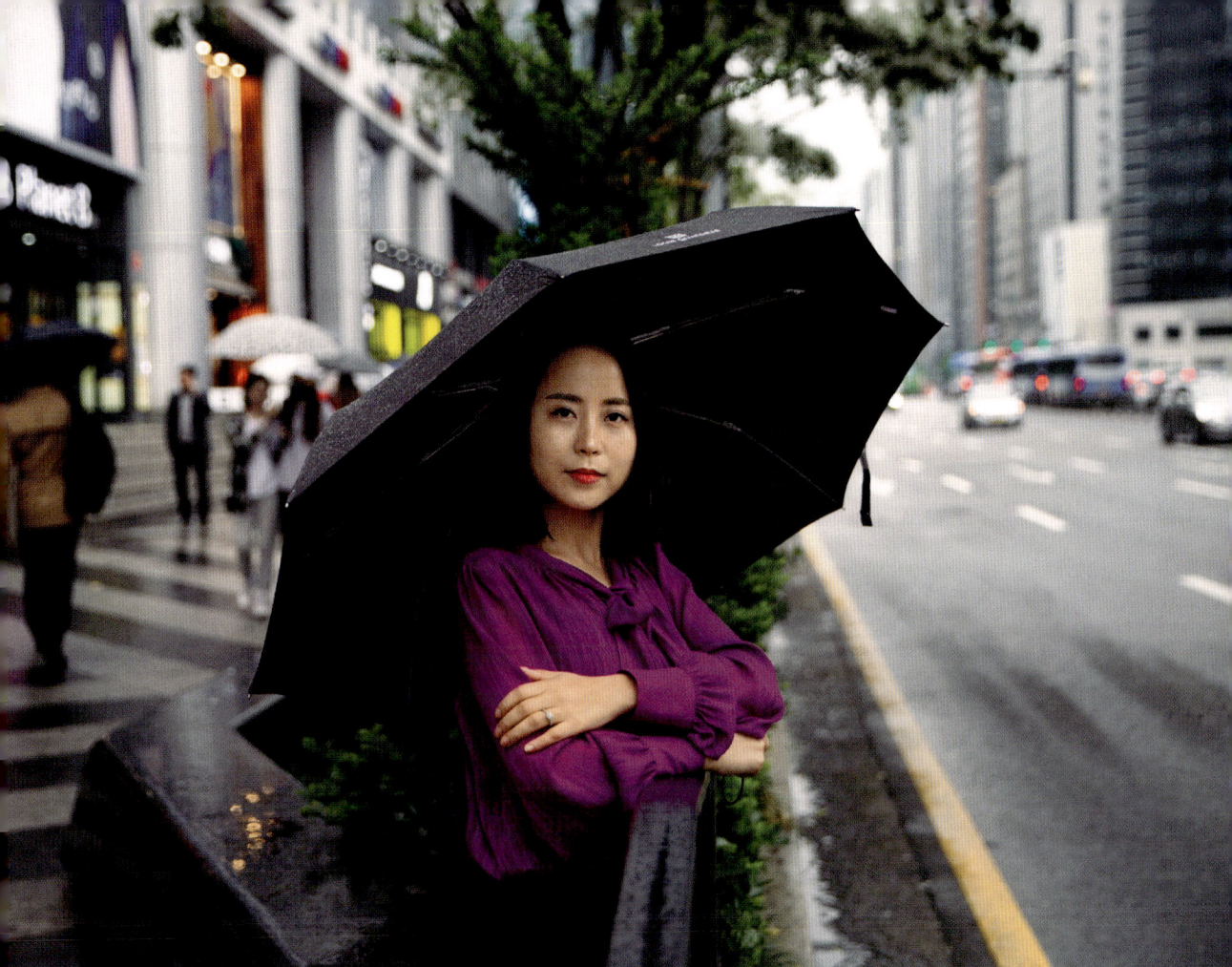

SEOUL, SOUTH KOREA

Song-Juok is a North Korean defector, and her journey to escape North Korea and finally reach freedom in South Korea is an incredible saga.

Song-Juok's father dreamed of escaping North Korea with his family, but he passed away when she was sixteen. Determined to fulfill their shared dream, Song-Juok successfully escaped the country three years later and made her way to China. However, she had to hide for more than a year in China since being discovered would result in deportation back to North Korea. Eventually, she managed to cross illegally into Myanmar and then Thailand, where she was finally allowed to seek asylum in South Korea.

It took Song-Juok two years to journey from North to South Korea, and she faced incredible challenges and risks along the way. Yet, she persevered, ultimately bringing her mother and sister to safety, as well, in yet another incredible saga.

Today, Song-Juok is a respected academic who studies politics and business, and she is the happy mother of two children. She sometimes misses the solidarity and simple friendliness of people in North Korea and the close ties between family members. But she still has nightmares about all the horrific things in the country, about the executions she was forced to see, and about her dangerous escape, which could have sent her in front of a firing squad. After witnessing so much suffering and hardship, Song-Juok tries to enjoy every moment of her new life.

BALI, INDONESIA

Here Jois is performing a ritual purification in the holy spring water of Tirta Empul, an astonishing Balinese Hindu temple. She often comes here in search of serenity and harmony.

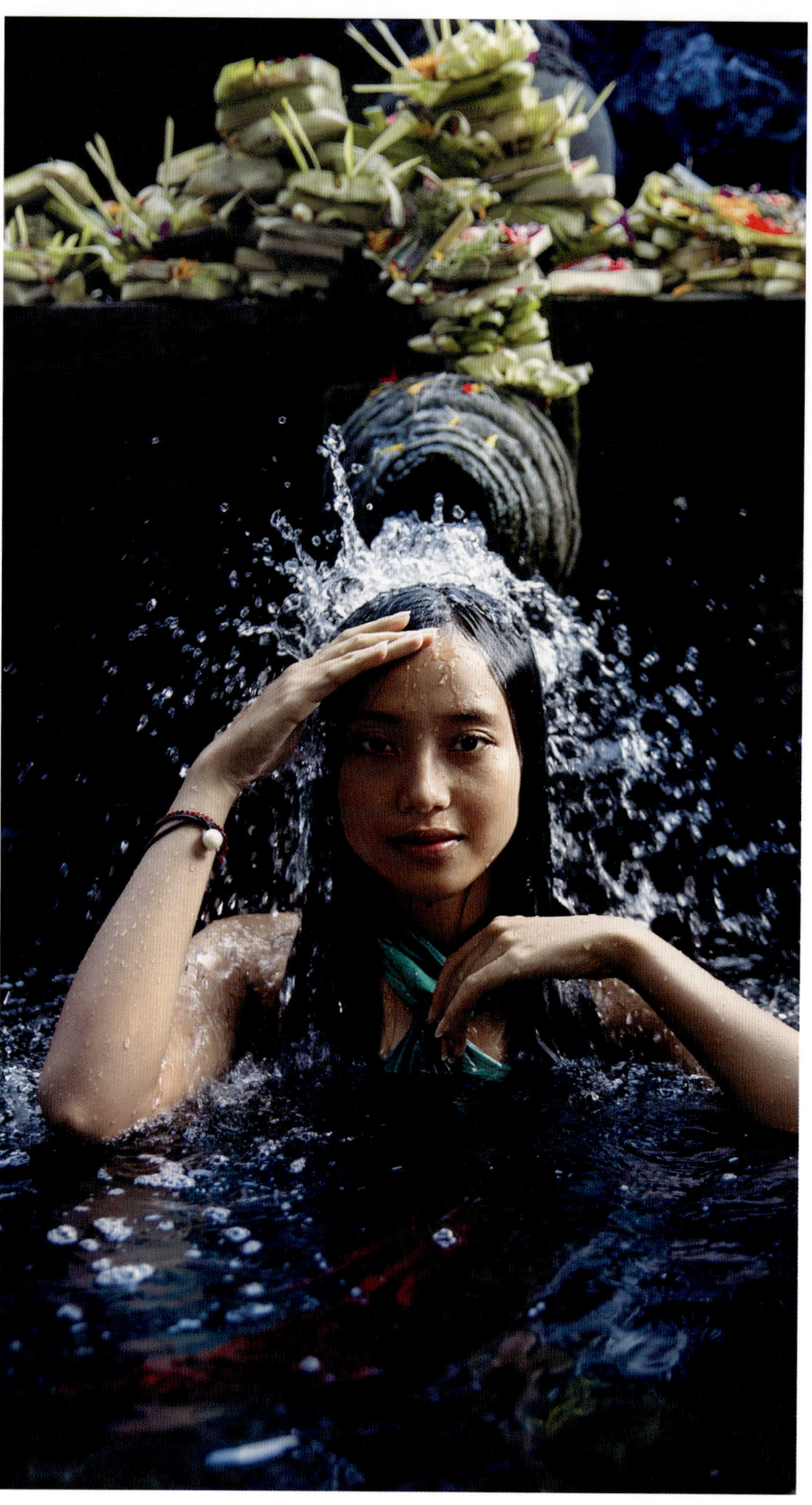

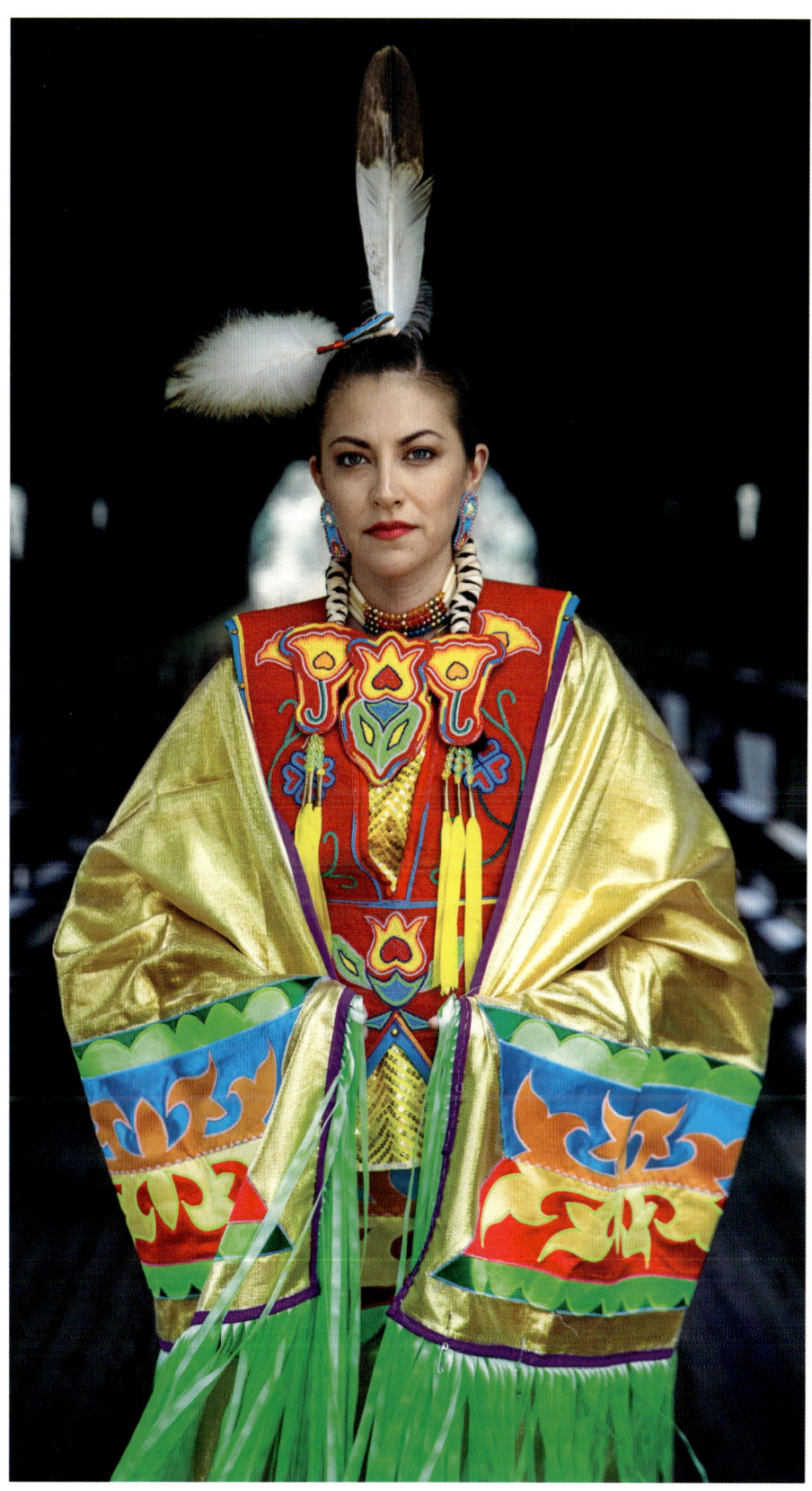

CHICAGO, UNITED STATES

On a typical day, Nicole works as a safety adviser at a truck company in Oklahoma. However, this was not a typical day.

Whenever she has the opportunity, Nicole actively participates in powwows, which are sacred social gatherings held by the Indigenous peoples of the Americas. This is her way of honoring her Native American ancestors, the Ho-Chunk. Nicole has been engaged in this meaningful tradition since childhood, and now her young daughter accompanies her, ensuring the continuation of this wonderful tradition.

BAGHDAD, IRAQ

Zahraa Ghandour had a tough childhood. Raised by an aunt who was a midwife, she witnessed women coming to their house to give birth. She remembers that when girls were born, there was often a feeling of disappointment for the parents. This experience followed her throughout her life, motivating her to prove its absurdity.

Zahraa became a celebrated filmmaker, actress, and women's rights activist. Her work broke barriers in Iraqi cinema. Her cultivated personality helped her capture things in a profound and noncommercial way.

She faces many misconceptions, with traditionalists accusing her of being a bad example for Iraqi women. However, she refuses to stop or leave the country. In 2020, when she had the chance to document the first-ever countrywide women's march with her camera, she understood that things are slowly changing, and someday there will be no more disappointment when a girl is born.

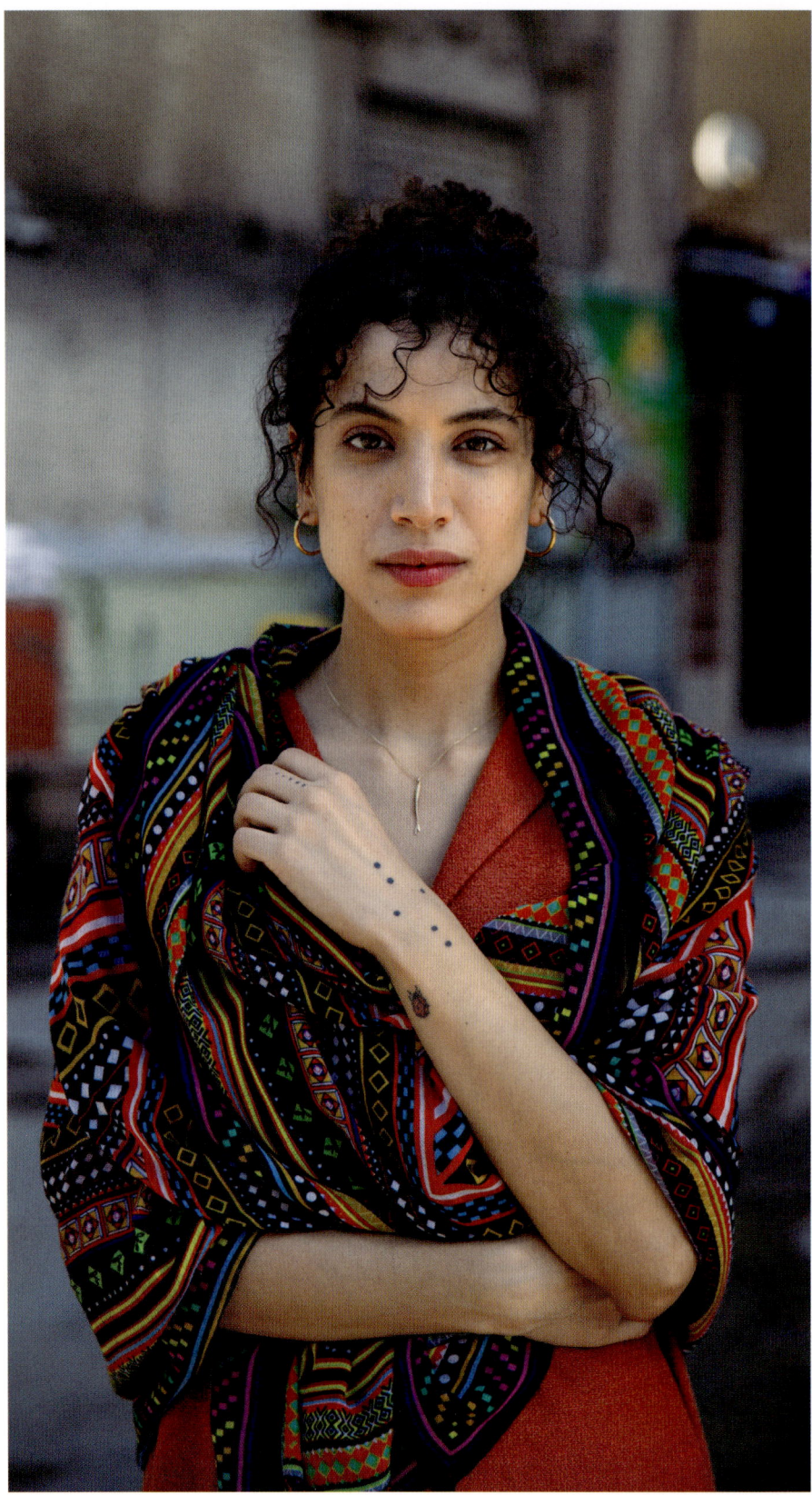

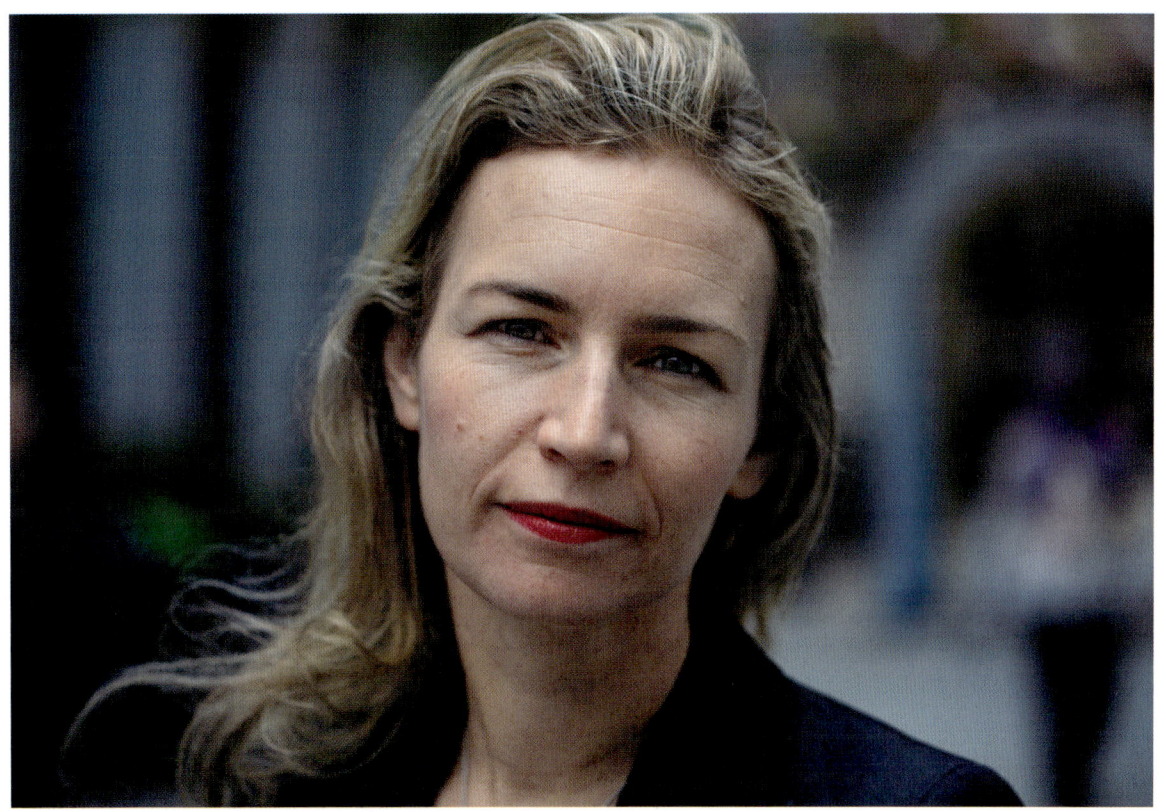

LONDON, UNITED KINGDOM

I photographed Lea Ypi in front of the London School of Economics and Political Science, where she is a professor of political theory. Widely considered one of the world's leading thinkers, her work goes deep into the concept of freedom.

Growing up in Albania, Lea experienced a radical transformation firsthand, living through both the communist and postcommunist eras. Initially, she grew up in one of the most isolated countries on Earth and the last Stalinist outpost in Europe. Shortages, political executions, and a constant presence of the secret police dominated daily life. Yet, despite the horrific realities of the regime, a strong sense of community and mutual support existed among the ordinary people.

The 1990s brought a dramatic shift. Freedom, at least in concept, seemed readily available. However, this new era came with its own challenges: mass migration, violent conflicts, and a period of significant instability.

Lea's memoir, *Free: Coming of Age at the End of History*, chronicles these formative years. Not just her memoir but also much of her work as a political theorist and philosopher tackles the multifaceted concept of freedom.

SOUTHERN ETHIOPIA

Acake was happy to see herself in this photo, as she was very proud of her new dress. It was a gift from her beloved son, who lives far away in the capital of the country.

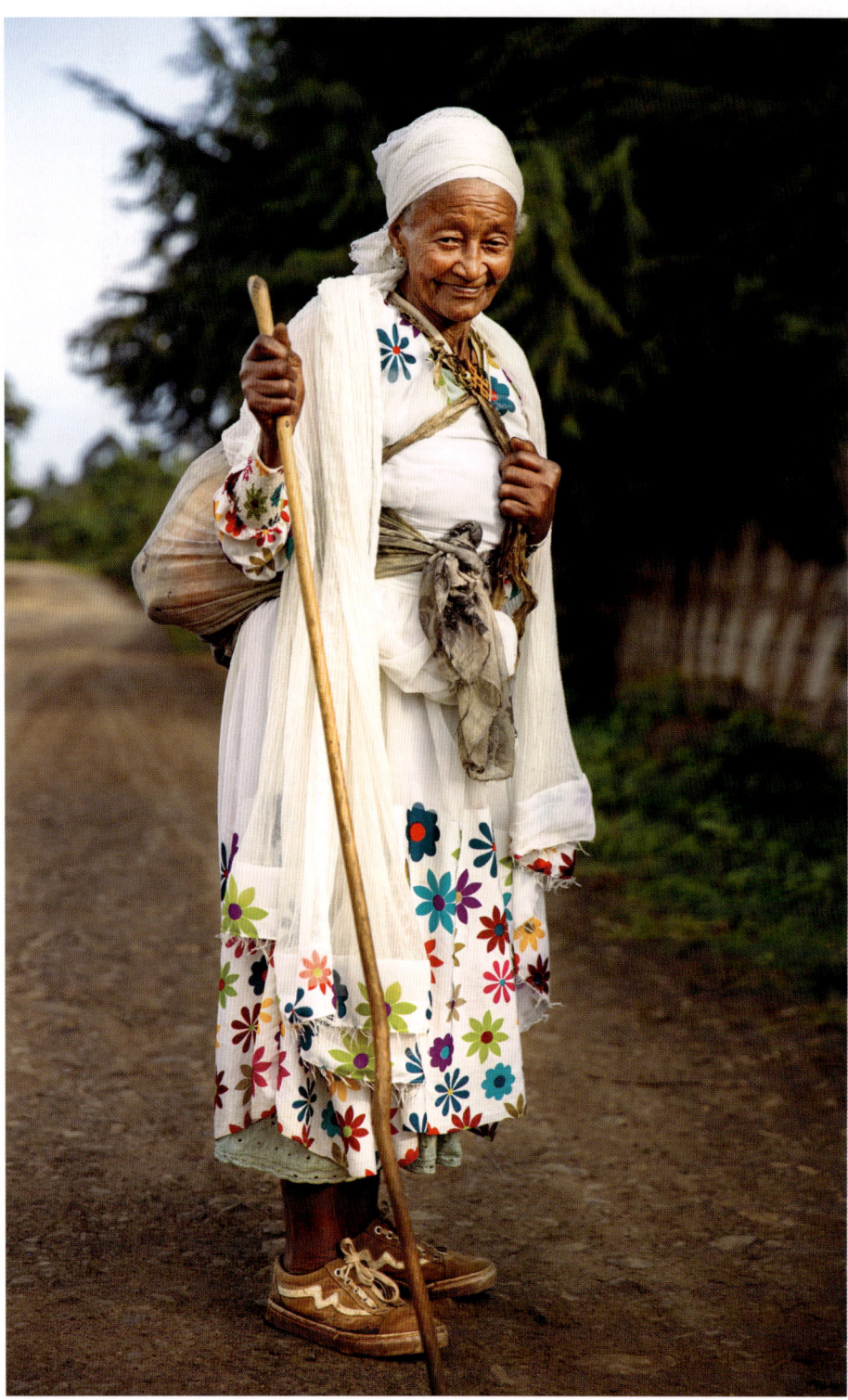

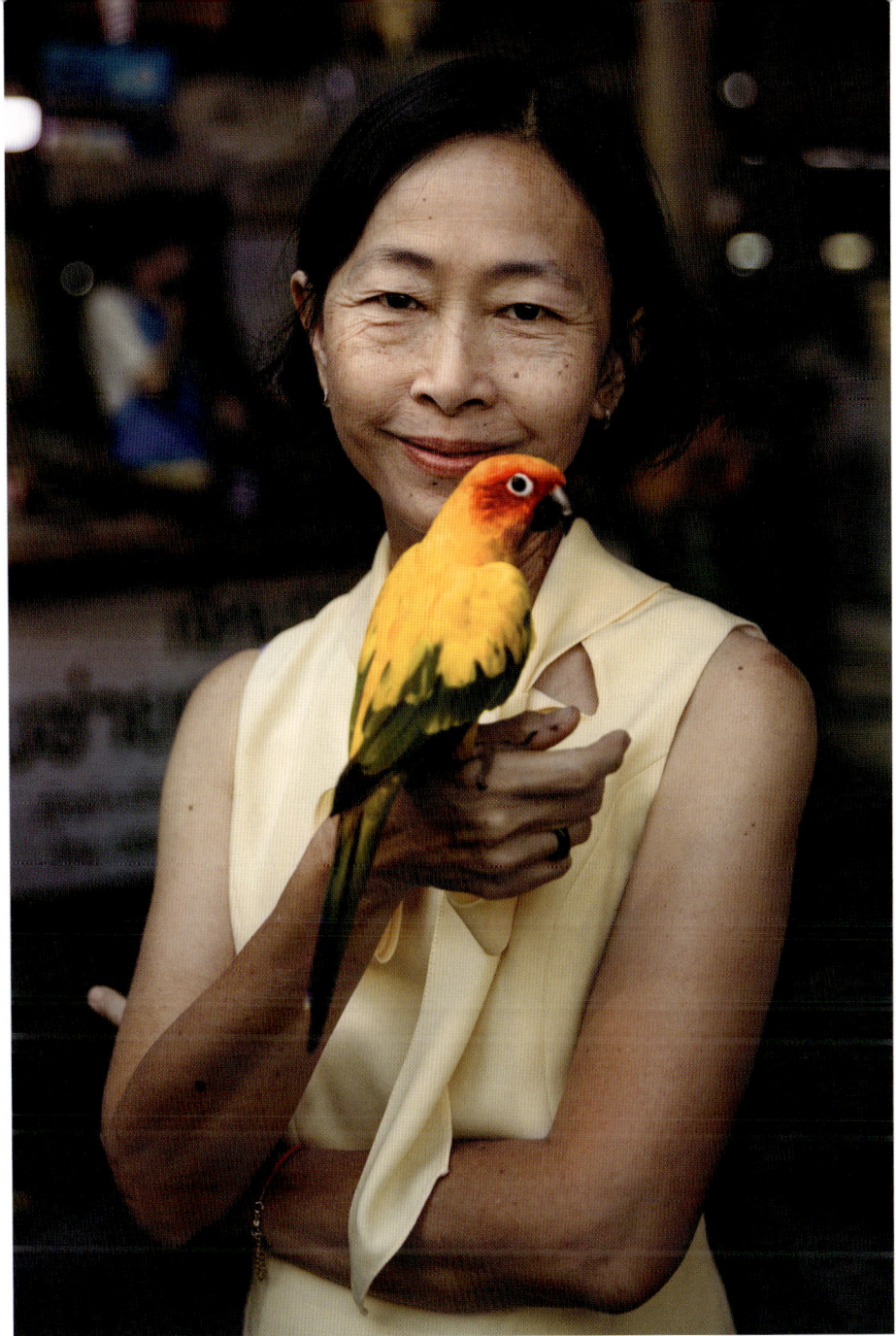

BANGKOK, THAILAND

I met these two best friends at a market. As a retiree, Neaw was feeling very lonely until she adopted Yaya, a loving female parrot. Now Neaw is very happy with her new friend. Yaya lives freely in the front of the house and asks Neaw to take her to their favorite place every day: the market.

This is the place where everybody knows and talks with them—no more loneliness with such a sociable parrot! Yaya is not a talking parrot, but she knows how to make herself understood. Neaw's life became suddenly more colorful—exactly like her best friend's plumage.

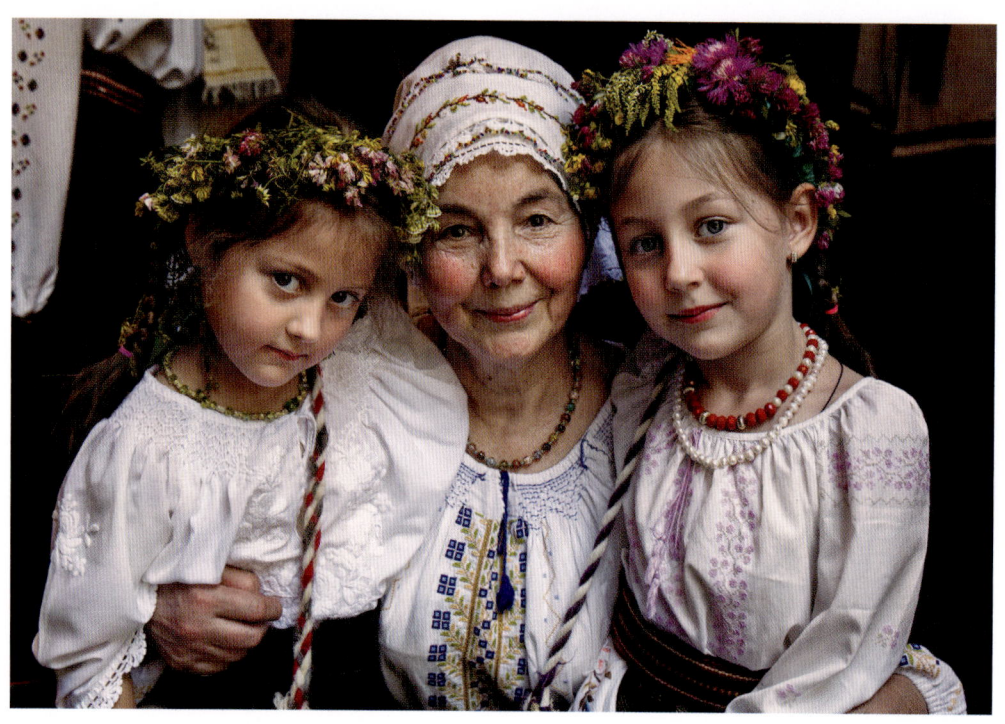

CHIȘINĂU, MOLDOVA

A grandmother with her granddaughters during a celebration.

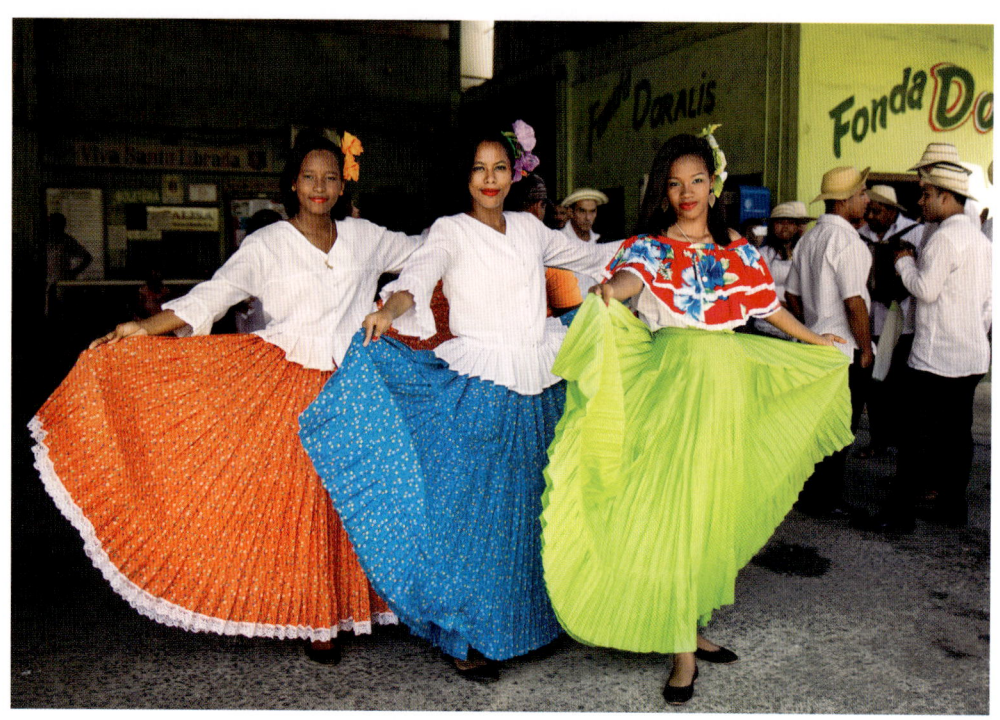

LAS TABLAS, PANAMA

These three women were taking part in a traditional festival.

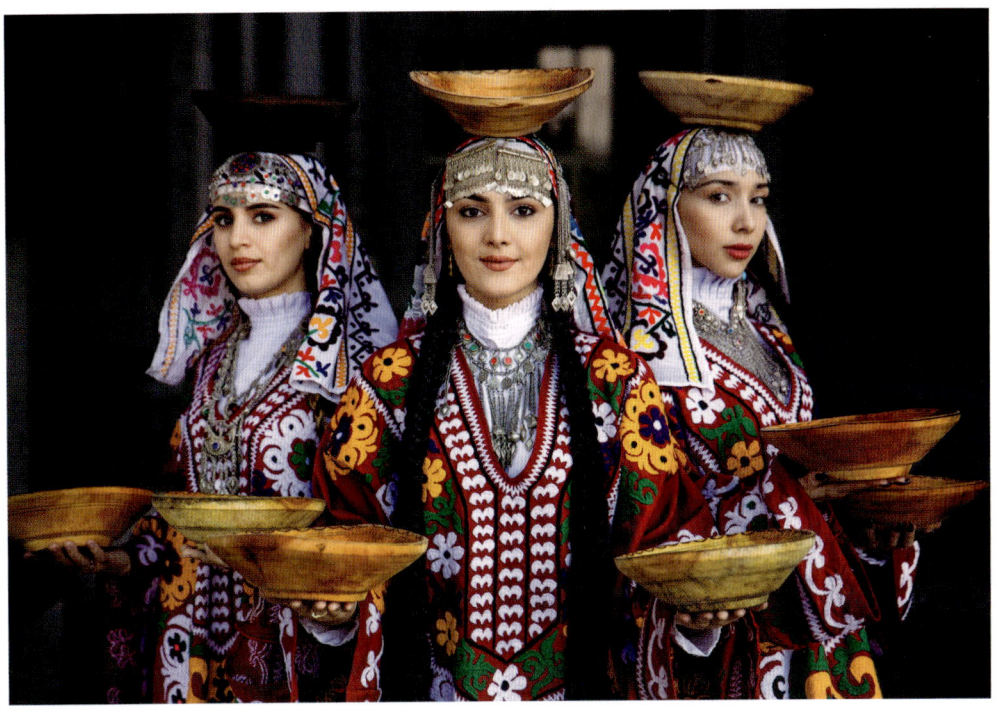

DUSHANBE, TAJIKISTAN

These three women are part of Padida, the country's most prestigious dance group.

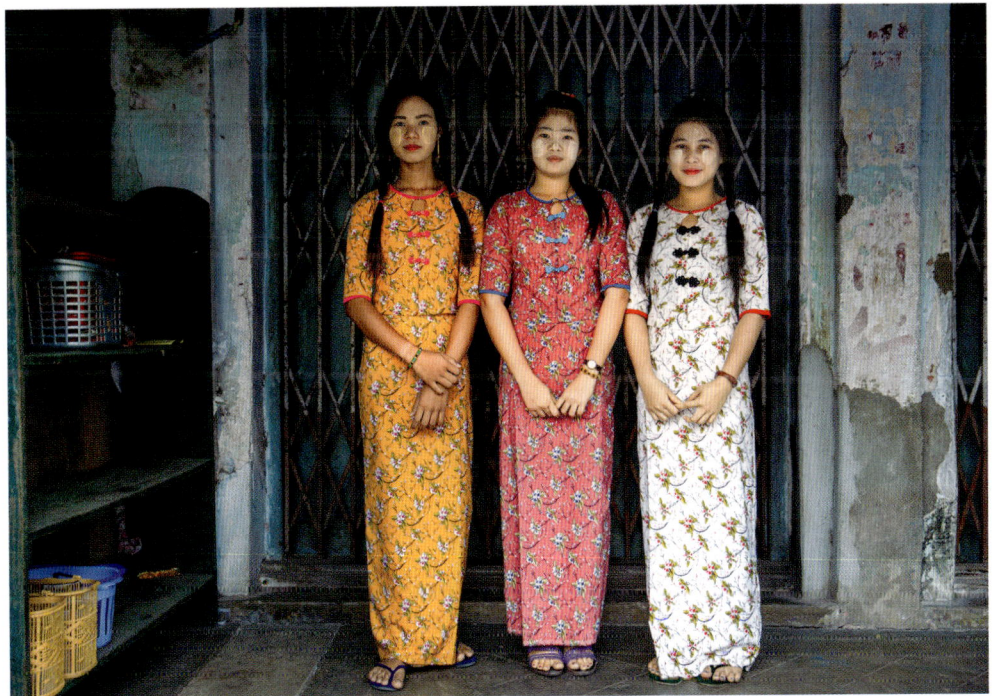

MAWLAMYINE, MYANMAR

These three young women were promoting the opening of a new shop.

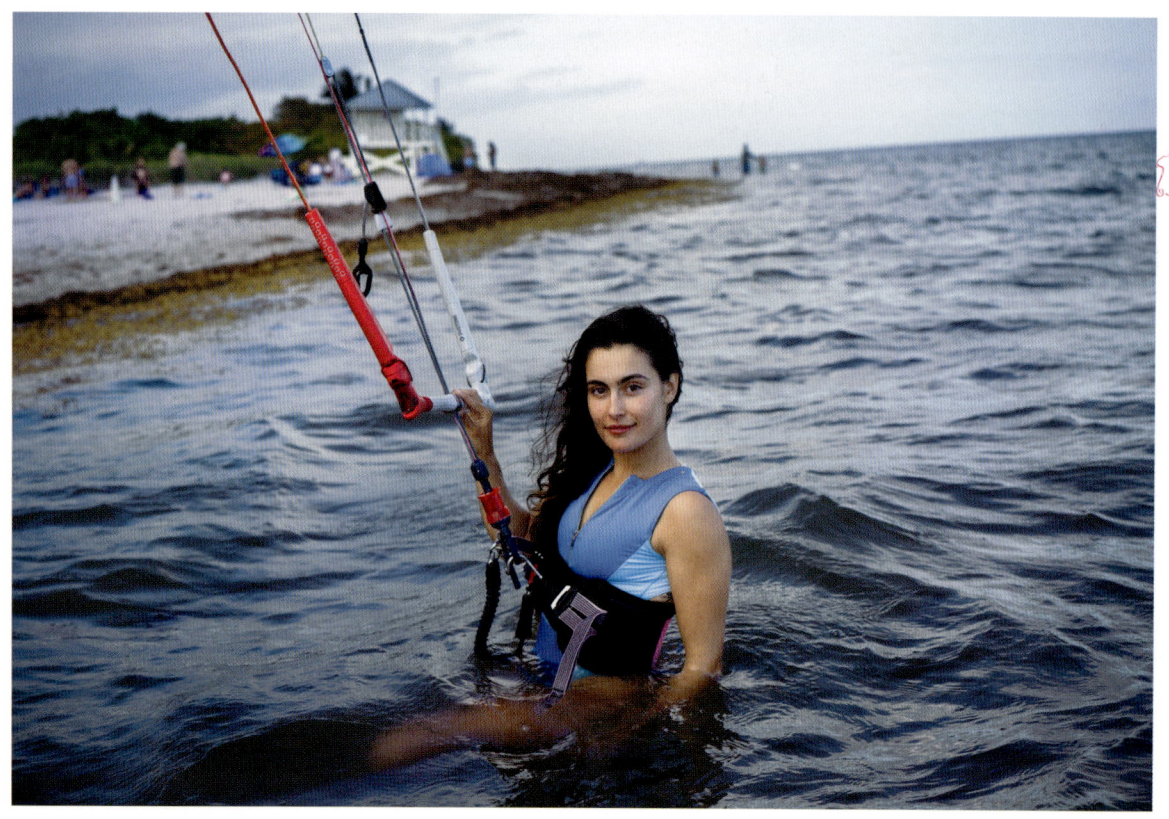

MIAMI, UNITED STATES *(Above)*

To pursue her passion for water sports, Sarah Dunick moved from Washington (one of the coldest states in the USA) to Florida (one of the warmest). Today, she works as a kite- and windsurfing instructor in Miami. In her free time, she drives her campervan in search of remote beaches with the best wind and waves.

JEDDAH, SAUDI ARBIA *(Opposite)*

Her country is well known for the desert, but she loves the water. Hold your breath! This is the fascinating story of a young woman who dives deep into the sea—deeper than any other woman in her country.

Salma Shaker breaks records and also stereotypes. Her father is a marine biologist, so Salma spent a lot of her childhood scuba diving in the sea. But she didn't like scuba diving very much. She felt constrained by the equipment. For her, going underwater was about freedom and serenity. So, she started free diving. Her free diving record stands at about 138 feet deep. Salma can hold her breath underwater for about four minutes and thirty seconds.

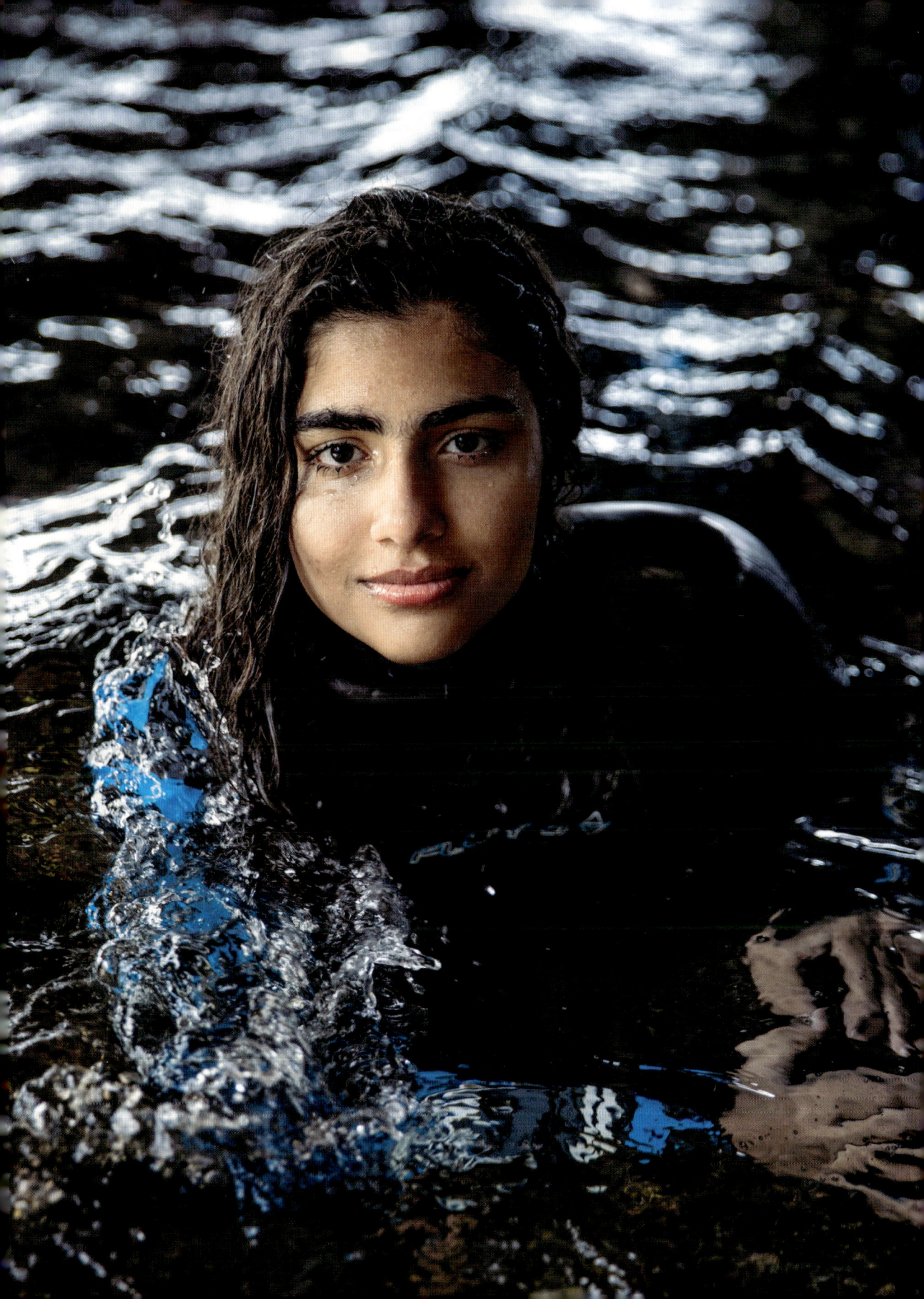

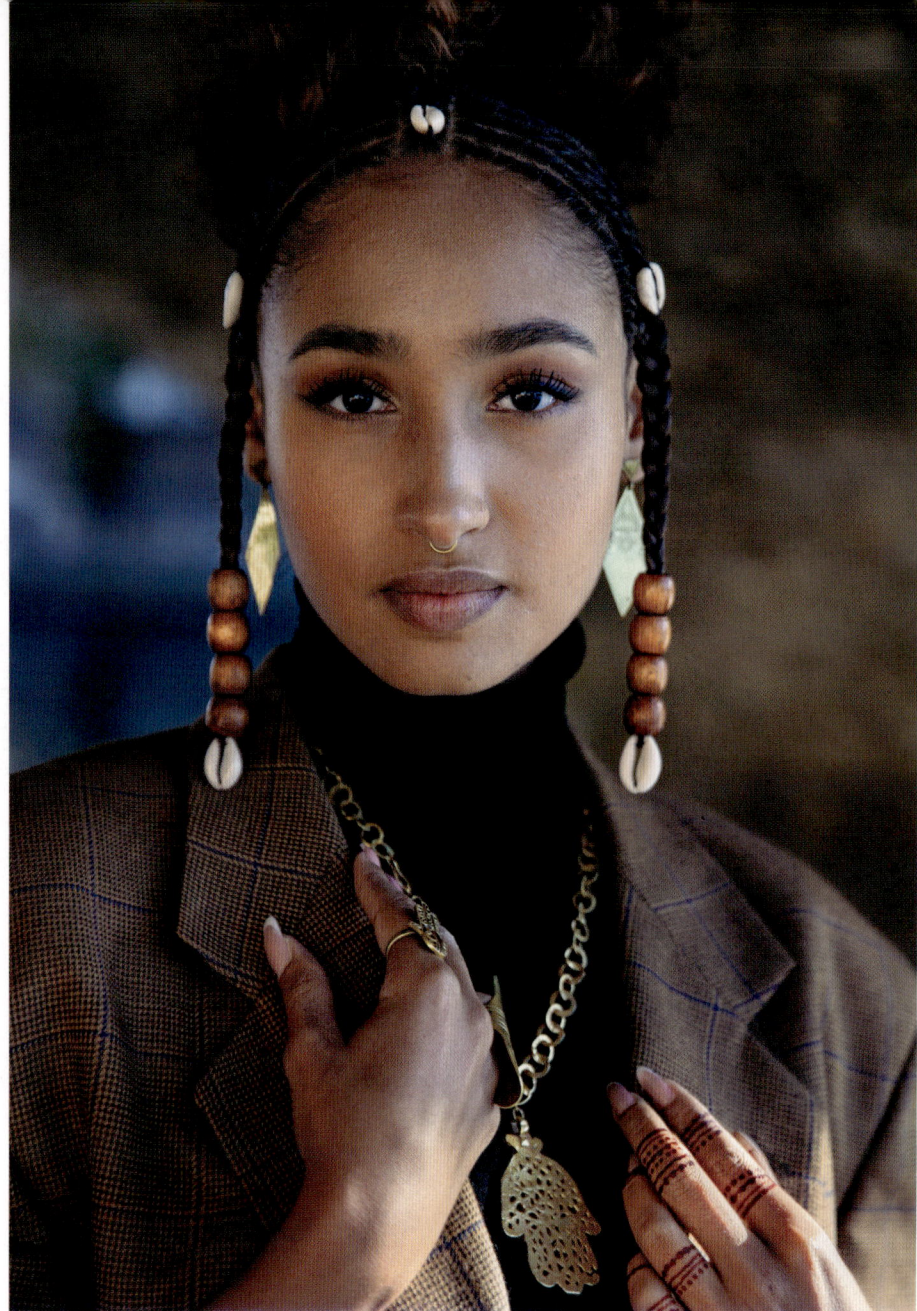

PARIS, FRANCE

Nawal Benali dedicates a huge part of her life to honoring her North African heritage. Born in Tunisia in a southern Amazigh community, she moved to Paris when she was a few months old with her Algerian French adoptive family.

Nawal received a good education in her family and pursued a career in journalism. However, she never forgot her roots. Every day, she celebrates Amazigh culture through her work but also through outfits, hairstyles, accessories, and tattoos. The Amazigh people have a remarkable history dating back millennia. In her ongoing quest for self-discovery, Nawal frequently travels to North Africa to immerse herself in the rich Indigenous culture of her birthplace.

OPUWO, NAMIBIA

Uaakoina was going from her small village to the market in a nearby town. Herero women have a great sense of style, but their outfits are about more than aesthetics; they are a statement of their identity and history.

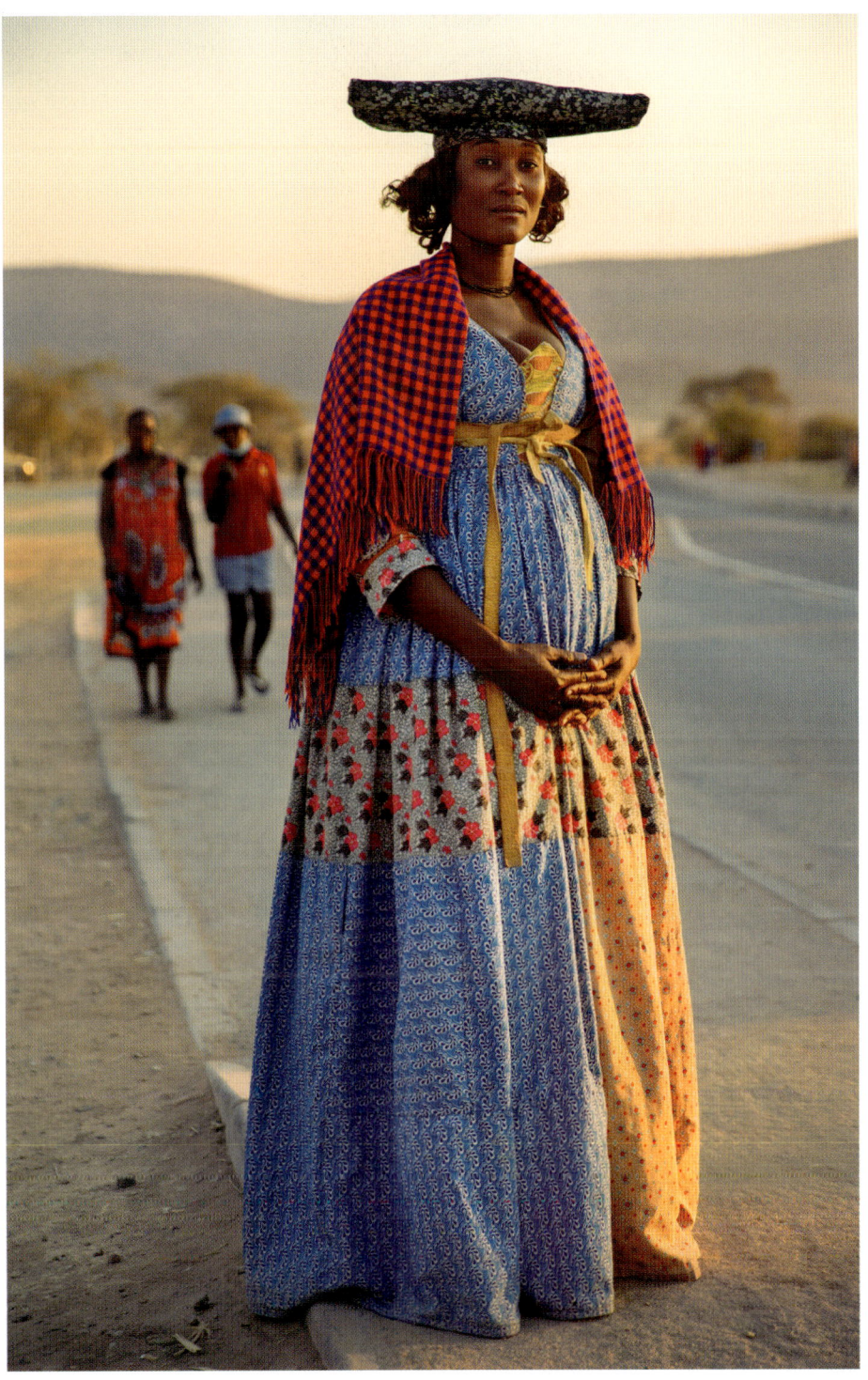

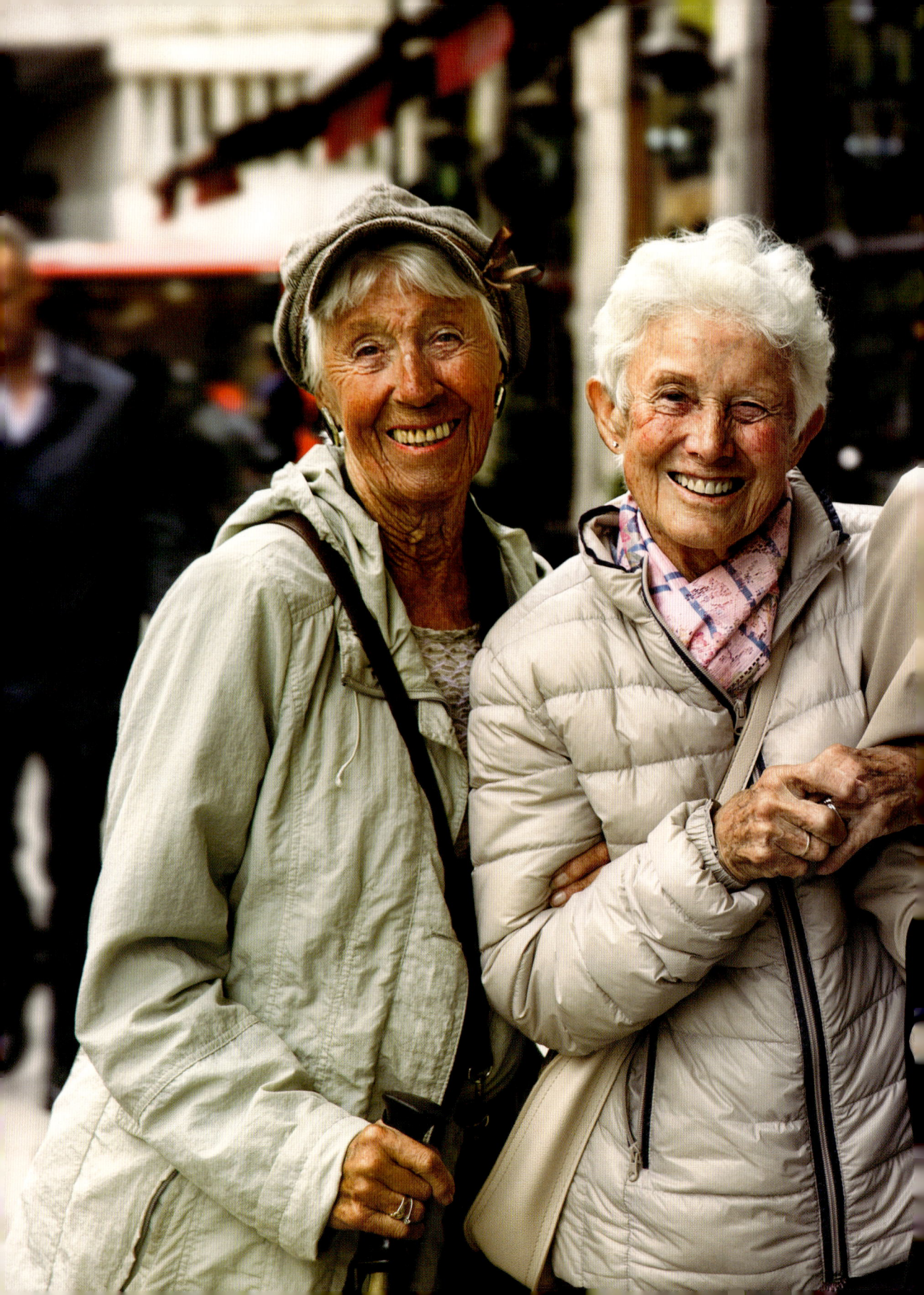

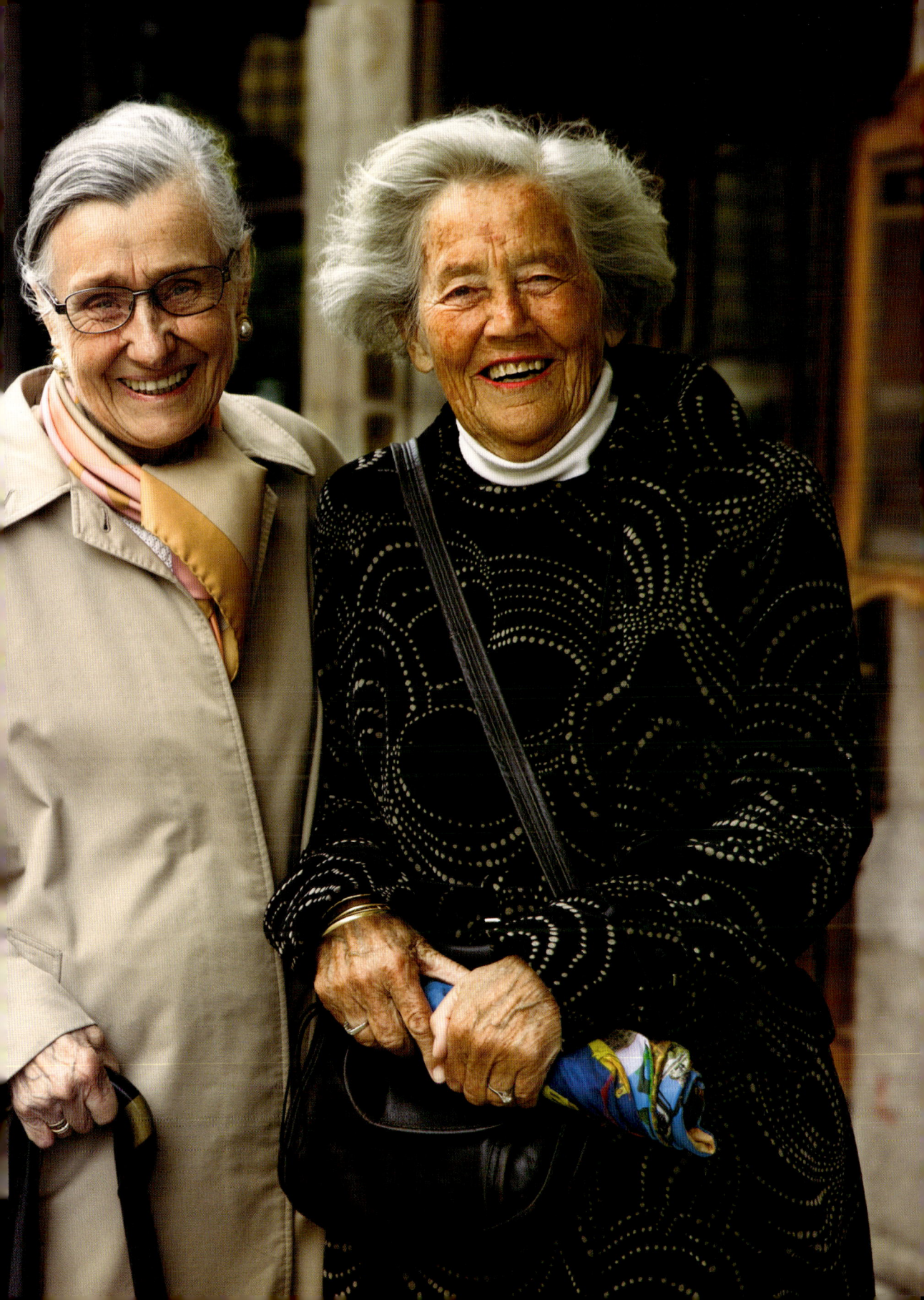

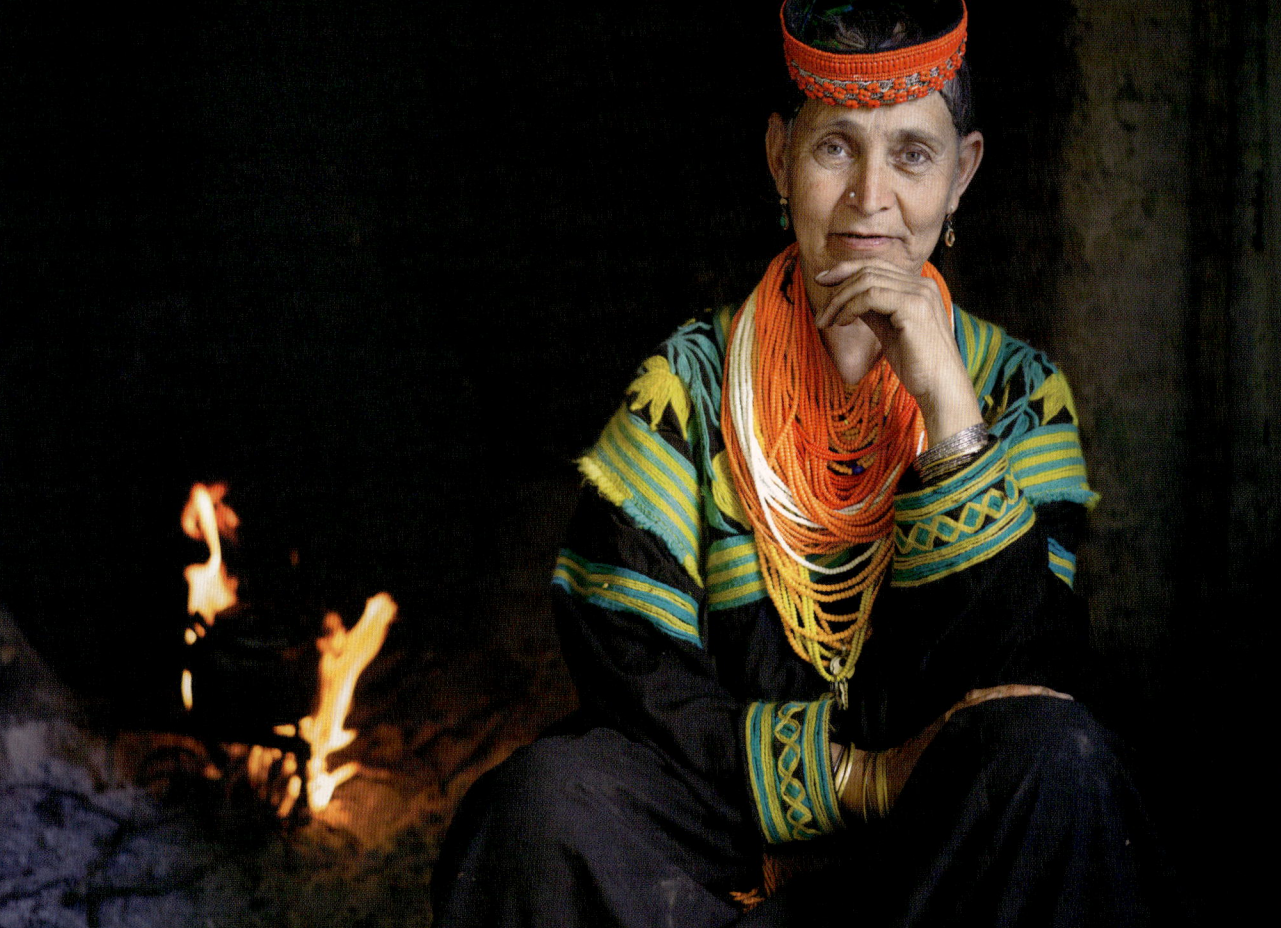

NORTHERN PAKISTAN

In her village, everyone knows Jamdana as the predictor. She uses an heirloom bracelet passed down from her mother and a unique pendulum to reveal the fortunes of villagers who seek her guidance.

OSLO, NORWAY *(Previous spread)*

The friendship between these lovely ladies began when they were in high school. About seventy years later, I encountered them on the streets of Oslo. It was a gloomy day, but they were shining. They told me that they were out "to celebrate old age." A beautiful age and a beautiful friendship!

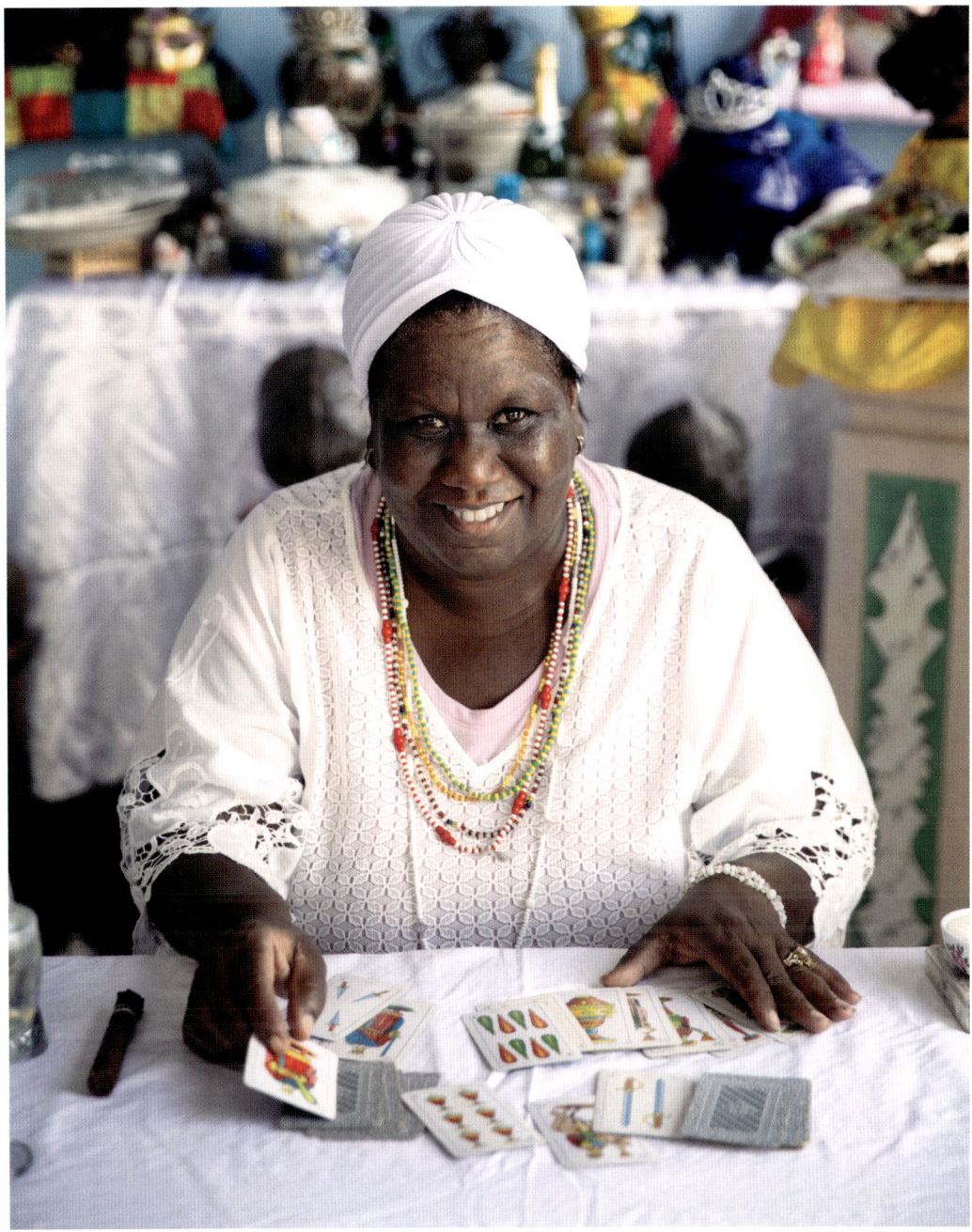

HAVANA, CUBA

Luisa is a Santería priestess. Santería is an Afro-Cuban religion born through a process of syncretism between the traditional Yoruba religion of West Africa, Christianity, and spiritism. In the Santería tradition, women have always held a significant role.

Every day, Luisa performs rituals in front of her altar and offers guidance to those who visit her. She's worked in a blood laboratory for many years, while her son has become a respected physicist in the United States. As much as she loves the physical and palpable world, she's always been drawn to the spiritual one.

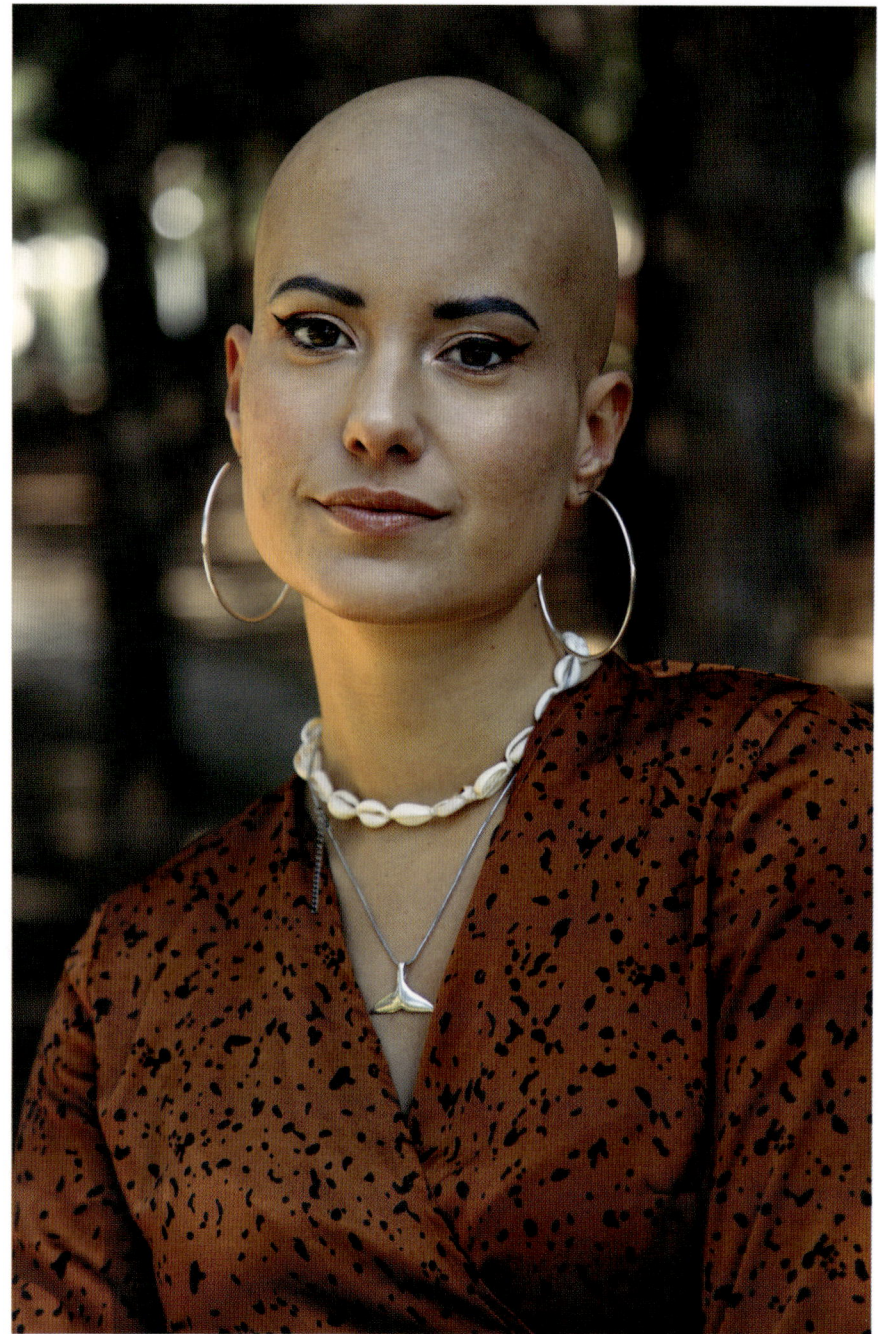

BARCELONA, SPAIN

Julia is passionate about surfing, so she travels the world in search of beautiful waves, finding seasonal jobs to support her passion in each new place. A few years ago, when she realized she had alopecia—an autoimmune condition affecting hair growth—she initially tried to hide it. Over time, she learned to embrace and love her new look and shifted her focus to what she loves most: the ocean.

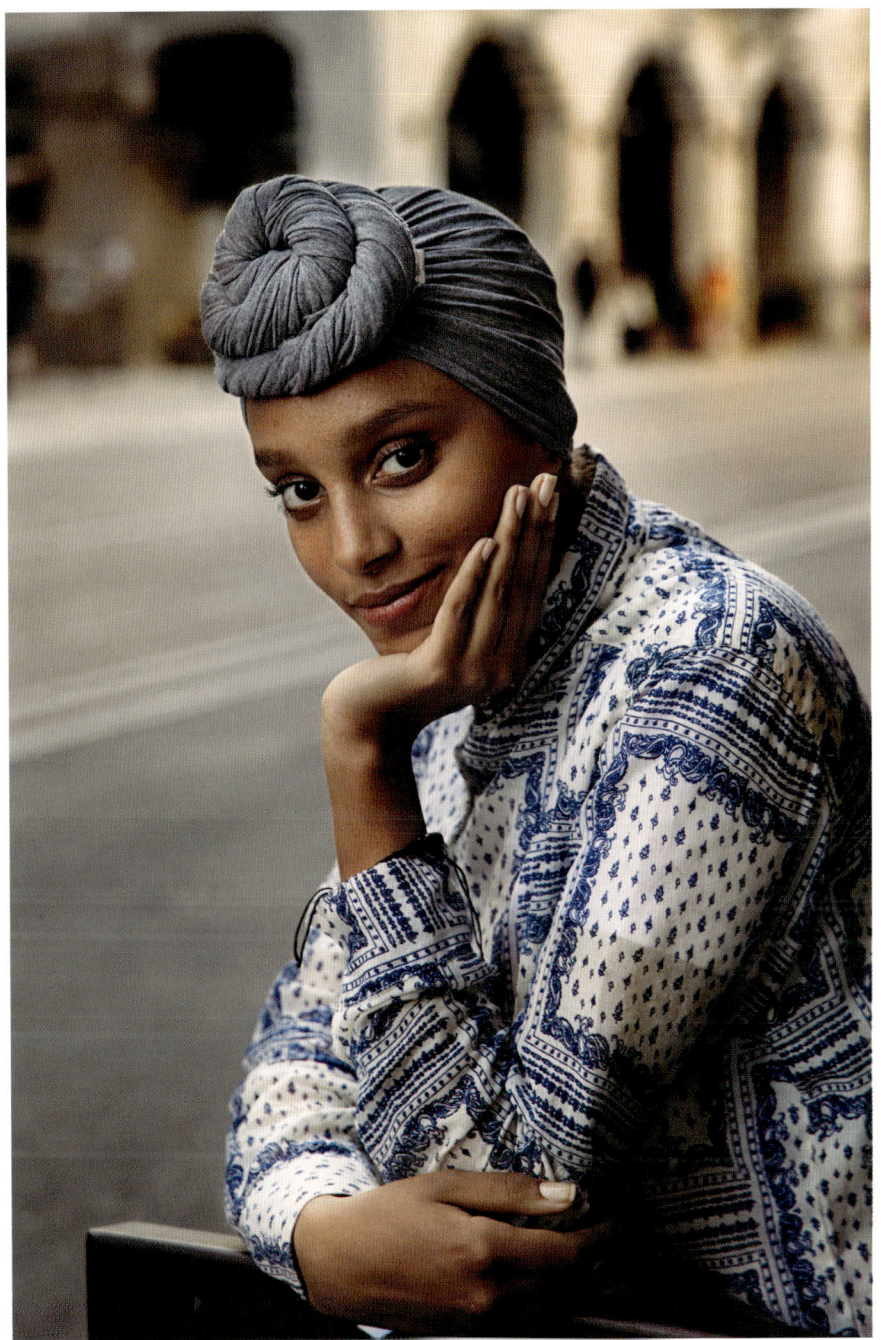

CASABLANCA, MOROCCO

Young Oumaima covers her head as part of her beliefs. But she also loves fashion, so she likes to play with the way she wears the scarves.

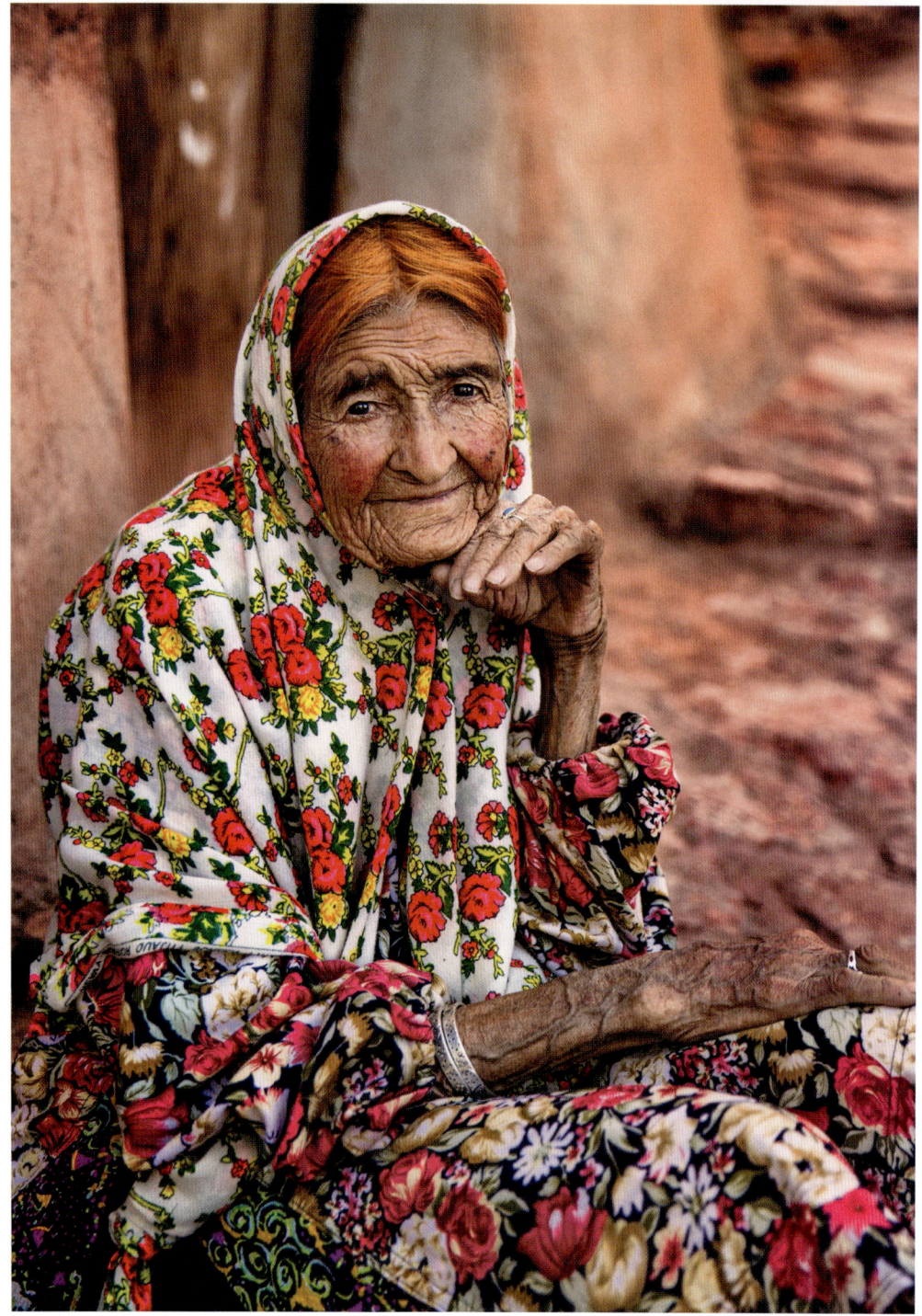

ABYANEH, IRAN

This lovely lady was relaxing in front of her home, curiously watching all passersby. We couldn't communicate through words due to the language barrier, but she happily agreed to be photographed. At the end of our short encounter, she gently held my hands in hers. Though we spoke different languages, we exchanged smiles, which broke down all barriers.

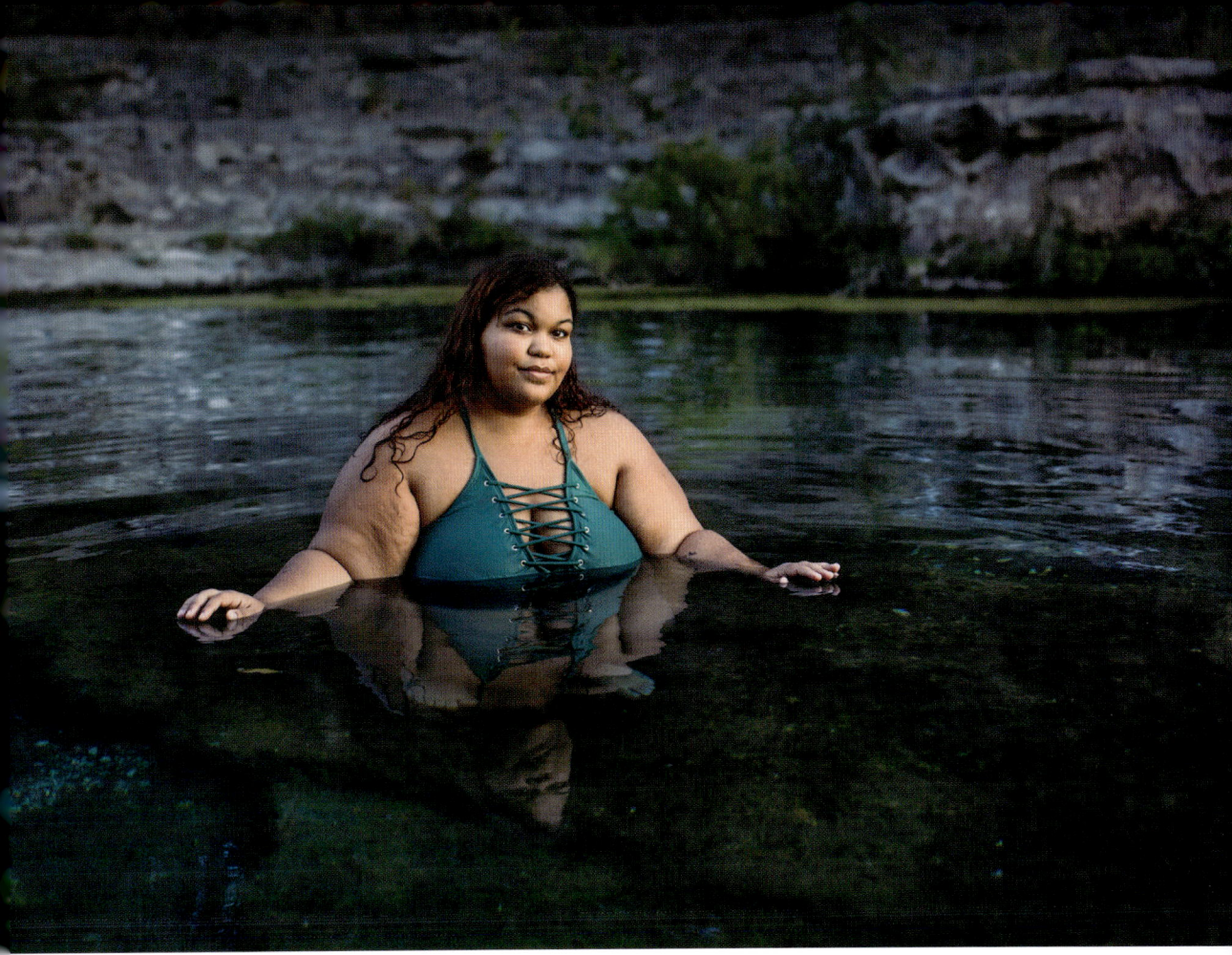

AUSTIN, TEXAS, UNITED STATES

This place, called Barton Springs Pool, offers a peaceful retreat for people in search of relaxation and swimming. Looking around at all those perfect bodies and the splendid scenery, one might feel as if they were on the set of a glamorous magazine photo shoot.

However, for me, beauty is so much more. When I noticed Veronize and her serene expression, I instantly knew I wanted to photograph her. Veronize was equally surprised and thrilled by my proposal. It happened to be the first time she had ever worn a two-piece swimsuit in her life. Sometimes things happen for a reason, and perhaps that's why I found myself there on that September day.

Veronize had just begun the journey of accepting her body, and wearing that swimsuit marked an important milestone for her. However, the road leading up to that moment was filled with years of struggle. Her parents had emigrated from the Dominican Republic to the United States, driven by the dream of providing a better life for their daughter. They created a unique name for her—a combination of their own names: Veronica and Ezekiel.

Veronize experienced bullying from a young age. At just twelve years old, someone started a false rumor in her school claiming she was pregnant. This was just one of many episodes when she faced humiliation because of her body.

Despite all the suffering, Veronize remained a kindhearted person by responding to hate with love. Today, she works at a holistic shop and embodies the nurturing nature of someone who takes care of her loved ones when they are in need.

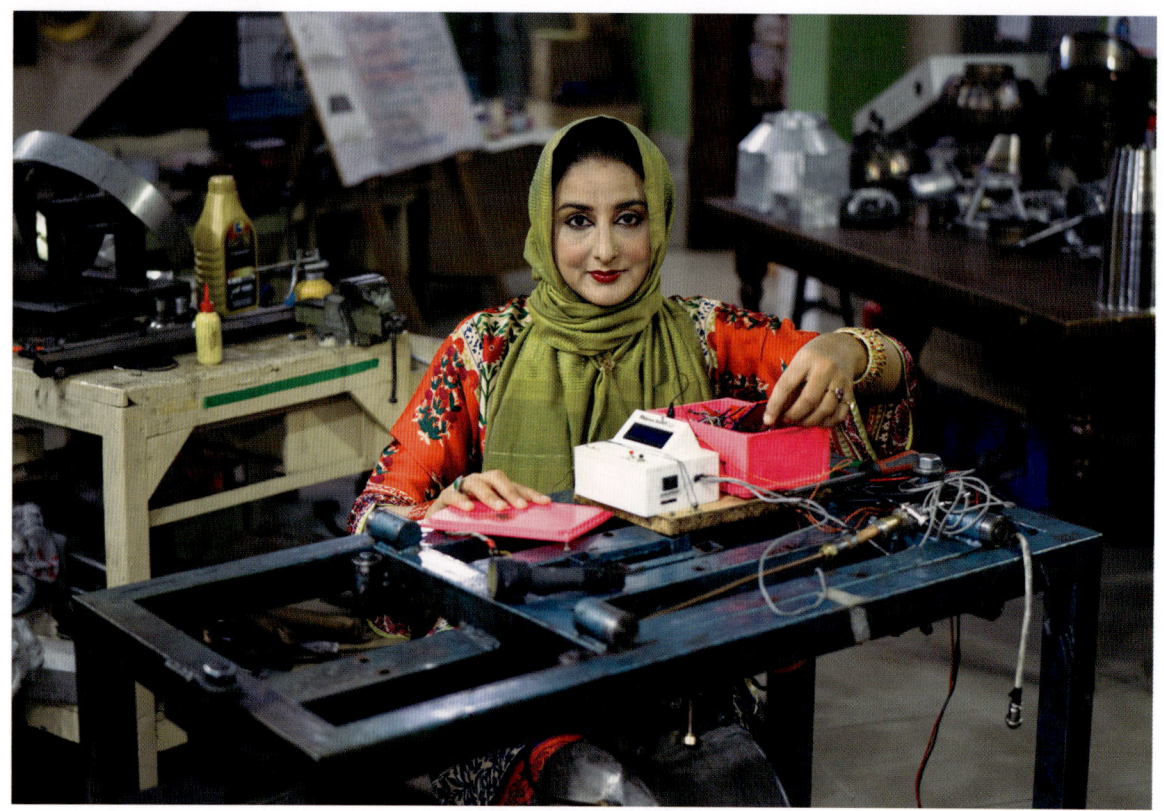

ISLAMABAD, PAKISTAN

Sarah Qureshi is an engineer, a pilot, an innovator, an entrepreneur, and a mother. Born into a family of scientists, she developed a passion for aviation from childhood. She loved assisting her father while he worked on engines and various machines. All those years made her dream big.

A while ago, Sarah made a groundbreaking innovation by designing the world's first eco-friendly engine, which is currently under development.

When you see a plane in the sky, it is always followed by vapor trails called contrails. Those trails contribute significantly to CO2 emissions. Sarah's revolutionary design eliminates contrails, and she hopes that her engine will be in use in a few years.

Sarah's country doesn't have a rich history in aerospace, but she is committed to changing that.

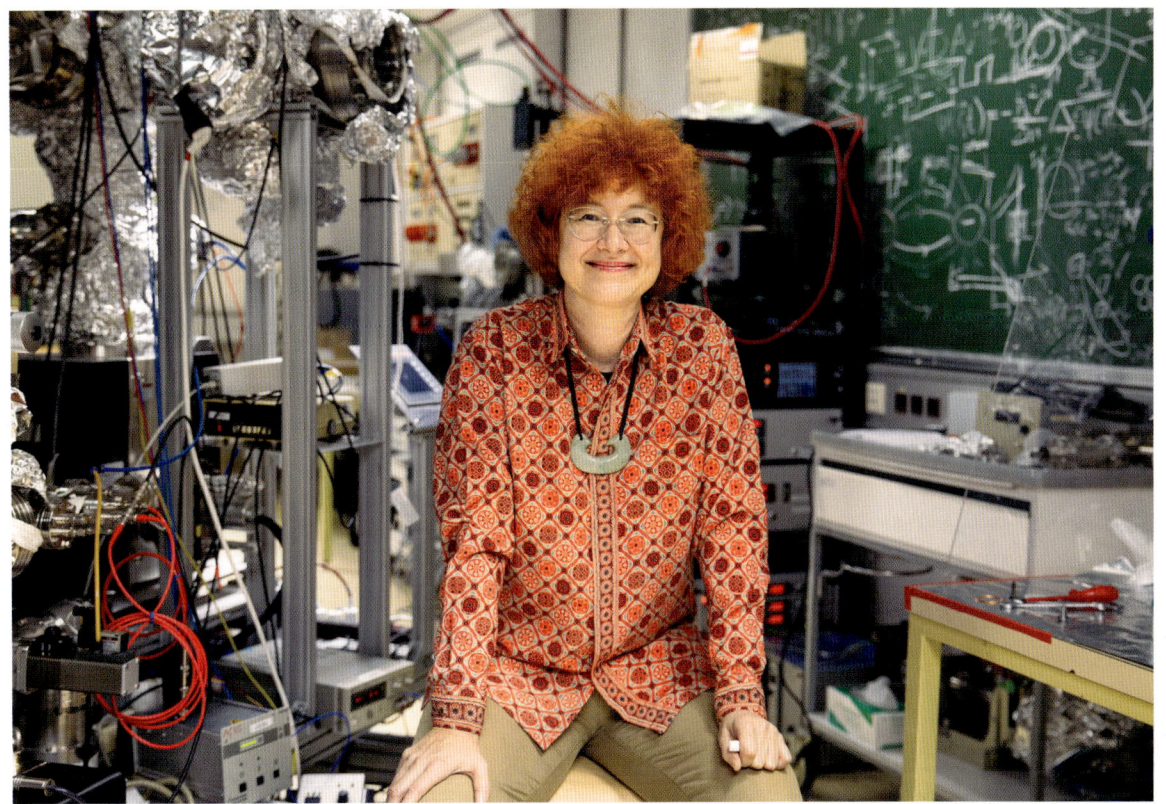

VIENNA, AUSTRIA

It was fascinating to step into Ille's fabulous universe, where the eminent physicist and professor studies the world on a scale of nanometers. To put it into perspective, a single strand of hair has a diameter of about eighty thousand nanometers.

Ille Gebeshuber's work extends beyond the boundaries of traditional physics, incorporating elements from biology, arts, and social sciences. Ille was born in the countryside, and that's how she became fascinated by nature.

After studying and working at Vienna University of Technology, she moved to Malaysia, where she has lived for seven years. Besides being a professor at the National University of Malaysia, she also studies the rainforest. During numerous jungle expeditions, she's been inspired by the remarkable properties of animals and plants. Ille believes that if we understand the whole complexity of nature, which has improved continuously via evolution over many millions of years, we can use it for positive technologies that address the global challenges faced by humanity.

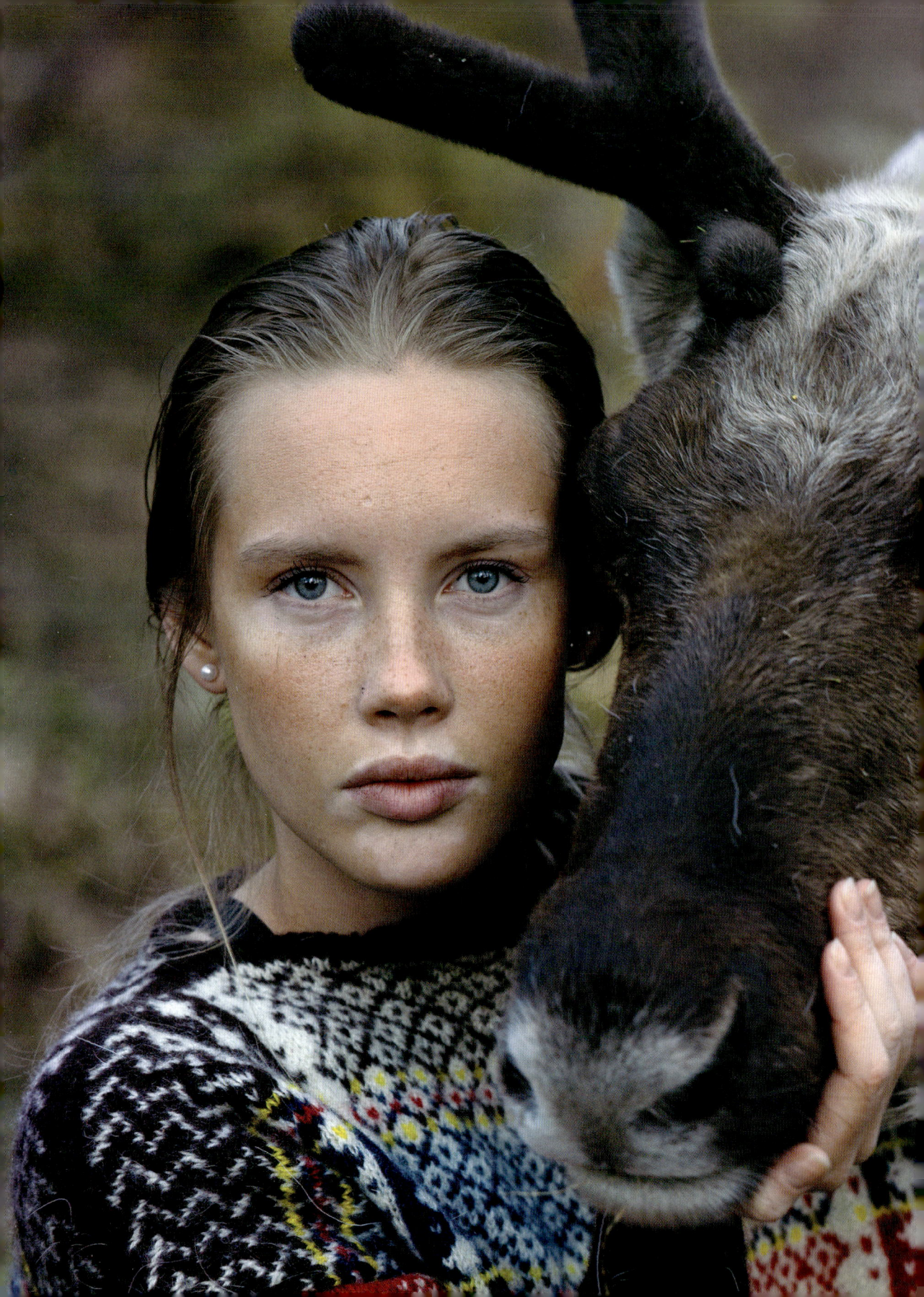

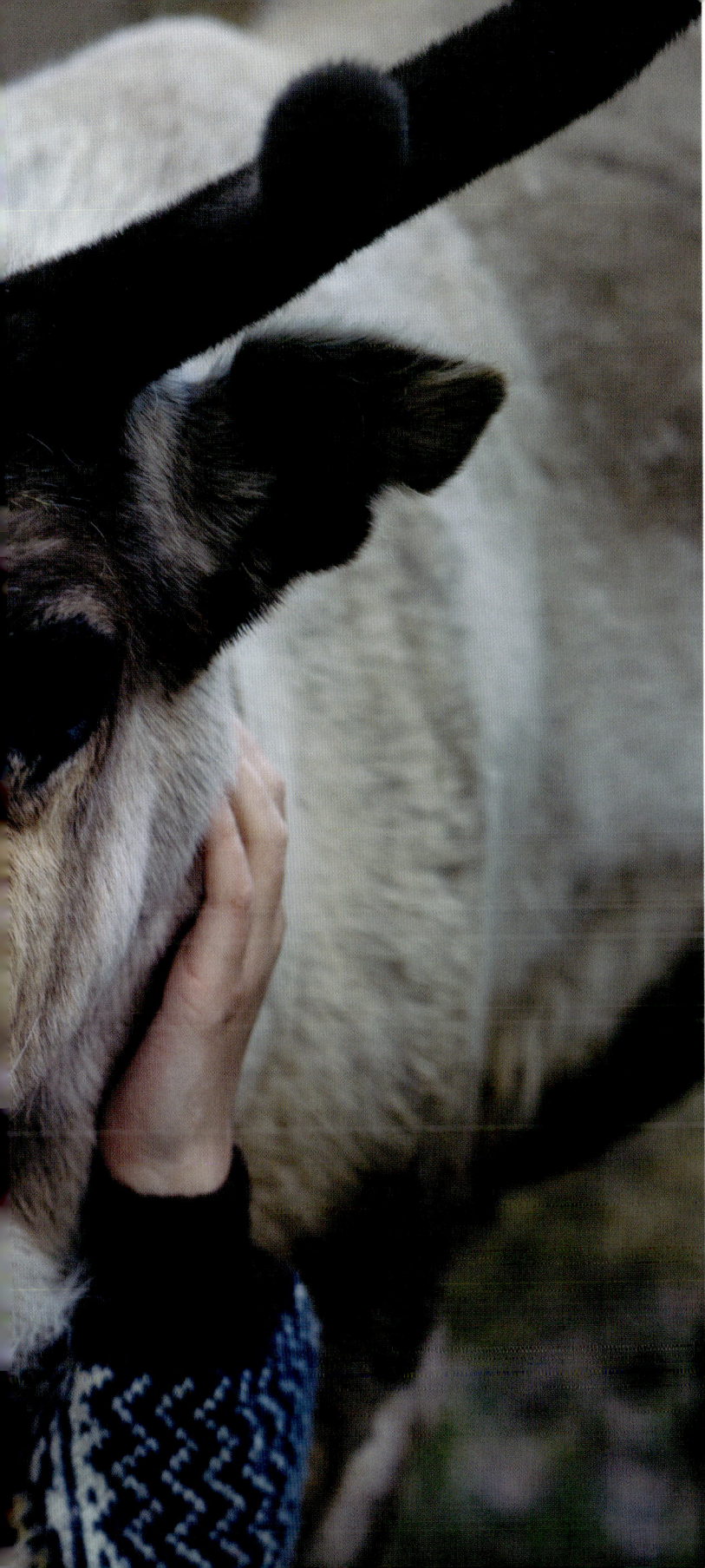

GLEN, SWEDEN

Deep in the forests of northern Sweden lies this small Sámi village with just a few houses. For outsiders, it may seem like the end of the road, but for Evelina Solsten, it's where the road begins.

The Sámi are an Indigenous people of northern Europe, traditionally reindeer herders, known for their unique languages and cultural identity. Evelina is passionate about preserving her people's traditions. Although she currently lives in the city to pursue her university studies, she dreams of returning to her village to raise reindeer and spread knowledge about Sámi culture and reindeer herding.

In Sámi culture, every newborn receives reindeer from family, and it is considered a sacred mission to care for them throughout their lives. Evelina is determined to educate others about Sámi culture and combat prejudices, ensuring her heritage is respected and understood.

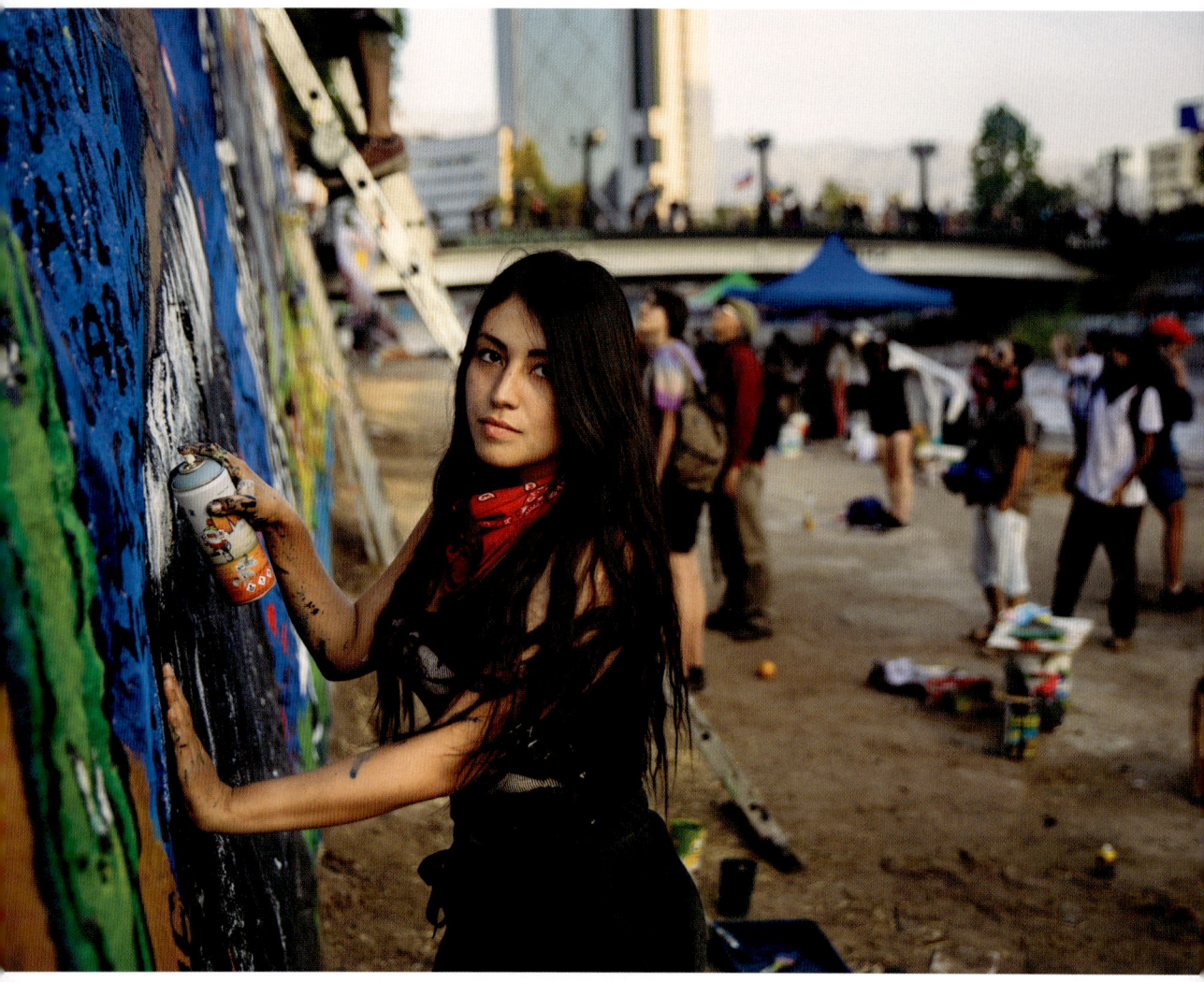

SANTIAGO, CHILE

Lesley was using street art to show her support for the protests against poverty and inequality in the country. She studied psychology at the university and made huge sacrifices to be able to pay for her studies. She hoped for a fairer system in Chile and for more opportunities to be offered to those in need.

BERLIN, GERMANY

Tayla Camp is an art critic. Although her greatest passion is classical art, she's definitely not a classical art critic. Tayla always liked to live and think outside the box. The young American experienced life in different parts of the world, like New York City, Tokyo, London, and Berlin.

Tayla loves to bring art closer to people—to make it more accessible and to decode the symbols and messages. Art is one of the most precious things in the world, a medicine for the soul, and I really love to see people like Tayla bringing it closer to the public.

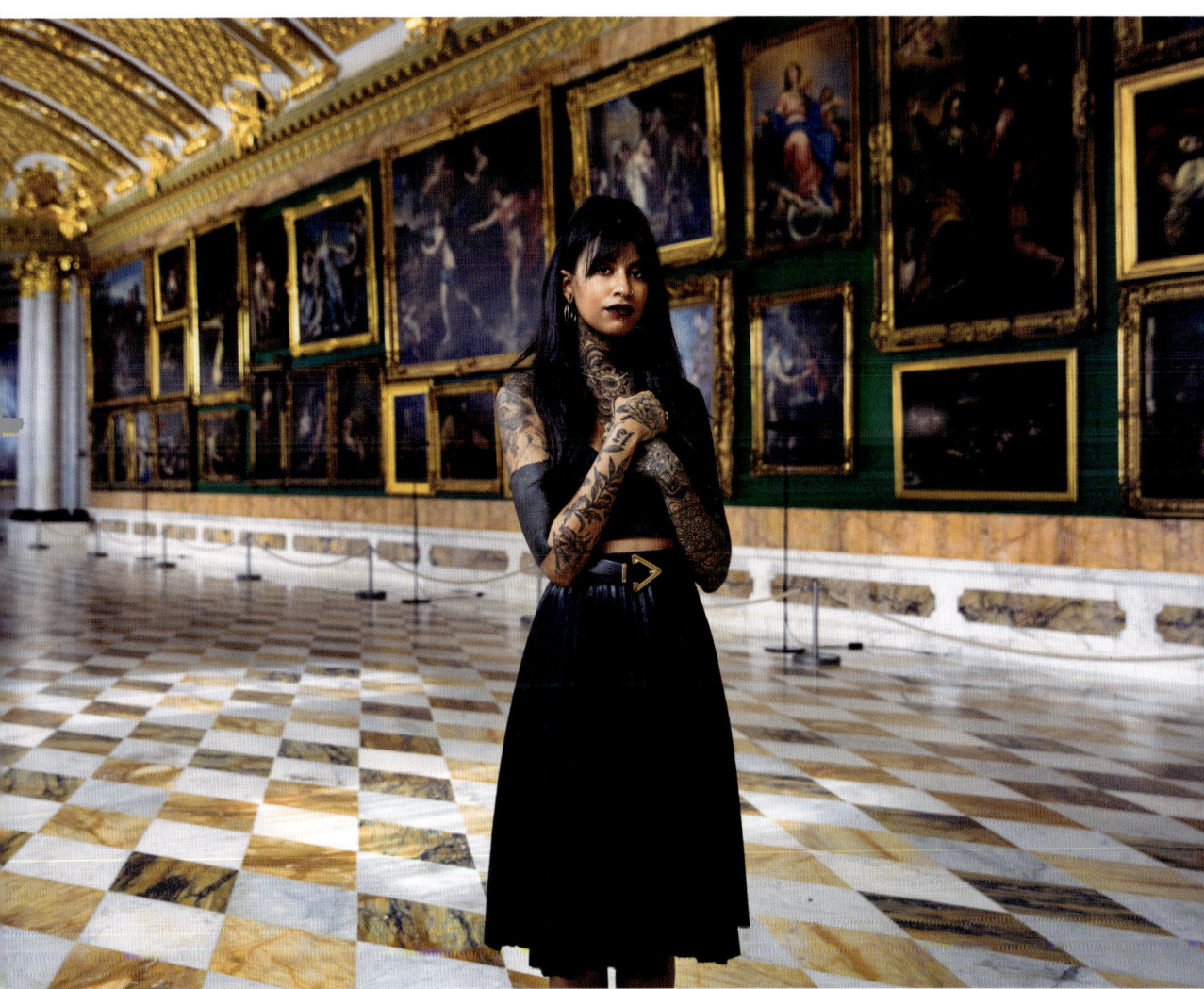

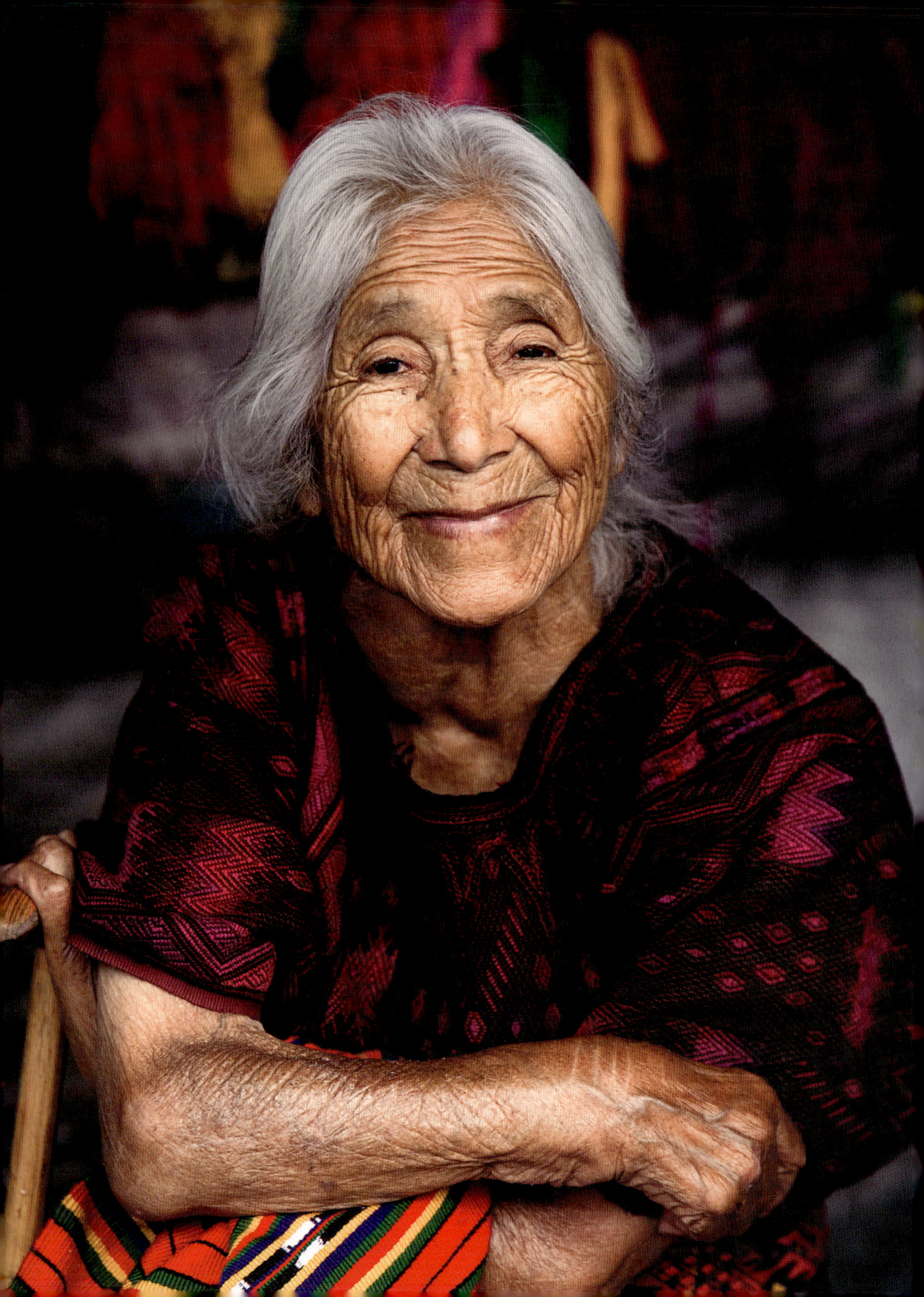

CHICHICASTENANGO, GUATEMALA

Jacinta's story begins many, many years ago. It was 1916 when a fifty-year-old woman in Guatemala decided to induce an abortion after believing herself to be too old to have another baby. However, the abortion failed, and, a few months later, Jacinta was born. This incredible lady was a survivor even before birth. When I met her, she was 103 years old.

Jacinta was the youngest daughter, so, according to tradition, she took care of her parents until they passed away. After, she married, but her husband was quite oppressive, and they didn't get along. She was seventy years old when he passed away. Jacinta admitted frankly: at age seventy, she finally started to enjoy herself for the first time in her life. She still felt young—and that the best time of her life was just beginning.

Jacinta lived by herself until she was ninety-nine years old when, after breaking a foot, she decided to move in with one of her granddaughters.

When I met Jacinta and her granddaughter, they were coming from an appointment during which Jacinta's hearing aid had been adjusted. She needs her hearing aid more than ever because she recently started learning Spanish. Although Spanish is the official language of the country, Jacinta has spoken only Quiché, her Indigenous native tongue, all her life. Now she watches TV programs in Spanish and asks her granddaughter about the new words she hears.

Jacinta's longevity secrets include her love for cooking traditional Mayan recipes, which her granddaughter used to open a restaurant. These recipes are sophisticated, meat is rarely used, and there's a rich combination of herbs.

I could go on with stories about this extraordinary woman, but 103 years of strength and beauty could never be fully captured in words. I hope this inspires you to always remain as young and beautiful in spirit as Jacinta.

TOKYO, JAPAN *(Below)*

Hundreds of umbrellas were moving quickly in Shibuya Crossing—one of the most crowded crosswalks in the world—during the rush hour. Makoto, a young hairdresser, stopped for a portrait and an exchange of contacts before rejoining the infinite flow.

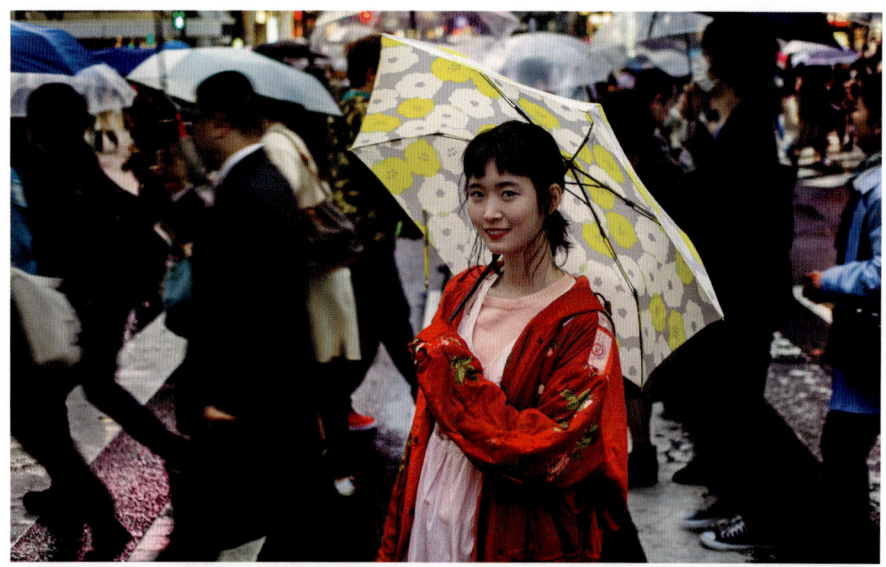

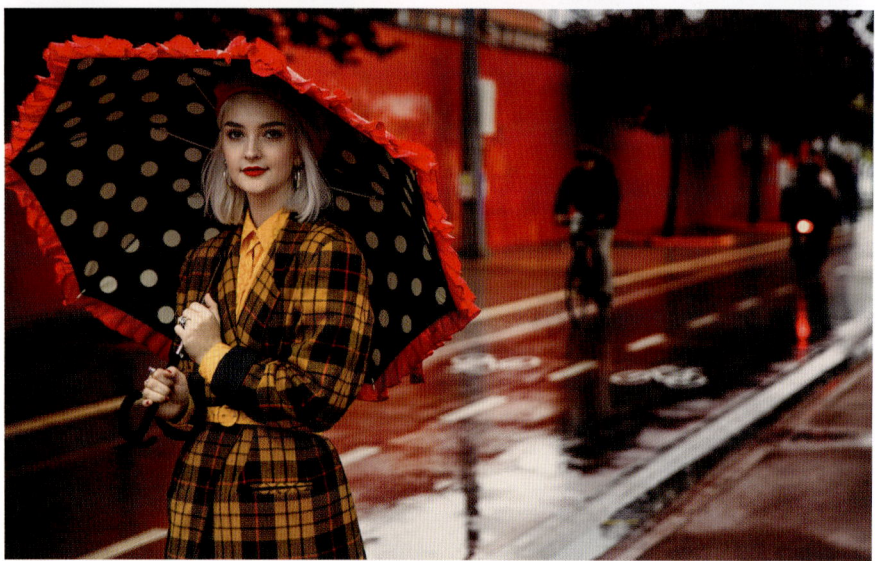

COPENHAGEN, DENMARK *(Above)*

For many years, Alice suffered from depression. It was a tough time for her until vibrant colors began to fill her life. A few years ago, she began creating comics and opened a secondhand clothing shop. She loved the fact that secondhand clothes are both environmentally friendly and marvelous.

Alice owns fewer clothes than ever before, yet her outfits are more beautiful than ever. Referring to her colorful daily clothes, Alice told me, "You can't have a bad day when you wear these."

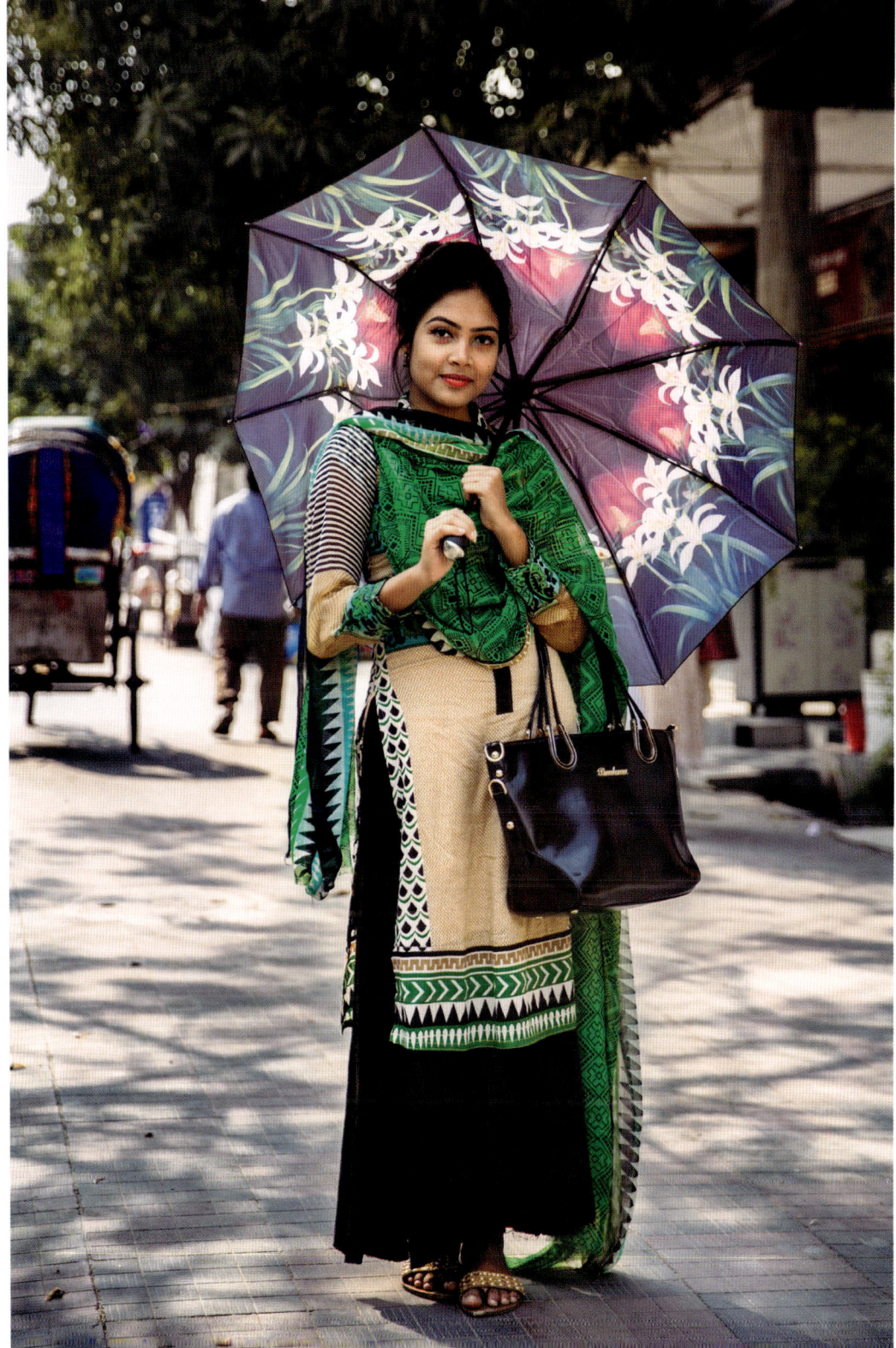

DHAKA, BANGLADESH

I met Tethe in the alleys of the New Market. Many imagine women in Muslim countries wearing only modest, dark-colored outfits, but I have never seen so many colorful clothes as I did here.

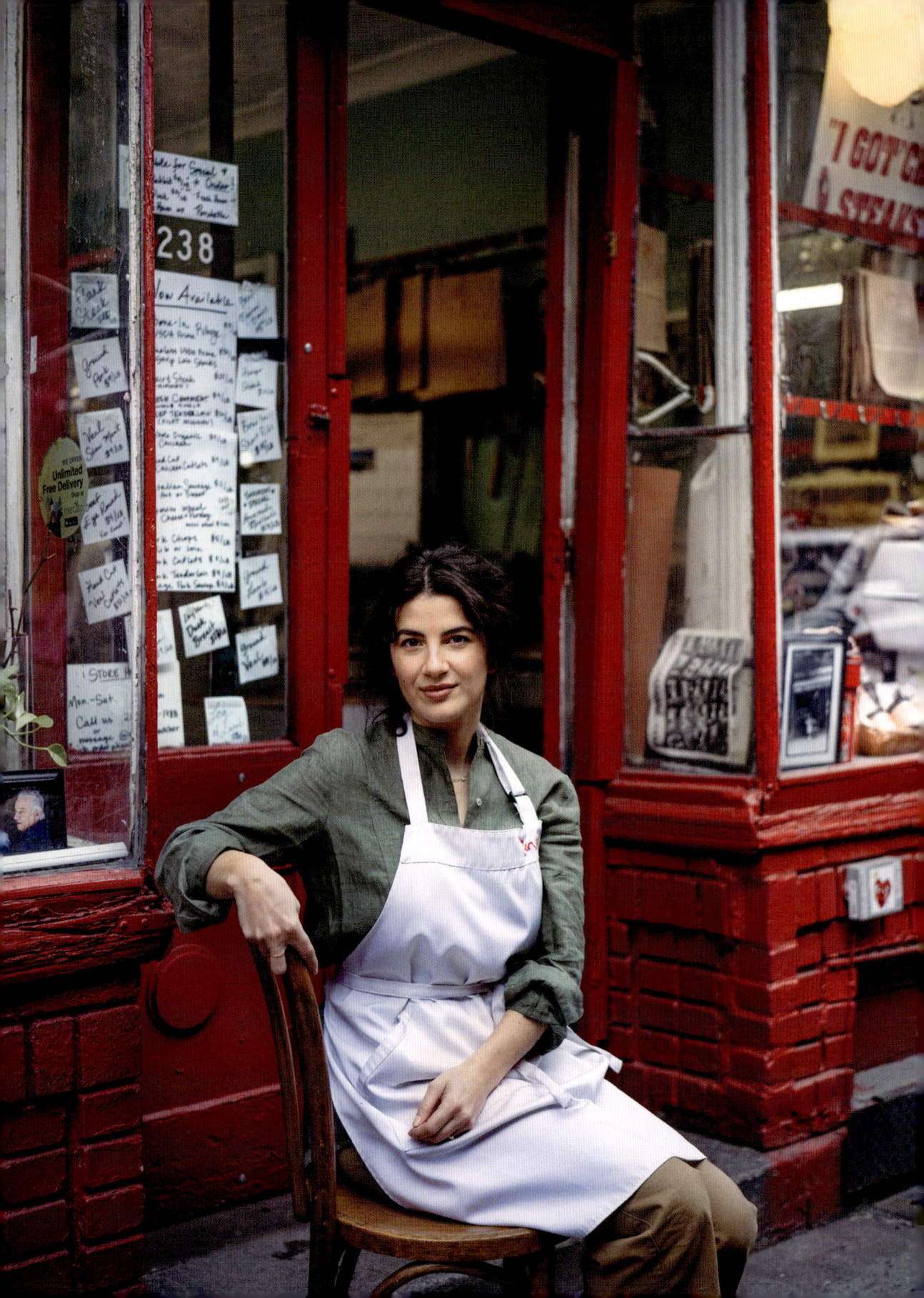

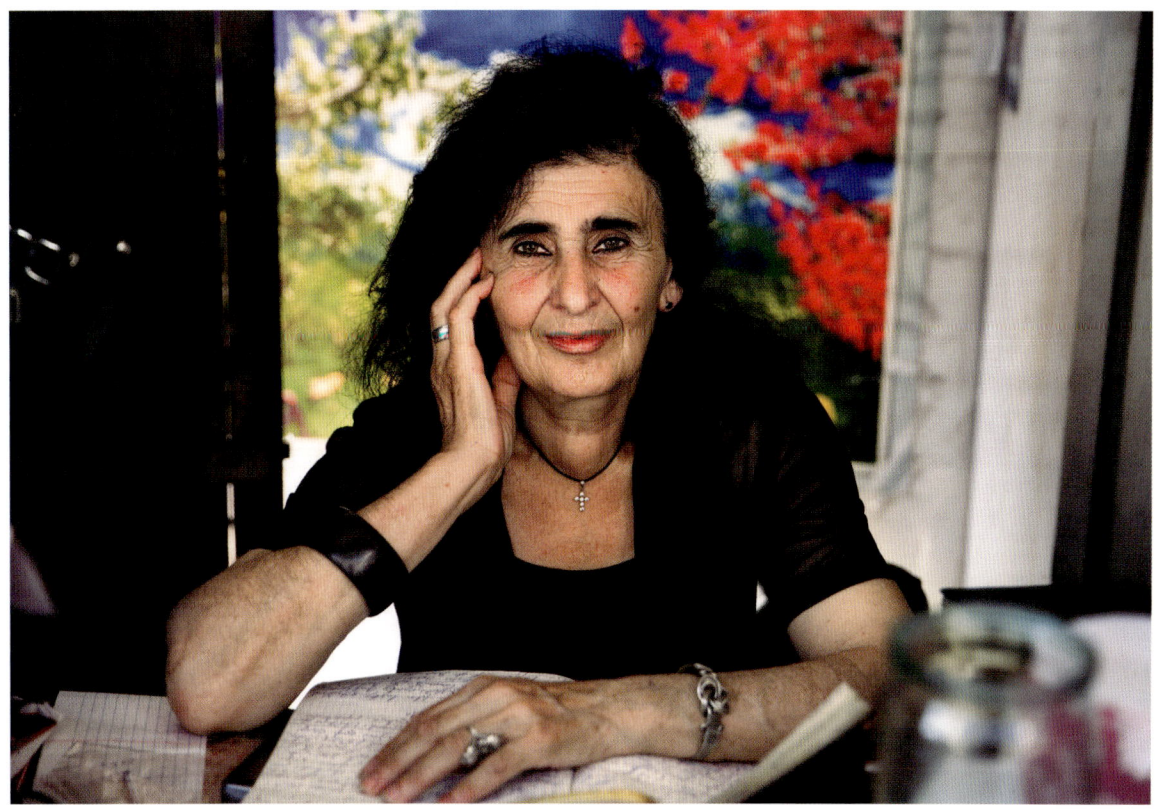

TBILISI, GEORGIA *(Above)*

I noticed Lila in her small grocery shop in 2017. I was amazed to learn that what she held in front of her was a diary and that she had been keeping one for almost forty years. She told me that she writes in it every day—otherwise she simply cannot fall asleep in the evening.

She always began her journal entries with a description of the day's weather and then continued with stories about herself, her family, and her friends. Lila wanted to leave these fascinating memories for her four children so they could be passed down through generations. A couple of years ago, I was so sad to find out that Lila passed away. But her meaningful diary remains—a beautiful legacy for her children and grandchildren. Rest in peace, dear Lila!

NEW YORK CITY, UNITED STATES *(Opposite)*

About a century ago, Jennifer Prezioso's great-grandparents opened this butcher shop in Manhattan's Little Italy. In 2017, Jennifer was following an acting career while her grandpa Moe was managing the shop alone. At the time, he was ninety-three, so Jennifer stepped in to drive him to and from work.

The driving gig turned into an apprenticeship. Today, Jennifer is the butcher and owner of this legendary shop. Or, as she likes to say, "half shop, half museum."

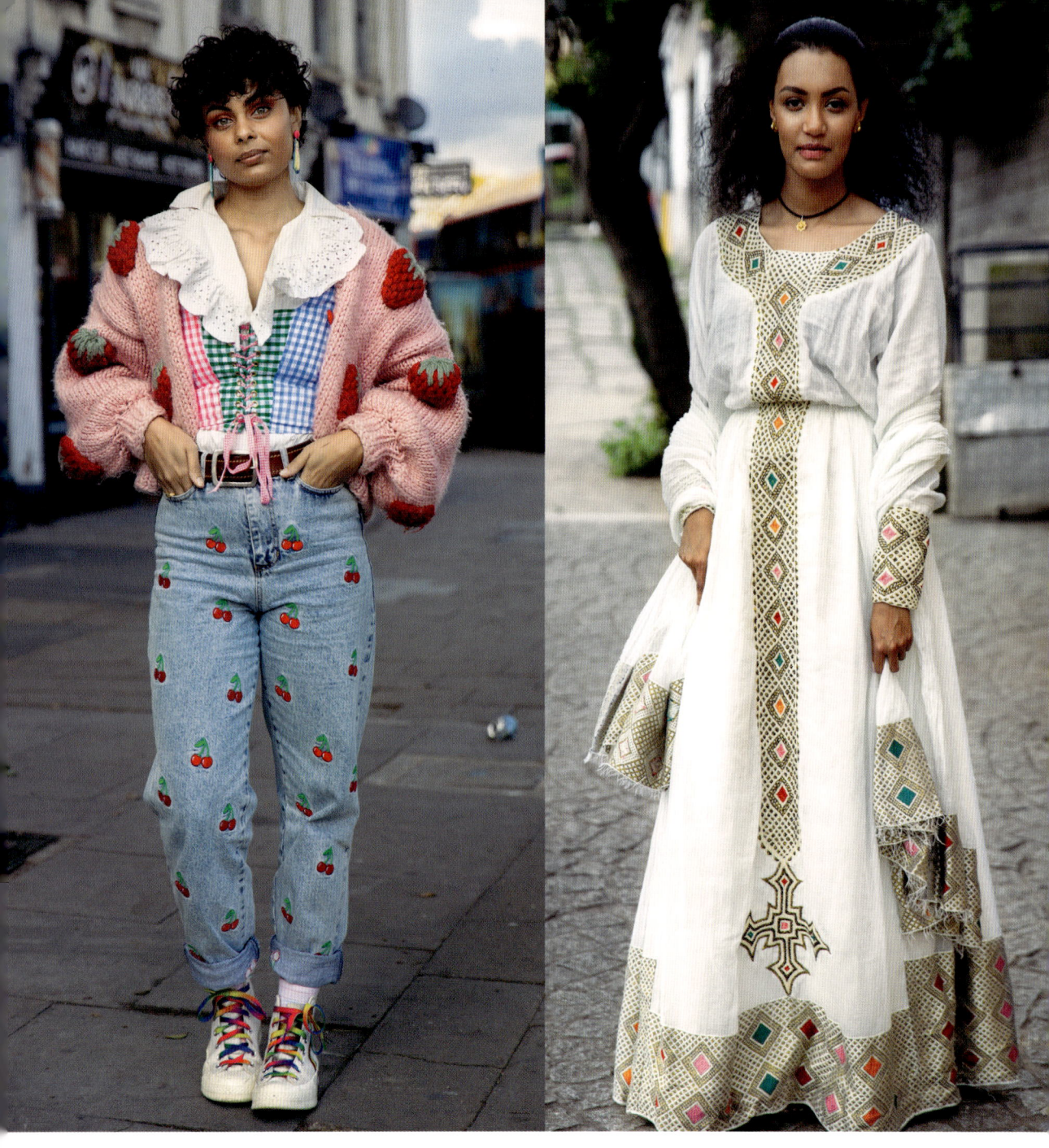

LONDON, UNITED KINGDOM

ADDIS ABABA, ETHIOPIA

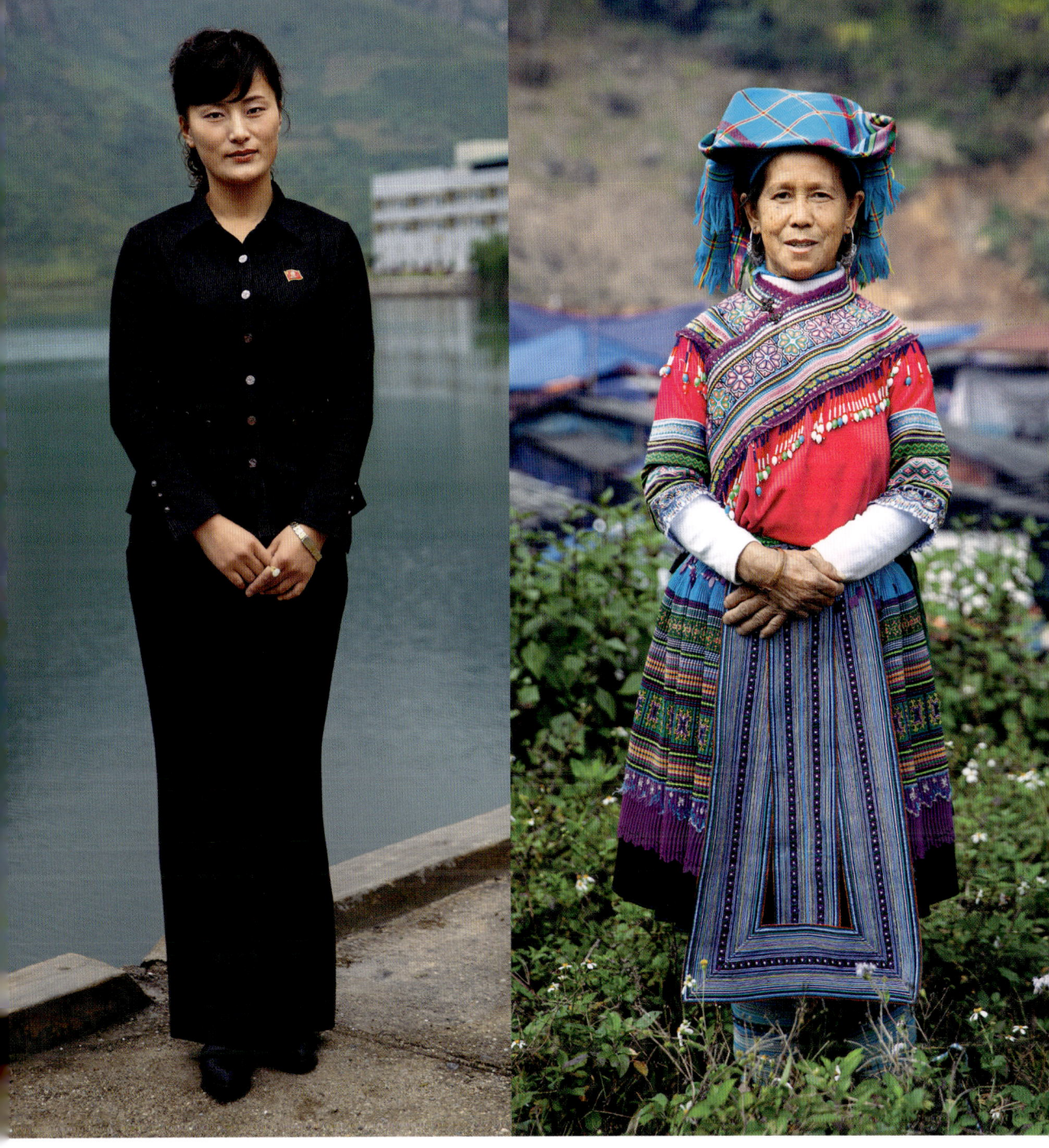

WONSAN, NORTH KOREA

SACRED VALLEY, PERU

ISLAMABAD, PAKISTAN

Karishma Ali is the first female professional soccer player in her town in northern Pakistan. When she was little, she used to watch soccer games on TV with her father. It's how she fell in love with the sport.

Later, when she started to play the sport herself, most locals disapproved of her passion, while her father fully supported her. When Karishma turned fifteen, she moved to a bigger city for professional training. More and more people found out about her unique story. Besides encouragement, she also received threats, but that didn't stop her on the pitch or outside it.

Against all challenges, Karishma founded a soccer club for girls back home. The first weeklong camp was intended for ten girls, but seventy girls ended up joining. The training pitch was set in the mountains, nearly a two-hour walk from town, in order to provide a safe place for the girls to play.

Karishma knows from her own experience that sports provide the greatest opportunity for girls to build self-esteem and dream big. Her own story is just the beginning.

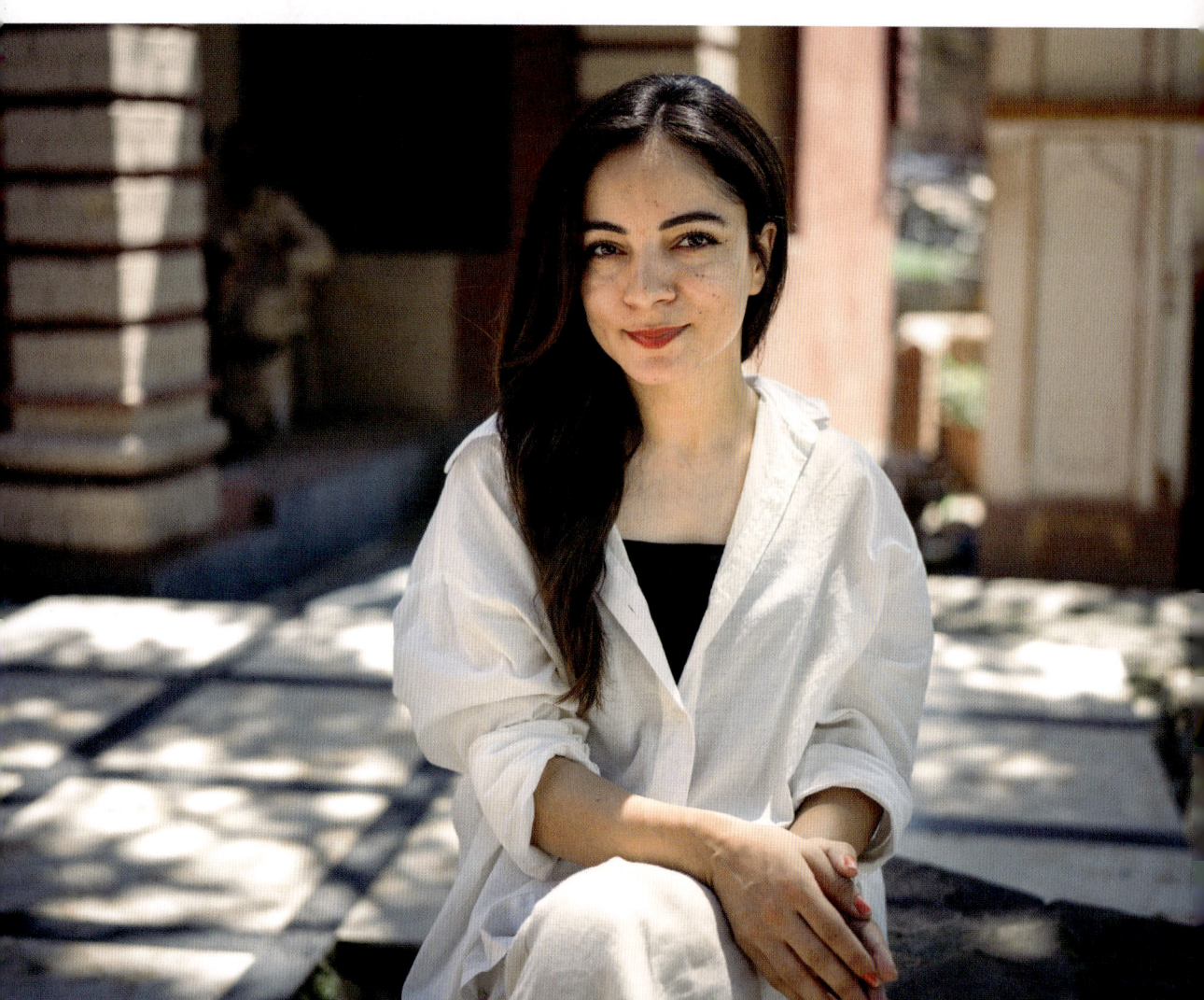

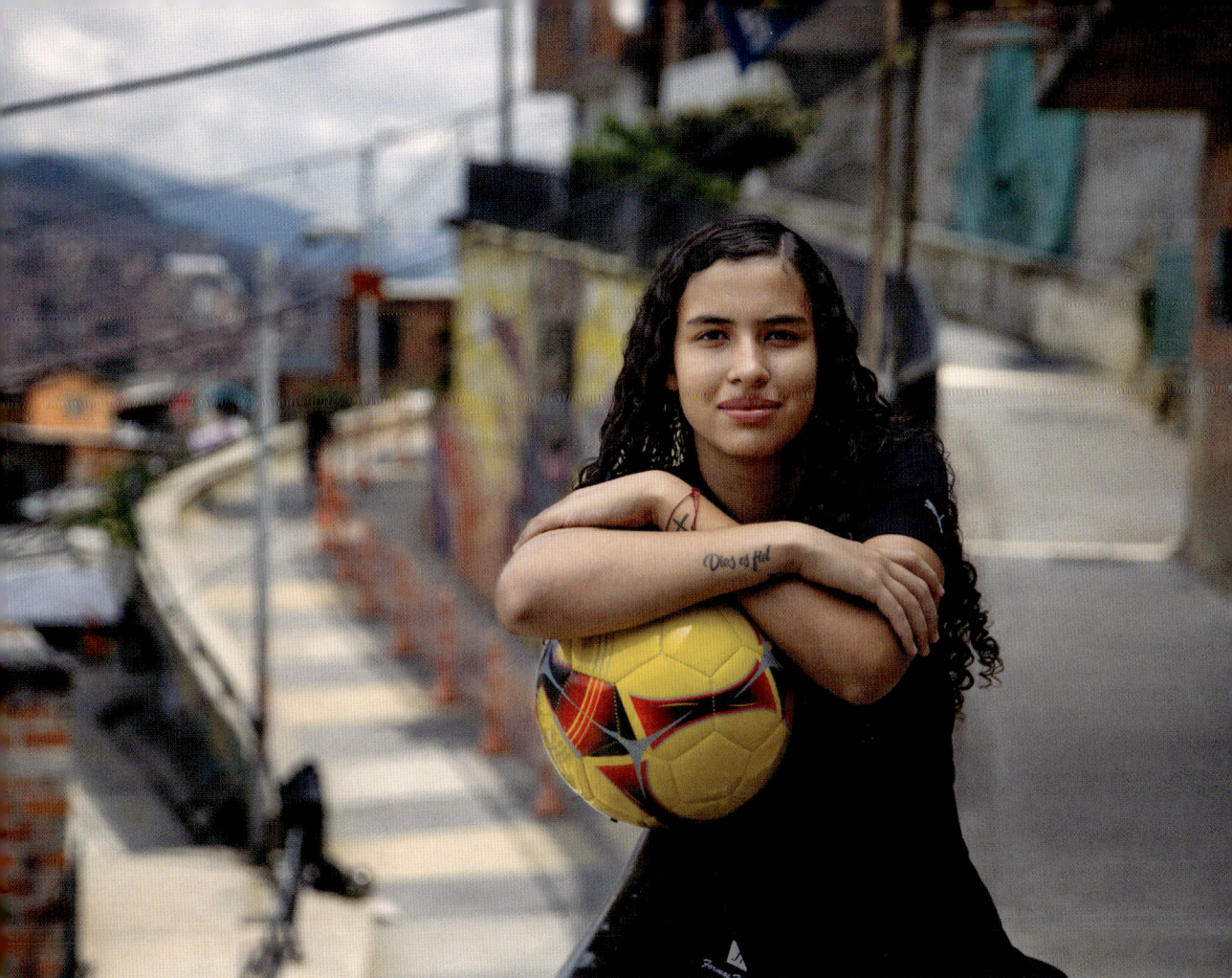

MEDELLÍN, COLOMBIA

Liced Serna grew up in a neighborhood known for violence, insecurity, and drug trafficking. She managed to stay out of trouble, unlike many teenagers in her community, thanks to the discipline she learned from soccer.

When I photographed her in 2020, Liced was training hard and dreaming about playing for the national team of Colombia—and also for a European club. Since then, both her dreams have come true.

LISBON, PORTUGAL *(Below)*

Tired of the stereotypes about women with short hair, Inês De Almeida Costa decided to cut her hair and challenge the standards of femininity. As an actress, this was seen as a risky move in her field, but she feels happy and confident about it.

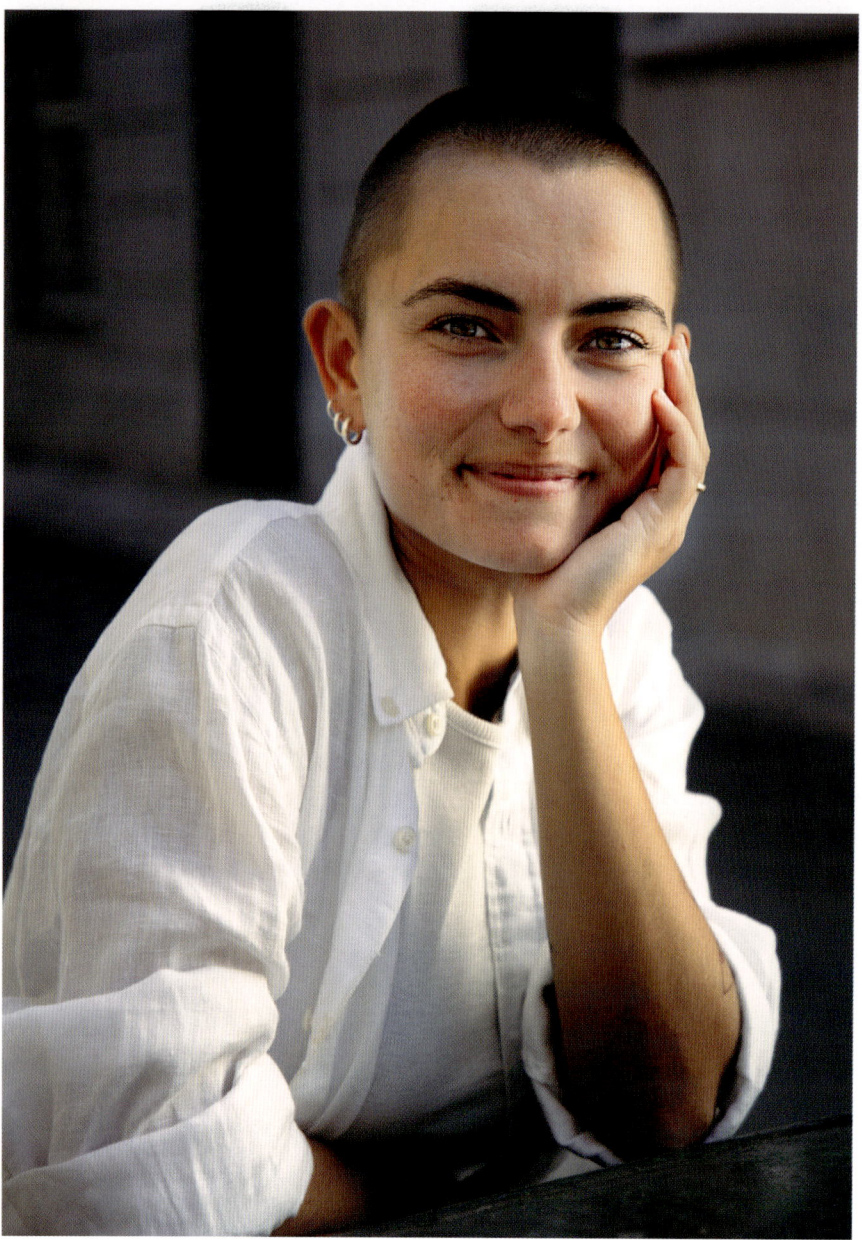

YANGON, MYANMAR *(Opposite)*

Yin Yin was coming from work when I noticed her on the streets of her city. I love to see Inês and Yin Yin on the same spread, as this is proof that women can be however they want to be.

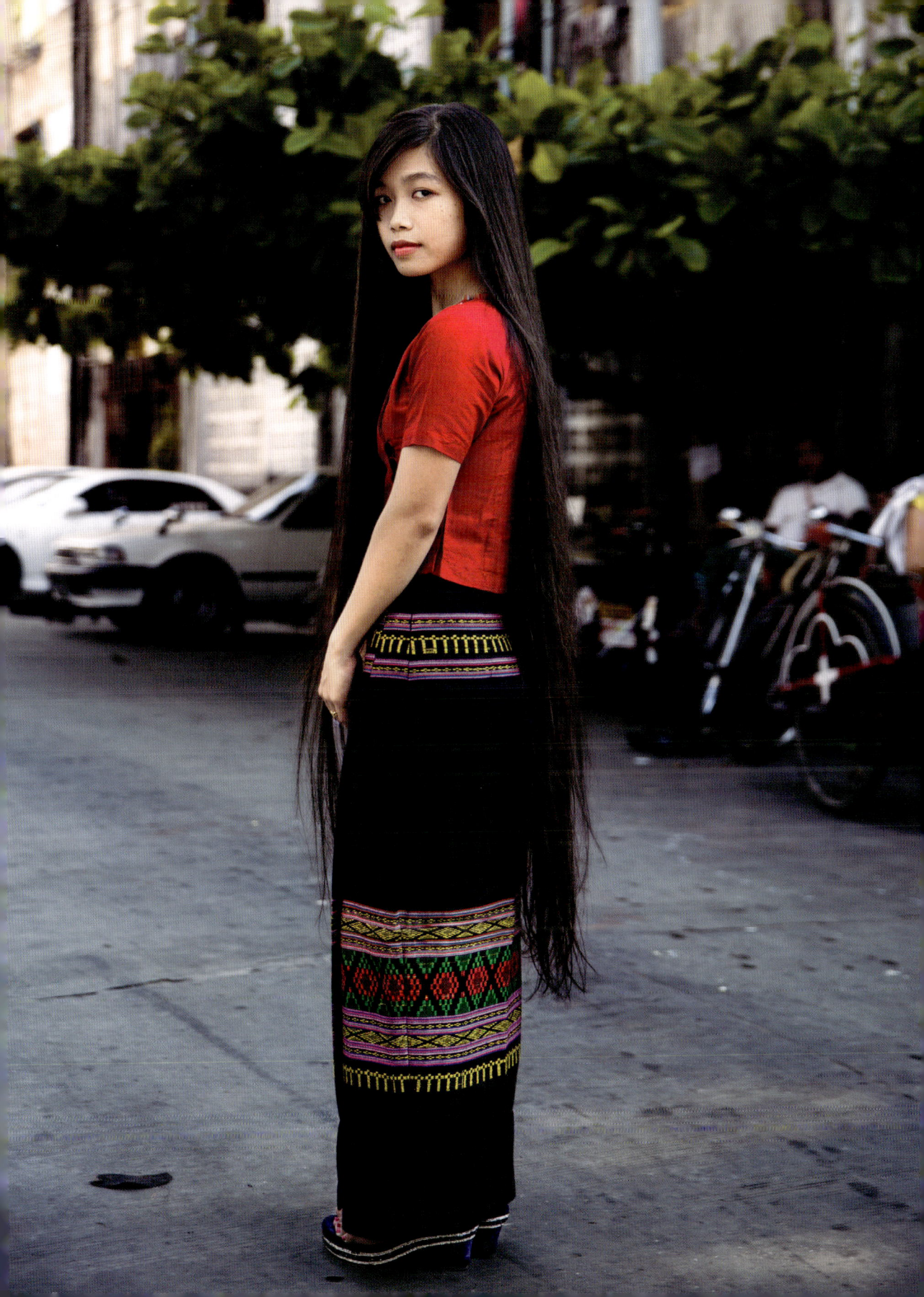

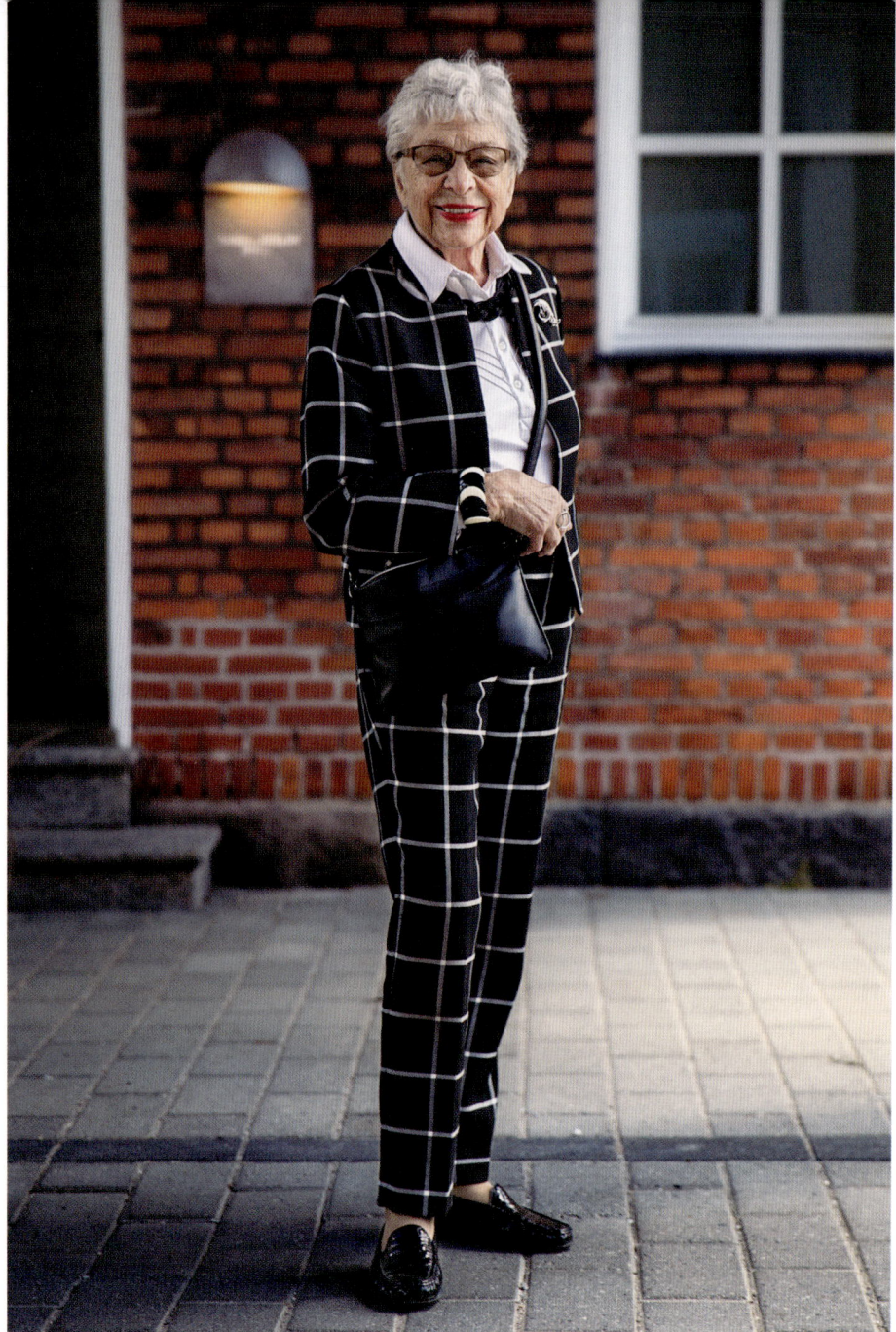

COPENHAGEN, DENMARK

Dressed in a charming outfit, this lady was hurrying through the streets of this picturesque city.

Alice is a physiotherapist. At eighty-four, she works with passion every day. She told me her patients would simply not want to work with another physiotherapist, so she doesn't plan to retire soon. When I met her, she was on the way to see a patient who is an auto mechanic.

"He fixes my car. I fix his back!"

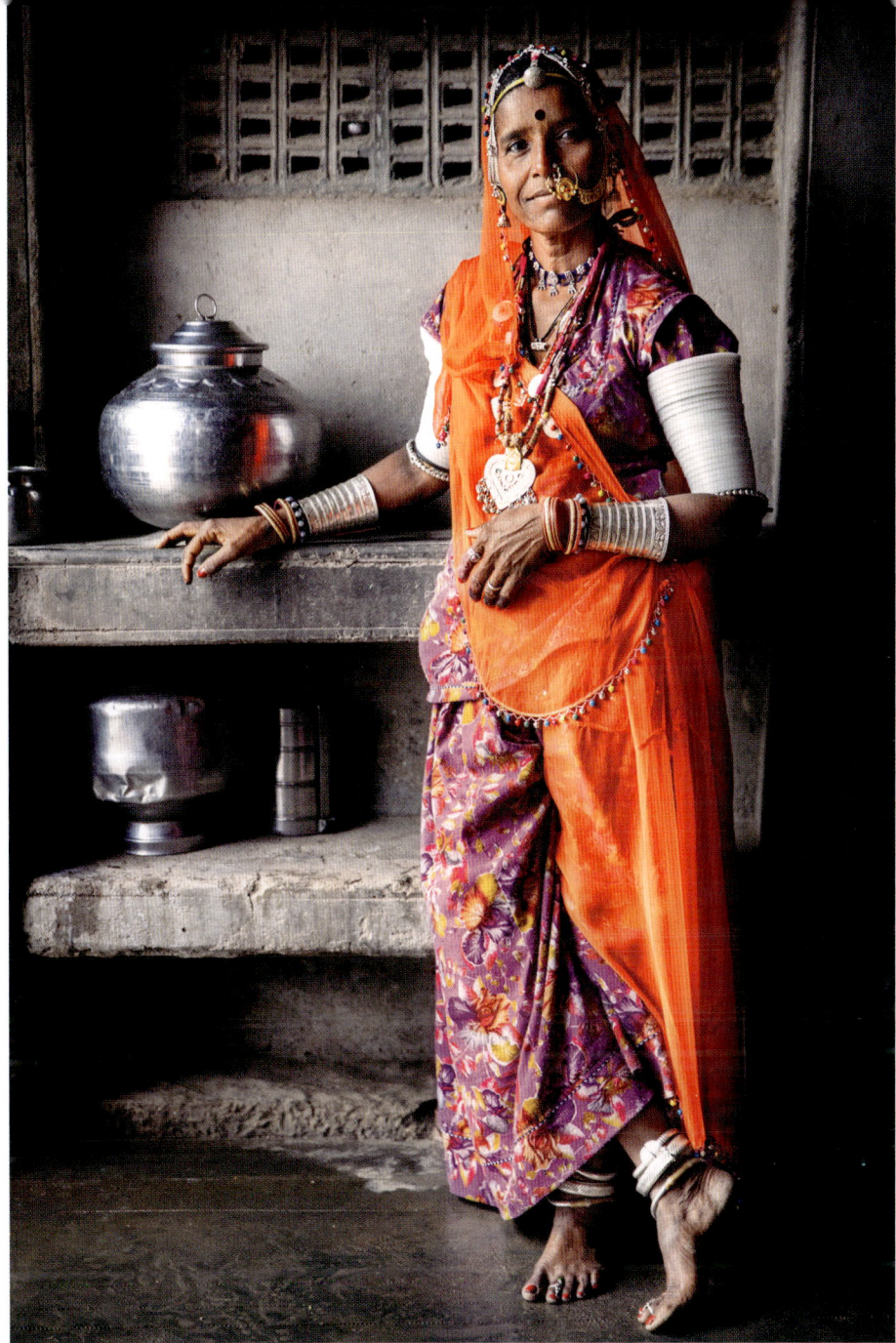

RAJASTHAN, INDIA

I photographed Gavri in her kitchen just after she finished cooking some chapati and a lentil curry. Looking at her spectacular outfit, you might think she was preparing for a celebration. But Gavri was not going outside that day

This is how most women in her region dress every day—even when they stay inside their homes.

COLOGNE, GERMANY

Vanessa Didam is a chimney sweep. She shared with me her vivid childhood memories of a chimney sweep visiting her house from time to time to clean the chimneys. His presence fascinated her, and his departure left behind a sense of security within the family. At the age of thirteen, Vanessa decided to become a chimney sweep, as well, and began learning the trade. She started to work in the field at the young age of sixteen.

Within her closely knit community, ancient traditions are still held dear. Vanessa's beautiful uniform not only provides fire protection but also serves as a representation of the ancient community to which she belongs. As I photographed Vanessa, people from the street approached her and asked for permission to touch the buttons on her clothing. According to local tradition, it brings good luck.

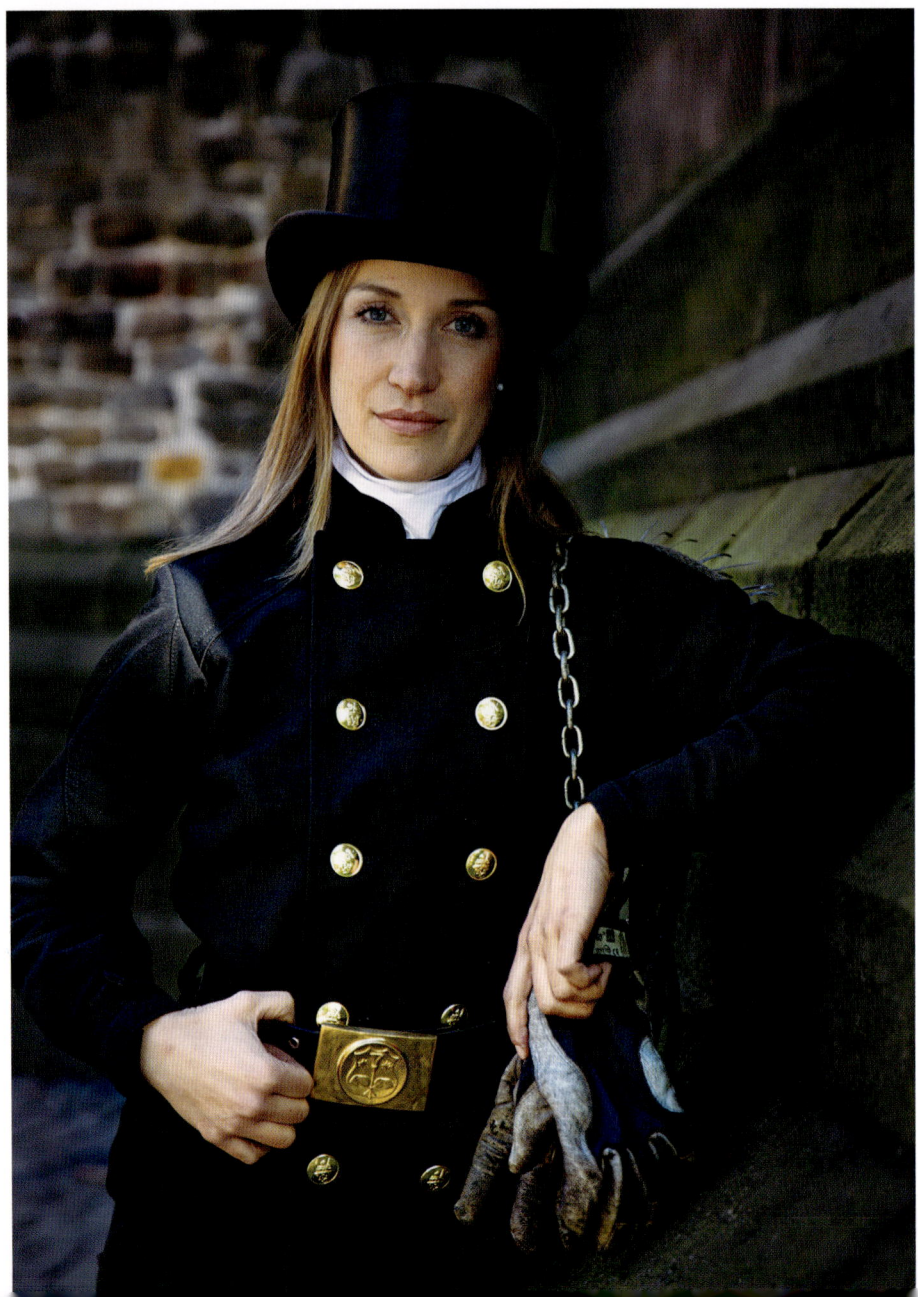

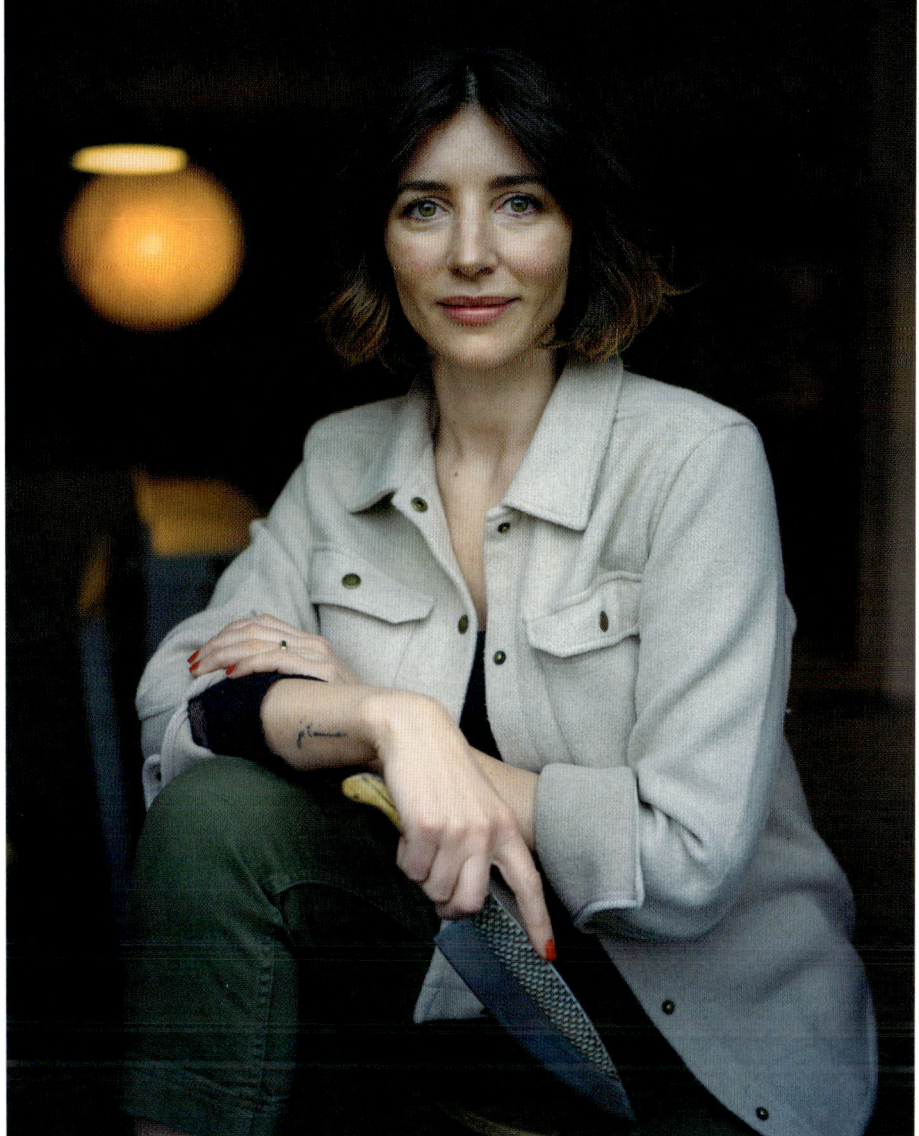

NEW YORK CITY, UNITED STATES

This beautiful knife, handmade by Chelsea, is a reflection of her captivating story. Growing up in rural Vermont, Chelsea Miller was homeschooled by her mother and life-schooled by her carpenter-blacksmith father. In this self-sustainable environment, she learned the value of natural resources from a young age.

Later, she moved to New York City, studied acting, and became a professional actor who performed on prestigious stages. When her father fell ill, Chelsea chose to return home and assist in his complex care during the last few years of his life.

During his illness, she spent a lot of time with her father, exploring his blacksmith workshop. Her father shared his knowledge from his crutches and wheelchair, and Chelsea discovered her new mission. Knife making became a place for self-discovery as well as an outlet for processing her father's illness and, ultimately, his death.

Today, Chelsea is back in New York City, sharing stories about beauty, exploration, and imperfection through each unique knife she creates.

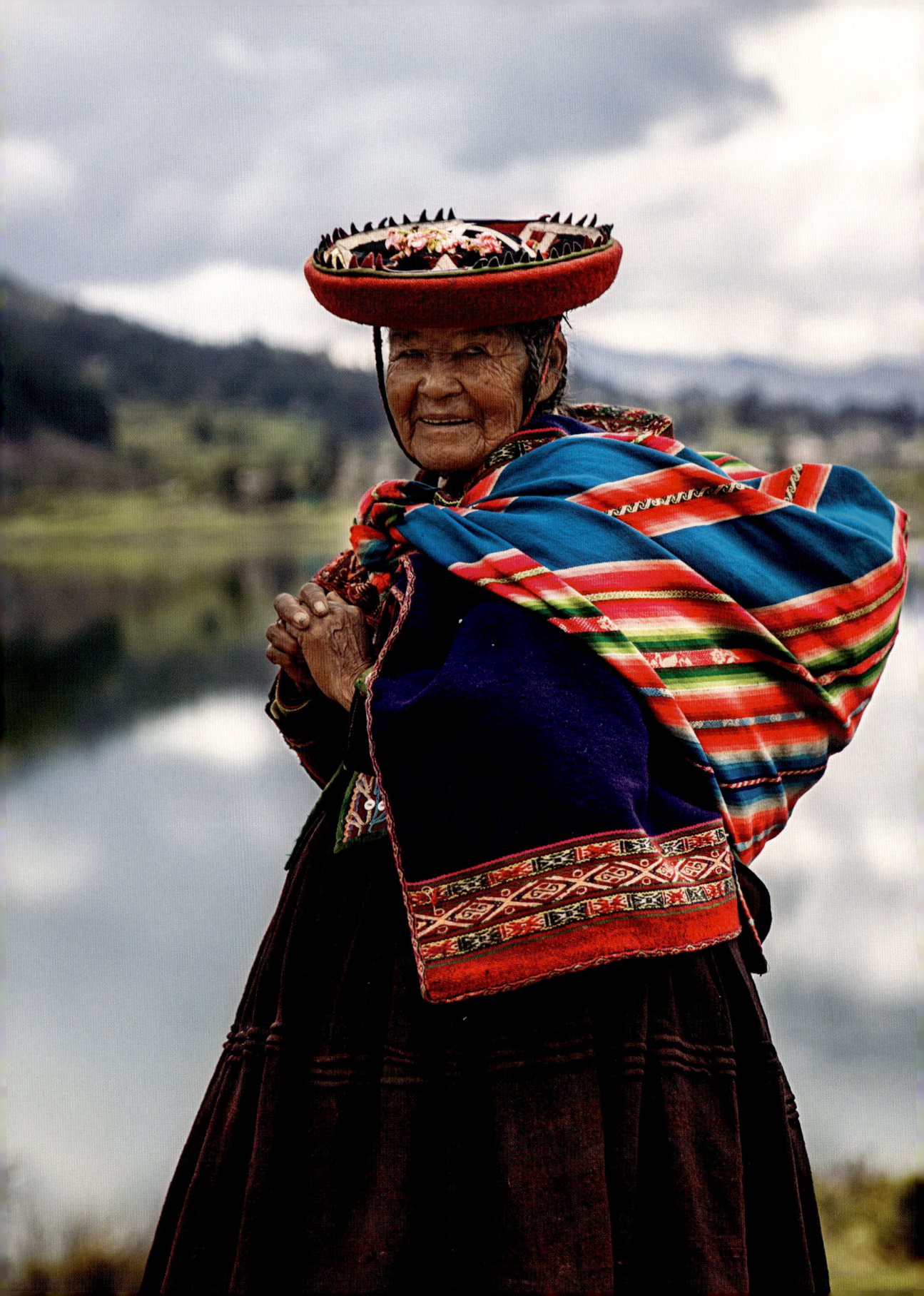

SACRED VALLEY, PERU

When I met her, Escolastica, eighty-eight years old, was walking home. She was joyful and energetic, full of humor and wisdom. She told me she has walked and walked all her life—on the steep slopes of this fascinating valley, between its isolated villages, and sometimes carrying heavy burdens exactly like her ancestors, the Incas.

In many places of the world, we go to the gym to stay in shape and buy tours to visit such breathtaking landscapes. But Escolastica has these for free. Without a doubt, life is very hard in this kind of place, but it comes with different kinds of rewards. And maybe this is the secret to Escolastica's bright and vivid spirit.

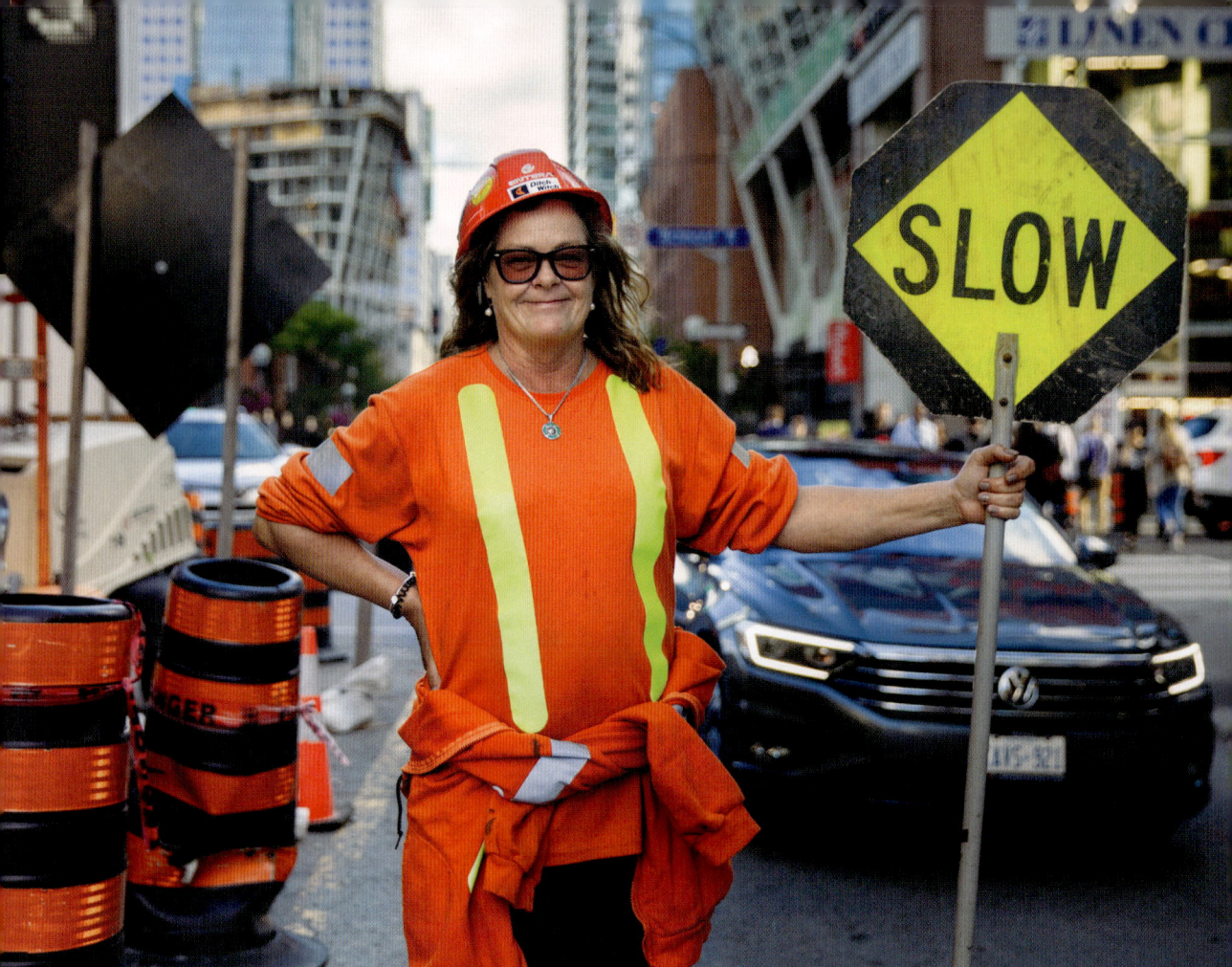

TORONTO, CANADA

When she was younger, Thea worked in an office at a bank, but she didn't like the sedentary lifestyle. For the past twenty years, she has been working in construction, and she loves it, because she is always outdoors, she gets to be physically active, and she enjoys the tangible results of her work. She is often the only woman on the team, but that has never bothered her.

LONDON, UNITED KINGDOM

How would you imagine a female stand-up comedian? Well, Fatiha El-Ghorri defies all stereotypes. Born in London to Moroccan parents forty-one years ago, Fatiha grew up in a family of thirteen siblings. Her life has been like a roller coaster, with many ups and downs.

She experienced the loss of her father at the age of six, went through two divorces, and even spent some time living in homeless shelters. However, she always overcame the challenges. After her second divorce, Fatiha searched for a way to start a new life. By chance, she found a course teaching the basics of comedy writing and performance. That course changed her life.

Today, she is a respected comedian who earns a living through her shows. Her sketches deal with everything from marriage and divorce to Islamophobia. With each performance, Fatiha defies misconceptions—proving that one can be both a proud Muslim woman and a successful stand-up comedian.

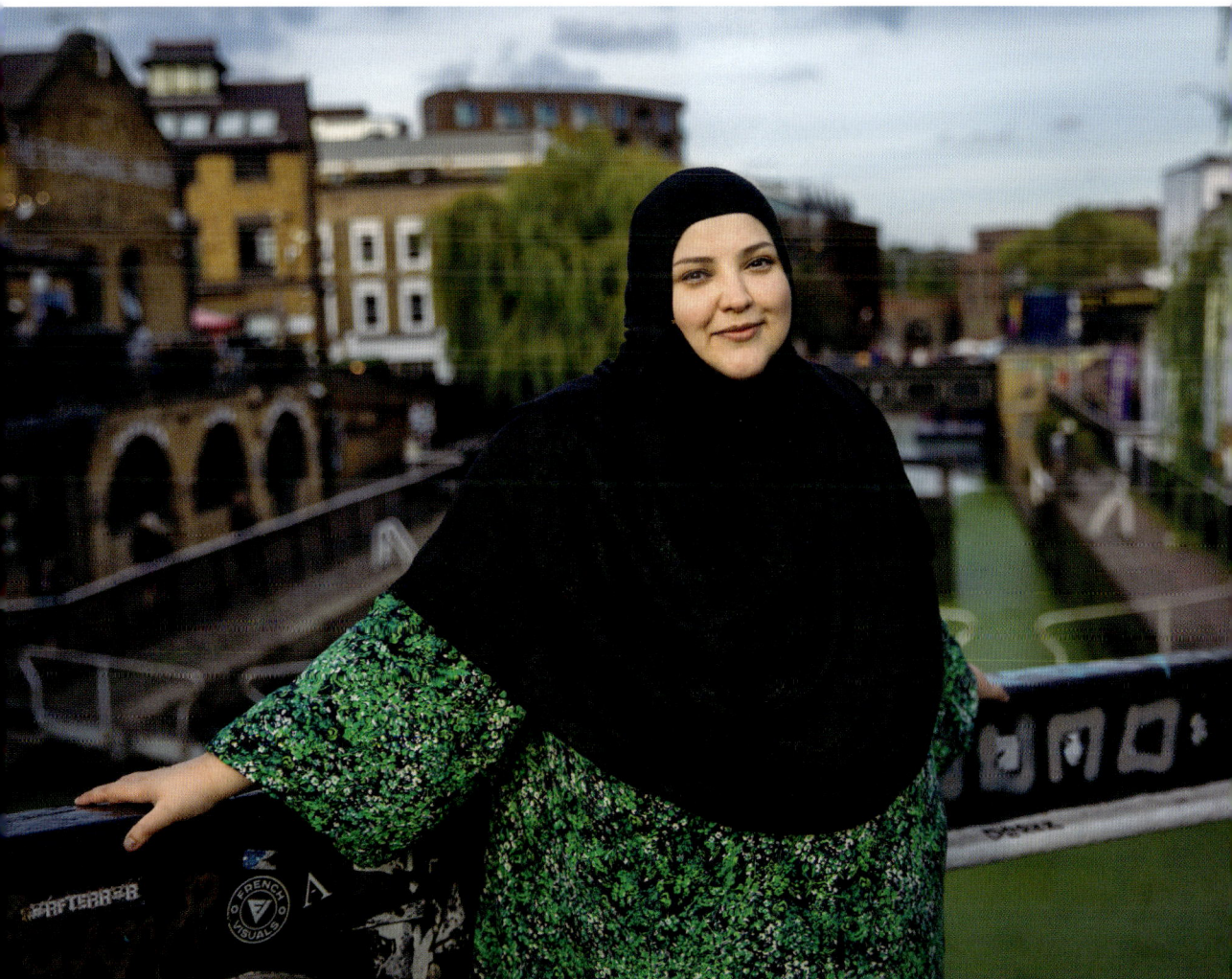

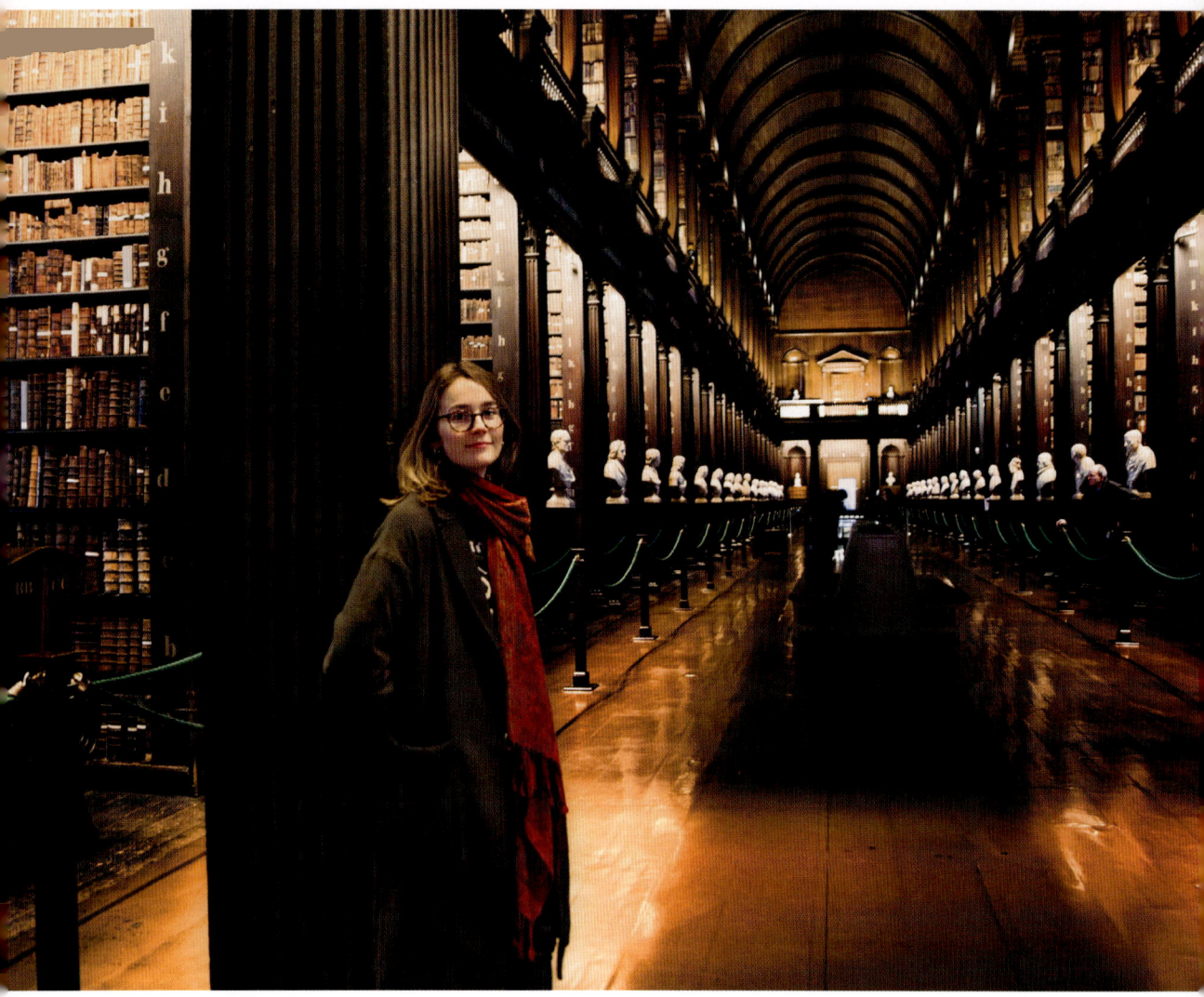

DUBLIN, IRELAND

Lyndsay is pursuing environmental studies at Trinity College Dublin. The college library is renowned as one of the most impressive in the world, and that's where I photographed her.

While exploring this remarkable place, I found myself surrounded by sculptures of great philosophers, writers, and other personalities. However, what struck me was that all these busts inside the library depict men.

For centuries, women had fewer opportunities than men in academic fields. Although there is still significant inequality worldwide, things are changing. People like Lyndsay, who recently won a prestigious global award in the earth and environmental science category, are challenging the old norms. A former provost of this prestigious college once said, "Over my dead body will women enter this college." Today, about 60 percent of the students here are women.

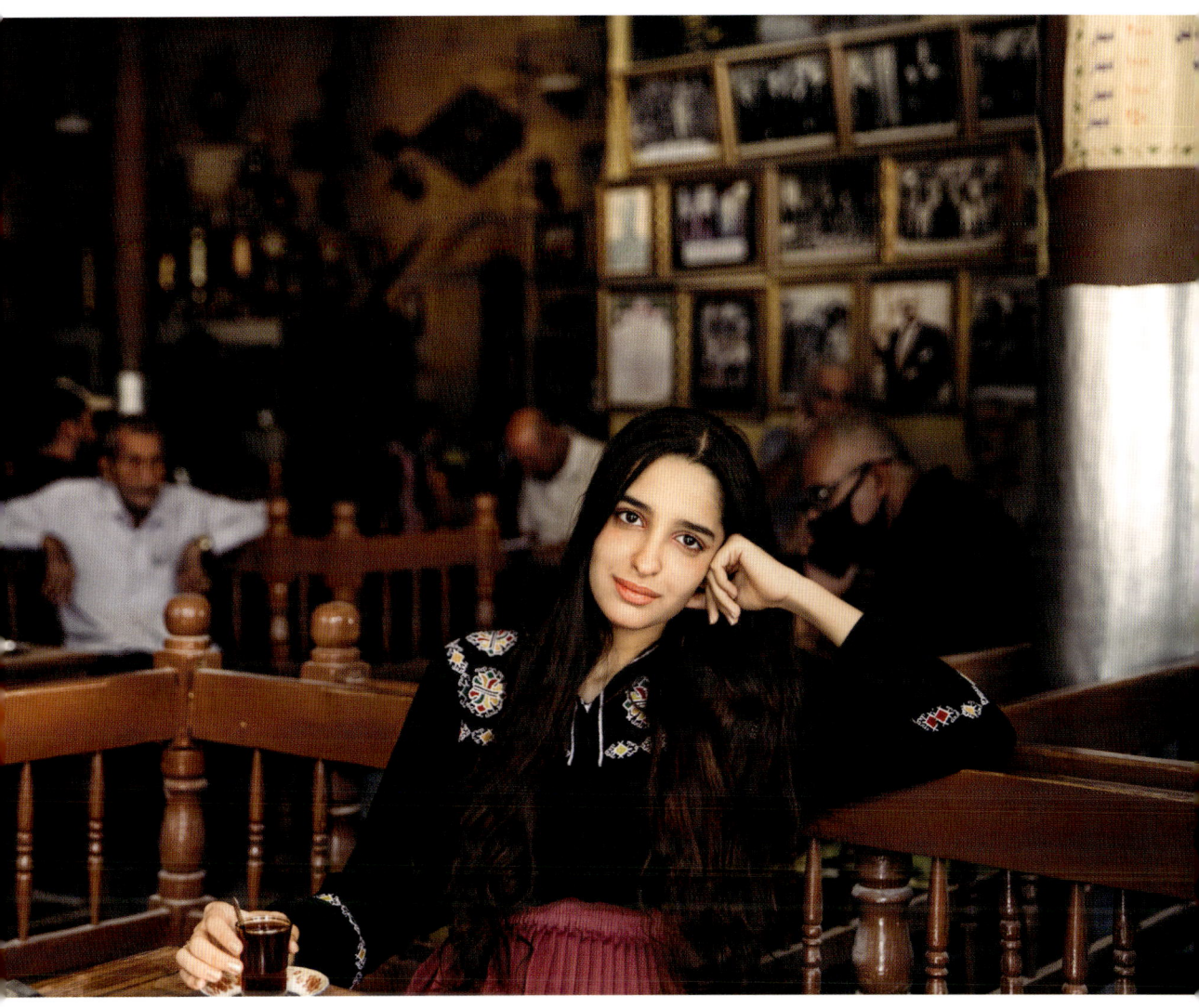

BAGHDAD, IRAQ

You will see only men in most coffee shops around Baghdad. But not in this coffeehouse, which is a symbol of freedom. Here, women like Mariam can come and relax with tea or coffee without the fear of being looked upon with misconceptions.

Shabandar Café, which has been open for more than one hundred years, is an iconic place for artists and intellectuals. This is probably the reason why the place was destroyed in a car bomb attack in 2007. But the café rose from its own ashes, continuing to be a symbol of freedom with young people like Mariam carrying on its heritage.

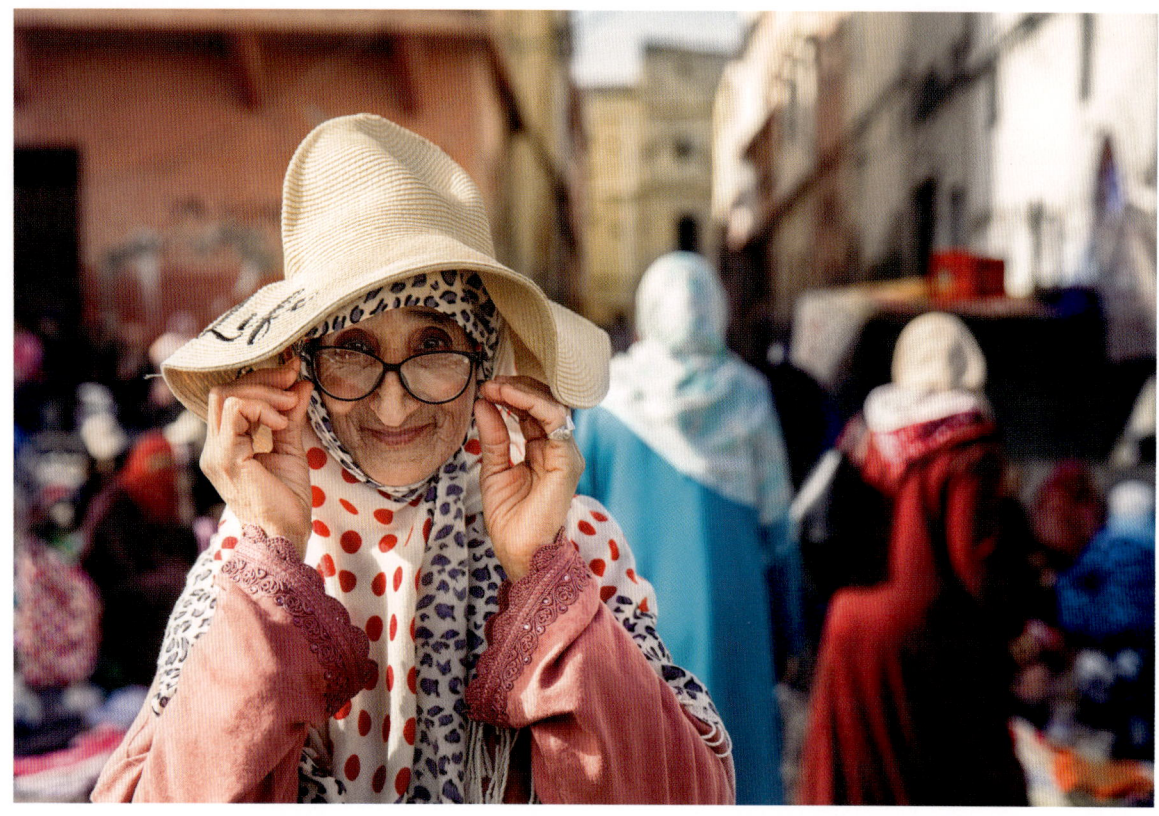

CASABLANCA, MOROCCO (Above)

I met this lovely lady in a crowded bazaar, where she was buying food, accompanied by her granddaughter.

I saw wisdom and positivity in her eyes and immediately wanted to know her life story. Zahra doesn't know her age because the notions of a birth certificate or a birth anniversary didn't exist in her region when she was growing up. She is the mother of seven children—all born at home.

For me, the birth of my only child in a modern maternity hospital seemed like the biggest challenge of my life. So, to me, women like Zahra are true heroines.

TOKYO, JAPAN (Opposite)

Emiko was on her way to a concert hall with her husband when I noticed her.

"He invited me to a Beethoven concerto and then to dinner."

Love was in the air—that's for sure—and without it, I couldn't have taken this picture. Initially, Emiko refused to be photographed, saying she's old and not beautiful, but her husband convinced her that's not true at all. And, indeed, Emiko is beautiful. Most importantly, Emiko is loved.

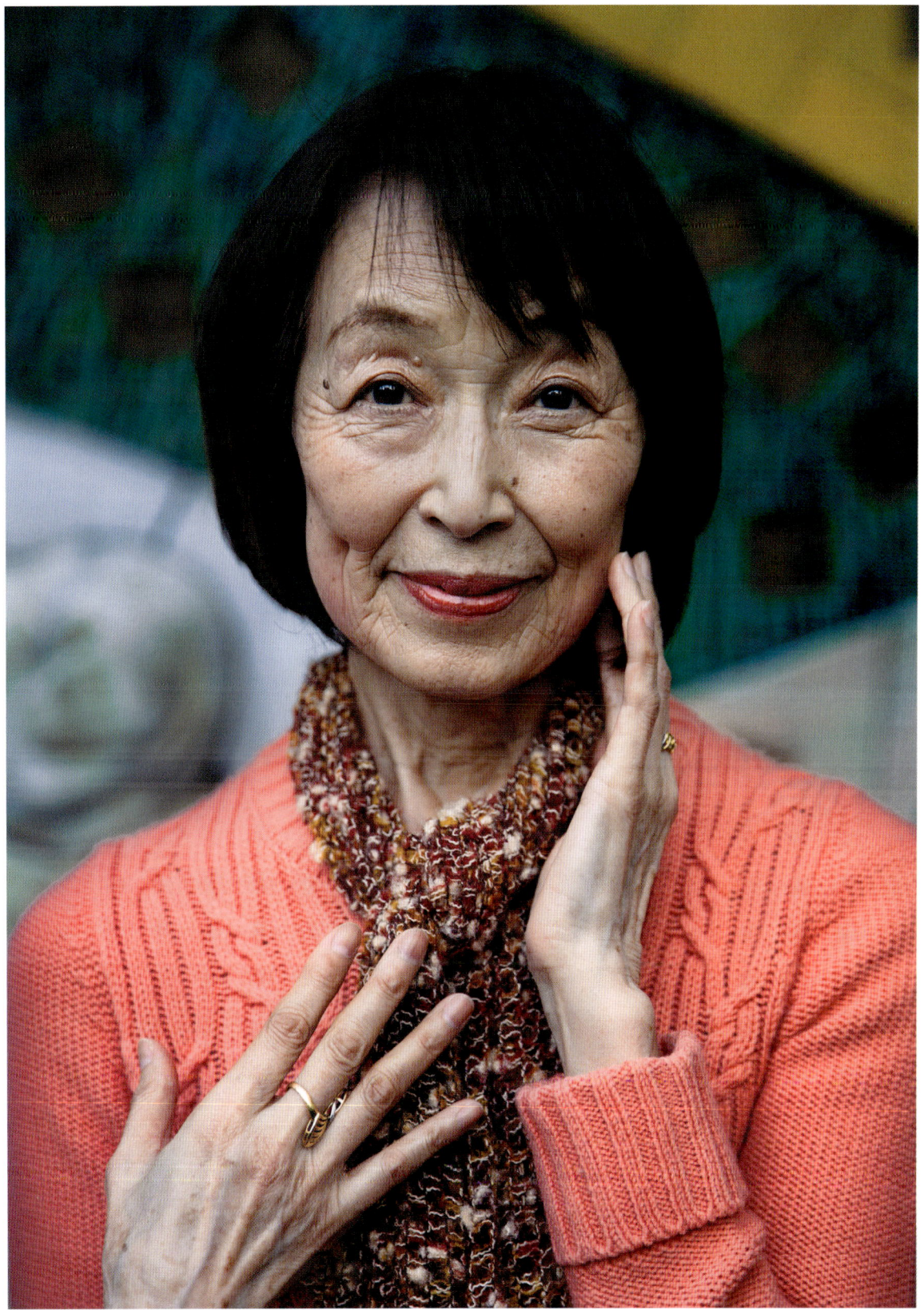

JEDDAH, SAUDI ARABIA

Nujood Alotaibi is a painter. From the beginning, she's been attracted to the visual side of life. Perhaps it's because, in childhood, she suffered from a hearing disability and had to learn how to lip-read.

Today, she wears hearing aids in both ears, and that makes her life much easier. She feels fortunate and wants to give back to those in need. That's why, besides painting, she also works with children who have learning disabilities. She knows from her own experience what they need most.

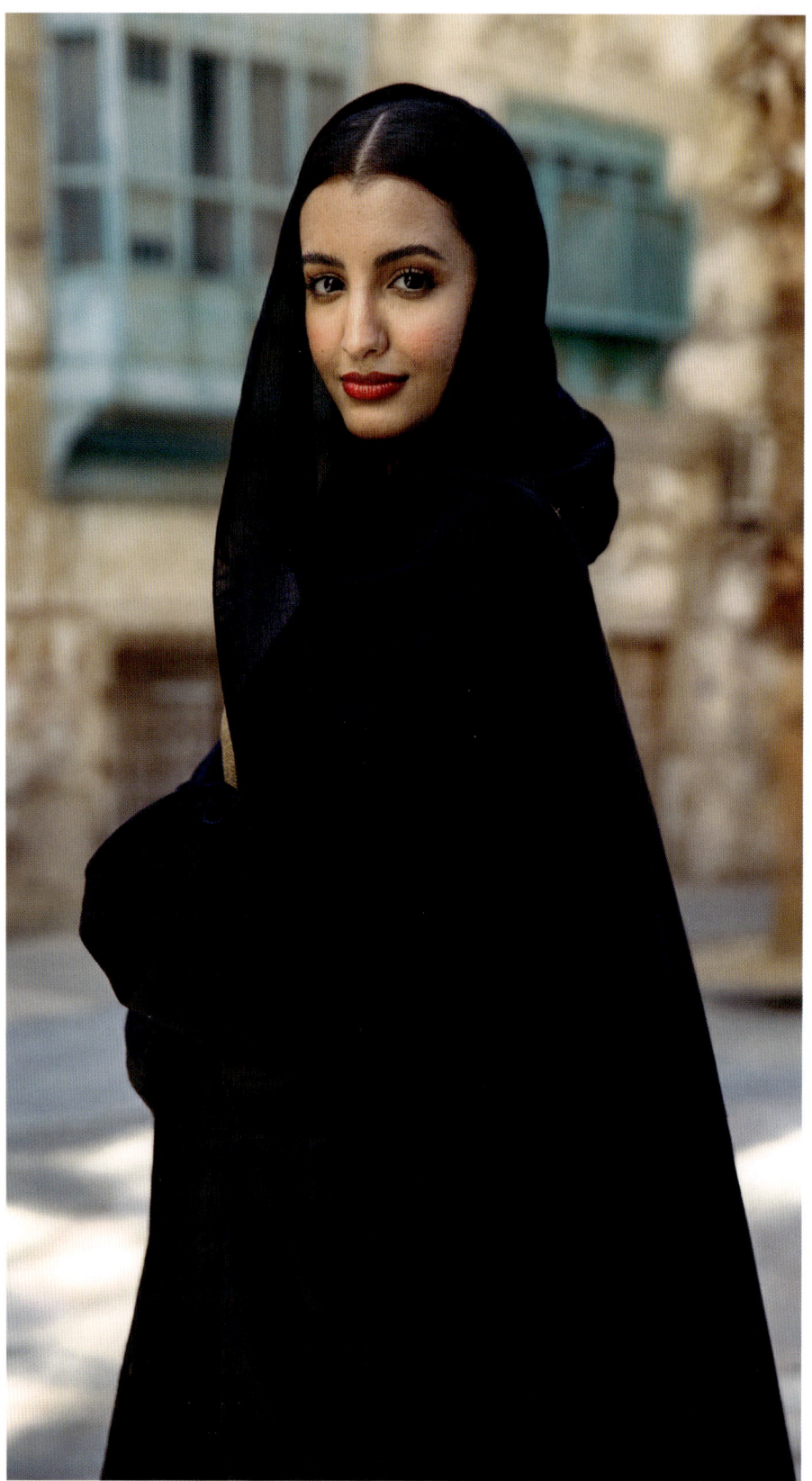

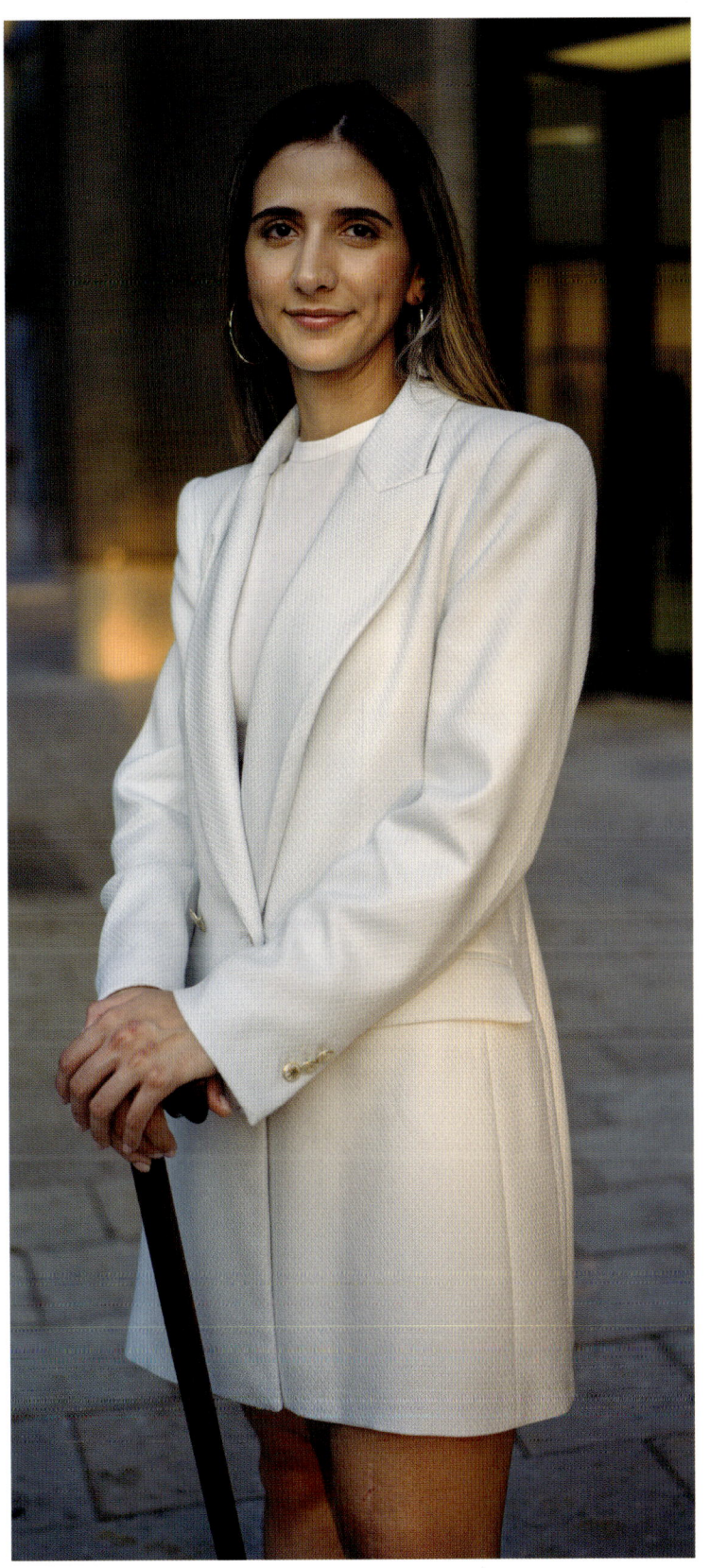

MIAMI, UNITED STATES

Paula Carozzo was born in Venezuela, and when she was five years old, she was admitted to the hospital to have surgery to remove her tonsils. What is normally a simple procedure transformed into a terrible event for Paula. She came out of surgery with a nontraumatic brain injury that would cause a disability for the rest of her life. Paula spent a few weeks in an induced coma. When she woke up, she couldn't move her hands or feet.

Paula's parents desperately searched for an answer all over Venezuela but couldn't find a solution. They decided to move to the United States in search of treatment. After many surgeries, Paula regained the use of her arms, but her gait was still affected.

During her teenage years, Paula faced comments like, "What happened to you?" and "Look, Paula doesn't walk very well," but she refused to let these negative remarks define her.

Step by step, she learned to open herself up to acceptance and to love herself as she is.

As a part of her self-discovery journey, Paula began sharing her daily experiences with disability on a blog and soon created a beautiful community of people who share similar lives. That's how Paula found her mission and became a disability activist who advocates for equity. Today, she also models and gives speeches about her experience.

Paula's journey with a cane is a manifesto for authenticity and real beauty. In her daily life, she uses different colorful canes that not only provide support but also make a statement about who she is. Looking back, she thinks thirteen-year-old Paula would be so honored to see where she is today.

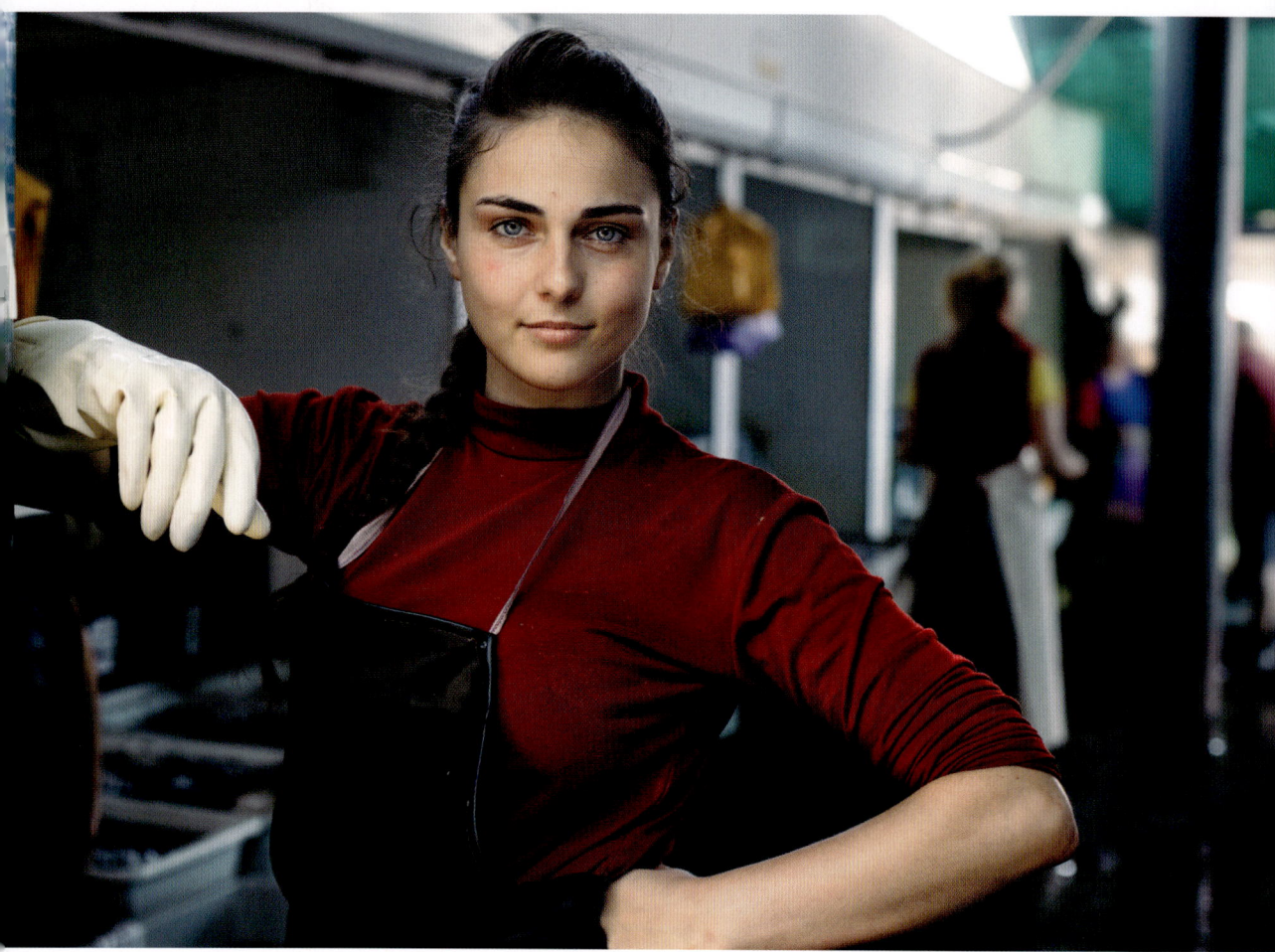

CHIȘINĂU, MOLDOVA

I noticed Mihaela in this city's biggest market. She started helping her parents with their small fish stall when she was six. Now this is her full-time day job.

Six days per week, she wakes up at three in the morning, opens the stall at five in the morning, and closes it fourteen hours later, at seven in the evening.

It's exhausting work, which also involves carrying heavy boxes in addition to selling to customers all day. But Mihaela is happy to be her own boss, have a decent income, and always be surrounded by other sellers who've become her good friends.

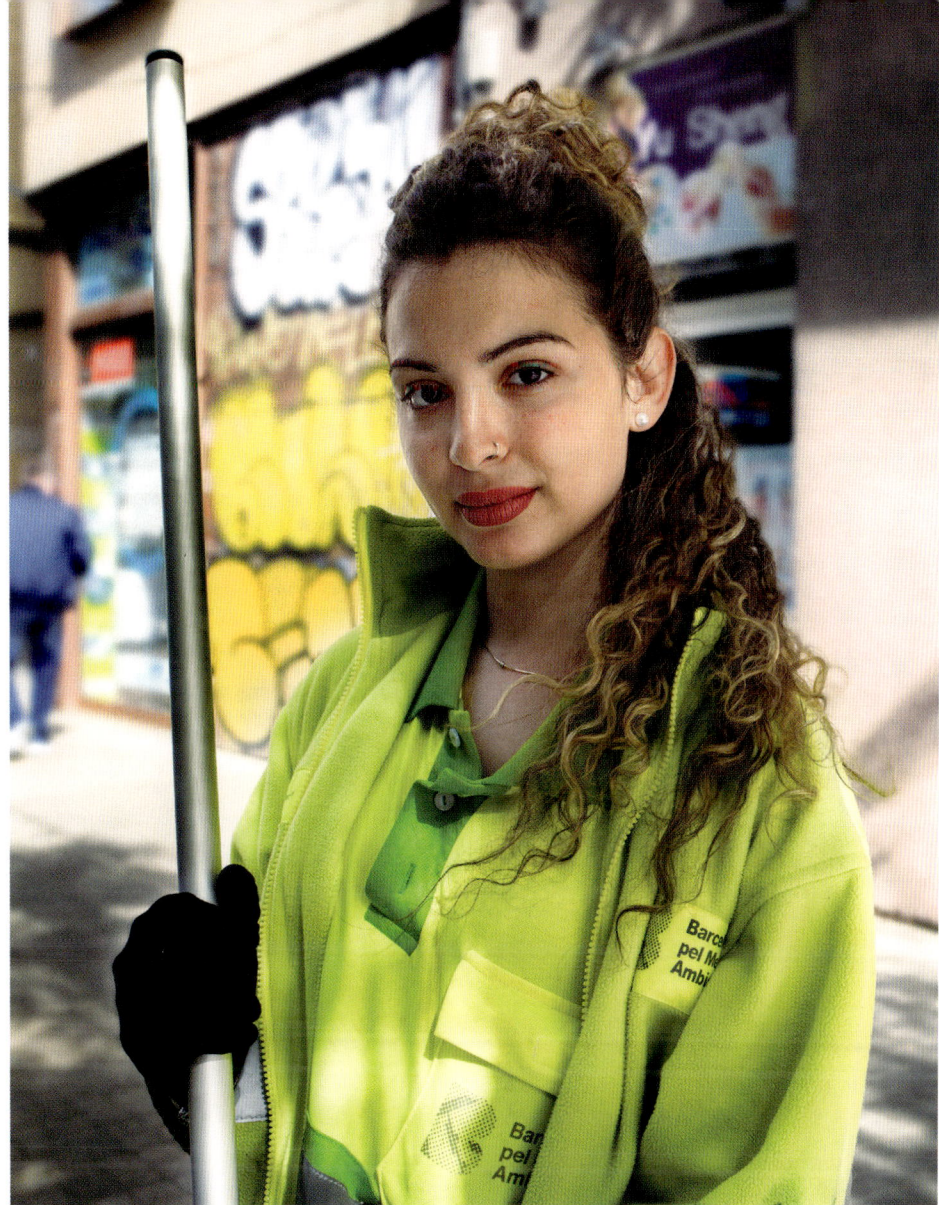

BARCELONA, SPAIN

Juncal was working hard when I noticed her. The life of this young street sweeper was never easy.

She's originally from the Basque Country, an autonomous community in northern Spain. When she was a child, her mother abandoned her, and her father died of cancer. After these terrible events, Juncal moved to Barcelona, where she was raised by an aunt.

She started this job two years ago, when she was only nineteen. While many other youngsters continue to live with their parents at this age, Juncal told me she is proud that she's financially independent and living on her own.

In this photo, it seems to me that Juncal resembles a heroine from a Japanese manga story. And I think people like her—who, despite all painful moments in their childhood, manage to grow up so beautifully—are indeed heroes.

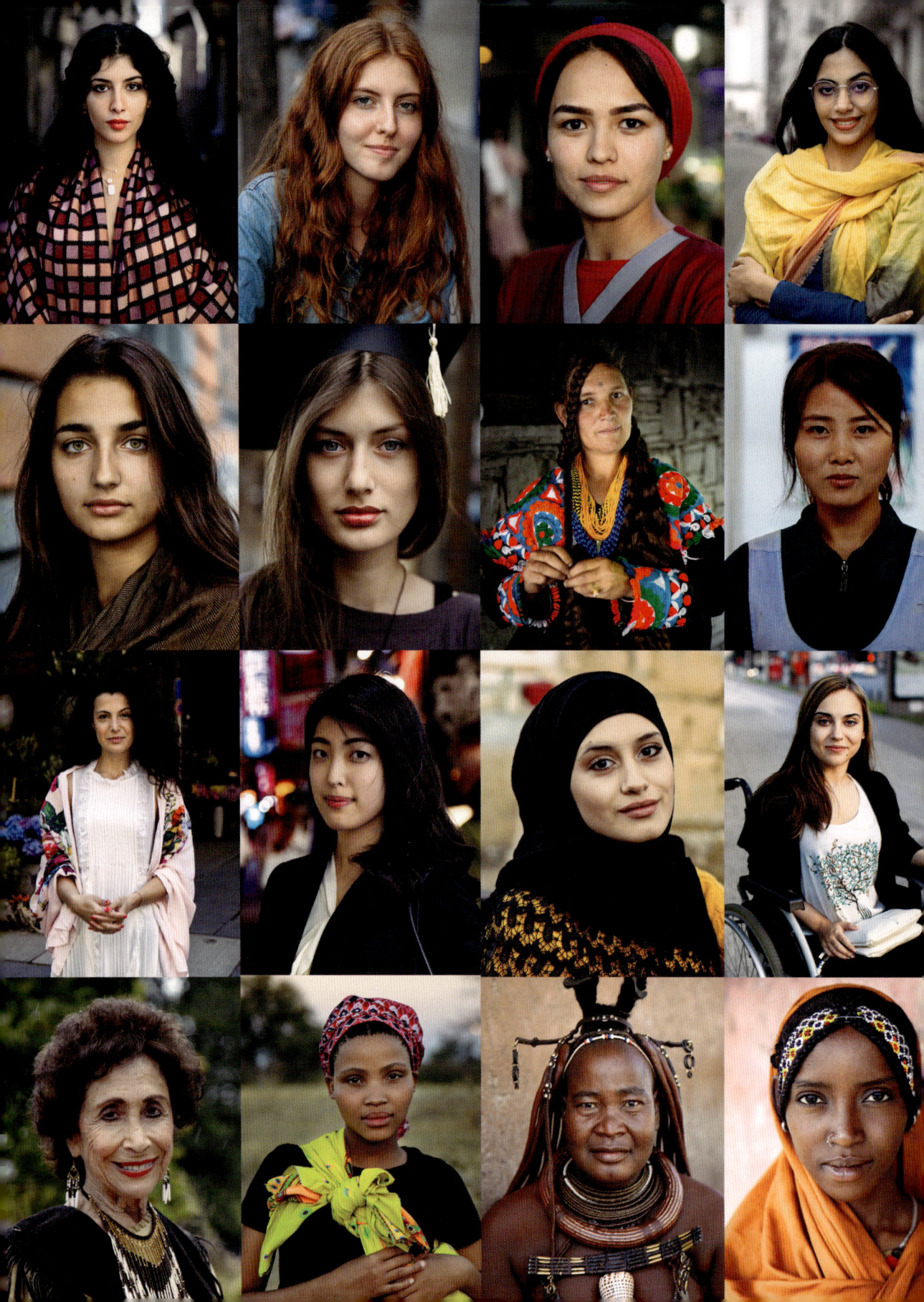

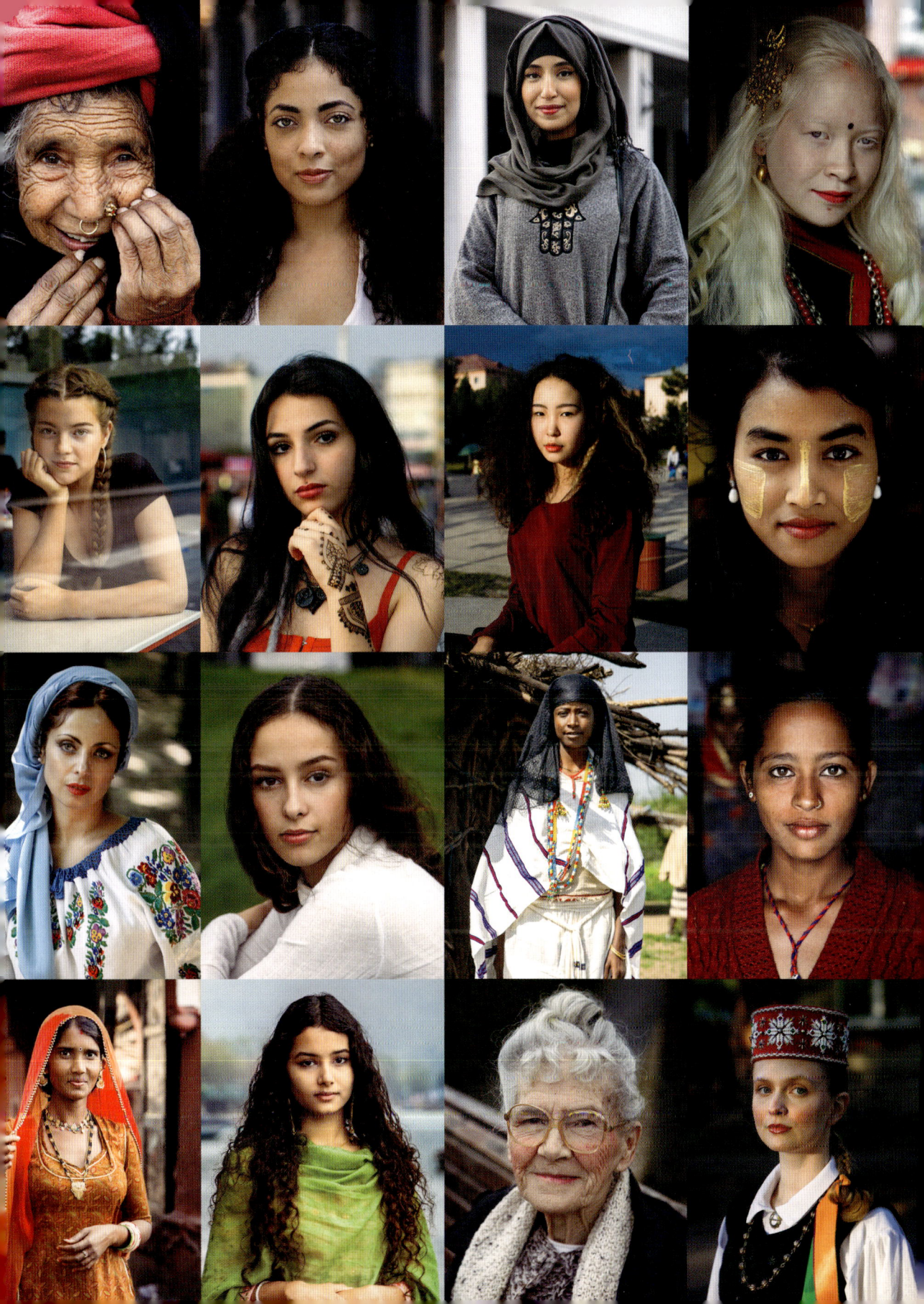

FREEDOM

It's 2021, and I find myself in Kabul, the capital of Afghanistan, amid a tense atmosphere. The American troops have commenced their withdrawal. There are widespread rumors that the city will soon fall to the Taliban. The Taliban already hold a significant part of the country, and today I must cross through some of their territory. My desire is to reach a small town to the north, but getting there will prove to be a formidable challenge. I intend to photograph some girls who practice sports in this small town, as it is an incredible example of resilience and defiance in Afghanistan.

To facilitate our journey, my guide provides me with a burqa to wear. For those unfamiliar, a burqa is a garment worn by many Afghan women that covers the entire body, including the face. This is the first time I'm wearing a burqa. I can only glimpse the outside world through a few tiny holes.

My guide advises me that if we encounter Taliban forces along the way, I must keep my face covered and pretend to be mute. Countless thoughts race through my mind, reflecting on the shooting of Malala Yousafzai by the Taliban for merely advocating for education.

Thankfully, we encounter no Taliban members during our journey. Days later, I return home to Europe, a place of safety and comfort. However, a couple of weeks later, news arrives that the entire country of Afghanistan has fallen under the control of the Taliban. The women who previously tasted glimpses of freedom are now left with nothing. They are denied the right to work and to pursue education.

If you are reading these lines, then it likely means you are enjoying far greater freedom than any woman living in Afghanistan. Yes, even in the most progressive nations, significant gender disparities persist. But, nevertheless, most women today—and people in general—experience greater freedom than ever before.

Yet, far too often, we take our freedom for granted. It's there until one day it disappears—even without constraints around us like the ones in Afghanistan. We sometimes unknowingly surrender our freedom simply because it seems more convenient or comfortable in the moment.

Freedom for me is the ability to chase a dream, to speak truth despite the fear, to choose a path even if it's unconventional or, on the contrary, totally conventional.

For me, freedom means I can travel the world and fulfill my dream of photographing women. For each woman I encountered, freedom held a distinct meaning. What does freedom mean to you?

Your journey might lead you to Everest, the highest peak on Earth, or to a cozy home where you live a simple life with an ordinary job and seek to share cherished moments with your family. What I learned from all the women I've met is that there are thousands of ways to live your freedom. It's not the magnitude of your dream that matters—it's being true to yourself and following your heart that matters. That, ultimately, is freedom.

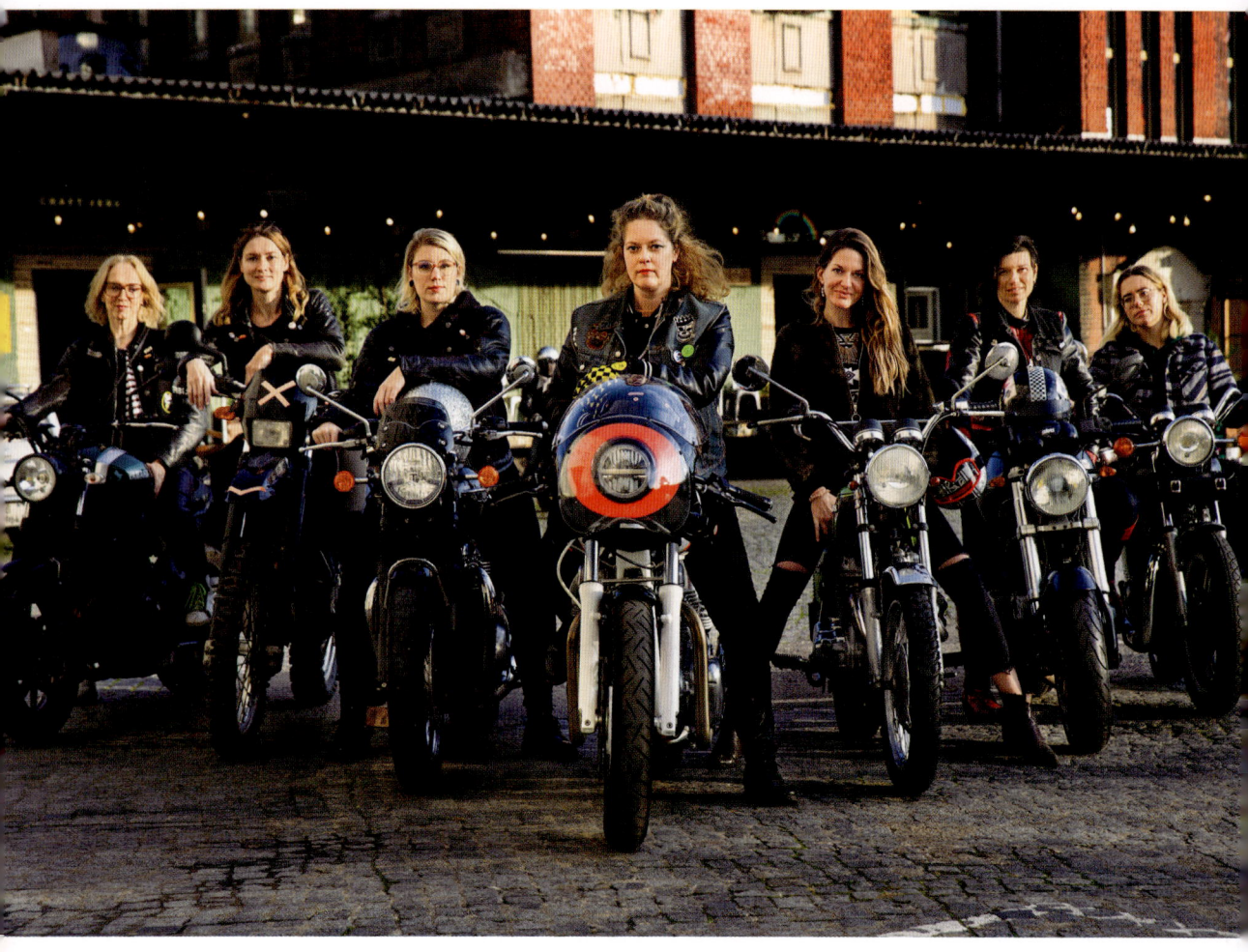

BERLIN, GERMANY

Meet the Curves, an all-female motorcycle group embracing the true meaning of freedom and shattering expectations in a field dominated by men.

Despite their growing size and popularity, the group remains tightly knit and resembles a family. Their love for motorcycles extends beyond riding—they are all passionate about mechanics, and some of them are building bikes and running mechanical workshops. For the Curves, no roads are impossible.

NEW YORK CITY, UNITED STATES

For more than two decades, Judaline Cassidy has worked as a plumber, and she loves every bit of her profession. She decided to inspire more women and girls to become skilled professionals. She gave public speeches about it, and a few years ago, she started a project called Tools & Tiaras to expose and mentor young girls and women about the trades.

She knows from her own experience the challenges women face when entering a male-dominated field, but she wants to break the barriers and reshape the way trades are perceived.

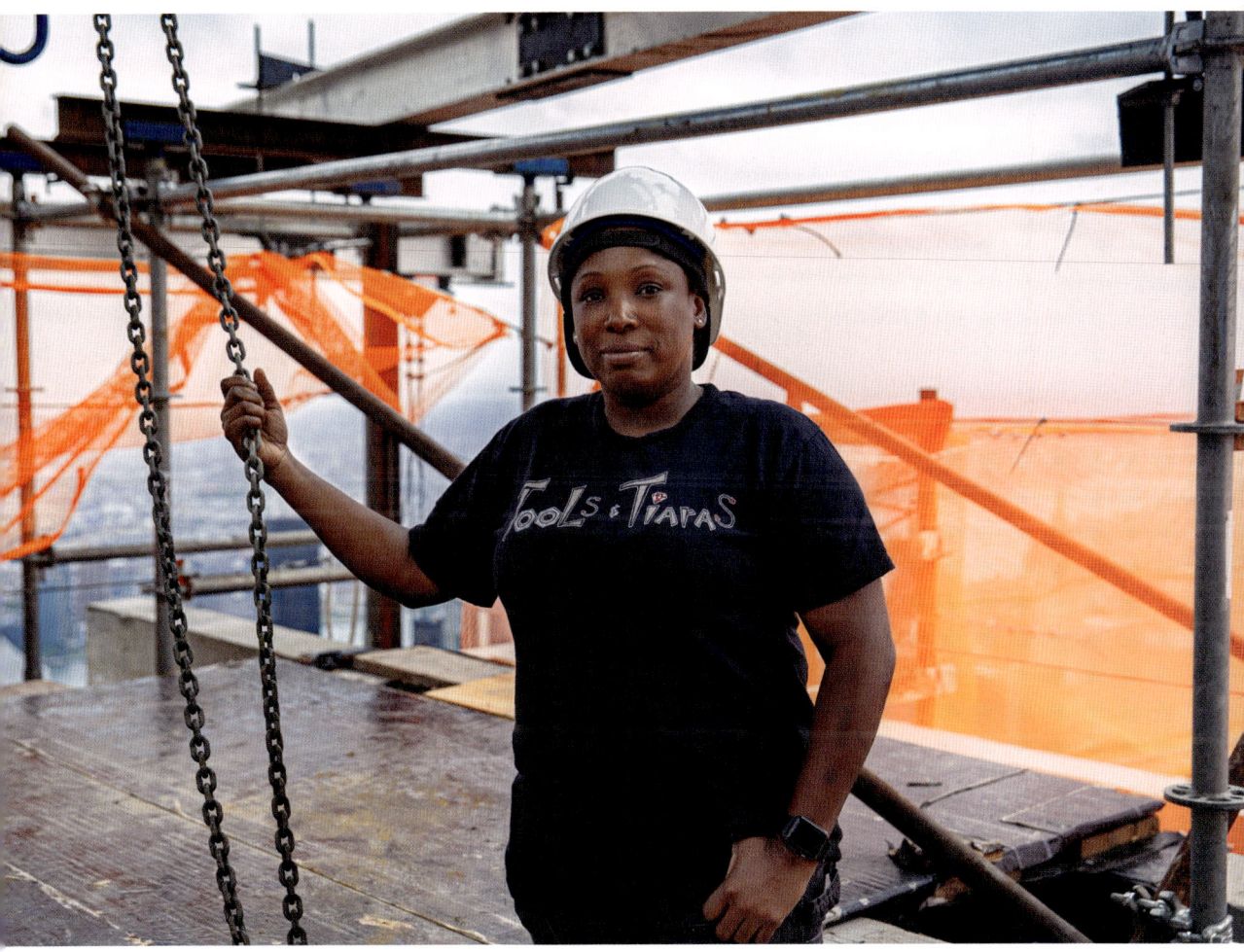

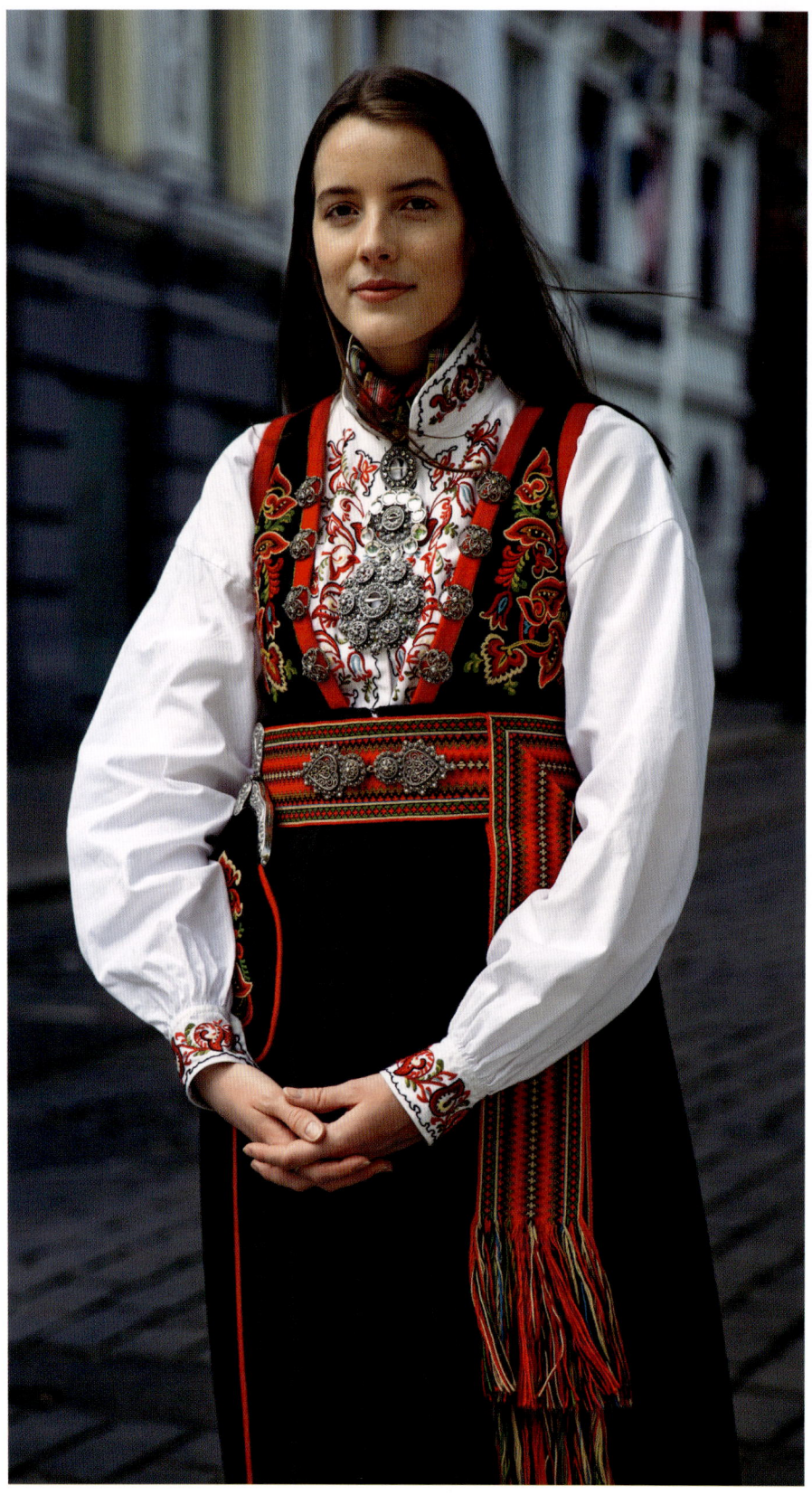

OSLO, NORWAY

Line wears her *bunad*, a sophisticated Norwegian folk costume, every year on Norway's national day. On this special day, as you walk the streets of Oslo, you'll find thousands of women wearing different kinds of *bunads*. The *bunad* often showcases handwoven fabrics and intricate embroidery. It is typically passed down from mothers and grandmothers.

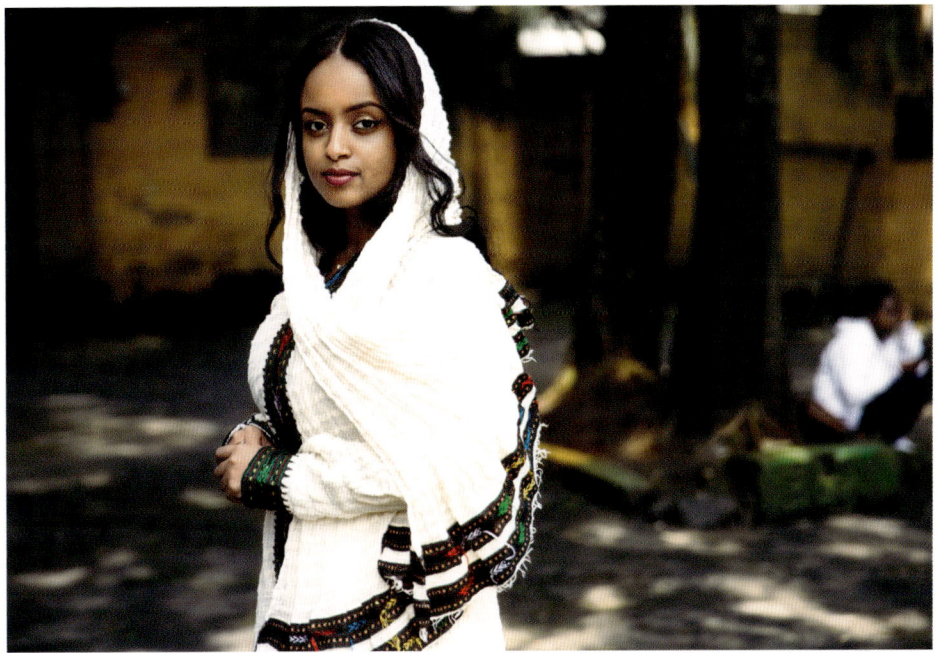

ADDIS ABABA, ETHIOPIA

On special occasions, Ruby proudly wears her traditional Ethiopian attire, called *habesha kemis*. This long dress is made from a thin white fabric called *shema*, which is handwoven from cotton. It's beautiful and delicate and keeps the body cool in this hot climate.

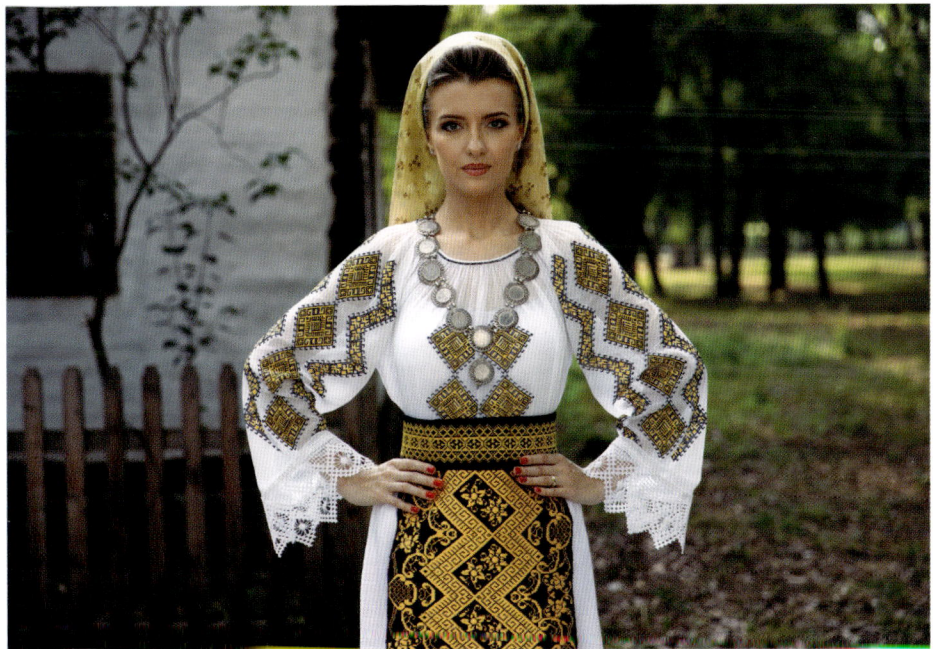

TIMIȘOARA, ROMANIA

Doriana is a singer. She fell in love with traditional music during her childhood, when she spent time vacationing at her grandparents' home in a traditional village.

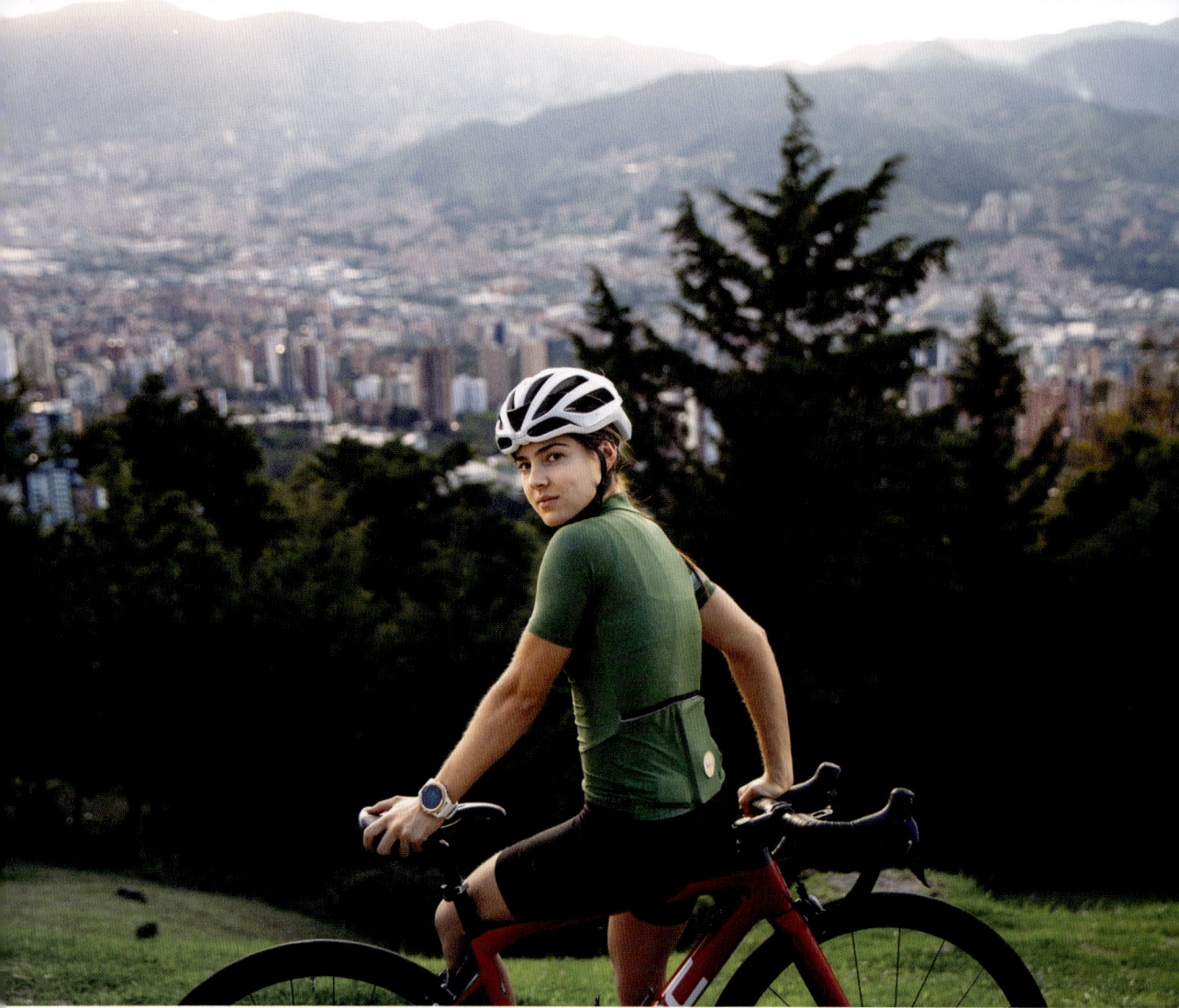

MEDELLÍN, COLOMBIA

Colombia gave the world some of the greatest cyclists. With such amazing and diverse landscapes, it's no wonder that so many Colombians are in love with cycling.

I photographed Cristina Franco next to Las Palmas Summit, a spectacular spot with a splendid view two thousand five hundred meters above Medellín, the country's second-biggest city.

You must ride through a hard nine-mile climb to get here by bicycle. For Cristina, it's no big deal now, but the first time she did it remains one of her most intense memories.

As a teenager, she dreamed of becoming a professional cyclist, but an accident changed her plans. A car hit her while cycling—her collarbone was broken, she suffered difficult surgeries, and she endured months of recovery.

Today, she is a semipro cyclist, and cycling is still her life. She sometimes goes to competitions, she leads cycling tours, and she also creates beautiful outfits for cyclists under her own brand.

While climbing, there are always more paths to the peak. You just have to find the one that suits you best.

MEXICO CITY, MEXICO

Escaramuza charra is Mexico's only female equestrian event. Teams ride horses in choreographed movements accompanied by music. It's a sport but also an art. It's traditional but still very popular in the modern world.

Celine has practiced the artistic sport since she was little. For fifteen years, she has been riding Golden, her beloved horse. She feels that they are in a perfect symbiosis, and this really makes a difference in a sport defined by details.

Dressing for a competition takes hours, and there are strict guidelines for all the costumes, which are inspired by female soldiers who fought in the Mexican Revolution. All embroidered details are sewn by hand, and the sombreros have a leather strap that sits under the chin.

Celine and all the other Mexican women who practice this unique sport prove that strength and elegance can go hand in hand.

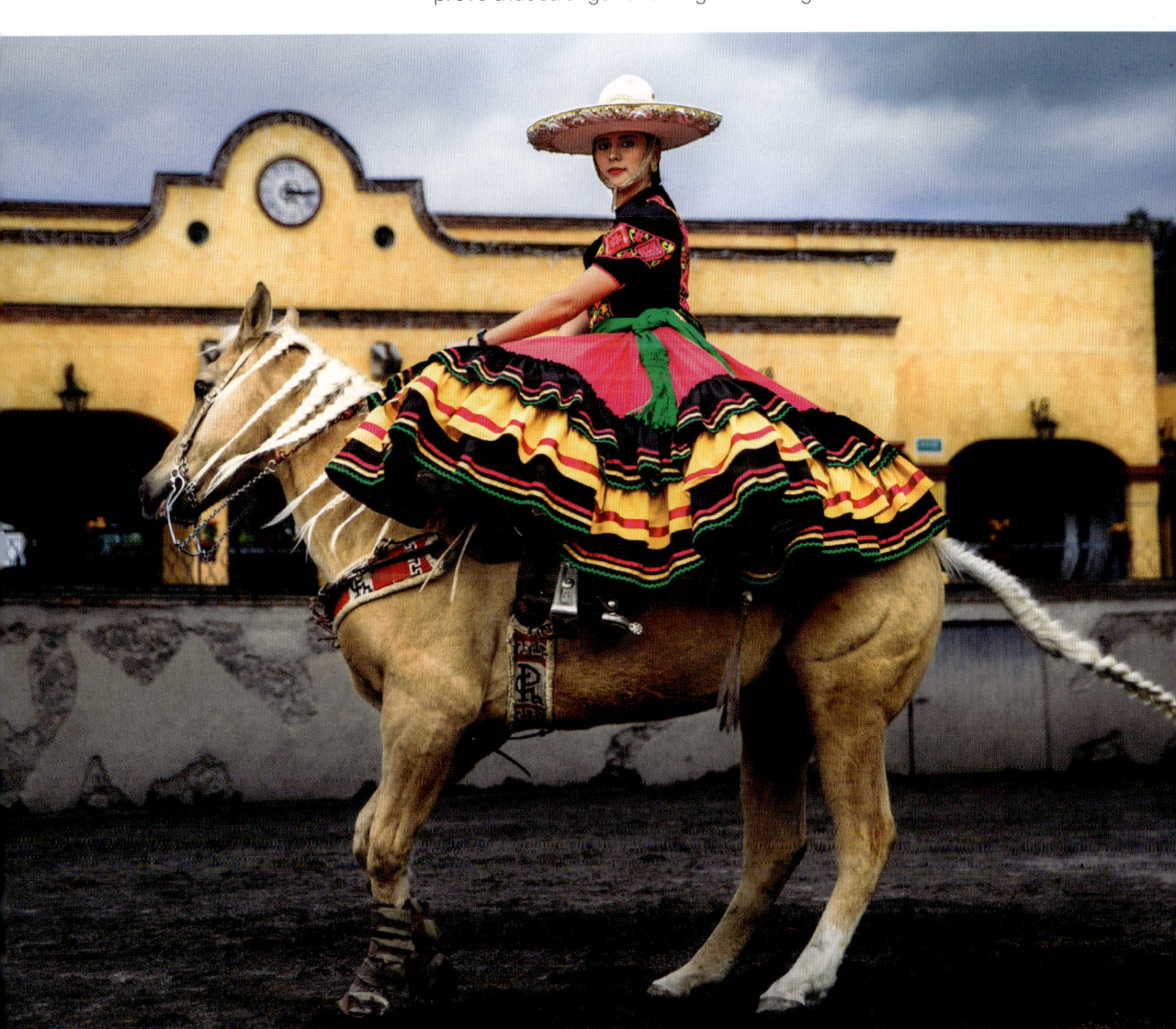

LAHORE, PAKISTAN

I was fascinated to find out that Farheen practices two very different arts, but after hearing her story, everything made sense.

Farheen Raza Jaffry's mother was a seamstress. While growing up, Farheen was always by her mother's side, witnessing this beautiful craft. But Farheen's mother was also passionate about singing.

Today, Farheen is an appreciated fashion designer and also a professional singer. Ghazal music, her favorite, is a highly popular genre in this part of the world, one inspired by ancient ghazal poetry.

Farheen has inherited both her mother's passions and taken them to the next level.

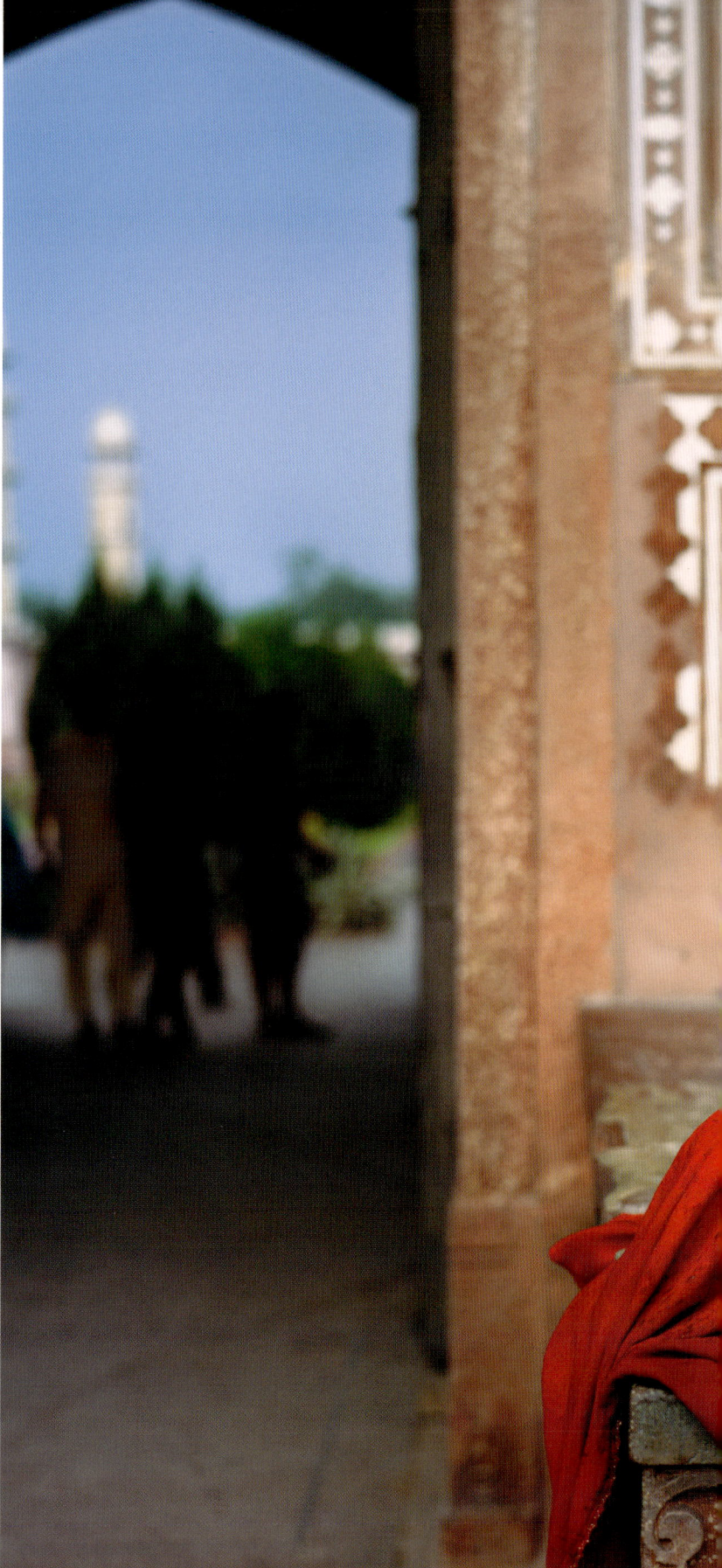

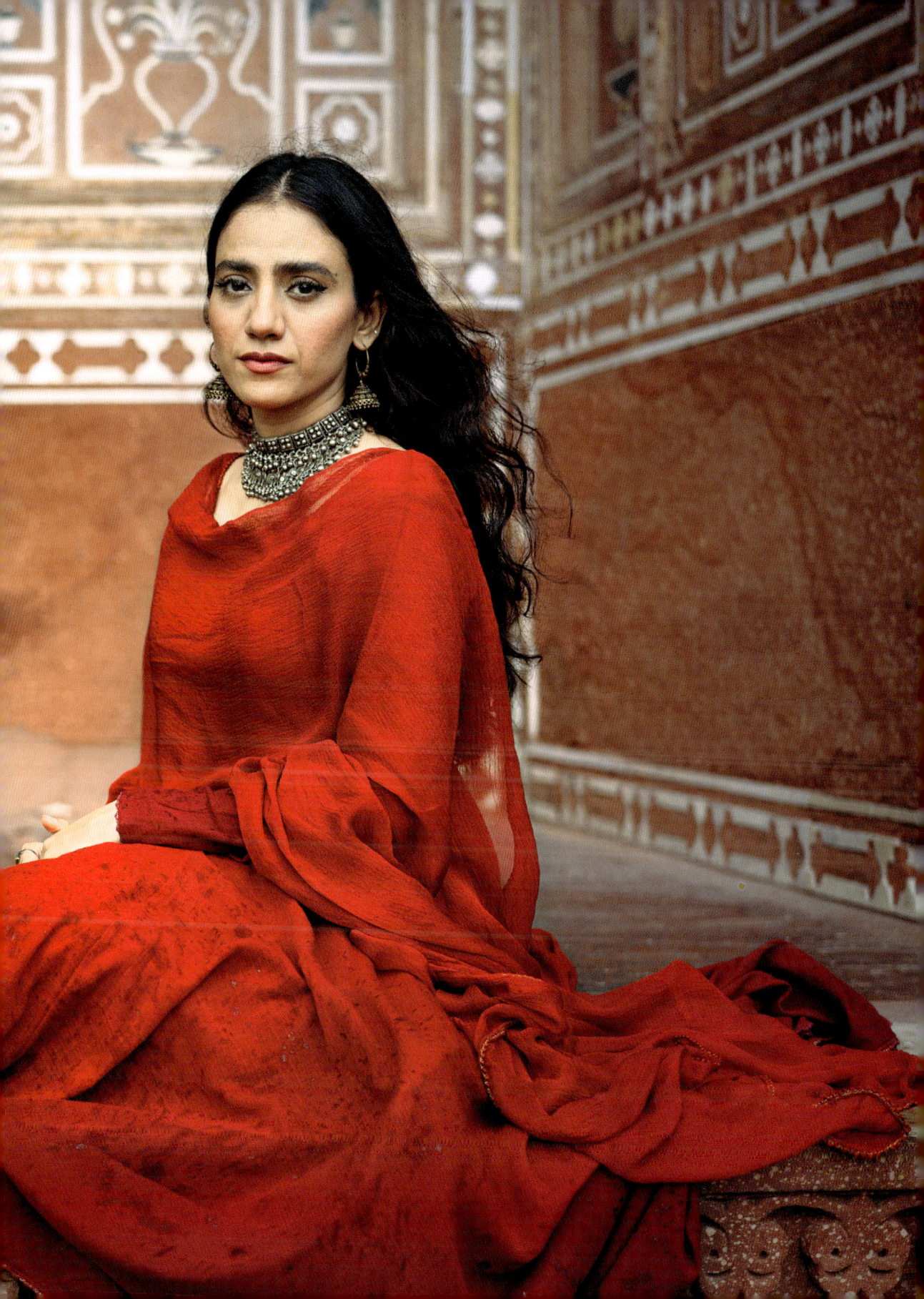

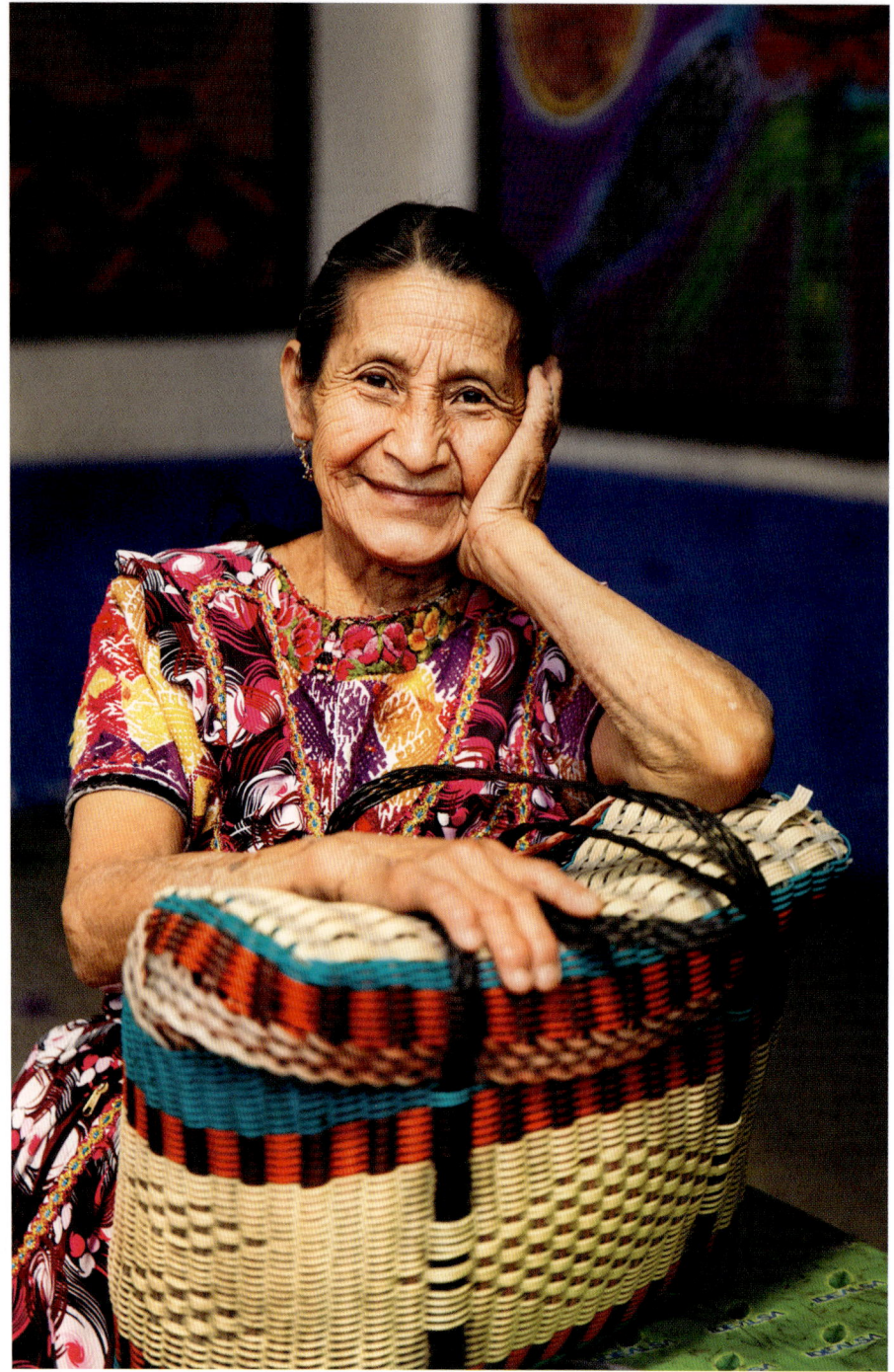

CHICHICASTENANGO, GUATEMALA

Maria is a cook who has owned her small village restaurant for almost half a century. When I met her, she was at the market buying ingredients. Despite her heavy bags, she moved quickly and radiated happiness about her work. She explained that her kitchen is like a playground where she feels free. Maria enjoys slow food and sometimes dedicates up to seven hours cooking a single dish.

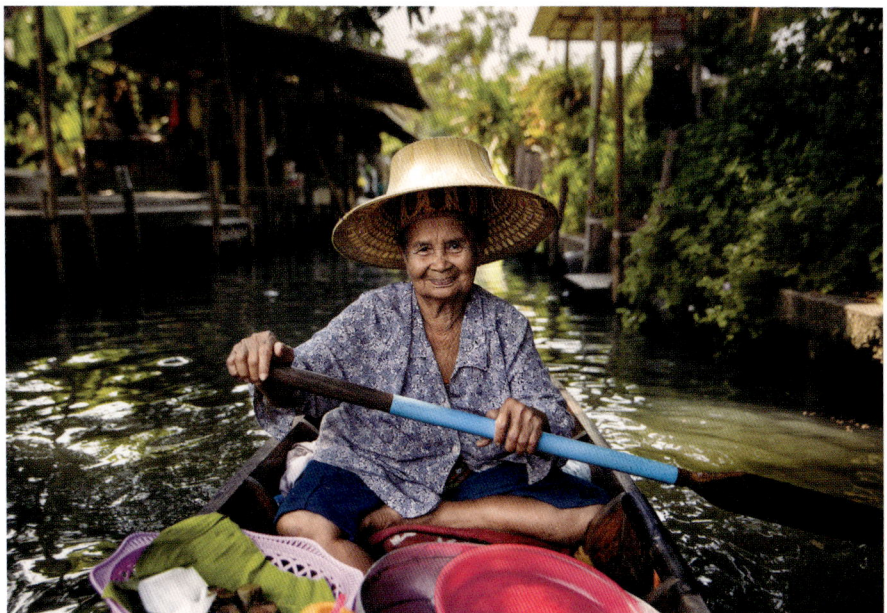

DAMNOEN SADUAK, THAILAND

Payao has been selling food in this floating market for more than fifty years. She lives in a nearby floating village and always uses her boat as both a means of transportation and a small takeaway restaurant.

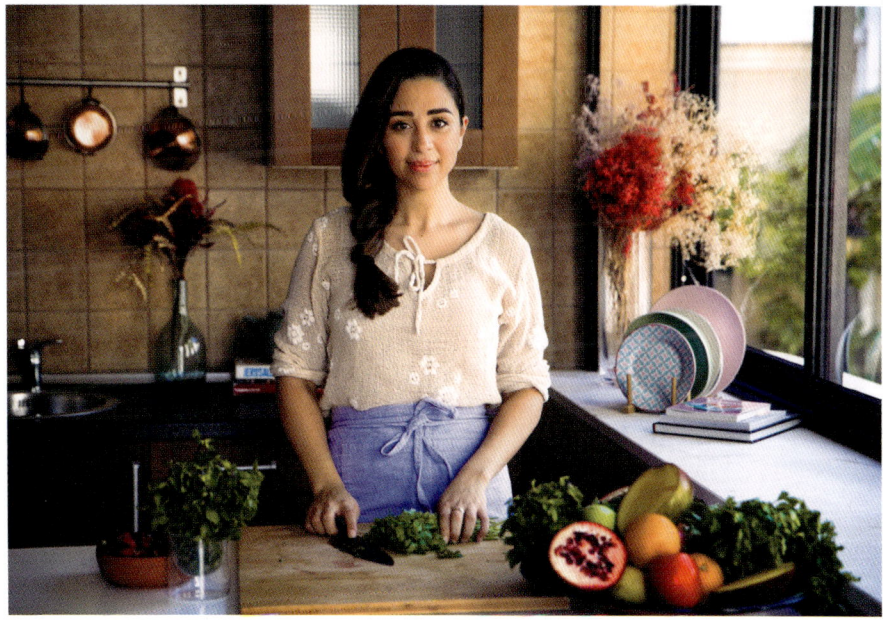

JEDDAH, SAUDI ARABIA

Although Nour Al Zaben studied finance abroad, she decided to follow her passion for cooking and return home. Today, she is a respected chef who creates fusions between Middle Eastern flavors and global influences. She aspires to elevate her country's cuisine to the top.

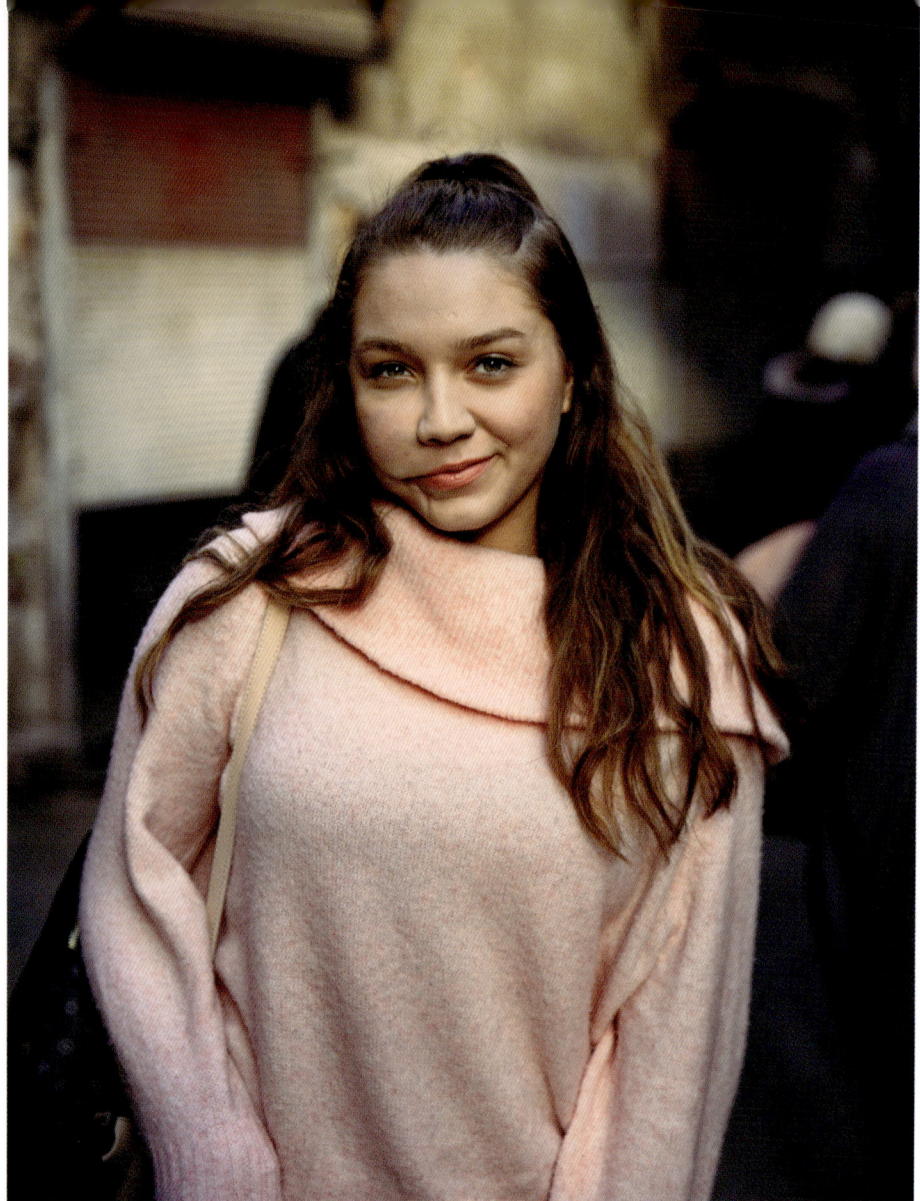

DAMASCUS, SYRIA

Because of some medical errors, Rafah Mothkal experienced a malformation during her birth process. Her childhood was very painful. She lost her father, who was shot during the war when she was only eleven. As she grew up, Rafah found it difficult to accept that she was different. During those years, she underwent forty-five repairing surgeries. She stayed home most of the time, and when she went outside, she always tried to hide her face in different ways.

Over time, due to the terrible physical suffering that followed the surgeries, she realized that the solution was not to change her face but to change her mindset. So, she decided to cancel all the surgeries. Today, she runs a blog where she promotes self-love. She has a supportive boyfriend and receives messages from people with similar experiences congratulating her on her initiative. This gives her even more strength and motivation.

Rafah's journey to discover her beauty was long and painful, but, today, her beauty shines.

LADAKH, INDIA

Tashi, Dolkar, and Wangmo are Buddhist nuns. They were out in the city for a walk. Besides the spiritual aspect, their nunnery also provides educational opportunities for many women in the region.

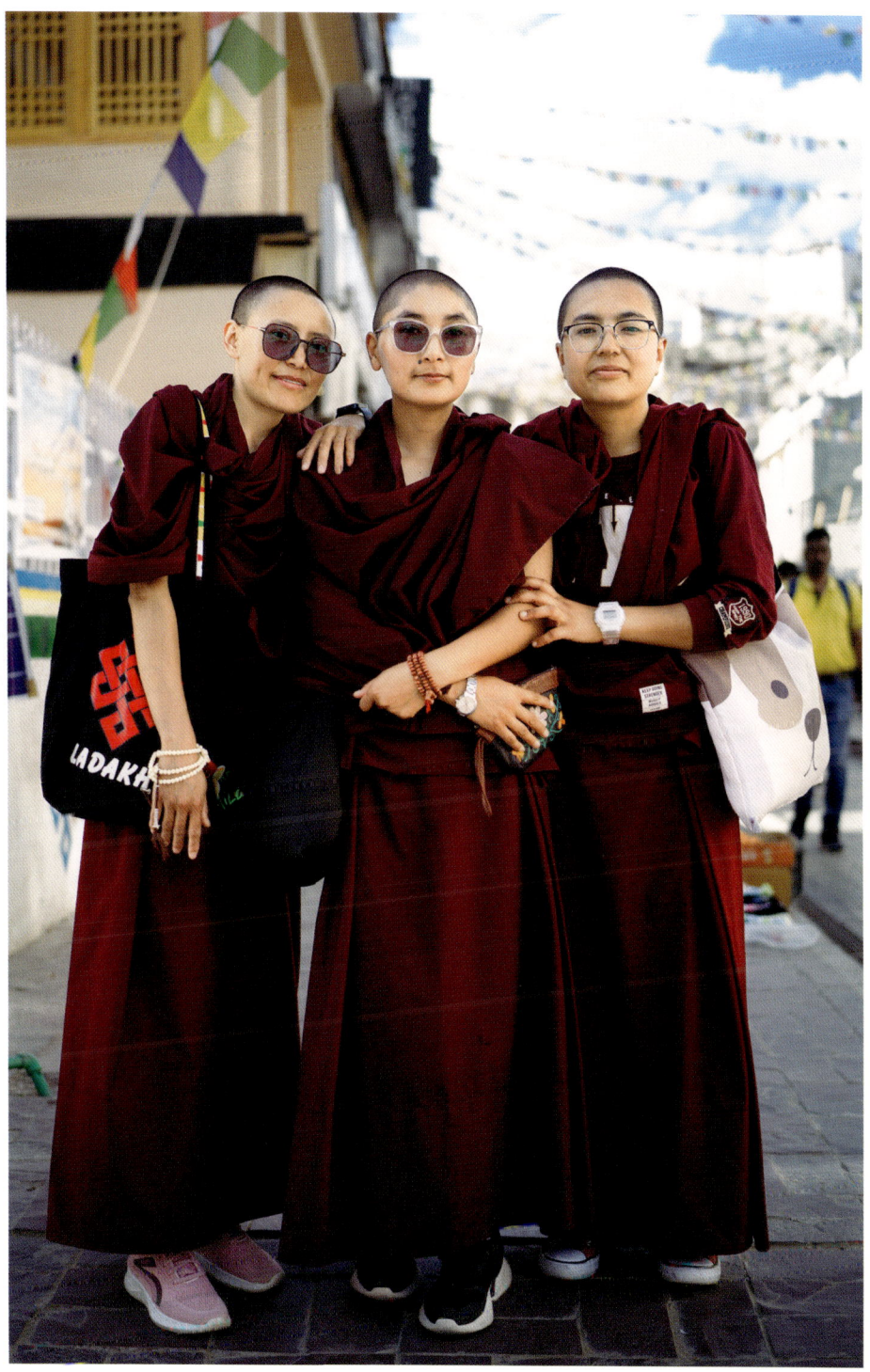

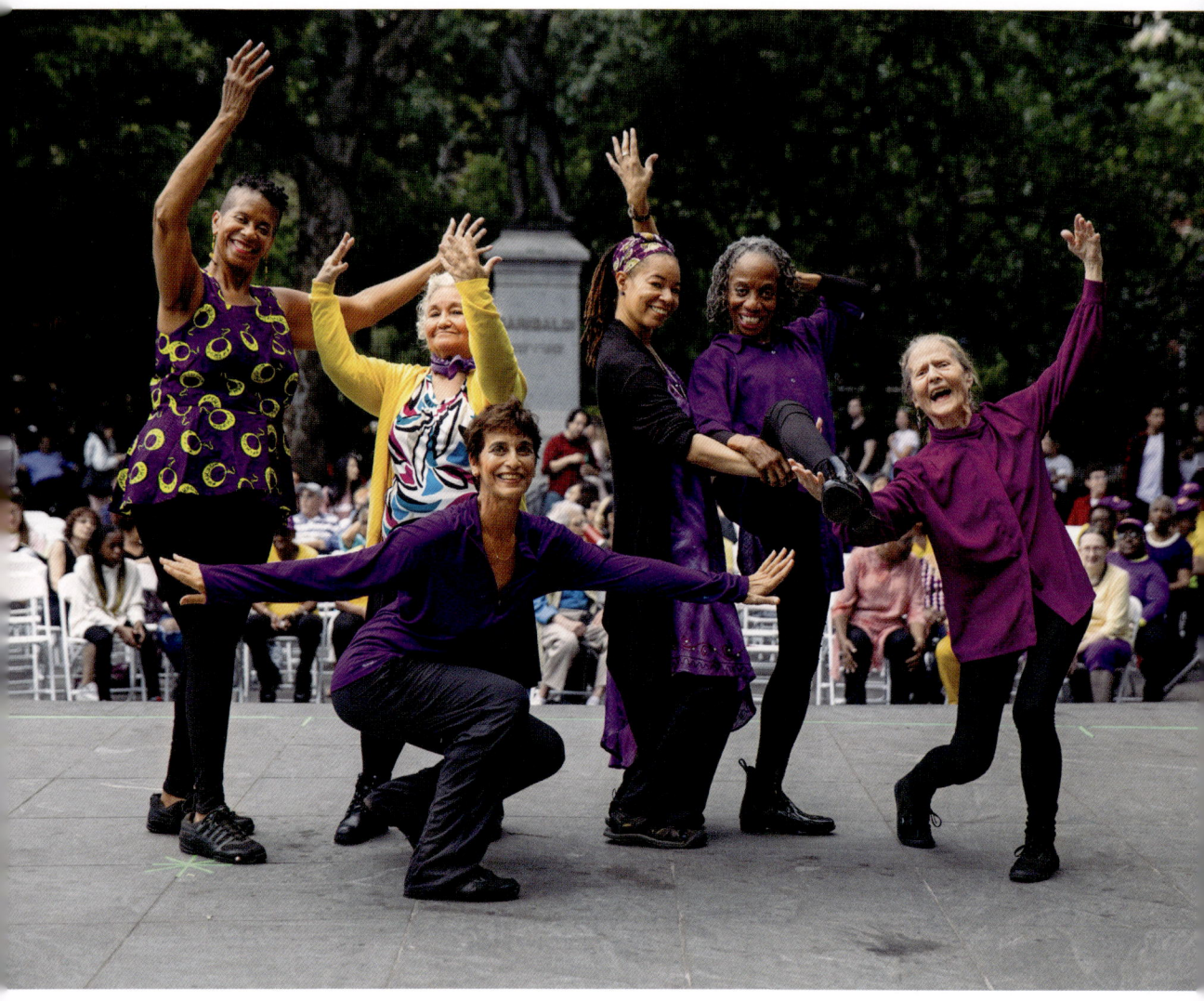

NEW YORK CITY, UNITED STATES

This community of dancers, called Revival, is breaking stereotypes about age and bringing the joy of dancing closer to the people. Under the guidance of professional choreographers, the senior dancers offer vibrant shows in the iconic Washington Square.

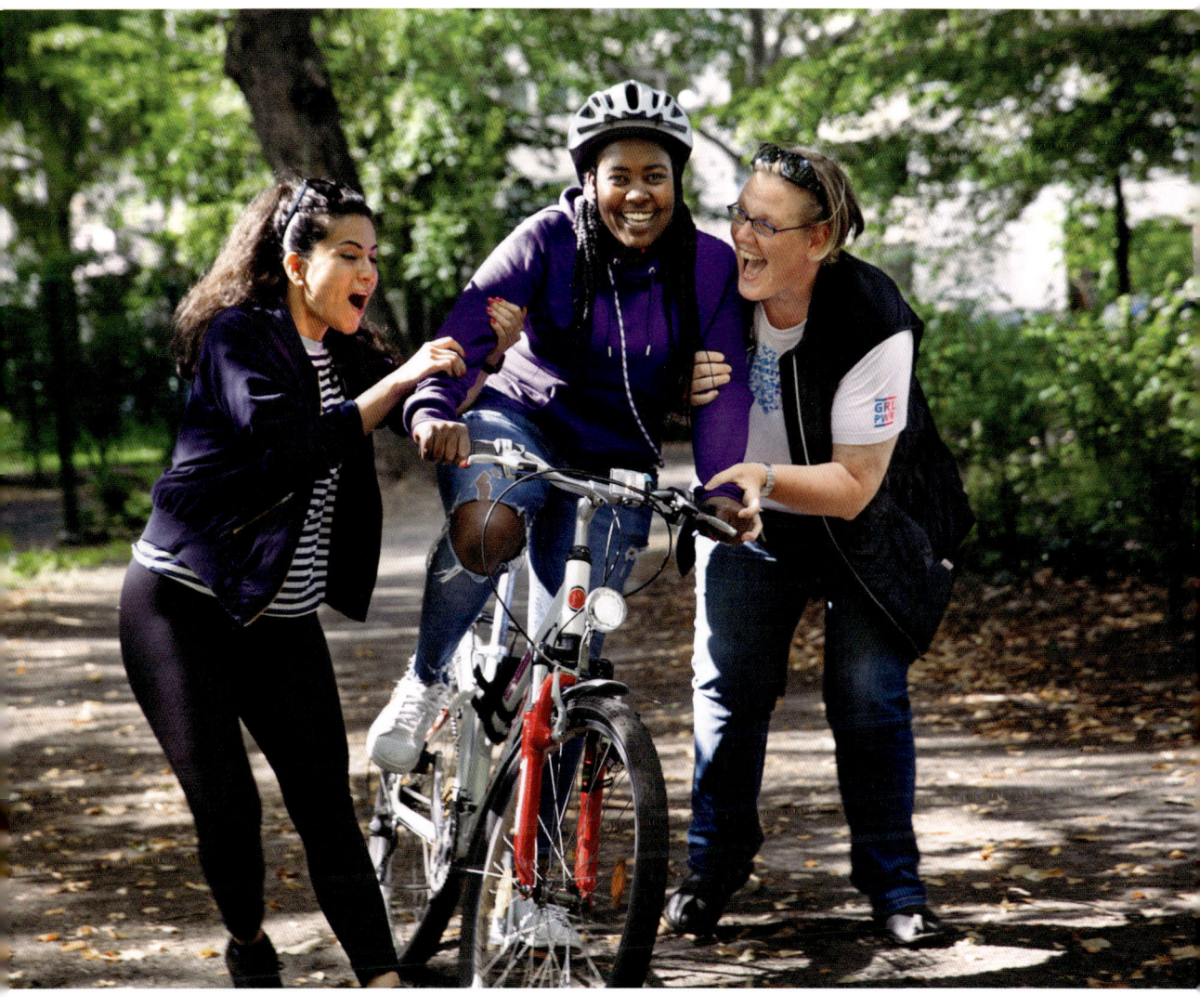

BERLIN, GERMANY

Many girls around the world don't get the chance to experience the joy of riding a bike during their childhood. But it's never too late to learn.

For many years, Annette Krüger (*right*) has been teaching refugee women in Berlin how to ride bicycles as well as repair the basics. In a city where bicycling is often the most effective means of transport, this brings many opportunities and much more freedom to these women. Through her project, called Bikeygees, Annette has gathered a team of soulful volunteers and empowered thousands of women and girls by helping them to become more mobile.

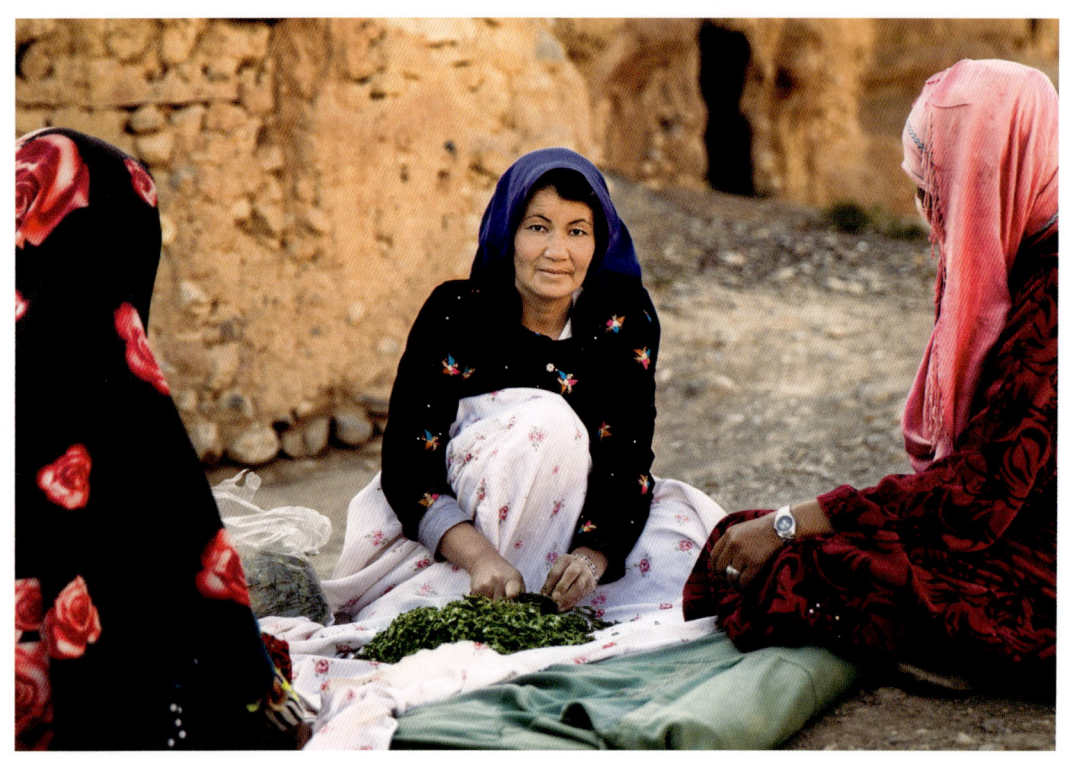

CENTRAL AFGHANISTAN

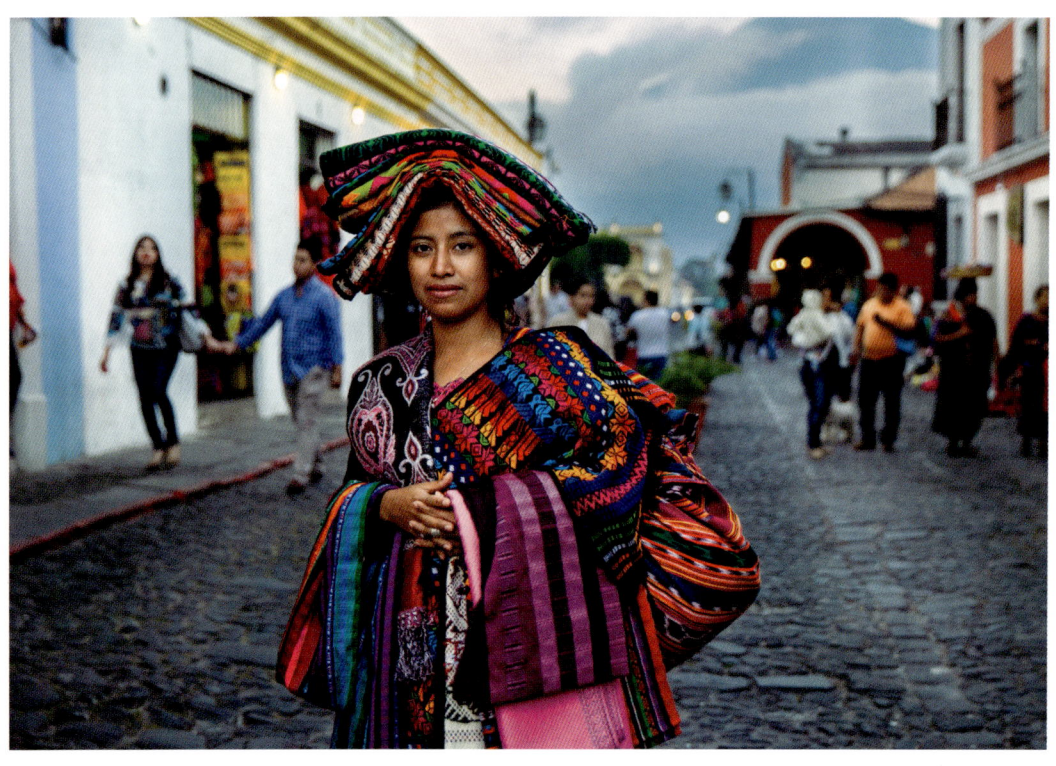

ANTIGUA, GUATEMALA

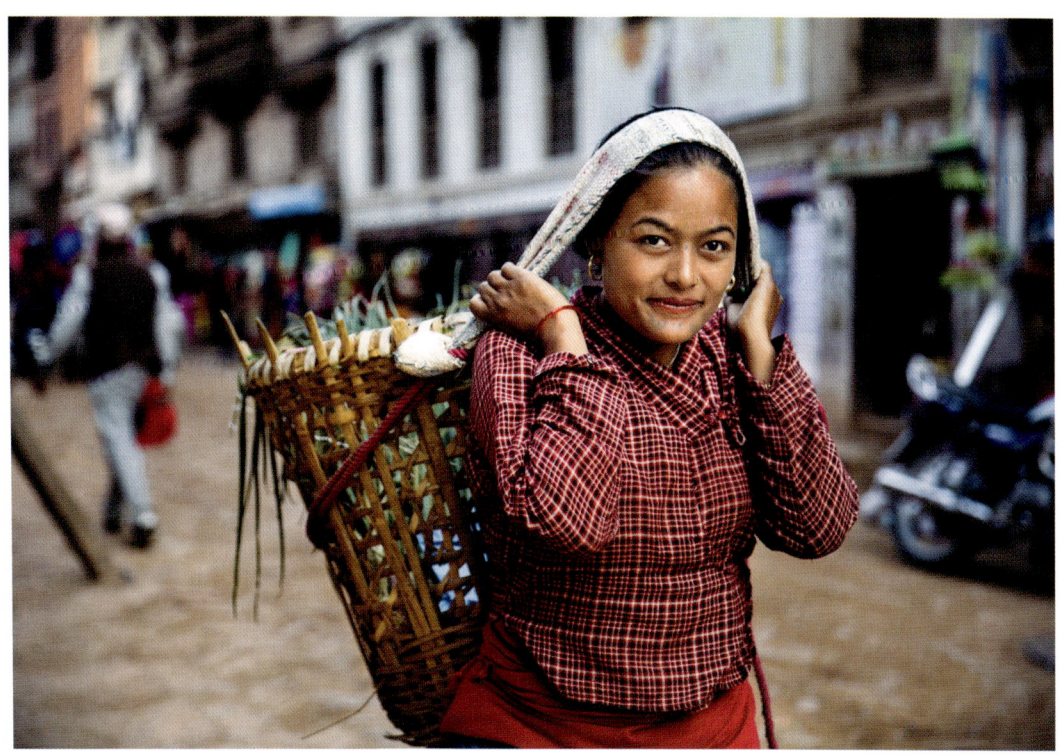

KATHMANDU, NEPAL

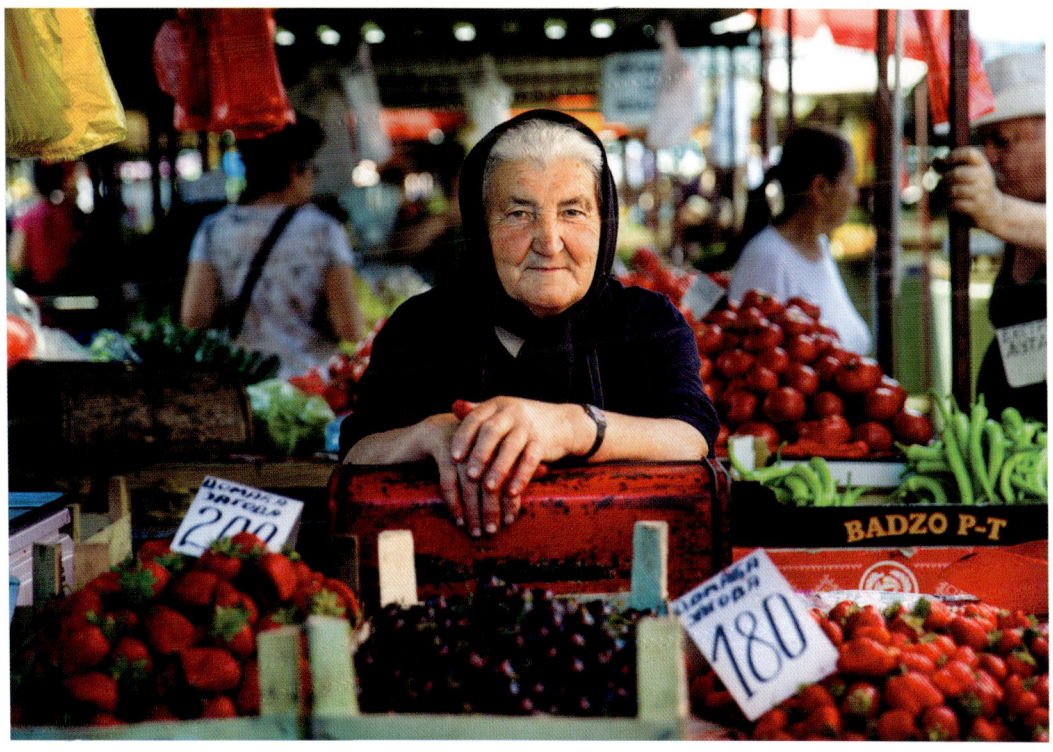

BELGRADE, SERBIA

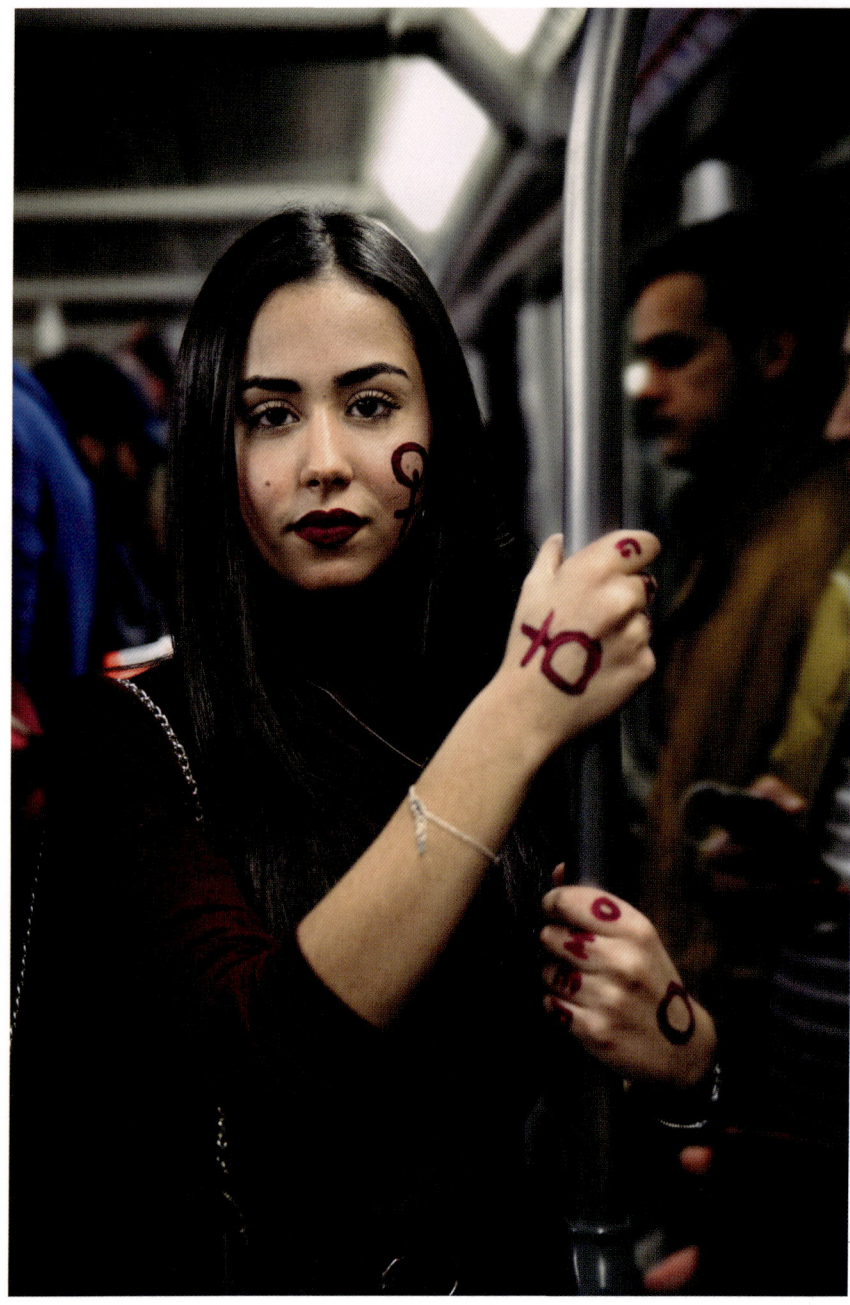

BARCELONA, SPAIN

When I first noticed her, Hajar was in the subway coming home from the Women's Day March. She told me that, for her, this special day is not a celebration but one of the 365 days when we should fight for equal rights.

Hajar was born in Spain to Moroccan parents and is studying law. She is passionate about human rights and has spent time with women in need, including refugees. She believes that first you have to know the rules of the game before improving them.

SIBIU, ROMANIA

She's just twenty-three but has already started a movement. Maïté Meeûs, who is of Belgian and Indian descent, lives in Brussels, the capital of Belgium, and was visiting this charming town in Romania when I met her.

In 2021, staff members of some bars in Brussels were accused of drugging and assaulting several young girls. What seemed like isolated cases proved to be a wide, horrible phenomenon. Many other denunciations followed, revealing hundreds of similar abuses around the city.

Maïté and many other people in Brussels took to the streets to protest against these despicable acts and show their support for the victims. But Maïté felt she could do more than that. So she started an Instagram page called @balance_ton_bar. Her purpose was to anonymously collect and share testimonials of drug-facilitated sexual assaults in bars around Brussels.

Maïté's idea was to give a voice to the victims and show them that they were not alone. Soon, the movement spread in other cities, and Maïté created pages for each new community. Today, there are more than sixty pages.

The testimonials collected through these pages proved that drug-facilitated sexual assaults are a wide phenomenon in many places. After raising such massive awareness about this systemic problem, Maïté hopes that authorities will do much more to stop it. Her message is clear: no, these are not exceptions; this is a widespread phenomenon that must be stopped.

For her unique project, Maïté won a prestigious prize offered by Amnesty International. But what's much more important for her is to continue her activism and help more people affected by sexual assaults. In the near future, she wants to move to India and extend the community there. The world needs more people like Maïté.

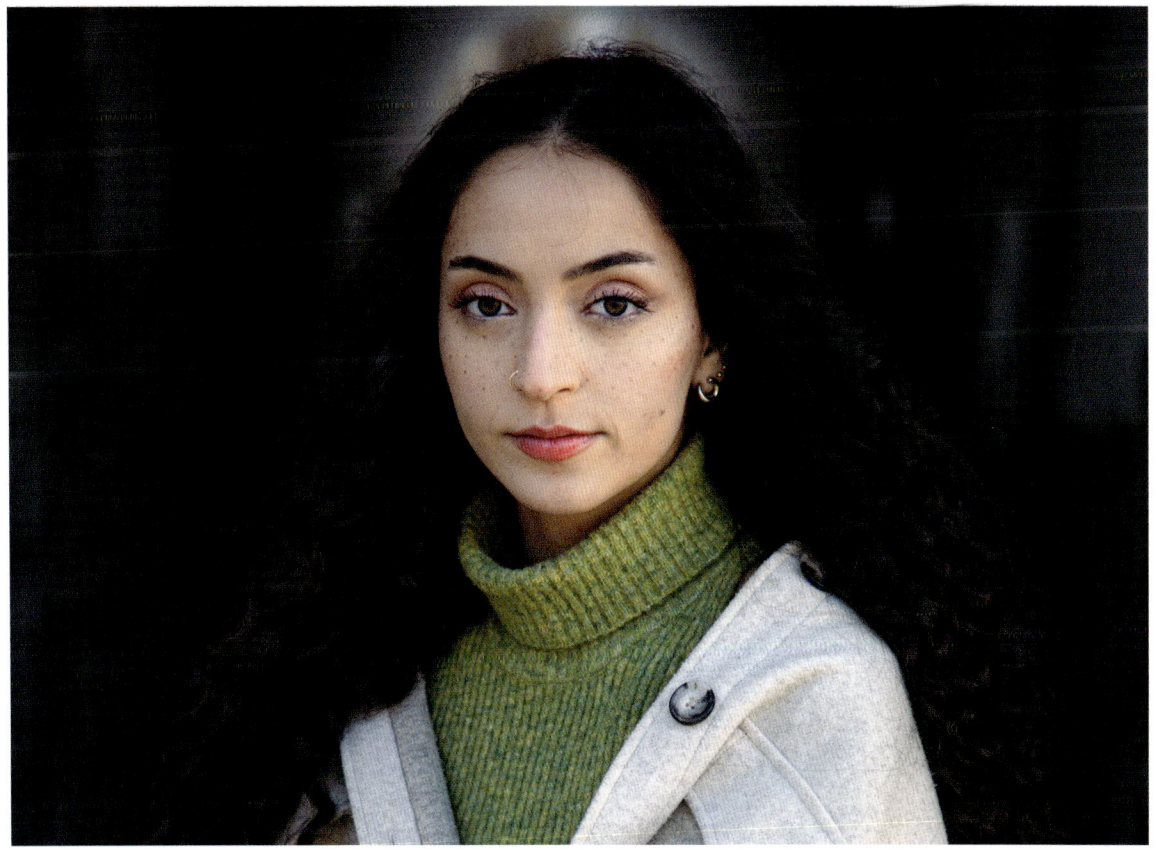

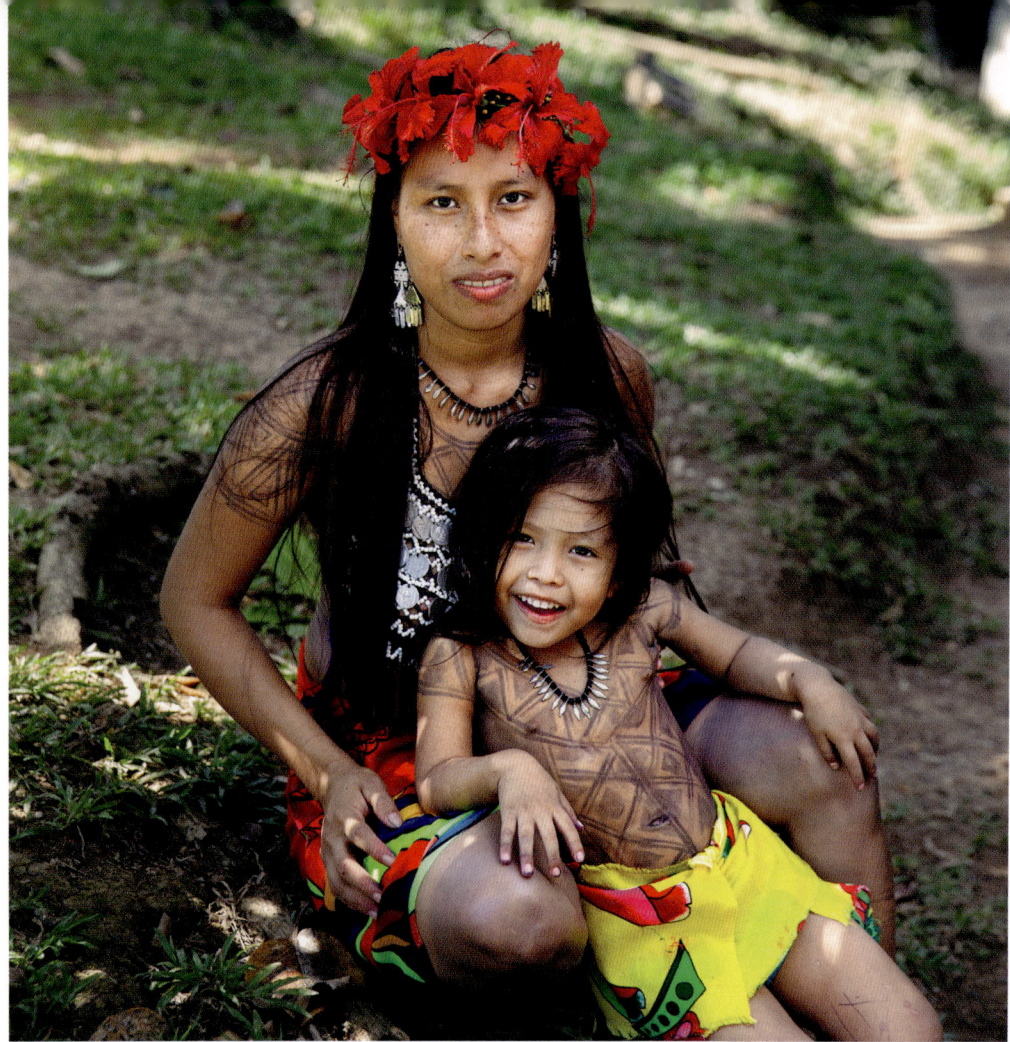

SOUTHERN PANAMA (Above)

This mother and son were playing when I visited their village. They are part of the Emberá ethnic group, one of the Indigenous communities of Panama. Emberá people usually live along the banks of rivers, as water plays a central role in their daily lives when it comes to fishing, bathing, and transport. Skin decoration is an important part of their culture. For this, they use the extract of a fruit known as jagua, or genipap, and the drawings generally last about ten days.

WESTERN ICELAND (Opposite)

Meet Andrea Geirsdóttir, an adventure guide, and her son, Benjamin. Iceland has some of the most spectacular landscapes in the world, which Andrea loves.

This strong and brave woman takes adventurous tourists onto the amazing glaciers of her country. It's a tough job with lots of responsibilities. Moreover, Andrea is a single mother, so each step on the glaciers means even more responsibilities.

But when you do what you love while also taking the necessary precautions, the sky is the limit. And Iceland has such a beautiful sky.

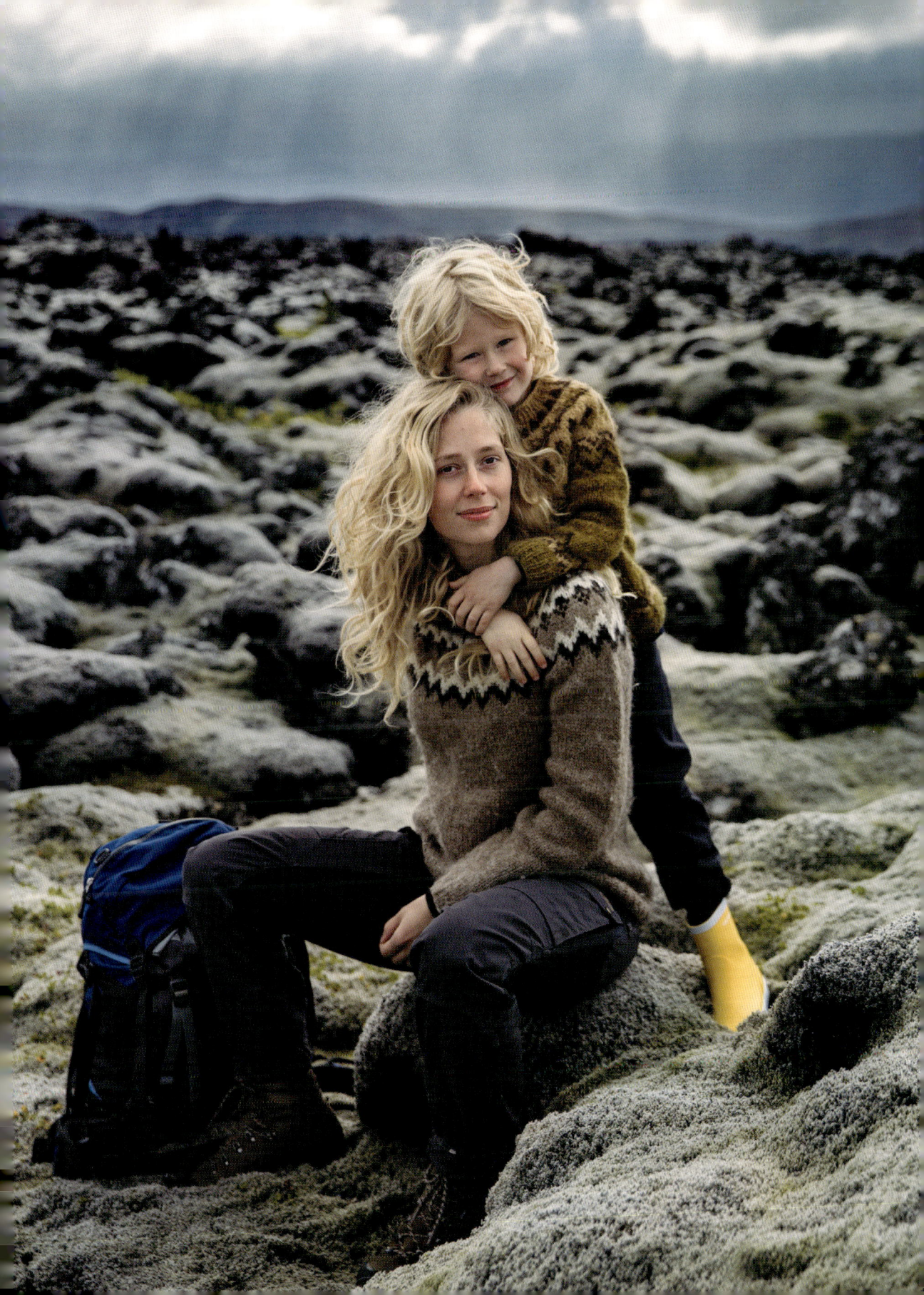

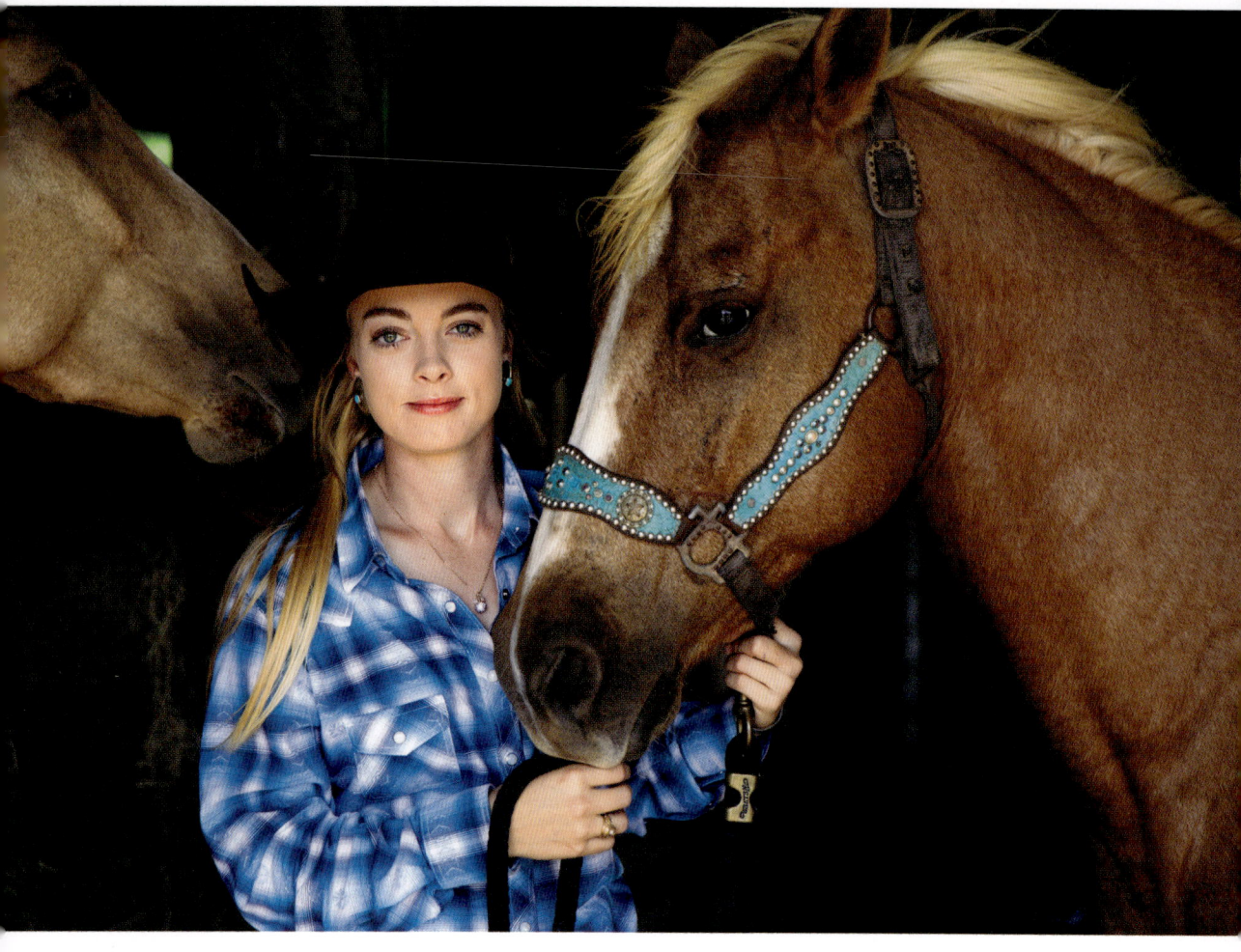

TEXAS, UNITED STATES

Jimmie Smith is a true cowgirl. She grew up on a farm in Texas surrounded by horses and stories about the rodeo. Today, she's one of the best barrel racers in the United States. Barrel racing is a rodeo event that involves a horse and a rider completing a timed pattern around preset barrels in an arena.

During my visit to Jimmie's farm, I was fascinated to witness her love for her horses and to listen to her adventures on the road. She sometimes travels for months, driving her truck across the United States from one rodeo event to another. She's fueled by her passion for this equestrian sport.

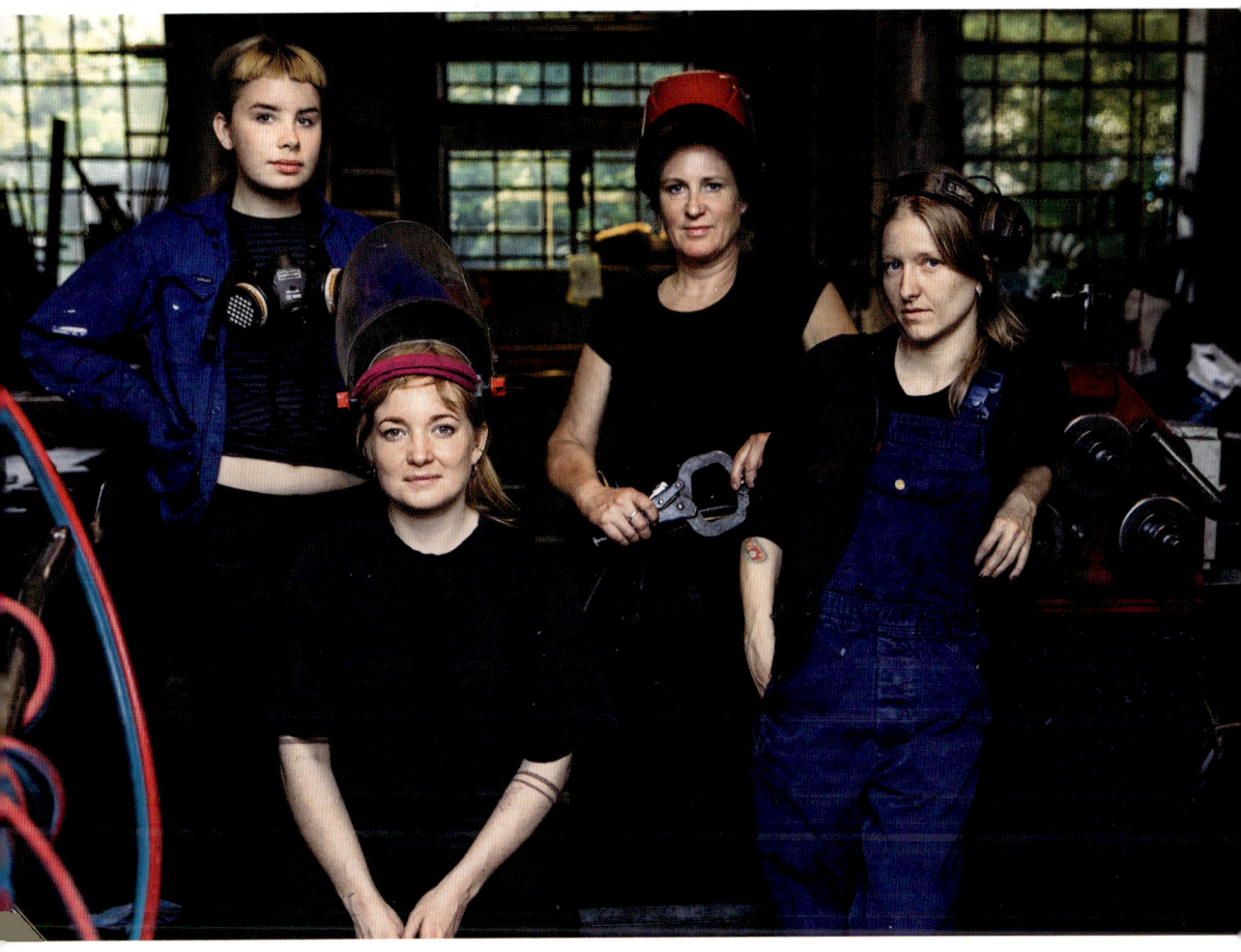

COPENHAGEN, DENMARK

This women-owned smithy is in the famous Freetown Christiania, an abandoned army base that was taken over by hippies in the seventies and which now hosts an intentional community. As I entered the workshop, I was immediately captivated by the strength and skills of these women as well as the genuine atmosphere. No wonder the smithy is well known for its high-quality craftsmanship and the design of unique pieces.

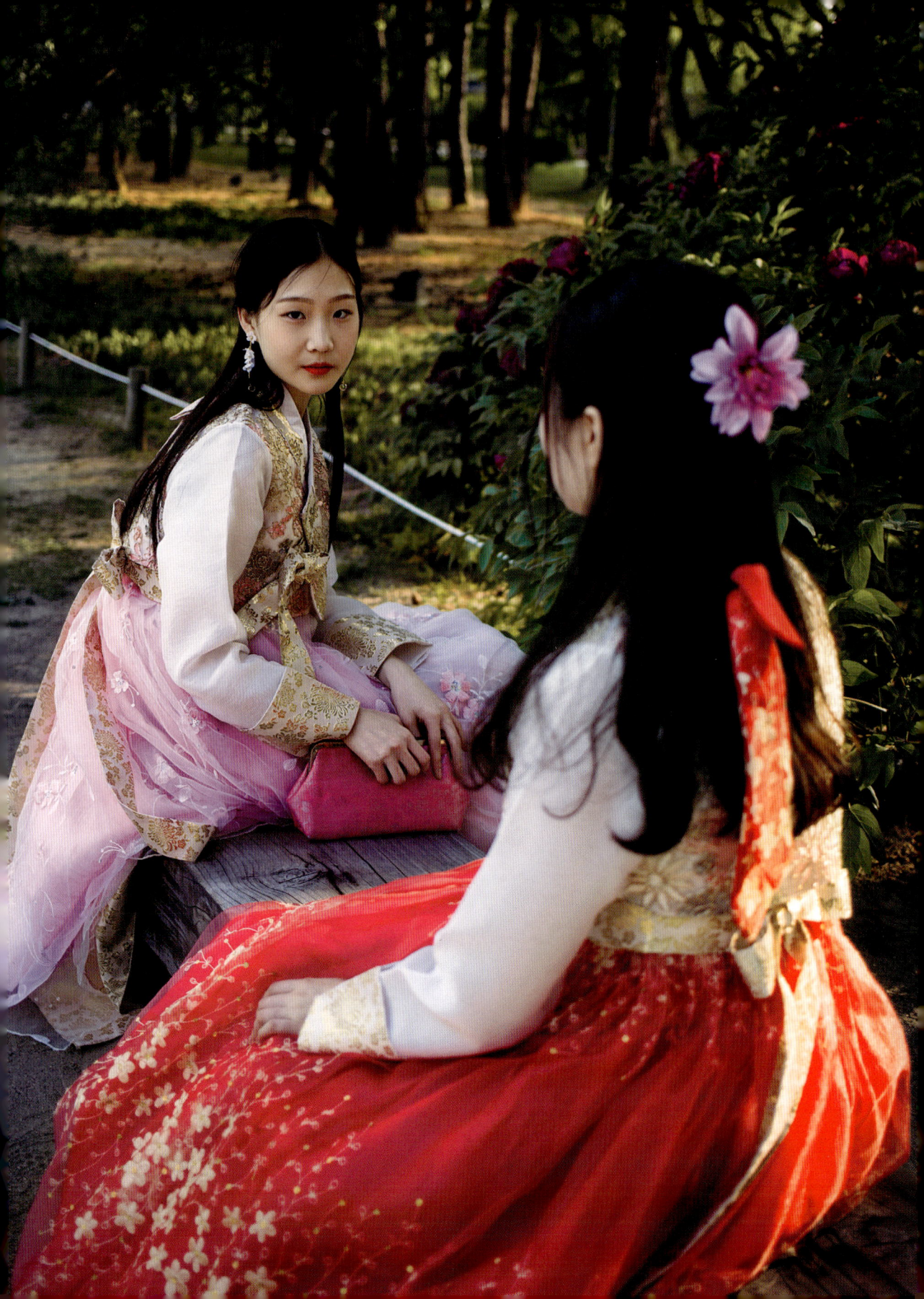

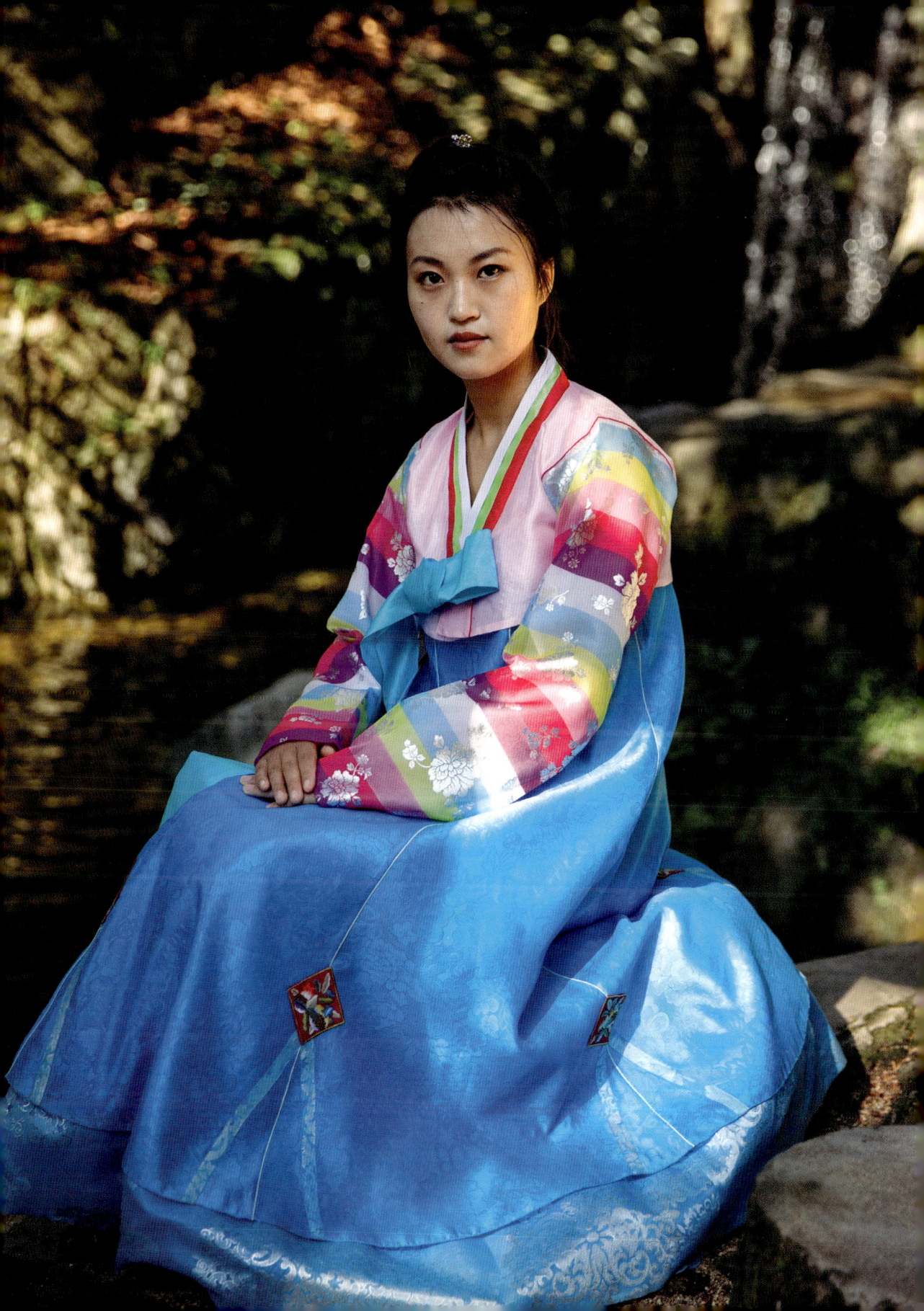

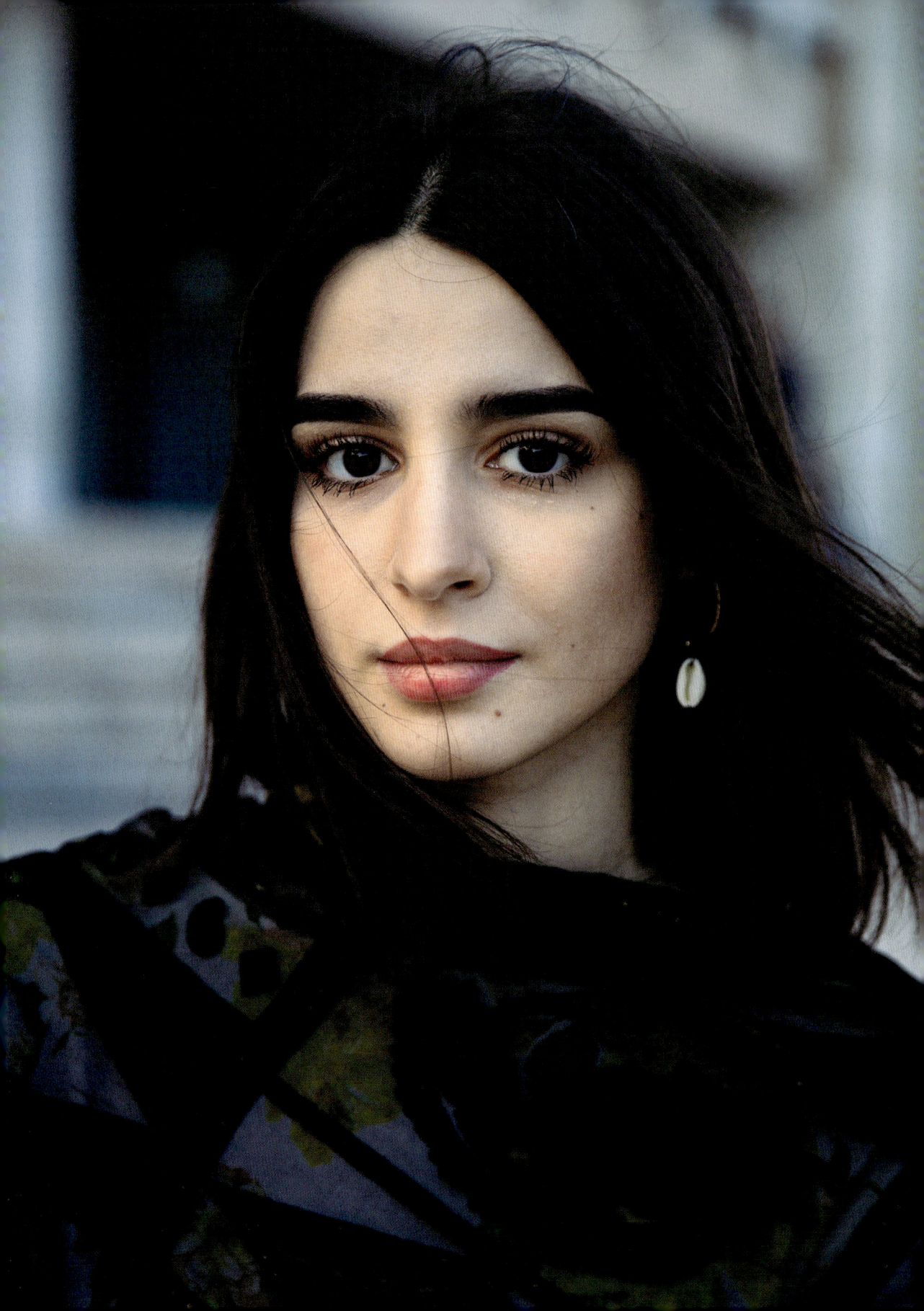

SEOUL, SOUTH KOREA *(Previous spread, left)*

Woojoo and June were relaxing after a long walk. During most warm weekends, thousands of South Korean women visit the beautiful gardens of the Gyeongbokgung Palace while wearing colorful traditional dresses, called *hanboks*, like their ancestors used to.

Looking around, you might feel as if you'd stepped into another era, but the latest generation of smartphones, which are capturing selfies all around, will remind you that you're in one of the most modern places on Earth.

SINUIJU, NORTH KOREA
(Previous spread, right)

While South and North Korea have taken very different paths, they were once a single country. You can still observe the shared heritage through the appreciation of the traditional costume, particularly among women. In North Korea, they use the term "*chosŏn-ot*" for the *hanbok*.

CRAIOVA, ROMANIA *(Opposite)*

Ruxandra is passionate about the languages of the world. Besides her native Romanian, she has studied English linguistics, competed in French language contests, and broadened her horizons by studying Japanese and Turkish.

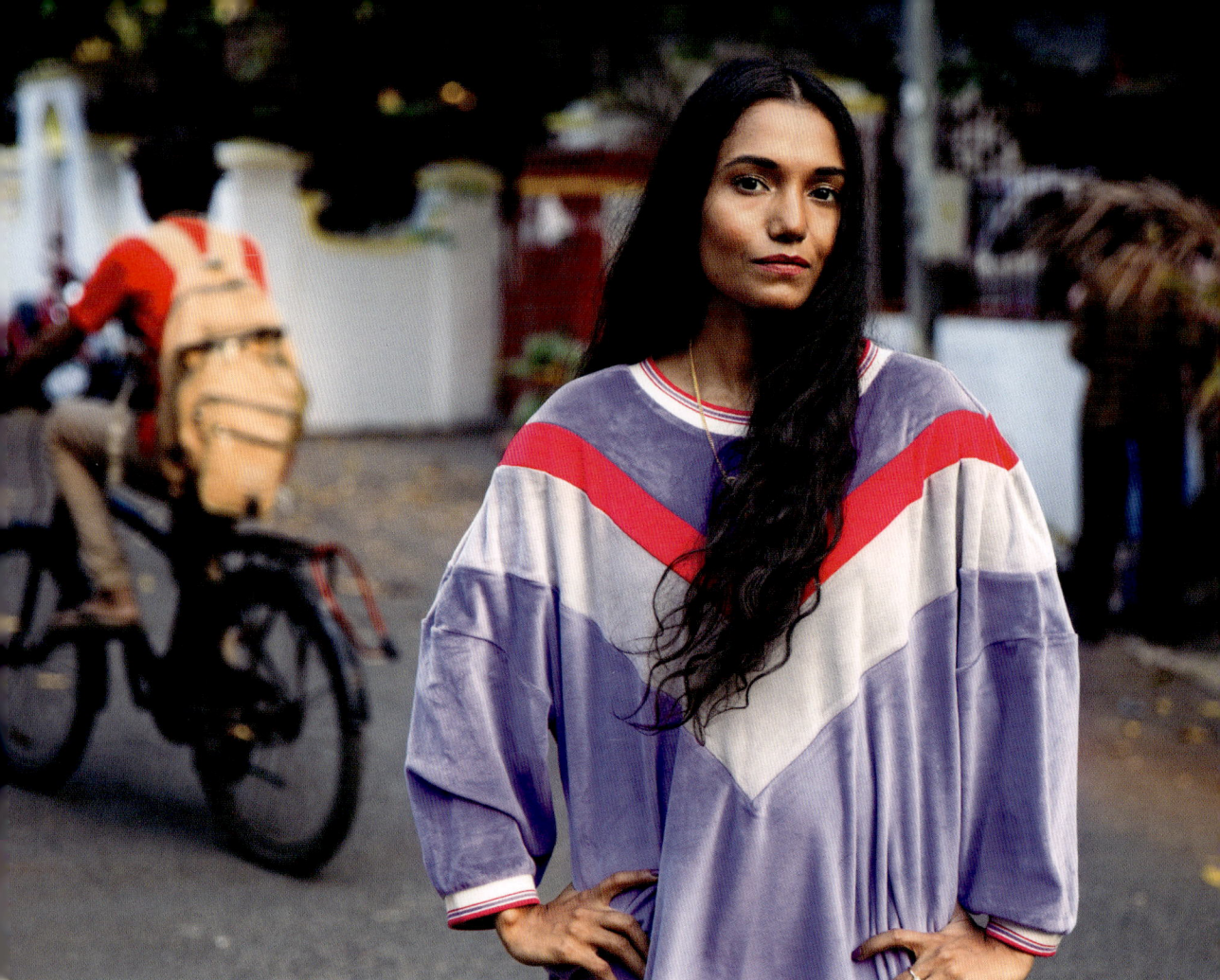

MUMBAI, INDIA

Deepa, known by her stage name Dee MC, is a pioneer in the Indian hip-hop scene. Born into a traditional family, Deepa's journey took an unexpected turn. She was involved in traditional music and dance from a young age, and the idea of becoming a rapper was far from her thoughts.

However, as she grew up, Deepa came across American hip-hop artists on TV. She found herself captivated and loved memorizing their verses and reciting them without losing her breath. In the beginning, her family regarded it as just a hobby that would pass, but gradually they learned to accept her passion.

Today, Deepa is an established artist, and her verses are empowering messages for women in India. Much of her words address the conditions of Indian women and express their struggles and dreams.

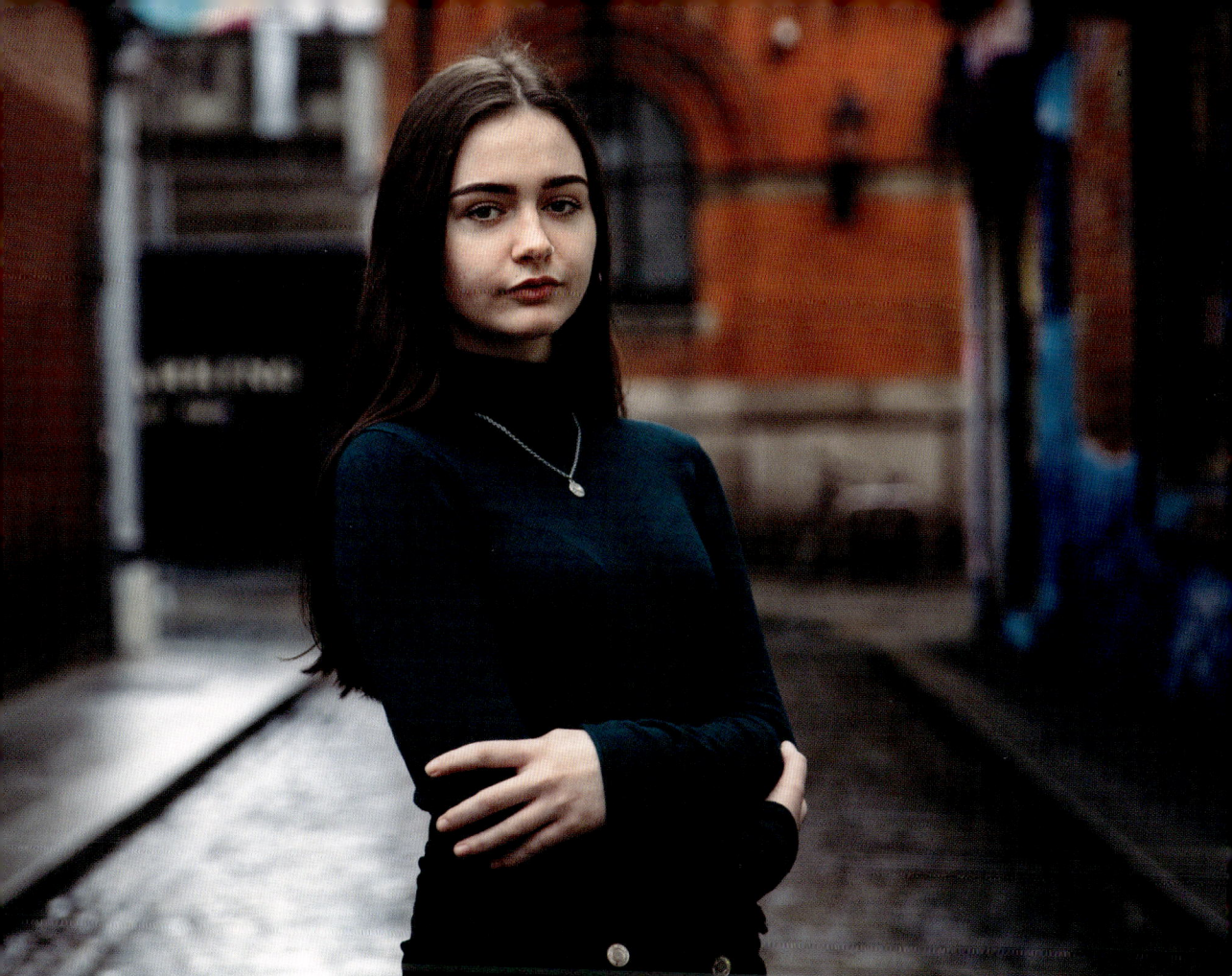

DUBLIN, IRELAND

After I photographed Natalya O'Flaherty on the streets of central Dublin, she recited one of her poems. Wow, what an incredible experience to hear her verses while witnessing her powerful performance.

Natalya is the type of poet whose art involves reciting her poetry. She's a spoken-word artist who masterfully combines boldness and sensitivity. "I can be soft and strong in the same breath," suggestively states one of her lines.

SOUTHERN GUATEMALA

When I met her, Antonia was carrying a sack of huipils she had woven herself, intending to sell them at a market. Huipils are traditional blouses worn by Indigenous women in Central America. Antonia has been crafting splendid huipils for the past fifty years. Despite the significant changes in the world over these years—with imported clothes becoming cheaper and cheaper—she keeps weaving.

Creating a single huipil requires months of complex work and creativity, in contrast to the few minutes it takes to produce a normal blouse in a factory. As the world changes, with technology and artificial intelligence having more and more influence on our lives, I love to search for inspiration in the natural intelligence and creativity of people like Antonia.

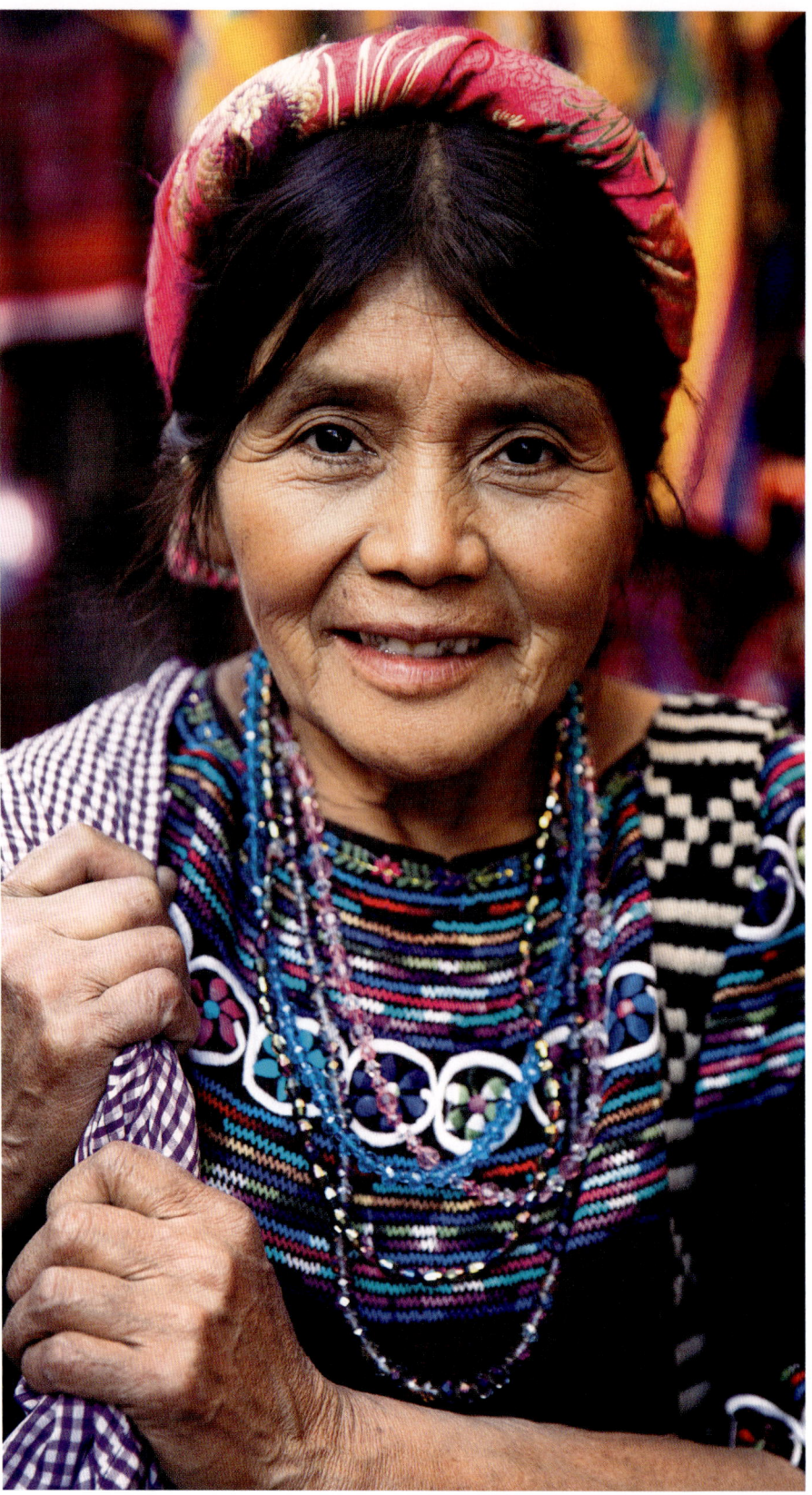

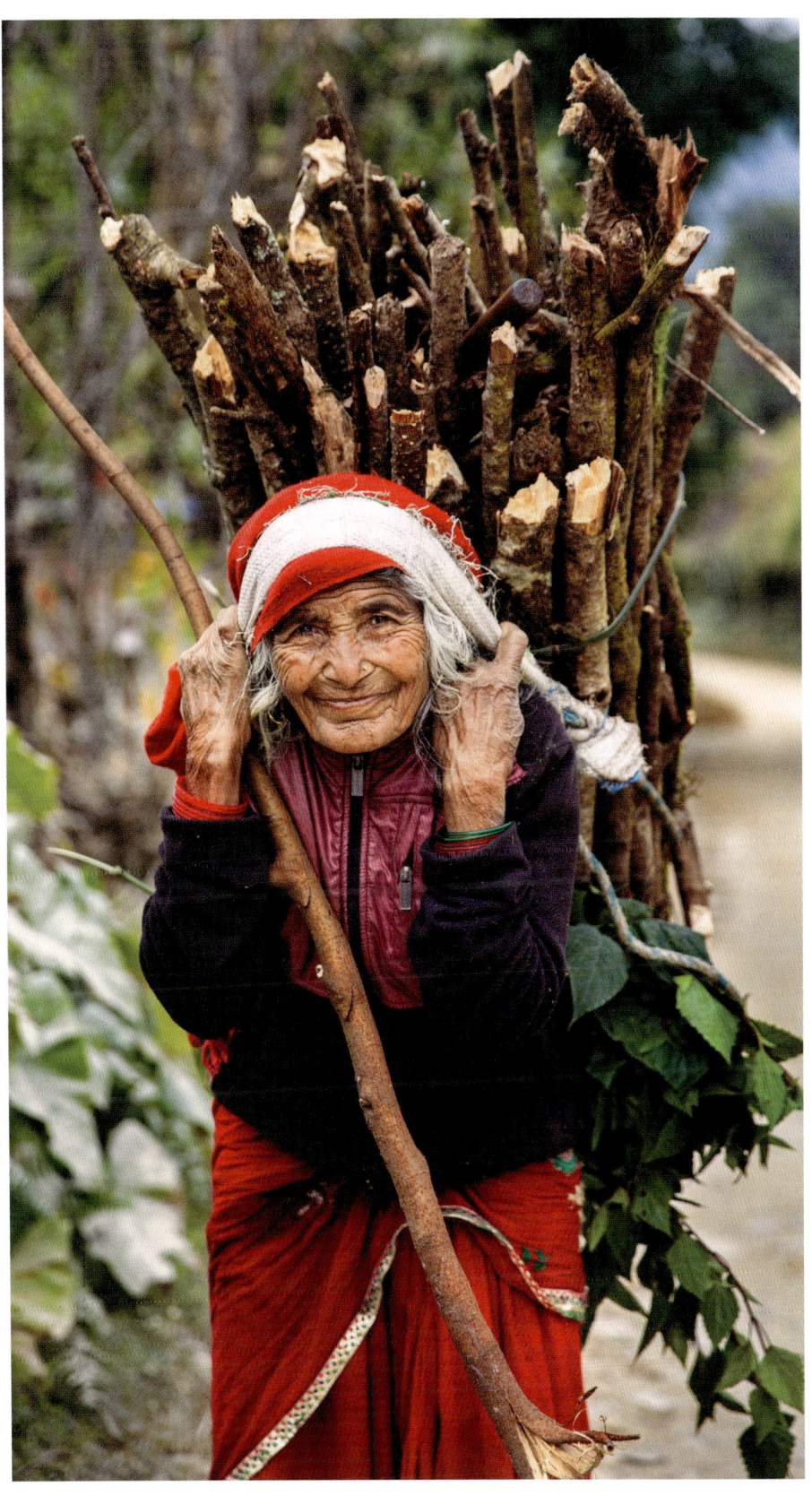

POKHARA VALLEY, NEPAL

The landscape here, with the huge Annapurna Mountains in the background, is just splendid. But what about the life of the locals?

Kunti is eighty-six years old and has always picked and carried wood for cooking and heating.

She invited me into her home. I tried to put the wood on my head to see just how heavy it is. Believe me, it felt massive. I'm young and healthy but couldn't carry it for more than a few seconds. She carried it for a couple of hours—and that was just today's haul.

People here carry burdens every day—both literally and figuratively. Still, there's beauty, kindness, dignity, and many genuine smiles all over the place.

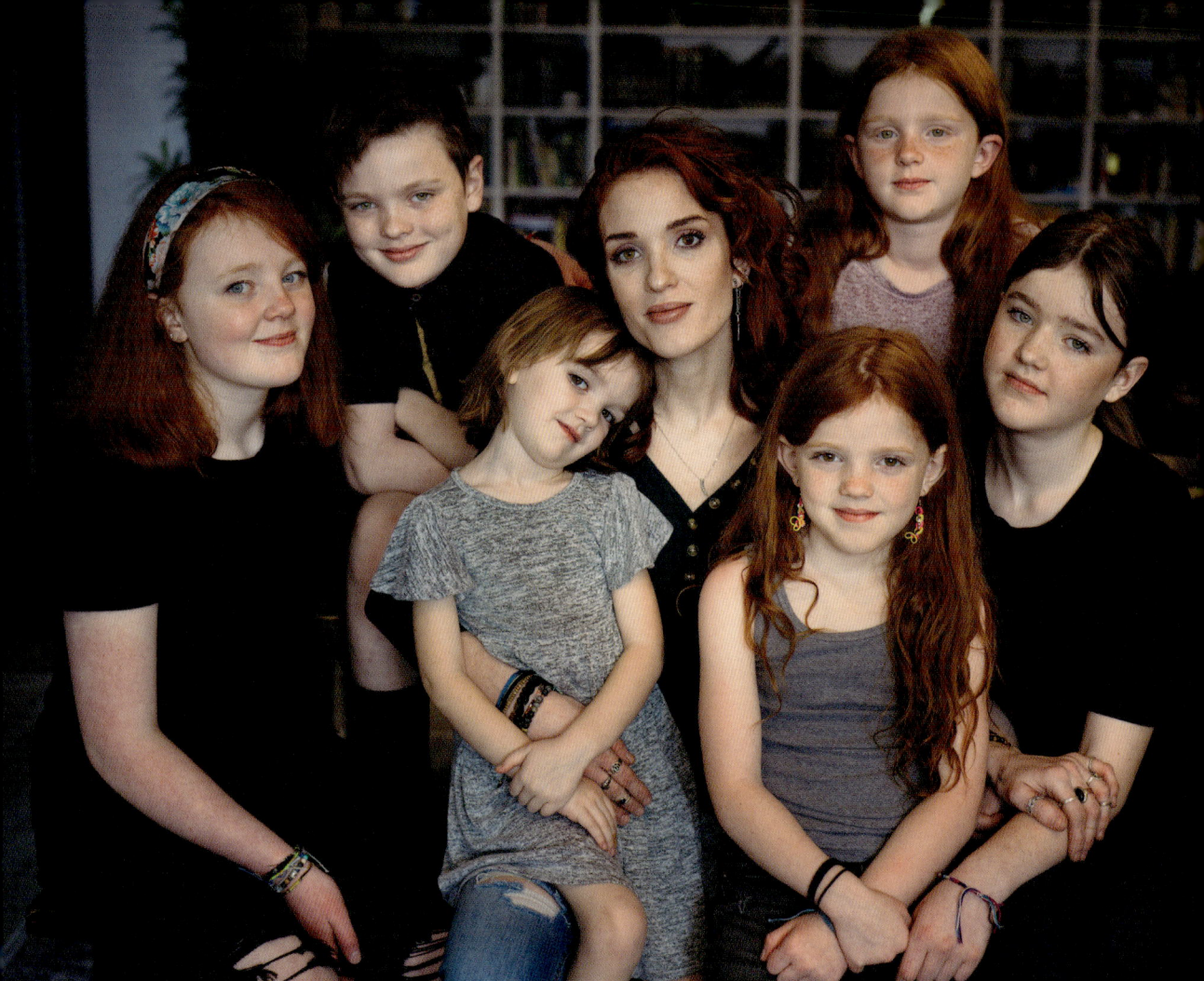

SALT LAKE CITY, UNITED STATES

This is Emily Meyers and her children inside their home. Emily's husband passed away after a terrible fight with cancer. For the sake of her family, Emily had to keep walking through the huge challenges of this tough yet fascinating story called life.

BUDAPEST, HUNGARY

Réka Pávó was a warrior with a smile—one of the most beautiful humans I have ever met.

While undergoing chemotherapy for leukemia, Réka started to document her experience through powerful self-portraits. She wanted to show that a bald woman fighting for her life can still be optimistic and beautiful. She started to post her meaningful series on social media as a way to give courage and hope to other people in similar situations. After finishing her first treatment, she continued her mission by photographing cancer survivors and sharing their stories on social media.

Réka battled leukemia six more times in the years that followed, but she went on with her mission of supporting other people fighting cancer.

As her family described, on Réka's last days, her soul was stronger than ever, but her body longed for rest. More than anything, Réka wished to raise awareness about the importance of blood and cell donation. As you read this, remember Réka's message: You, too, can save a life!

Dear Réka, your beauty lives on eternally.

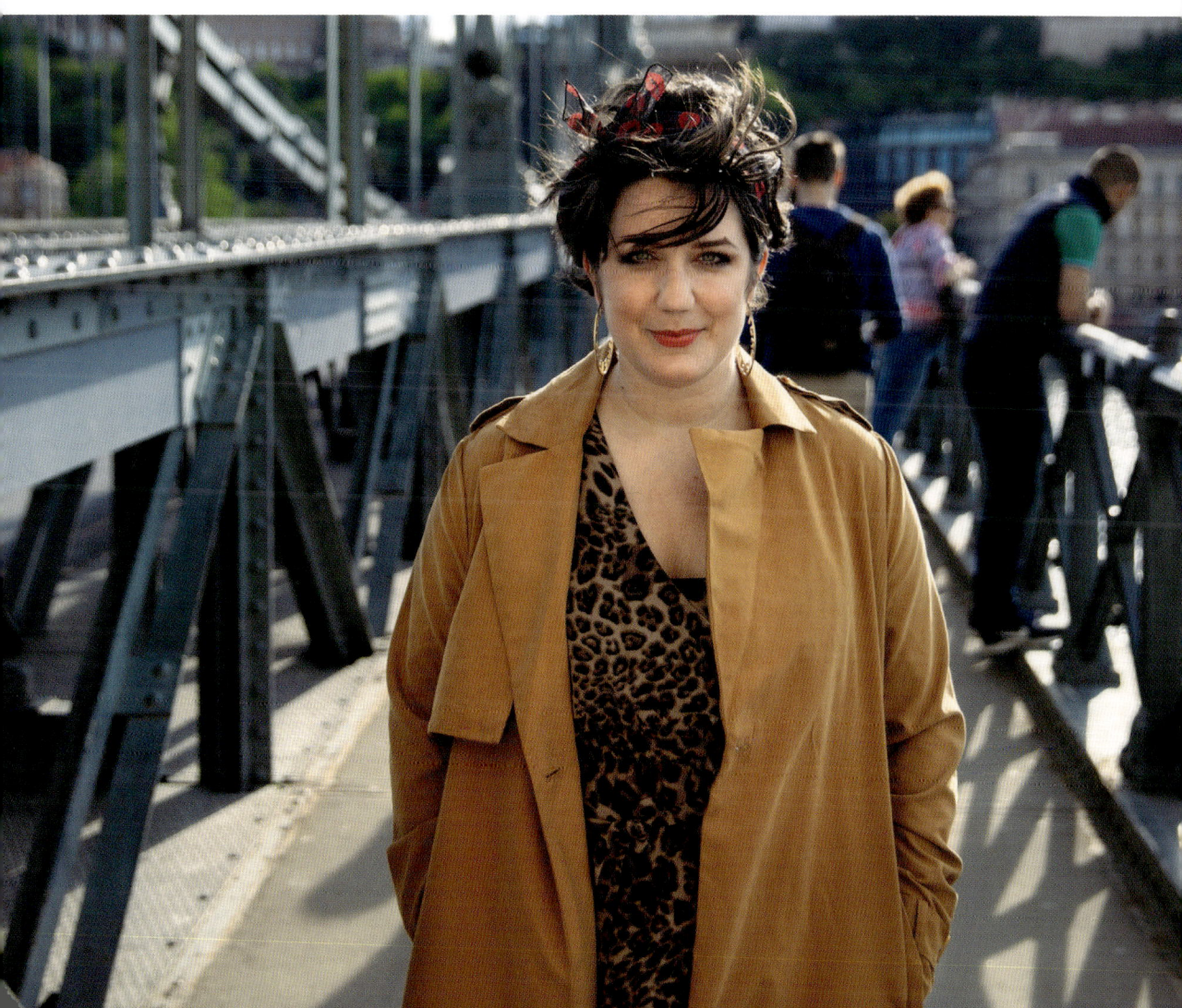

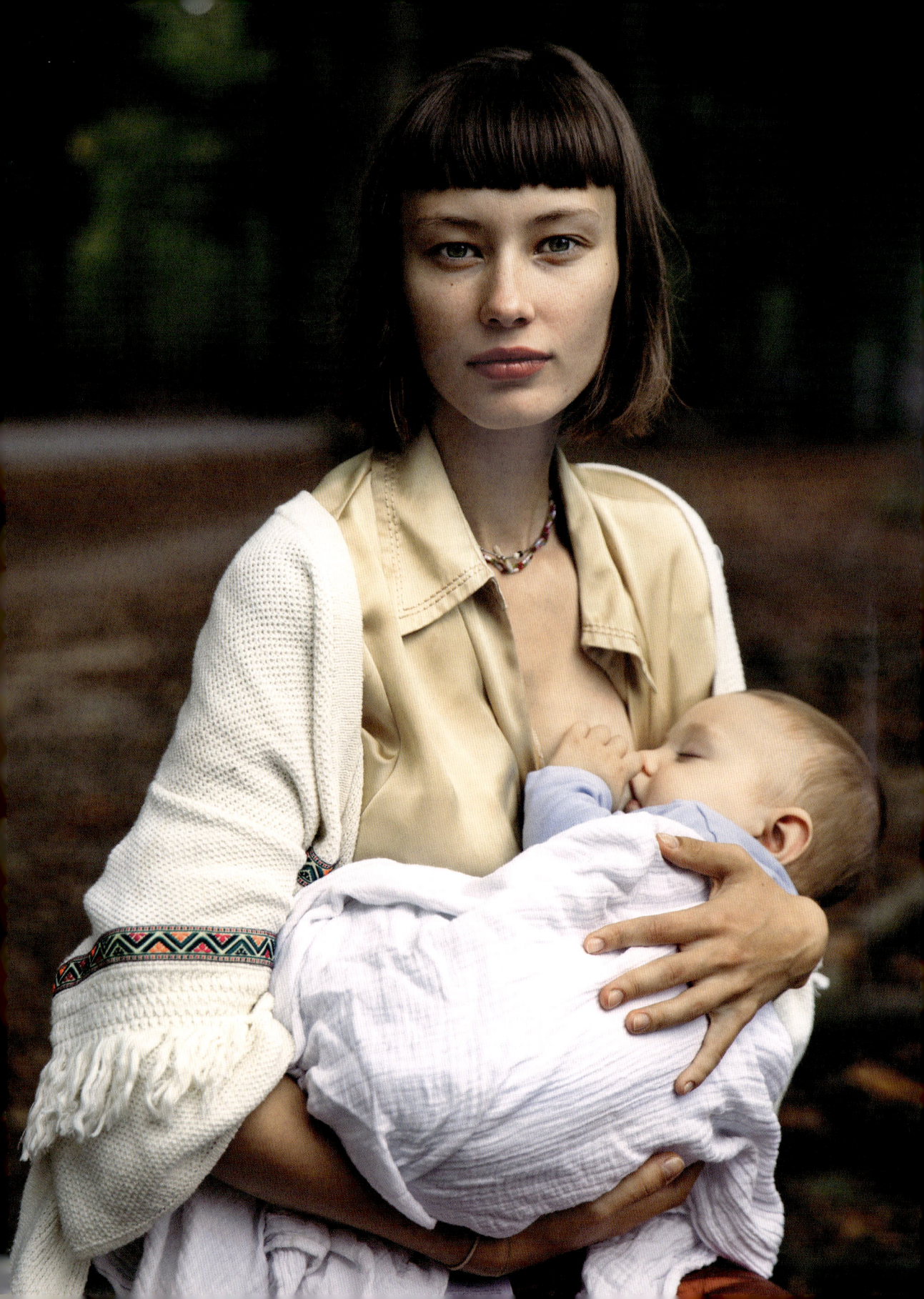

BERLIN, GERMANY *(Opposite)*

Masha and her son, Gaspar.

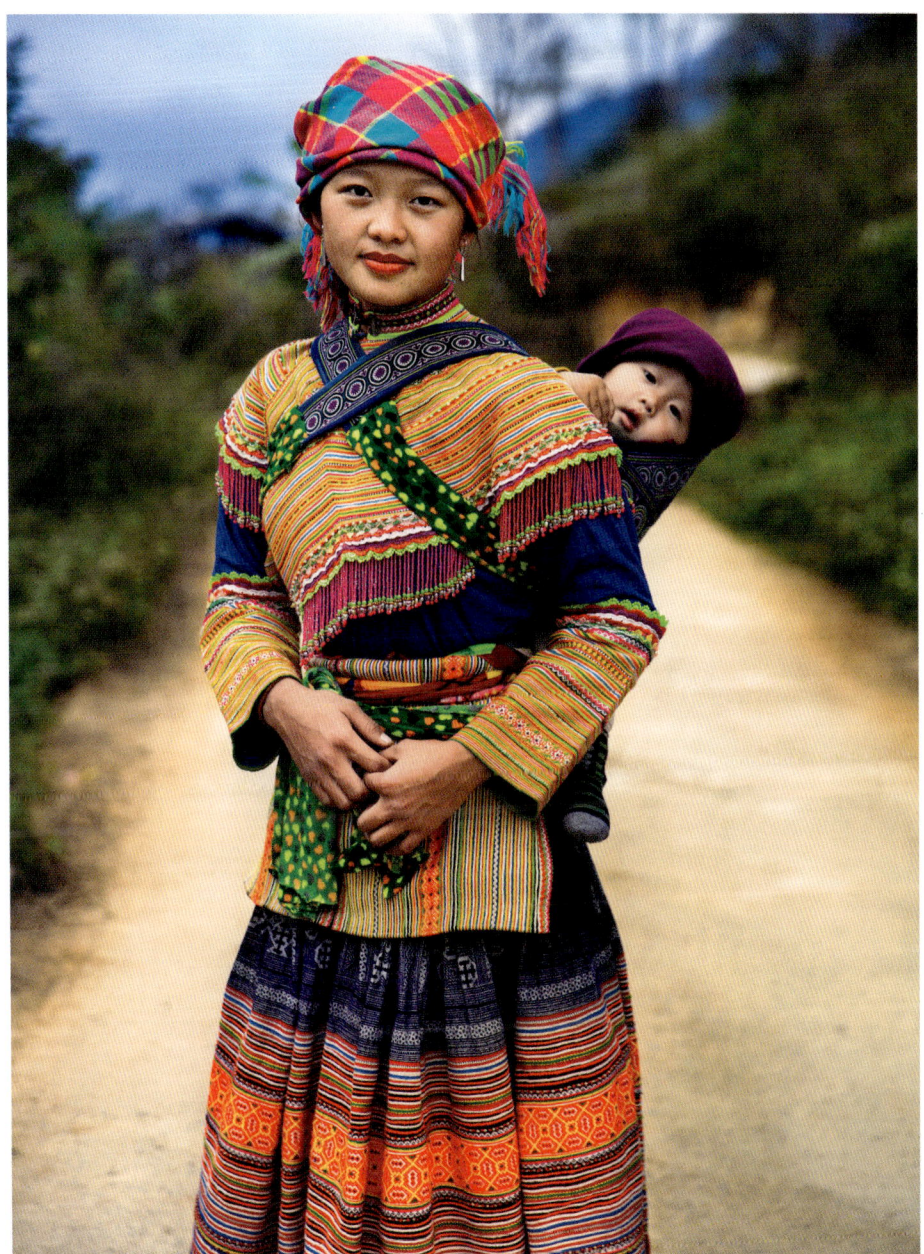

NORTHERN VIETNAM *(Above)*

This is Gâu and her son, Khoi. There are many differences between the cultures of the world when it comes to raising a baby. Throughout my travels, I've noticed that the ways a newborn is fed, carried, or educated can differ greatly. But what's similar all over the world is the intense love of a mother. Just like real beauty, real love has no bounds nor standards—it comes from the inside.

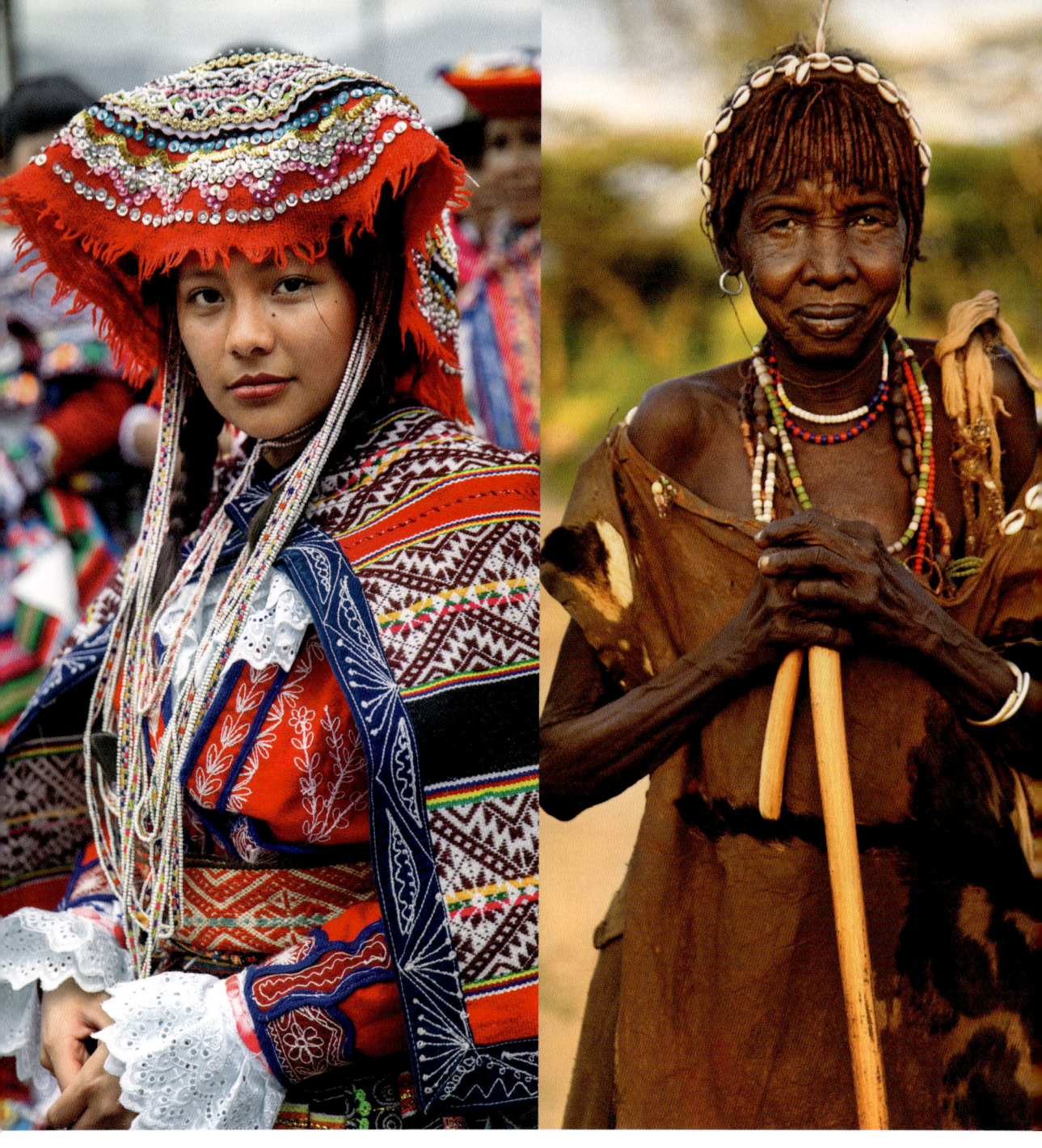

SACRED VALLEY, PERU

OMO VALLEY, ETHIOPIA

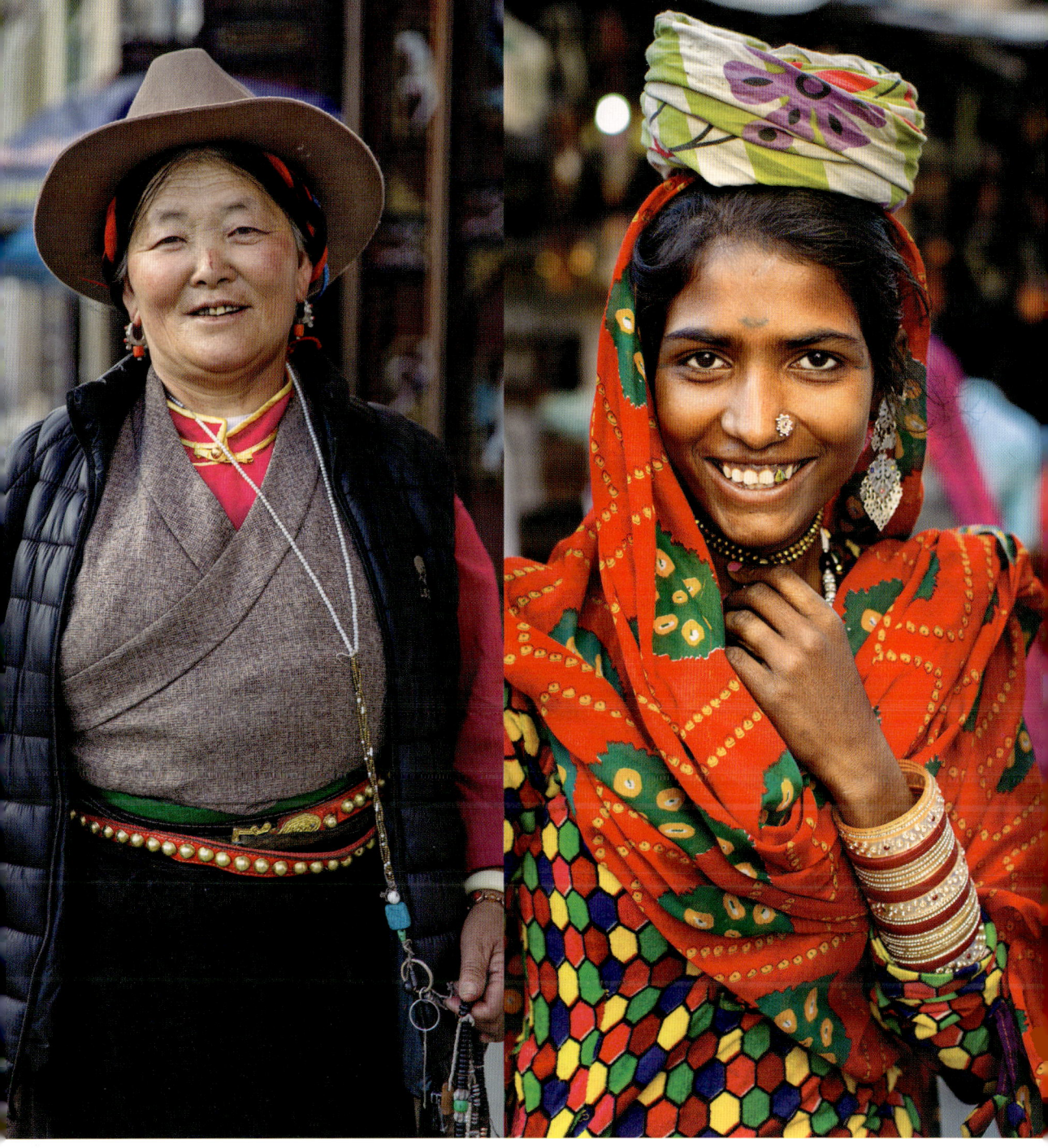

SICHUAN, CHINA

PUSHKAR, INDIA

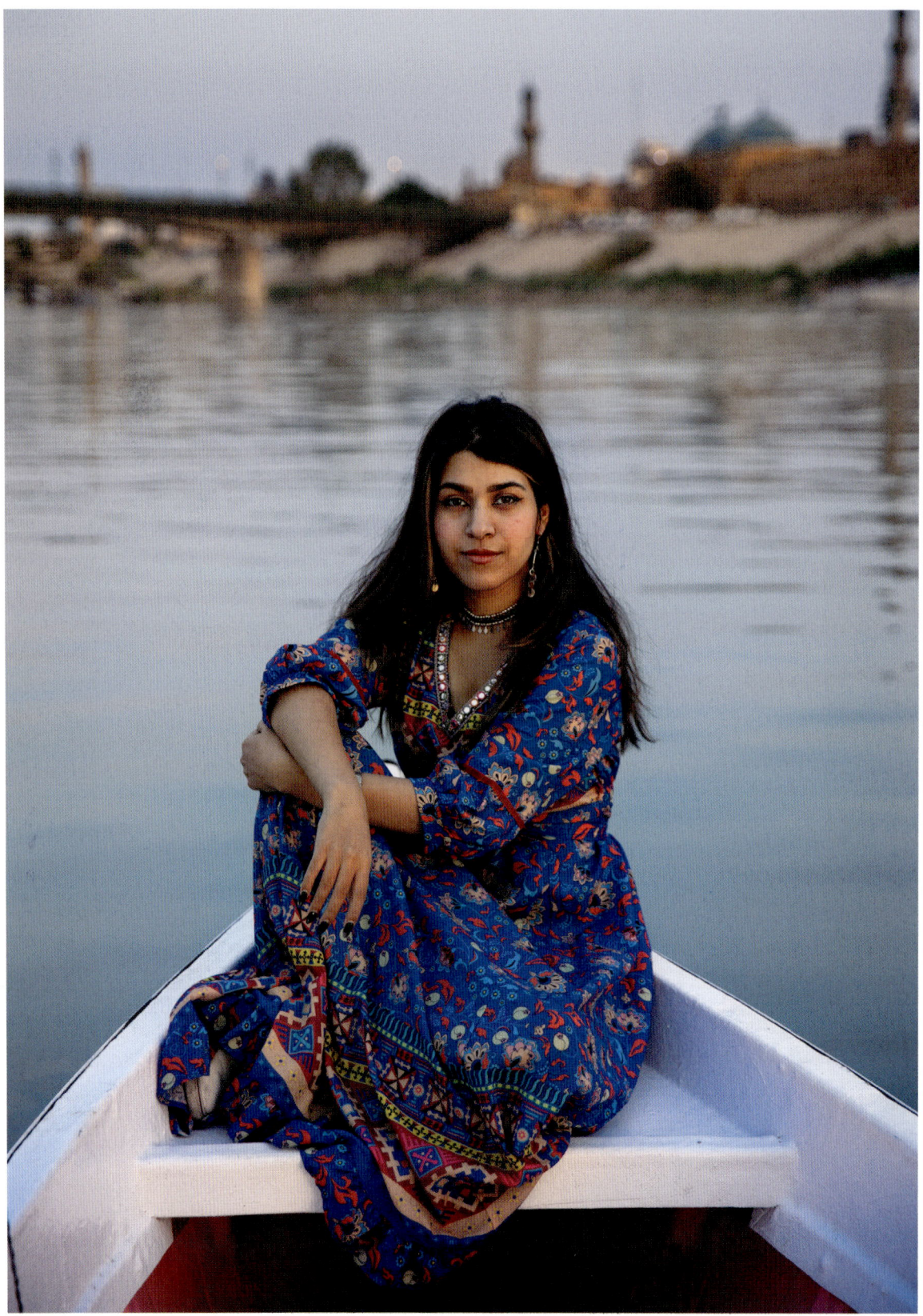

BAGHDAD, IRAQ *(Opposite)*

Aya Mansour is a remarkable person—a great example of strength and kindness. Although she studied mathematics at university, she dedicated most of her life to writing. Aya is still very young, but she's already a respected poet, writer, and journalist, and her work has been featured in prestigious media outlets.

Growing up in a country devastated by war, Aya has seen it all: the lifeless bodies of children, the agony of hostages, and the pain and despair of an entire nation. The weight of these experiences led to years of insomnia for her.

All that suffering made her decide to become a journalist so she could let the world know about the tragedies but also have a voice to make a change. She often receives threats because of her work, but she never thinks of quitting.

Aya's love for her country and its people is profound and impressive. She is on a permanent mission to make Iraq a better place, and I know that nothing can stop her.

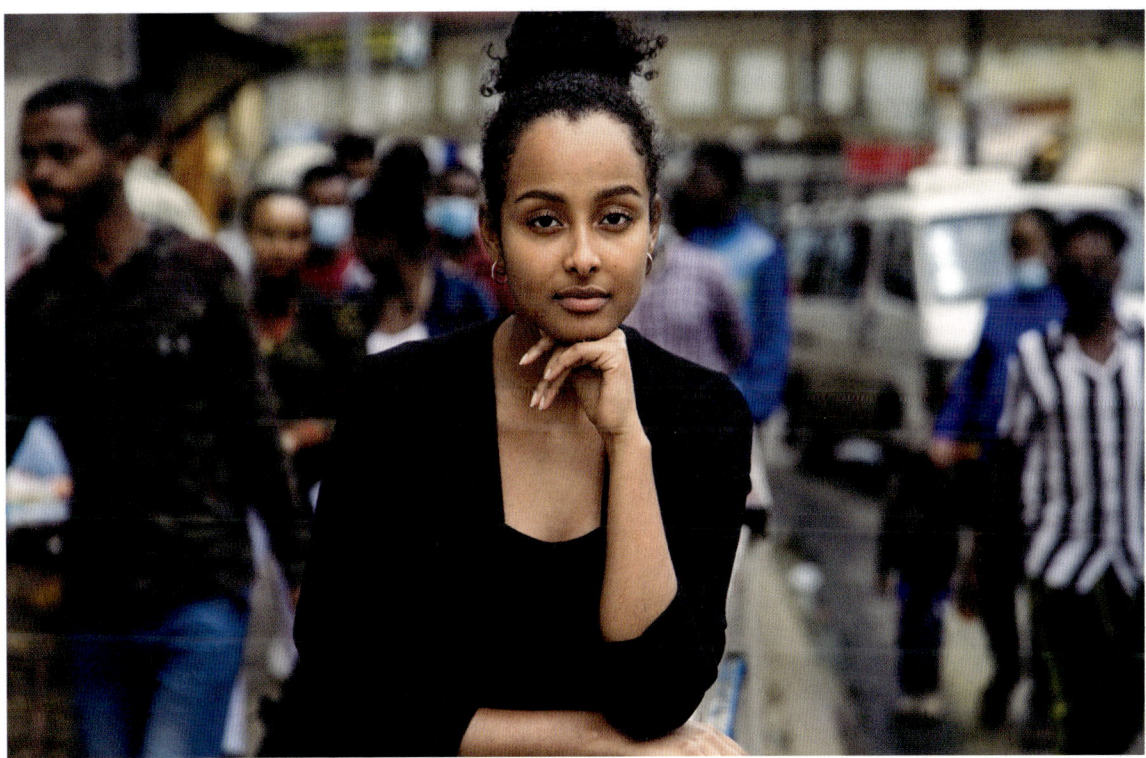

ADDIS ABABA, ETHIOPIA *(Above)*

Lydia Mengesha grew up in Germany within an Ethiopian family and has always had strong ties to her country of origin. Throughout her childhood, she frequently accompanied her father to Ethiopian villages, where he provided assistance to communities in need.

With a profound love for Ethiopia in her soul, Lydia returned to the country as an adult in order to contribute to its development. At the time of our meeting, she was employed by the International Organization for Migration, and she was living in her grandmother's humble house without modern amenities. Although far away from her comfortable life in Germany, she was feeling at the right place in the right moment of her life.

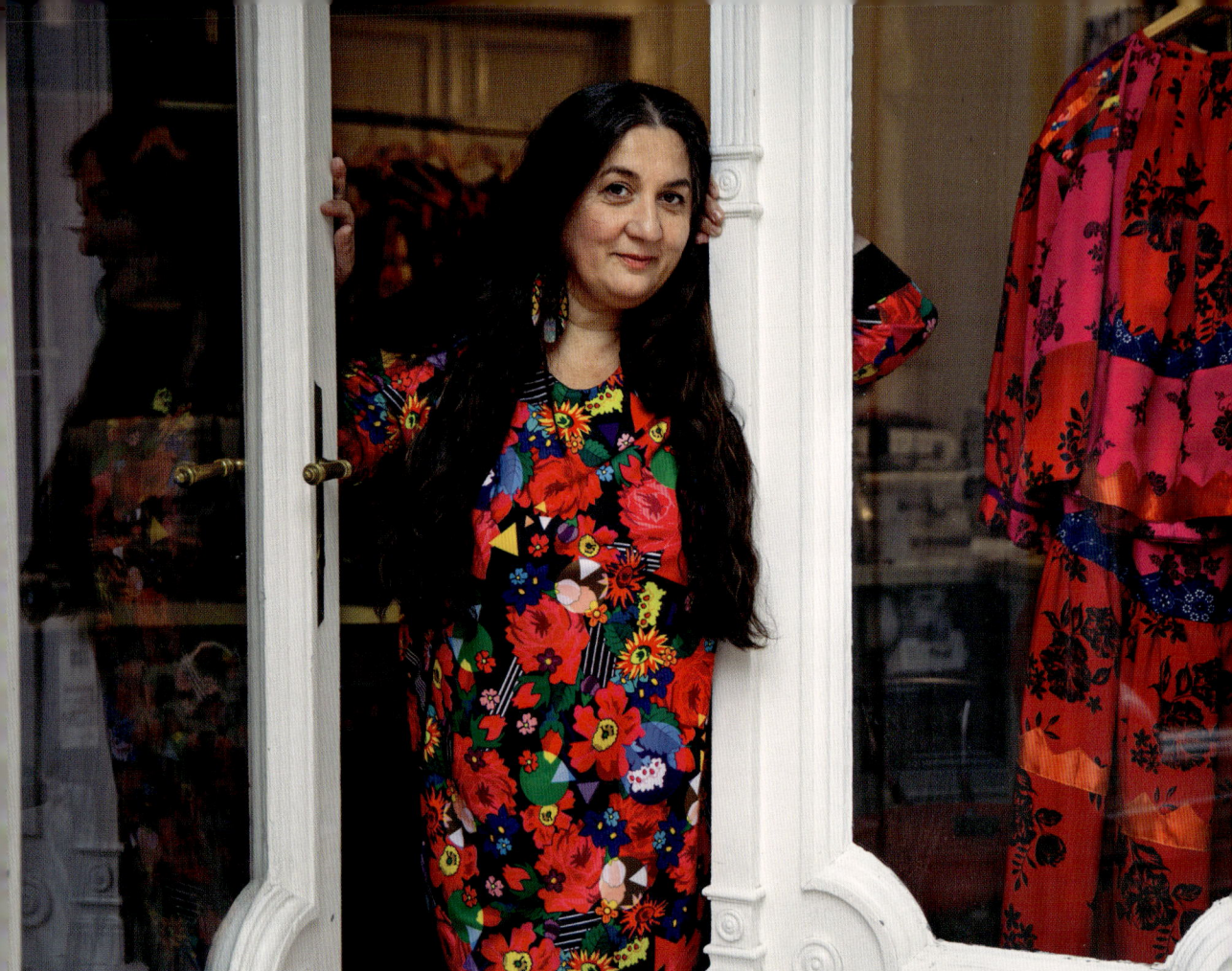

BUDAPEST, HUNGARY

I met Erika Varga in her vibrant workshop,
which is full of colorful outfits. She is a Roma
designer who is reshaping norms and bringing
Romani culture to a contemporary setting.
Historically marginalized Roma communities
across Europe often suffer social and
economic exclusion, discrimination, and
poverty. Through her label, which is called
Romani Design, Erika is defying misconceptions
while embracing and promoting her heritage.

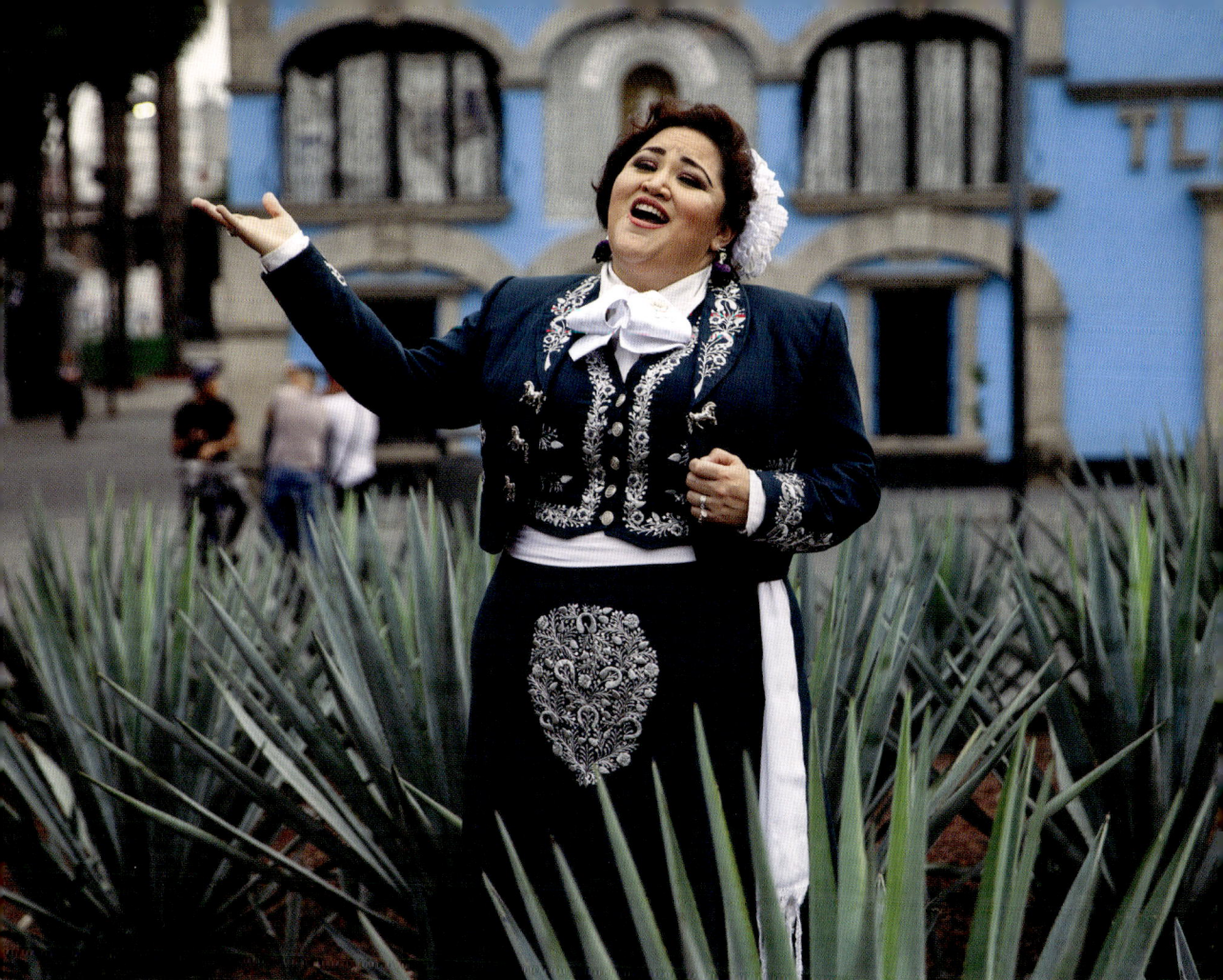

MEXICO CITY, MEXICO

Vanessa Velasco is one of few mariachi women. In Mexico, "mariachi" refers to groups of musicians that play a type of traditional music. Initially, Vanessa studied opera, as there were no female mariachi performers at the time. However, she later made her breakthrough in this male-dominated world by becoming a mariachi singer.

Today, Vanessa's voice is powerful—both onstage and in everyday life. She runs a prestigious mariachi school right here in Plaza Garibaldi, which is the vibrant epicenter of mariachi culture.

NEW YORK CITY, UNITED STATES

At the age of fifty-three, Karen Williams decided to return to modeling and became an advocate for greater representation of aging women from all backgrounds. Her gray hair is a manifesto for authenticity and freedom. She has always felt inspired by her mother—a woman who embraced every stage of her life with ease and grace.

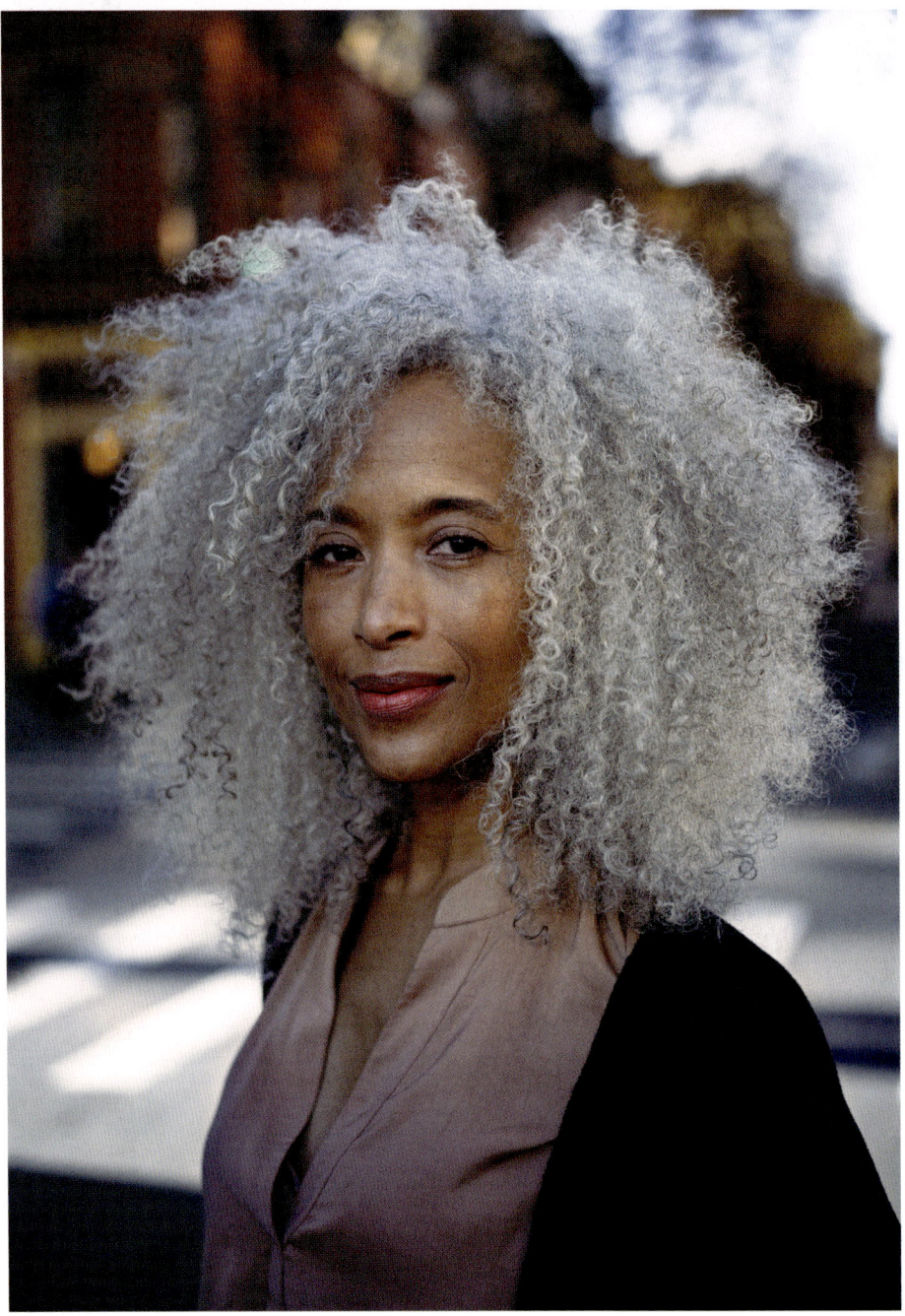

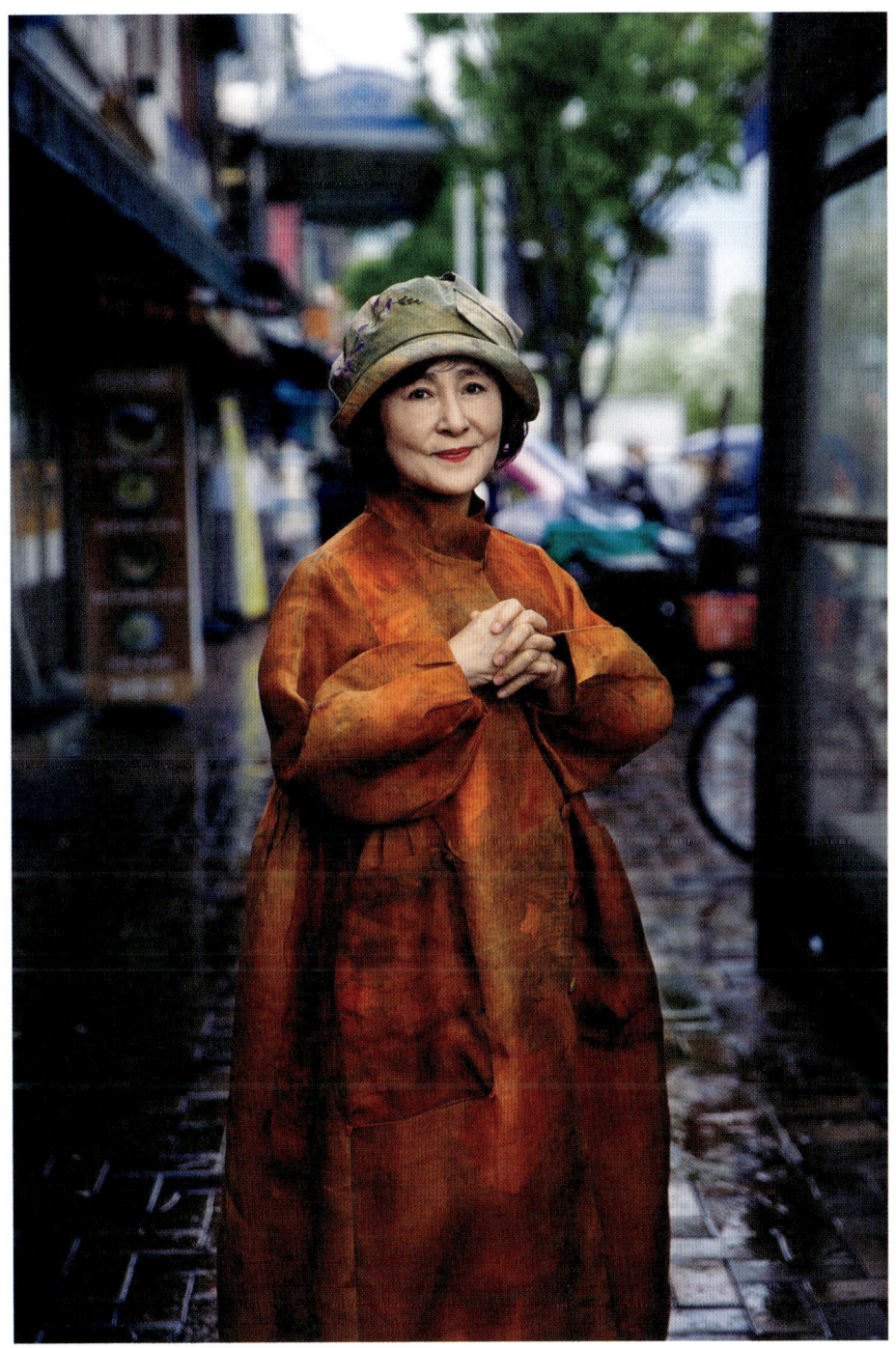

SEOUL, SOUTH KOREA

Yea-Eun designs clothes for stylish seniors. She wears her own creations in this photo.

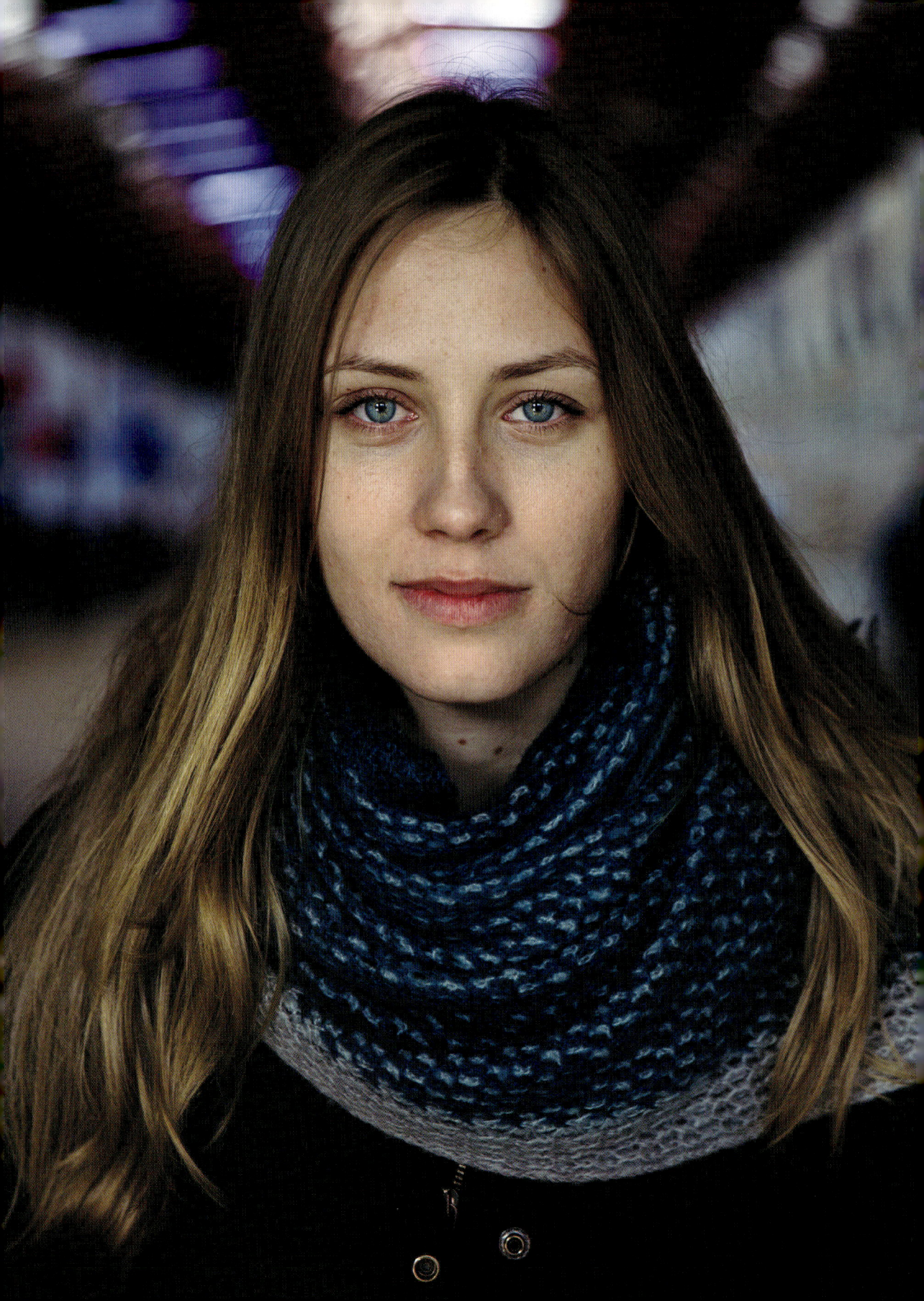

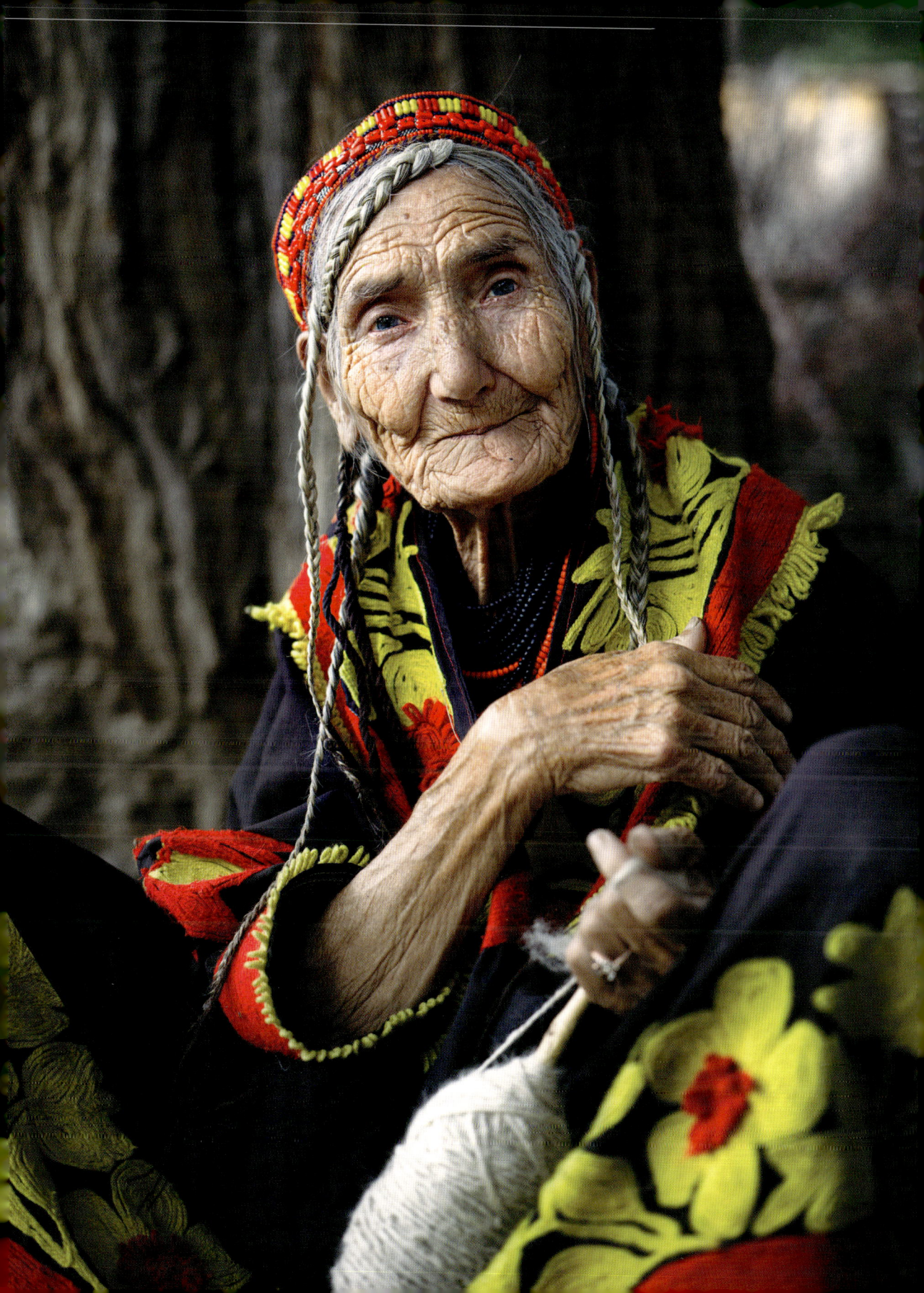

BUCHAREST, ROMANIA *(Previous spread, left)*

I photographed Simina Cernat in a train station. During her time at university, she was a successful student, and after graduation she easily could have found a good job. But she wanted something else. She wanted to discover the world.

She started traveling throughout Asia—accompanied only by her backpack. She taught English and French. She lived off a few dollars per day. She learned Indonesian and a bit of Hindi. She helped people in need as a volunteer. She had dengue and typhus. She explored the wilderness and reached places where locals had never seen a foreigner. She fell in love. She climbed challenging peaks in the Himalayas. She opened a restaurant in India. And she recently gathered her memories and published a book about her experiences as a solo female traveler. She called it *Samsara*.

Samsara is a fundamental concept in Indian religions and refers to the belief that all living beings go through cyclical births and rebirths. Figuratively, Simina already went through births and rebirths, but she did it in one single life. And that's just the beginning—she's only twenty-six.

KALASHA VALLEYS, PAKISTAN
(Previous spread, right)

The Kalash people have a captivating and distinct culture. A splendid hallmark of their culture is the traditional attire worn by women in every moment of their lives.

Shahardana spends her summer days spinning wool next to a field. At her age, she can't work in the field anymore, but she loves to stay close to it. Here she can socialize with the younger people of the village who work in the field. This way she never gets bored, and she also has the chance to share some of her wisdom with the younger generation. In the end, this is one of the ways culture and tradition are passed down through generations.

TEHRAN, IRAN *(Opposite)*

Setareh is passionate about poetry. She is studying for a PhD in Persian literature while having a love affair with Italian literature at the same time.

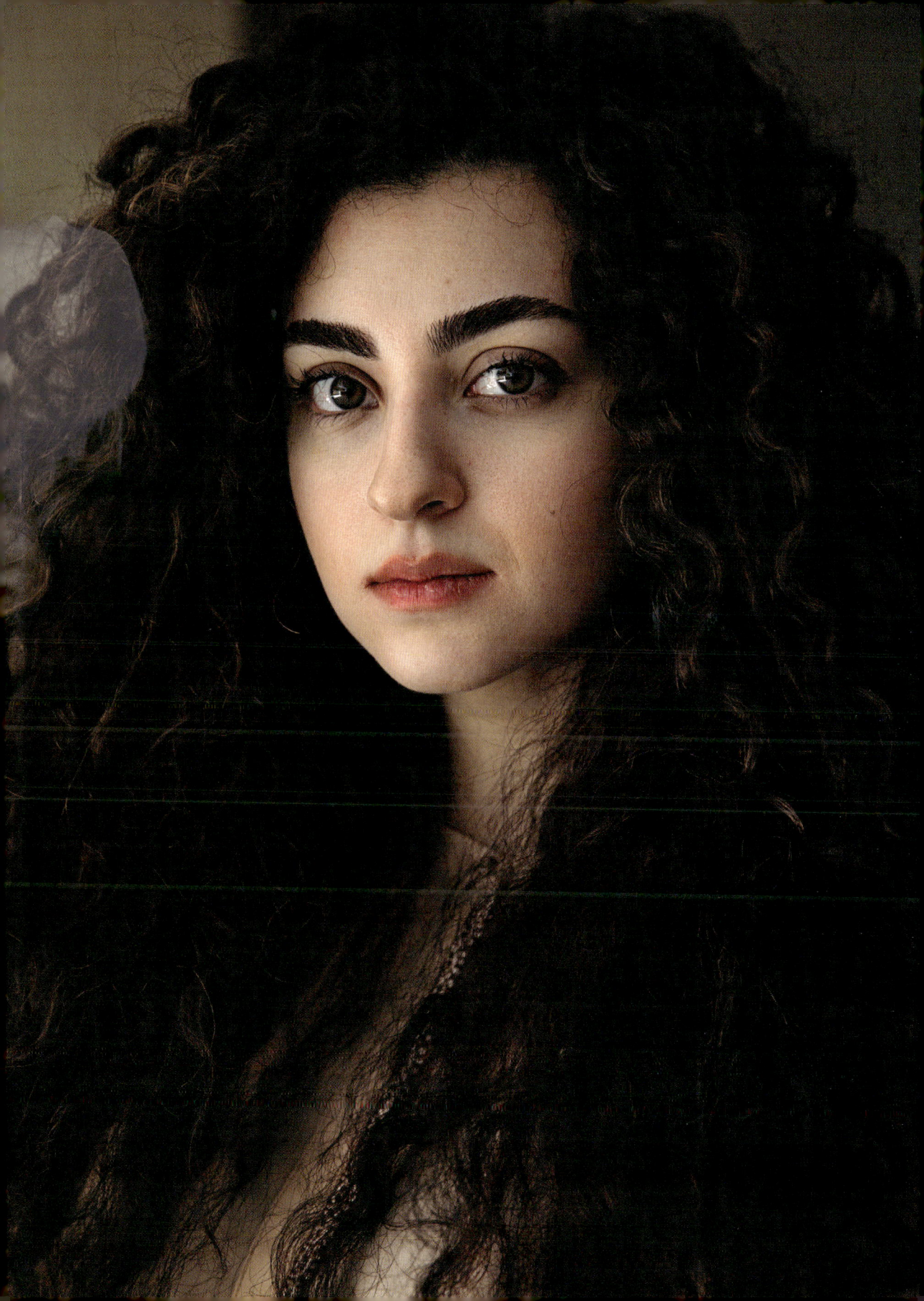

KYOTO, JAPAN

When she was fifteen years old, Yuka joined a *maiko* school in the Miyagawacho district of Kyoto. A *maiko* is an apprentice geisha in western Japan.

As a teenager, Yuka lived in a closed environment with strict rules, and that's when she realized how much she loves freedom. Very rarely after school, she was able to visit different coffee houses and observe the coffee preparation—it was fascinating.

Right before becoming a *geiko*, which is what geisha are called in western Japan, Yuka decided to change her path. Today, she's a barista, but her work is so much more than just preparing coffee. Yuka has transformed the coffee-preparation process into a real performance art by adding the moves, the grace, and the outfits of a geisha.

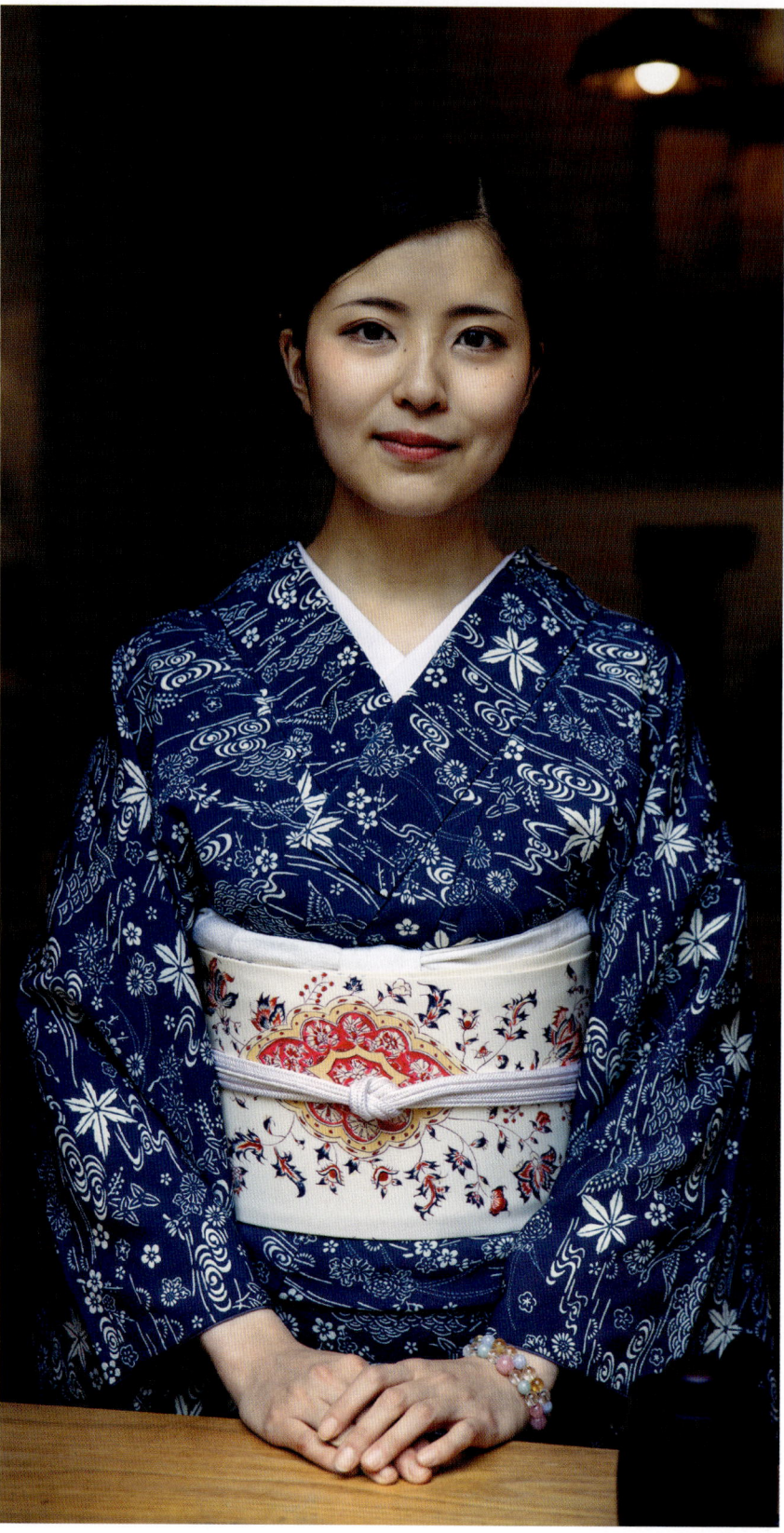

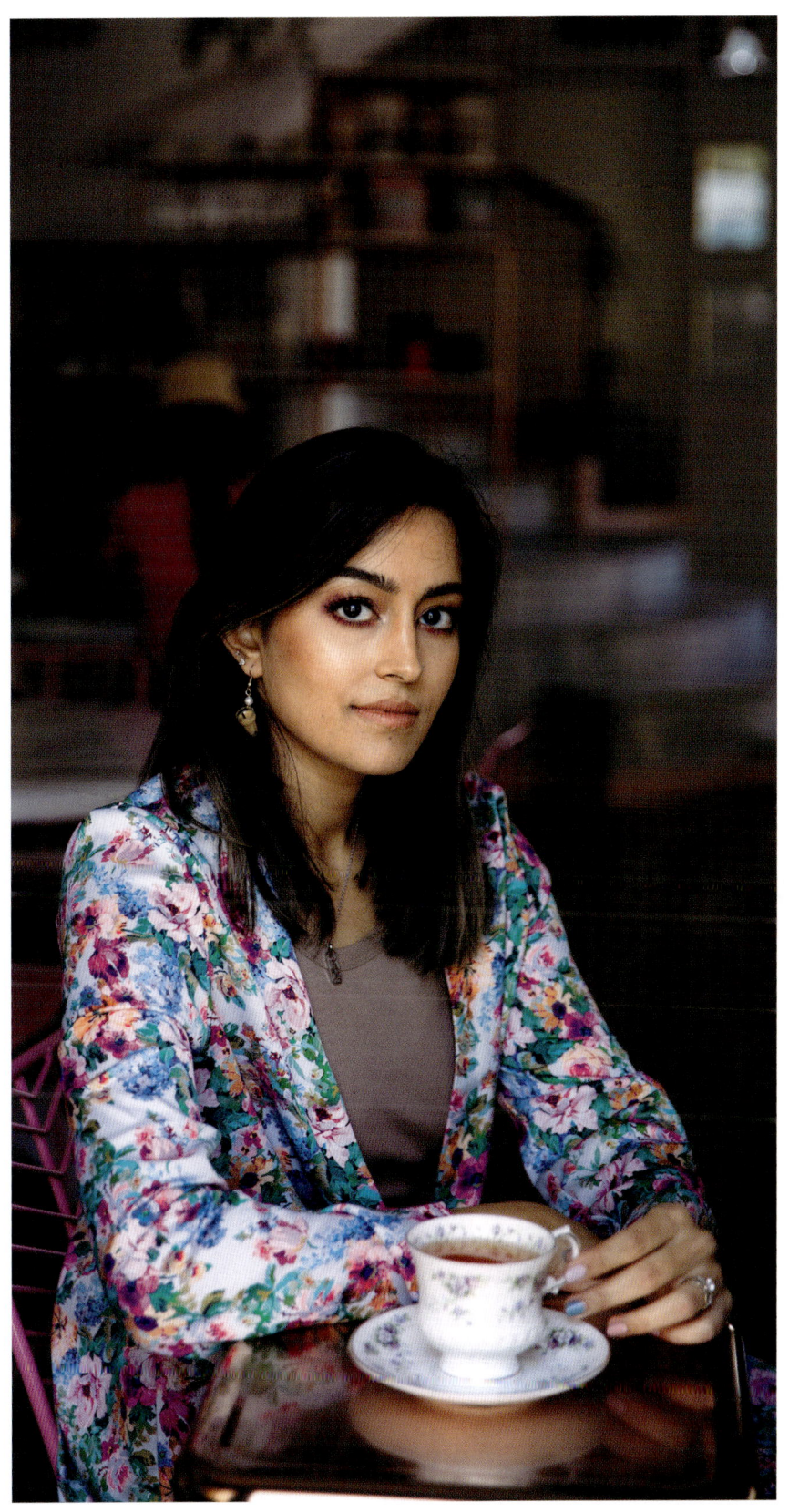

DUBAI, UNITED ARAB EMIRATES

Tania Lodi is originally from Pakistan and has been living in Dubai for almost two decades. A few years ago, she was diagnosed with an autoimmune condition called fibromyalgia, which causes chronic pain and tenderness throughout the body. Initially, she managed the horrific pain with painkillers, but, over time, she realized the long-term use of painkillers would ruin her life.

So, for years she searched for cures and solutions. She discovered meditation and poetry, studied psychology, and understood how important mindfulness and gratitude are for the health of the body. She then discovered the healing properties of tea.

Today, Tania owns a beautiful tea shop, where she creates unique blends for different needs. That's exactly where I photographed her. In a world where coffee is trendier than ever, she believes tea is very underappreciated and wants to change that. Her own example is relevant. For many years, she has been managing her challenging autoimmune condition without relying on painkillers—all while viewing life with positivity.

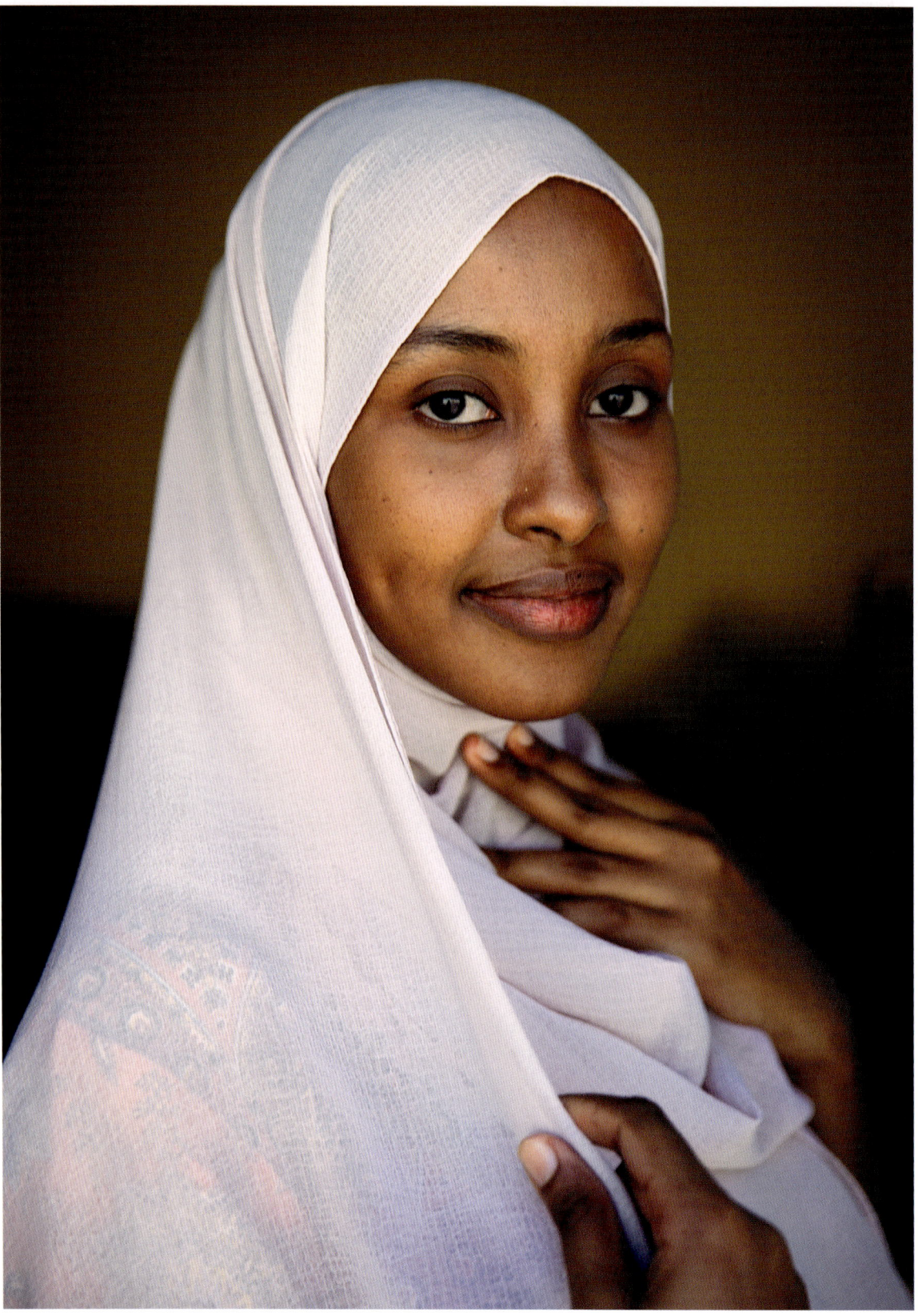

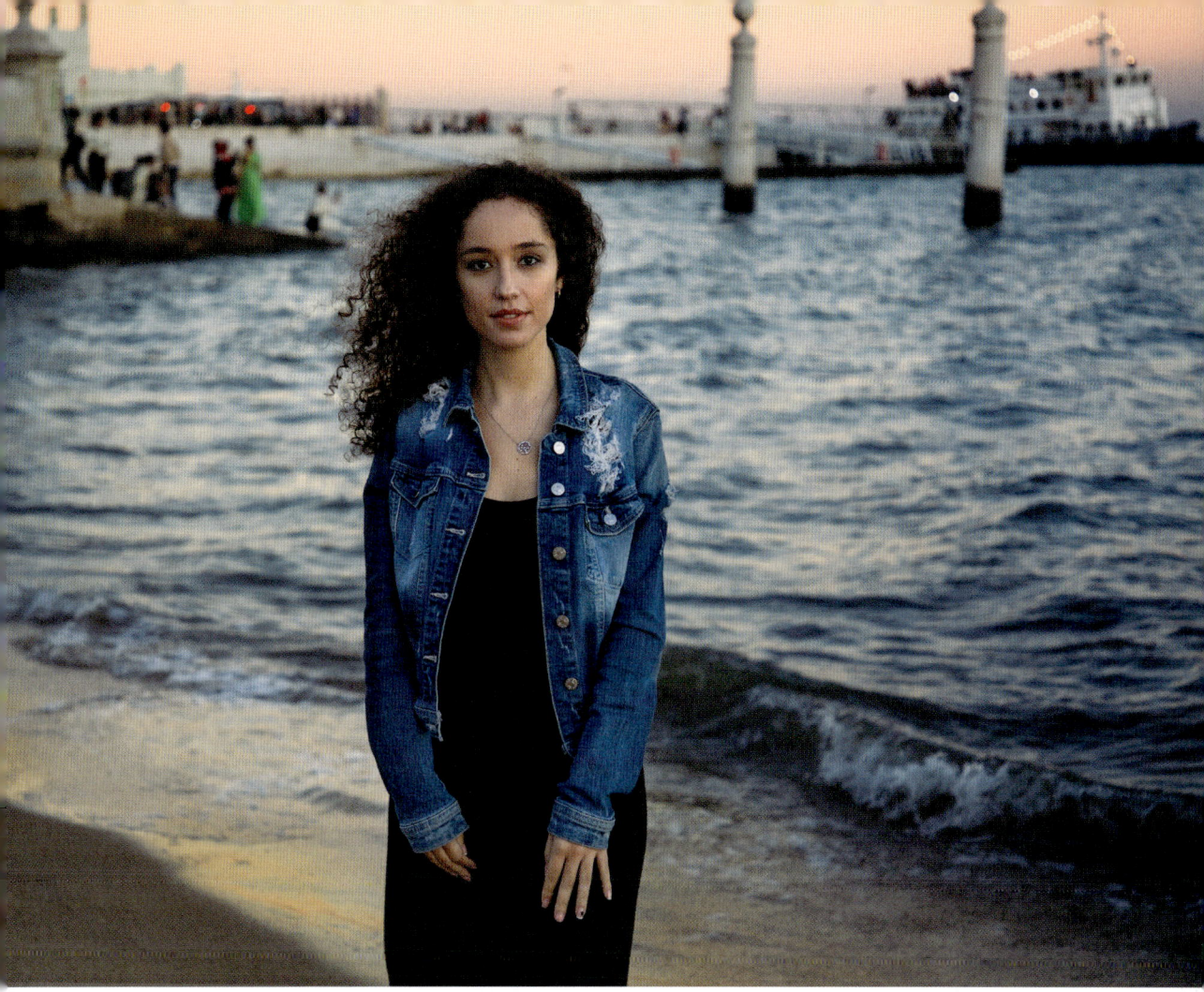

LISBON, PORTUGAL *(Above)*

Joana Almeida is a fado singer who performs the melancholic and soulful music that is
a trademark of Portugal. She first discovered fado during childhood, when her father
used to sing every day for fun. But back then, Joana was not particularly interested in
fado. When she started to sing during adolescence, Joana explored very diverse musical
genres, from pop to choral and even metal. But once she tried fado, she instantly knew it
was her calling. What was just a passion for her father evolved into a profession for Joana.

HARGEISA, SOMALILAND *(Opposite)*

Mushtaq, a biomedical engineer, is the only woman
in her office. She dreams to someday have her own
company, and to motivate and support more girls in
this part of the world to become engineers.

METEHARA, ETHIOPIA

It was market day in this small town. Most people here are Karrayuu, an ethnic group of pastoralists living in the area.

For Alu, a young Karrayuu woman, this was just an ordinary day at the market. For me it was extraordinary to witness the local traditions, to taste the local food, and to admire handmade outfits like Alu's.

I love to visit the markets of the world. For me, they are the core of many communities.

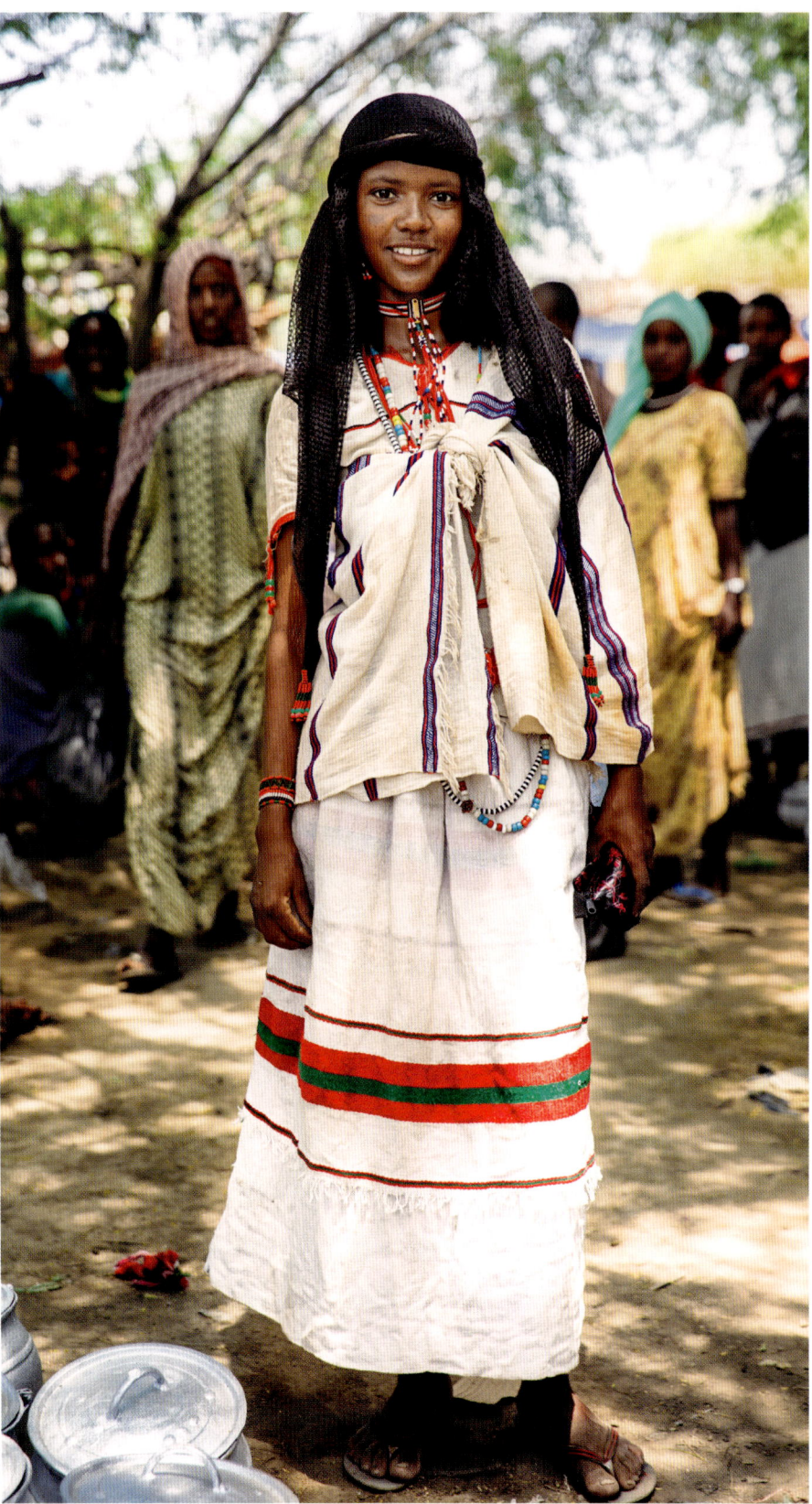

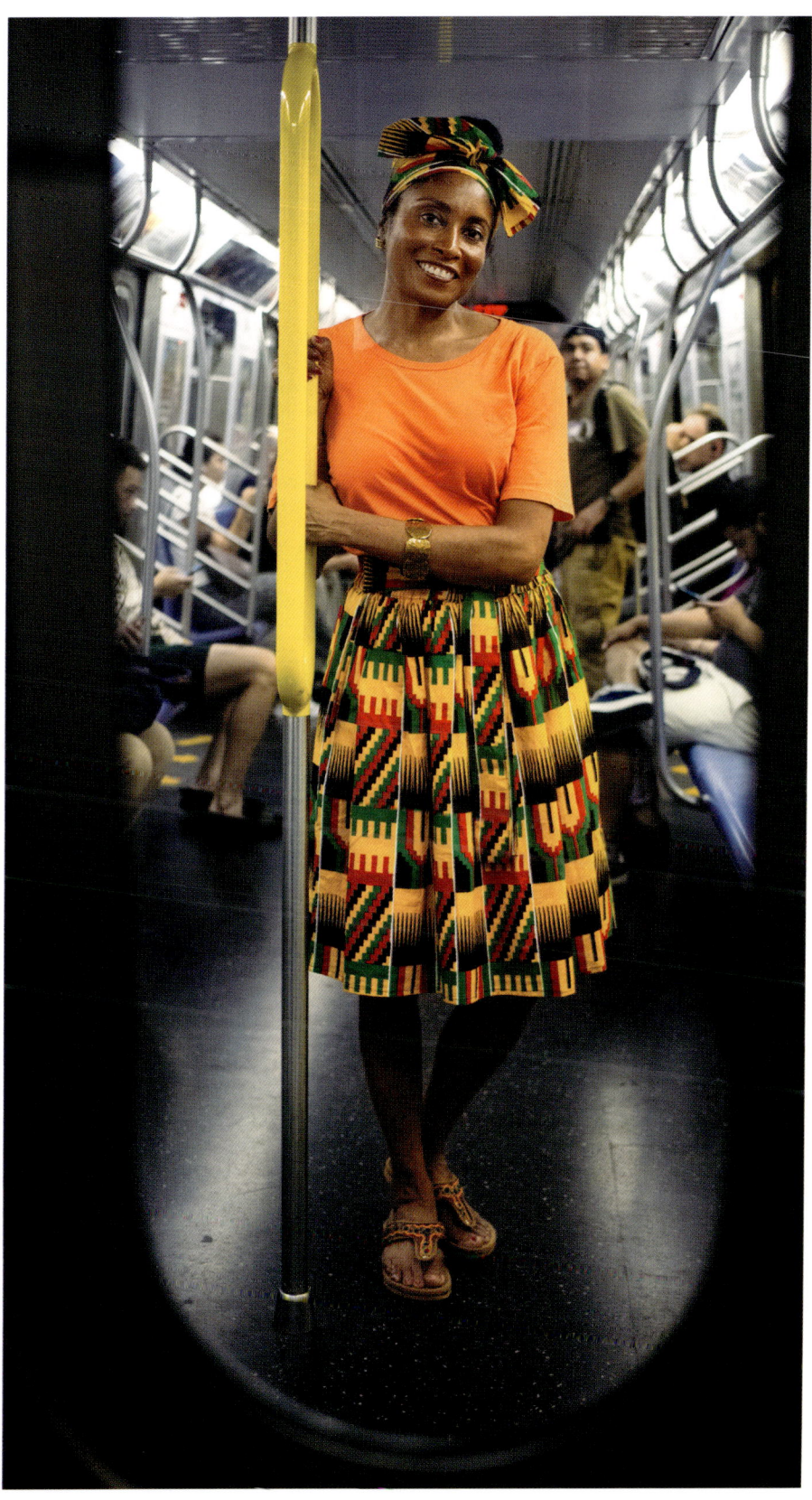

NEW YORK CITY, UNITED STATES

I noticed Vania in the subway. She has African, Native American, and European roots, and she's in love with diversity. She was born in Colombia but decided to move to New York City because she believes this is the best place to experience the diversity of the world.

Each day she dresses differently and celebrates different cultures. The day I met her was dedicated to Africa, and the previous day to Asia.

She was coming from the hospital, where she works as a psychiatrist, and was going to a tango lesson. What a colorful life, lived in colorful outfits, celebrating a colorful world.

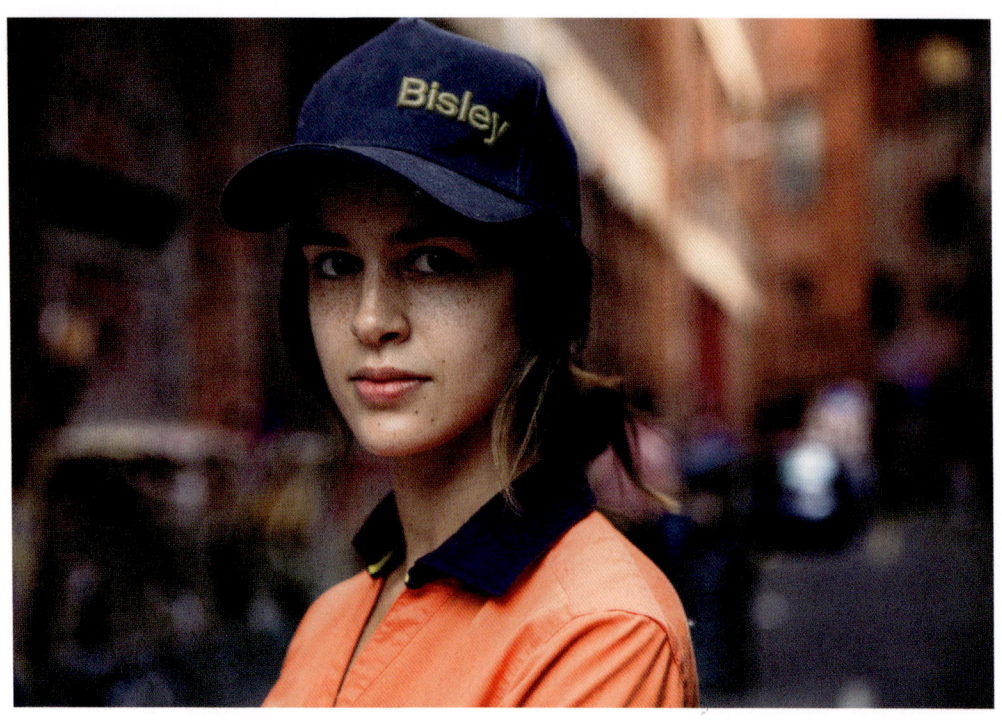

MELBOURNE, AUSTRALIA

Catie is a tiler.

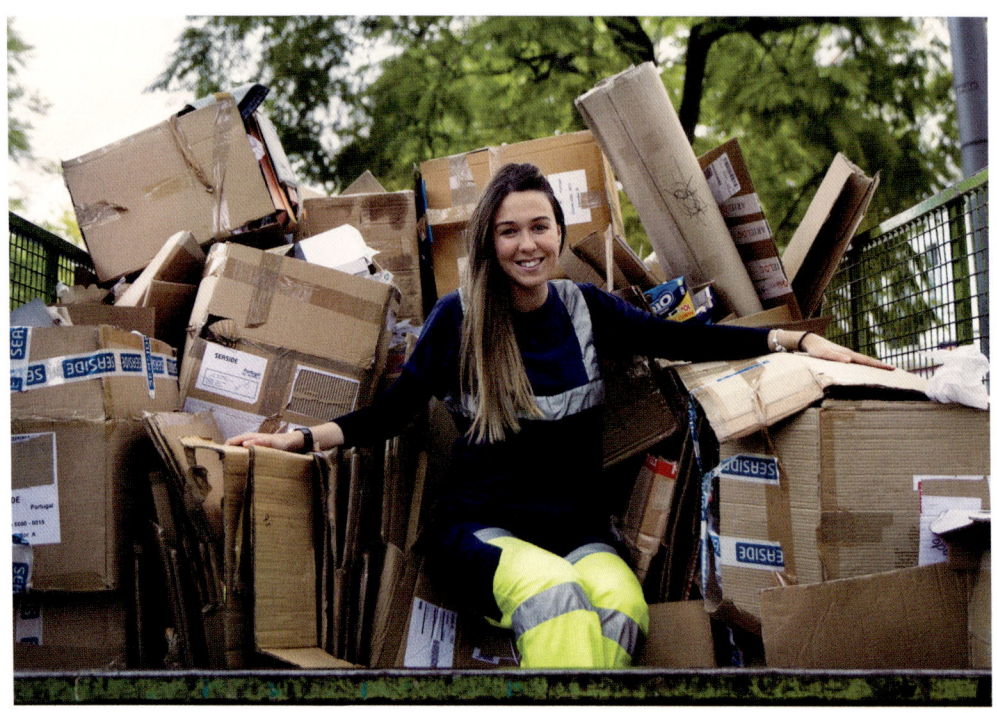

LISBON, PORTUGAL

Barbara is a waste collector.

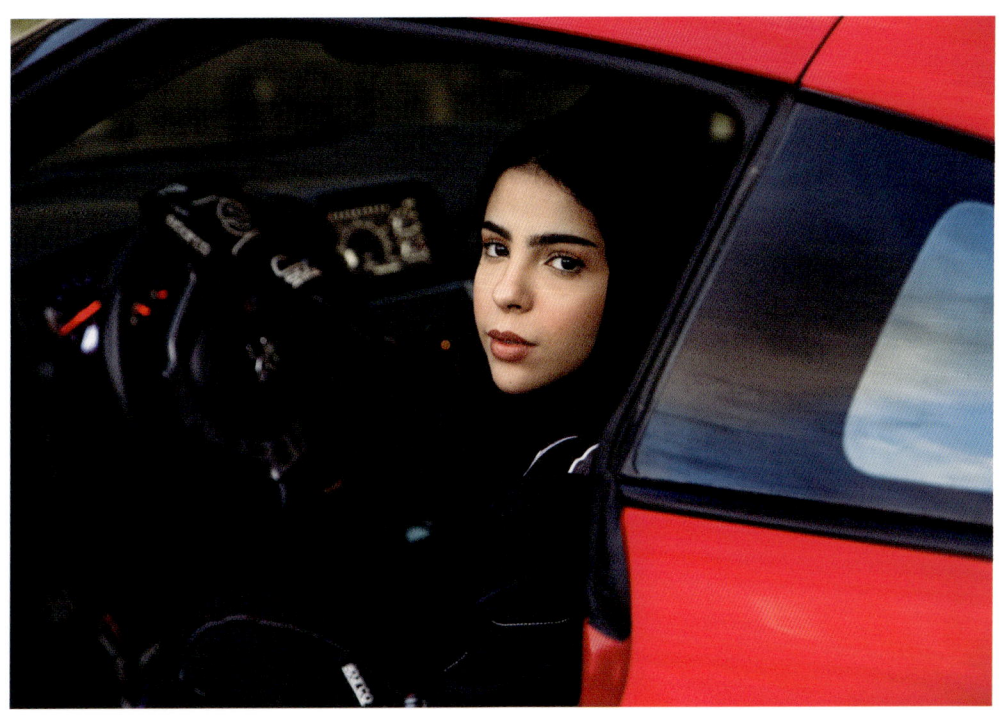

JEDDAH, SAUDI ARABIA

Reem is a racing driver.

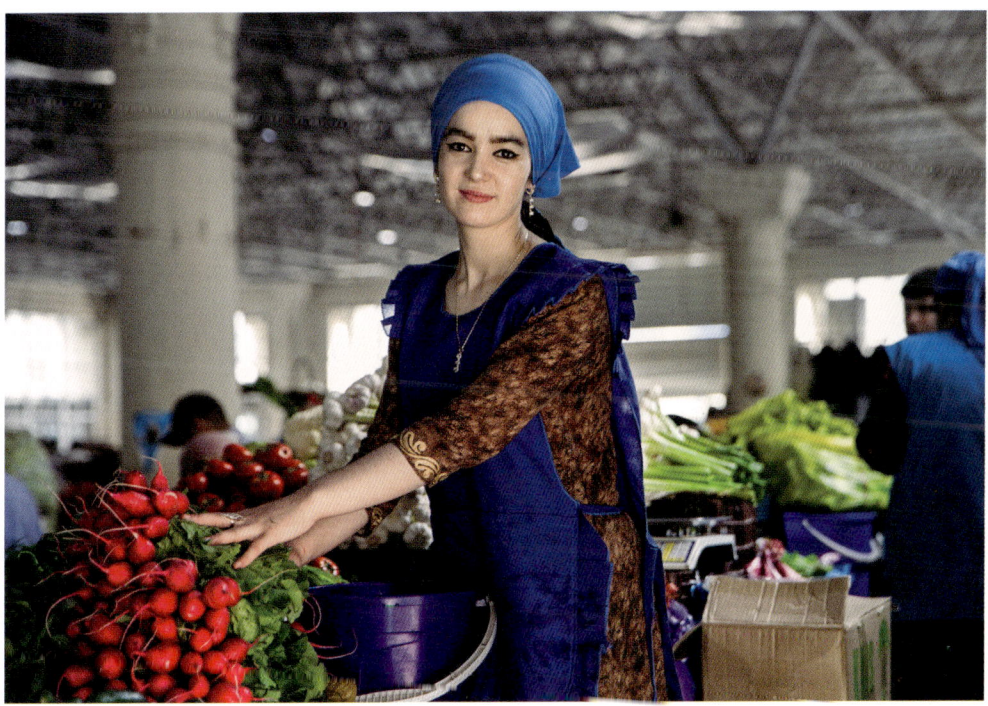

DUSHANBE, TAJIKISTAN

Shamigul is a seller.

HAVANA, CUBA

Her name translates to "dove" in Spanish, and after enduring many hardships, she learned how to soar above all the suffering.

Paloma was born without a left hand, yet she never considered this a disability. At the young age of twenty, when she gave birth to a baby girl, she became a joyful and devoted mother. However, a tragic event shattered her world. Due to a severe infection, her baby passed away. Through immense pain, Paloma found the strength to heal and became a mother once again. Her boy is two years old now, and Paloma is raising him by herself. I was amazed to find out how she changes diapers with one hand and how she does her own manicures using her feet.

Paloma makes her living as a seller in a souvenir shop. Although she studied informatics and was one of the best in her class, she didn't find a job in this field because employers deemed her unfit. However, Paloma proves every day that they were wrong.

I asked her, "Isn't all of this overwhelmingly difficult?" And she told me that nothing in life is difficult compared to losing a child. All her daily challenges mean nothing—as long as she has a healthy and happy child.

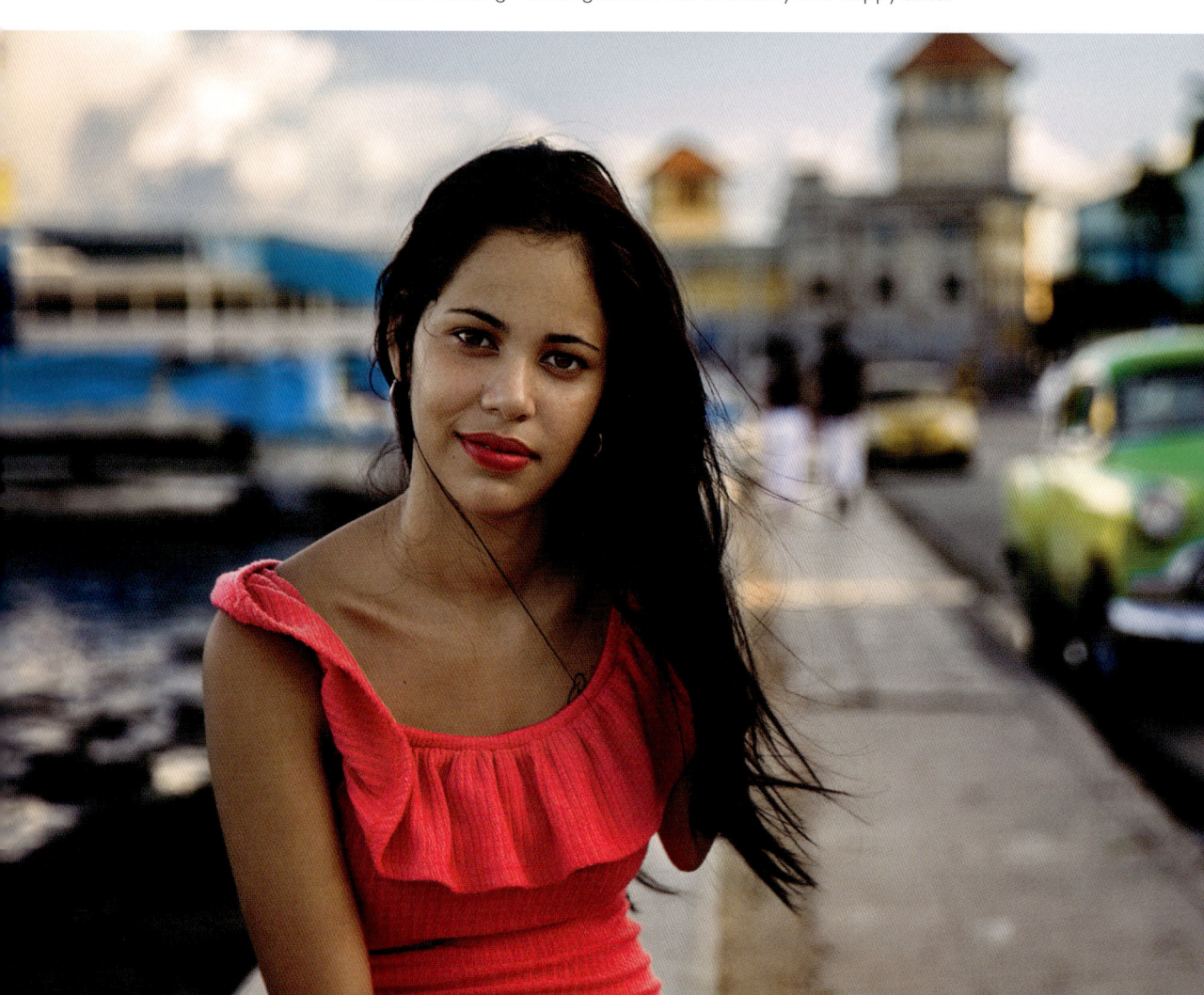

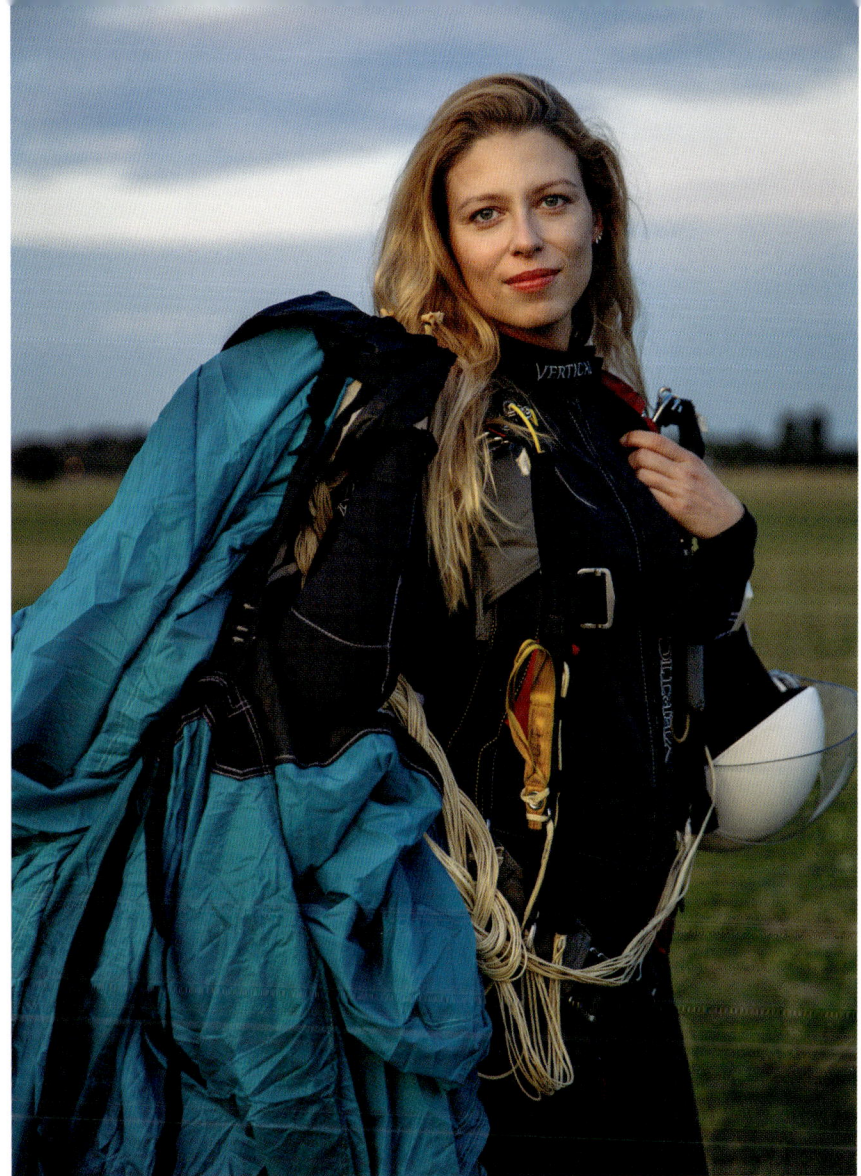

BERLIN, GERMANY

A few years ago, Lisa got pregnant. She was thrilled and spent time preparing to become a mother. However, during the fifth month, she lost her baby due to pregnancy complications. The stillbirth left her traumatized. She felt her life had lost its meaning. After a long period of depression, Lisa discovered skydiving.

Her first jump was filled with fear, but it served as a wake-up call, making her realize her strong desire to live. Lisa found that skydiving was therapeutic for her, so she started practicing it regularly.

With jump after jump, Lisa grew stronger and recovered her enthusiasm and optimism. She realized that if she can do skydiving, she can do anything.

She shared that being up in the sky made her understand how small she is in this beautiful and vast world. And if you know how small you are, your problems become smaller, as well.

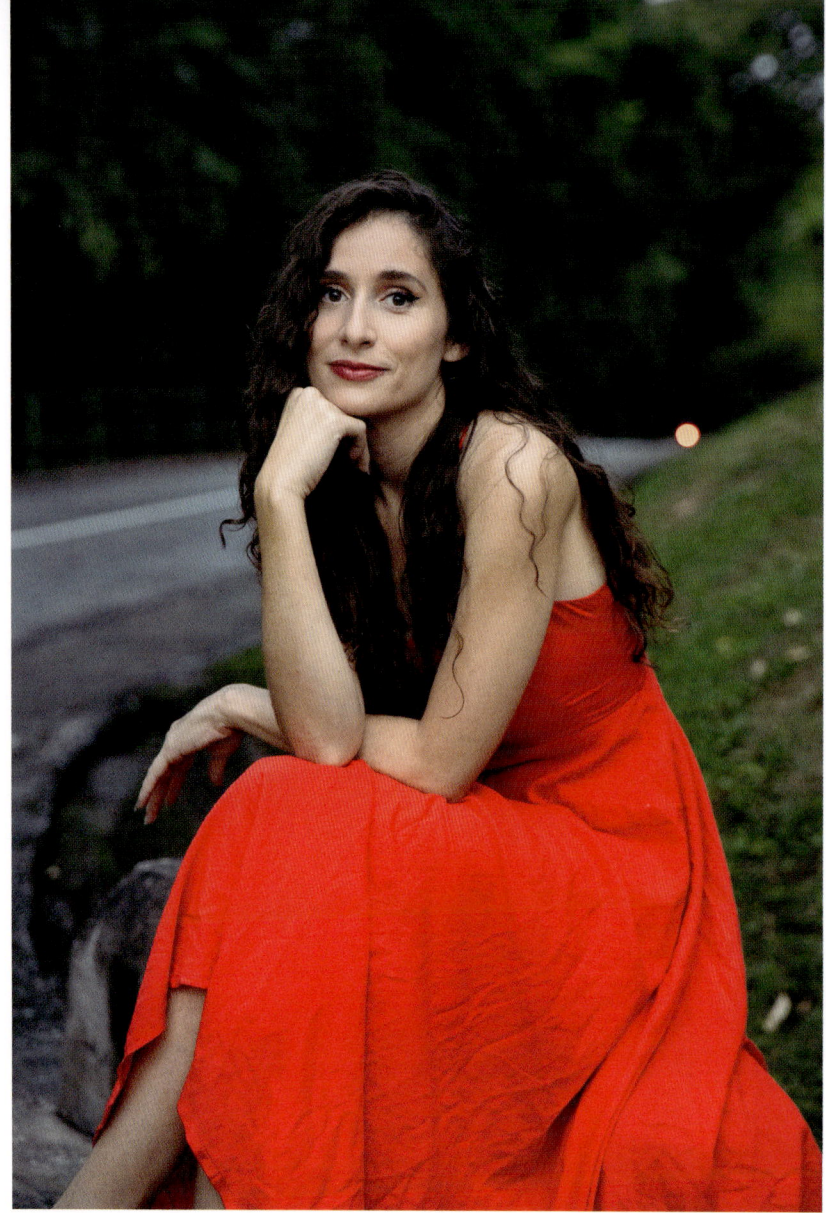

SINGAPORE

Alyne Tamir is a global citizen. In recent years, she has traveled to and lived in many different countries. Alyne grew up in a very conservative environment in the United States and married at a young age. After a few years, she realized she wanted a different path in life. She chose to divorce, which led her on a journey of self-discovery around the world.

That's how Alyne founded an online community to address issues such as female empowerment, healthy eating, and animal welfare. She also founded a Facebook group with more than one hundred thousand members called Girls Gone Global, which provides a safe space for women worldwide to connect and share their thoughts. Alyne knows from her own experience that there are many places around the world where women can't really speak out, and she wants to amplify the voice of every woman.

BARCELONA, SPAIN

Natalia studied biology and has always been fascinated by exploring the world and nature. She has just returned from a journey in the Philippines and India. She's selling some of her belongings at a flea market and preparing to begin a new journey to Canada. For Natalia, life is an adventure in which places and people are much more important than mere objects.

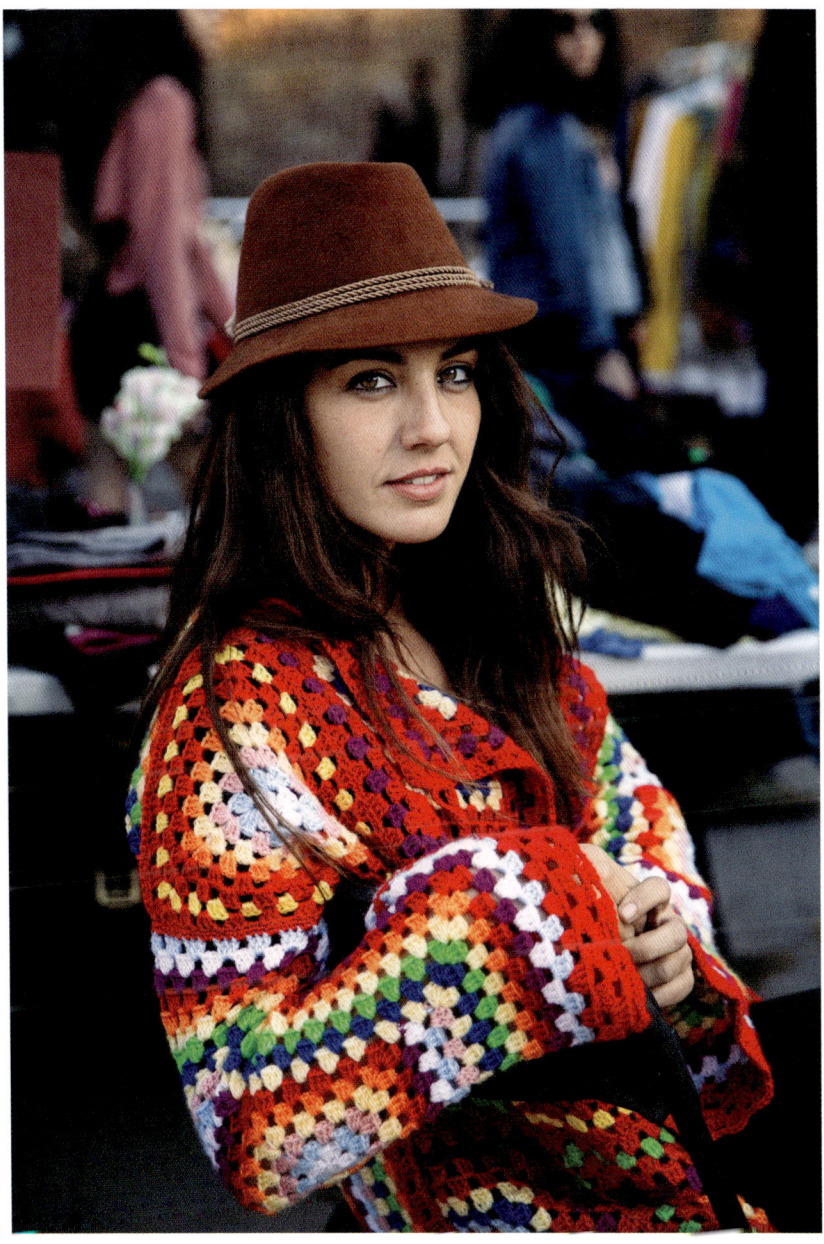

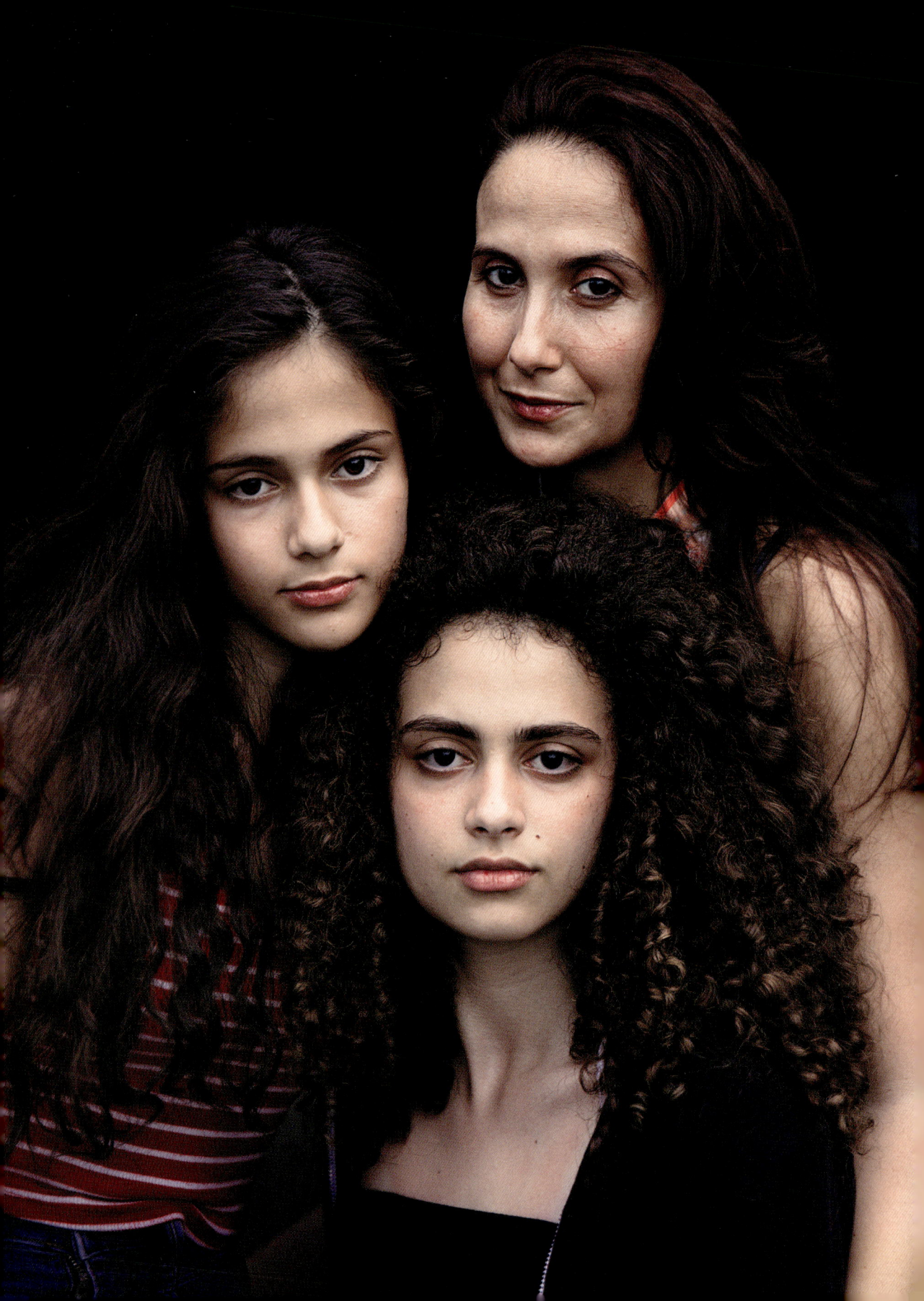

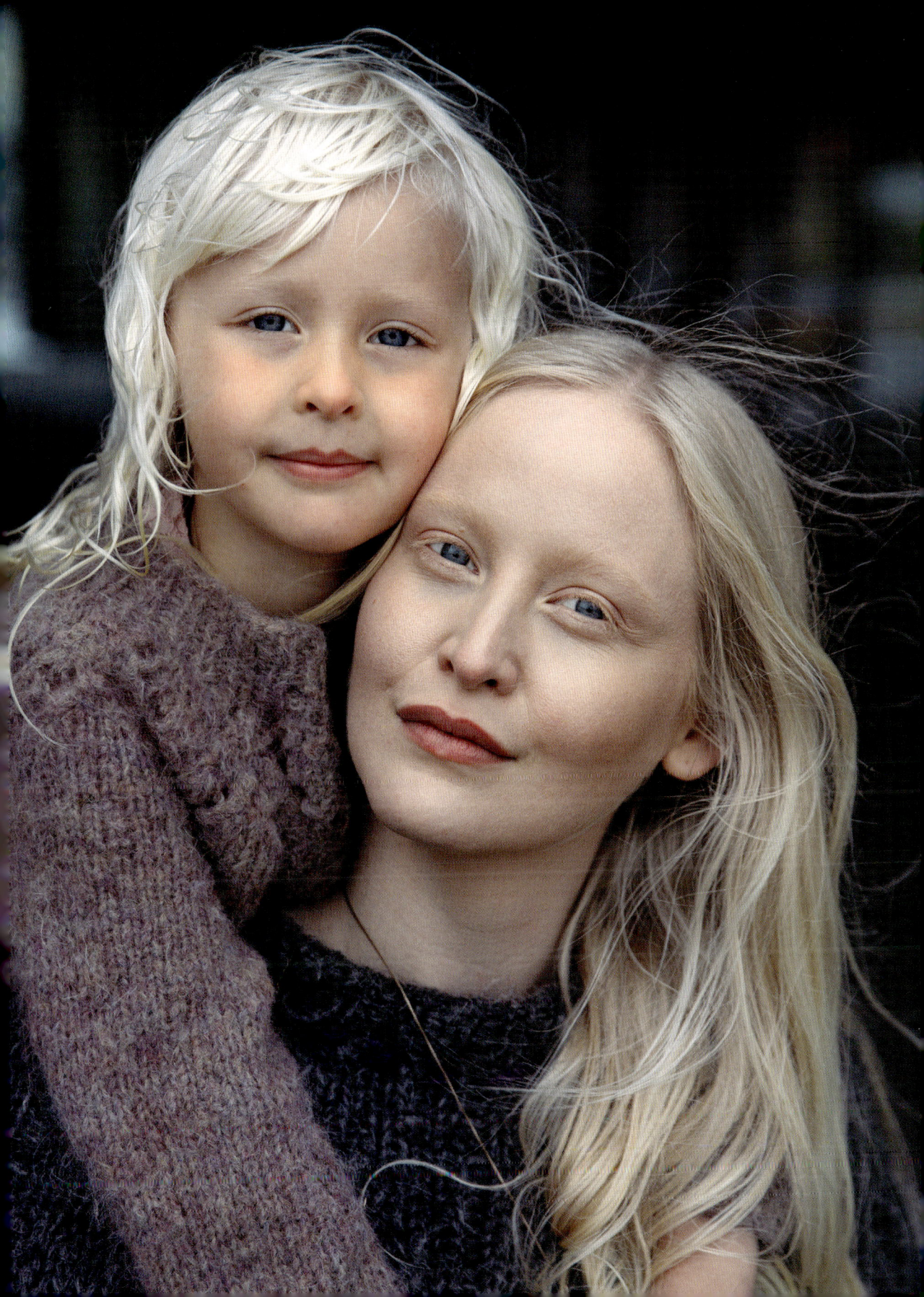

BUCHAREST, ROMANIA *(Previous spread, left)*

It's always fascinating to capture the incredible bond between mothers and their children. Carmen is Romanian, while her daughters, Ranya and Zara, also have Middle Eastern roots.

REYKJAVÍK, ICELAND *(Previous spread, right)*

Meet Tanja Björk, along with her daughter Bergdísi. When we met, she had just returned from Los Angeles. Despite the cold August weather in Iceland, Tanja considered it perfect, as she was finally back home. As a single mother, Tanja was successfully raising two children while also pursuing her acting career and traveling to different parts of the world for her work.

Our meeting was very inspiring for me, a new mother. It confirmed to me that despite all the challenges, one can still follow their passion, explore the world, and be a dedicated mother simultaneously.

CHIȘINĂU, MOLDOVA *(Opposite)*

She is Victoria, whose name means "victory" in Romanian. Her own life represents a victory of hope over suffering. Victoria Suruceanu was born with a disability in one of her legs and spent most of her childhood and adolescence in hospitals. Whenever she was home, other children would mock her by stealing her crutches. Those years were marked by constant suffering.

At the age of twenty-one, after a successful prosthetic implant, she learned to walk without crutches for the first time in her life. This moment became the happiest one for Victoria, shining a light after years of darkness. However, she still felt a sense of shame about her prosthetic and always kept it hidden.

Over time, things started to change. Through therapy and self-learning, Victoria learned to love every inch of her body, including the prosthesis. She even adorned it with a tattoo of a blooming peony to celebrate the beauty of life. Meanwhile, Victoria also found the love of her life, and when I photographed her, she was preparing to become a mother in less than a month—a happy, confident, and victorious mother.

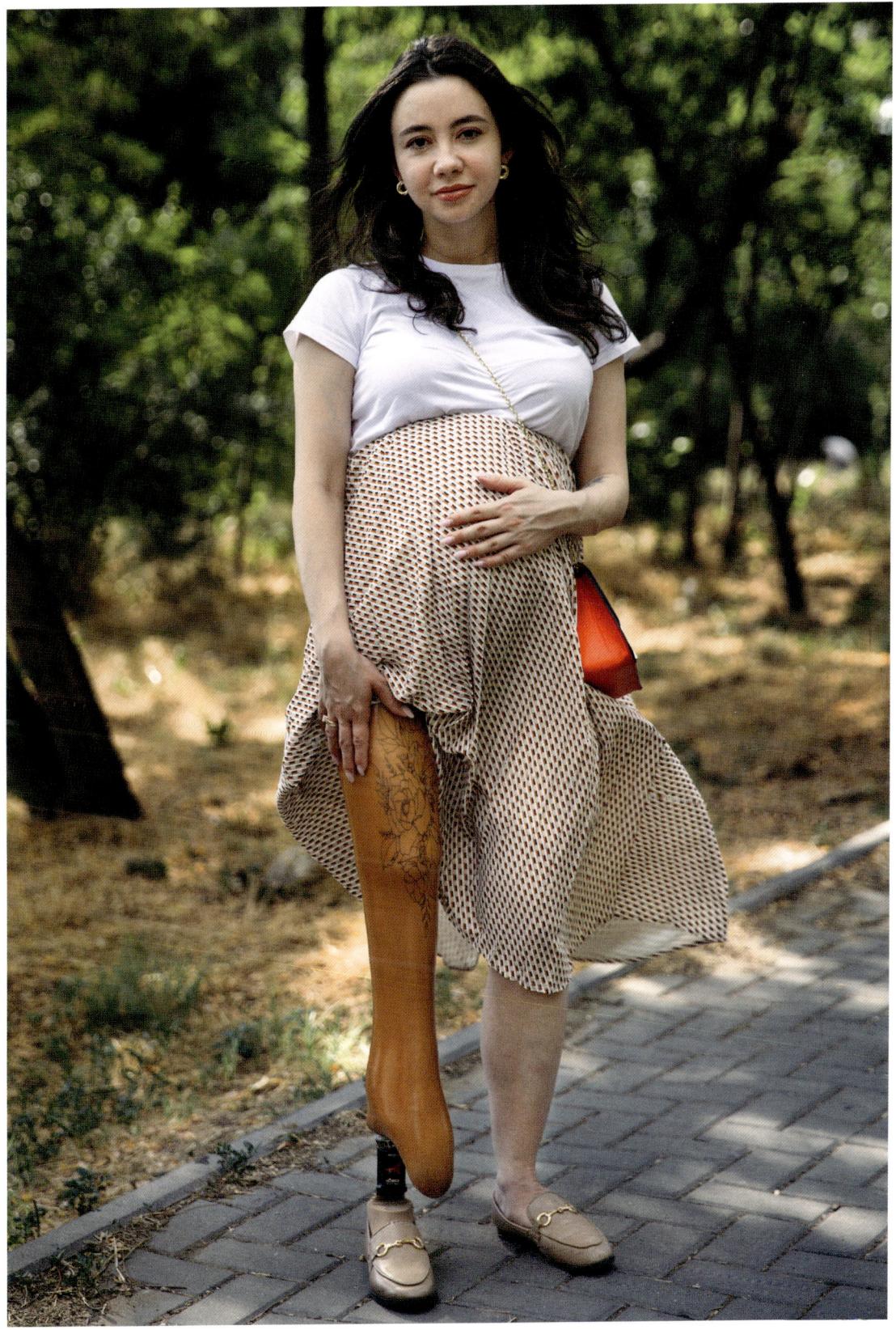

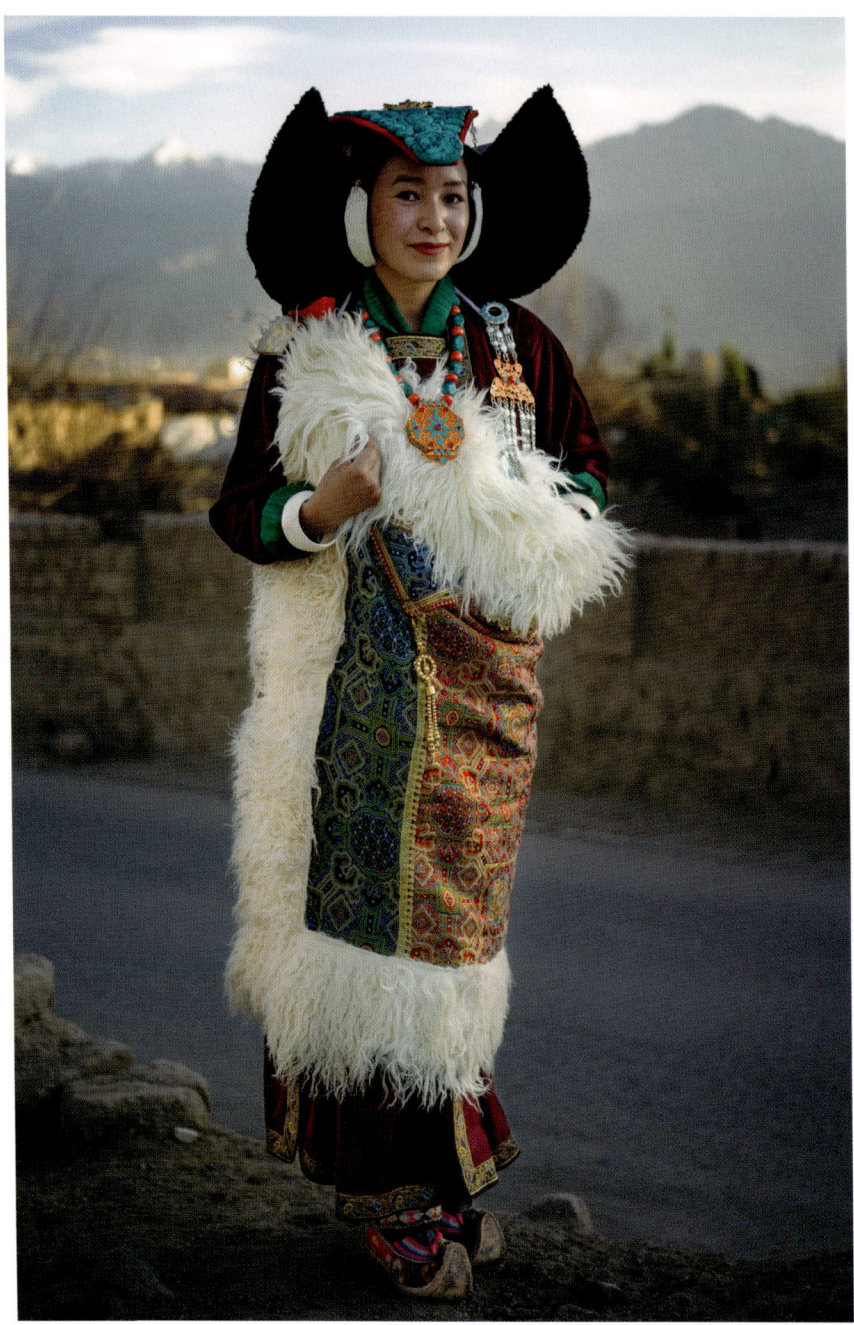

LEH, INDIA

Nimoo is a dancer in a traditional Ladakhi group. Ladakhi people have a beautiful culture that shares similarities with their Tibetan neighbors. The Ladakhi traditional outfits are some of the most sophisticated in the world. Nimoo's shoes, for example, are called *pabu* and are made of woven yak hair. Her headdress is called a *perak* and is studded with gemstones; it's a precious symbol of status passed down from mother to daughter.

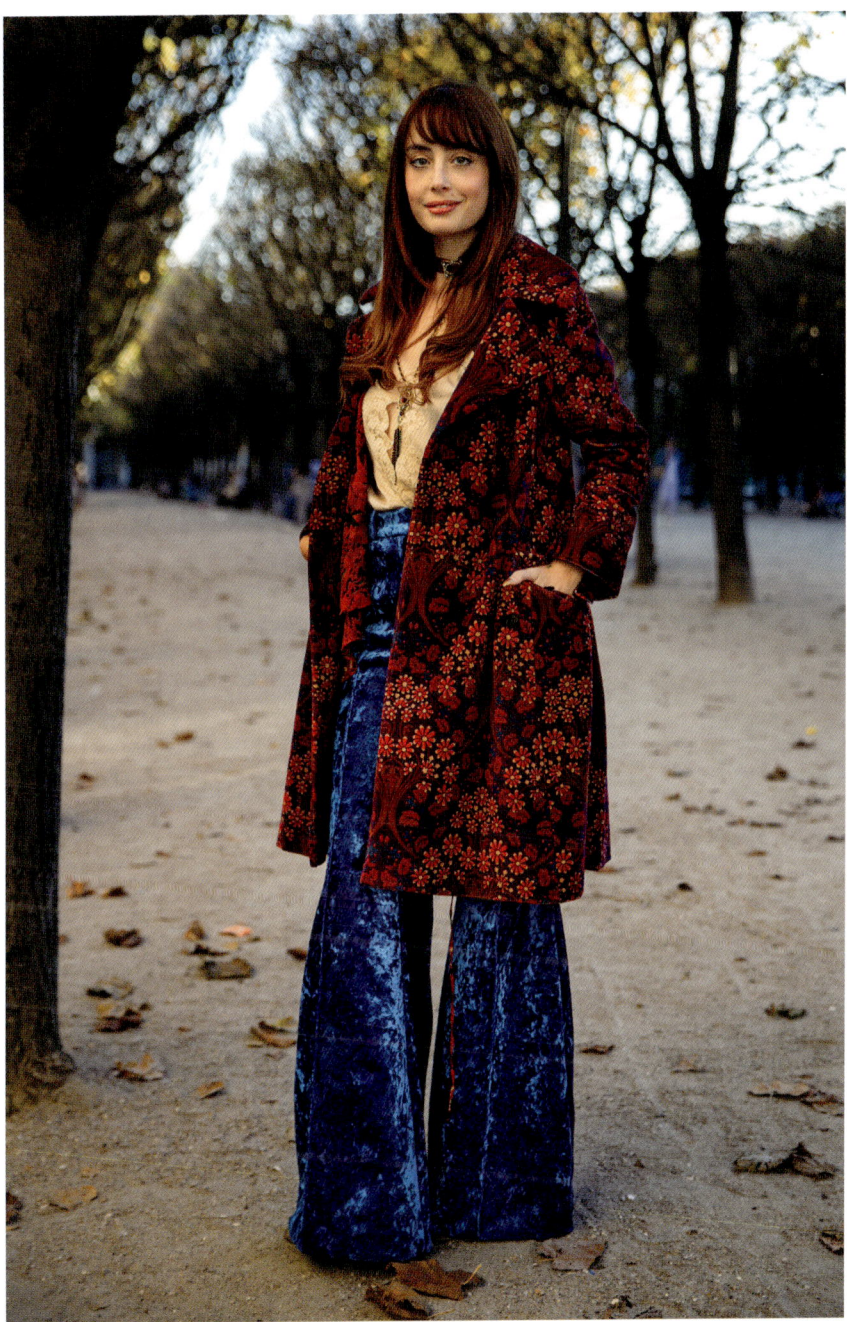

PARIS, FRANCE

After studying art history, Louise Ebel started a blog showcasing her passion for art, history, travel, and style. She enjoys highlighting the forgotten women of history, a theme she explores in her book describing the destinies of lesser-known women artists in the nineteenth century. Louise has also lived in Japan, where she worked as a journalist and a TV presenter for many years. Her multidisciplinary approach is ultimately the best way to explore the complex art and cultures of the world.

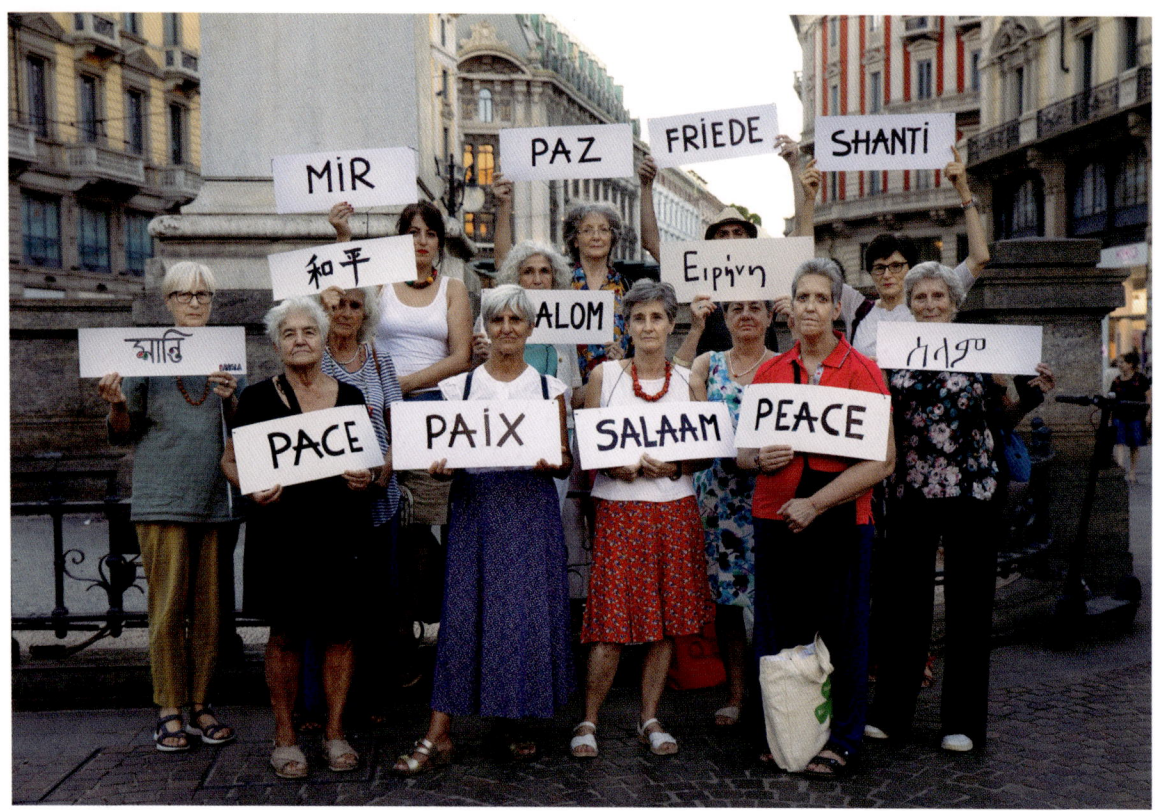

MILAN, ITALY

These women were meeting once per week in the center of the city to raise awareness about conflicts around the world and make an appeal for peace. They were holding placards with the word "peace" written in different languages.

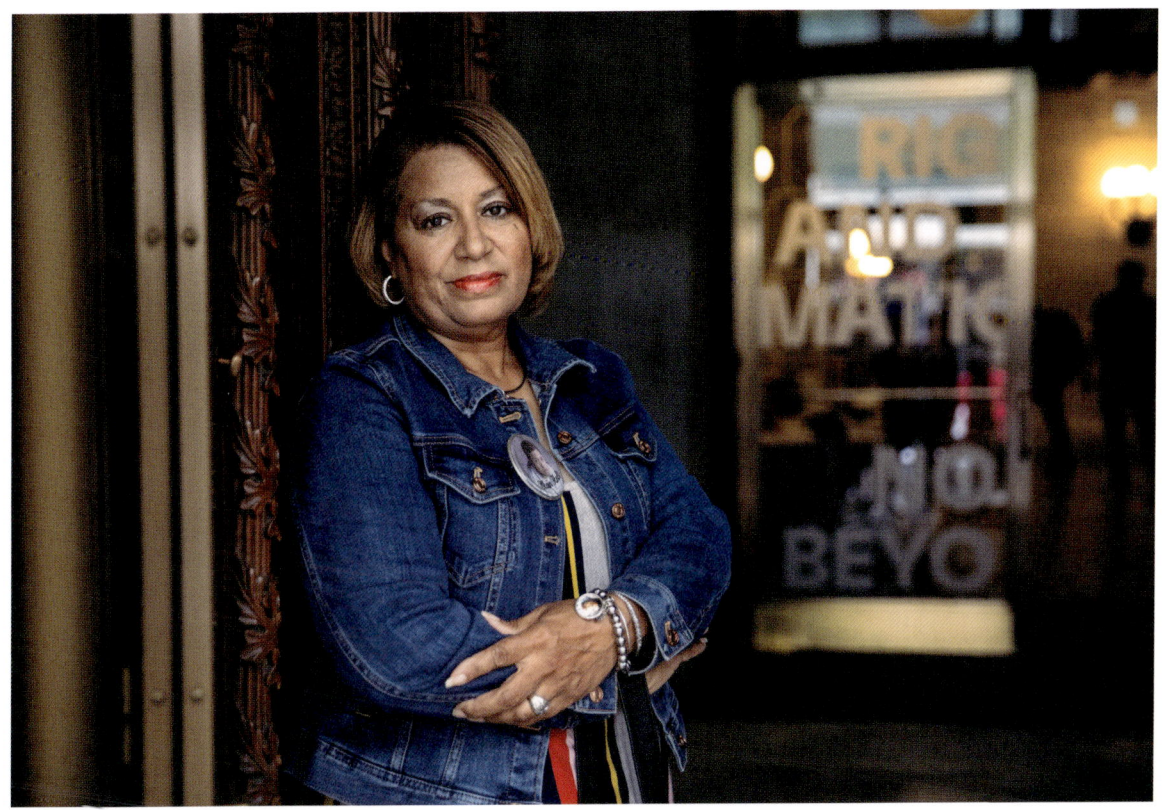

CHICAGO, UNITED STATES

Annette Nance-Holt is the first African American woman to run the Chicago Fire Department. Unfortunately, the moment I met this brave and courageous woman, she was focused on something else.

She was coming out from the inauguration of a memorial dedicated to victims of gun violence. Her own sixteen-year-old son was shot and killed in 2007 while trying to shield a friend after a gang member opened fire on a bus.

Annette is a strong advocate for victims of gun violence, and this memorial was a project she cared deeply about. She wants her son and other victims to be remembered as real people with real stories—not as anonymous statistics featured in the daily news.

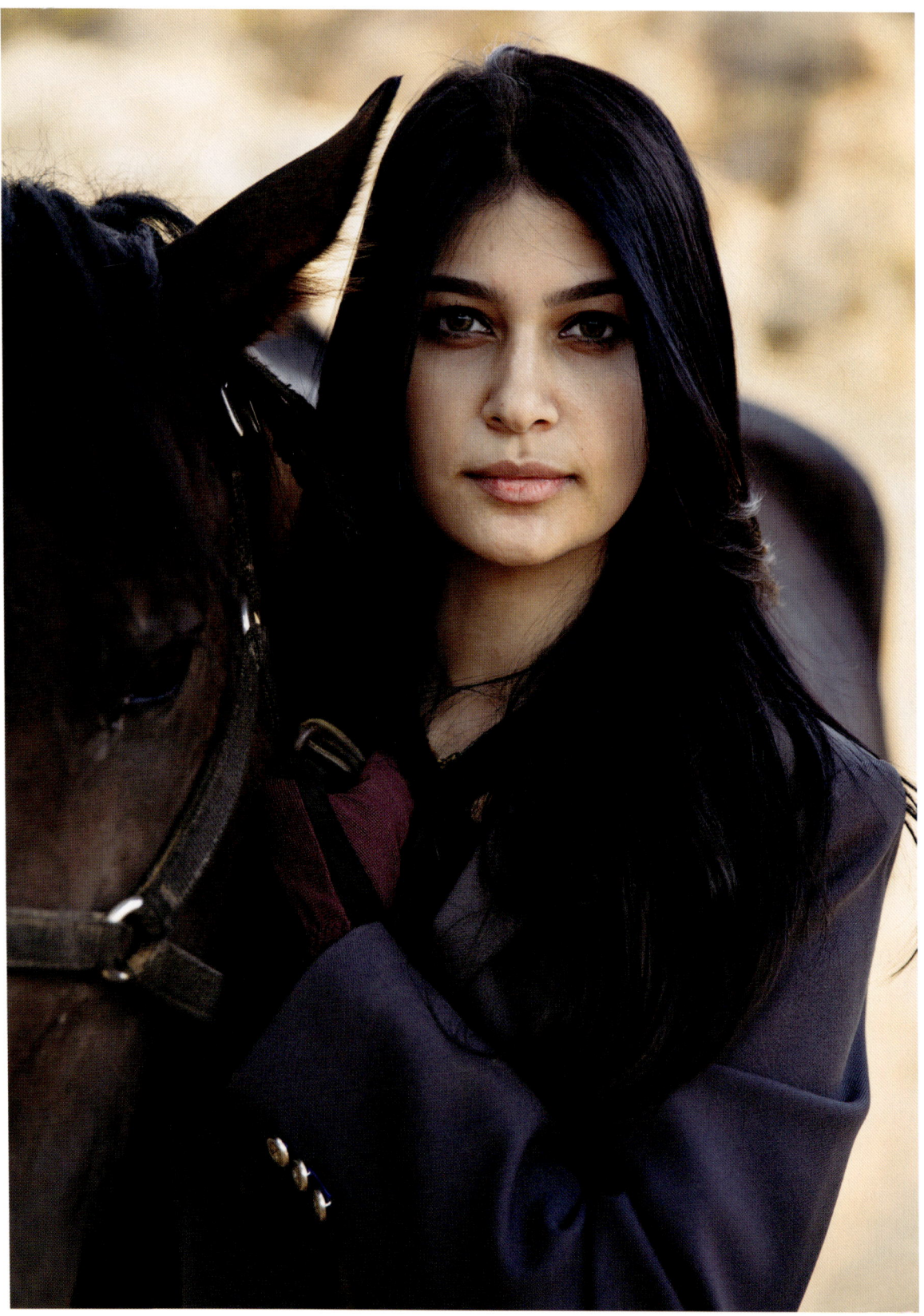

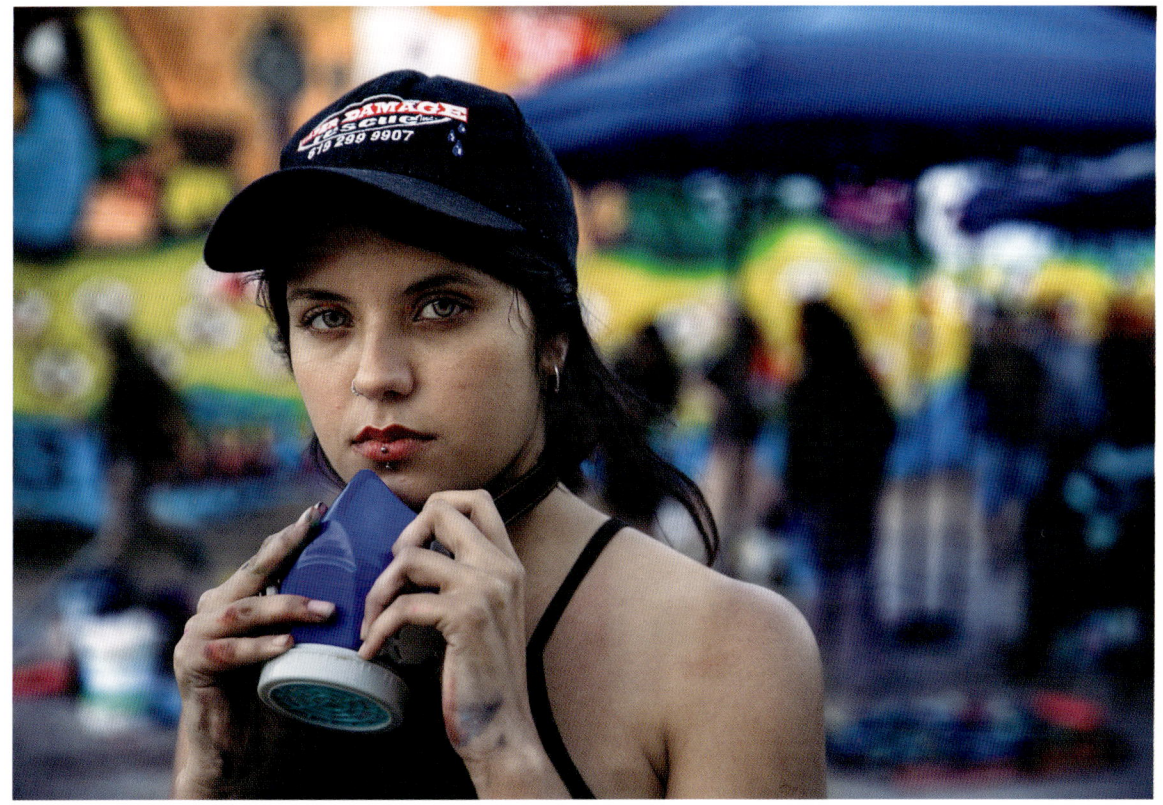

SANTIAGO, CHILE (Above)

Constanza was taking part in the huge protests against poverty and inequality in her country. The police were constantly throwing tear gas, so most protesters were prepared with special masks.

BAALBEK, LEBANON (Opposite)

Guitta Mcheik often returns to her hometown, high in the mountains, to ride and enjoy the surroundings. She grew up on a farm here and was surrounded by strong and powerful people who always inspired her.

For her, riding symbolizes freedom and strength—values she has consistently fought for. Her life is now based in Beirut, the capital of the country, where she studied law and actively participated in the Lebanese revolution in 2018

She used unconventional ways, such as street performances during protests, to make powerful statements. She also documented street abuses and offered free legal support to those in need. She was abusively arrested, as well, but that didn't stop her from fighting for a better Lebanon. In addition to law, Guitta is also involved in journalism today, and she uses her diverse skills to make her country a better place.

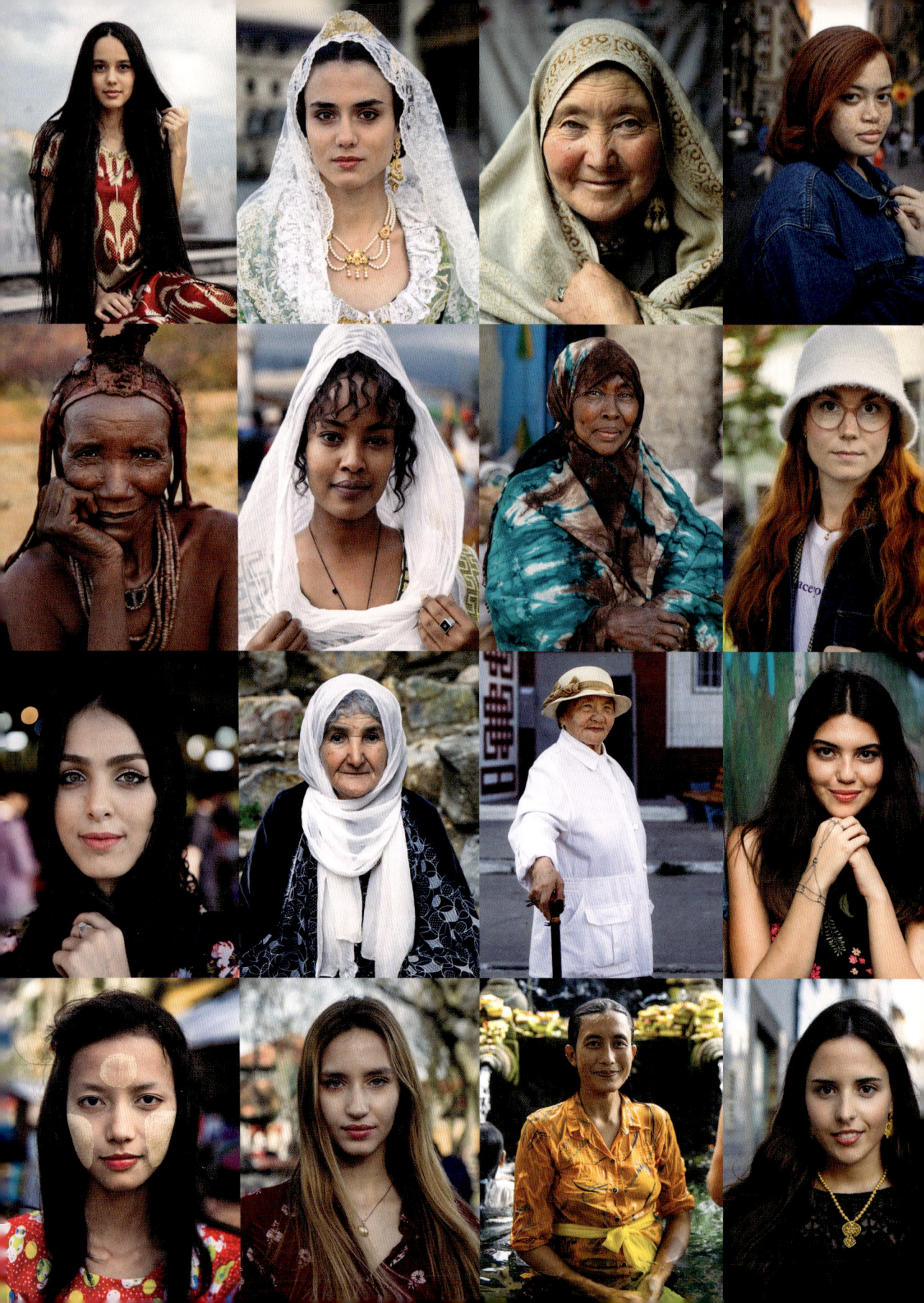

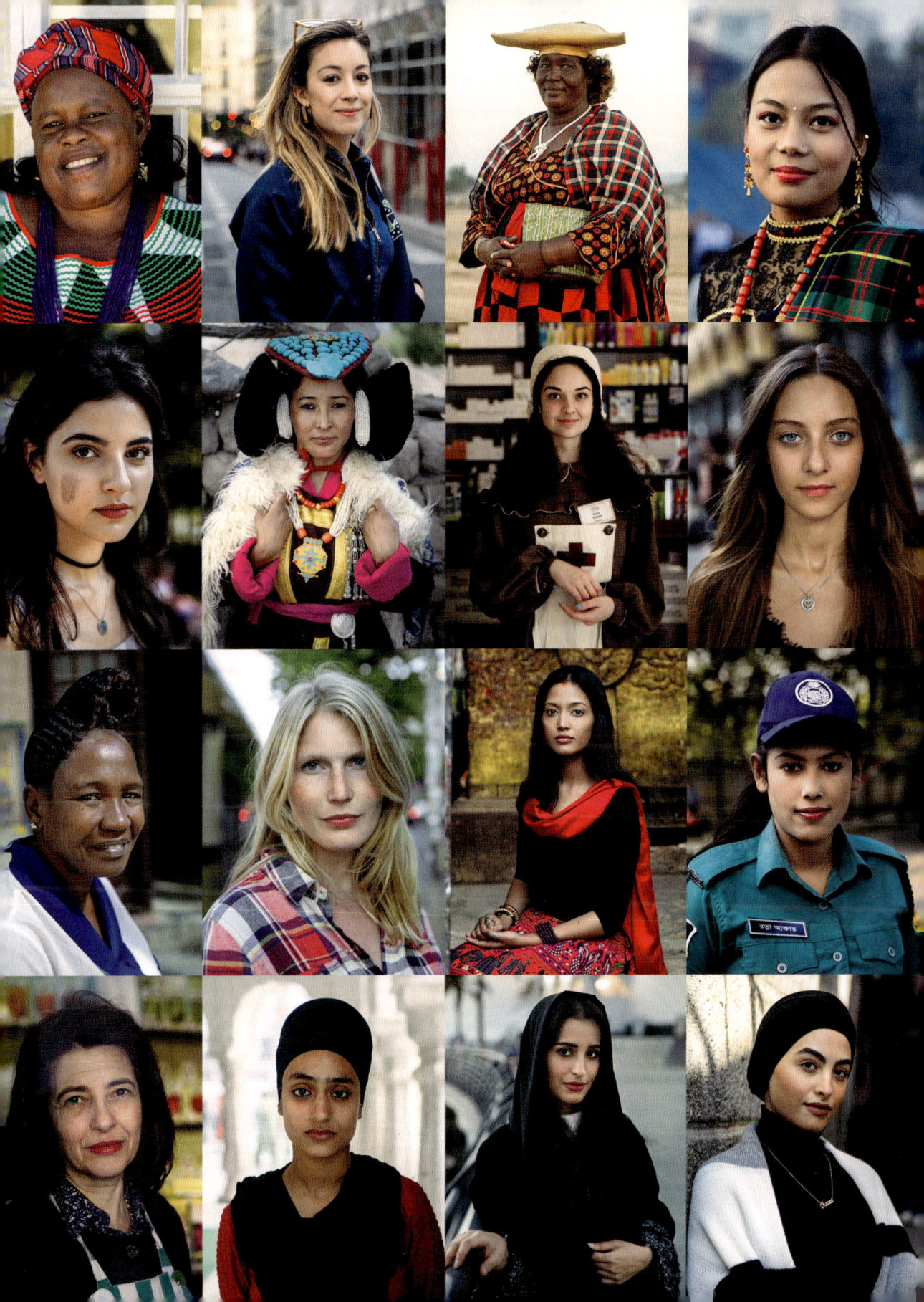

LEGACY

It's a cold and dark November day, and my father's funeral has just ended. There's darkness all around, and there's darkness in my soul. Yet, suddenly, amid the darkness, memories of him flood my mind, bringing warmth and light.

My father was a painter. In his workshop, when I was little, I learned the magic of colors. As I enter his home, it feels strange not to find him there. But the walls are adorned with his paintings. In a way, he is still there, and he always will be. His art is a part of his legacy.

But his legacy extends beyond his art. As we gather with friends and relatives after the funeral, we feel the absence of his jokes and his bright personality. Each one of us will always carry a glimpse of his humor and positivity, and that's also a part of his legacy. And then there's my work. He gave me my first camera and taught me about color. All my work as a photographer is a part of his legacy, as well.

In the weeks and months following the funeral, a question haunts my thoughts more than ever before: Life passes so quickly, we are so small, and we're suddenly gone—so why are we here? What's the purpose? The legacy seems the only reasonable answer to me. Whether you're a religious person, a spiritual person without religion, an agnostic, or an atheist, legacy is part of the answer, I think. But everyone has a different interpretation of legacy. I will tell you about mine, which has developed after years of traveling around the world.

During my work on the Atlas of Beauty project, I encountered women with remarkable legacies. The legacy of a teacher in her amazing students; the legacy of a doctor in her hundreds of patients who live because of her; the legacy of a mother in her children, whom she raised with great sacrifices; the legacy of a scientist in her groundbreaking discoveries; and the legacy of an engineer in her projects that changed lives for good.

But what I've realized is that you don't necessarily need to be a doctor, a teacher, a parent, an artist, a scientist, or an engineer to leave a valuable legacy. You don't need to be famous or successful, either. Every small gesture in which you use your power for good becomes your legacy. Every small gesture multiplies, creating another small gesture, and another one, like a ripple effect. From planting a tree to inspiring a friend, from making someone smile to reconditioning a house, legacy comes in many forms. And all these acts are not just about what happens after you're gone. They collectively form the beauty that you share with those around you, enriching your life every single day and helping you overcome the challenges.

I believe that legacy isn't solely about smiling all day long or being kind every second of our lives. While that would be remarkable, most of us don't possess this power. There are moments when we feel sad, angry, envious, or frustrated, and during those times, legacy is often the last thing on our minds. However, there are countless other moments when we're in a better mood, and it's during those times that we can reflect on our unique power and work toward shaping our legacy.

Legacy is about consistency, as well. If one small act can make a significant impact, imagine the potential of thousands of acts throughout your lifetime. But even if you haven't begun consciously building your legacy, it's never too late to start. Ultimately, you are your legacy.

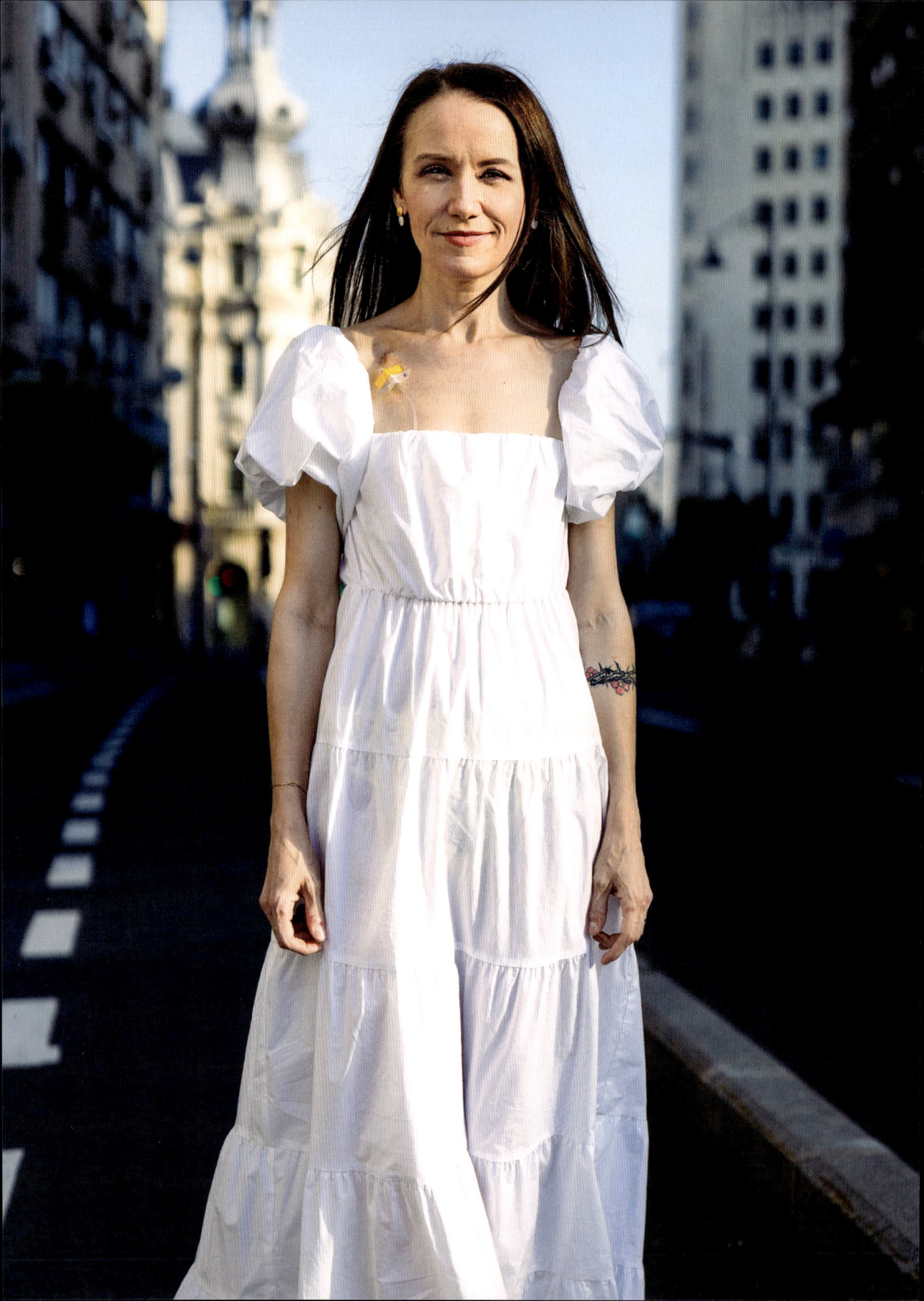

BUCHAREST, ROMANIA *(Opposite)*

At twenty-five years old, Adelina Toncean had a comfortable corporate job—then a newspaper article changed her life forever. After reading that article, she adopted a boy abandoned in a hospital with an incurable disease. Then, when she adopted another boy in a similarly dire situation, she miraculously found a treatment and saved his life. But she didn't stop there.

She founded an organization and saved many other children. Adelina raises funds and arranges special flights to send children in desperate medical situations to specialized hospitals around the world, where they will have a chance of survival.

Meanwhile, Adelina herself was diagnosed with an incurable disease, but she refuses to give up. She's on a mission to save more children, because angels never stop flying.

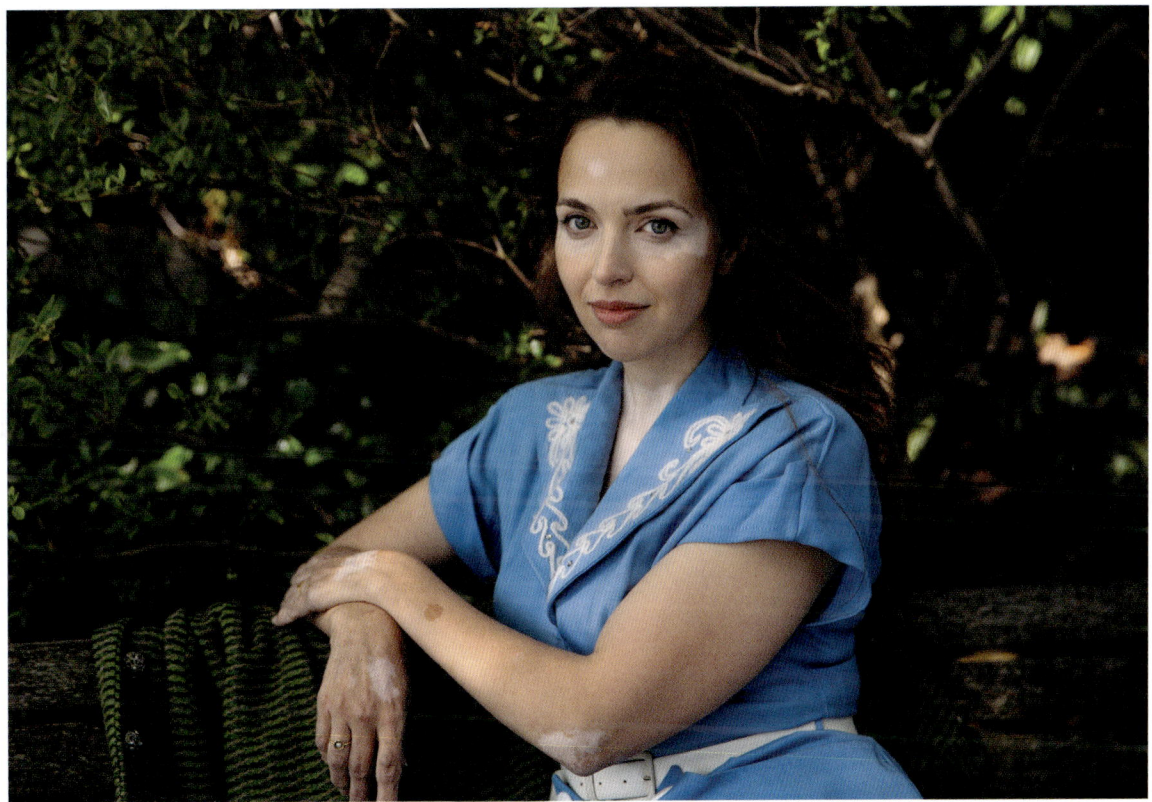

COPENHAGEN, DENMARK *(Above)*

When she was fifteen years old, Marie found out that she has psoriasis, an autoimmune condition that affects the skin. As a teenager, she was devastated by the diagnosis. Though she initially felt ashamed about her skin, she eventually learned to love herself and her body exactly as it is.

Not only did she overcome her shame about her appearance, but she also started a blog where she shares her passion for vintage clothes and pictures of herself.

Since psoriasis has a hereditary component, Marie is on a mission to educate her two young daughters about loving every inch of their bodies just the way they are. If one of them inherits the condition, Marie knows they will not feel the same pain she did.

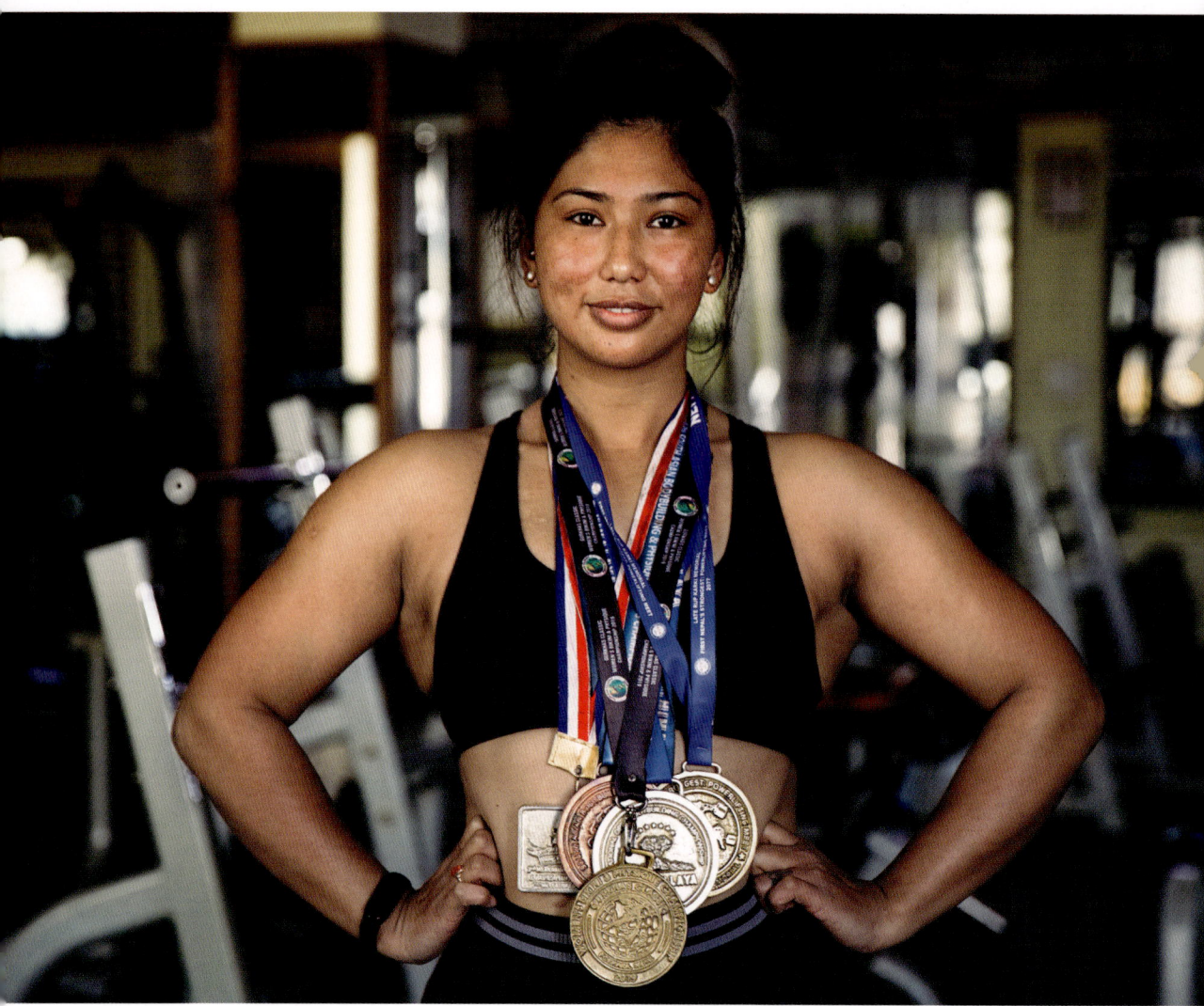

KATHMANDU, NEPAL

After finishing her career as a basketball player, Sujita Manandhar
searched for new ways to stay fit. That's how she discovered bodybuilding.
In Nepal, it is very rare to see women practicing this sport, but she didn't
care about misconceptions. Her new path was extremely challenging, but
after years of hard work and discipline, she became one of the best in her
country—just as she had been in basketball.

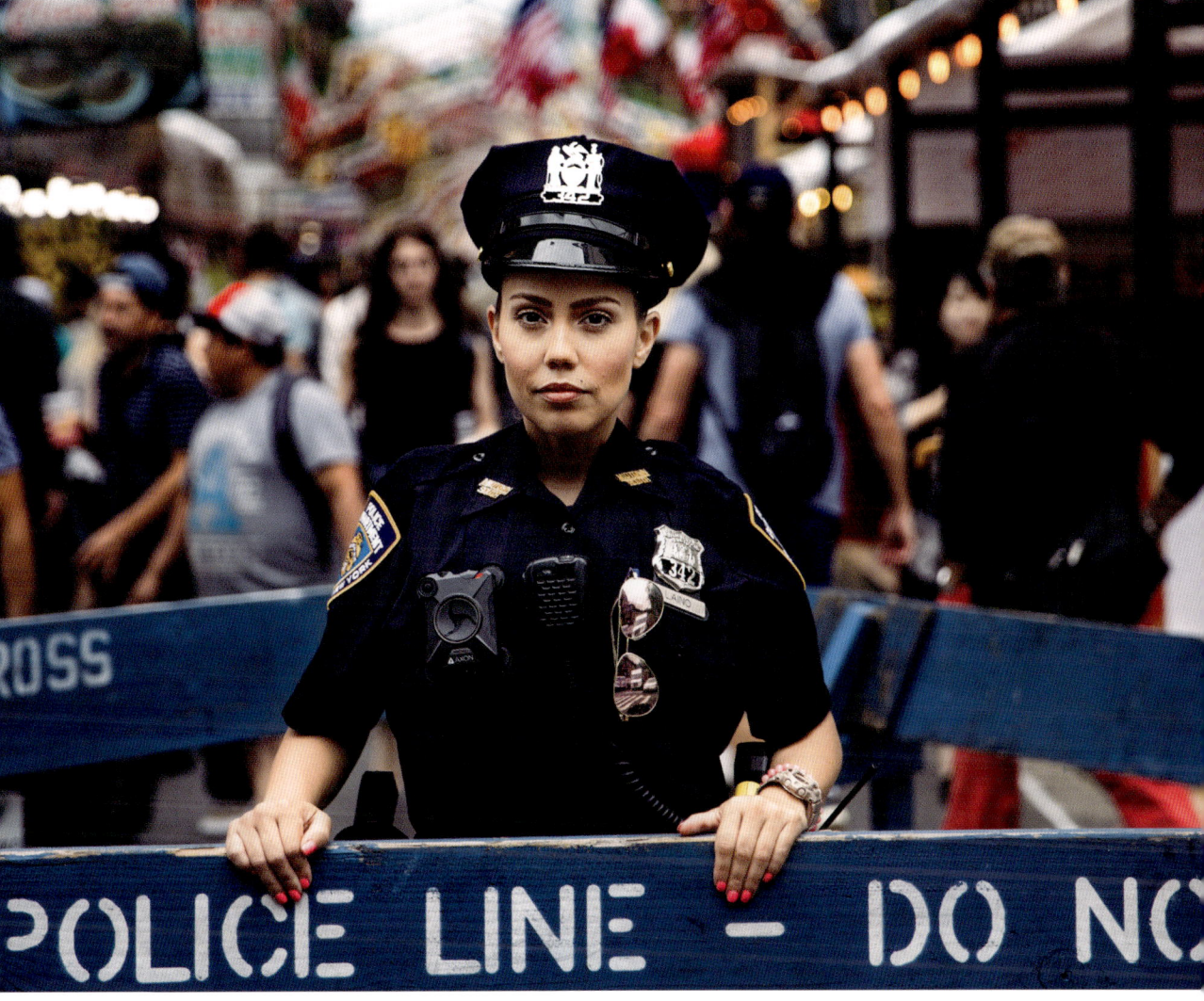

NEW YORK CITY, UNITED STATES

Just a few years ago, Camila was a housewife taking care of her two little children. One day, without any prior notice, her husband decided to leave her for a younger woman.

Camila found herself alone in her thirties with two children, no money, and no prospects. Was she brokenhearted? Of course, who wouldn't be? But Camila decided to move on rapidly, when so few would have had the strength to do so.

She had been holding on to a dream for a long time, and now was the moment to fulfill it—she applied to the NYPD Police Academy and was accepted. Camila was the oldest in her class, a woman in a field dominated by men. But all that made her even more ambitious.

Now, at thirty-seven, after years of struggles, she is a respected police officer, and she can afford to offer what's best to her children.

SIBIU, ROMANIA

Anna is from Germany. A few years ago, she joined an ancient community of crafters. She is traveling the world and stopping in different places to undergo her apprenticeship in carpentry. In German, she is referred to as a "*gesellin*."

As a "*gesellin*," Anna must wear a specific uniform and follow an ancient code of rules. For instance, she is required to craft her backpack and to always use a special walking stick, and she is not permitted to pay for transportation or accommodation.

Anna had been on the road for three years, and her apprenticeship was nearly completed, when I encountered her on the streets of this town in Transylvania. It was fascinating to hear about her incredible adventures around the world.

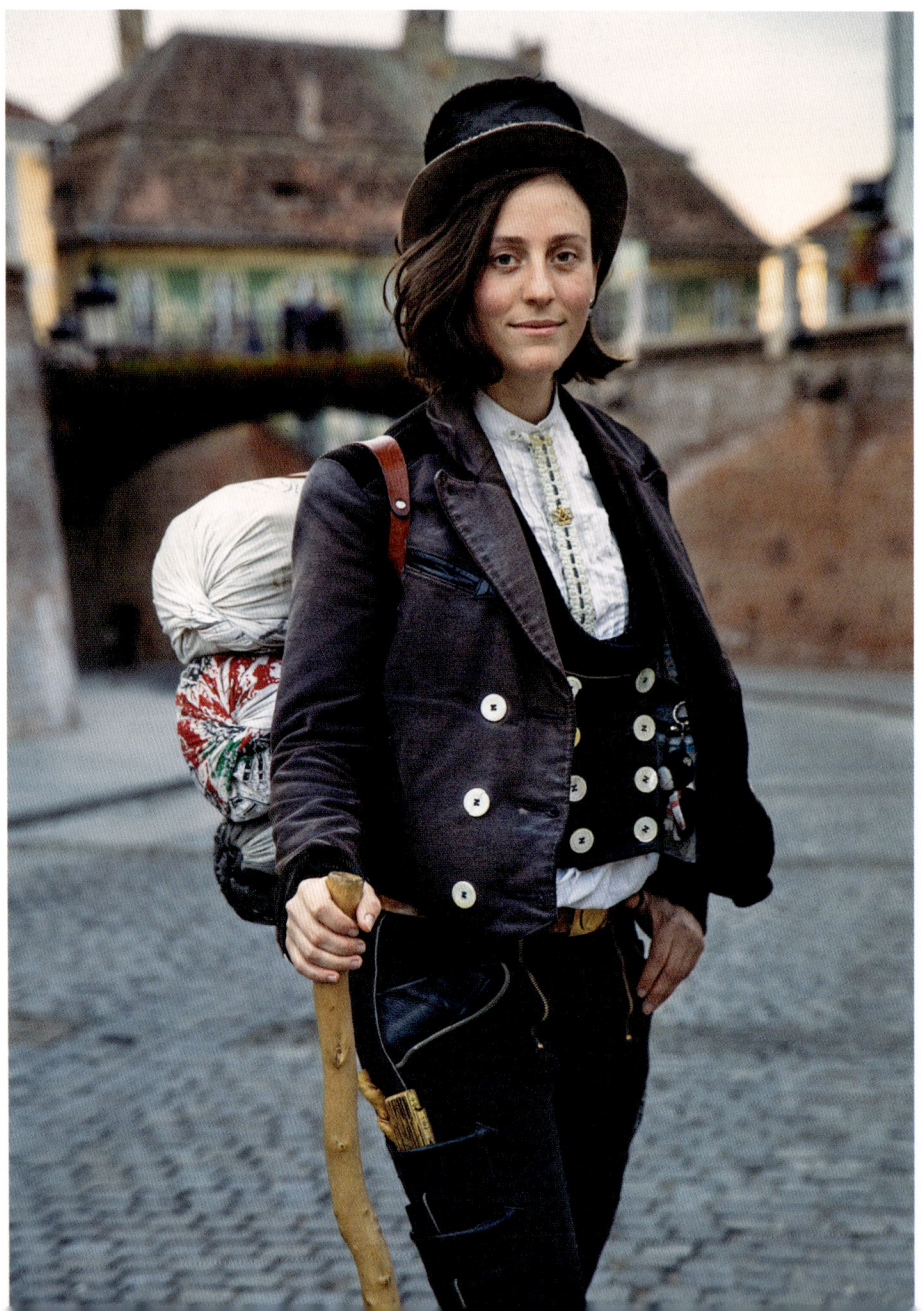

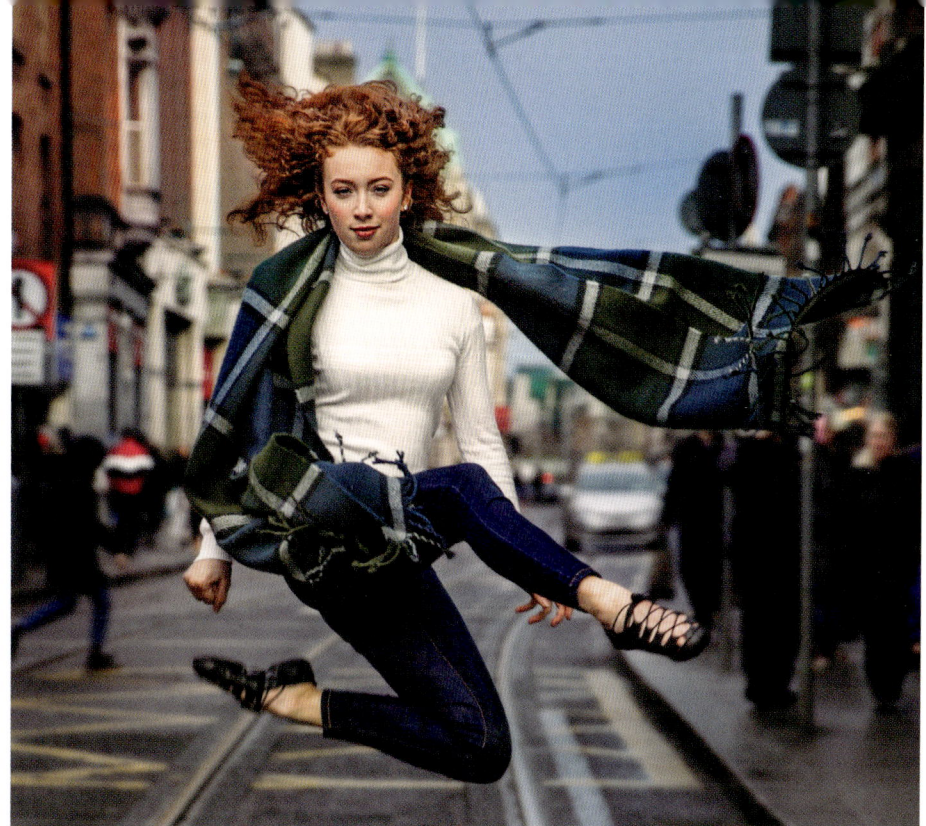

DUBLIN, IRELAND

When Amy-Mae Dolan started to show me a few Irish dancing steps, it felt to me as if she were flying. She made it look so simple, but behind the skill were years of effort and sacrifices.

Amy-Mae started to practice Irish dancing when she was only two years old. Growing up in the countryside meant she had to travel long distances to attend a reputable dance school. Although she was deeply passionate about dancing, she never imagined herself becoming a professional. In high school, inspired by personal experiences, she decided to become a doctor. However, life had other plans in store for her. When she was preparing to start university and study medicine, Amy-Mae received a life-changing phone call—it was an invitation to join the prestigious *Riverdance*.

Riverdance is one of the most renowned shows in the world, a legendary production that combines traditional Irish music and dance. Initially, Amy-Mae joined the show as a troupe dancer, and soon she found herself literally and figuratively soaring across stages worldwide. But that was only the beginning.

After some time, she was invited to take on the lead role in the show. Her life, already amazing, transformed into something truly extraordinary.

Reflecting on her journey, Amy-Mae believes that she may not have possessed as much natural talent as others, but she worked tirelessly and was driven by an immense passion for her craft. She shares that whenever she hears music from the show, her heart starts racing, and she feels the adrenaline flowing through her body.

Amy-Mae still plans to become a doctor in the future, but in the meantime her dancing is her therapy for us, the audience.

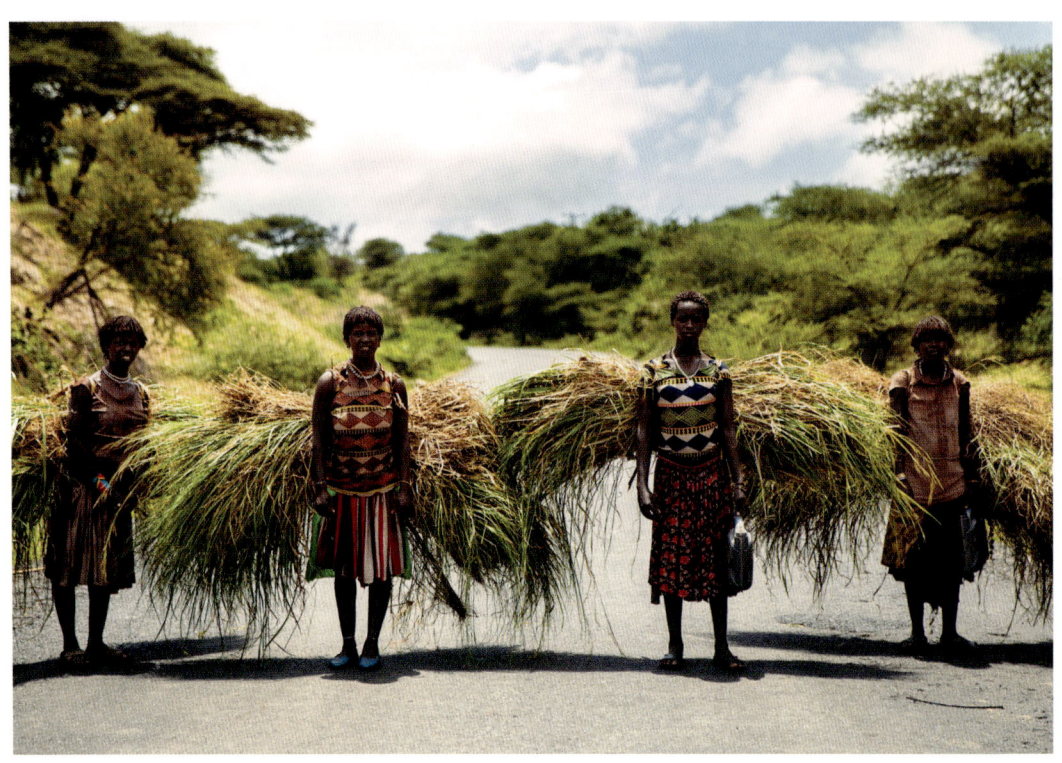

OMO VALLEY, ETHIOPIA

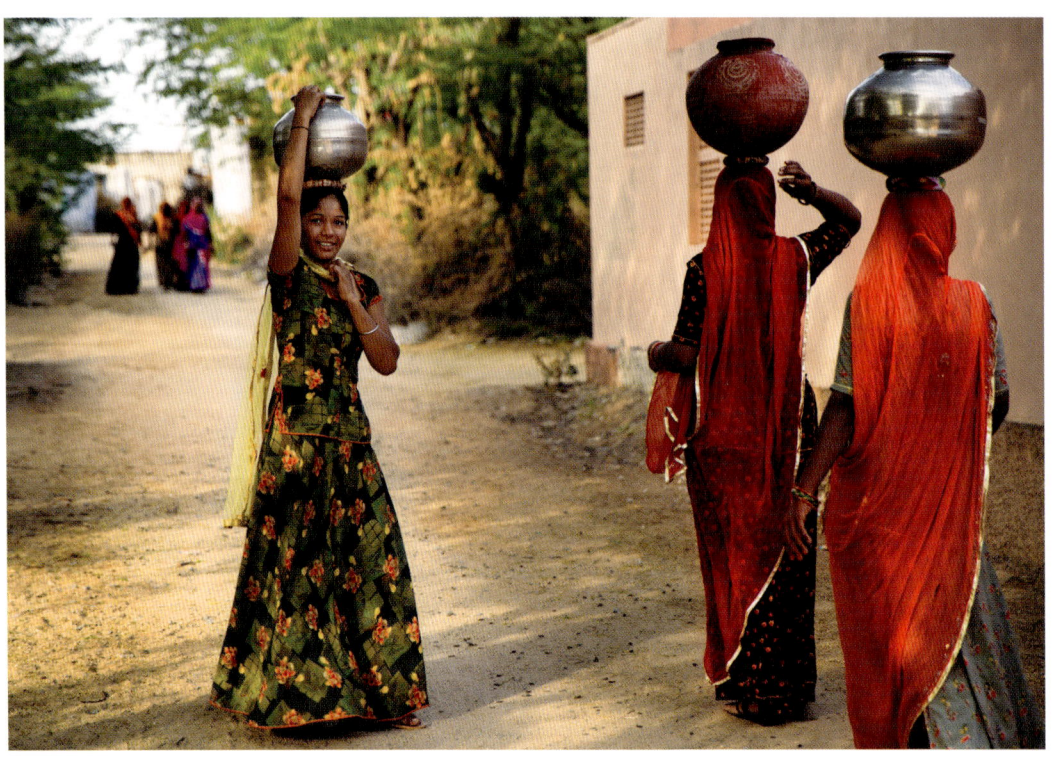

RAJASTHAN, INDIA

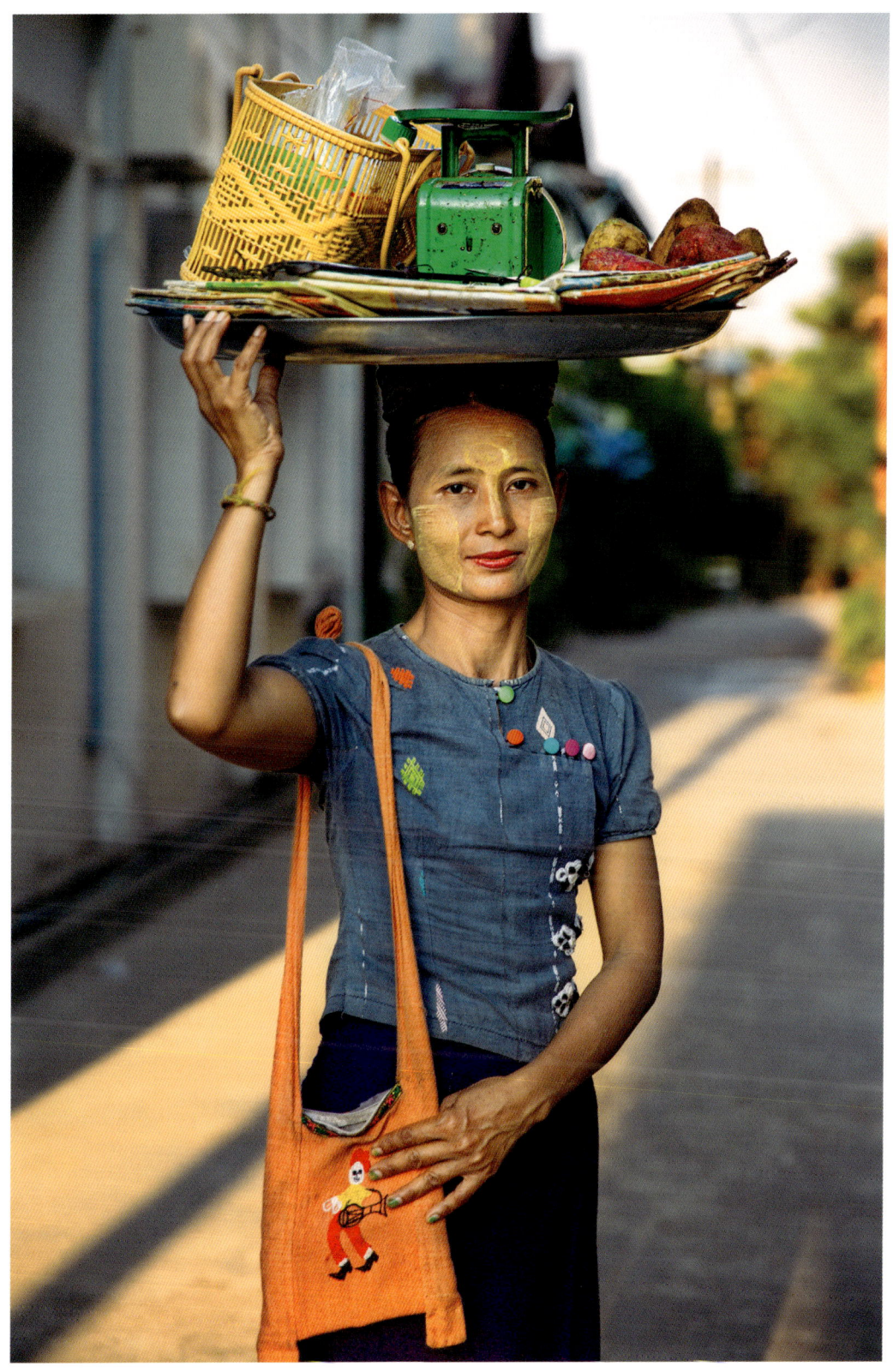

MAWLAMYINE, MYANMAR

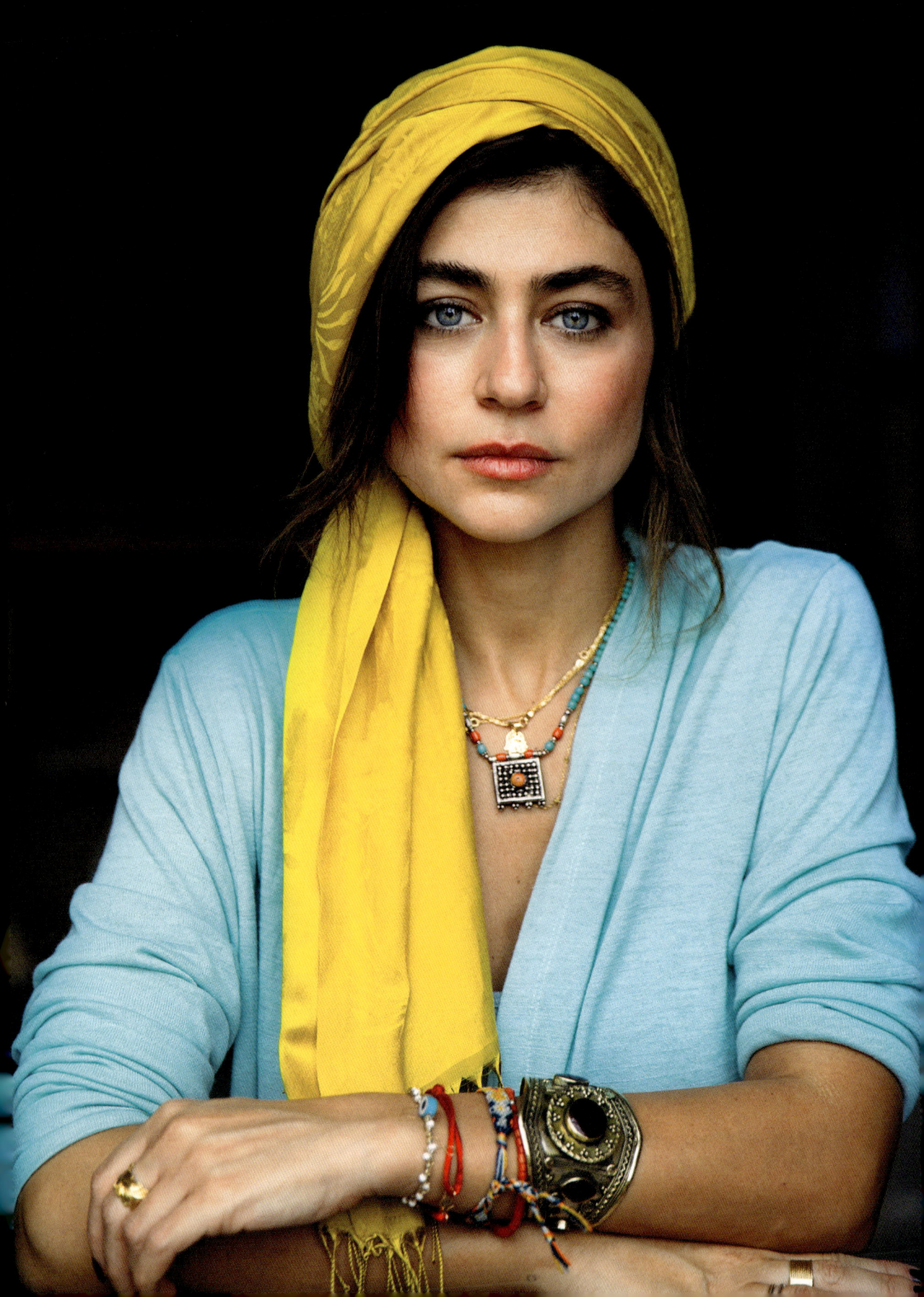

BEIRUT, LEBANON (Opposite)

As a humanitarian worker, Bathoul Ahmed has dedicated her life to helping those in the most desperate situations. When I met her, she was working for the United Nations's refugee agency.

Bathoul grew up as a refugee in the United Kingdom. She began volunteering to assist other refugees while she was in secondary school. Over the past decade, while working in different conflict zones, she has realized that refugees are often reduced to numbers that come and go in the media. However, behind those statistics are real, terrible, and unknown stories.

In Yemen, Bathoul has witnessed mothers struggling to produce enough milk to feed their babies due to malnourishment. She has heard the cries of severely malnourished children. She listened to a boy recount how he lost a leg and a hand in a landmine explosion that also took the life of his best friend. Even with tireless work, day and night, Bathoul felt she couldn't do enough.

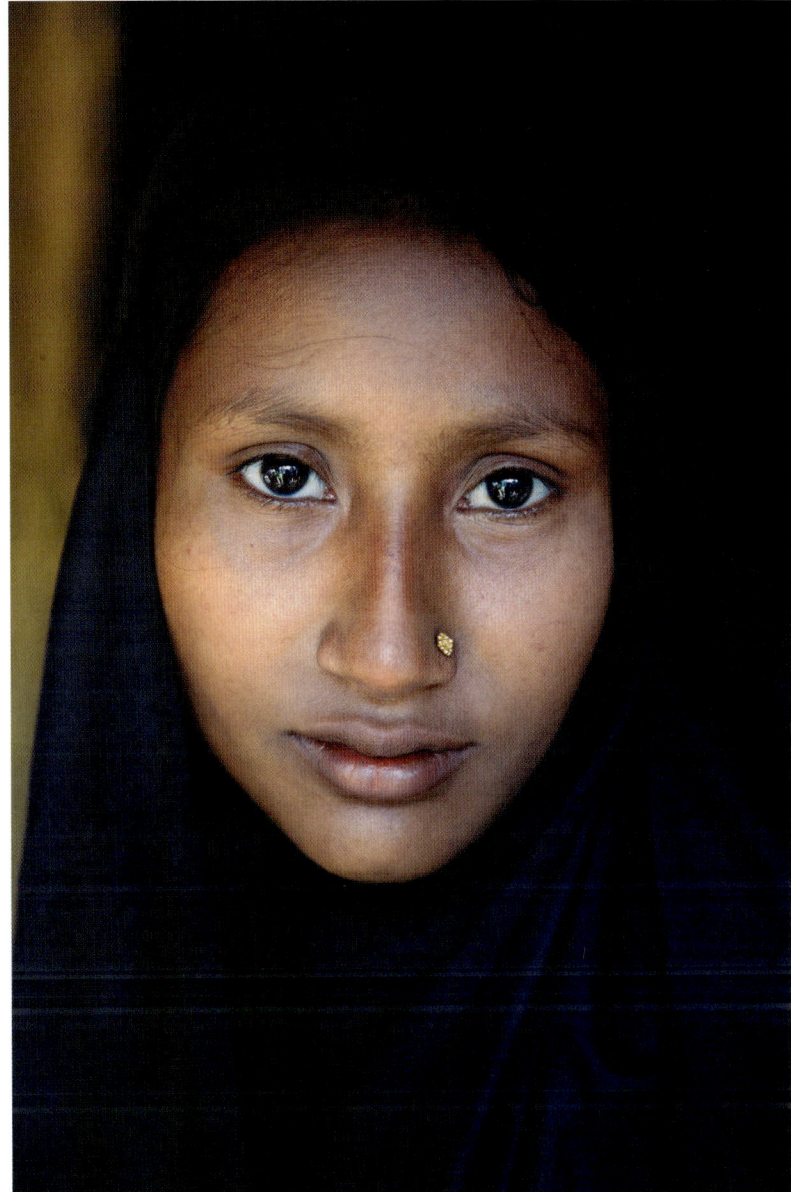

KUTUPALONG REFUGEE CAMP, BANGLADESH (Above)

I met Norizan, who was pregnant, in the world's largest refugee camp. I was pregnant, as well. Hundreds of thousands of Rohingya, who fled from neighboring Myanmar to escape a massacre, were living here. I have been in many refugee camps, but nothing compared to Kutupalong. The conditions were horrendous, with widespread disease and the constant danger of deadly landslides due to heavy rains.

While photographing Norizan, I looked deep into her eyes and saw a reflection of myself. We were two pregnant women in such different situations. And I wondered: Had I done enough to help people like her? Had we all done enough?

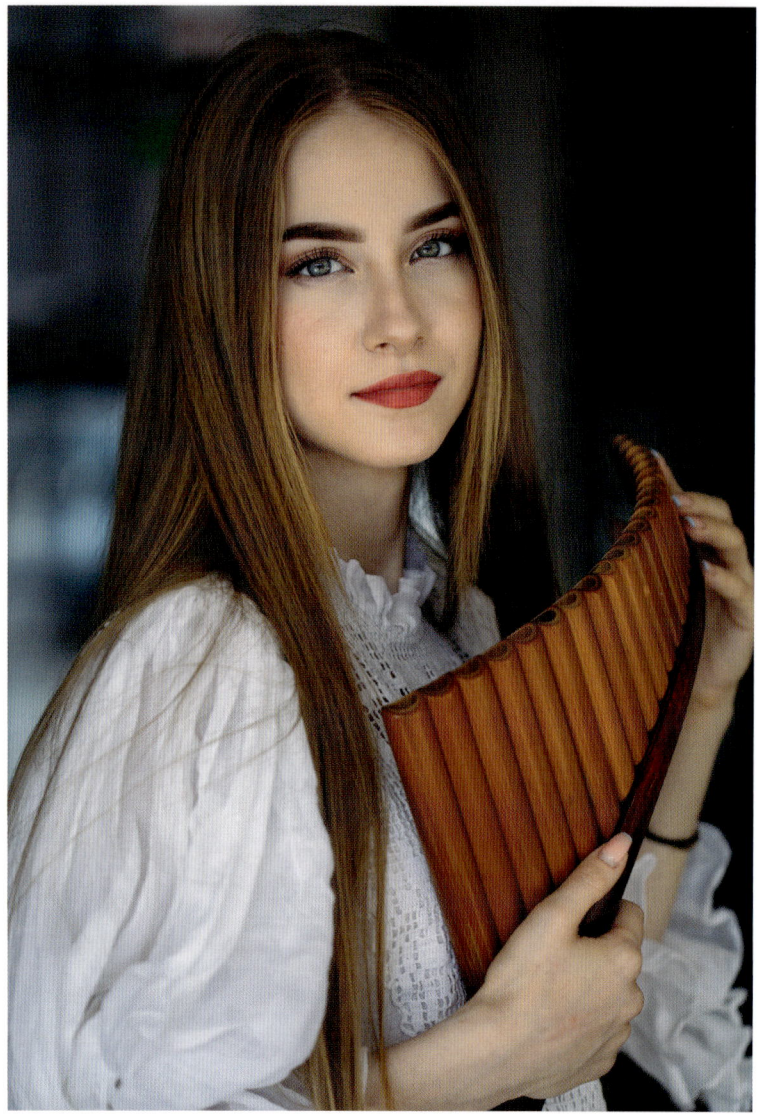

CHIȘINĂU, MOLDOVA

Adriana Babin plays the *nai*, a traditional Romanian pan flute. Her skills and ability to approach a variety of genres, from traditional to classical and jazz, have made her a successful instrumentalist. Adriana performed on prestigious stages worldwide and achieved financial independence at the age of sixteen, but all these successes came with great sacrifices.

Adriana has worked hard from a young age while spending a lot of time away from her family and from typical childhood activities. Yet this is most of the time the only path to becoming a skilled instrumentalist.

While reflecting on the journeys of an esteemed instrumentalist, some would question whether it was all worth it. But when Adriana is onstage, sharing the unique sound of her *nai* with the audience, she feels complete and knows she is exactly where she belongs.

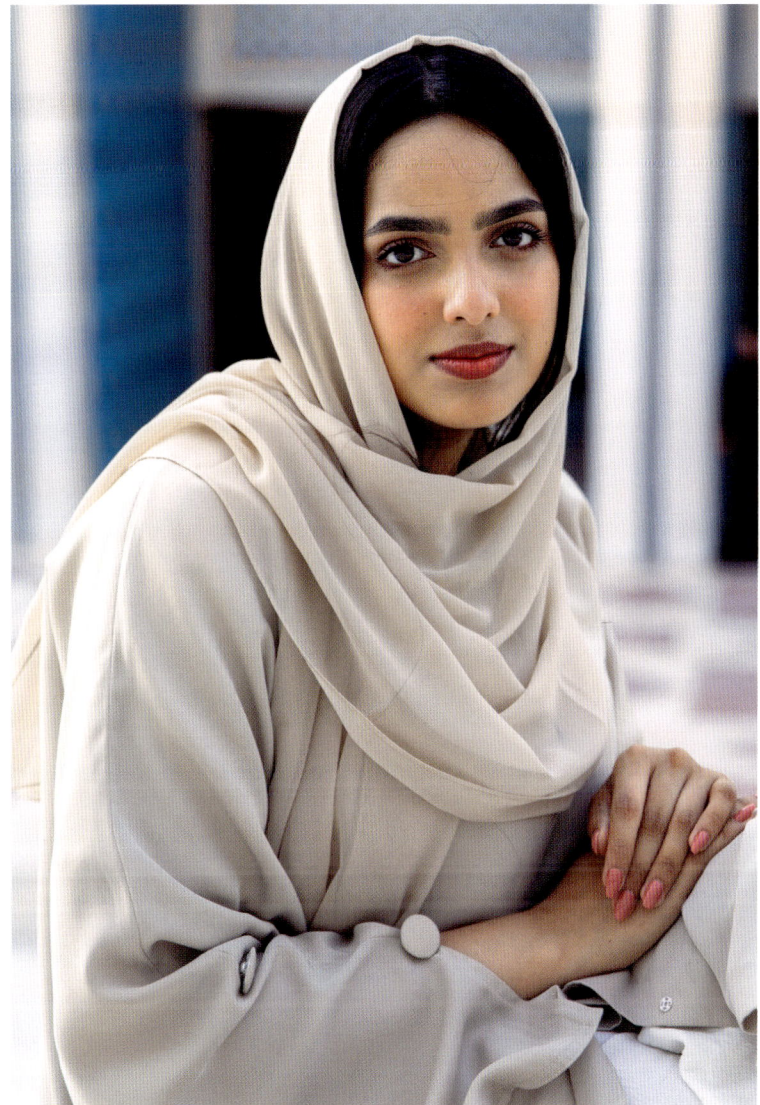

ABU DHABI, UNITED ARAB EMIRATES

I photographed Reem Almenhali at the Cultural Foundation, a place she often visits to get inspiration and create her own pieces of art. Reem chose an unconventional path for this part of the world—one that is also challenging. She is a playwright who uses poetry to explore the condition of women in the region. She draws inspiration from her own experiences and the experiences of her family.

Reem's plays feature female protagonists, which is pioneering in this part of the world. She is a bold woman who is using her art to challenge prejudices and give a voice to women in her community.

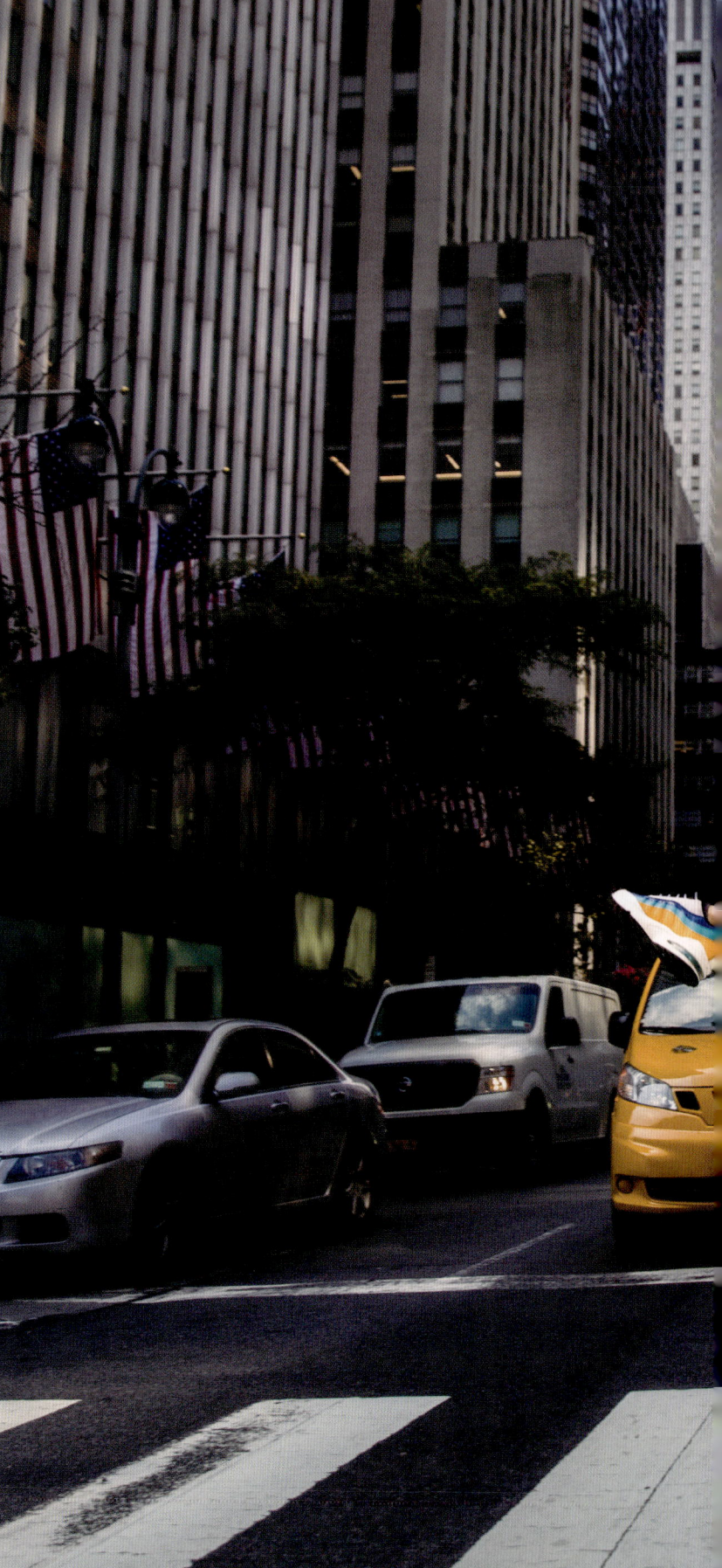

NEW YORK CITY, UNITED STATES

Erica Lall, a ballerina at the prestigious American Ballet Theatre, makes the grand jeté seem effortless. Yet years of dedication and passion lie behind each graceful leap.

Ballet has fascinated Erica since she was little—in her eyes, it was the most challenging form of dance. During those years, she was usually the only dark-skinned girl in class in her Texas hometown. She was constantly advised to avoid the sun so she would not get too tanned. It must have felt terrible to hear such comments, but Erica kept soaring higher and higher. Her efforts and talent didn't go unnoticed.

When she was fifteen, she left home and moved to New York City on her own, where she was invited to study ballet with some of the best teachers in the world. Malicious comments didn't stop, though. At the end of the day, all those painful comments make her even more ambitious.

Besides performing for the American Ballet Theatre, she also mentors young dancers. She wishes to encourage more children and teenagers from disadvantaged communities to join ballet. Like her, they can soar over all the challenges and prejudices.

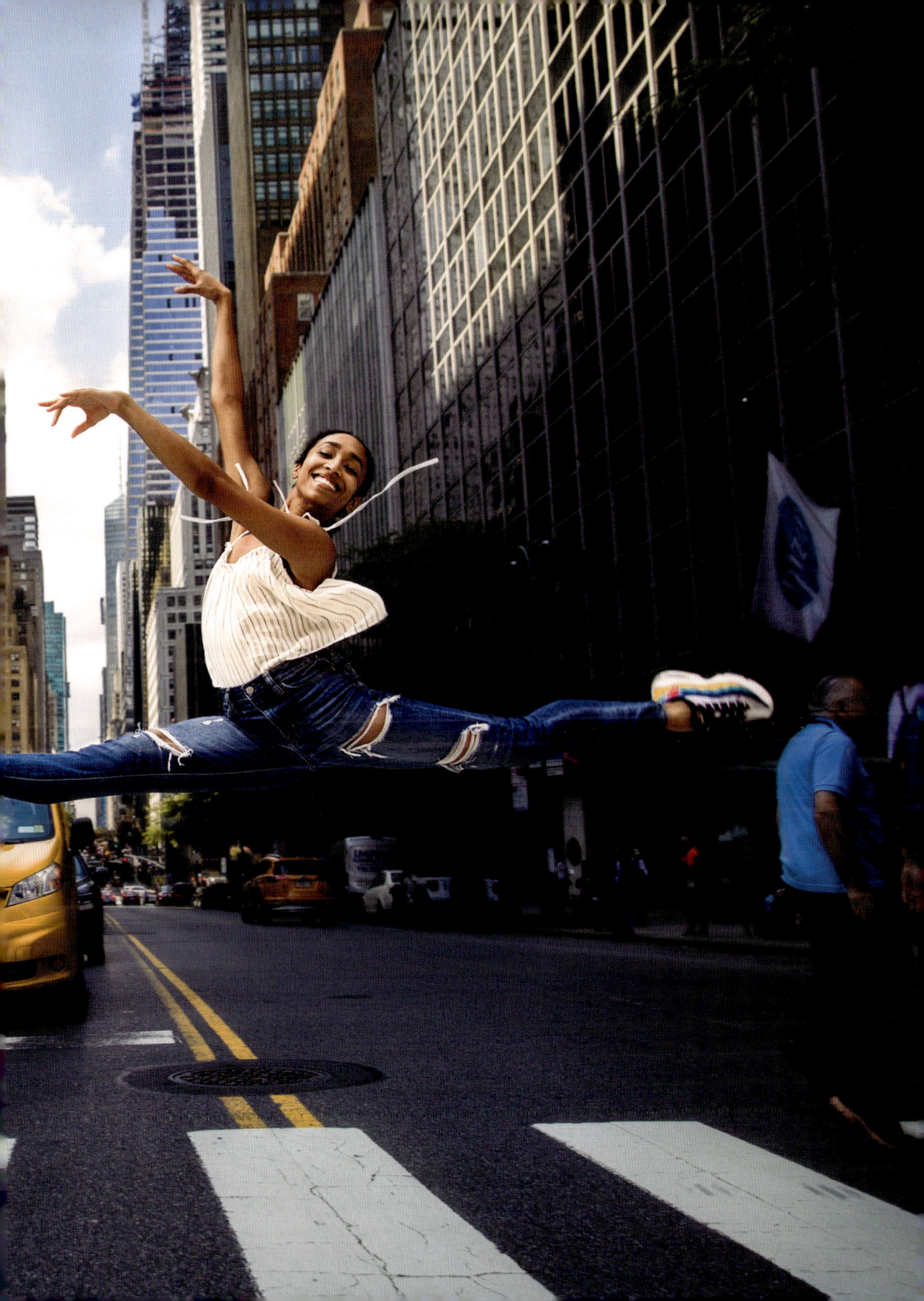

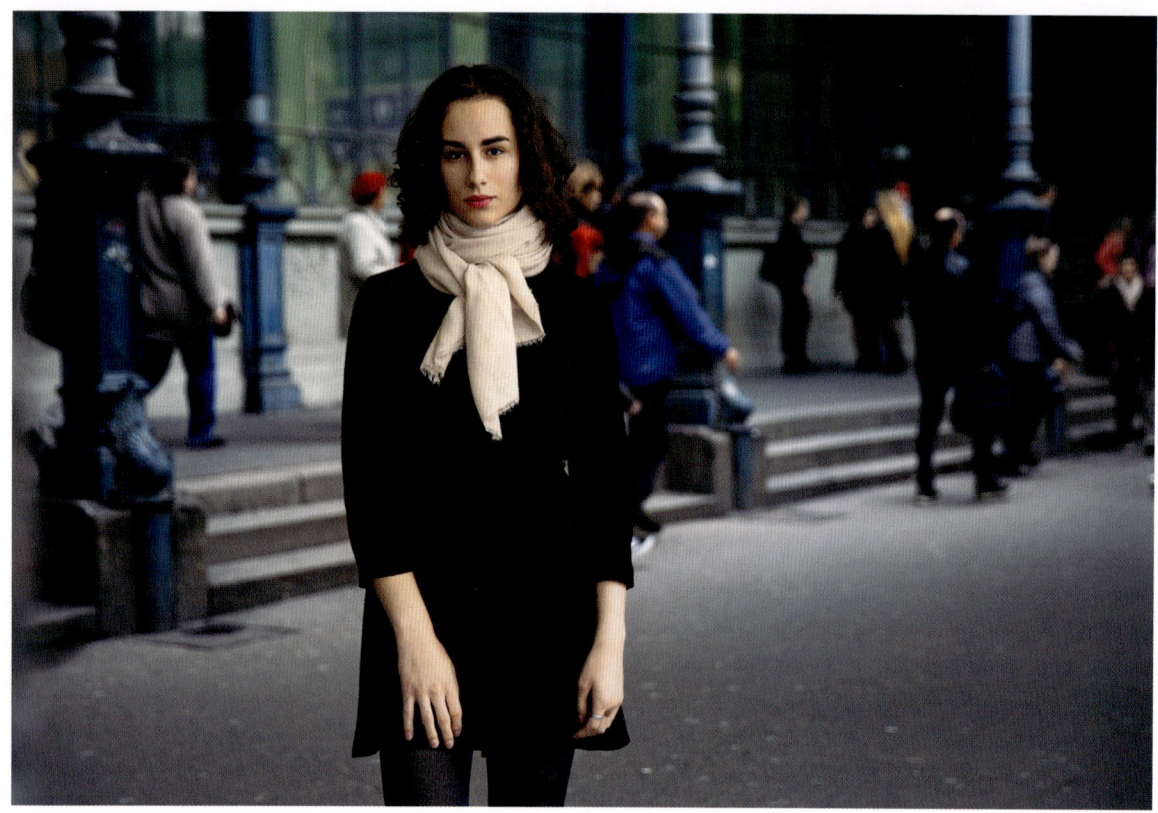

BUDAPEST, HUNGARY *(Above)*

I photographed Adél Onodi at the Nyugati railway station.
She shared with me her many struggles as both an artist and
a transgender woman. As a singer and actor, she dreamed of
building a career in Berlin and living a life free from intolerance.

COLOGNE, GERMANY *(Opposite)*

Lisa Pah lost beloved family members to cancer. After
much suffering, she found relief in two distinct activities.
She is a self-taught painter, using watercolors to
express her deepest feelings. At the same time, she
works as a researcher at one of the most prestigious
institutes in the world, where she studies cancer. The
impact of her losses has fueled her commitment to
understanding and combating this terrible disease.

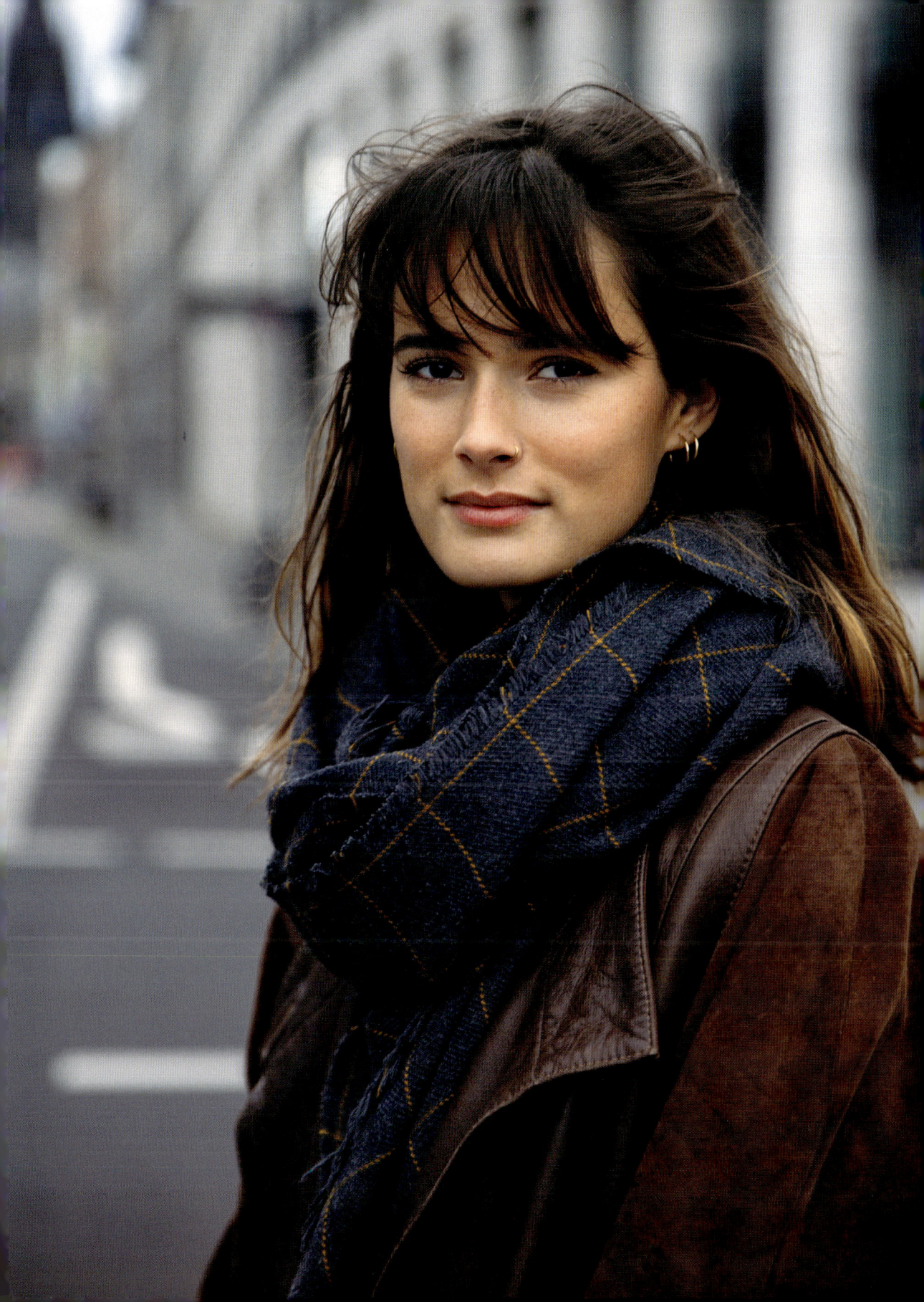

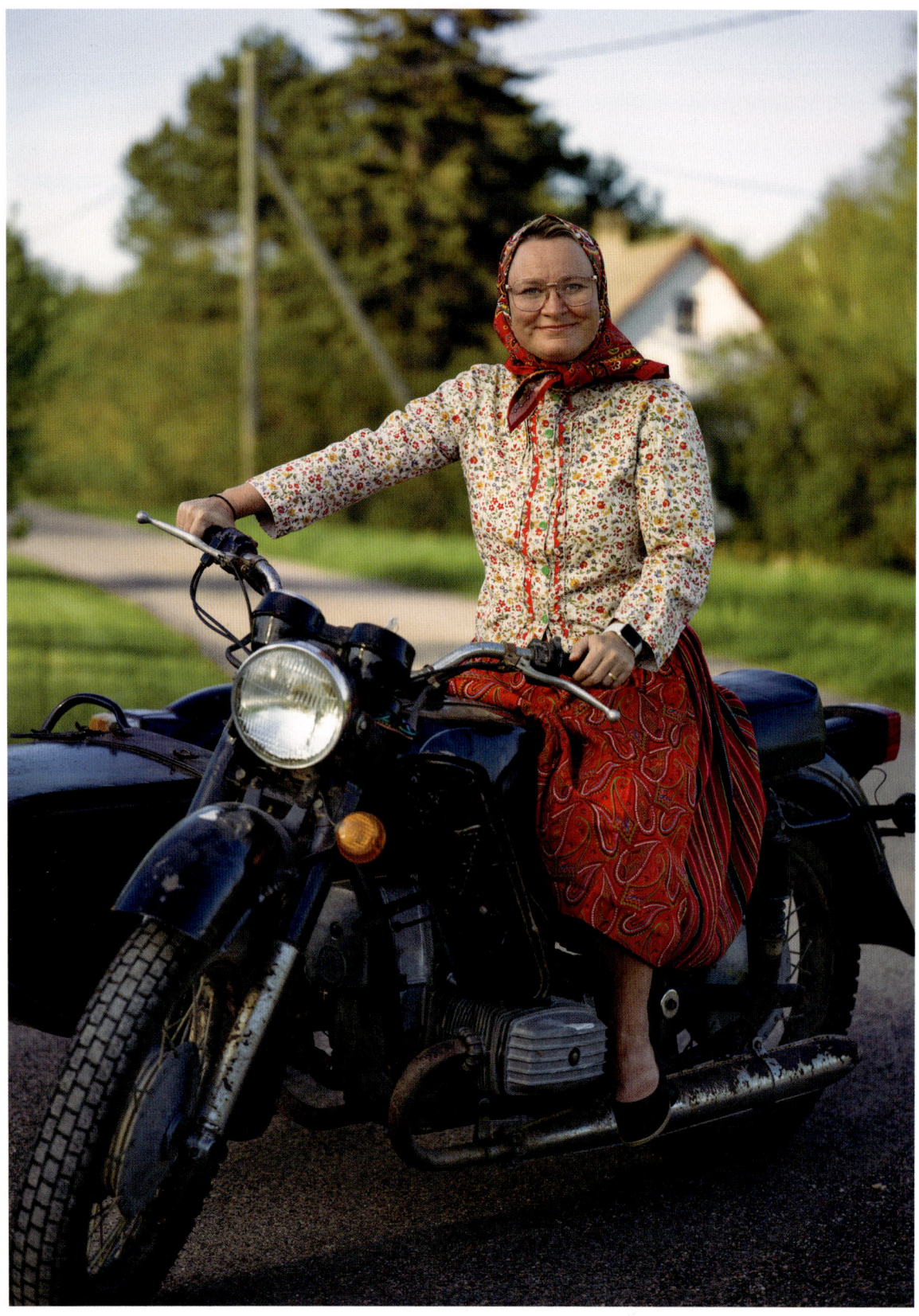

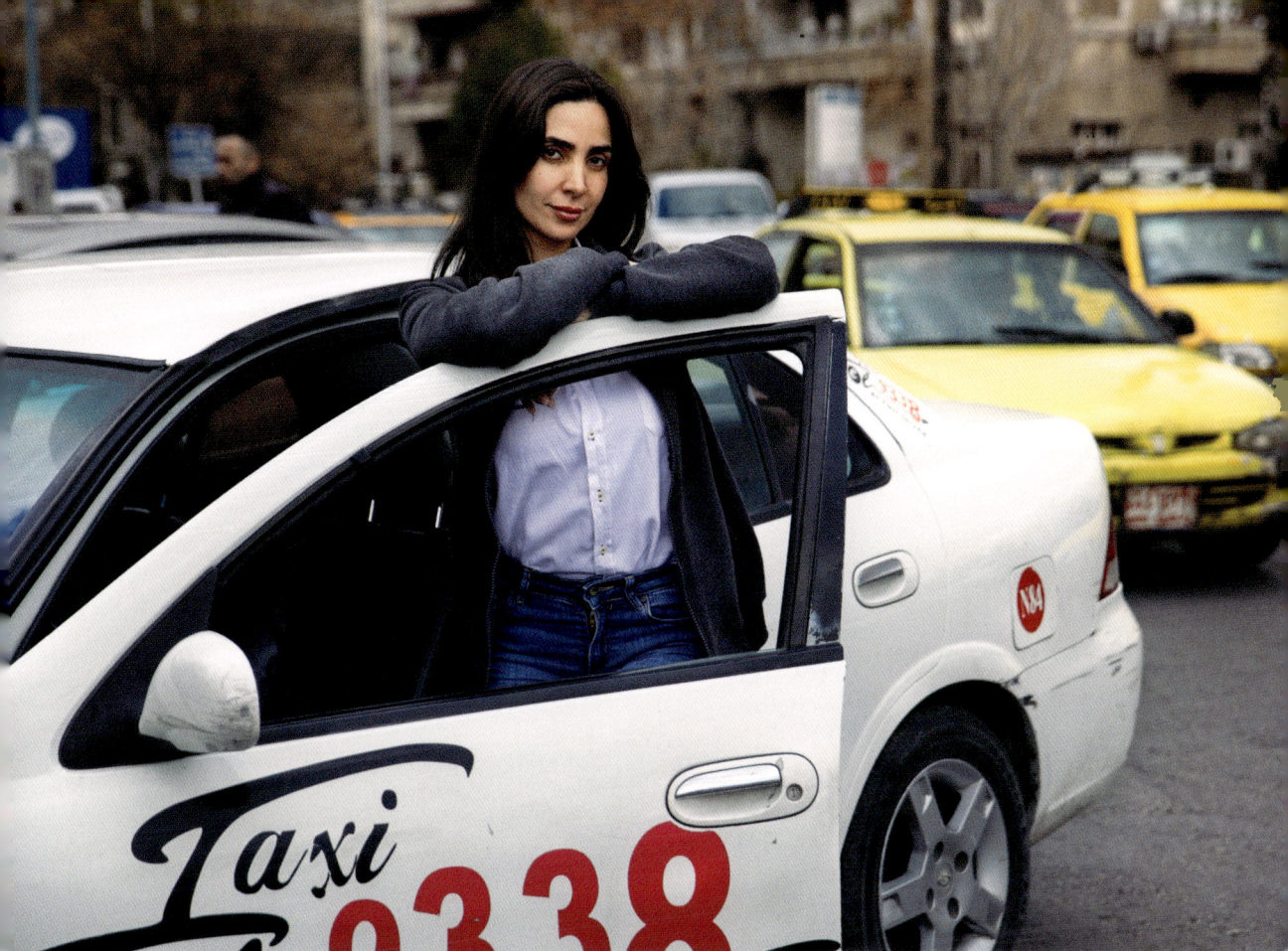

DAMASCUS, SYRIA *(Above)*

Driving in the chaotic traffic of Damascus is a real challenge. But not for Kinana, who feels like a fish in water. Every morning, she goes to the gym, and then she navigates her cab through the crowded streets of Damascus. In this intense traffic, there are often arguments and conflicts, but I was fascinated to see how Kinana handles the chaos with confidence and ease.

KIHNU ISLAND, ESTONIA *(Opposite)*

On this fascinating island, you can see that women truly can do anything. Due to a history of men being at sea, Kihnu women have become masters of adaptation.

Mare is a central figure in preserving Kihnu's traditional culture. Her life is dedicated to promoting and protecting Kihnu's rich cultural heritage. She is an eminent intellectual, but she also leads a simple life on the island, living in harmony with nature.

She's the mother of four children, a lighthouse keeper, and a passionate motorcycle driver. She believes that it's important for communities not to forget how to grow their own food, make their own clothes, and be able to survive if, for example, one day there's no electricity or modern amenities. For Mare, a traditional life is not just a symbol of the past but also a way to survive if the world changes someday.

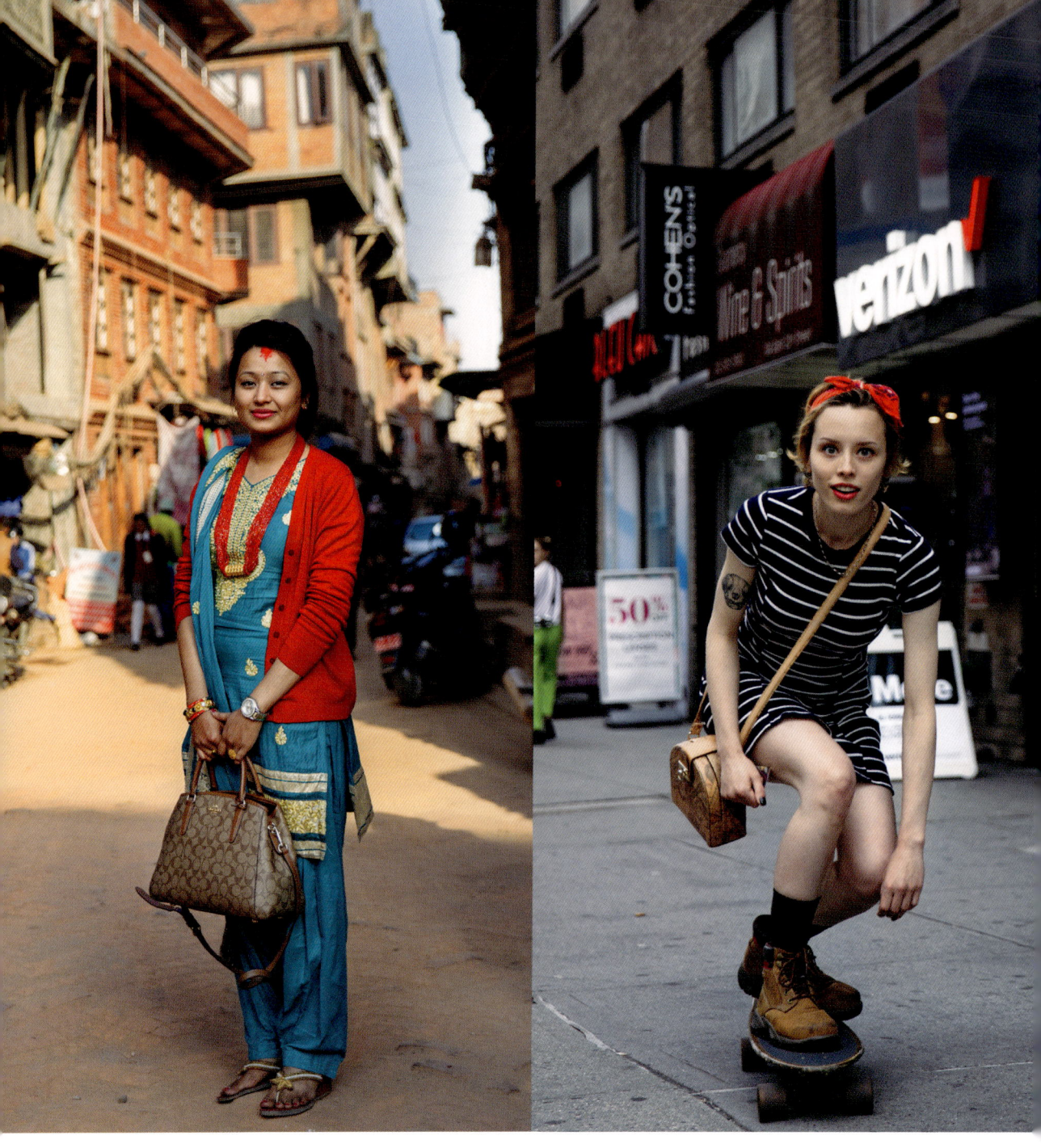

KATHMANDU, NEPAL

NEW YORK CITY, UNITED STATES

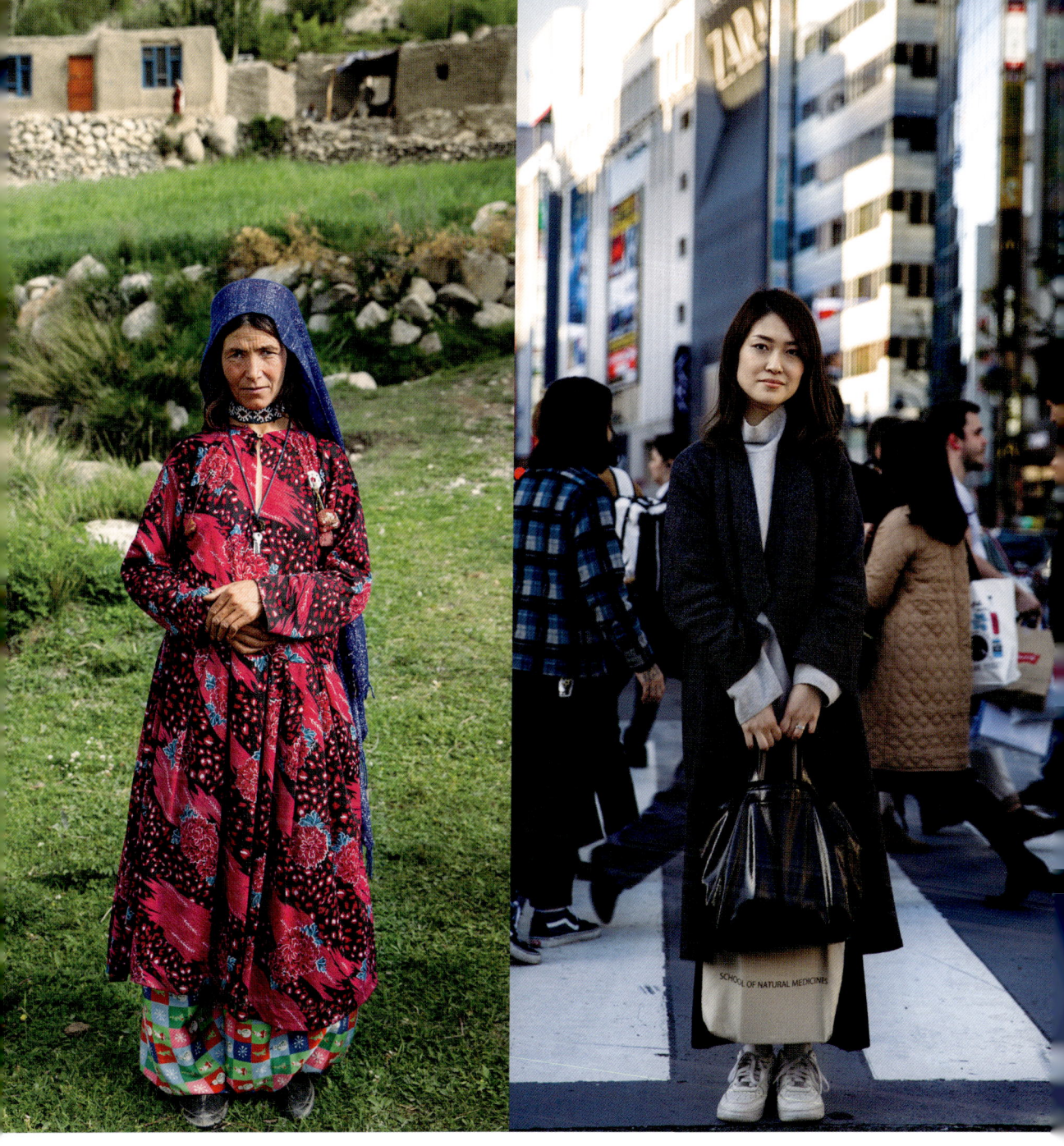

NORTHERN AFGHANISTAN

TOKYO, JAPAN

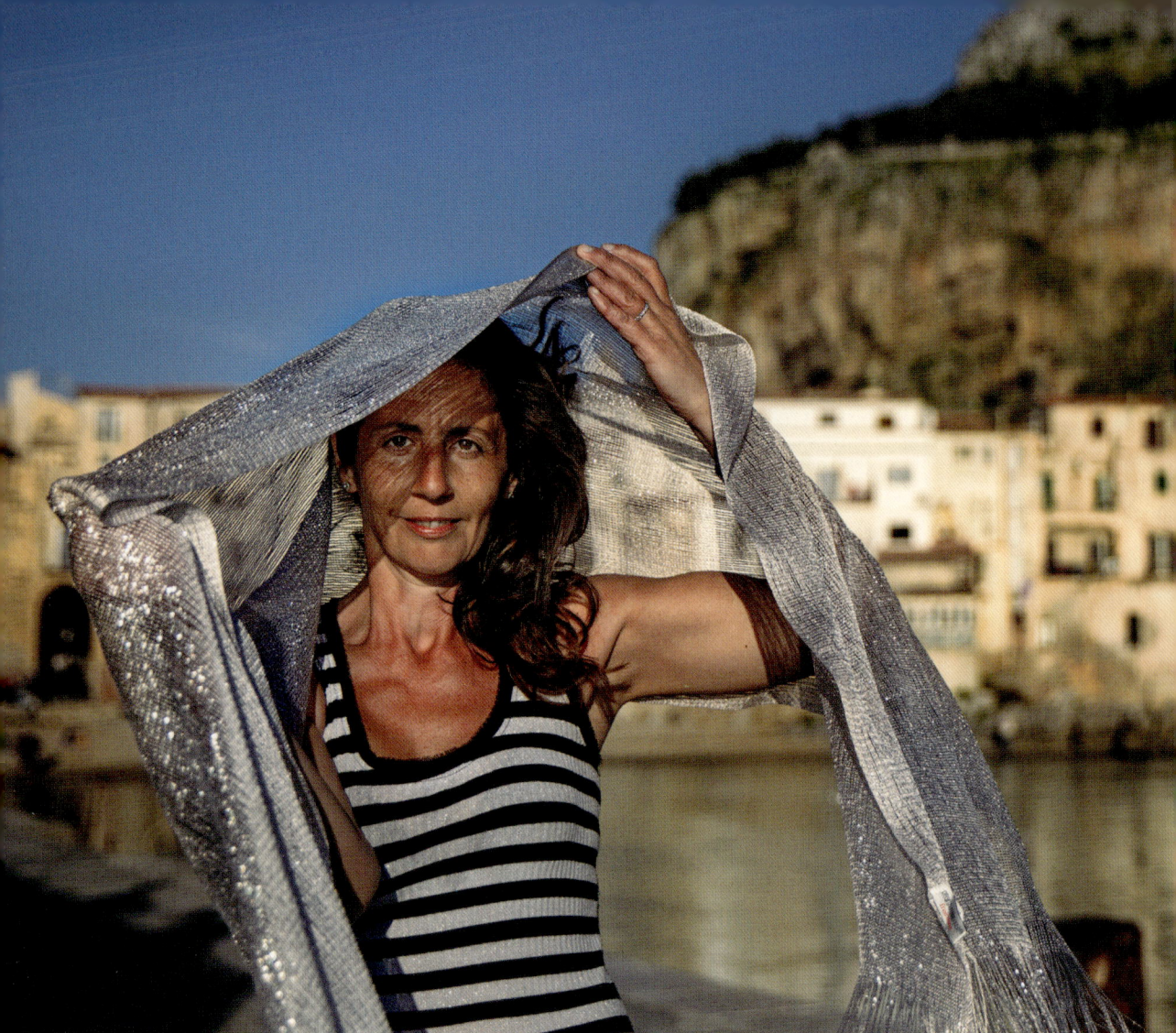

CEFALÙ, ITALY

Born in this charming seaside town in Sicily, Cancetta's life was always related to the sea. She was born in a family of fishermen and later became a lifeguard on this picturesque beach.

She was always fascinated by the beauty of the sea, but she was also aware of its formidable force. She experiences this fascinating duality every day, and that's why being a lifeguard is much more than a job for her.

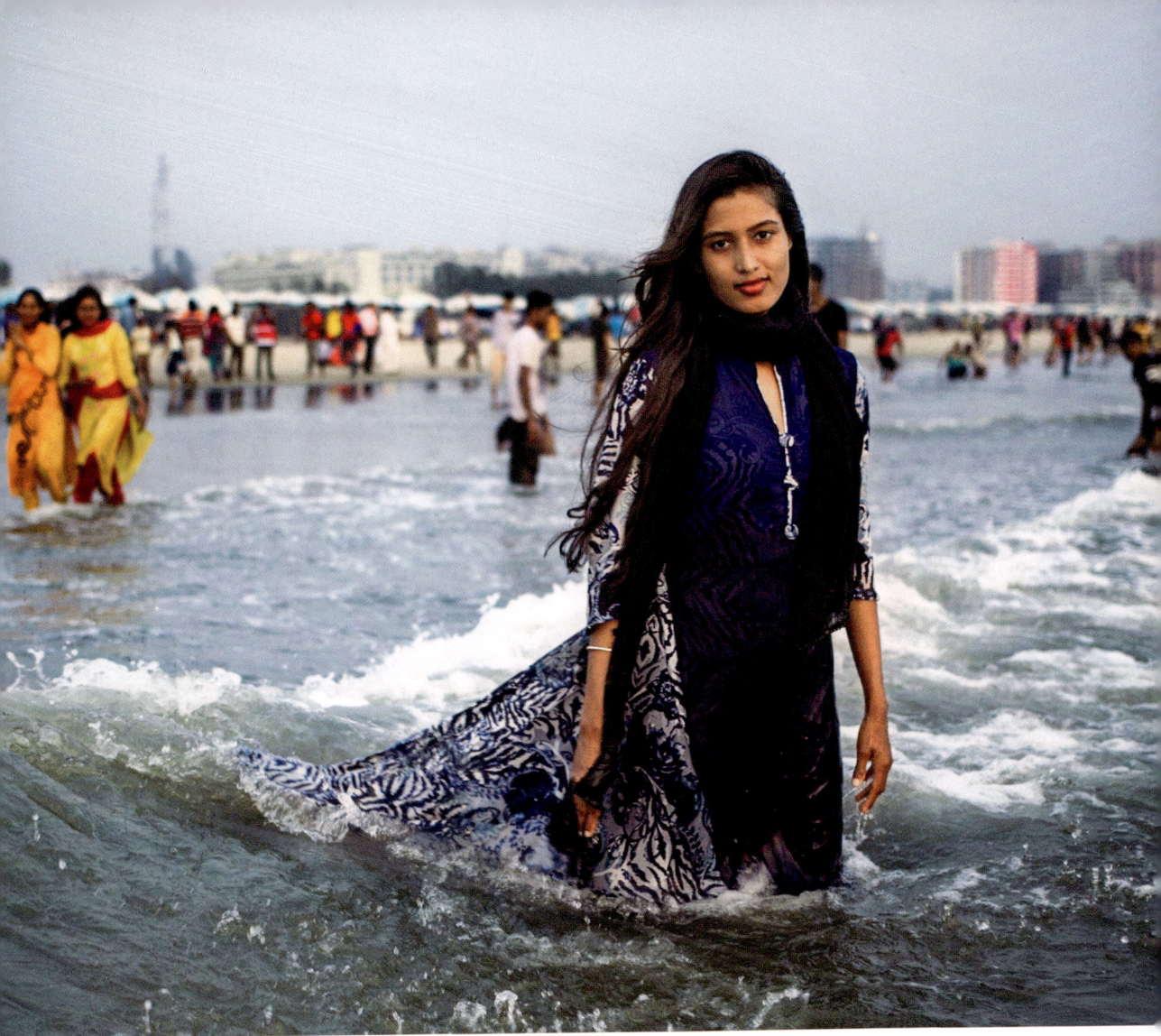

COX'S BAZAR, BANGLADESH

It was a beautiful day in March when I visited Cox's Bazar Beach, renowned as one of the longest beaches in the world. Bangladesh is a very traditional country, so it's common for both men and women to bathe while fully clothed. However, it is uncommon to encounter a female lifeguard. Luckily, I was fortunate enough to meet one.

Just before sunset, I noticed Sabina. She was relaxing after a day of work—right at her workplace. She shared with me her deep-rooted love for the sea. It was a feeling she had cherished for as long as she could remember. At that time, she was pregnant. Coincidentally, so was I. I felt a beautiful connection between us: two women, from different corners of the world, driven by passion in their professions while eagerly awaiting the arrival of their firstborns.

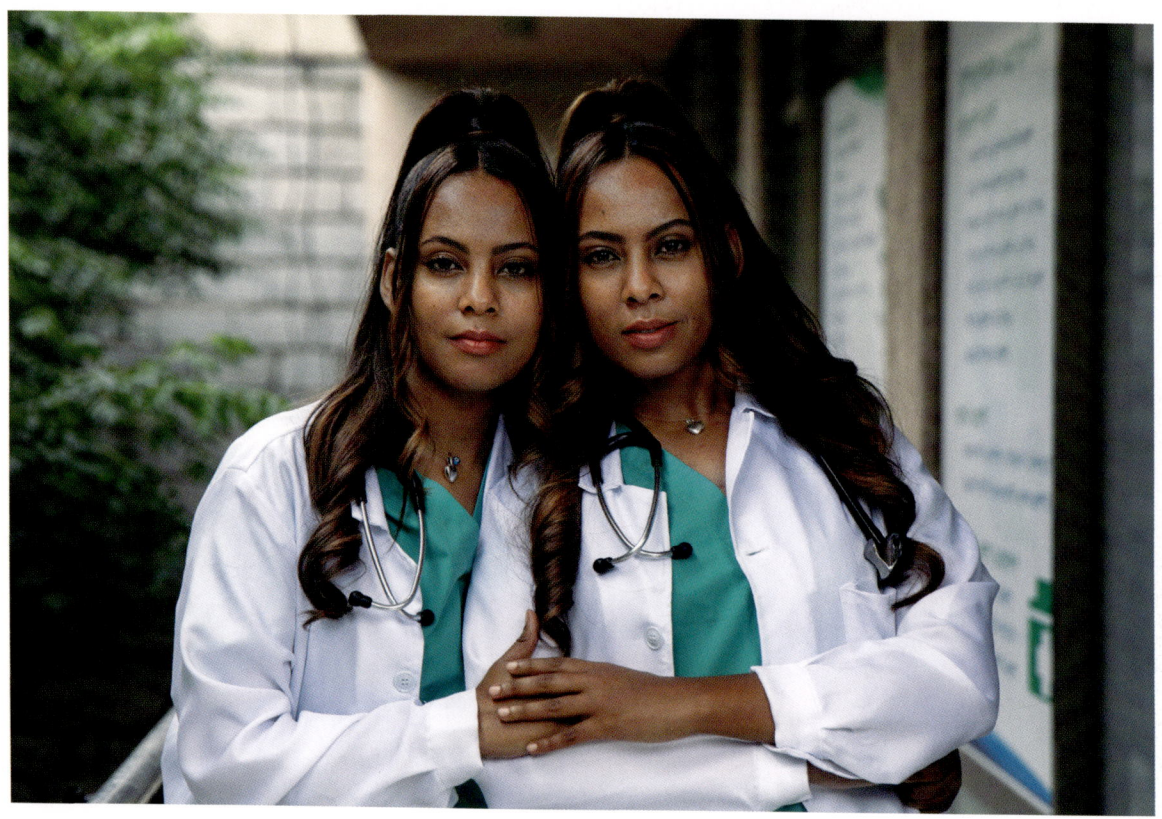

ADDIS ABABA, ETHIOPIA *(Above)*

Meet Jerusalem and Kalkidan, twin sisters who are general practitioners. Their childhood was tough—they lost their father when they were only one year old. As a result, the sisters grew up with a strong determination to solve medical problems. Today, they run their own clinic, which is dedicated to serving the local community with love and compassion.

VIENNA, AUSTRIA *(Opposite)*

Sisters Vlada and Victoria live in Kyiv, Ukraine, but took a few days off for a short vacation in Vienna. It took them twenty-four hours by train to get here, but they were happy to finally enjoy a few days of calm and peace after months of war.

Their city was no longer on the front line, but air raid sirens sounded every day, which indicates the danger of a missile strike and that residents should seek shelter. Soon after our encounter, Vlada and Victoria were back home, dreaming about something that most of us take for granted: peace.

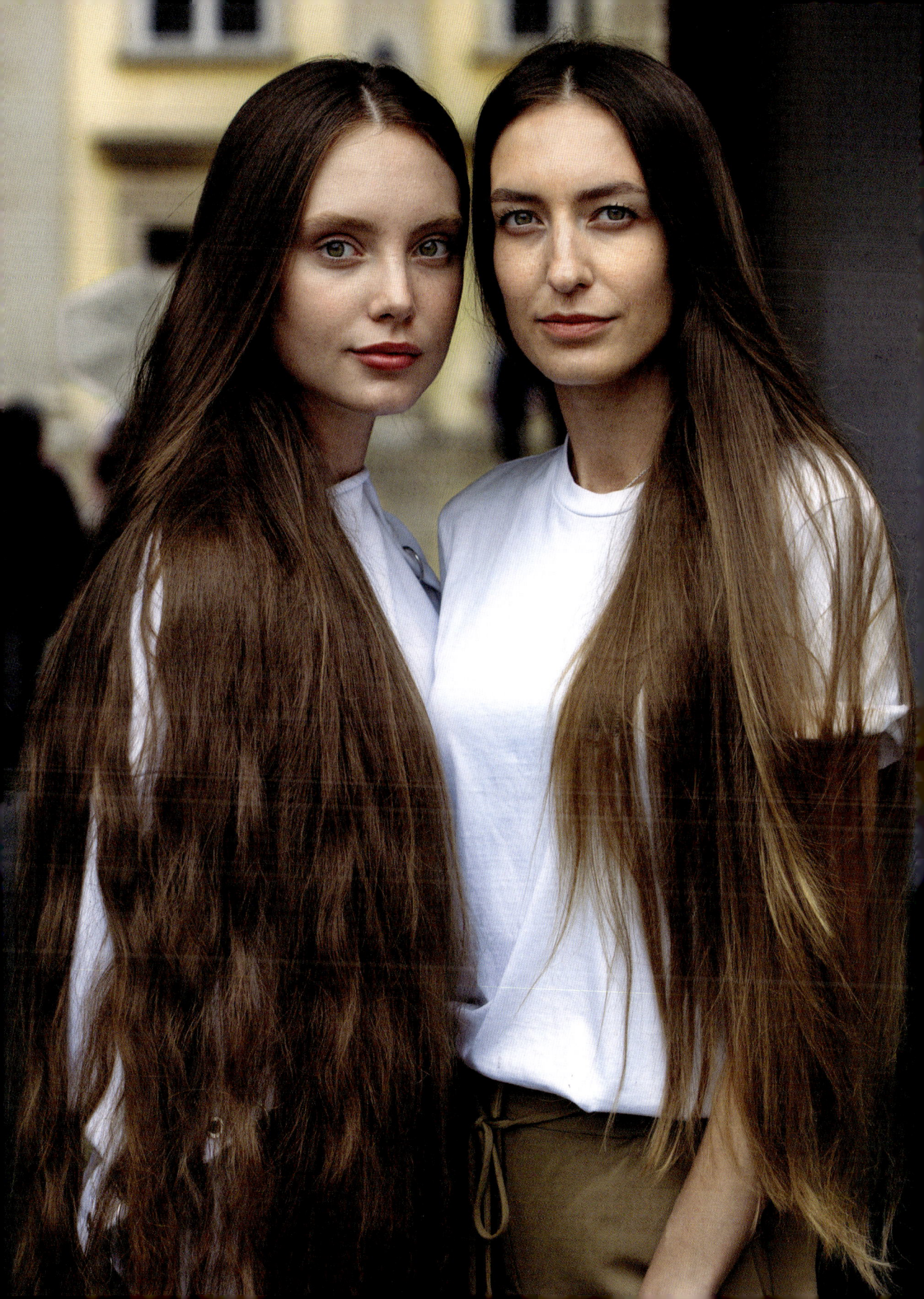

MOLDOVA

Marina grows some of the tastiest blueberries I have ever tried. She started this small business with her husband in their village.

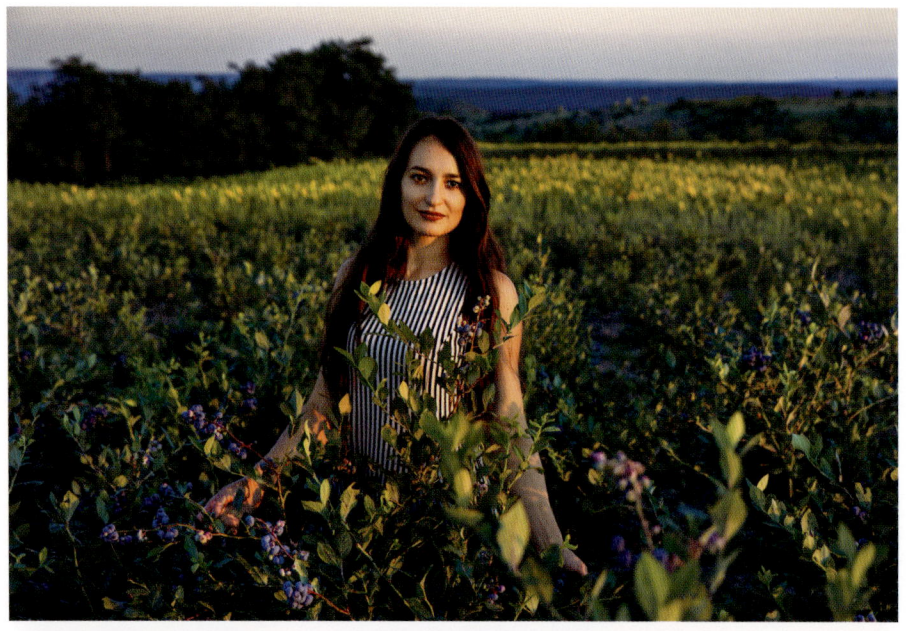

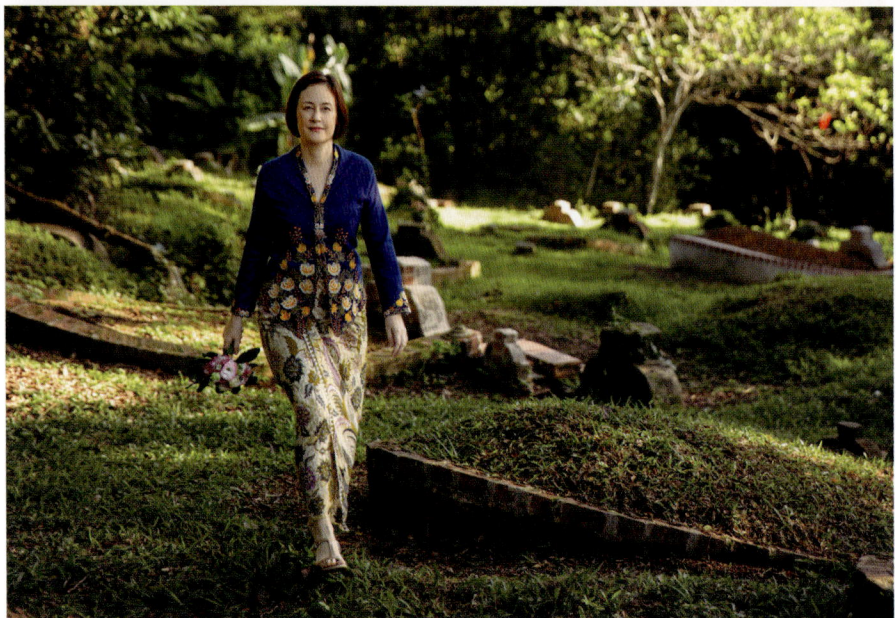

SINGAPORE

Inspired by the splendid tiles she found on the tomb of her great-grandparents, Jennifer Lim started a program called the Singapore Heritage Tile Project. Working with more than one hundred volunteers, she restored and documented thousands of rare decorative tiles in this cemetery. For Jennifer, the diverse designs of the tiles she restored illustrate Singapore's diverse heritage and her own, as well.

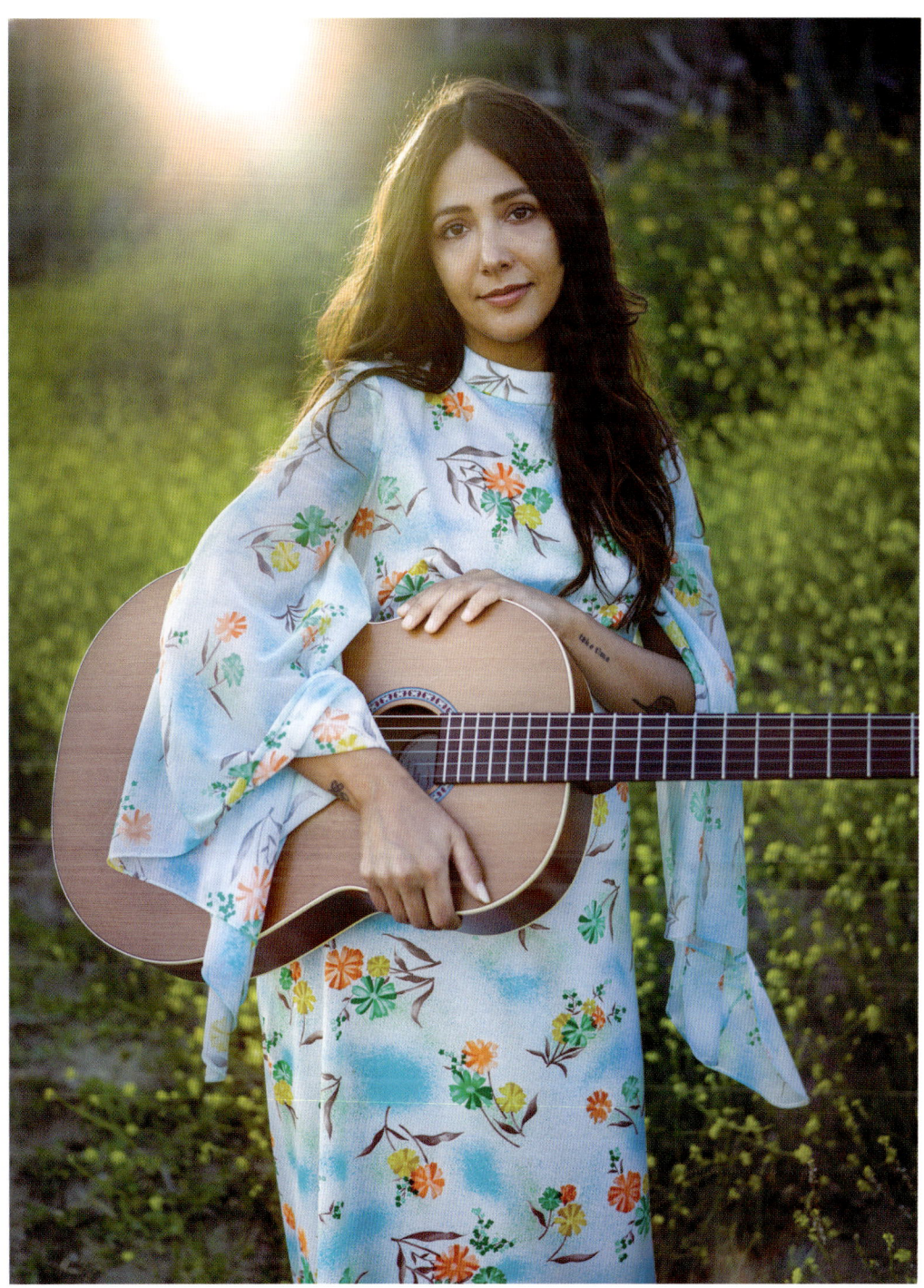

LOS ANGELES, UNITED STATES

At age thirteen, Lisa Houdei started to write her own music. Besides being a musician, she also paints and sculpts. Her soulful art is warm and dreamy.

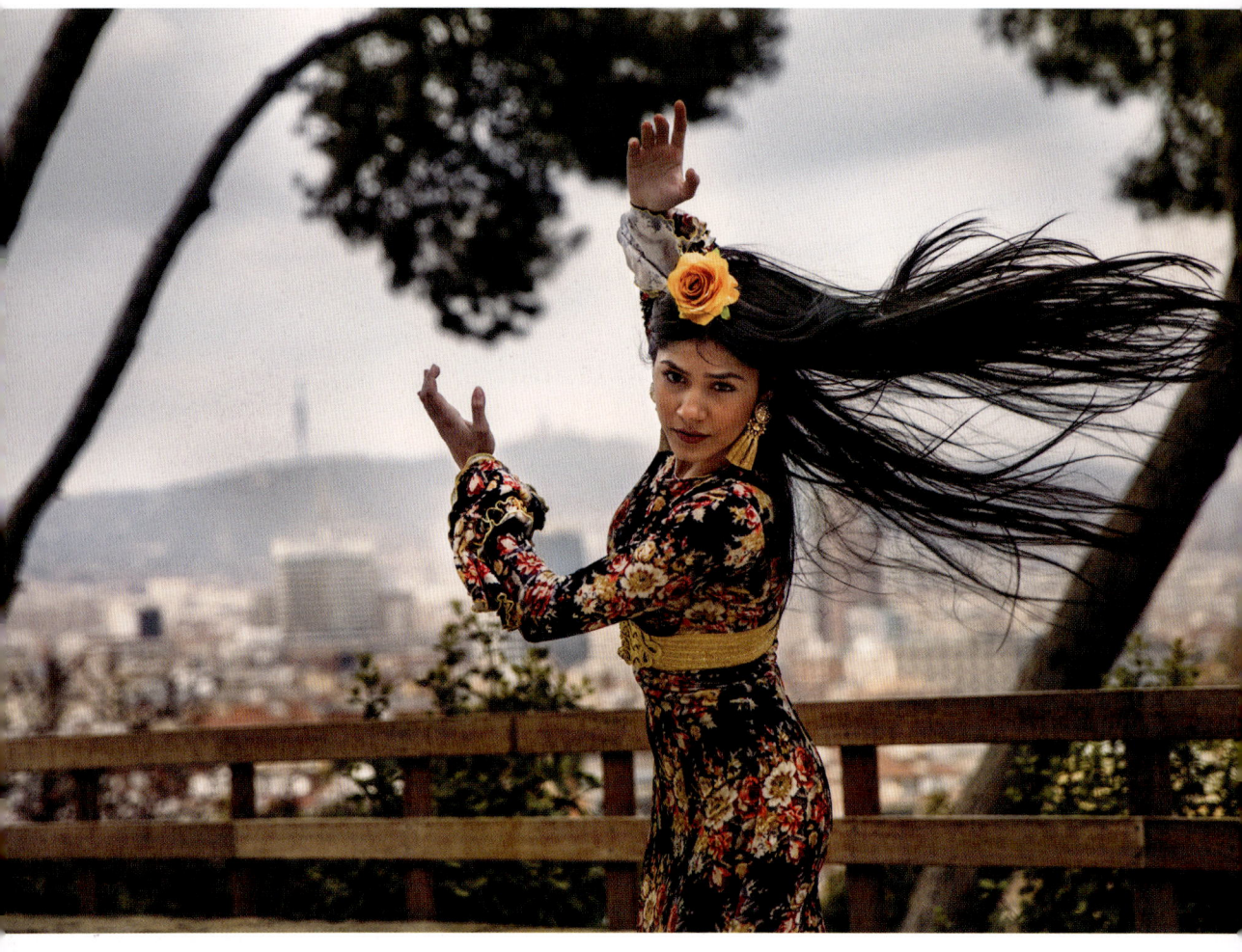

BARCELONA, SPAIN

I photographed Gema, a flamenco dancer, in front of the *tablao* where she performs. A *tablao* is a venue where flamenco shows are performed. Let me tell you—it's such an incredible experience to witness the passion, the power, and the charisma of great flamenco artists. Originally from the region of Andalusia, flamenco has been influenced by and associated with the Romani people in Spain.

Gema herself comes from a Romani family deeply connected with this mesmerizing art. Gema's great-grandaunt, Carmen Amaya, was one of the greatest flamenco dancers of all time. Some say Carmen was the first woman to truly master flamenco footwork, previously reserved for the best male dancers due to its speed and intensity. She used to be called a human tornado. Now, almost a century later, her great-grandniece carries on the tradition.

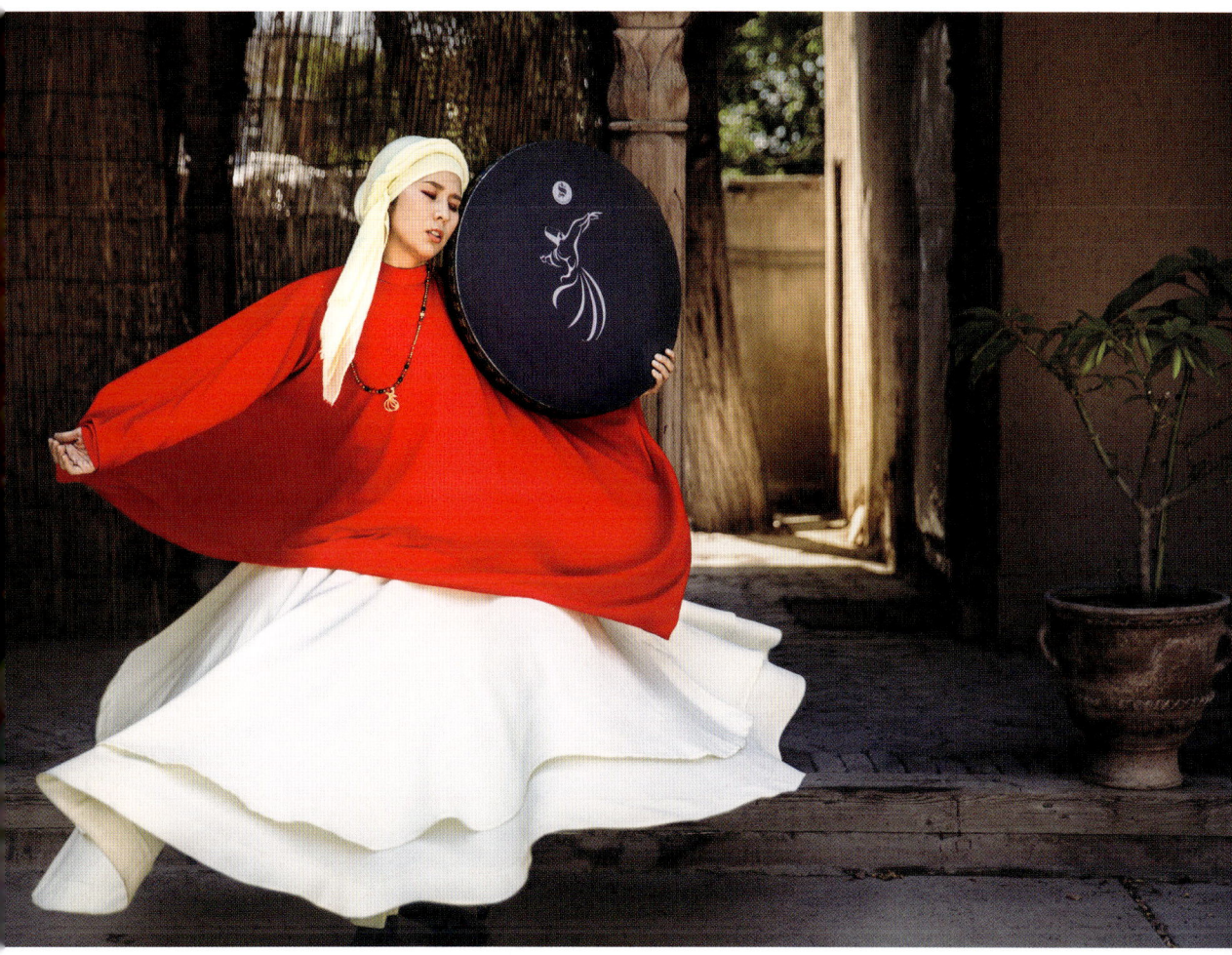

KABUL, AFGHANISTAN

For many years, Fahima was likely the only female mystical dancer in Afghanistan. In a society in which any form of dance is widely considered taboo for women, she defied stereotypes. But her motivation wasn't to prove something or satisfy her ego; it was simply to pursue what she loved most.

This dance is a part of Sufism, a mystical form of Islam that emphasizes the inward search for God. The continuous whirling is a form of meditation that allows the dancer to transcend the ego and focus on God. Fahima wanted to share this unique experience with other Afghan people, so she established a school for it. Unfortunately, soon after our meeting, Kabul fell to Taliban forces, which forced her to leave Afghanistan. Fahima has a great gift, and I'm sure that she will find a way to share it with the world eventually.

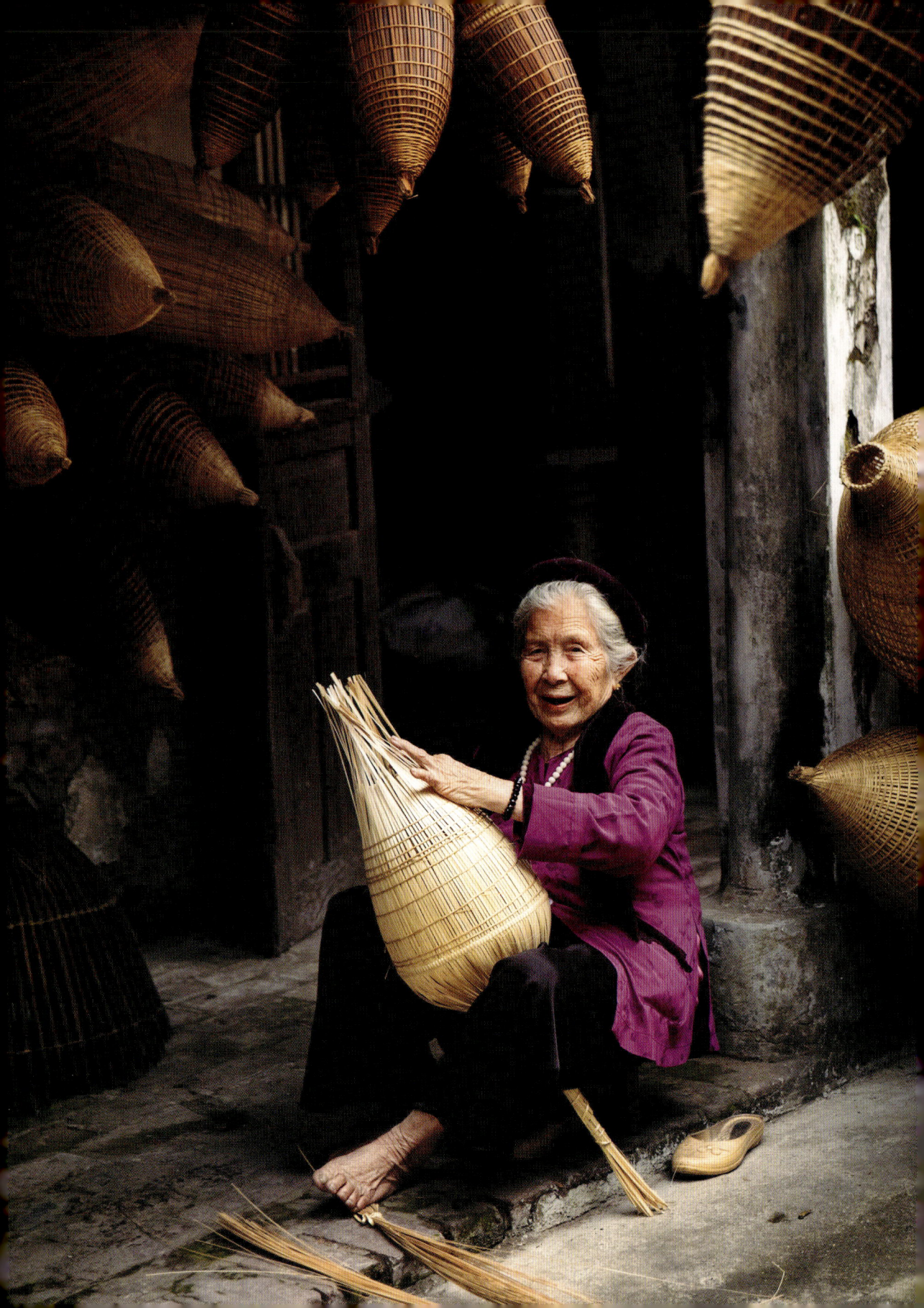

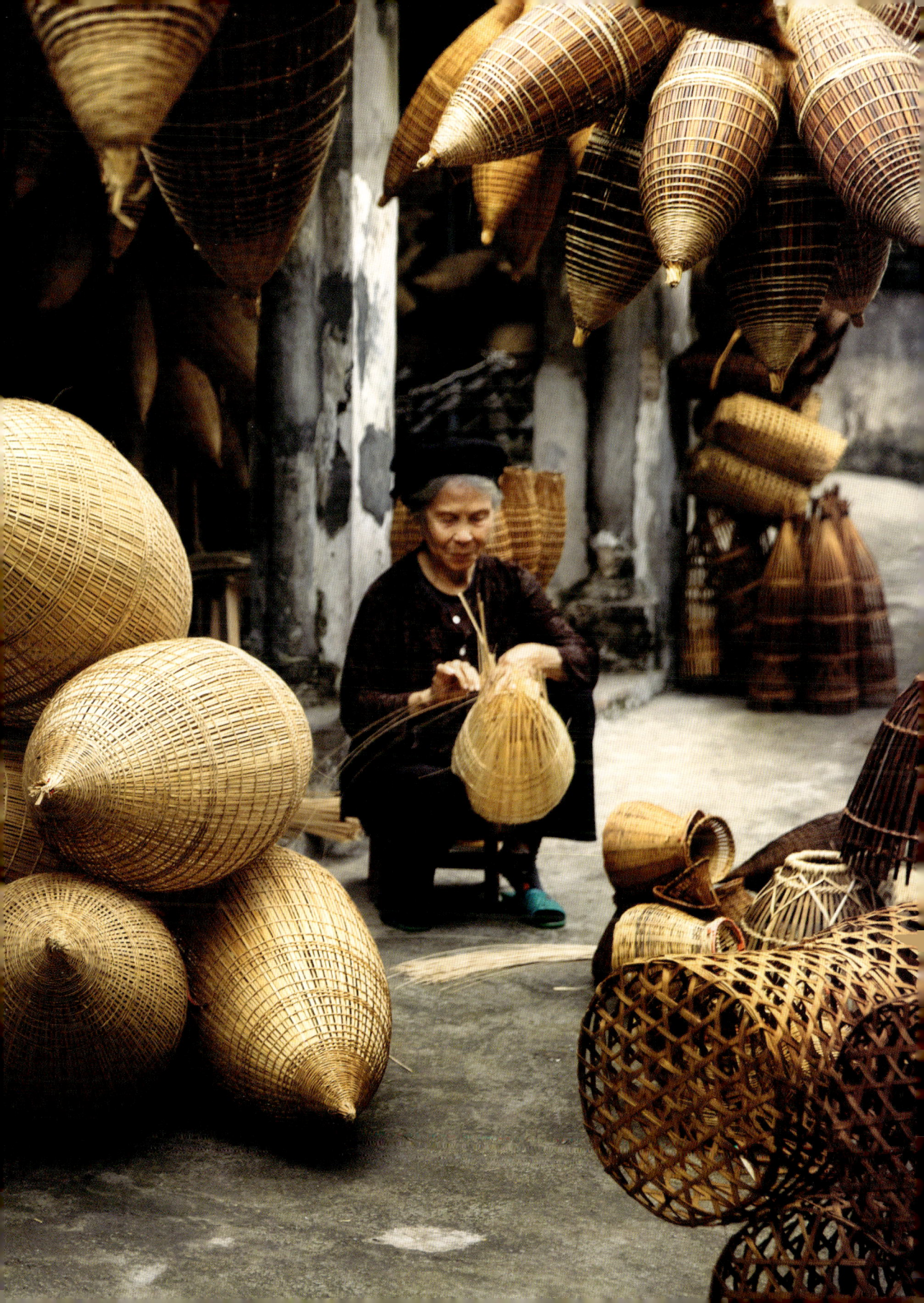

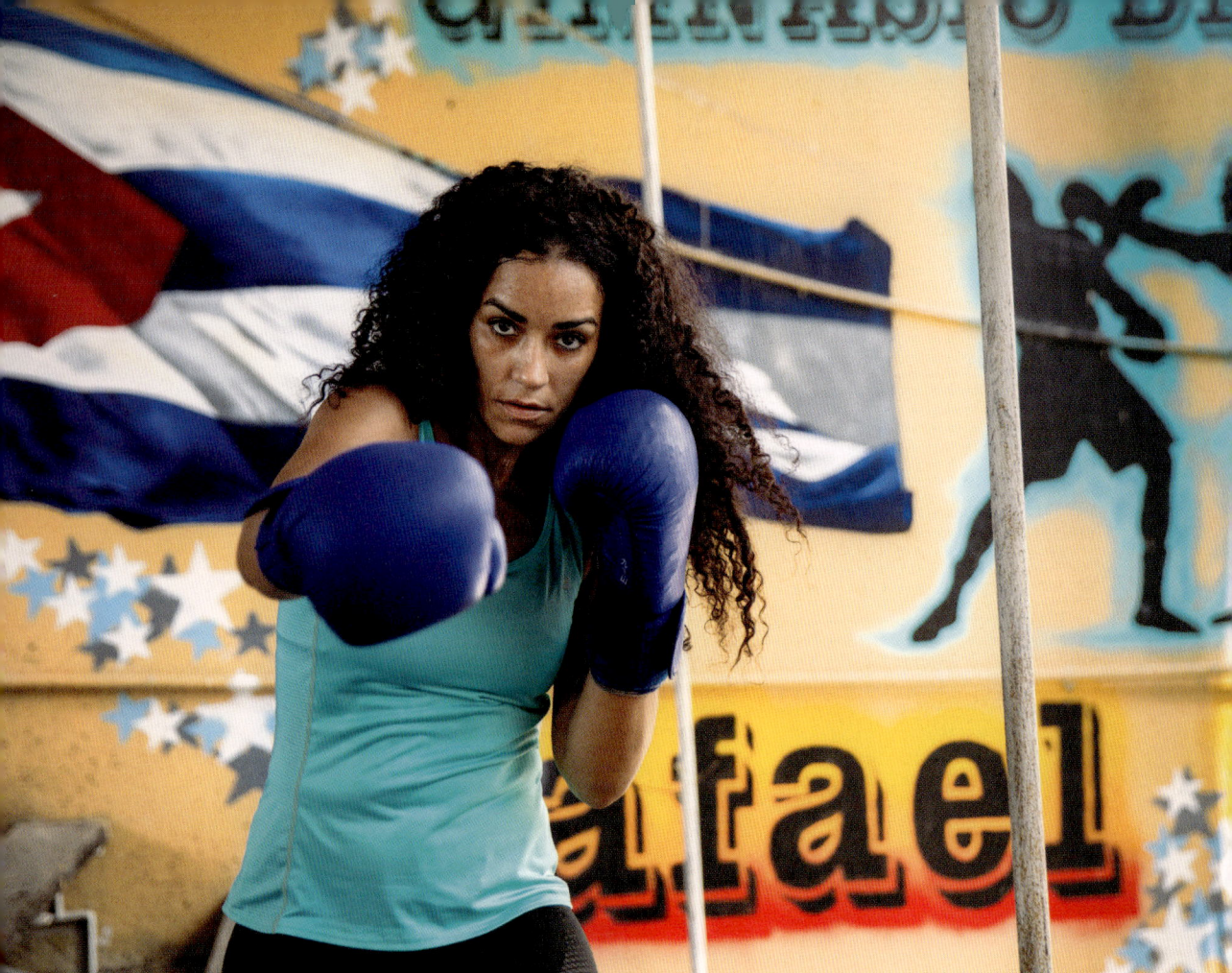

HAVANA, CUBA

Anabelle wanted to inspire her two young boys to try sports, so she began practicing boxing with them. Eventually the boys decided to quit, but Anabelle persisted and continued to improve. Cuba has a rich tradition in male boxing, but until recently women were prohibited from participating in competitive and even sparring matches. Anabelle, along with other Cuban women, are now challenging the norms.

HANOI, VIETNAM *(Previous spread)*

For the past eighty years, these two cousins have been crafting bamboo fishing traps in the very same place. The world around them has changed much, but they are still here, keeping this ancient tradition alive.

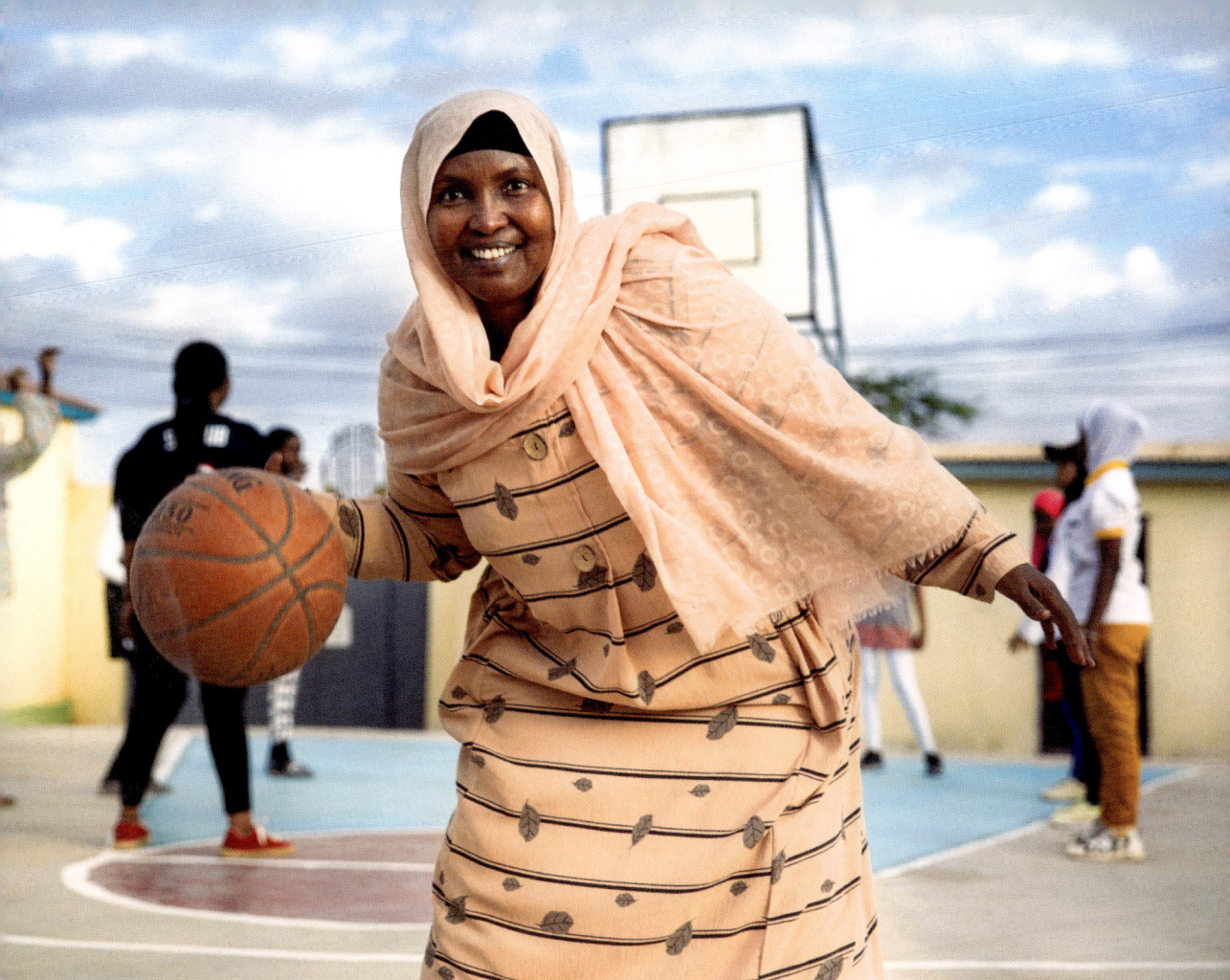

HARGEISA, SOMALILAND

When Khadra was a teenager, she excelled as a star athlete. At that time, when her country was under the rule of a cruel dictator, she could play basketball in public, but her freedom to practice her religion was restricted.

Later, the political regime changed, and the situation took a turn in the opposite direction. Khadra found herself able to practice her religion freely, but she was no longer permitted to play sports in public.

Khadra has always been religious and has always been an athlete. But unlike many people in Somaliland, she believes that there is no contradiction in being a devout Muslim and a woman athlete.

After her retirement, Khadra wanted to inspire new generations of young women through sports. Some years ago, she bought her own piece of land and built a wall around it to create a safe space for women and girls to play basketball.

Today, she has about fifty students, proving that women can find their voice and power against all misconceptions.

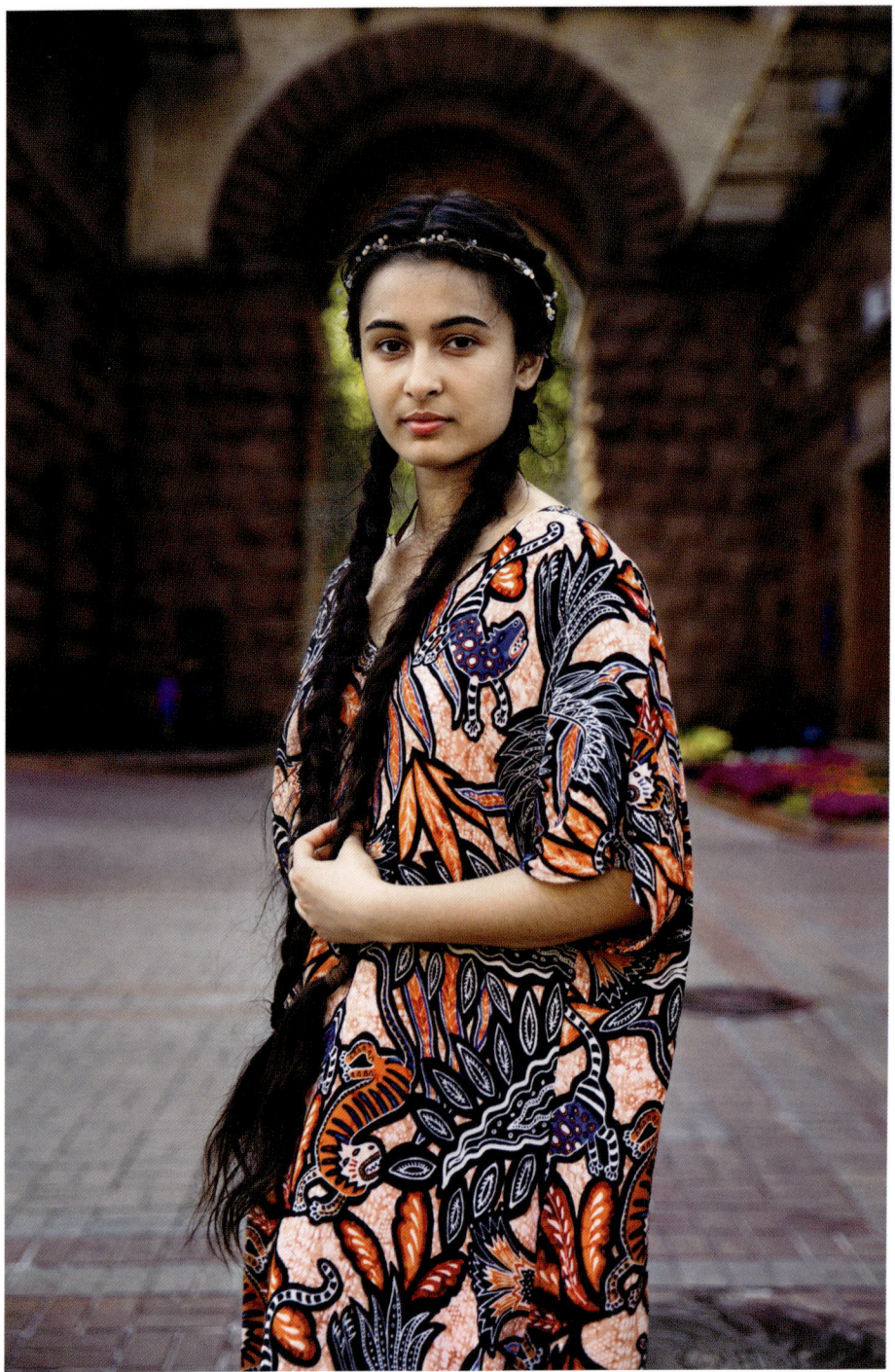

KYIV, UKRAINE

Grace was born to a Ukrainian mother and an Indian father. She grew up in Ukraine and was studying journalism in Canada when I met her in 2018. "I feel like a member of Mother Earth," she told me.

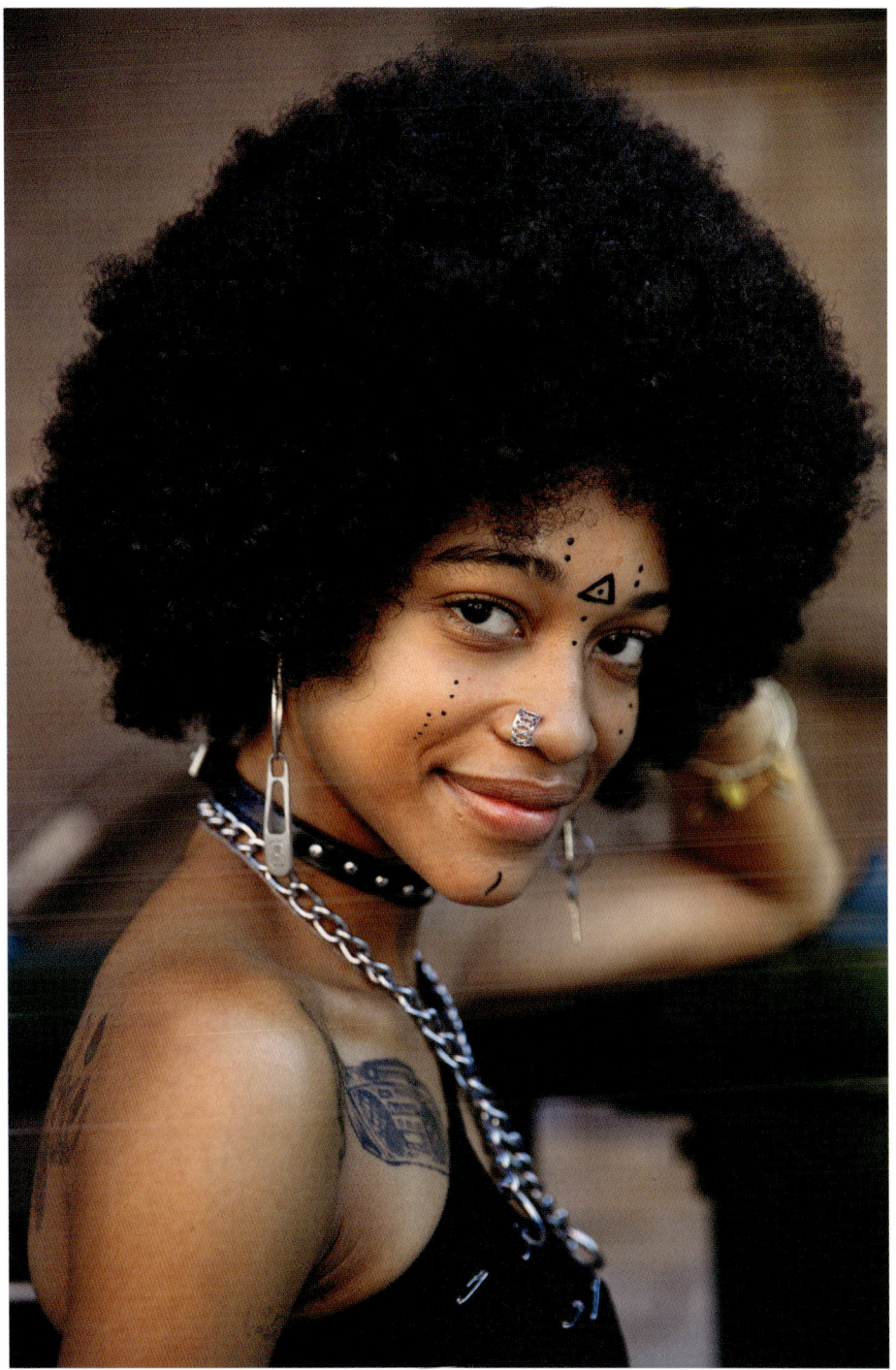

NEW YORK CITY, UNITED STATES

Ooniku was on her way to the hairdresser when I met her on the streets of the Bronx. She loves African American rock music and takes pride in her African heritage. There are days, like the one when we crossed paths, when she loves celebrating this through face drawings.

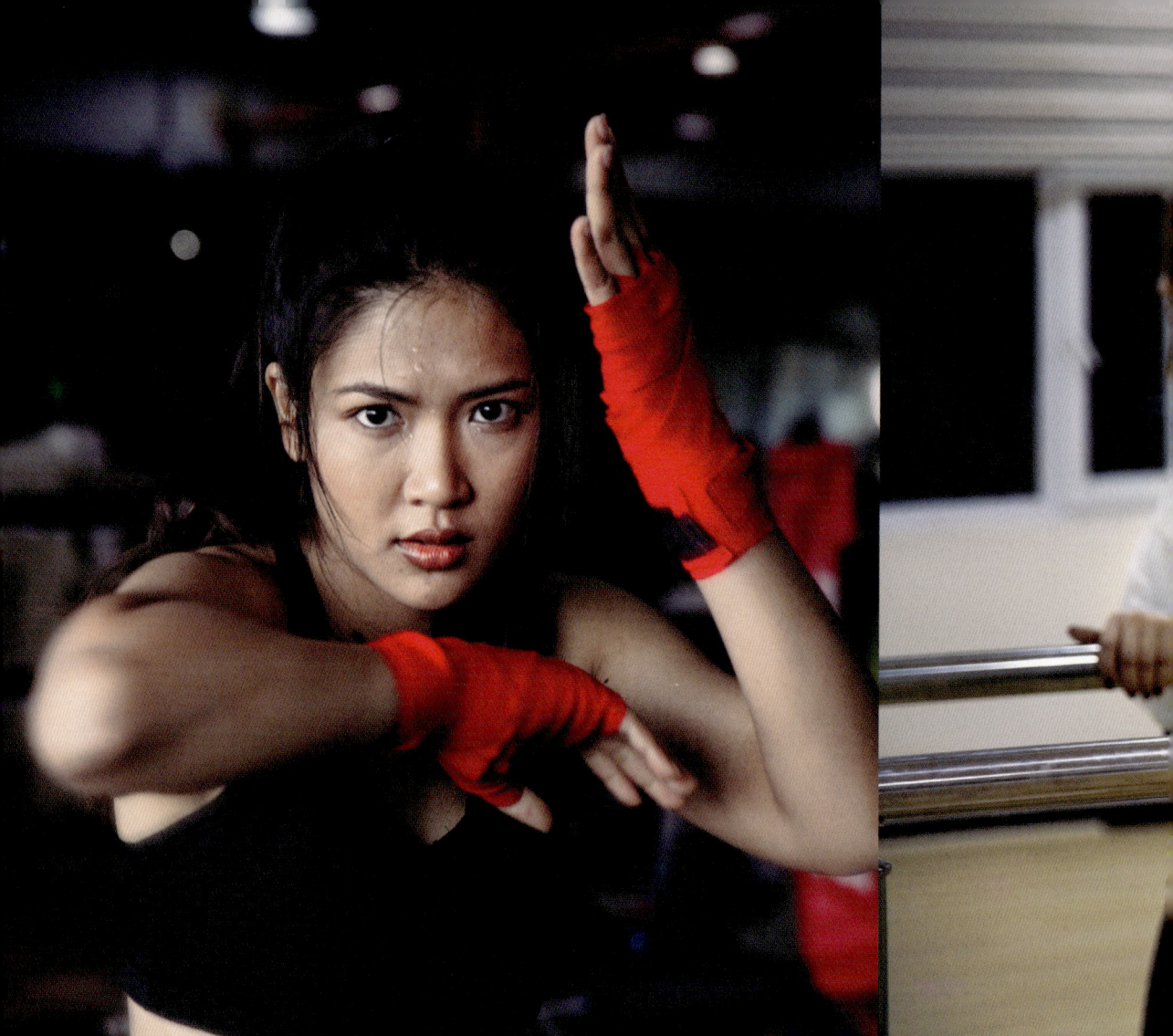

BANGKOK, THAILAND

Angsana Kamhanphol is a smart, elegant, and educated woman. She has an English degree and works as a marketing specialist. Zaza Sor Aree is a tough fighter, having competed in more than forty-one professional combats. She is also a former Thai boxing champion. No, I'm not talking about two different women. Zaza Sor Aree is Angsana's ring name.

Angsana was always in love with sports, and at fifteen years old, she started Muay Thai, also known as Thai boxing. She trained hard, she made sacrifices, and eventually she became a world champion. But in all that time, she never neglected school. Today, she is a champ in the ring but also in real life—two beautiful sides coexisting in one amazing woman.

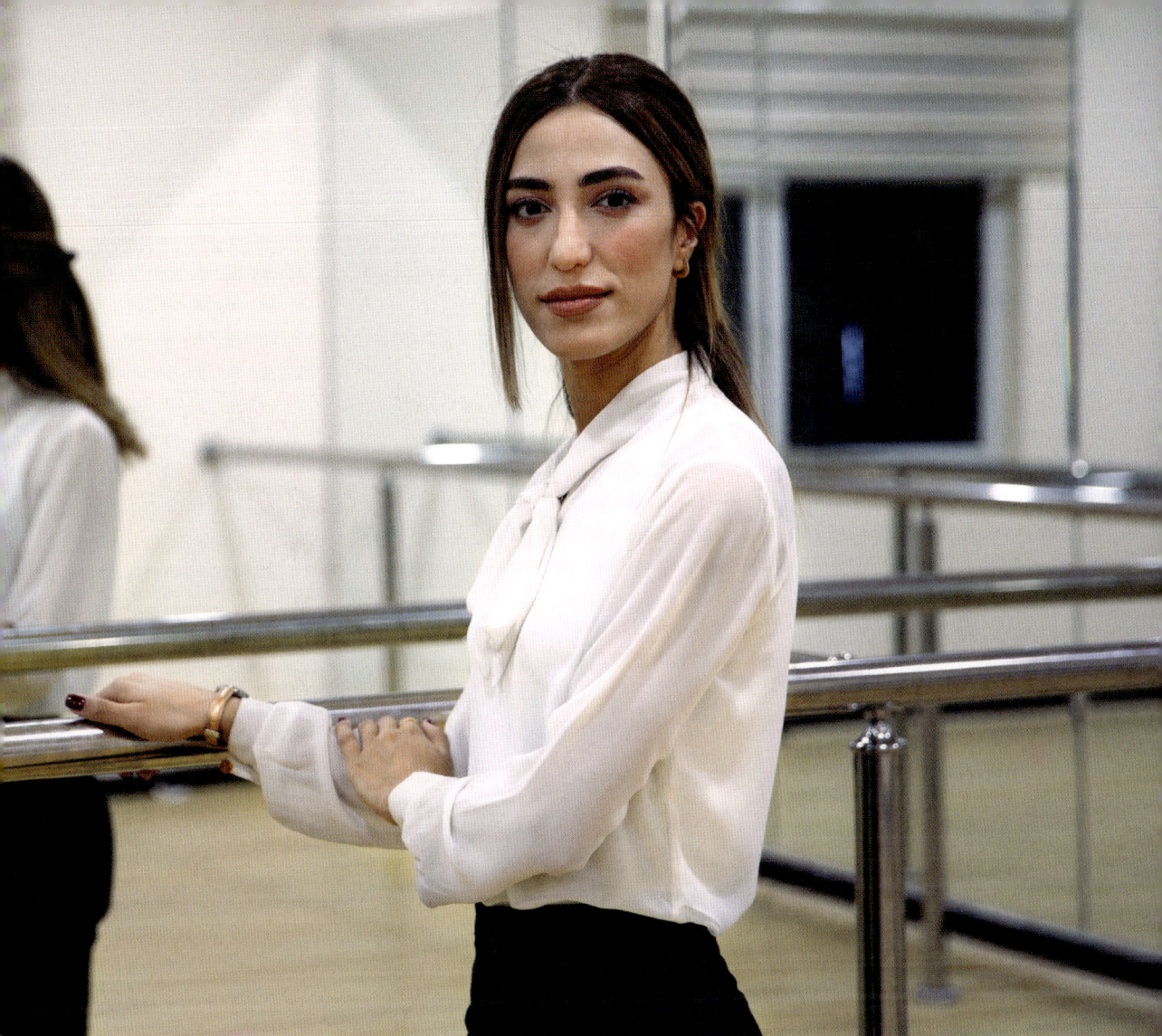

BAGHDAD, IRAQ

Leezan Salam is an amazing Iraqi ballerina who is teaching a new generation of dancers despite opposition from conservatives and hard-liners. Leezan faced many challenges when opening her ballet academy, but, today, she has more than thirty students.

She clearly remembers her academy's first show. The father of one of her best students would not allow his daughter to participate because he feared people would perceive it as something shameful. In the end, the father agreed, and, today, he eagerly asks about the next shows.

When Leezan is dancing, she can disconnect from all the problems of the world. She wants to share that feeling with all her students.

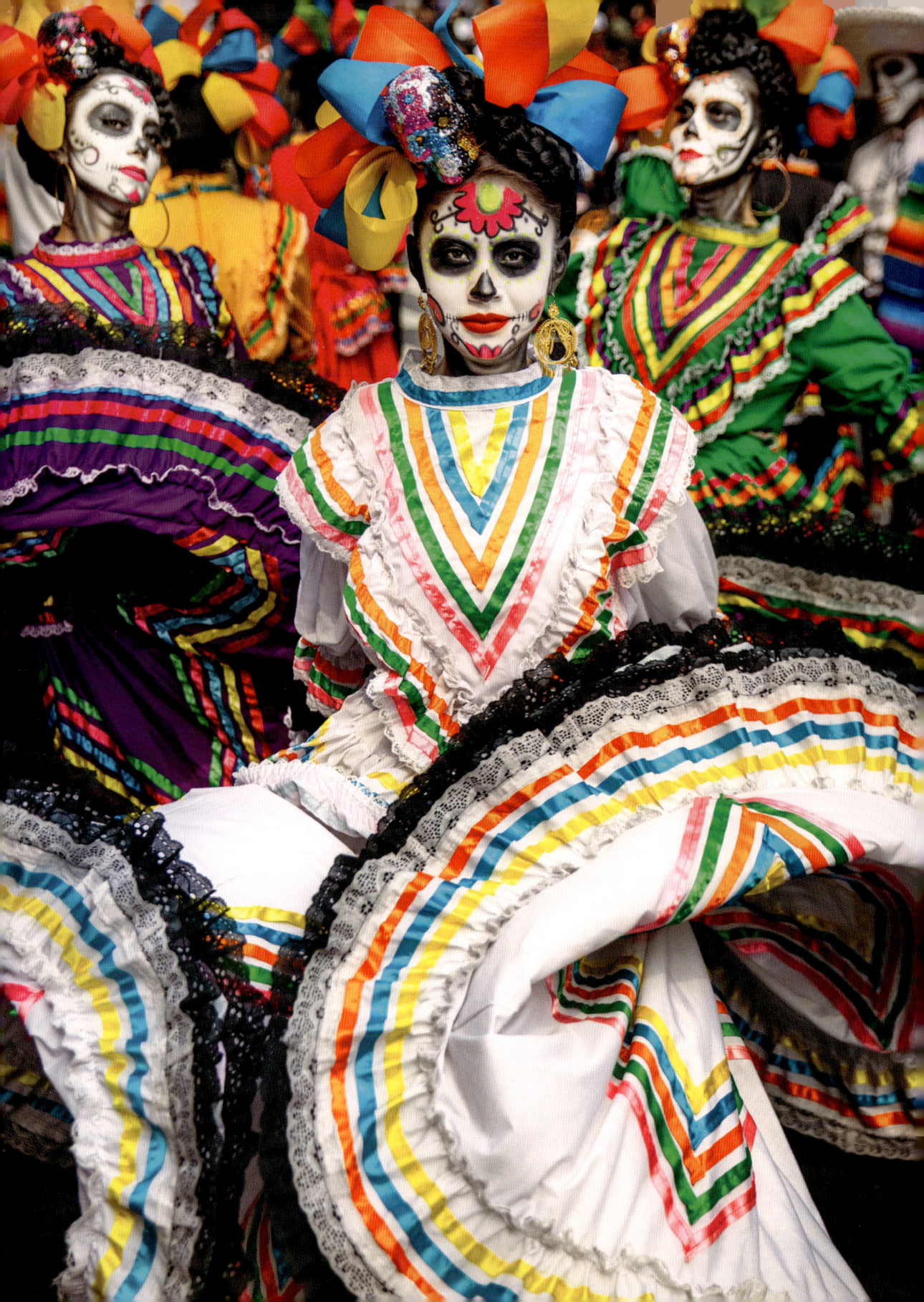

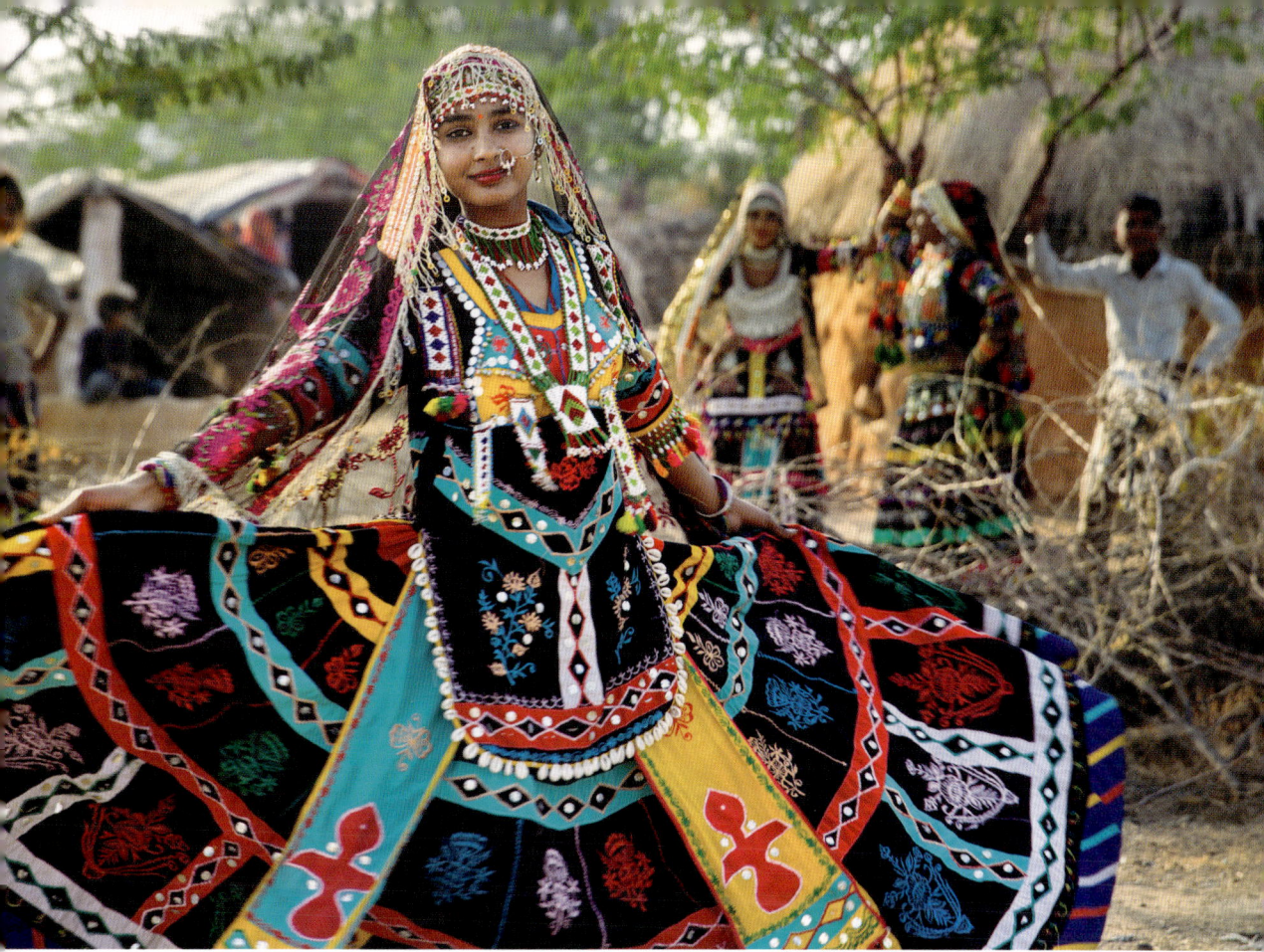

RAJASTHAN, INDIA (Above)

To me, the Kalbelia are one of the most fascinating ethnic groups of the world. During their history, they've faced discrimination and lived a harsh life—but they keep singing and dancing.

Here Saheba is performing a dance that replicates the movements of a snake. For hundreds of years, the lives of Kalbelia have revolved around snakes. They used to catch and raise snakes and trade their venom.

When this activity was forbidden by law, performing arts became the group's main occupation. In the old times, if a snake happened to enter a home, a Kalbelia would be called to catch the serpent and take it away without killing it. Today, Kalbelia are usually called upon to perform their unique dance at celebrations.

MEXICO CITY, MEXICO (Opposite)

These women spent hours preparing for *el Dia de Muertos*. This Mexican celebration might remind you of Halloween, but it's in fact a totally different tradition.

These spectacular makeovers are inspired by skulls, but they're not intended to be scary. The Day of the Dead is not a somber occasion at all but a colorful celebration. People give offerings to the souls of loved ones who have passed away. This gesture helps them feel a little closer.

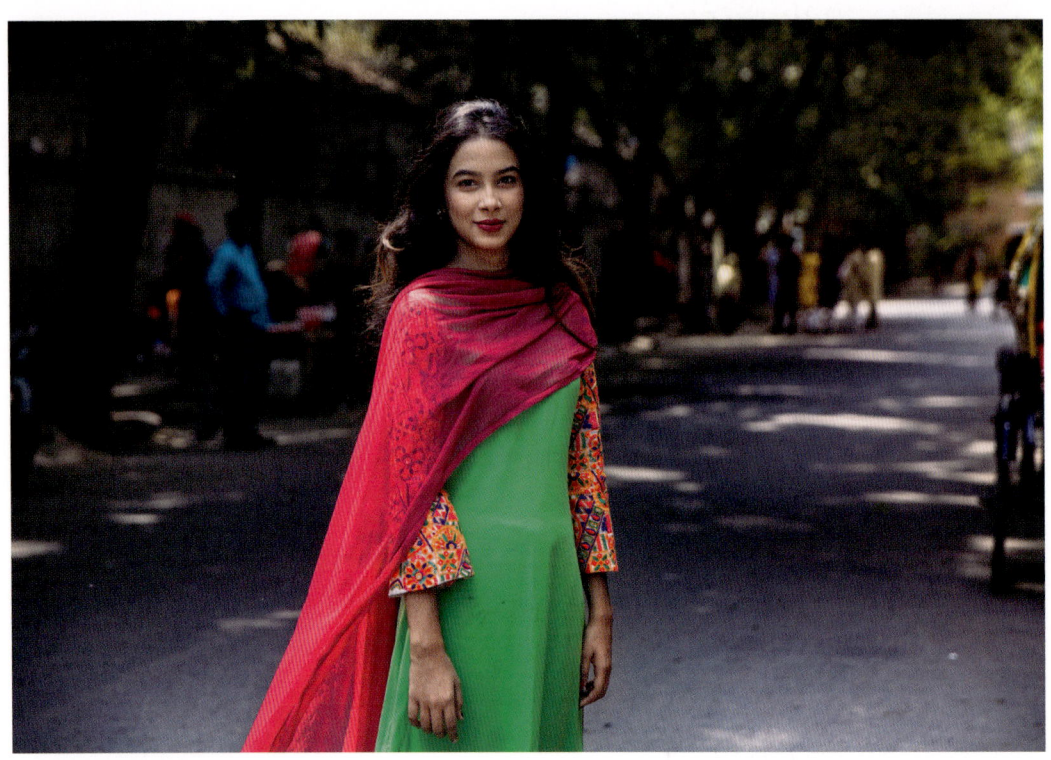

DHAKA, BANGLADESH

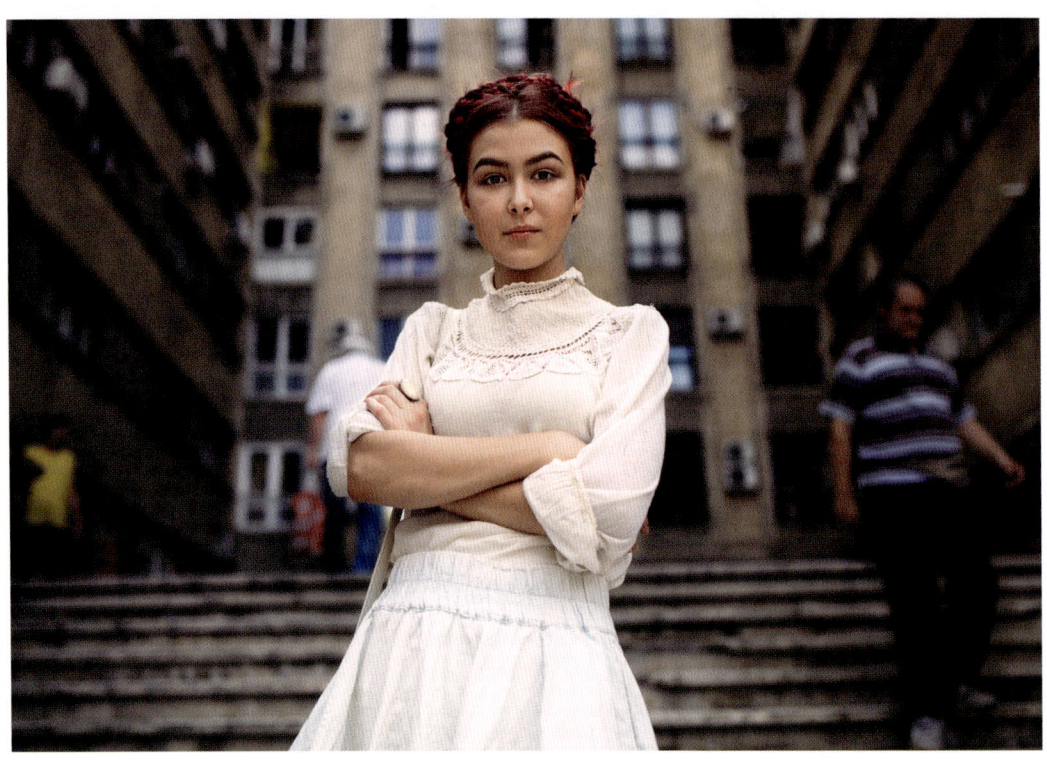

BUCHAREST, ROMANIA

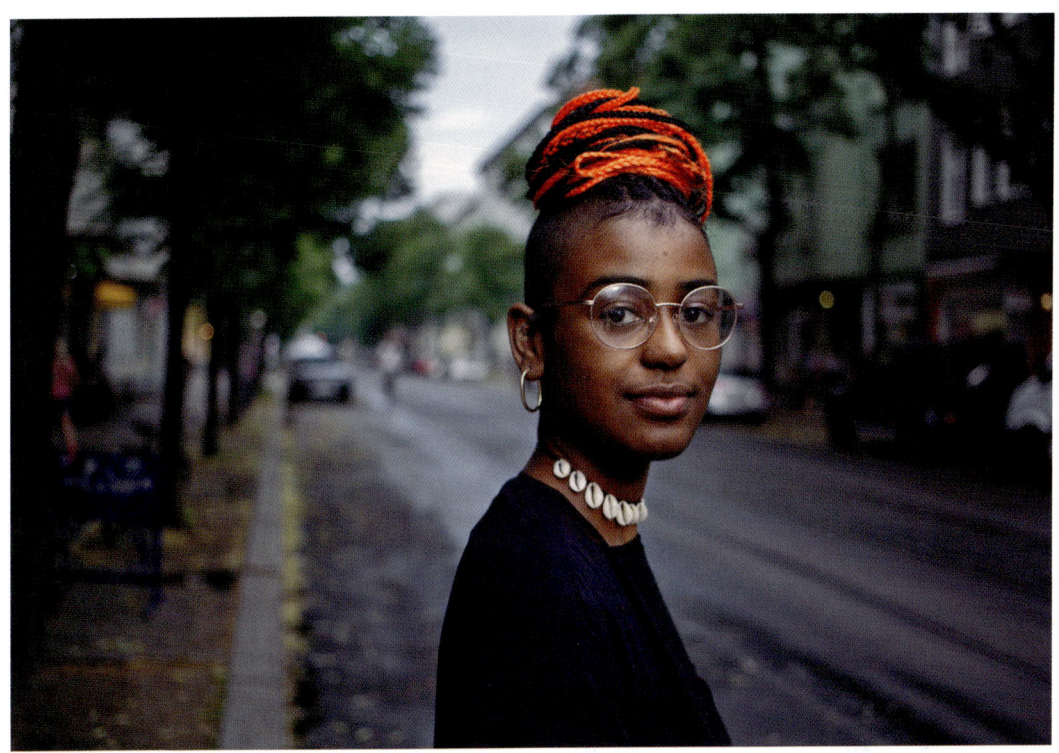

BERLIN, GERMANY

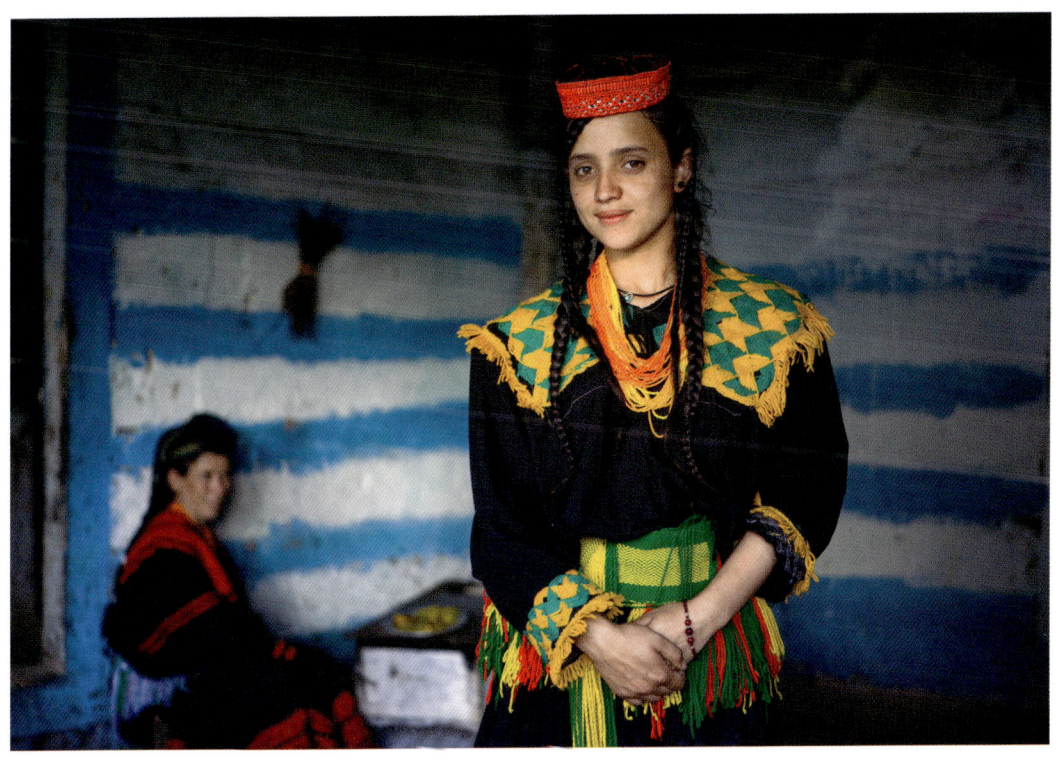

KALASHA VALLEYS, PAKISTAN

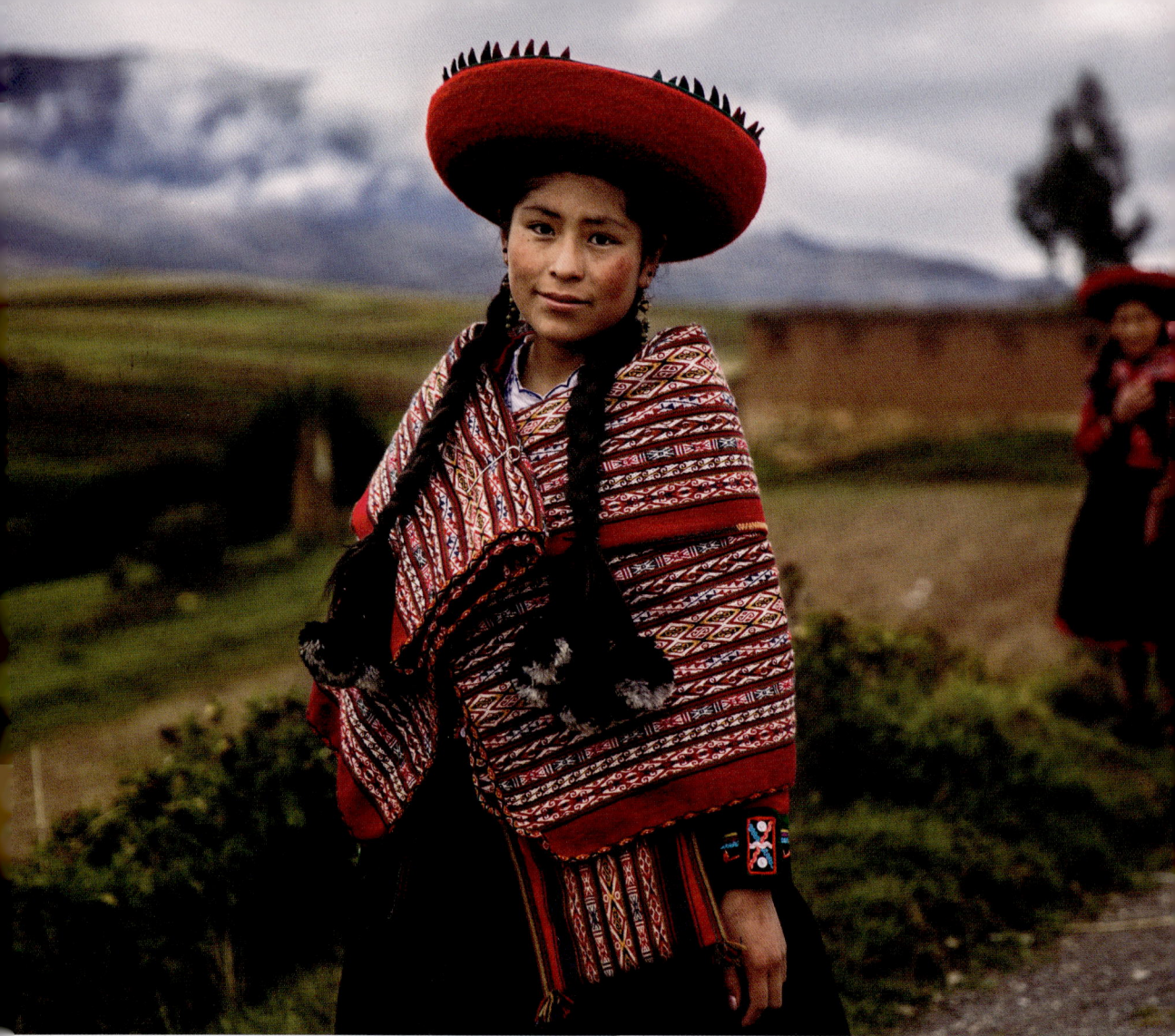

ANDES MOUNTAINS, PERU

High in the mountains in a land that was once part of the Inca Empire, you'll find some of the most beautiful outfits in the world. Killa, together with other women from her community, weaves and sells these traditional costumes.

"Killa" means "moon" in Quechua, her native language. And sometimes the moon is still in the sky, watching her, when she starts the long path to the market early in the morning. She was close to her destination when we met, but the lengthy day of work was just beginning.

On that small road were more spectacularly dressed women, and the scene was looking like a catwalk. Not a common one, like those from Milan or New York City, but a magical one where the models are also designers and sellers. Yes, you'll see a lot of style on a fancy street in Paris, but nothing so genuine as here.

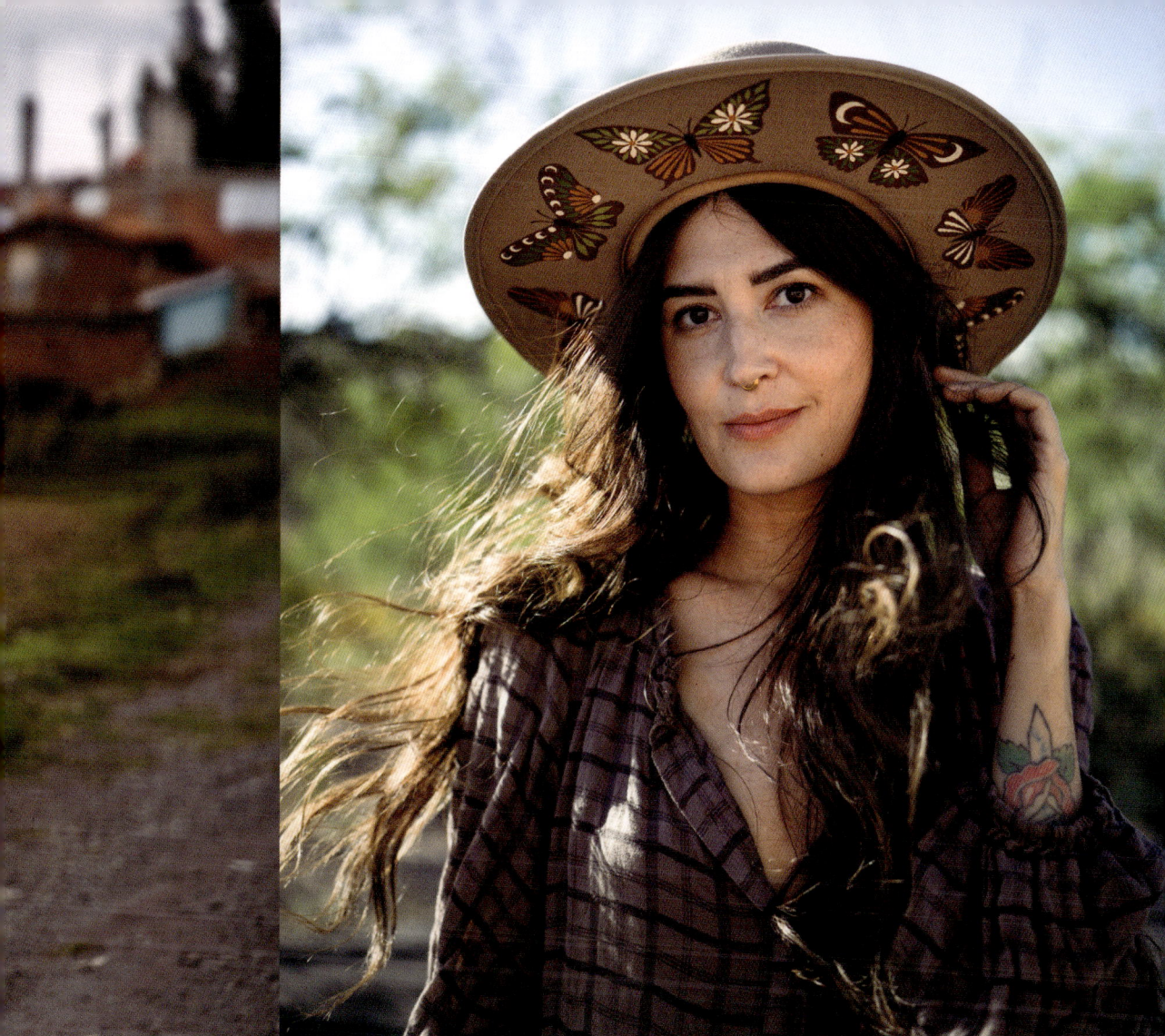

ARIZONA, UNITED STATES

Jenny Wantland is a self-taught artist who creates fascinating hats. Living with her husband and three daughters deep in the Sonoran Desert, she draws inspiration from the magical wildlife that surrounds her. The Sonoran Desert is incredibly rich in fauna and flora, and each hat, thoughtfully designed and hand-painted by Jenny, is a unique celebration of this splendid place.

BEIRUT, LEBANON

Ghenwa Nemnom is bringing her *qanun* to today's music after years of rigorous studies both in Lebanon and the United States. She is one of the few women to have mastered this ancient Middle Eastern instrument that originated three thousand five hundred years ago.

Some perceive the *qanun* as something old-fashioned or limited to traditional Middle Eastern music. However, Ghenwa takes her instrument to a different level by blending its unique sound with various musical genres.

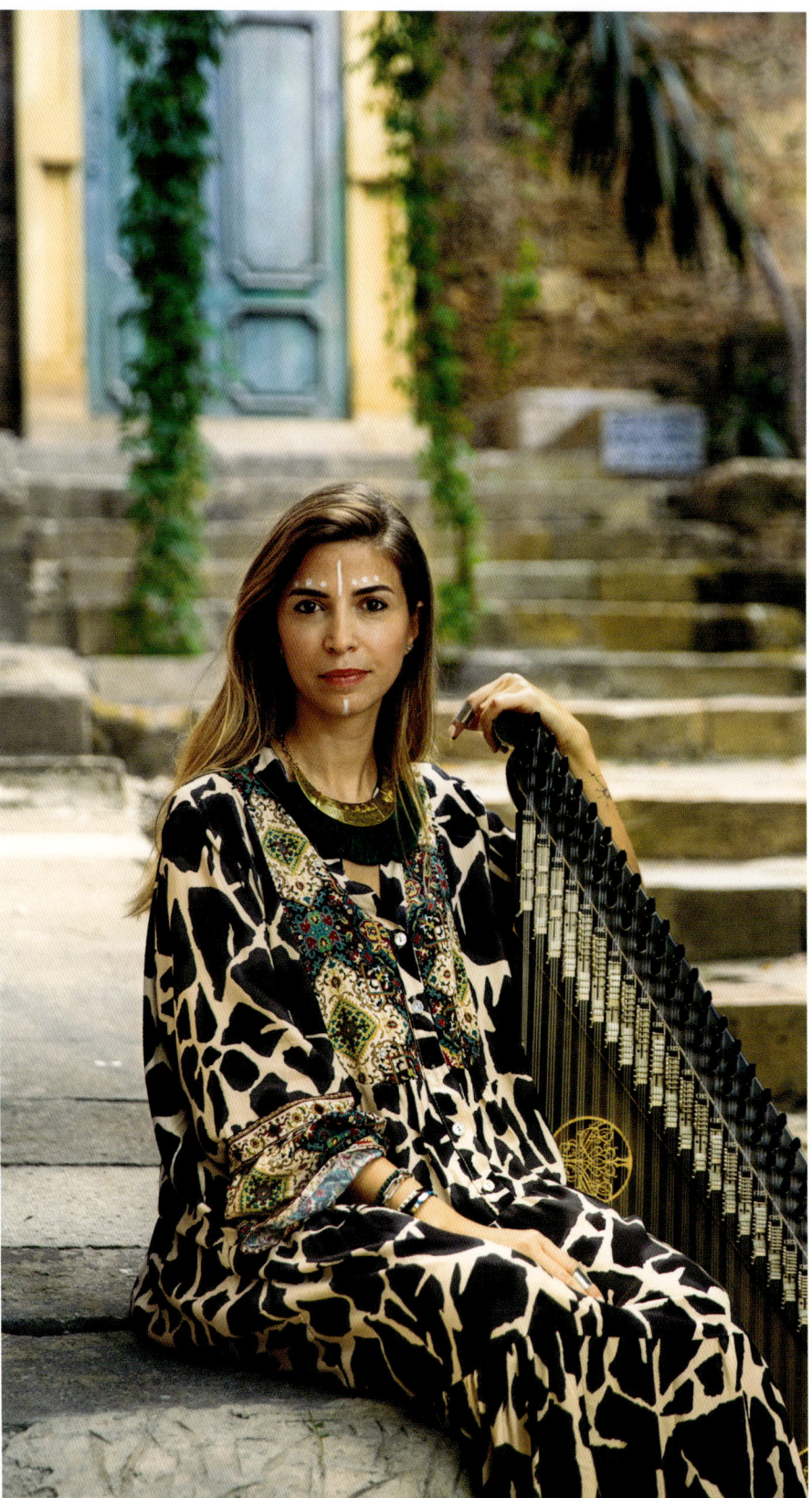

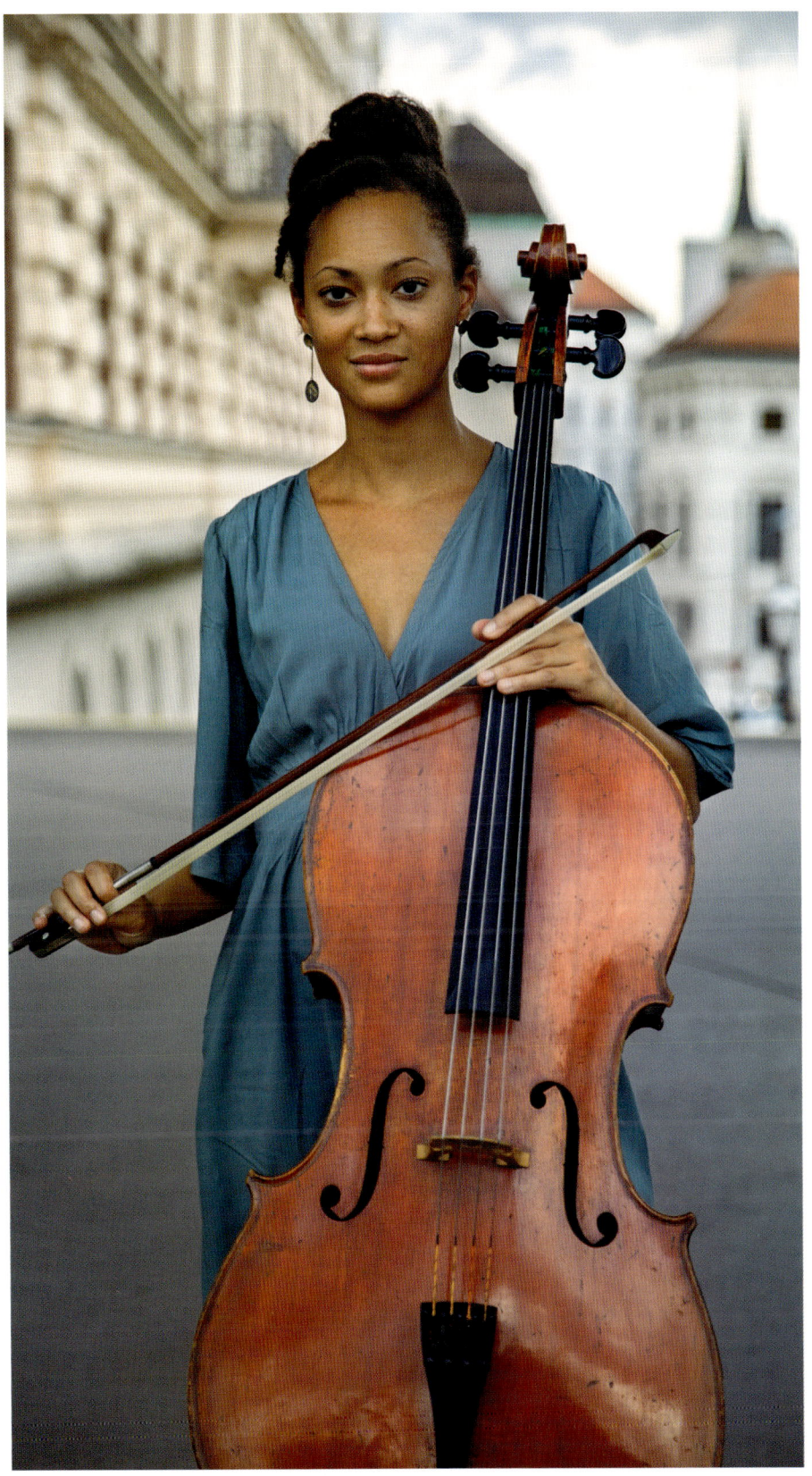

VIENNA, AUSTRIA

As a versatile cellist, Marie Spaemann moves with ease within the genres of classical, pop, or jazz. Besides being a cellist, she is also a singer-songwriter and experiments every day with the endless diversity of music.

LADAKH, INDIA

I have captured thousands of portraits all around the world, but Tsering Tsomo is the only woman with two husbands who I had the chance to photograph.

Nestled deep in the mountains of Northern India, in the Aryan Valley, lives one of the most captivating ethnic groups on the planet. Most refer to them as the Brokpa, but they prefer to be called Aryans. Their remarkable traditional attire, worn during festivals and celebrations, is unique in the world. What's even more intriguing is that within this community, both men and women sometimes have multiple spouses.

Historically, this practice was primarily aimed at consolidating land—a group of brothers would marry the same woman to prevent land disputes and divisions. However, this custom has become increasingly rare, and Tsering Tsomo is one of the last women in the community with two husbands. She is the mother of four children and has always felt fortunate about her unique family.

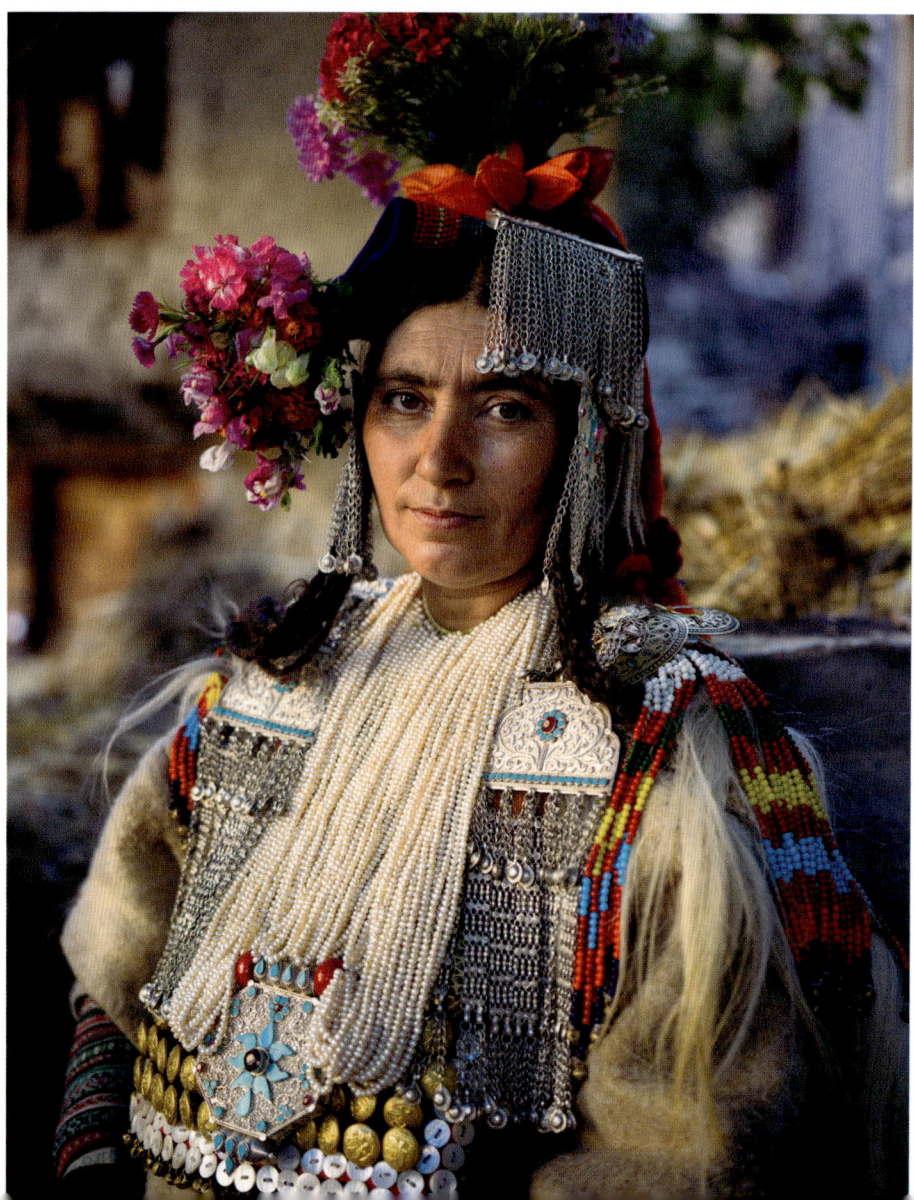

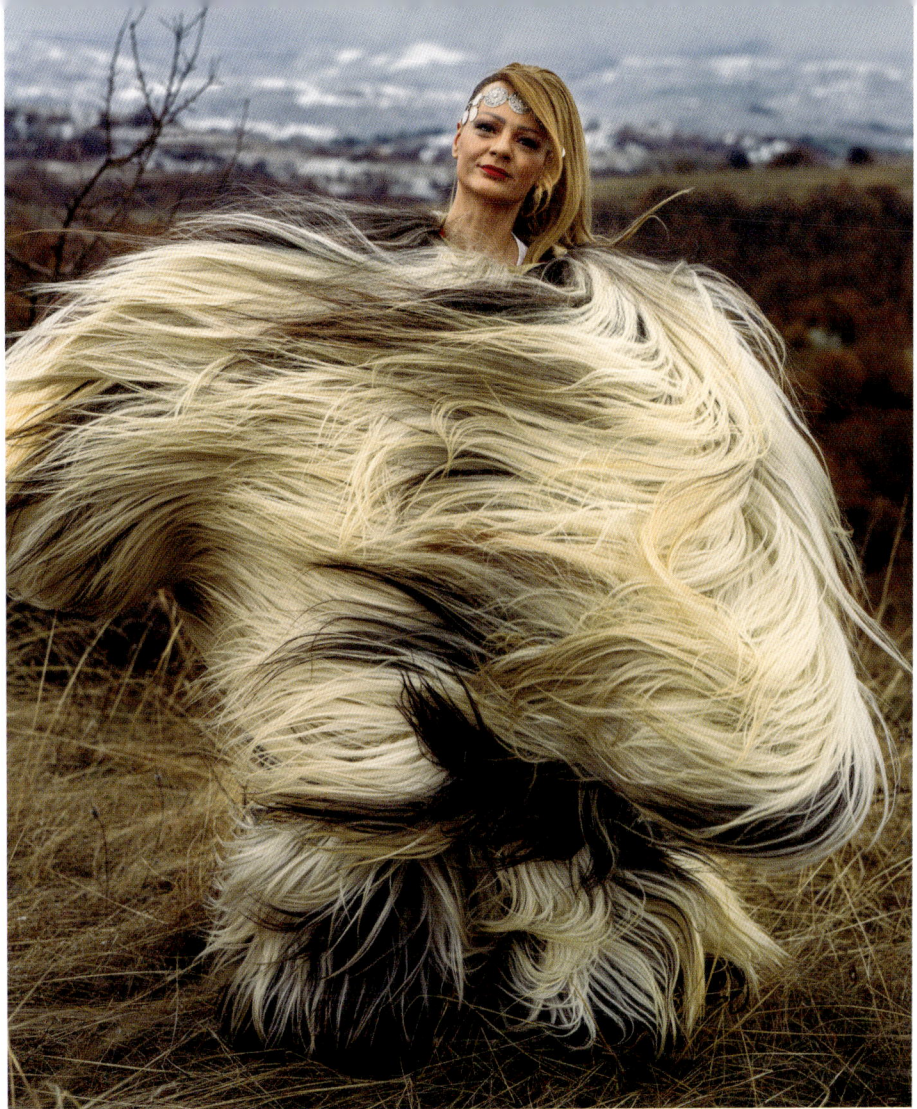

BLAGOEVGRAD, BULGARIA

I have witnessed many traditions all over the planet, but this one in Bulgaria is one of the most fascinating and enigmatic, with roots dating back thousands of years.

Desislava, a border police officer, holds a deep passion for the Bulgarian tradition of Kukeri. Kukeri are costumed people who perform traditional rituals during the winter months, aimed at driving away evil spirits, bringing good luck, and ensuring a bountiful harvest for the coming year.

Desislava inherited her love for Kukeri from her father, who passionately worked to preserve the tradition during communist times, when many traditions were suppressed. Once exclusively practiced by men, Kukeri is now practiced by women, as well, with Desislava being one of the first female Kukeri dancers.

The costumes are masterpieces, often weighing up to one hundred seventy-five pounds and requiring immense strength to wear. The fantastical masks and the enigmatic dance movements complete this captivating tradition, which thrives again thanks to dedicated people like Desislava and her father.

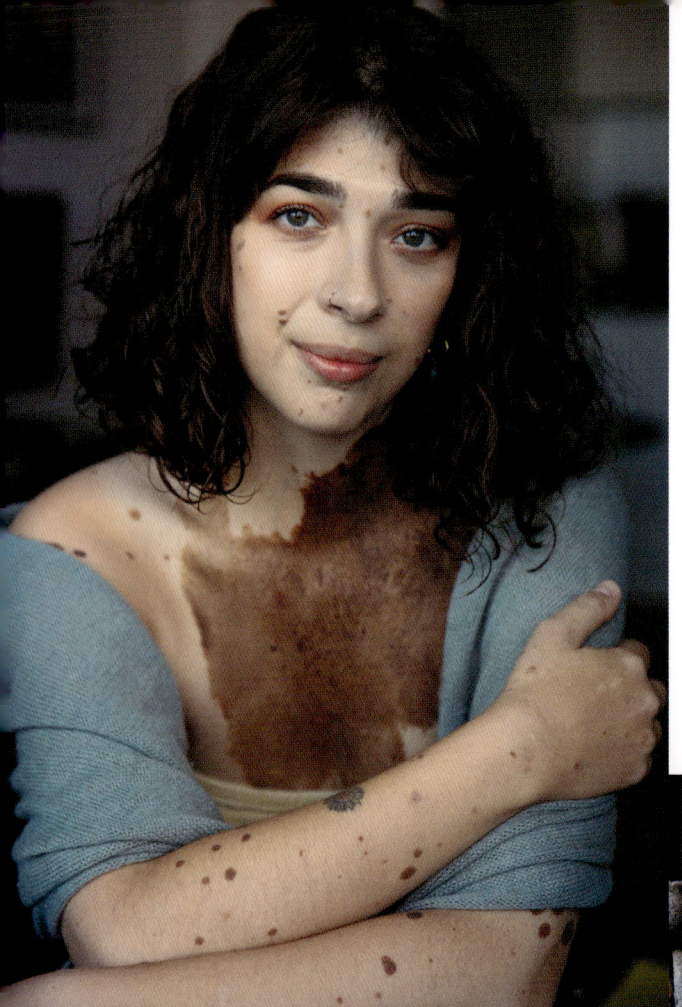

LONDON, UNITED KINGDOM (Left)

Gemma Whyatt was born with a rare skin condition known as congenital melanocytic nevus (CNM). Her journey to self-acceptance was long, yet the destination was incredibly rewarding. Today, besides being a doctor, Gemma champions self-love and raises positive awareness of CNM.

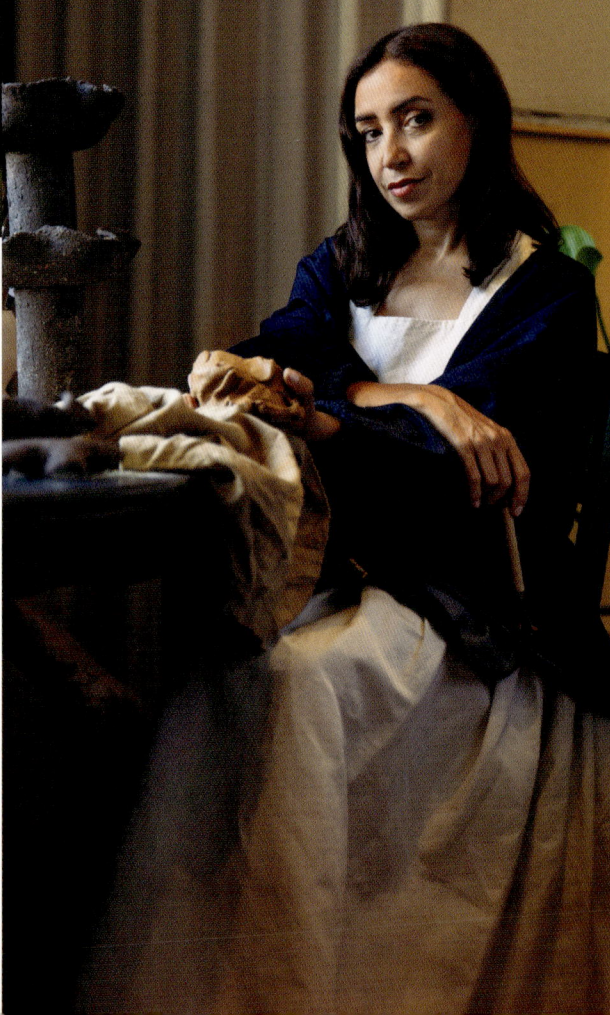

MILAN, ITALY (Right)

Besides running a prestigious design studio, Elena Pelosi is also in love with ceramics. Her pieces are always crafted to be functional while telling a powerful story. Elena often travels to different parts of the world to gather various raw materials and study different styles of craftsmanship across diverse cultures.

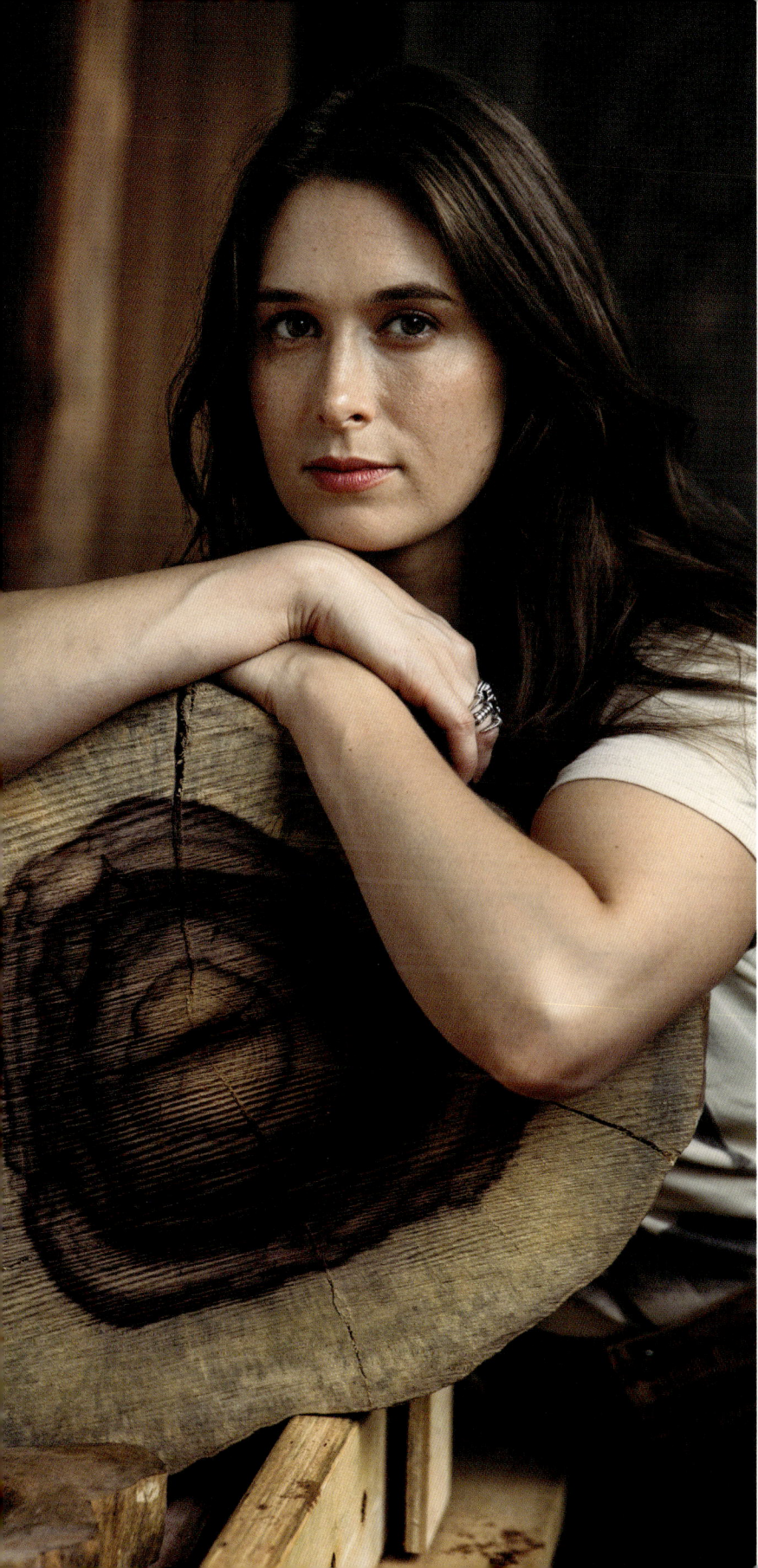

NEW YORK CITY, UNITED STATES

Alexandra Climent's story is about love—love for nature. A self-taught woodworking artist, Alexandra makes expeditions around the globe to gather rare and spectacular species of naturally felled lumber from the depths of various jungles. Back home in New York City, she creates splendid pieces of sculptural and functional art from the found lumber. She believes that the trees in the rainforest are the rulers of the jungle, and she feels a responsibility to showcase their beauty through her work—but only after the trees have lived their full lives.

Everything started in 2009 during a trip to Central and South America. Alexandra visited the rainforest for the very first time and instantly fell in love with it. She was fascinated by its beauty and power but was equally worried about its deforestation. She decided to express those feelings through art.

Today, Alexandra is involved in programs that combat deforestation while also aiding the reforestation of the jungles with endangered species of native trees.

When the hands, the mind, and the soul work together in such a beautiful way, humans and nature can truly live together in harmony.

PANAMA CITY, PANAMA

This mother and daughter are from an ethnic group called Guna, and they were visiting the capital of the country to sell some goods. Guna families are deeply traditional, practicing matrilineal and matrilocal customs. This means the groom moves in order to become part of the bride's family, and he also takes the last name of the bride.

The contrast between these traditional women and the modern skyscrapers in the background tells the complex and complicated story of our world.

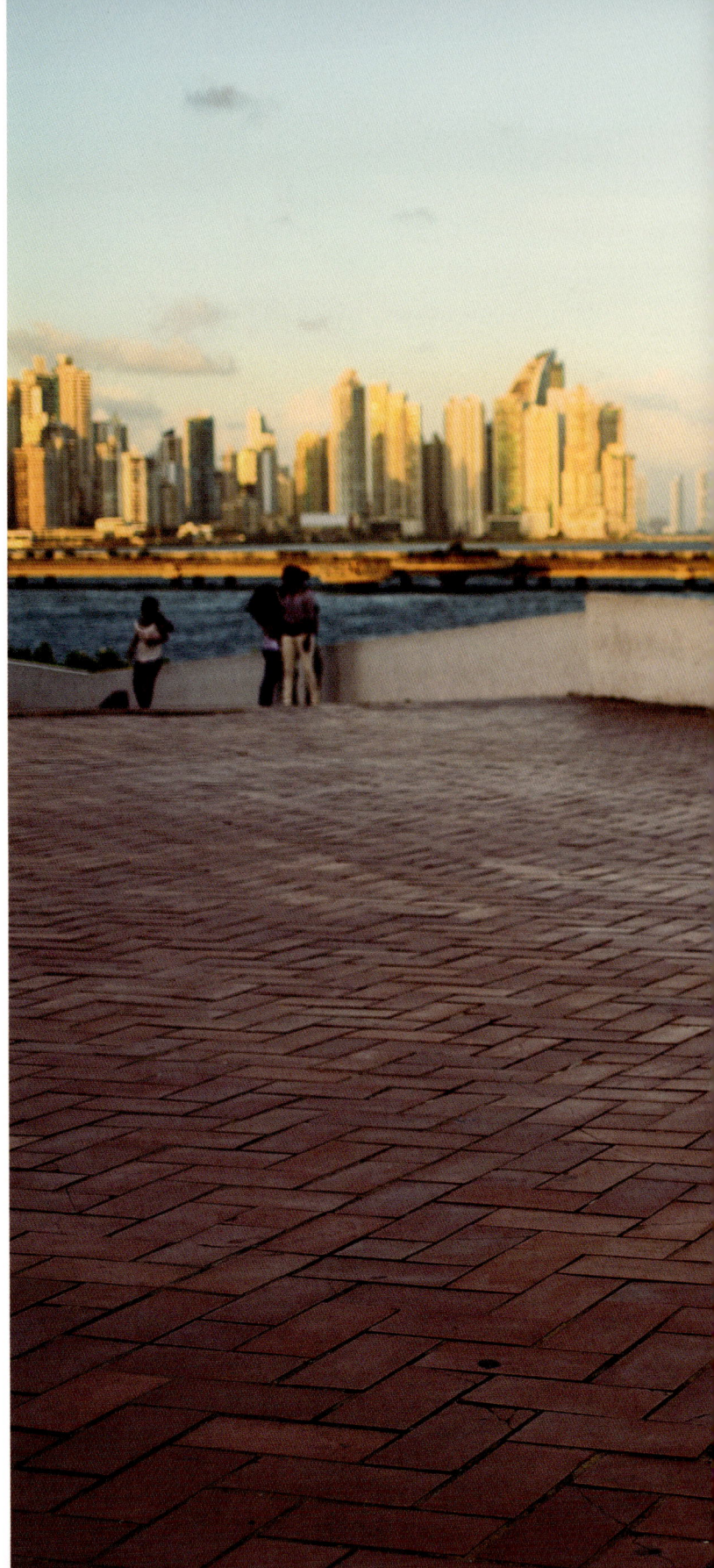

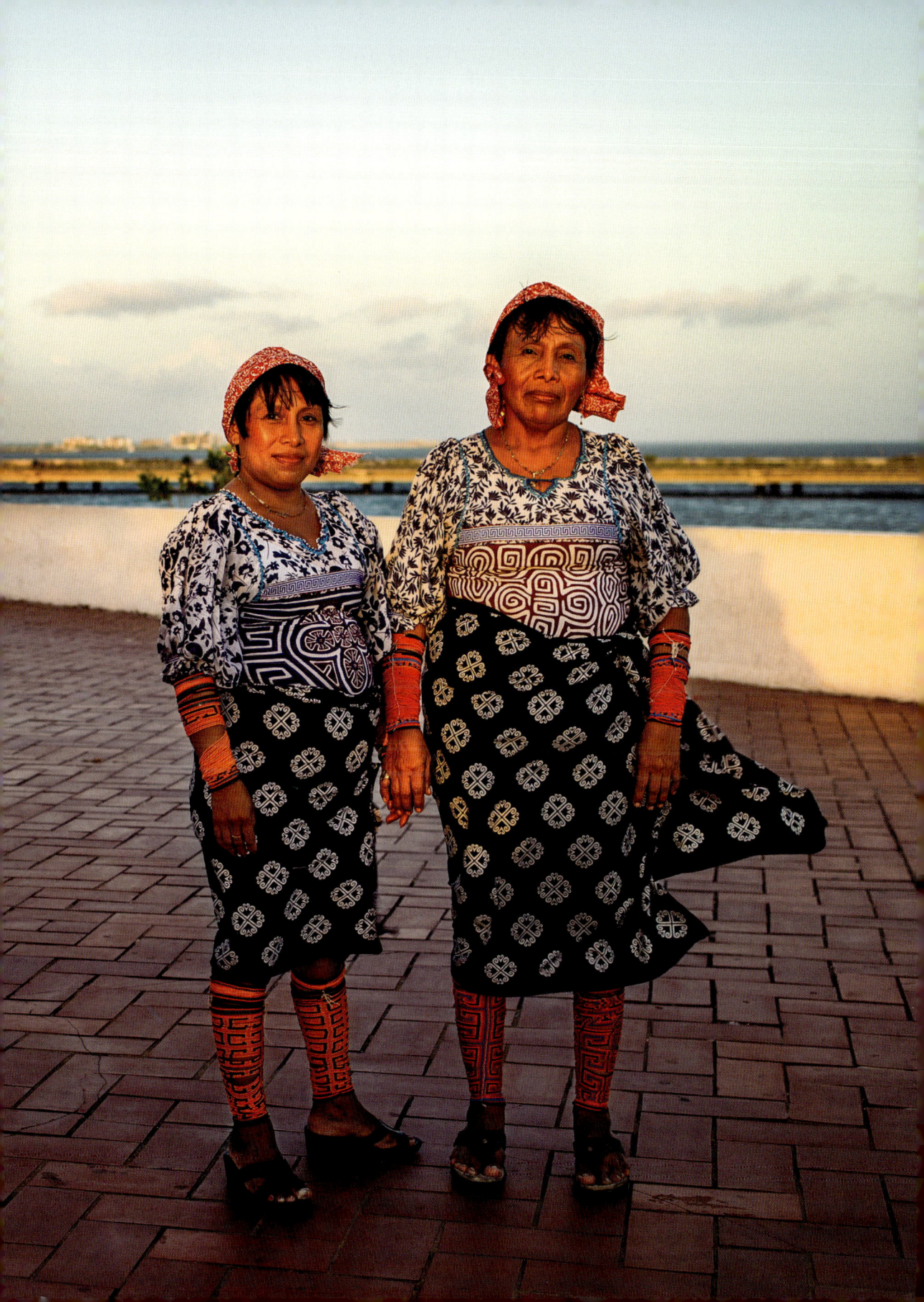

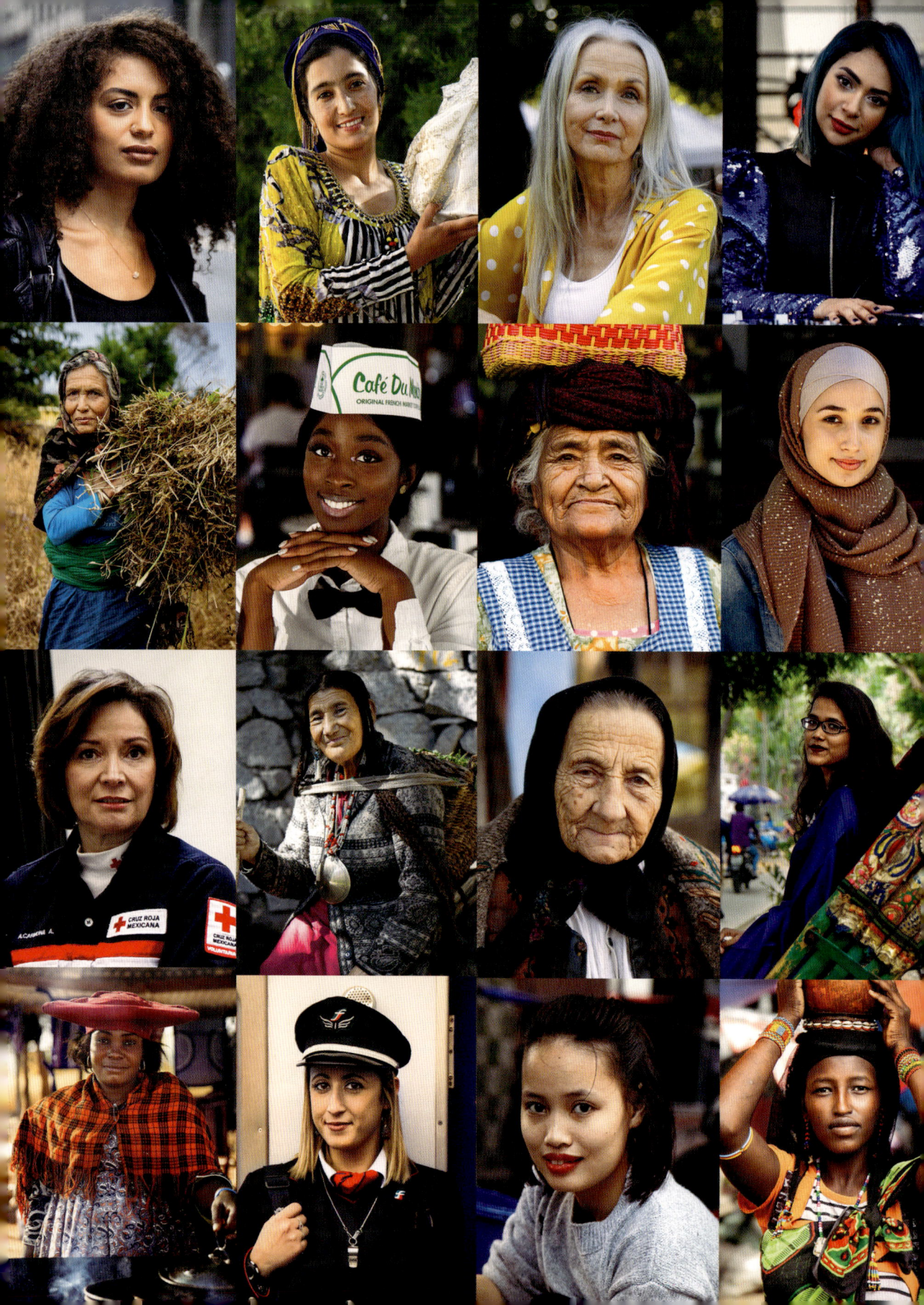

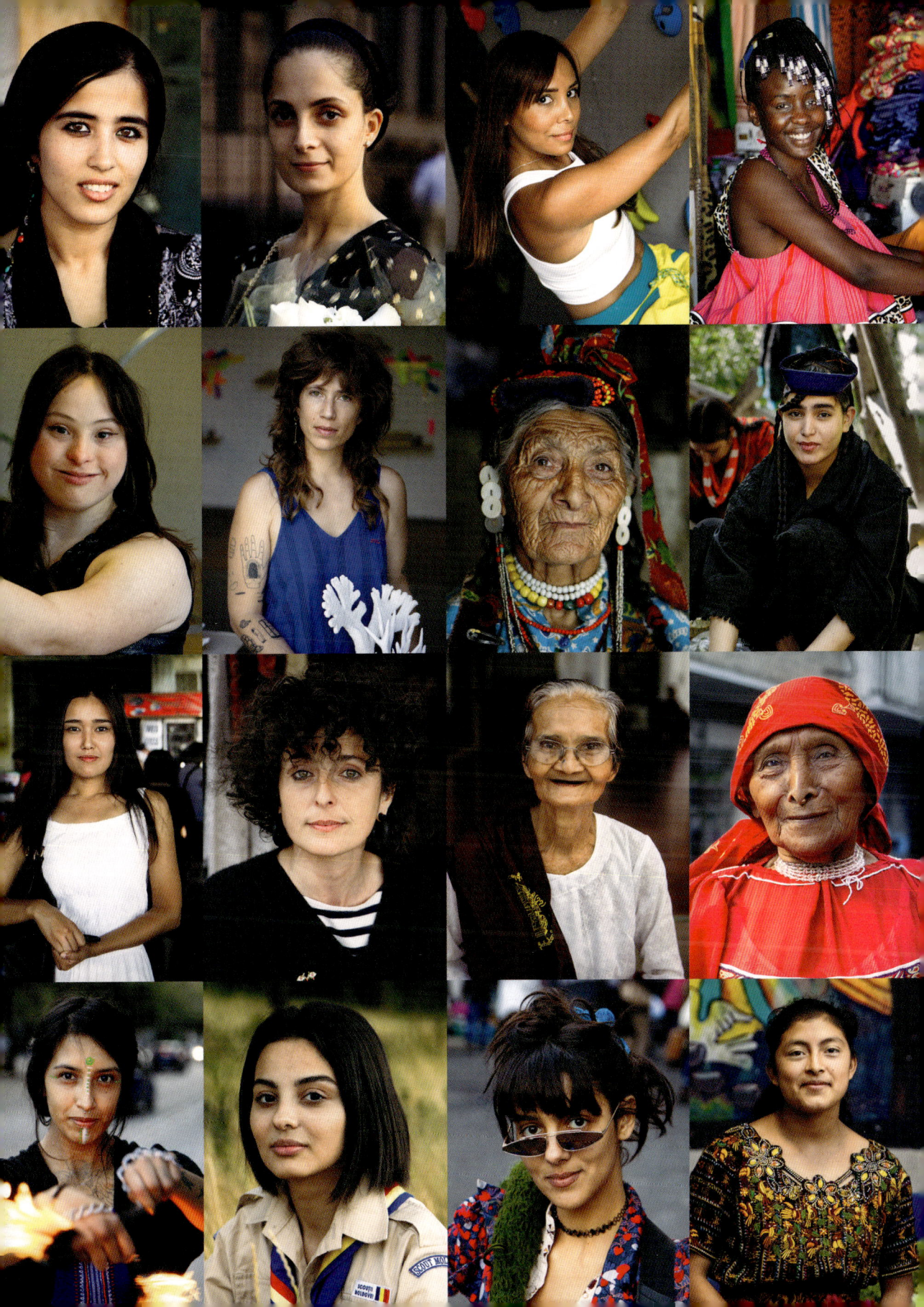

ACKNOWLEDGMENTS

I hope you enjoyed this vibrant journey around the world. For me, it took eight years of intense work and challenges. Despite the difficulties, the beauty I encountered made every second worthwhile, and I'm deeply grateful for this incredible experience.

First, I want to thank all the incredible women who agreed to be photographed and shared their stories with me. Without them, this book simply would not exist.

Thank you to my dear dad. You passed away too early, but I will always celebrate your bright spirit and optimism through my work. Thank you, my beloved husband, for your enormous contribution to who I am today. Thank you to my mom, and thank you to my parents-in-law and sister-in-law.

Thank you to my literary agent, Brian DeFiore, for making a new dream come true. Thank you to Patty Rice, Julie Barnes, Danys Mares, Elizabeth Garcia, Kayla Overbey, and to all the wonderful team at Andrews McMeel Publishing. It was so amazing to work together again. Thank you to Aubre Andrus for fine-tuning the text.

Thank you, Elisa Marcon from Yalea Eyewear. Thank you, Raluca Gavra, for your support. Thank you to all my friends in Sibiu.

Last but not least, I want to thank all those who donated for *The Atlas of Beauty*. It's difficult to express in words how much your contributions, both financial and emotional, meant to this book. Thank you, a million times. Here are just a few of those who supported *The Atlas of Beauty* through donations:

Andra Paraschiv, Ileana Nitu, Jennifer Boscardin-Ching, Sonia Martin Lewis, Rotary Club Udine, Zhou Fang, Atlas Adaline Tompkins, Hassina Sayad, Alexandra Serban, Angela Cramariuc, Sabine Van Staden, Asociatia Civic Help, Ursula Nicol, Anca Enache, Marc Smith, Karyn Wagner, Sarah Whitehouse, Knute Michael Steen, Luca De Pauli, Sharvi and Shaivi Kalwani, Susanne Schmid, Merinda Robert, Constantin-Dorinel Preoțescu, Anja Gräf, Yasmina Kechida, Loredana Padurean, Seraina Amstutz-Hertig, Andrina Stan, Angela and Mircea Dragoi, Leandra Scharnhorst, Katharina Wolf, Maja Miljenovic, Kazuko Funakoshi, Janine Nakotte, Barbara Meier, Isa and Alex from @travel_neverland, Sorina Luca, Helga Beck, Tina Lundberg, Victor Marian Puscas, Samra Sarkol, Angelica Racareanu, Crini Lău, Marta Moslw, Celesta Hubner, Ozkan Ego, Laura García del Olmo, Elaine Chu, Francesca C., Maria Hrytsuk, Theresa Ehsani, Alina Vacaru, Chen ya Chang, Danny Jasiczek, Maja Knobel, Radhika Jagdeep, Marion Roussel, Keshini Palenthiran, Ionuț Vasiliu, Sibylle Fleischmann, Zara Salam, Laurens Bohlen, Gülce Postaci, Karolin Suemengen, Sorina Mashhadi, Loulwa Sleiman, Clémence Derennes, Oana Nechifor Dogan, Yulia Brodskaya, Manuela Kubenka, Alina Dumitrașcu, Natalia Maticiuc, Daniella Raj, Kayode Williams, Naomi Calmatuianu, Alina Marin, Stephanie Nichole LeVeque, Raluca-Maria Sandu, Georgiana Buturoiu, Sandra Linton, Andrea Mălina Titieni-Schuhmann, Jan Roos, Alessia Piazza, Debby Ladouceur, Iulia și Ovidiu Gherman, Valentina Buzdugan, Roxana Collet, Vera Gottschall, Sine Medom Vorre, Alexandra Hamilton, Nurşen Öğütveren-Armea, Jason Sozo, Andreea Ileana Lazar, Claudia Dora Matei, Ela Verman, Violeta Stefan, Joana Raquel Monteiro da SIlva, Sabine Baulig, Susanne Schmid, Paul Adriaanse, Aura Botorog,

Ada-Julie Görne, Alessio Zaghini, Pedro Szot, Anabela Neves, Stefano, Simona and Paolo Crosta, Floriana Ionescu, Niels Stauffenegger, Patience Shutts, Ana Maria Cuculescu, GoThru Media, Gitte Grundsøe, Wanjing Ji, Shahrun Moinizadeh, Sierin Lim, Carrie Brownlee, Irina Constantin, Marieve Saji, Cécile Nourry, Marie Daffe, Kerstin Eikel, Francine Torres, Caterina Colomer, Viorica Pacurar, Valerie Sara Tonolli, Annika Burneleit, Benita and Alicia, Andreea Niculcea, Cindy Puah, Cristina Domuta, Miriam Koschowski, Valeria Avramenko, Carmella Hart, David Cummings, Ladislav Lihan, Fred Lentz, Joanna Mary Delargy, Robin Smith-Trequesser, Florentina Negrutiu, Adriana Zeciu, Kate Tonkin, Anamaria Zauchenberger, Eman Salem, Adriana Costache, Roger Castillo, Soumya Banerji, Reina Irena, Ozan Akgül, Namiko Numao, Jördis D, Daniela Lungu, Kay Wai Ki Poon, Lim Junxiang, Mirjana Gegenbauer, Valérie Blanchard, Wendy Thomson, Milton Jang, Anca Davidoiu, James Chien, Raïs De Weirdt, Gabi John, Thomas Rogers, Simona Chitoiu, Adele and Mateo Sapienza, Ovidiu Bodea, Susan Caston, Miriam Castro, Javed Akhtar Mohammed, Claire Gosselin, Raluca Elena Paraschiv, Alexandra Townsend, NhaVinh Tran, Goran Plišić, Mary D. Healy, Irina Obukhova, Faith Sweet, Nina and Mihaela Tunaru, Kathleen Stone, Richard Johnson, Eva, Ana si Arnaud Boata Daniele, Amira Ioana Shaat, Luciana Bulato, Stefanie Lenze, Yasmin Naghash, Marina Trinca Vespan, Bruce Miller, Laura Dwight, Diane Condon, Kim Naidu.

In memory of Lisa Duvall.

Title page photo: Mihaela Noroc and her daughter, Natalia, in Sweden.

COLLAGE IMAGE LOCATIONS (from left to right, top to bottom):

PAGE IV: Namibia, Ethiopia, Australia, Ethiopia, Germany, France, Lebanon, China, Mongolia, Kyrgyzstan, Bangladesh, India, Portugal, Iran, Nepal, Iraq.

PAGES 64 TO 65: Romania, Tajikistan, United States, Morocco, Chile, Nepal, United States, Saudi Arabia, Romania, Ethiopia, Chile, Unites States, Afghanistan, France, Nepal, Ethiopia, Norway, Guatemala, Portugal, Somaliland, Cuba, Moldova, Hungary, United States, Pakistan, Ukraine, Romania, Turkey, Mongolia, Turkey, United States, Kyrgyzstan.

PAGES 144 TO 145: Peru, Canada, Syria, Morocco, Nepal, United States, Nepal, United States, Namibia, Australia, Namibia, Belgium, Romania, Vietnam, Guatemala, Romania, Ethiopia, Guatemala, Somaliland, Spain, Iceland, Moldova, Bangladesh, Pakistan, South Korea, Bulgaria, Iran, Bangladesh, Myanmar, Montenegro, Albania, Bangladesh.

PAGES 214 TO 215: Syria, Canada, Tajikistan, Morocco, Nepal, United States, Morocco, Nepal, Bulgaria, Romania, Pakistan, North Korea, Sweden, Turkey, Mongolia, Myanmar, Bulgaria, Japan, Syria, North Macedonia, Moldova, Norway, Ethiopia, India, United States, Namibia, Namibia, Ethiopia, India, Nepal, Ireland, Latvia.

PAGES 286 TO 287: Tajikistan, Spain, Afghanistan, United States, Namibia, France, Namibia, Nepal, Namibia, Ethiopia, Somaliland, Sweden, Turkey, India, Ukraine, Georgia, Iran, Iraq, Mongolia, Turkey, Cuba, Finland, Nepal, Bangladesh, Myanmar, Portugal, Indonesia, Portugal, Portugal, India, Saudi Arabia, Syria.

PAGES 340 TO 341: Canada, Tajikistan, Canada, Saudi Arabia, Tajikistan, United States, Saudi Arabia, Namibia, Nepal, United States, Mexico, Bosnia and Herzegovina, Hungary, United States, India, Pakistan, Mexico, India, Romania, Bangladesh, Kyrgyzstan, Italy, Myanmar, Panama, Namibia, Italy, Vietnam, Ethiopia, Mexico, Moldova, Portugal, Guatemala.

Andrews McMeel Publishing
a division of Andrews McMeel Universal
1130 Walnut Street, Kansas City, Missouri 64106

www.andrewsmcmeel.com

25 26 27 28 29 TEN 10 9 8 7 6 5 4 3 2 1

ISBN: 978-1-5248-9479-5

Library of Congress Control Number: 2024944549

Editor: Patty Rice
Art Director: Julie Barnes
Production Editor: Elizabeth A. Garcia
Production Manager: Julie Skalla

ATTENTION: SCHOOLS AND BUSINESSES
Andrews McMeel books are available at quantity discounts
with bulk purchase for educational, business, or sales promotional use.
For information, please e-mail the Andrews McMeel Publishing
Special Sales Department: sales@andrewsmcmeel.com.